Having completed his PhD at Mar⟨ Perrin is Professor of New Testamen of Biblical Studies at Wheaton Graduate School (Wheaton, IL), where he also served as Dean (2012–17). He is author of numerous articles, co-edited volumes, and books, including *Lost in Transmission: What We Can Know about the Words of Jesus* (Thomas Nelson, 2007), *Thomas, the Other Gospel* (SPCK and Westminster John Knox, 2007) and *Jesus the Temple* (SPCK and Baker Academic, 2010). In addition to his academic responsibilities, he has served as founding chair of Covenant Classical School (Naperville, IL) and, as an ordained Presbyterian, has pastored several churches in the USA and in the UK. Nick lives in Wheaton with his wife Camie.

JESUS THE PRIEST

NICHOLAS PERRIN

Baker Academic
a division of Baker Publishing Group
Grand Rapids, Michigan

© 2018 by Nicholas Perrin

Published by Baker Academic
a division of Baker Publishing Group
PO Box 6287, Grand Rapids, MI 49516-6287
www.bakeracademic.com

Baker Academic edition published 2018
ISBN 978-0-8010-4859-3

Previously published in 2018 in Great Britain by SPCK

Printed in the United States of America

Library of Congress Control Number: 2018955794

Unless otherwise indicated, Scripture quotations are from the New Revised Standard Version Bible: Anglicized Edition, copyright © 1989, 1995 National Council of the Churches of Christ in the United States of America. Used by permission. All rights reserved.

Scripture quotations labeled NIV are from the Holy Bible, New International Version® (Anglicised). NIV®. Copyright © 1973, 1978, 1984, 2011 by Biblica, Inc.™ Used by permission of Zondervan. All rights reserved worldwide. www.zondervan.com. The "NIV" and "New International Version" are trademarks registered in the United States Patent and Trademark Office by Biblica, Inc.™

In keeping with biblical principles of creation stewardship, Baker Publishing Group advocates the responsible use of our natural resources. As a member of the Green Press Initiative, our company uses recycled paper when possible. The text paper of this book is composed in part of post-consumer waste.

For Camie

Uxor carissima

Contents

Preface   xiii
List of abbreviations   xvii

Introduction   1
  Treasures from the scrapheap   1
  A tale of two Jesus scholars: Schweitzer and Bultmann   1
  Schweitzer and Bultmann revisited   5
  A few notes of explanation   7
  A word on method   11

1 The prayer of Jesus   17
  Introduction   17
  The meaning of 'Father': a historical-critical conundrum   20
  Naming Yahweh as 'Father' in early Christianity and Judaism   28
    Naming Yahweh as 'Father' in early Christianity   29
    Naming Yahweh as 'Father' in Judaism   32
    Synthesis   36
  The exodus narrative as backdrop to God-as-Father   36
  The Lord's Prayer: a consistently eschatological prayer   38
    First petition: 'Hallowed be your name' (Q 11.2b)   39
    Variations on a priestly theme: petitions two through seven 44
      Second petition: 'Your kingdom come' (Q 11.2c) 44
      Third petition: 'Your will be done on earth as it is in heaven'
      (Matt. 6.10b–c)   46
      Fourth petition: 'Give us each day our daily bread' (Q 11.3) 47
      Fifth petition: 'And forgive us our sins, for we ourselves
      forgive everyone indebted to us' (Q 11.4a–b)   48
      Sixth petition: 'And do not bring us to the time of trial'
      (Q 11.4b)   50
      Seventh petition: 'but rescue us from the evil one'
      (Matt. 6.13b)   51
  Summary   52

2 The baptism of Jesus   54
  Introduction   54
  John's baptism   56
  Baptism and theophany as history   58
    A review of the sources   59
    Questions surrounding the theophany   61

Back to the theophany 63
The meaning of Jesus' baptism according to Mark 1.11 par. 67
  The sources of the scriptural quotation (Mark 1.11 par.) 67
  The meaning of the scriptural quotation (Mark 1.11 par.) in
  the light of Second-Temple reception 70
    Psalm 2 in Second-Temple Judaism 70
    Genesis 22 in Second-Temple Judaism 73
  Synthesis 76
Jesus' baptism in the context of the synoptic narratives 77
  Mark 77
  Matthew 80
  Luke 84
  Synthesis 88
Summary 88

3 **The kingdom of Jesus** 91
The apocalyptic framework of the kingdom: the parable of
the sower (Mark 4.4–9) 92
  Interpreting the parable of the sower: a first pass 93
  The pattern of apocalyptic expectation in three precursor 'seed
  texts' 98
    Jubilees 99
    Apocalypse of Weeks (*1 En.* 93.1–10; 91.11–17) 100
    Book of Dreams (*1 Enoch* 83—90) 101
    Synthesis 103
  The parable of the sower *redux* 103
    'A sower went out to sow seed' 104
    'Some seed fell beside the path' 105
    'Other seed fell on rocky ground' 105
    'Other seed fell among thorns' 106
    'Other seed fell into good soil' 108
  The parable of the sower and the historical Jesus 109
The future trajectory of the kingdom: the parable of salt
(Matt. 5.13//Mark 9.50//Luke 14.34–35) 112
  Matthew's parable of salt (Matt. 5.13) 114
    The Matthean context 115
    Priestly salt 117
    Salt in Matthew 118
  Luke's parable of salt (Luke 14.34–35) 119
    The Lukan context 119
    Salt in Luke 122
  Mark's parable of salt (Mark 9.50) 124
    The Markan context 124
    Salt in Mark 125
  The parable of salt and the historical Jesus 126

The present contours of the kingdom: the Beatitudes (Q 6.20–21)   128
   The meaning of the Beatitudes   131
     The social grammar of blessing   131
     The redemptive-historical grammar of blessing   135
   The 'poor' and the historical Jesus   137
   The Beatitudes and the historical Jesus   139
   Summary   140

4   Jesus Son of David   **143**
Jesus as 'Son of David'   144
   Jesus as the Son of David in early Christian tradition   144
   Son of David and the historical Jesus   147
David and the 'Son of David' as priestly figures   152
   David and Solomon's priestly activity   153
   Towards an explanation for David and Solomon's exceptional
   priestly status   157
     The united confederacy as a condition for legitimate
     royal-priestly rule   157
     The priestly David and 'Son of David' according to Psalm 110   160
Jesus the priestly Son of David   163
Summary   164

5   The identity of the Son of Man   **166**
The identity of the Son of Man in Daniel   168
   The cultic orientation of the book of Daniel   168
   Backgrounds to the Danielic Son of Man   169
   Who are the 'holy ones'?   179
   Synthesis   181
The historical Jesus and the Danielic Son of Man   182
   Preliminary considerations   182
   The healing of the paralytic (Mark 2.1–10 par.)   184
Summary   188

6   A re-envisaged priesthood   **190**
Sabbath-day liturgies: the grainfield controversy
(Mark 2.23–28 par.)   191
   The grainfield controversy according to Mark   193
     Jesus as a type of David   195
     The temple elite as a type of Abiathar   197
     The grainfield meal as a sacred meal   199
   The historical Jesus and the grainfield controversy   200
     Towards an explanation of Mark's handling of the grainfield
     meal   200
     Jewish conceptions of the present and future Bread of the
     Presence   201

Synthesis 204
Summary 207
Contrasting priestly approaches: Jerusalem's powerbrokers and
Jesus' peripatetics (Q 9.58 = Matt. 8.20//Luke 9.58) 207
  The homeless Son of Man 208
    Common interpretations of Q 9.58 208
    Reviving an overlooked reading: Q 9.58 as socio-political
    critique 210
    Intertextual allusions in Q 9.58 212
    Adam, Jacob and the Son of Man 216
  An alternative ethic: an excursus on the double commandment
  (Mark 12.28–34 par.) 218
  Synthesis 221
Inclusive table practices: the parable of the children in the
marketplace (Q 7.31–35 = Matt. 11.16–19//Luke 7.31–35) 223
  Hearing Jesus' voice behind the traditions 225
  Wisdom and her works (Matt. 11.16–19) 226
    The 'works' of Wisdom – whose works anyway? 226
    The complex interaction between Jesus, John and their
    disciples 227
    The double helix of Wisdom and Spirit (Matt. 11.5) 229
  Wisdom and her children (Luke 7.31–35) 231
    Luke's parable of the children in the marketplace in context 231
    The meaning of Luke's Wisdom 232
  Synthesis 234
Summary 236

7 Final confrontations 239
Introduction 239
The tribute tax for Caesar (Mark 12.13–17 par.) 240
  Problems with the standard readings of Mark 12.13–17 241
  The significance of the image and inscription 243
  The 'things of God' in Daniel 248
    The 'deep and hidden things of God' in Daniel
    (Dan. 2.20–23) 248
  The 'things of God' in Paul (1 Cor 2.1–14) 252
  The 'things of God' in Mark 255
    The 'things of God' in Mark 1—8 (Mark 8.33) 255
    The 'things of God' in Mark 12.17 257
  The 'things of God' in the setting of Jesus 260
The trial of Jesus (Mark 14.53–65 par.) 261
  The trial narrative in its Markan context 262
  The trial as a historical problem 266
  The verbal exchange at the trial 269
    Questions surrounding Jesus' final statement (Mark 14.62) 269

Contents

The interrogation (Mark 14.55–59)   272
The nature of Jesus' blasphemy (Mark 14.62)   273
Summary   280

Conclusion   **282**

Bibliography   291
Index of ancient and biblical sources   325
Index of modern authors   336
Index of subjects   343

Preface

One of the great paradoxes of the history of biblical interpretation is the fact that the study of the historical Jesus began to take flight in a particular moment of intellectual history when many of the words and actions attributed to Jesus were suddenly being called into question. Indeed, it was precisely this tension, between the extraordinary events reported by the Evangelists and the Enlightenment's commitment to the critical sifting of fact from fiction that would eventually occasion the rise of various 'criteria of authenticity'. Had it not been for the Enlightenment, it is unlikely that scholars would have ever developed rules for adjudicating the historical reliability of things reportedly said and done by Jesus. In this respect, the discussion over historical method, which has dominated historical Jesus research even down to this day, retains the indelible genetic code of this intellectual revolution – for better or for worse, or perhaps for a little bit of both.

Of course, it hardly bears stating that the Enlightenment is a historically situated intellectual movement with its own distinctive agenda and set of assumptions. With this in mind, many over the years have objected that the Enlightenment's presuppositions about the nature of reality are *a priori* incompatible with theological positions which the Church has adopted since antiquity. Time and again, such theologically minded objectors have asked, 'But if Jesus really is divine as well as human, then hasn't the historically oriented quest of the historical Jesus started us off on the wrong foot by asking us to construct a Christology from below, as opposed to a Christology from above?' While a question like this is certainly valid on some level, I wonder if the very framing of the question in these terms – if the very categories of 'Christology from below' and 'Christology from above' – are actually not themselves highly distortive, owing more to Western dualism than to the milieu in which the Jesus movement first took shape. What if, more specifically, in the theologians' very attempt to save Jesus from the treacherous jaws of the 'downstairs' of empirical history by making his primary space the 'upstairs' of metaphysical speculation, they have unwittingly aggravated matters? What if the dualism standing behind the upstairs–downstairs framework for discussing Jesus actually obstructs our vision of his self-understanding and aims?

While there are at least a handful of motivations for my having written this book, one of these has to do with my conviction that, though first-century Judaism ordinarily maintained a strict Creator–creature distinction, it would not have been implausible for a high priest of that time and place to have considered himself – under the right conditions – as a human participant in the divine. This should come as no surprise. Israel's priests, much like the temples they served, were the liminal space separating the divine realm from the human realm. As such, they straddled both worlds, dynamically functioning as both the ceiling to our post-Enlightenment 'downstairs' (phenomena) and the floor to our unseen 'upstairs', and that without contradiction.

Needless to say, if the high priest was a kind of third category in which the human and divine converged, and if Jesus also regarded himself as Israel's rightful eschatological high priest, it follows that our Christology need no longer be necessarily dictated by rigid categories of 'from above' and 'from below'. The present book *largely* assumes (though not without some warrant) rather than sets out to prove the former of these two conditions: the quasi-divine character of the priesthood. It is the latter premise, Jesus' self-identity as priest, which is the main concern of this book. As I will labour to show in the pages to follow, once we locate Jesus in the role of priest *ex officio*, we are able to make much better sense not only of certain otherwise perplexing Gospel texts, but also of the historical Jesus himself. If Jesus really saw himself as a priest on the terms that I am claiming, this begins to open a third path somewhere between the two broad options currently on offer in so much of historical Jesus studies: a secular, Arian-style Jesus (Jesus was just a man – nothing more) and, on a more popular level, a vaguely docetic, Apollinarian-style Jesus (Jesus was a God-man but his humanity did not extend to his cerebral cortex). This is not to say that the results of the present project have been driven by a certain theological agenda, but rather that by doing *better* history, as I hope to do here, we will also – as a fringe benefit – be poised to do better theology.

At its core, this book is a historical work, written for historians and students of history. I will have more to say about my historical method below. But in the meantime, suffice it to say that if history matters at all, then doing history on Jesus must also matter. I am quite aware that Jesus' first biographers were hoping to register some pretty remarkable claims about their hero. I am also aware that precisely this agenda has often been taken as warrant for stretching a long swathe of yellow tape around early first-century Galilee and Jerusalem, as if to say, 'Non-History Line: Do Not Cross'. (All the while, ironically, some of the same dispensers of such yellow tape are not the least deterred from offering a highly speculative sociological reconstruction of the so-called Q community or a detailed mirror-reading of Ephesians.) For my part, I wonder if this hermeneutical trend, sustained to some extent in North America as a reaction to simplistic fundamentalist readings of the Gospels, may itself be liable to the charge of being another kind of fundamentalism.

History, like life itself, is complicated and messy. Faced with this messiness, we can either throw up our hands before we've even started (consoling ourselves with the thought that we were never meant to get 'behind the text' of the Gospels anyway); or we can attempt to construct a holistic portrait, knowing that even if some of its parts may be tentative or even flat-out wrong, there's always hope that the whole, once organized in a coherent and compelling paradigm, may have an evidentiary value that outweighs the sum of the parts. At this place in the woods of Jesus scholarship, I am no longer sure whether the path bending behind the undergrowth of the Gospel text is the road less travelled or the road more travelled – I'm not in the habit of counting noses. I am convinced, however, that neither the events of Jesus' life nor the Gospel writers' interpretations of the same are extraneous to reconstructing Jesus' aims, as these have often been made to be. Unlike most books in the historical Jesus genre, the present volume will dedicate relatively considerable space to figuring out what the Evangelists meant, even as it seeks to secure the final goal of figuring out what Jesus meant. In my judgement, in stark disagreement with the classic form critics, penetrating to the story 'behind the text' can hardly be accomplished without some sense of what is going on, compositionally, 'in the text'. No doubt that will irritate the purists among the narrative critics as well as the purists among the Jesus research guild, and for that I apologize but not necessarily with repentance. Meanwhile, for those who have been steeped in a counsel of despair when it comes to synthesizing all things dominical, may this book be one of those which says, 'Take heart!'

This volume would not have been possible without a number of people. I am grateful, first of all, to my doctoral students and certain other student friends who have been involved – from compiling the Bibliography to offering sage editorial input – in the project: Nicholas Piotrowski, David Broughton, Rhett Austin, Greg Thellman, Jeremy Otten, Susan Rieske, Peter Green, Jarrett Van Tine, Caleb Friedeman, Nathan LeMahieu and Tyran Laws. Special mention also goes to my friend and close fellow pilgrim Bryan Eklund, who willingly read chapters with extremely helpful comment; other friends I remember eagerly responded to invited elevator-speech versions of the same: Rick Richardson, Dan Treier, John Powell, David Vinson, Joan Brown and Doug Koenigsberg. Then there were my two administrative assistants over the past five years, who in the process of having this project inflicted on them now deserve honorary doctorates of their own: Valerie Austin and Jessica Tate. In the broader academy, I think of the encouragement and input of colleagues like Simon Kingston (SPCK), Jeannine Brown, Greg Beale, Wendy Cotter, Edmondo Lupieri, David Moffitt, Elizabeth Shively, Mark Alan Powell, Nathaniel Perrin, Michael Barber, Leroy Huizenga, Scott Hahn, Ben Gladd, Mark Strauss, Jon Pennington and Warren Carter – I'll stop there with trepidation, almost certain there are others I am forgetting. Especial thanks go to Tom Wright and Brant Pitre, both of whom have been great encouragers along the way; and also to Crispin Fletcher-Louis, who kindly reviewed a draft of the first half of the book and whose name is approvingly cited throughout my footnotes with almost embarrassing frequency. Philip Law also gets very honourable mention for hanging in there with me when the book became overdue (several times over).

Finally, my deepest debt of gratitude is to my immediate family: my two sons, Nathaniel and Luke, who do me so proud, and most of all, my wife

Camie. After 25 years of marriage, I have never been more grateful for her unwavering love and tireless support. With fond thoughts of her cheering me over the finish line of yet another book project, I dedicate this book to her.

Wheaton, Illinois

Abbreviations

Abbreviations for the titles of ancient sources other than the Bible follow SBL conventions.

AB	Anchor Bible
ABRL	Anchor Bible Reference Library
AGJU	Arbeiten zur Geschichte des antiken Judentums und des Urchristentums
AnBib	Analecta biblica
AnOr	Analecta orientalia
ANRW	*Aufstieg und Niedergang der römischen Welt*
AOTC	Apollos Old Testament Commentary
ASNU	Acta Seminarii Neotestamentici Upsaliensis
AThR	*Anglican Theological Review*
AYBRL	Anchor Yale Bible Reference Library
BAR	*Biblical Archaeology Review*
BASOR	*Bulletin of the American Schools of Oriental Research*
BBR	*Bulletin of Biblical Research*
BBRSup	Bulletin for Biblical Research Supplements
BECNT	Baker Exegetical Commentary on the New Testament
BETL	Bibliotheca ephemeridum theologicarum lovaniensium
Bib	*Biblica*
BibInt	*Biblical Interpretation*
BibS(N)	Biblische Studien (Neukirchen, 1951–)
BIS	Biblical Interpretation Series
BJS	Brown Judaic Studies
BN	*Biblische Notizen*
BTS	Biblical Tools and Studies
BTZ	*Berliner Theologische Zeitschrift*
BU	Biblische Untersuchungen
BW	The Bible in Its World
BWANT	Beiträge zur Wissenschaft vom Alten und Neuen Testament
BZAW	Beihefte zur Zeitschrift für die alttestamentliche Wissenschaft
BZNW	Beihefte zur Zeitschrift für die neutestamentliche Wissenschaft
CBQ	*Catholic Biblical Quarterly*
CBR	*Currents in Biblical Research*
CGTC	Cambridge Greek Testament Commentaries
CH	*Church History*
CHANE	Culture and History of the Ancient Near East
ConBOT	Coniectanea biblica: Old Testament Series

CRHP	Cahiers de la Revue d'histoire et de philosophie religieuses
CSCD	Cambridge Studies in Christian Doctrine
DSD	*Dead Sea Discoveries*
Ebib	Études bibliques
EJL	Early Judaism and Its Literature
EKKNT	Evangelisch-katholischer Kommentar zum Neuen Testament
EncJud	*Encyclopaedia Judaica* (1971)
ETL	Ephemerides theologicae lovanienses
EvQ	*Evangelical Quarterly*
ExAud	*Ex auditu*
ExpTim	*Expository Times*
FAT	Forschungen zum Alten Testament
FoiVie	*Foe et vie*
FRLANT	Forschungen zur Religion und Literatur des Alten und Neuen Testaments
HBT	*Horizons in Biblical Theology*
HeyJ	*Heythrop Journal*
HSCP	*Harvard Studies in Classical Philology*
HSS	Harvard Semitic Studies
HTKAT	Herders theologischer Kommentar zum Alten Testament
HTKNT	Herders theologischer Kommentar zum Neuen Testament
HTR	*Harvard Theological Review*
HTS	*Harvard Theological Studies*
HUCA	*Hebrew Union College Annual*
HvTSt	*Hervormde teologiese studies*
IBC	Interpretation: A Bible Commentary for Teaching and Preaching
ICC	International Critical Commentary
Int	*Interpretation*
ISFCJ	International Studies in Formative Christianity and Judaism
JAAR	*Journal of the American Academy of Religion*
JAJSup	Journal of Ancient Judaism Supplement
JANER	*Journal of Ancient Near East Religions*
JBL	*Journal of Biblical Literature*
JBTh	*Jahrbuch für biblische Theologie*
JETS	*Journal of the Evangelical Theological Society*
JGRChJ	*Journal of Greco-Roman Christianity and Judaism*
JJS	*Journal of Jewish Studies*
JSHJ	*Journal for the Study of the Historical Jesus*
JSJ	*Journal for the Study of Judaism in the Persian, Hellenistic, and Roman Periods*
JSJSup	Supplements to the Journal for the Study of Judaism
JSNT	*Journal for the Study of the New Testament*
JSNTSup	Journal for the Study of the New Testament: Supplement Series

JSOT	*Journal for the Study of the Old Testament*
JSOTSup	Journal for the Study of the Old Testament: Supplement Series
JSP	*Journal for the Study of the Pseudepigrapha*
JSPSup	Journal for the Study of the Pseudepigrapha: Supplement Series
JTS	*Journal of Theological Studies*
JudAnc	*Judaïsme Ancien*
LBS	Library of Hebrew Bible/Old Testament Studies
LD	Lectio divina
LNTS	Library of New Testament Studies
LSTS	Library of Second Temple Studies
LtSp	*Letter & Spirit*
MSU	Mitteilungen des Septuaginta-Unternehmens
NAC	New American Commentary
NedTT	*Nederlands theologisch tijdschrift*
NICNT	New International Commentary on the New Testament
NICOT	New International Commentary on the Old Testament
NIGTC	New International Greek Testament Commentary
NovT	*Novum Testamentum*
NovTSup	Supplements to Novum Testamentum
NSBT	New Studies in Biblical Theology
NTAbh	Neutestamentliche Abhandlungen
NTL	New Testament Library
NTM	New Testament Monographs
NTS	*New Testament Studies*
NTTS	New Testament Tools and Studies
OBO	Orbis biblicus et orientalis
OTL	Old Testament Library
PNTC	Pillar New Testament Commentary Series
PrTMS	Princeton Theological Monograph Series
PTMS	Pittsburgh Theological Monograph Series
RB	*Revue biblique*
RelSRev	*Religious Studies Review*
RevExp	*Review and Expositor*
RivB	*Rivista biblica italiana*
RSPT	*Revue des sciences philosophiques et théologiques*
SBEC	Studies in the Bible and Early Christianity
SBG	Studies in Biblical Greek
SBL	Studies in Biblical Literature
SBLDS	Society of Biblical Literature Dissertation Series
SBLEJL	Society of Biblical Literature Early Judaism and Its Literature
SBLMS	Society of Biblical Literature Monograph Series
SBLSP	Society of Biblical Literature Seminar Papers
SBS	Stuttgarter Bibelstudien
SBT	Studies in Biblical Theology

ScEs	*Science et esprit*
SCS	Septuagint Commentary Series
SHJ	Studying the Historical Jesus
SJ	Studia judaica
SJCA	Studies in Judaism and Christianity in Antiquity
SJLA	Studies in Judaism in Late Antiquity
SNTSMS	Society for New Testament Studies Monograph Series
SOTSMS	Society for Old Testament Studies Monograph Series
SPAW	Sitzungsberichte der preussischen Akademie der Wissenschaften
SPB	Studia post-biblica
SR	*Studies in Religion*
STDJ	Studies on the Texts of the Desert of Judah
Str-B	Strack, Hermann L., and Paul Billerbeck, *Kommentar zum Neuen Testament aus Talmud und Midrasch*. 6 vols. Munich: C. H. Beck, 1922–61
StudBL	Studies in Biblical Literature
SUNT	Studien zur Umwelt des Neuen Testaments
SVTP	Studia in Veteris Testamenti pseudepigraphica
SWBAnt	Social World of Biblical Antiquity (second series)
TANZ	Texte und Arbeiten zum nutestamentlichen Zeitalter
TB	Theologische Bücherei: Neudrucke und Berichte aus dem 20. Jahrhundert
TBei	*Theologische Beiträge*
TBN	Themes in Biblical Narrative
THKNT	Theologischer Handkommentar zum Neuen Testament
TRu	*Theologische Rundschau*
TSAJ	Texte und Studien zum antiken Judentum
TynBul	*Tyndale Bulletin*
TZ	*Theologische Zeitschrift*
VT	*Vetus Testamentum*
VTSup	Supplements to Vetus Testamentum
WBC	Word Biblical Commentary
WMANT	Wissenschaftliche Monographien zum Alten und Neuen Testament
WTJ	*Westminster Theological Journal*
WUNT	Wissenschaftliche Untersuchungen zum Neuen Testament
ZAW	*Zeitschrift für die alttestamentliche Wissenschaft*
ZNW	*Zeitschrift für die neutestamentliche Wissenschaft und die Kunde der älteren Kirche*
ZTK	*Zeitschrift für Theologie und Kirche*

Introduction

Treasures from the scrapheap

In the provocatively titled documentary *Who the *$&% Is Jackson Pollock?*, we are told the story of a 73-year-old retired lorry driver named Teri Horton whose life suddenly took a very curious turn. One day while browsing in a local charity shop in California, Horton put down five US dollars cash for a large, brightly coloured painting – just the thing, she thought, to cheer up a despondent friend. When it later became obvious that the artwork wouldn't fit inside her friend's trailer, Horton took the painting back home and put it in front of her house in hopes of making at least a few dollars back on it. Before the day was over (with no luck moving the canvas), an art teacher happened to stroll by and mused that the piece might be the handiwork of the abstract-expressionist Jackson Pollock. Even though at the time Horton had no idea who Jackson Pollock was, she decided to follow up on the suggestion by doing a little research. To make a long story short, at least if the analysis of certain forensic art experts is to be believed, the art teacher was correct: the item was – and is – a Jackson Pollock original. The 'trash' Horton had purchased for $5 has since commanded offers as high as $9 million. And thus the aphorism: 'One person's trash is another person's treasure.'

For the purposes of introducing the present book, the story of Teri Horton may serve as a parable. In response to the question 'What is the kingdom of historiography like and to what should we compare it?', one answer might go something like this: 'It is like a woman who bought a piece of artwork from a charity shop. She thought it was insignificant, but it turned out to be treasure.' Though not nearly as memorable as any of Jesus' parables, such a parable just might illustrate the truth that the study of history tends to advance not so much through the fresh discovery of new data but through a fresh re-evaluation of that which has been set aside.

A tale of two Jesus scholars: Schweitzer and Bultmann

The principle certainly applies to one memorable passage from Albert Schweitzer's 1906 classic, *The Quest of the Historical Jesus*. Here, in his dialogue with the Old Liberalism of Albrecht Ritschl's school, Schweitzer takes his interlocutors to task for their neglect of Jesus traditions relating to predicted suffering. For these colleagues, lamentably so, 'the prediction of suffering has as little to do with objective history as the prediction of the parousia'.[1]

---

[1] Schweitzer 2001 (1906): 329.

Yet, according to Schweitzer, the widespread assumption of this material's inauthenticity had more than a little to do with the fact that Jesus' anticipation of suffering did not integrate well with the standard reconstruction of Old Liberalism:

> Consequently, none of the Lives of Jesus which follow the lines of a natural psychology, from Weisse down to Oskar Holtzmann, can make anything of it. They either strike it out, or transfer it to the last 'gloomy epoch' of the life of Jesus, regard it as an unintelligible anticipation, or put it down to the account of 'community theology', which serves as a scrap-heap for everything for which they cannot find a place in the 'historical life of Jesus'.[2]

With this poignant metaphor of the 'scrap-heap', powerfully descriptive as it is penetratingly insightful, Schweitzer explains how and why the nineteenth-century Lives had sanitized the 'Jesus story' of suffering. At the turn of the twentieth century, Schweitzer had the perspicacity to recognize that the discussion surrounding the historical Jesus had been unduly constrained by a Kantian idealism which left little room for such larger-than-life portraits of Jesus, dripping with dark premonitions and gloomy experiences. Even if Ritschl's heirs could find it within their hearts to grant authenticity to these foreboding streaks on the canvas of the Gospels, they wouldn't know what to make of them. Steeped in their zeitgeist, such thinkers did not have the categories for even countenancing the possibility that Jesus' experience and anticipation of suffering were actually the very method of his madness.

Parting company with his interlocutors at this juncture, just as he had parted ways with Old Liberalism's eschatology by insisting that Jesus was indeed looking forward to the imminent transformation of the cosmos, Schweitzer assigned considerable significance to the Jewish background of the 'Great Tribulation'. For our Alsatian author, it was precisely this anticipated event, a scenario of apostasy and suffering leading up to the messianic dawn, that explained not only Jesus' determination to 'turn his face towards Jerusalem' but also his willingness to accept the grim fate awaiting him. However, as Schweitzer's reconstruction would have it, Jesus would in the end experience sharp cognitive dissonance between his expectation of events and the reality which actually unfolded. As Jesus expires on the cross, he realizes that the much-anticipated tribulation had not climaxed in the way he had hoped. God had neither come to the rescue nor brought about the kingdom, leaving Jesus to die a disillusioned man.

But what if Schweitzer was essentially right about Jesus? What if Jesus did expect God to install a new cosmic order in a moment of crisis? How are we to reconcile this with his ethical teachings, which seem to imply their own ongoing relevance? At this juncture one might have expected Schweitzer, given his distinctive understanding of Jesus' eschatology, to

---

[2] Schweitzer 2001 (1906): 329.

2

attribute the Gospels' ethical materials to later ecclesial redaction. But instead our author boldly declares that these teachings are but an 'interim ethic', a kind of *ad hoc* measure temporarily implemented in preparation for the end of the present world order. And so: historical problem solved. But then this reconstruction creates problems of other sorts, namely, that since the 'interim' on Schweitzer's scenario could have only been a matter of months, we can hardly suppose that these same makeshift norms would have had anything meaningful to say to the great moral questions of his day – much less ours. On Schweitzer's reading, Jesus was far more interested in announcing his apocalyptic vision than in conveying a well-ordered set of moral teachings; consequently, the master's ethical materials quickly consign themselves to theological irrelevance.

Perhaps like Shakespeare's queen who 'protests too much', the initial reception of *The Quest of the Historical Jesus* was overwhelmingly negative; Schweitzer's reviewers subjected his methods and conclusions to withering criticism. Today, with the luxury of more than a hundred years of hindsight, we can still agree that a number of these initial criticisms were justified. But by the same token, the clarity afforded by time has also allowed us to see that Schweitzer had become an *enfant terrible* in his day largely because he had, very unconventionally, smeared paint strokes on the conventional portrait of Jesus. The result was a portrait that raised serious questions about Jesus' theological relevance. (What after all could be more irrelevant than a historical figure who was flat-out wrong in regards to his central conviction?) Equally troubling was Schweitzer's representation of a wild and woolly, if not capricious, Jesus, one who ultimately defined himself by contingent crises, persecution and suffering. Neither good taste nor Kantian idealism had much tolerance for such things.

Notwithstanding the furore provoked by the *Quest*, Schweitzer's recourse to ancient Jewish apocalyptic as a way of explaining Jesus' vision of suffering has retained an enduring historical plausibility. The account has proven to be so plausible in fact that nine decades later N. T. Wright was able to declare that the *Schweitzerstraße*, one of two major avenues for twentieth-century Jesus research, was still open to considerable traffic. But the *Schweitzerstraße* would have never become anything more than a bramble-covered footpath, had Schweitzer not retrieved Jesus' suffering from the scrapheap of history. Contemporary critics of Schweitzer may continue to doubt the authenticity of this piece, even as some art critics continue to doubt the authenticity of Horton's alleged Pollock, but no matter. The point has been made and is still very much on the table, awaiting further discussion. A critical mass of Jesus scholars have come to agree that suffering occupied a prominent place in Jesus' consciousness, but we have not sufficiently explored why.

The great Rudolf Bultmann was among the next generation of Jesus scholars obliged to engage Schweitzer's thesis directly or indirectly. Publishing his *Theology of the New Testament* a half-century and two world wars after Schweitzer's epic contribution, Bultmann was convinced of an apocalyptic Jesus in principle, but was careful to stipulate – against his predecessor's thoroughgoing apocalypticism – that Jesus' vision really pertained neither to the end of the current order nor to the ushering in of new political realities. Instead, on his reconstruction, Jesus had transposed the apocalyptic moment into a call for decision, requiring the individual to stand before God in a posture of absolute dependence and radical obedience. In taking this approach, Bultmann was attempting to distance himself from two fronts. Against, on the one side, the Jesus of Old Liberalism, depicted now by the likes of Adolf von Harnack (for whom the kingdom was largely a matter of personal formation) or Walter Rauschenbusch (for whom the kingdom was a renewed social-political order), the Marburger insisted that the historical Jesus' message was characteristically apocalyptic; against, on the other side, those who like Schweitzer emphasized Jesus' apocalypticism, he was equally firm that the synoptic reports of Jesus' rabbinic-style ethical concerns could not have very well been tacked on by the same Church which declared him as Risen Christ. Yet like Schweitzer, Bultmann also believed that the only finally convincing account of the historical Jesus was one which maintained a basic unity between his eschatology and his ethics. Such unity was forthcoming, so he argued, on the premise that all of Jesus' ethical teachings were eschatological in the sense that they were backed by the timeless demand of God on the individual. Thus, for Bultmann the existential crisis remained paramount: 'All that man can do in the face of the Reign of God now breaking in is this: Keep ready or get ready for it. Now is the *time of decision*, and Jesus' call is the *call to decision*'.[3]

Though Bultmann would also eventually distance himself from his friend and Marburg colleague Martin Heidegger, the former's emphasis on individual decision had been much influenced by the latter. In the period between the wars, the sense of alienation generated by overwhelming socio-economic and political forces spawned the felt need for a fresh philosophical assertion of human freedom, much as Heidegger's existentialist philosophy was able to provide. Now, in his post-war *Theology of the New Testament*, Bultmann sought to apply the same existential grid to Jesus. This was plausible at first blush simply because, as our author points out, the Gospel records are replete with indications that Jesus was constantly calling his hearers to *decide*. And although the call to ethical decision was certainly not absent from Old Liberalism's moral suasion theories of Jesus, these accounts did not come close to explaining, as Bultmann had so magnificently done, the sense of urgent crisis pervading the dominical materials. Like Schweitzer before him, Bultmann had at least recognized the inherent persuasiveness of a vision that could do justice to the breadth – apocalyptic and sapiential wisdom material alike – of the synoptic tradition. But in order to achieve such a vision, it would be necessary to rescue not Jesus' suffering but his call for decision from

---

[3] Bultmann 1951: 9.

the scrapheap of history. Once again: one Jesus scholar's trash is another Jesus scholar's treasure.

In offering their respective unified theories of the Jesus traditions, both Schweitzer and Bultmann were each in their own way attempting to resolve what is perhaps *the* central problem of historical Jesus studies: the tension between Jesus as sage (speaker of universal truths) and Jesus as apocalyptic prophet (predictor of future cataclysmic events). We barely need to restate the problem. If the historical Jesus' principal concern was ethics, how could his moral teaching have been conceivably informed by the end of the space–time continuum (unless we are to suppose, lamely, that Jesus lingered on these looming eschatological realities merely to convey a little extra urgency)? Conversely, if Jesus' main interest was in the apocalypse, then what lasting relevance could there have been in moral ruminations? While one common strategy (before and after the period of Schweitzer and Bultmann) for solving this dilemma has been to assign the apocalyptic material to one stage in the formation of the synoptic tradition and the sapiential material to another, neither writer was willing to go this route. (Perhaps they both sensed the inevitable circularity of an argument which conveniently escapes through the back door of a traditions-history argument wherever the paradigm incurs counter-indications.) For his part, Schweitzer's solution to this dilemma was to reframe Jesus' ethical message as a subsidiary crater of the imminent eschatological crisis, an event which finally turned out to be the great non-event. By contrast, Bultmann's solution was to redefine (demythologize) the eschatological moment as the everlastingly present moment, which had the effect of severing moral reflection from one's location in the time–space continuum. Despite coming to radically different conclusions regarding the nature of Jesus' programme, both Schweitzer and Bultmann instinctively sensed that the best solution to the problem posed by the ethics and eschatology of Jesus is one which effectively integrates both.

Schweitzer and Bultmann revisited

The present book is, among other things, an attempt to revisit the same integrative project undertaken by Schweitzer and Bultmann. In doing so, I propose to retrieve certain components of their reconstructions, components which, though seemingly now right back on the scrapheap in more contemporary Jesus scholarship, deserve serious reconsideration. For the purposes of my project, I look to each writer in two respects. First, with Schweitzer I intend to take seriously the crucial importance of the tribulation within the self-understanding of the historical Jesus. Second, again alongside Schweitzer, I will entertain the possibility that Jesus was not so much interested in promulgating a universal norm ('universal' in the sense of being true at all times, for all persons and in all places) but rather in conveying an ethical message which, though eventually lending itself well to being principalized in different directions, was in the first instance intended to apply to the specific conditions occasioned by the tribulation. Issued as a guide for negotiating the current trials in the current eschatological crisis, Jesus' teachings were fundamentally eschatological in nature. Third, with Bultmann I will agree that Jesus' message implicated its hearers in a crisis of decision, demanding urgent response. The very nature of his challenge, implicit in his teachings, left no room for aloof detachment or hedging deferment: the time was now. Fourth and finally, again with the author of *Theology of the New Testament*, I will maintain that this enjoined decision was a totalizing and self-involving decision. Jesus' instruction was not offered as a bit of for-what-it's-worth advice but a call for absolute self-surrender. The only platform for working out that self-surrender was the controversial, even socially scandalous, community now taking shape around Jesus.

So much for my disclosed points of agreement with Schweitzer and Bultmann, but there are also critical junctures at which I will also disagree. First, Schweitzer's account of tribulation is far too rough and unpolished a fixture to function properly within Jesus' mental apparatus. While this book does not undertake a thorough critique of Schweitzer on this point, it can be said for now that there is no evidence that ancient Judaism coupled tribulation and divine intervention with the same chronological tightness that Schweitzer's Jesus did.[4] Consequently, to make my second point, as ingenious as Schweitzer's theory of the 'interim ethic' may be, it turns out to be entirely unnecessary. I can agree that 'interim ethics' may be a fitting description for Jesus' moral teachings, so long as we can stay flexible on the duration of 'interim', which for Jesus was an indefinite period. Third, whereas I agree with Bultmann on the critical nature of Jesus' call for decision, I will disagree on the substance of that decision. Against the Marburger, who believed that both Jesus' call and the enlisted response were individualized transactions easily abstracted from the historical context, I maintain that Jesus' call to decision was his summons to join his society, with its own distinctive ways of thinking and doing. True, Jesus' invitation was extended to the individual, but it was an invitation which demanded as an initial step personal solidarity with a specific social reality, the Jesus movement itself. Fourth, on a related note, though Bultmann's Jesus has far more to say about the individual's vertical commitments than their horizontal commitments, I believe that the historical Jesus' conception of absolute surrender had a vertical *and* a horizontal aspect, demanding that self-surrender unto God be expressed through self-surrender unto the community – and vice versa. The notional intersection between these axes was nothing less than the vocation Jesus imposed.

Gleaning the most promising insights of both Schweitzer and Bultmann, while setting aside the less promising, I intend to renew their project of integrating eschatology and ethics. The key to this integration begins by

---

[4] The definitive book on Jesus and the tribulation is still Pitre 2005.

describing Jesus in *priestly terms*. By stating that Jesus was 'priestly', I am not proposing that he laid claim to an officially sanctioned Levitical or Zadokite or Hasmonean office, but rather that he represented himself as taking on certain priestly *functions* notwithstanding his lack of conventional qualifications. These functions pointed to the onset of a divinely initiated process through which Jesus would become and in some sense already had become the eschatological high priest.

In maintaining Jesus' sacerdotal self-understanding, I do not rule out the possibility that he also thought of himself as a prophet and messianic king. Indeed, although I won't take the time to make a thorough argument to this effect, in my view – as will become clear – it is highly likely that Jesus considered himself to be both. My relative neglect of the messianic category in particular is not meant to indicate its relative (un)importance in Jesus' mind. Yet I am writing this book to offset a particular problem: while scholars will regularly sling around terms like 'messiah' or 'messianic', and then unselfconsciously shift over to seemingly interchangeable terms like 'king' or 'royal', we still have hardly begun to elucidate how the Jewish messianic concept, variegated as it was, *brought together the royal aspects and priestly aspects*. To anticipate myself, I am convinced that in many a first-century mind the ultimate significance of the promise of Davidic restoration lay not in its implications of political autonomy (as important as autonomy might be) but in its cultic entailments, for as pressing as the problem of Roman occupation might have been, even more acute was the festering defilement of the temple. Along the same lines, in the imagination of the first-century pious, the final significance of the expected messiah was not in his vanquishing of Israel's political foes (again, as important as this piece might have been) but in his renewing of temple space. The point is hardly extraordinary. I trust it will come as no shock when I suggest that the Jews of Jesus' day did *not* stand in the streets of Jerusalem, chanting the Aramaic equivalent of 'Liberty, Equality, Fraternity'. Likewise, I hope that it would not be the height of scandal if I were to suggest that ancient Israel never held out political autonomy as a moral end unto itself. For Israel the point was not political autonomy but its chief concomitants: a politically unified theocracy unburdened by the authority and ideology of foreign gods – crucial pieces for a finally functioning temple. As important as Jesus' royal messianic aspect may be, the evidence suggests that he subordinated his royal identity to his primary identity as priest. Jesus sought to implement not a theocracy but a hierocracy under the God of Israel.

A few notes of explanation

For those conversant with contemporary historical Jesus studies, the account which I am proposing – if not the very title of this book, *Jesus the Priest* – may come as something of a surprise. After all, while Jesus' self-consciousness of his messiahship has been both touted and denied, neither the affirmers nor the deniers on this issue have been generally willing to identify Jesus in priestly terms. 'Jesus as priest' may be a well-worn concept for students of the biblical book of Hebrews; not so much for those in the historical Jesus trade. For this reason, even in writing this book, I confess to feeling a little like Paul on the way to the Areopagus (Acts 17), half-expecting that some half-incredulous readers will pick up the book whispering to themselves, 'What is this babbler trying to say?', while others will consider my basic argument with a critical open-mindedness, as if to say, 'May we know what this new teaching is that you are presenting?' But in arguing for Jesus as a priest, I am not so much making a brand-new argument as making an argument that has not yet, for whatever reason, received the traction that it's due.

With that in mind, it may be helpful to speak not only to the context of the present project, but also to certain contemporary socio-historical contexts that may help us better understand a 'whatever reason' here and there. In writing the current book, I am offering the second instalment of a three-volume trilogy. In the anticipated third book, *Jesus the Sacrifice*, I intend to explore Jesus' death and the meaning – to tip my hand on this point already – which Jesus assigned to it. I mention this as part of a caveat: while some readers of the present tome may be frustrated by my occasional use of words like 'atonement' without fully explaining what I mean, I beg their patience ahead of time with the good hopes of their seeing the full case face to face in volume three. Meanwhile, in my earlier book *Jesus the Temple* (2010), I advanced a case similar to but not identical with the one being made here. To summarize the first book in this trilogy, I argued that the Jesus movement was a counter-temple movement whose most defining moment occurred with the so-called cleansing of the temple. In addition, I maintained that various activities characteristically attributed to Jesus in the tradition, including exorcism, healings and feedings, are best interpreted as counter-temple activities. While the present volume is a continuation of the project which began with *Jesus the Temple*, my argument here does not materially depend on the arguments marshalled there. Making minimal recourse to the first volume, *Jesus the Priest* offers a different argument on a different trove of evidence. As will become clear enough to readers of *Jesus the Temple*, the present book also retains a somewhat different thrust and methodology. In terms of scope of materials, the principal difference between this book and its predecessor is that while the earlier volume focused primarily on Jesus' actions, the current book concerns itself more with Jesus' words (with the exception of Chapter 2 which focuses on Jesus' baptism, in which case we are dealing with the alleged voice from heaven). In terms of focus, while *Jesus the Temple* was principally concerned with Jesus' quest for renewed sacred space, this present volume will attend more to how he and his followers self-consciously functioned as proleptic priests within that quest. I would like to think of the two books as complementary, sometimes overlapping but far from redundant.

That the essential argument of *Jesus the Temple* has been reviewed but unrebutted, I trust, provides initial warrant for the basic premise of *Jesus the Priest*. But as I have already hinted, in taking up this line of argument I am hardly standing alone in the field. Others have written persuasively on this topic. For some, the particulars of their arguments and/or their conclusions are somewhat different from mine; for others, the overlaps are quite close.[5] Still others have written on the topic and I share many of their judgements. Perhaps like Teri Horton, who was emboldened by the musings of an art teacher passing by, I too have been encouraged by the musings of other scholars who are now seeing many of the same things I have been seeing. In writing this book, as well as its prequel, I am hoping to set out (for many) a new and (for some) an unusual portrait of Jesus for both a semi-popular readership and the guild alike.

Even so, perhaps an explanatory word or two is in order as to why the particular angle I am exploring appears to be such a *novum*. I think there are a number of complex reasons for this, but I will try my hand at naming a few of them. In the first place, I believe that ancient Judaism's long-overdue makeover, set into motion by E. P. Sanders' *Paul and Palestinian Judaism* and continuing in discussions surrounding the New Perspective on Paul, has yet to make its full impact on historical Jesus studies.[6] If Sanders insisted that the twentieth-century study of Paul had been warped by its reliance on inaccurate and fundamentally anti-Judaistic portrayals of ancient Judaism, the sub-discipline of Pauline studies seems to have heard the implicit call to repentance. In recent years, I notice that when the same set of concerns is raised in historical Jesus studies, it regularly appears in connection with allegations of supersessionism or replacement theology, that is, a reconstruction which envisions the Church as a replacement for Israel. While I have been accused by at least one reviewer of peddling a form of supersessionism in publishing *Jesus the Temple* (and may perhaps receive the same criticism in relation to *Jesus the Priest*), I dispute the charge but nevertheless find a certain irony in the fact that it has been the anti-Judaistic tendencies latent within so much twentieth-century scholarship that has long impeded the very thesis I am seeking to advance. Here we need to go no further than Bultmann's above-discussed *Theology of the New Testament*, where he not uncharacteristically writes:

> Polemic against the temple cult is completely absent from the words of Jesus. As a matter of fact it, too, had essentially lost its original meaning in his time; for Judaism was no longer a cultic religion, but had become a religion of observance.[7]

---

[5] All this will become clear enough in the footnotes. For now, see Friedrich 1956; Sanders 1985; Meyer 1992; 2002 (1979); Chilton 1992; 1996; Wright 1996; Fletcher-Louis 1997b; 2000; 2006; 2007b; Tan 1997; Bryan 2002; Pitre 2005; 2008; 2015; Klawans 2006; Barber 2013b. This isn't even to touch on the burgeoning literature on the centrality of the temple in the Old Testament; see, e.g., the collection in Morales 2014.

[6] Sanders 1977.

[7] Bultmann 1951: 17.

With the disparaging phrase 'religion of observance' Bultmann of course means that Judaism had devolved to a religion of meaningless externalities. Accordingly, the day-to-day operations of the cult and the life of the temple had become nothing more than a trifling legal formality – and therefore virtually irrelevant not only to many pious Jews who deserve better but also to Jesus himself (good neo-Kantian that he was). Sentiments such as Bultmann's are exactly the kind of thing Sanders has in mind when he draws up his excoriating and broad-sweeping indictment. But sentiments such as these also explain why the vast bulk of Jesus scholarship has neglected the temple, despite clear indications in the Second-Temple literature of its utmost significance, in its reconstruction of Jesus. Is it going too far to suggest that the current disregard of Israel's cultus within contemporary Jesus studies is at least indirectly related to the anti-Judaistic (and therefore anti-cultic) paradigm instantiated in Bultmann? I think not. For my part, I believe, hope and trust that the current project actually stands near the culmination of guild-wide effort to escape the (conscious or unconscious) anti-Judaism of our academic forebears and to allow Jesus to be a fully fledged Jew of his time.

If anti-Judaistic thinking has been one of the scandalous skeletons in New Testament scholarship's closet, the other remaining set of bones – and perhaps, to cite Philip Jenkins' title, 'the last acceptable prejudice' – is the anti-Catholic tenor of the last two hundred years of Protestant-dominated scholarship.[8] This point, I think, is commonly enough observed that it hardly needs demonstrating.[9] As a Protestant scholar, I suspect that much of the inertia surrounding Jesus' interest in the cultic has at least something to do with Protestants' characteristic disinterest in the same topic. I am not alone in this suspicion. In her book *Anti-Cultic Theology in Christian Biblical Interpretation: A Study of Isaiah 66:1–4 and Its Reception*, Valerie A. Stein speaks to this point when she comments how it is

> evident that Protestant anti-cultic theology is reflected in interpretations of Isa 66:1–4 in the Modern Era, including in historical-critical scholarship. The anti-cultic attitude is rooted in the theology of Martin Luther. Protestant scholars have dominated modern biblical scholarship until recently. This is especially true for German scholarship of the late 19th and early 20th centuries, which is still influential today. Aversion to ritual dominates this scholarship. Sometimes these attitudes take the form of a preference for prophetic and Deuteronomistic material (which is often identified closely with Christianity) over Priestly material (which is identified with Judaism).[10]

Stein's remarks pertaining to the reception history of Isaiah 66 may perhaps, with only slight modification, be extended to the modern-day quest of the

---

[8] See Jenkins 2003.
[9] For an overview of literature investigating anti-Catholic urges in nineteenth-century culture and thought, see Drury 2001.
[10] Stein 2006: 4.

historical Jesus. Is it far-fetched to imagine that, despite all its pretensions of scientific objectivity, Protestant-dominated Jesus research for the past two hundred years has unconsciously yet systemically downplayed Jesus' priestly aspect? Hardly. If studies show that business recruiters tend to hire people like themselves again and again, Protestant Jesus scholars have likewise been unconsciously attracted to a very Protestant Jesus again and again.

As readers we can hardly extract ourselves from our own social locations, but with a little self-awareness we can at least put *some* critical distance between our scholarship and our culturally conditioned biases, just as we can reflect self-critically on our pre-theoretical assumptions. Call me naive, but I am enough of a modernist to believe that, with a measure of intellectual honesty, escape from solipsism remains possible. As responsible readers of history, we are not entirely doomed to the vicious circle of our self-referential universe. My hope in writing this book is no different from the hope of any author: that its readers will be able to set aside constraining prejudices (not least anti-Catholic and anti-Judaistic biases) and judge its merits by the overall strength of the argument.

A word on method

At the present moment, many sense that the quest of the historical Jesus is lurching towards a cul-de-sac which will soon be requiring us to wheel around and try a different route. The present impasse is both methodological and substantive, fraught with unresolved issues involving criteria and interpretative judgements, stymied by controverted questions of 'How can we know?' and 'What do we know?' Confidence in the once tried-and-true tools of critical scholarship has eroded; conventional methodologies, like an old bridge failing the engineers' annual inspection, are no longer being trusted to bear the evidentiary load they once had carried.[11] For some, such developments sound like the final tolling of the bells for historical Jesus scholarship. I demur. As long as we can agree that Jesus of Nazareth existed in time and space, we should continue to work towards a mutually agreed-upon means by which we might access this figure historically. Obviously, the old positivistic approaches will no longer do. But it is equally obvious that a radical scepticism regarding the possibility of retrieving meaningful facts about Jesus is simply the reverse side of the coin of this old positivism. Then there are those who oppose historical Jesus studies out of a theologically high-minded commitment to the canonical text, over and against any attempted reconstructions behind the text. I find such a posture unconvincing. To deny the possibility of meaningful reflection on the historical Jesus in principle is to commit oneself ahead of time to a version of Docetism.

Nevertheless, convinced that we will soon need some new options on

---

[11] See, e.g., Sanders 1998; Holmén 2002; Rodríguez 2009; Wedderburn 2010: 161–82; Allison 2010: 3–30; Keith and LeDonne 2012.

both fronts, I attempt in this book to go in a new direction by offering a microhistory of Jesus. By undertaking a microhistory I intentionally restrict myself to a very limited number of source texts, largely undisputed as reflecting the setting of Jesus, all the while seeking to ask, in the words of Charles Joyner, 'large questions in small places'.[12] There are inherent advantages to such selectivity. First, by relying on materials which the critical consensus has already assigned to the dominical setting, I stand a better chance of convincing the full breadth of my readers, including those who are relatively reluctant to credit Jesus with material ascribed to him in the Gospels. Accordingly, as I approach the authenticity of the various pericopae, I will normally be able to get by with little more than a nod to the trump cards of scholarly opinion. In the few places where I rely on a controverted tradition (Chapter 4), I intend to play out the hand by the current rules of the game. In this way, I hope to demonstrate that my case can be successfully established on the so-called 'critical minimum' of authentic Jesus tradition – without requiring lines of evidence that some would, for source-critical or form-critical reasons, regard as dubious. And so, just as Paul sought to make his point at the Areopagus on the basis of a very few but very well-accepted texts, I will be employing a fairly limited range of texts as a baseline, involving not many more than a dozen passages from the Jesus tradition. The added benefit of this approach is that it avoids the methodological quagmire that even sometimes taxes the patience of professional Jesus scholars. I justify this approach to the historical Jesus in the hope that the famous dictum of Ludwig Mies van der Rohe will prove true: 'Less is more.'

Second, by limiting the number of texts under consideration, I also hope to avoid the all-too-common mistake of rushing isolated texts (pericopae, sub-units, etc.) on and off the stage, impressing them into a chorus of 'standard' but sometimes misguided readings, and all the while failing to do exegetical justice to any of them. And so, compared to many of its counterparts in the genre, this book will offer a relatively deep reading of the biblical texts. This will involve synthesizing the web of insights garnered from composition criticism, redaction criticism, socio-historical backgrounds, and the study of the Hebrew Bible. While negotiating the relationship between these vertices will be complicated enough, I will be particularly interested in exploring Jesus' voice as a centralizing theme behind synoptic variation, as well as in reconstructing the dialogue between Jesus' sayings and their invoked scriptural traditions. If we allow for the possibility that Jesus, along with the Jews of his day, gleaned from these scriptures a roughly coherent narrative, the main talking points of what Schweitzer calls a 'dogmatic history', this puts us in a position to interpret Jesus' aims in the light of that narrative. I am fully aware that for some of my dialogue partners this approach will draw charges of 'metanarrative' (the great bogeyman of postmodernity) and

---

[12] Joyner 1999: 1.

'maximalist reading'. But then again, it is too often these same critics who either refuse to advance a constructive account of their own (and in this sense may be cheerful consistent minimalists but are nonetheless contributing nothing positive to the discussion), or sneak in a hopelessly maximalist reading on another front, involving, say, some highly detailed social agenda on Jesus' part, or well-detailed 'Q community', or something of the sort. My basic defence and the premise of my argument is that Jesus took the Hebrew scriptures extremely seriously, and to the degree that contemporary accounts of the historical Jesus fail to take this point seriously, I believe, they will be all the more off point. I therefore also believe that in order to understand Jesus' aims, we must be willing to engage in a deep but historically disciplined reading of the Scriptures.

My argument proceeds on two concurrent levels: one largely cumulative and the other linear. In the cumulative thread of my argument, I provide a fresh reading of the aforementioned blocks of Jesus tradition by paying attention to certain – often seemingly minor – textual details, presumably reflective of Jesus' oral utterances. Focusing first on the Lord's Prayer and its scriptural subtexts, I set forth a working hypothesis that Jesus identified his movement as a priestly movement, tasked with ushering in the renewed cultic space promised in Ezekiel 36 (Chapter 1). In subsequent chapters, this hypothesis is then tested with reference to other dominical texts; moving from the peripheral textual detail to the big picture, my approach remains inductive throughout. Meanwhile, the unearthing of new clues gives rise to new questions, leading to the acquisition of even more clues, followed by a new set of questions, and so it goes across the chapters – all, I hope, in growing support of my overall argument.

In principle, this approach is not unlike the one adopted by the Italian microhistorian Carlo Ginzburg, who justifies his method as follows:

> Historians cannot help sometimes referring back (explicitly or by implication) to comparable series of phenomena; but their strategy of finding things out, like the volumes in which they present their work, is basically about particular cases, whether concerning individuals, or social groups, or whole societies. In this way history is like medicine, which uses disease classifications to analyse the specific illness of a particular patient. And *the historian's knowledge*, like the doctor's, *is indirect, based on signs and scraps of evidence, conjectural.*[13]

For physicians and murder-mystery detectives alike, as well as for historians of Christian origins, sometimes the surest path to discovery begins not with a grand theory but with a journey that looks carefully at the isolated parts one at a time in the hopes of finding a connective thread. Likewise, in undertaking a text-centred microhistory of the Jesus tradition, I find that certain deceptively inconsequential details of the tradition eventually force

---

[13] Ginzburg 1980: 16; emphasis added.

some major questions about the historical Jesus' cultic interests. On 'the systematic gathering of these "small insights"' (to quote Ginsburg quoting the great eighteenth-century art historian J. J. Winckelmann), drawn from passages which are regularly regarded as conveying not just the words but the very pulse of Jesus, I seek to trace a series of lines from the capillaries of isolated textual phenomena back – often by an admittedly circuitous route – to the main arteries of Jesus' aims, and on to the heart valves of his movement.[14] There is a theory behind this approach. In penetrating the thought world of a bygone age, it is often the implicit assumptions *behind* the surviving texts rather than the assertions *within* them that proves most useful. To be sure, a microhistorical approach to Jesus is not unencumbered by the potentially problematic issue of selectivity (why are we talking about *this* saying or episode rather than *that* one?), but concerns over the privileging of certain data and the implicit demotion of other data (inevitable in any historical study) should be somewhat mitigated as the clues begin to take on a voice of their own. Once the authentic tradition's cultic metaphors and narratives are properly coordinated, the case for a self-consciously priestly Jesus becomes compelling.

The second and more linear layer of my two-fold argument also begins in Chapter 1. My point of departure begins with noting the evidentiary weakness for the traditional explanation for Jesus' identification of God as 'Father'. Against the commonly held theory that Jesus called on God primarily on the basis of inward personal experience or feeling, I suggest that Jesus' distinctive naming of the divine was occasioned by a redemptive-historical analogy, operationalized by Jesus himself, between his persecuted disciples and the exodus generation persecuted under Pharaoh. Just as the trials (*peirasmoi*) of the exodus would be the means by which Israel, precisely as son of god (Exod. 4.22–23), would actualize its elect role as a 'kingdom of priests' (19.6); so too, Jesus' followers were to realize their sonship and priesthood through suffering. This observation lays the groundwork for Chapter 2, where I find evidence that when Jesus was identified as the 'son of God' at his baptism, this title was intended to convey his function as imminent high priest. Then, building on Chapter 3, Chapters 4–6 attempt to resolve how Jesus' filial status relates to his alleged title as 'Son of David', as well as to his also alleged title 'Son of Man': here I will argue that both of these titles denote a priestly function that has thus far been seldom appreciated. Finally, in Chapter 7, history testifies to the confrontational quality of Jesus' identification with the Son of Man.

The book closes out with a recapitulation of some of the most important implications of my argument, historical and theological. For those who take up this book out of a purely historical interest, I hope I will have provided an intriguing new point of departure for understanding Jesus. For those whose

---

[14] Ginsburg 1989: 105.

primary interest lies in the sphere of theology, there will probably be more than a few points of relevance along the way, that is, after a little connecting of the dots on the theologian's part. Meanwhile, I hope and trust that those who read this book out of both a historical and a theological concern will be well served on both fronts. If Jesus is the priest and was so in his lifetime, the historical and theological ramifications are far-ranging indeed. Whether I have successfully established this thesis I will leave to the reader to judge.

1

The prayer of Jesus

Introduction

It is a truth universally acknowledged that any single, young faith-tradition in possession of at least a few adherents and some longevity must be in want of marrying itself to certain defining practices. The early Church is no exception. Judging by our sources, the most central of these must have been baptism and the Lord's Supper. But right up alongside these two was yet another practice integral to the life of the Church: the recitation of the *Pater Noster* (*PN*) or the Lord's Prayer. The late first-century *Didache* called for the repeating of the Lord's Prayer three times a day (*Did.* 8.2). The second-century church father Tertullian summarized the petition as an 'abridgement of the entire gospel', and summoned believers to preface their own personal prayers with the words of this prayer (*Or.* 1). A third-century Carthaginian bishop by the name of Cyprian labelled it as 'a compendium of heavenly doctrine' (*Dom. or.* 9). Finally, the late fourth-century *Apostolic Constitutions* (7.44) required that the Lord's Prayer be uttered while standing, much as Jews for centuries had recited the Amidah. Even though the canonical writings record no instance of the early Church reciting the Lord's Prayer, by the post-apostolic era the repeated words had already become well entrenched in its liturgical life.

The broad and enduring reception of the Lord's Prayer in the early Church provides a convenient point of departure for assessing its significance in the life of the historical Jesus. Whether it was Matthew and Luke who more accurately preserved the petition as they found it in Q or whether, as is more likely, both fell back on a shared oral tradition, it is noteworthy that this is the only prayer which Jesus is recorded as having enjoined upon his disciples. This in turn provides the best explanation for the theological and liturgical prominence of the Lord's Prayer in the life of the early Church: the disciples, having received the prayer directly from Jesus and having committed themselves to repeating it dutifully on a regular basis, set the standard for subsequent church practice. In following years, the prayer would continue to be sustained in ecclesial memory through regular, communal repetition – as it is even today. This does not mean that Jesus' full prayer can be confidently reconstructed on an exact word-for-word basis as he first gave it in the Aramaic (occasional difficulties in the Greek together with obvious differences between the Matthean and Lukan versions render this project problematic). Nevertheless, given good reason to believe that a verbal core of the Gospel accounts goes directly back to the historical Jesus, a reconstruction of the original becomes feasible.[1] This judgement is hardly controversial – even the most sceptical of historical Jesus scholars would agree.[2]

Yet for our purposes it is not enough to infer that the Lord's Prayer was repeated early, far and wide: there must also be some significance in its having been regarded as a convenient précis of the gospel itself. Undoubtedly, the summative function which the early church fathers assigned it could not have endured apart from a high degree of interpretative interest in Matthew 6.9–13//Luke 11.2–4. While many today think of the *PN* as a kind of formulaic 'toss in', recited mechanically and unreflectively in liturgical settings, this does not seem to be how the early Church thought of it. Indeed, the evidence suggests that there were at least some influential thinkers who correlated the Lord's Prayer with cardinal points of doctrine. This collective interest helped solidify the prayer's function as a theological outline.

The impetus for this trend is worth pondering. In theory, the continual repurposing of the Lord's Prayer in the patristic era could be chalked up to, as much as anything, the theological creativity of the fathers, who were keen to offer whatever notional support they could to such a central component of the Great Church's liturgy. But another, more attractive option is to suppose that the broadly held vision of the Lord's Prayer as an all-encompassing prayer – a prayer, both literally and figuratively, to end all Christian prayers – is to be traced to its first reception among the disciples. This is not to say that the likes of Peter and John would have interpreted the prayer exactly in the manner of the Didachist and Tertullian (certainly they did not), but rather that the early second-century interpreters' tendency to ascribe the prayer such extraordinary status was an inherited tendency. Ultimately, the weightiness of the *PN* is to be related back to the historical Jesus himself. Since history records Jesus enjoining one prayer and one prayer only, it would not be surprising for him to have carefully formulated it as a kind of executive summary of his programme. Indeed, I believe that a proper understanding of this prayer will confirm this to be the case. In this chapter, I shall consider both the opening address ('Father') and the subsequent petitions in the hope that the prayer, when viewed through the appropriate lens, may shed more light than we have heretofore realized.

On comparing the opening line of the Lord's Prayer in Matthew (6.9b) and Luke (11.2b), we find that the Lukan version omits the modifiers 'our'

---

[1] As classically presented in Burney 1925: 113. Despite offering an extraordinarily speculative source-critical explanation for the Sermon on the Mount as a whole, Betz and Collins (1995: 375) remain sceptical in principle when it comes to the task of reconstructing the prayer. I will be following the conventional view that the scope of the prayer is best represented by Luke (with passing comment on two petitions usually credited to Matthew); see Carruth and Garsky 1996.

[2] Contra Mell 1994. The Jesus Seminar (Funk and Hoover 1993: 148–9) ascribes the first, second, fourth and fifth petitions to Jesus; it remains mildly dubious on the sixth ('lead us not into temptation/test') petition and thoroughly sceptical on the third ('your will be done') and seventh ('deliver us from evil') petitions.

and 'who is in heaven'. The variation may be due to the modulation of tradition that comes with repeated performance (compare how the wording of 'institution' of the Lord's Supper is variegated across the earliest witnesses), or it may simply have to do with changes which occurred at an editorial level, that is, Matthew choosing to add the phrases in accordance with his theology and literary style. In the latter case, this would mean that Luke's version more closely reflects the original wording. But all such matters negligibly impact the focal point here: the curious fact that Jesus addresses the divine being as 'Father' and encourages his disciples to do the same.

In the Lord's Prayer and elsewhere, there is little doubt that Jesus did in fact call God 'Father'.[3] This is demonstrable, simply and quite convincingly, by the frequency with which the Gospel tradition ascribes such language to him. In an overwhelming number of instances in which Jesus speaks of divinity, he uses the term 'Father'.[4] In Jesus' prayers, 'Father'-laden language is standard; the sole exception is the cry of dereliction (Mark 15.34//Matt. 27.46), an exception which essentially proves the rule.[5] Jesus' habit of referring to his community in familial terms corroborates our suspicions: for the historical Jesus, the preferred term for the divine was 'Father'.[6]

Of course in the ancient world, comparisons between deities and 'father' were not unheard of. Perhaps this is not surprising. Given the array of ancient cosmogonies which include a personal creator, it would only be natural to think of these creating deities in paternal or maternal terms, as the case might be. Both in Ancient Near Eastern (ANE) and Greco-Roman contexts, the one who gave birth to humanity is not infrequently designated 'Father' or 'Father of humankind' or the like, and this in relation to both humanity as a collectivity and individuals alike.[7] On one level, Jesus fits hand in glove with the first-century world.

At the same time, it would be short-sighted to leave off there. Jesus' usage of 'Father' in addressing the divine is indeed distinctive, and this is clearly so for at least three reasons. First, as suggested directly above, Jesus' use of 'Father' (as an appellation of God) is notable for its frequency. Whereas other texts or figures from antiquity may be found addressing God in paternal terms here and there, Jesus has neither predecessor nor contemporary who calls God 'Father' with anything approaching his frequency and consistency.

---

[3] Despite the objections of D'Angelo (1992a; 1992b).

[4] Examples abound: 'Father' *simpliciter* (Matt. 11.25–27; 24.36; 28.19; Mark 13.32; 14.36; Luke 10.21–22; 22.42; 23.34, 46; John 4.23; 5.19, 20; *passim*), 'my [heavenly] Father' (Matt. 6.21, 32–33; 11.27; 12.50; 15.13; 16.17; Luke 10.22; 22.29; 24.29; John 5.17; 6.32, 40; 8.19; etc.), and 'your [heavenly] Father' (Matt. 5.16, 45, 48; 6.1, 4, 6, 8; Mark 11.25; Luke 6.36; 12.30; John 20.17; etc.). Although the Evangelists' redactional activity may have much to do with the precise wording ascribed to Jesus, the point remains that variations are merely that – variations on a consistent theme.

[5] Matt. 11.25, 26, 27 par.; Mark 14.36 par.; Luke 22.34, 46; John 11.41; 12.28; 17.1, 5, 11, 21, 24, 25.

[6] See, e.g., Mark 3.31–35 par.

[7] See Fensham: 1971: 129; Marchel 1963: 134. I am indebted to Susan Rieske for these references.

This is not simply a function of the size of the database of sayings ascribed to Jesus, for on any audit of the Jesus tradition 'Father' is a distinctively recurring motif. Second, for Jesus the term is virtually his exclusive way of naming God. While those texts that speak of divine fatherhood will invariably also use other names for the deity, this is not really the case for Jesus. When it came to speaking of God, Jesus invariably fell back to the same term over and over again: 'Father'. Third, on considering the evidence of the early Church, we have the strong impression that the primitive Christians adopted Jesus' familial language in a highly self-conscious way.[8] Although this point will be argued more fully below, suffice it to say for now that early Christianity seemed to have taken on the fatherhood of God as a kind of distinctive trademark. The best explanation for this self-conscious use of the term involves tracing a trail back to Jesus' frequent and virtually exclusive use of 'Father'. While there may be more going on here (undoubtedly there is), at the very least the early Church must be seen as tipping its collective hat in Jesus' direction every time they uttered the term in connection with God. Some modern scholars may doubt that Jesus' father-language was distinctive; the early Church was not of the same opinion. Jesus did not simply call God 'Father', but did so conspicuously and purposefully.

Given the importance of 'Father' in Jesus' vocabulary, it stands to reason that in unpacking this term both in the Lord's Prayer and in the larger Jesus tradition, we might reasonably hope to acquire substantive insight into what made him tick. Indeed, if the historical Jesus' concept of the 'kingdom of God' is like a reconstructed house, then the meaning of 'Father' is its foundation. And for that reason the task becomes all the more burdened: no matter what the angle, one's interpretation of this address largely defines – and in turn will largely be defined by – how one understands the sum and substance of his message. Considering the various approaches to the problem at hand, it is clear that getting at the significance of 'Father' is easier said than done.

The meaning of 'Father': a historical-critical conundrum

So then, what did Jesus mean when he called upon God as 'Father'? Was this a carry-over from Greco-Roman divine-naming practices? Or is the context more directly Jewish? And if it was Jewish, was this a substantive departure from antecedent theological tradition or of a piece with it? Alternatively, if Jesus invited others to share in his own particular way of speaking about God, did he do so without intending any profound theological entailments, that is, without meaning to revise current beliefs about the God of Israel? To summarize all these questions: how, if at all, does Jesus' naming God as 'Father' stand in continuity with his own religious trajectory?

To this last question there have been several standard responses. In the late

---

[8] Rom. 1.7; 6.4; 8.15; 15.6; 1 Cor. 1.3; Eph. 1.3; 2 Tim. 1.2; Heb. 2.11; Jas. 1.17; 1 Pet. 1.2–3; 2 Pet. 1.17; 1 John 1.2; Rev. 1.6; *1 Clem.* 8.3; Ign. *Eph.* 4.2; etc.

nineteenth century and the first half of the twentieth century, a good number of writers alleged a radical discontinuity between Jesus' God-talk and that of his contemporary Jews – and this discontinuity was the genius of his message. For example, Wilhelm Bousset writes: 'It is in the proclamation of God as heavenly Father that we meet the most original and truly creative aspect of Jesus' preaching'.[9] Bousset's heirs in the *Religionsgeschichteschule* would follow suit.[10] According to this line of scholarship, Jesus' emphasis on the fatherhood of God stood at the core of his revolt against Judaism – whether in its nationalism (e.g. Heitmüller) or in its supposedly legalistic trammels (e.g. Bosworth, Warschauer).[11] Here, too, one finds recurring statements to the effect that Jesus' filial language flowed out of his own personal intimations of divine fellowship; his invitation to address God as 'Father' – in the Lord's Prayer and elsewhere – followed on his own experience of God's father-like presence and care.[12]

This last line of interpretation is of course still very much alive and well today, and this is in part due to the highly influential writings of Joachim Jeremias. Paying special attention to the Aramaic term *Abba* ('father'), Jeremias emphasizes the radical discontinuity between Jesus' prayer and the prayer of his contemporaries, and writes that prior to Jesus it 'would have been irreverent and therefore unthinkable to call God by this familiar word'.[13] Moreover, according to Jeremias:

> [w]e are confronted with something new and unheard of which breaks through the limits of Judaism. Here we see who the historical Jesus was; the man who had the power to address God as Abba and who included the sinners and the publicans in the kingdom by authorizing them to repeat this one word, Abba, dear father.[14]

For the Göttingen scholar the essential genius of Jesus was in his flouting religious convention of his day and daring to name God with such an intimate term; it was this divinely directed address *Abba* and its connotations of childlike trust that defined both him and his movement. It was also the use of this word that set him apart from first-century Judaism as a whole. For Jeremias, *Abba* provided the much-needed window into Jesus' inner life which the Liberal tradition after Schleiermacher had been requiring.

There are admittedly some serious problems here.[15] First, given *Abba*'s sparse attestation both in the Gospels and in the first-century milieu, we

---

[9] Bousset 1892: 41 (reference is originally cited in Thompson 2000: 14). The translation is my own.

[10] The most famous of these heirs, Bultmann, recognized the essentially Jewish roots of Jesus' father-language (see Bultmann 1958 (1934): 191–4), but also insisted that the 'stark simplicity of "Father"' in Jesus' prayers stood in contrast to the 'over-loaded' forms of address in Jewish prayer practices (Bultmann 1951: 23).

[11] Heitmüller 1913; Bosworth 1924; Warschauer 1927: 172–3.

[12] Manson 1951 (1931): 102–8; McKnight 1999: 61–2; Dunn 2003: 717–8; Keener 2009: 271–2.

[13] Jeremias 1965: 21.

[14] Jeremias 1965: 30.

[15] See especially Thompson 2000: 25–34.

have a right to be suspicious that it was really the recurring catchphrase Jeremias makes it out to be. Within the Jesus tradition, the term occurs only once (Mark 14.36); prior to the time of Jesus, it is completely unattested. Of course, it is possible that behind each instance of the Greek word 'Father' (*patēr*) in the Gospel tradition we hear Jesus uttering *Abba*, but this would be nothing more than speculation. Other lexical options, including Hebrew vocatives (Hebrew was the standard language of prayer for many Jews of the period), are plausible. That Jesus used *Abba* at least on occasion is, I believe, likely. That Jesus used *Abba* in reference to Yahweh at all places and at all times cannot easily be demonstrated.

Second, as James Barr noted in the title of his well-known essay: *Abba* does not mean 'Daddy'.[16] The term is neither childish (as if it were restricted to the domain of little children) nor even specifically connotative of prepubescence. This portion of Jeremias's argument is simply mistaken, a fact which he himself later acknowledges.[17] While this does not rule out the possibility that the term entailed a sense of intimacy, there is no reason to think that it would have conveyed any more or any less intimacy than the Greek equivalent (*patēr*). The Aramaic utterance cannot hold the lexical freight Jeremias assigns to it; the word *Abba* is certainly too fragile a foundation on which to establish Jesus' consciousness of God.

Third, and perhaps most problematically, Jeremias bracketed out consideration of sources from the Diaspora and restricted his query to the very limited lexical evidence of Palestinian Judaism. The added value of this move, so far as Jeremias' thesis was concerned, was that it effectively quarantined instances of 'Father' which might have otherwise put his argument at risk. In the 1960s when Jeremias first set out his position, such a move appeared legitimate, since biblical scholarship tended to imagine that Diaspora Judaism and Palestinian Judaism occupied two separate silos. However, over the past half-century scholarly opinion has moved on and the alleged hermetic seal separating Palestinian Jews from their confreres in the Diaspora is now no longer as airtight as we once imagined. If the ascription of father-imagery to God was acceptable in the Diaspora, it was almost certainly also acceptable in Jerusalem. In that case, Jeremias' exclusion of Diaspora texts from consideration is unwarranted.

Against Jeremias's approach, it must be acknowledged that the Jewish scriptural tradition was by the first century already comfortable with the concept of Yahweh as Father. We might consider the following passages drawn from a handful of pre-Christian texts written within several hundred years of Jesus' lifetime:

> O Lord, *Father* and Master of my life, do not abandon me to their designs, and do not let me fall because of them! Who will set whips over my thoughts,

---

[16] Barr 1988.
[17] Jeremias 1971: 67.

and the discipline of wisdom over my mind, so as not to spare me in my errors, and not overlook my sins? Otherwise my mistakes may be multiplied, and my sins may abound, and I may fall before my adversaries, and my enemy may rejoice over me. O Lord, *Father* and God of my life, do not give me haughty eyes . . .[18]

But it is your providence, O *Father*, that steers its course, because you have given it a path in the sea, and a safe way through the waves . . .[19]

He has shown you his greatness even there. Exalt him in the presence of every living being, because he is our Lord and he is our God; he is our *Father* and he is God for ever.[20]

The willingness to call God 'Father' is also attested in older Hebrew scriptures as well (Isa. 63.16; 64.8; 1 Chron. 29.10 LXX). Furthermore, it was an ancient trajectory that continued down to the first century CE and beyond. If the reports concerning the first-century Hillelite Yohanan Ben Zakkai or Rabbi Abiba (*m. Soṭah* 9.15; *m. Yoma* 8.9) are accurate enough, Jesus' own contemporaries would have cheerfully embraced the epithet.[21]

The implications of this should be clear enough. Because Jesus' father-language has more precedent than Jeremias would have us believe, this interpretative approach has naturally failed to consider the possibility that Jesus, rather than sitting askance to Hebrew traditions of divine fatherhood, is in fact engaging them. Moreover such evidence throws up serious obstacles to any attempt to explain Jesus' filial term as being motivated by his personal religious experience. For once it is admitted that the concept of God as Father was in place within Judaism both well before and after the time of Jesus, and that this concept has no discernible link with the subjective experience of God as Father, then the common explanation that Jesus' fatherly God-talk was a unique expression of *his* subjective experience – well, all this suddenly begins to look thin. Given the data on the table, the 'experiential view', as I might call it, is unsupportable.

One way out of this dead end (and as far as I can see, the only way out) is to drum up support from some insight into Jesus' consciousness. But the problem here is that that is exactly what we do not have. Marianne Meye Thompson states the issue succinctly:

The problem, of course, is that the Gospels recount nothing that purports to be a 'report' from Jesus of his 'experience' or 'subjective consciousness.' We do not know, because we have no evidence for it, that Jesus considered his understanding of God as Father an aspect of his inner experience or that he 'experienced' God as Father. The Gospels do not portray Jesus as explaining whence he derived this designation for God. It may have arisen from his personal or inner experience, but to posit personal experience as the origin of

---

[18] Sir. 23.1–4; emphasis added.
[19] Wisd. 14.3; emphasis added.
[20] Tobit 13.4; emphasis added.
[21] 'On whom can we stay ourselves? – on our Father in heaven'.

the designation and then to argue that Jesus' use of Father gives us direct access to his experience of God is simply a circular argument.[22]

Indeed, to maintain that Jesus' personal experience was the fulcrum on which his Father-God language rested is to maintain a point which cannot be deduced from the Gospel tradition itself. Suppositions regarding Jesus' consciousness of God are the stuff of unsupported premises, not the logical consequence of an argument.

In fact, arguably, the closest we come to Jesus' consciousness, surfacing in the recorded witness to his prayers, leads us in a quite opposite direction. For when Jesus does pray 'privately' as a Son to the Father, he is regularly praying as a Son in a unique sense, occupying an inimitable role. One might consider, for example, a prayer preserved in Matthew and Luke; Matthew's version reads as follows:

> [25]At that time Jesus said, 'I thank you, Father, Lord of heaven and earth, because you have hidden these things from the wise and the intelligent and have revealed them to infants; [26]yes, Father, for such was your gracious will. [27]All things have been handed over to me by my Father; and no one knows the Son except the Father, and no one knows the Father except the Son and anyone to whom the Son chooses to reveal him.'[23]

While scholars are divided as to whether or not Jesus spoke these words, all should be able to agree that we have at least an unambiguous and early articulation of a collective memory of Jesus reaching back at least as far as the putative Q source. Verse 27 makes clear that Jesus sees his own status as 'Son' in unique terms: he alone, precisely as the Son, has been entrusted with 'all things'. In this instance, Jesus' consciousness of his sonship is tightly bound up with his perceived role as exclusive recipient and mediator of revelation. Again, at least in this context, when Jesus speaks of God as 'Father', it is a way of speaking that *cannot* be shared with his disciples or even translated into their terms.[24]

While some would object that the interpretation of Jesus' sonship in Matthew 11.25–27 par. is a post-Easter – and therefore theologically overwrought – misinterpretation of his intentions, we have other instances where Jesus uses Father–Son language in an exclusive sense. For example, there is a relevant passage from John 5; it reads as follows:

> Therefore the Jews started persecuting Jesus, because he was doing such things on the sabbath. But Jesus answered them, 'My Father is still working, and I also am working.' For this reason the Jews were seeking all the more to kill him, because he was not only breaking the sabbath, but was also calling God his own Father, thereby making himself equal to God.[25]

---

[22] Thompson 2000: 31.
[23] Matt. 11.25–27.
[24] 'God and his unique agent belong intimately together' (Hagner 1993: 321).
[25] John 5.16–18.

Whether or not this particular event actually occurred (or occurred exactly as the Evangelist reports it) is beside the point. Nor, if the episode is historically rooted, is there any need to quibble over the Evangelist's interpretation of each party's motives. Assuming that the author of the Fourth Gospel is writing near the close of the first century and has a pastoral eye on mounting tensions between the local communities of believers and their detractors in the nearby synagogues, we must surmise that his description of the Jews' offence bore at least some semblance to reality. While it cannot be denied that the Gospel writer was interested in casting Jesus' opponents in a negative light, this does not mean that he would have invented wholesale the flashpoints that marked out the lines of debate between the messianic communities and the synagogues. On the contrary, unless the Evangelist was willing to undermine completely his own elucidation of Jesus' sonship (John 5.19–47), framed as a response to his opponents' suspicions, the account in John 5.16–18 must have plausibly portrayed contemporary sensitivities on this point for the sake of his audience who knew very well what was – and what was not – acceptable God-talk in the Judaism of the day.[26]

According to John, Jesus' invocation of God as 'Father' was understood by some as implying his own equality with God. Assuming that the likes of Tobit and Ben Sira did not imply their own co-equality with God when they named the divine in paternal terms, one infers that it wasn't simply Jesus' invocation of 'Father' that caused offence, but rather his claim to be 'the Son' in a unique way. In the narrative leading up to John 5.18, the theological anxieties of Jesus' doubters would have been quickly dispelled on their being assured that Jesus was not claiming to be 'a son' in any unique or especially theologically loaded sense. What makes the remainder of the chapter all the more surprising, then, is the very fact that John's Jesus, rather than downplaying his own filial status, actually exacerbates the tensions by claiming for himself two responsibilities normally reserved for Yahweh: the giving of life and the issuing of final judgement (5.20–30). If modern readers might wonder what all this business of raising the dead and offering judgement has to do with Jesus' co-equality with God (5.18), we must remind ourselves that both Jesus and his opponents would have thought of divine co-equality in primarily functional rather than metaphysical terms. At issue, then, was not the question of Jesus' divine substance or essence (as would later preoccupy the framers of the Nicene Creed); the issue was the authority of John's Jesus to serve as Yahweh's agent. In this respect, the Johannine witness, much like the synoptic tradition, makes a principle distinction between Jesus' sonship and any sonship that might be claimed by the disciples.

And so we have come face to face with a paradox within the tradition.

---

[26] Likewise, Paul's statement in Phil. 2.6 ('who, though he was in the form of God, did not regard equality with God as something to be exploited') would border on the absurd if (the apostle himself were not persuaded that) the earthly Jesus had controversially asserted his co-equality with God.

On the one hand, we have Jesus referring to Yahweh as 'your Father' and inviting his followers to pray, '[Our] Father'; on the other hand, we have, according to the same Gospel tradition, Jesus claiming a unique filial identity. To put this in theological terms, there are apparently communicable and non-communicable aspects to Jesus' Sonship/sonship. Just how these aspects related to each other and on what basis is not merely a problem for post-Chalcedonian theologians; students of the historical Jesus are also on the hook. It is a problem which must admit at least some level of resolution, a way forward.

One path forward, to get back on the road travelled by Old Liberalism, proceeds first by flattening out any principle distinction between Jesus and his followers, and second by suggesting that any and all categorical distinctions between Jesus and his disciples were smuggled into the Gospel tradition at a late stage. In this vein, the originality of the historical Jesus consisted in his inviting humanity to join him in calling on the Creator God as the common Father, and to consider fellow human beings as siblings within the family of humanity. In this case, the thrust of Jesus' message could perhaps be summarized in the words of the German Romantic poet Schiller, immortalized through the chorus of the last movement of Beethoven's Ninth Symphony:

> Be embraced, you millions.
> This kiss is for the whole world!
> Brothers, over the starry canopy
> Must a loving Father live!

This is a viable route in theory. But unless we are willing to jettison indications of Jesus' unparalleled sonship as the greasy fingerprints of the post-Easter Church, as a comprehensive model it will not do. More far-reaching objections to this view have to do with its still needing to prove, against the grain of the evidence, either that Jesus' use of 'Father' was altogether innovative (which is belied by the above-cited Jewish sources) or that Jesus' true innovation lay in his consciousness of God (which is indemonstrable because this consciousness is fundamentally inaccessible). On this issue, the Old Liberal Jesus seems to tell us more about Romantic sentimentalism than it does about the historical Jesus.

Another possibility, breaking off from this one, is to maintain that Jesus' filial language was a function of his inner piety, but to insist too that Jesus also claimed to be '*the* Son' in a unique and quite separate sense. On this view, it may be supposed that Jesus called on God as Father in an exclusive sense, even as he encouraged his disciples also to call on God as Father on a different basis and on far more democratic terms. To its credit, this solution avoids one of the burdens of the previous approach, namely, the need to strip away sundry Christological references like an old layer of outdated wallpaper. Yet economy on one level exacts an inordinate price at another, for now there is a certain awkwardness in explaining how Jesus' (upper-case) Sonship relates to the generic sonship of the disciples. If Jesus objectively holds the role of 'Son' and is privy to an accompanying set of 'son-like' subjective experiences, is it only the latter that is extended to the disciples? And in this case, are we to suppose that Jesus' identity as 'the Son' has no logical relationship to his communicable experience as Son, so that it is virtually a matter of coincidence that his identity and experience happen to be summarized with one and the same word? In addition to harbouring such unsatisfactory entailments, this approach shares the same basic weakness of the drill of Old Liberalism: it makes an unknown quantity its point of departure. So far as the origins of Jesus' father-language are concerned, it makes no sense to begin with a background we cannot hope to have (the religious musings of Jesus' heart), all the while setting aside backgrounds we do have, namely, the naming of God as 'Father' in early Christianity and pre-Christian Judaism.

Before attending to those traditions, it bears stating that notwithstanding the weaknesses of Jeremias's argument, he deserves our praise and consent on two important points. First, as Jeremias insisted, Jesus did use *Abba* at least once. Even if the occurrence of *Abba* at Mark 14.36 represents an isolated instance, there is no reason to doubt the authenticity of this word, reflecting the moment at Gethsemane (assuming the historicity of the Gethsemane event itself) or other moments which might have given rise to this utterance.[27] This might seem a rather small gain, but in this complex business of Jesus research we are grateful for such little mercies.

Second, Jeremias was also right to maintain that Jesus' usage was distinctive. This follows not so much on any lexicographical evidence surviving from Palestinian Aramaic texts, scarce as it is, but on the evidence of early Christianity's own theological reflection. Writing in the 50s, the apostle Paul indicates that the believers' invocation of God as '*Abba* Father' was an eschatological privilege, reserved for those who possessed the Spirit, that is, those who had put their faith in Christ (Rom. 8.15; Gal. 4.6). Mark's decision to preserve the Aramaic wording of Jesus' prayer (Mark 14.36) only corroborates the distinctiveness of the title '*Abba* Father' within the Christian community. Taken together, the Pauline and Markan evidence suggests that the Aramaic word, even if not necessarily exclusive to Christian worshippers, was at least a characteristically Christian prayer term. And if praying to *Abba* was a practice distinctive of the early Jesus movement, it was almost certainly distinctive of Jesus' prayers as well. After all, while Jesus' willingness to call God '*Abba*' was not necessarily inconsistent with the Judaism of his day, there must be some historical explanation for how and why early Christianity came to define itself over and against surrounding Judaism by imitating Jesus on this score. Given the transition from Jewish invocation of Yahweh as 'Father' to early Christian cries of '*Abba* Father', all this must have at least *something* to do with the historical Jesus. But what?

---

[27] So, e.g., Pesch 1976–80: 2.391; Grassi 1982; Gnilka 1997: 262; Dunn 2003: 716; etc.; contra D'Angelo 1992b: 160; Collins 2007: 678.

At this point, perhaps a restatement of the problem I am flagging up would be helpful. In this chapter, I have sought to challenge the very common argument that Jesus' use of father-language simply issued from his personal experience of God as father – all in reaction against Judaism as he knew it. As I see it, this approach has two basic weaknesses. First, because Jesus' naming Yahweh as 'Father' is not nearly as original as we have often been led to believe, it becomes difficult to argue that his doing so was a groundbreaking way of seeing God. At best one might argue that Jesus emphasized God as father *more* than his contemporary Judaism, but then this would only suggest a difference of degree. Second, there is no salvaging the experience-of-God-as-father argument on the basis of some alleged insight into Jesus' consciousness. Not only are the inner workings of Jesus' mind more or less impenetrable to us, but also, when we do have such fleeting glimpses, we find a figure who thinks of himself as a Son in a way that his followers could never hope to be.

This leaves us with several questions. First, if Jesus saw himself as *the* Son in a specialized sense, how, if at all, does this relate to his ascription of sonship and daughtership to his disciples? Second, granting that there was something distinctive about the father-language of Jesus and the early Church, how do we describe that distinctiveness? The first of these questions is rather looming and will need to be left aside for now; the second question will detain us for the remainder of this chapter.

Naming Yahweh as 'Father' in early Christianity and Judaism

Rather than insisting against the evidence that *Abba* originated out of Jesus' interior experience with God, I suggest a more promising line of interpretation begins with parsing the context in which *Abba* and God-as-Father language occur. The 'Jeremias model' has maintained that Jesus' filial prayer-language was virtually unparalleled and thus constituted a fundamental break with Judaism. I believe that the extant pre-Christian prayers referring to God as 'Father' speak against this conclusion. Now I propose that when the relevant texts both pre- and post-Jesus are properly considered, there emerges a common theological grammar, shared both by Jesus' forebears in Judaism and by his followers in early Christianity. To put a sharper point on it, whereas Old Liberalism had assumed that Jesus' habit of addressing God as 'Father' followed from his forming an unprecedented judgement about God (God is like a father), I would argue instead that these invocations had much more to do with his conviction that he and his followers had been called to a special role within the eschatological scenario, a role already anticipated by the redemptive story *par excellence*: the exodus. Towards demonstrating this, we should start not with the historical Jesus but with early Christianity, on one side, and Second-Temple Judaism, on the other. If the early Christians had a special place in their heart for the term *Abba* (and, as far as we can tell, they did), and if this estimation also stood in conceptual continuity with Judaism's use of the terms, then we might expect Jesus' bias for father-language to stand in continuity with both.

Naming Yahweh as 'Father' in early Christianity

On comparing the three New Testament texts which incorporate the term *Abba* (Rom. 8.15; Gal. 4.6; Mark 14.36), one discovers striking points of commonality. In each case *Abba* is associated with suffering (persecution in particular), which itself is interpreted within an eschatological framework and described with language tracing back to the exodus narrative. To return to the notion of 'grammar', one might say that so far as the early Christian witness is concerned, limited as it is, the word *Abba* presupposes an ongoing experience of trials that not only is analogous to the exodus but stands in fulfilment of it.

While in the purview of post-Reformation interpretation, Paul's letter to the Romans is not normally considered a text centrally concerned with suffering, the immediate co-text of Romans 8.15 – itself within the climactic chapter of Romans 8 – suggests that the apostle himself might have seen it differently:

> For you did not receive a spirit of slavery to fall back into fear, but you have received a spirit of adoption. When we cry, 'Abba! Father!' it is that very Spirit bearing witness with our spirit that we are children of God, and if children, then heirs, heirs of God and joint heirs with Christ – if, in fact, we suffer with him so that we may also be glorified with him. I consider that the sufferings of this present time are not worth comparing with the glory about to be revealed to us.[28]

As has been shown elsewhere, Paul's language of 'inheritance' here betrays solid links with the stories of exodus and conquest.[29] For the apostle, the proof of this exodus-like inheritance is forthcoming in the believers' experience of the Spirit, more exactly, the Spirit's inducing believers to cry out (*krazō*) 'Abba!' in the midst of tribulation (Rom. 8.15).[30] For the apostle, then, the utterance 'Abba' encapsulates a familiar narrative in which believers, despite their experience of persecution in the present age (Rom. 8.35–36), may expect a full inheritance, their due right as 'sons', on the other side of such opposition. In this context, the word *Abba* is a watchword, reminding the Roman Christians that they are not only participating in the experience of

---

[28] Rom. 8.15–18.
[29] De la Potterie 1976: 219–28, esp. 225; Wright 2013: 2.659; but especially extensive discussion in Keesmaat 1999: 55–77.
[30] As Wu (2015: 108–9) observes, *krazō* is 'frequently found in the Psalms to refer to fervent and passionate prayer in the face of suffering (e.g., 21:3, 6, 25; 106:6, 13, 19, 28 LXX)'; more to the point, such crying out characterizes righteous sufferers seeking deliverance from their enemies (cf. Exod. 5.8).

the sin-bearing Son (Rom. 8.3), but are also (in the same sacerdotal key) re-enacting the trials of the exodus with hopes fixed on the 'inheritance' to come. *Abba* is at once a familiar tune and the first strains of music from a farther room.

In Galatians 4, undertones of tribulation are not far beneath the text.[31] Following Paul's reminder that the fullness of time has come and that God had sent the Spirit which cries out 'Abba! Father!' (Gal. 4.6), he goes on to allude to the pains of childbirth which he experiences on behalf of the Galatian believers (v. 19). As commentators will readily note, the metaphor of birth pains was standard for Jewish descriptions of national tribulation.[32] In this case, Paul's pains are not simply personal, but rather eschatological.[33] If those who joined Paul in holding the line against the circumcision party shared in his persecution (1.7; 4.29; 5.11), the apostle has interpreted this as part and parcel of the 'present evil age' (1.4), the age of tribulation. Within this context as well, the cry of 'Abba' sustains the believers and confirms their approaching inheritance (3.29—4.7) in spite of and indeed precisely through their trials. In both instances of 'Abba' in the Pauline literature, the term is associated with eschatological hope in the midst of persecution, framed in vocabulary reminiscent of the exodus.

Turning to the use of 'Abba' in Mark 14.32–42, one finds the same pattern. Earlier in the narrative, James and John had approached Jesus with the petition to sit at his right and left hand once he had come in the fullness of his messianic glory (10.37). They request, in other words, to share the corner office in the eschatological inheritance of Israel. After assuring them that they were out of their depth, Jesus asks whether they would be able to drink his cup, only next to promise them that they will in fact drink from his cup (10.38–39). Later, in Gethsemane, it is this time Jesus who pulls James and John aside (along with Peter) as he returns to the subject of the 'cup' (14.36). Since the 'cup' that Jesus wishes to forgo is parallel to the equally abhorrent 'hour' (14.35), it is unlikely that either have to do with suffering in a generalized sense. After all, in speaking about 'the hour', Mark's Jesus is drawing upon the Danielic 'hour', which is nothing less than the hour of tribulation when the saints are handed over to the wicked.[34] This is *the* much-anticipated tribulation, the divinely appointed season of darkness before the proverbial dawn.[35] While 14.32–42 contains no explicit mention of redemption, James and John's earlier query about their eschatological future, together with the Evangelist's

---

[31] For an able argument that the Galatians' suffering is front and centre for Paul, see now Dunne 2013.
[32] See also Chapter 3 below.
[33] So e.g. Gaventa 1990; Eastman 2007: 89–126.
[34] So, rightly, Pitre 2005: 482–5; cf. Dan. 8.19; 7.25; 11.6, 35, 40, 45; 12.1, 4.
[35] It is this same tribulation (*peirasmos*) which Jesus wishes to put on the disciples' radar screen, front and centre, when he admonishes: 'Watch therefore, so that you do not fall into apostasy when persecution comes after you next' (v. 38, my own paraphrase). Of course, despite Jesus' warning, in Mark's account persecution does come and in short order the disciples apostasize, at least for a time (14.66–72).

subsequent account of the resurrection (16.1–8), show that the dark clouds of Gethsemane retain, after all, the silver lining of new creation. Notably, it is in one of the few Markan passages dedicated to Jesus' anticipation of tribulation that he calls out 'Abba, Father' (14.36). This suggests that for Jesus, as he looks ahead to the cross, the tribulation is already underway. The Evangelist clearly exhibits the same pattern as Paul: the prayer of 'Abba' is again closely associated with divinely ordained tribulation, the non-negotiable stepping stone leading up to redemption.

The Markan account of Gethsemane is also salted with images of exodus. First, Mark's Jesus repeatedly instructs his disciples to 'keep watch' through the night (14.34, 37, 38), just as Passover was a 'night of vigil' (Exod. 12.42). Second, in exhorting his disciples not to cave in to the pressures of the *peirasmos* ('trial') (Mark 14.38), Mark's Jesus is employing precisely the same term applied to the plagues (Deut. 4.34; 7.19; 29.2 LXX), not least the plague against the firstborn which struck at midnight (Exod. 12.29).[36] The invocation coheres with Mark's Christological thrust. As Mark conceives it, Jesus is not only the Zechariahan 'smitten shepherd' (see Mark 14.27) but also the firstborn 'Son of God' (1.1; 3.11; 5.7; 15.39) who was about to absorb the midnight blow of the *peirasmos*. Eventually, the disciples would also have their turn at the 'cup' of tribulation (10.35–34; 13.1–32), as will too, we suspect, Mark's readers. Faced with the awful realities before him, Jesus prays that the hour might '*pass by* from him' (*parelthē ap'autou*) (14.35), the very verb used to describe Yahweh's 'passing over' (*parechomai* in the LXX) the blood-stained lintels of obedient Israel.[37] This also anticipates the 'blood of the covenant' (14.24), granted at the Last Supper by Jesus, clearly to be understood against the context of the Mosaic covenant's ratification (Exod. 24.8).

Given these three uses of *Abba* in the New Testament, it is difficult to resist the conclusion that the Aramaic vocable was a kind of technical term for the early Christians. It spoke to the circumstance of tribulation, which Jesus has already undergone in the Passion and which too Jesus' followers could expect to experience as his witnesses. By crying out '*Abba* Father', the early Christians were reminding God as much as themselves of the eschatological inheritance which awaited them on the far side of tribulation. In each case, the cry is not simply a white-knuckled holding on for dear life, but a verbal commitment to remain faithful in the light of one's exodus-like calling and future inheritance. Although the pattern holds for a limited set of data, it holds without exception.[38]

---

[36] On this point see especially Gray 2008: 167.

[37] Evans 2001: 411.

[38] We see hints of the same in other passages which though lacking the precise term nevertheless speak to a process of becoming 'sons of God' through a process of persecution. See, e.g., Matt. 5.44–45 ('Love your enemies and pray for those who persecute you, so that you may be children of your Father in heaven') and Heb. 5.8 ('Although he was a Son, he learned obedience through what he suffered').

Naming Yahweh as 'Father' in Judaism

On considering the use of 'Father' in the prayer-language of the Second-Temple literature, we find a similar pattern. For example, in the (second-century BCE) Tobit, Yahweh is named 'our Father' and 'our God . . . for ever' (Tobit 13.4), but this within the context of the faithful suffering affliction in the midst of exile (13.1–5).[39] By acknowledging Yahweh appropriately, Tobit intends 'to show his power and majesty to a nation of sinners' (13.6), much as Israel's emergence through the plagues was calculated to 'show the power' of Yahweh to Egypt.[40] To be sure, Tobit 13 has a particular interest in Deuteronomy 32 (including Deut. 32.6 where Yahweh's fatherhood is invoked), but Tobit's hymn actually invokes the entire Deuteronomic recapitulation of the exodus as a way of talking about return from exile.[41] For Tobit, as for many Jewish texts of antiquity (not least Deuteronomy 32 itself), return from exile was a kind of second exodus.

In the same century, the author of Sirach prays to God as 'Father' (Sir. 23.1, 4) as a response to the 'insults' and 'bloodshed' stemming from persecution (22.24). Later, Ben Sira prays: 'Lord, you are my Father; do not forsake me in the days of trouble, when there is no help against the proud' (Sir. 51.10.).[42] The 'proud' are not merely behaving snootily; the verse envisages injustice or persecution of some kind. Calling on Yahweh as 'Father' was for Ben Sira an appropriate response to persecution from the Gentiles.[43]

The (first-century BCE) text of 3 Maccabees provides a handful of relevant instances. First, recalling the story in which Ptolemy IV prepares to enter the Holy of Holies despite the protests of the faithful, the author records the prayer of Simon the high priest and the subsequent intervention from above: 'Thereupon God, who oversees all things, the *first Father* [*propatēr*] of all, holy among the holy ones, having heard the lawful supplication, *scourged* [*emastixen*] him [Ptolemy] who had exalted himself in insolence and audacity' (3 Macc. 2.21; emphasis added). Only two chapters later, the Jews again raise their prayers to the 'merciful God and Father' of heaven in order to 'avert with vengeance the evil plot against them and in a glorious manifestation rescue them from the fate now prepared for them' (5.8.). Still later, the Jews find themselves once again on the brink of destruction at the hands of Gentiles, when Eleazar the high priest prays: 'Look upon the descendants of Abraham, O *Father*, upon the children of the sainted Jacob, a people of your consecrated

---

[39] This obtains only in the Greek versions; the Aramaic and Hebrew have lacunae here.
[40] Exod. 9.16; cf. Deut. 4.34, 37; 26.8; 34.12.
[41] On the parallels with Deut. 32, see Weitzman 1996; on the broader reference to Deuteronomy, see Schüngel-Straumann 2000: 167–8, 169–70.
[42] The Greek has 'Father of my Lord' here.
[43] J. Corley (2002: 36–8) helpfully picks up on the connection between Ben Sira's Father-directed prayers and Yahweh's mercy, but retains a kind of God-of-the-attributes approach instead of appealing to the biblical narrative. This prepares for, in my view, rather distant and unhelpful comparisons with pagan prayers appealing for mercy.

portion who are perishing as foreigners in a foreign land' (6.3; emphasis added). Then, drawing an analogy between their own desperate situation and that of Israel at the exodus (not to mention Daniel and Jonah), Eleazar remembers that 'you, Father, watched over and restored [him] unharmed to all his family' (6.8).[44] Clearly, in these instances from the Hellenistic period, the invocation of 'Father' is tied to contexts involving imminent danger from persecuting Gentiles, as well as the hope of deliverance.

Admittedly, there are also instances in which the pattern I have been describing is not immediately clear-cut. But then on closer inspection the text yields up the same structural markers. For example, in *Jubilees* (second century BCE), the Lord speaks to Moses about a forthcoming day:

> And I shall cut off the foreskin of their heart and the foreskin of the heart of their descendants. And shall create for them a holy spirit, and I shall purify them so that they will not turn away from following me from that day and forever. And their souls will cleave to me and to all my commandments. And they will do my commandments. And I shall be a *father* to them, and they will be sons to me. And they will all be called 'sons of the living God'.[45]

Drawing on the scriptural texts of restoration (Deuteronomy 32; Jer. 31.9; Hos. 1.1), the author of *Jubilees* links the elect's sonship with their proleptic obedience. However, within the broader co-text, Yahweh's announcement of these tidings is only in response to Moses' earlier prayer that God's people be released from exile:

> Do not abandon your people and your inheritance to walk in the error of their heart. And do not deliver them into the hand of their enemy, the gentiles, lest they rule over them and cause them to sin against you.
>
> (*Jub.* 1.19)

In short, the promise of sonship is again issued in direct response to the faithful's prayer to be released from the oppressive Gentiles. For the author of *Jubilees*, this oppression of exile is interpreted as nothing less than a recapitulation of the oppression borne by the Sinai generation.

The *Testament of the Twelve Patriarchs* may also be relevant, though it would admittedly be of an uncertain relevance, since the text is regularly regarded as problematic due to the strong possibility of late Christian interpolation.[46] Here the patriarch Levi foresees the period of exile and the climactic apostasy

---

[44] Croy (2006: 99) aptly summarizes: 'Eleazar's petition rehearses prominent events in Israel's salvation history, beginning with Pharaoh, the archetypical example of Gentile arrogance'; thus, 'the author makes an explicit connection between the present crisis and Israel's past'.

[45] *Jub.* 1.23b–25; emphasis added.

[46] Many years ago, Jonge (1960; 1962; 1980) strenuously emphasized Christian interpolation within the document, a direction resisted by Philonenko 1960; Braun 1960; Kee (1983: 777); and most recently by deSilva 2013. For the purposes of my argument here, I admit this as an essentially Christian document. See Davila's introduction to *Aramaic Levi* in Bauckham, Davila and Panayotov 2013: 121–41.

to follow: 'In the seventh week there will come priests: idolators, adulterers, money lovers, arrogant, lawless, voluptuaries, pederasts, those who practice bestiality' (*T. Lev.* 17.11). In response, Yahweh will send 'a new priest' who will supplant the old priesthood (18.1–2). At that time, the heavens will be opened 'and from the temple of glory sanctification will come upon him, with a fatherly voice, as from Abraham to Isaac' (18.6).[47] The priest in turn will 'give the majesty of the Lord to those who are his sons in truth forever' (18.8). In scriptural terms, divine 'majesty' comes in the form of both the pillar cloud of divine presence (Exod. 16.10; 24.16; etc.) and the consuming judgement of Yahweh against his enemies at the exodus (Exod. 15.7). For this author, Yahweh's direct response to Israel's apostasy and tribulation was the raising up of a priestly figure who (along with his followers?) would be addressed by God in filial terms. A similar kind of prediction is issued in the *Testament of Judah* 24.1–6, where the elect, following their enslavement by the Gentiles in exile (23.1–5), will be called 'sons in truth' (24.3). Even if Christian hands shaped this recension of the *Testament of Levi*, that this document should share the phrase 'sons in truth' with *Testament of Judah*, and that within a context of struggle, may be significant.

Within the broad expanse of the Qumran corpus, outside the biblical material, there is only one instance in which Yahweh is identified as Father. This occurs in 1QH in a prayer of lamentation. The hymnist reflects on his suffering at the hands of his oppressors:

> I can give a reply to who (*sic*) wish to devour me and a rebuke to who (*sic*) wish to cast me down. I have pronounced my own verdict as unjust, but your judgment I have pronounced just, for I know your truth. I have chosen my judgment, I have been pleased with my afflictions, because I hope for your kindness.[48]

Confident that God will come through on his behalf, the writer continues:

> until old age you take care of me. For my father did not know me, and my mother abandoned me to you. Because you are father to all the [son]s of your truth. You rejoice in them, like her who loves her child, and like a wet-nurse you take care of all your creatures on (your) lap.[49]

Here one need not over-read the comparison between Yahweh and a father. Obviously, the paternal metaphor is driven by Psalm 27.10, which speaks to the failure of the psalmist's earthly parents and the contrasting goodness of God, who is as a surrogate parent in their stead. Thus, for the Qumran author, the metaphor may simply be illustrating the providence of Yahweh. At the same time, the very fact that the author identifies the faithful covenanters as

---

[47] This is obviously a reference to the Aqedah (Gen. 22), an event which I will cover in more depth in Chapter 2.
[48] 1QH[a] 17.8–10. This and all subsequent translations are from García Martínez and Tigchelaar (2000).
[49] 1QH[a] 17.34–36.

'sons of your truth', while the remainder of humanity is assigned the status of foster children, suggests that the community members saw themselves as retaining sonship to God in some specific and unique sense. It is quite possible that the hymnist's experience of sonship, along with his calling on Yahweh as 'Father', is not unconnected with his experience of his beleaguered position. The usage is not inconsistent with the pattern in view.

The last pre-Christian text of the intertestamental period is Wisdom (first century BCE), which includes several interesting passages. The first recounts the imagined thoughts of the wicked who lie in wait for the righteous with resentful musing:

> We are considered by him as something base, and he avoids our ways as unclean; he calls the last end of the righteous happy, and boasts that God is his *father*. Let us see if his words are true, and let us test what will happen at the end of his life; for if the righteous man is God's child, he will help him, and will deliver him from the hand of his adversaries. Let us test him with insult and torture, so that we may find out how gentle he is, and make trial of his forbearance. Let us condemn him to a shameful death, for, according to what he says, he will be protected.[50]

Here 'God's child' has nothing to do with any sentimental notions or subjective experience but is applied to a situation of tribulation in which one expects divine deliverance. Even according to the unrighteous, proof of sonship is in the act of divine deliverance. Yet later, in an apparent exception to the pattern I have been tracing, God is identified as 'Father' and that in connection with his providential oversight of a sailing craft:

> For it was desire for gain that planned that vessel, and wisdom was the artisan who built it; but it is your providence, O *Father*, that steers its course, because you have given it a path in the sea, and a safe way through the waves.[51]

While the ascription of fatherhood to Yahweh may be intended to under-score divine superintendence of the universe, it may equally have to do with the fact that the speaker of these words is Solomon, who is after all the 'son of God' in a special sense. It is impossible to be sure one way or another.

Still, within all these instances there is a prevailing pattern: the identification of God as Father (and/or the praying individual's self-identification as Yahweh's son or child) regularly has to do with deliverance from oppression. The one possible exception to this rule is the last-discussed Wisdom 14.3, but it is an exception which may also admit some explanation. Judging by the sources predating the time of Jesus, one might go so far as to say that, from each supplicant's point of view, it is precisely in his deliverance that Yahweh is proven to be Father; it is also through faithful perseverance that the pious

---

[50] Wisd. 2.16–20; emphasis added.
[51] Wisd. 14.2–3; emphasis added.

prove themselves as Yahweh's sons. The recurring subtext remains that of the exodus.[52]

Synthesis

In the early Christian and pre-Christian Jewish literature, we do not find many instances in which God is named as 'Father'. But where they do occur, it is inevitably in connection with the experience of suffering and the expectant hope of redemption, all typically rendered in terms of the exodus. In my view, it would be asserting too little to say that these tribulations were, from the ancients' perspective, merely *like* those of the exodus. Given the atoning significance which ancient Judaism often ascribed to the suffering of the righteous, one suspects that the pious regarded their oppression as being in some sense a recapitulation or fulfilment of the exodus. By setting particular and present-day instances of suffering within the context of Israel's foundational story, these authors were attaching deep theological significance to their own experience. Their point: however random the oppression of the righteous might appear, such suffering would somehow lend itself to a process culminating in redemption. The Jewish prayer to God as Father was a prayer of hope, turning the mind's eye from the immediacy of dark tribulation to the eschatological light at the end of the tunnel.

The exodus narrative as backdrop to God–as–Father

The recurring appeal to Israel's foundational story of redemption in early Christianity and Second-Temple Judaism makes sense because the exodus is at bottom a story in which identity and calling emerge out of suffering. And this identity and calling centre on worship. In this connection, the point of departure is Yahweh's call to Moses:

> And the LORD said to Moses, 'When you go back to Egypt, see that you perform before Pharaoh all the wonders that I have put in your power; but I will harden his heart, so that he will not let the people go. Then you shall say to Pharaoh, "Thus says the LORD: Israel is my firstborn son. I said to you, 'Let my son go *that he may worship me* [*wĕya'abdēnî*].'"'[53]

Israel was Yahweh's son, and as such the people were collectively called to worship or to serve (*'bd*) their vassal king. This was Israel's *raison d'être*. Accordingly, the overarching goal of the exodus was not simply to achieve

---

[52] This pattern is also sustained (albeit inconsistently) in the rabbinic literature, which has relatively few instances of 'Father' as a divine ascription. For example, in reference to tortures and executions endured for the sake of maintaining purity, Rabbi Nathan comments: 'These wounds caused me to be beloved of My father in heaven' (*Mek.* 20.6). Speaking of the tribulation leading up to the return of the messiah, R. Eliezer repeatedly warns that in such times Israel can only hope to stay itself 'on our Father in heaven' (*Soṭah* 9.15). See also *Exod. Rab.* 34.1.

[53] Exod. 4.21–23; emphasis added.

freedom for its own sake (a peculiarly Western notion), but to enable Israel to realize its specific purpose: to worship Yahweh the Creator God. Because this concept of sonship entails both relational and functional aspects that cannot be finally separated, it is only in discharging this calling that Israel becomes the son of God in the fullest sense. The same fusion of priestly function and identity is equally implicit in Yahweh's pronouncement that Israel is a 'kingdom of priests' (Exod. 19.6, NIV) and Yahweh's 'treasured possession' (*sĕgullâ*) (19.5, NIV). In Jewish covenant thinking, it would have been inconceivable for Israel to remain Yahweh's 'treasured possession' without faithfully offering worship; it would have been equally inconceivable for Israel to be God's son apart from the faithful discharging of its priestly responsibilities.[54]

The precise meaning of 'kingdom of priests' (*mmlkht khnym*) in the Hebrew text of Exodus 19.6 remains something of an open question. However, when we consider the Greek LXX translation *basileion hierateuma*, the options begin to narrow, leaving us inevitably with the sense of a 'royal priesthood'.[55] In the LXX the term *hierateuma* (Exod. 19.6; 23.33; 2 Macc. 2.17) refers to a priestly office. Thus in the Second-Temple period, the term 'royal priesthood' envisaged a leadership constituted by priests who also have a royal status. This ideal set forth in Exodus 19.6 probably explains why more than 200 of the leading men of Judea, according to the historian Diodorus Siculus, insisted to the first-century BCE Pompey that their nation be ruled not by a king but a high priest.[56] On the assumption that Jesus shared this framework, this would lead us to expect his vision of a new exodus to involve the establishment of a new priestly class charged with the sacred service of leading a renewed holy nation.

Sacred service requires sacred ground. The destined venue of Israel's priestly service was to be the land of 'inheritance', the geographical *telos* of the entire exodus narrative. Just as Israel could hardly have been conceived of as the son of God apart from its appointed cultic role, neither of these could be imagined apart from the proper stage: the land of inheritance, an inheritance which followed logically on the idea of Israel as the 'son of God'.[57] The land was not simply a place to settle; it was purposed first and foremost as a sacred space. The centre of that sacred space would of course be the temple where Yahweh would plant 'them on the mountain of your possession, the place, O LORD, that you made your abode, the sanctuary' (Exod. 15.17).[58]

---

[54] The post-exilic prophet Malachi understood it no differently: 'They [the righteous] shall be mine, says the LORD of hosts, my *special possession* [*sĕgullâ*] on the day when I act, and I will spare them as parents spare their children [i.e. sons] [*bĕnô*] *who* serve them' (Mal. 3.17; emphasis added).
[55] So, e.g., Kooij 2007: 258; Wevers 1992: 246.
[56] *Bib. hist.* 40.2; see the fuller argument in Kooij 2007.
[57] Inheritance was the expected right of the firstborn; see Stuart 2006: 146, 150.
[58] Scriptural tradition identifies the 'holy mountain' as Zion (Isa. 11.9; 27.13; 56.7; Ps. 74.2; Ezek. 17.22–23). Note especially the parallelism between 'inheritance' and 'temple', for example, in Ps. 79.1: 'O God, the nations have come into your *inheritance*; they have defiled your *holy temple*; they have laid Jerusalem in ruins' (emphasis added).

Inheritance is as integral to sonship as sacred space is to the priestly office.

Yet the ancient Jews were well aware that the consecration of God's people and God's space would have never occurred, were it not for the series of tribulations leading up to the exodus. In their annual reflection on the first Passover event (Exod. 13.14–16), generations of the gathered faithful would have taken to heart that the terrifying tribulations of their ancestors in Egypt, including Pharaoh's recurring obstinacy and the firstborns' brush with death, were not in vain. In retrospect such tribulations proved to be not only a catalyst for Israel's role as a kind of corporate 'priest' to the nations, but also Yahweh's appointed means of organizing – with lambs' blood as in the consecration of Exodus 24 – Israel's priestly class.[59] Ironically, the oppression of Yahweh's son became the very mechanism through which Israel's sonship was to be fully realized. John Davies' comments are apt:

> It should be noted that this designation of Israel as Yhwh's son is chiefly found in the Hebrew Bible in contexts dealing with the Sinai and exodus experience or with the return from exile in texts which may echo the exodus account (Jer. 3.19; 31.9, 20; Hos. 11.1) . . . This declaration regarding Israel's distinctive status thus takes on a more programmatic role and its prominent position fosters the idea that the divine intervention in the plagues has as one of its purposes the privileging of Yhwh's 'son' in relation to the Egyptians.[60]

Yet the distinctive nature of that 'privileging' is the convergence of priesthood and suffering, for as Davies also observes: 'If Christian interpreters have tended to see priesthood in terms of missionary service, a typically Jewish reading is to see it in terms of suffering.'[61] In the thought world of ancient Judaism, then, to suffer on Yahweh's behalf was to assume a priestly posture. Likewise, by faithfully maintaining their respective roles in the midst of the Passover tribulation, Israel and Israel's firstborn sons proved their filial and hereditary status. It is against this background that the early Christian and Second-Temple Jewish divine-naming practice begins to come into sharper focus.

The Lord's Prayer: a consistently eschatological prayer

Given this recurring pattern in the Jewish texts, it now remains to be asked whether Jesus' address of 'Father' in the Lord's Prayer is to be understood along similar eschatological lines. In other words, does the *PN* provide evidence that Jesus saw himself and his disciples as 'priests' whose suffering would be used to leverage redemptive purposes? Towards answering this question, a closer inspection of the remainder of the prayer is in order. But perhaps it is best to take this one step at a time. If the first petition can be shown to have a sacerdotal thrust, then this provides good initial support for

---

[59] Levenson 1993: 43–8.
[60] Davies 2004: 108.
[61] Davies 2004: 96.

my reading of 'Father', coming – as I claim – off the lips of a very Jewish and very beleaguered Jesus. In this respect, the first petition may serve as a kind of test case.

First petition: 'Hallowed be your name' (Q 11.2b)

On the face of it 'hallowed be your name' is a priestly phrase, for 'hallowing' or 'consecrating' (*hagiazō*) is normally done through priestly agents.[62] Of course Yahweh also consecrates and is the ultimate source of all that is holy.[63] Whether the verb *hagiasthētō* ('hallowed') in Q 11.2 is a divine passive (making Yahweh the subject of the hallowing activity), or simply a passive verb which allows for substantial human responsibility, is a standing exegetical puzzle. Jewish usage points us in either direction, just as the history of interpretation has also gone both ways.[64]

For some commentators, one factor which tilts the scales in a God-ward direction is the aorist aspect of *hagiasthētō* matched by the parallel aorist verbs in the prayer.[65] Such an approach sees the aorist as implying punctiliar action so that the hallowing in view is not a gradual process but rather a once-for-all event. If valid, this would, on the one hand, militate against a commonly held interpretation that Jesus is inviting prayer for ongoing hallowedness of the faithful, and, on the other hand, support a reading which finds here a meteoric moment of divine intervention. Exegetical decisions at this early juncture will in turn shape one's reading of the rest of the prayer. It is one thing if Jesus intended the first petition first and foremost as a request for divine enablement for day-to-day obedience; it is quite another if it was initially intended as a plea for God to arise in a dramatic eschatological in-breaking.[66] While I think the latter option is to be preferred for reasons below, one must guard against putting more evidentiary weight on the Greek aspect than it can reasonably bear – especially when we finally have to deal with the Aramaic subtext.[67]

A more certain approach begins with the assumption that Jesus is praying

---

[62] Moses assumes a priestly role when he consecrates the people at the foot of Sinai (Exod. 19.10, 14; cf. Ps. 99.6) and later consecrates the tabernacle furnishings (Exod. 40.1–11); the same goes for Solomon when he, as priest-king (see Davies 2011: 47–9), consecrates the temple (1 Kings 8.64; 9.3). Otherwise, the task of consecration fell to the Aaronic priests: 'Aaron was set apart to consecrate the most holy things, so that he and his sons for ever should make offerings before the LORD, and minister to him and pronounce blessings in his name for ever' (1 Chron. 23.13).

[63] Exod. 31.13; Lev. 11.44.

[64] See Luz 1989–2005: 1.316–17.

[65] So Brown 2010 (1961): 292–3.

[66] The latter, eschatological reading is preferred by Brown 2010 (1961); Dupont and Bonnard 1966; Jeremias 1971: 193–203; Davies and Allison 1988–97: 1.593–4.

[67] If, as Campbell (2008: 84) maintains, the negative aorist imperative (found in the parallel petition of Q 11.4) involves nothing more than 'a specific agent performing action within a specific situation', this would not necessarily speak to the petitions as punctiliar events. On the other hand, it would support the notion that Jesus' prayer was situation-specific, precisely as the eschatological reading is wont to argue.

within the context of the Scriptures, which is to say that he is 'praying out' the Scriptures. In the Hebrew Bible there are two places in which Yahweh's *name* is sanctified: Isaiah 29.23 and Ezekiel 36.23.[68] The context of the former verse (Isa. 29.22–24) involves the third of three transformations envisaged for Jacob, a scenario in which the people will be restored to proper reverence before Yahweh. Ezekiel 26.23 also refers to a restoration of worship, although in more explicit and thorough terms, and in the context of a return from exile. The verse and its subsequent context read as follows:

> [23]*I will sanctify my great name*, which has been profaned among the nations, and which you have profaned among them; and the nations shall know that I am the LORD, says the Lord GOD, when through you I display my holiness before their eyes. [24]I will take you from the nations, and gather you from all the countries, and bring you into your own land. [25]I will sprinkle clean water upon you, and you shall be clean from all your uncleannesses, and from all your idols I will cleanse you. [26]A new heart I will give you, and a new spirit I will put within you; and I will remove from your body the heart of stone and give you a heart of flesh. [27]I will put my spirit within you, and make you follow my statutes and be careful to observe my ordinances. [28]Then you shall live in the land that I gave to your ancestors; and you shall be my people, and I will be your God.[69]

The parallel between 'hallowed be thy name' (Q 11.2b) and the phrase 'I will hallow my great name' (Ezek. 36.23), generally accepted by commentators, does not rule out the possibility that Jesus' prayer was inspired less by Ezekiel and more directly by first-century prayers modelled on Ezekiel. A parade example of the latter would be the Qaddish, a prayer which, like the *PN*, pairs the hallowing of the (name of the) God of Israel with the coming of the kingdom.[70] In my judgement, while Jesus may have been mindful of prayers similar to his own formulation, a more directly biblical backdrop makes better sense for several reasons. First, as Klein first observed over a century ago, a number of words and concepts in the Lord's Prayer, beginning with the first petition, notionally correspond to various elements in Ezekiel 36.23–29 – and that in roughly sequential order.[71] Even if the alleged parallels are not

---

[68] The person of Yahweh is sanctified in Lev. 10.3; Ezek. 38.23; the name is profaned in Ezek. 39.7; Lev. 22.32.

[69] Ezek. 36.23–28; emphasis added.

[70] One version reads as follows: 'Great and hallowed be his great name! Amen! In the world, which he has created, according to his will, may his kingdom come in your lifetime and in your days' (my own translation of the Hebrew provided by Lehnardt 2002: 21); the dependence of this family of prayers on Ezek. 36.23 and 38.23 is well established (Lehnardt 2002: 41, 256–9).

[71] Klein 1906: 45–6; followed by Friedlander 1969 (1911): 163–5; Swetnam 1972. The parallels are as follows: 'hallowed be your name' (Matt. 6.9c//Luke 11.2b) > 'I will sanctify my great name' (Ezek. 36.23); (2) 'Your kingdom come' (Matt. 6.10a//Luke 11.2c) > 'I will . . . bring you into your own land' (Ezek. 36.24); (3) 'Your will be done, *on earth* [*epi gēs*] (Matt. 6.10b)' > 'you shall live *in the land* [*epi tēs gēs*]' (Ezek. 36.28); (4) 'Give us this day our daily bread' (Matt. 6.11//Luke 11.3) > 'I will summon the grain and make it abundant' (Ezek. 36.29); (5) 'forgive us our debts' (Matt. 6.12//Luke 11.4a) > 'On the day . . . I [will] cleanse you from all your iniquities' (Ezek. 36.33); (6) 'rescue us from the evil one' (Matt. 6.13//Luke 11.4b) > 'I will save you from all your uncleannesses' (Ezek. 36.29).

all equally convincing, the accumulation of plausible parallels fulfils one of the standard criteria for determining intertextual resonances, the criteria of volume and recurrence.[72] Second, if we follow many scholars in supposing that the historical Jesus was centrally concerned with Israel's restoration, and consider too that this echo of Ezekiel 36.23 (and the surrounding text of Ezekiel 34—37) stands as the lead-off petition within a series of programmatic petitions, then we are inclined to imagine that Jesus had directly, creatively and substantively engaged the prophetic text. In other words, because Jesus is offering this prayer as a distinctive prayer, uniquely characteristic of his own movement, it is less likely that he is simply mimicking the synagogue prayers of his day on a purely formal level; it is more likely that he is appropriating standard prayer-forms as familiar scaffolding for a fresh interpretation of the foundational text. Third, if Jesus' prayer is indeed to be understood on analogy with other Jewish prayers which claimed Yahweh's paternity in the midst of tribulation, then Jesus could hardly have done better than to begin his prayer formula with a nod to Ezekiel 36. The address of 'Father' alongside a call-out to a well-known vision of return from under the Gentiles' thrall (Ezek. 36.24) constitutes a perfect match with the profile of prayers set out in this chapter. Jesus' appropriation of Ezekiel 36 in the formulation of his own prayer shows every sign of being highly intentional.

Just what Jesus intends with the words 'hallowed be your name' is another question. A splendid point of departure here would be to ask just how Ezekiel 36 could be informing the prayer. For the sake of concision, I will limit myself to four potentially relevant observations on Ezekiel's text. The passage is first of all striking in its invocation of Edenic conditions and language of inheritance. According to the prophet, the land will be emphatically fruitful (Ezek. 36.8); it will also provide a renewed stage for Israel's destiny to 'increase and be fruitful' (v. 11), thus renewing the Edenic mandate to 'be fruitful and multiply' (Gen. 1.28).[73] Moreover, Yahweh's address to the land ('I will lead people upon you – my people Israel – and they shall possess you, and you shall be their inheritance' (Ezek. 36.12)) clearly hints to the era of the conquest. In Ezekiel's description of the restored land, the collocation of Edenic imagery with images of the (not-yet-profaned) land draws attention to the *tertium comparationis* that unites both settings: their status as purified cultic space.[74]

Second, in Ezekiel's vision Yahweh promises to 'sprinkle clean water upon you' (Ezek. 36.25). The sprinkling of water represents not simply cleansing in a generic sense. Rather, it replicates the initial stage of the ordination ceremony of the Levitical priests as they prepared to take up their sacred

---

[72] See Hays 1989: 30.
[73] In v. 35 the comparison with the Garden of Eden is explicit: 'And they will say, "This land that was desolate has become like the garden of Eden"'.
[74] Block 1997: 334.

calling.[75] Ezekiel was in effect promising that those priestly responsibilities which in an earlier era were reserved for an elect priestly class would one day be extended to the nation as a whole. Anticipating a consecration nationwide in scope, Ezekiel joins the chorus of prophetic witnesses that speak to a reinvigorated priestly role in the eschaton.[76]

Third, in the same verse, Ezekiel is confident that the same water of consecration will have the added effect of cleansing Israel from its idols (Ezek. 36.25). This is consistent with the above two points. Even if the land were to be restored to pristine cultic conditions, and even if Israel were to undergo a far-ranging consecration, all this would do little good apart from the effective removal of that which sent Israel into exile in the first place: the nation's idols. So long as the core of Israel's worship was to give the one true God proper allegiance, then those things which competed with that allegiance had to be eradicated.[77]

Fourth, and finally, Ezekiel promises the granting of the spirit (Ezek. 36.26–27), which would empower the nation to keep Yahweh's decrees. The giving of the spirit was of course broadly understood as part and parcel of the much-anticipated new covenant.[78] Israel had failed in the past, but Ezekiel and the broader prophetic tradition held out the spirit as a firm basis for future hope. In order to remain faithful in their new priestly calling, the remnant of Israel would have to make room for the new heart and new spirit which Yahweh had promised.

In summary, Ezekiel's vision of restoration anticipated at least four realities: (1) the renewal of the land; (2) the people's purification from idols; (3) the consecration of a new priesthood; and (4) the indwelling of the spirit. None of these should come as a surprise: all four elements could be considered important, even crucial, puzzle pieces as exiled Israel wistfully imagined life after captivity. One might say that any one and all of these points are both necessary and sufficient conditions for the restoration.[79] Interestingly, for Ezekiel restoration was only indirectly of 'political' significance: the primary significance of the return consisted in its cultic implications – a renewal in the worship of Yahweh.

So much for Ezekiel's theology. But on the assumption that Jesus had Ezekiel 36.23 in mind in the very introduction of his prayer, just how much of this can we expect to have been incorporated in the first petition? It is a difficult question which will receive some resolution later in my argument.[80]

---

[75] Num. 8.5–13, especially v. 7. So too, e.g., Zimmerli et al. (1979: 2.248–9): 'When reference is made here to "sprinkling with clean water" . . . we should see behind this image a ritual act of sprinkling with water for the purpose of cultic purification.'

[76] Isa. 25; Jer. 31.31–37; Joel 2.28.

[77] Block 1997: 344–5.

[78] Isa. 59.21; 61.1; Ezek. 37.14; 39.29; cf. Jer. 31.31–37.

[79] That the hallowing of the name involved the (re)consecrating of the temple space as a prerequisite step to divine indwelling makes sense, since it was the temple which housed 'the name' (1 Kings 9.3, 7 par. 2 Chron. 7.16, 20).

[80] See Chapter 3 below.

But for now, if there is any promising path forward, it is in seizing on Jesus' distinctive coupling of two important narratives: the exodus story, embedded as it is in the term 'Father' (Q 11.2a), and the Ezekielian vision of restoration, incorporated in the phrase 'hallowed be your name' (Q 11.2b). As I have argued, by calling on God as 'Father', Jesus and his disciples were asking Yahweh to do in their own time what God had done in the exodus, namely, repurpose the machinations of the wicked for atoning ends. So, then, by praying just this prayer, Jesus and his disciples were going on record before God that they were prepared to accept this appointed suffering, thereby exercising their newly acquired priestly role. Next, in encouraging his disciples to pray 'Hallowed be your name', Jesus was exhorting them, on the logic of Ezekiel 36, to participate in the ushering in of the eschatological conditions: the reconsecration of sacred space and the restoration of God's people. Following the lead of this newly ordained priesthood, the members of remnant Israel would eschew their idols and embrace the spirit, even as they would be poised to serve Yahweh anew. After all, return from exile meant not a return to business as usual, but a fresh start characterized by an unprecedented experience of the divine presence.

So when Jesus and his disciples prayed, 'Father, hallowed be your name!', they were not so much enlisting divine grace for long-term obedience; instead, they were asking Yahweh to effect the eschatological restoration of Israel's priestly office and cultic space in their very midst. In this respect, Jesus' prayer sets itself apart from the Qaddish through its distinctively self-involving thrust. When Jesus imagined the practical outworking of Ezekiel 36, he imagined his own movement's unique involvement in redemptive history – in the present hour and through divinely appointed persecution (as the address 'Father' makes clear). This was not simply a matter of enlisting Yahweh's involvement in some future bye and bye. The reality was that God was already acting through this new order of priests.

In this connection, it may be no coincidence that in the Jewish sources the hallowing of Yahweh's name refers not only to human moral effort in the general sense but also to the more specific context of martyrdom.[81] The link between hallowing and martyrdom is fairly obvious. If the blood of animals had the power to effect atonement and consecrate the temple apparatus, how much more, so it was thought, would the blood of the righteous serve the same purposes. This prompts the question as to whether Jesus' prayer 'Hallowed be your name' amounts to a verbal commitment to martyrdom. A number of factors make this very plausible. First, if we interpret the first petition in martyrological terms, then this can be related to the ample attestation that Jesus himself anticipated his death and would have naturally interpreted this in martyr-like terms.[82] Second, it is certainly plausible that

---

[81] Cf. Str-B 1.411–18; Ben-Sasson 1972.

[82] Mark 9.31; 10.45; Luke 22.35. For an excellent survey of scholarship arguing that Jesus anticipated his death, see McKnight 2005: 47–75.

Jesus considered martyrdom as a necessary step to restoration, since this very notion is already instantiated in the period.[83] Third, the subsequent mention of 'tribulation' (Q 11.4) is indication that severe suffering is already at least on the horizon when Jesus first issues the prayer. Fourth, in the Gospel of John, Jesus asks the Father to 'glorify your name' through his own death (12.28). If glorification is roughly synonymous with sanctification (cf. Lev. 10.3), then John's Jesus took for granted that his death would sanctify the name and thereby accomplish the goals of Ezekiel 36 (cf. John 17.1–3).[84] Whether or not this Johannine sentiment traces back to the historical Jesus, my point is simply that one of Jesus' earliest biographers interpreted Jesus' death as a culminating act by which he hoped to secure the promises of Ezekiel 36. If Jesus intended the first petition as essentially a martyr's prayer, then he could not have been entirely surprised eventually appearing before Caiaphas hours from his death. I will return to this point below; for now it is enough to recognize that the vocative 'Father' coupled with the imperative 'Hallowed be your name' positions Jesus and his movement at the crosshairs of God's redemptive purposes.

Variations on a priestly theme: petitions two through seven

I am aware that I may seem to be drawing some pretty far-reaching conclusions on the basis of a very small set of words. Of course if the *PN* is in fact a crisply worded outline that, much like a contemporary 'vision statement', captures in a handful of strokes Jesus' overall agenda, we should expect to have to do this kind of decompression.[85] Still, the argument I have been making would be considerably strengthened were the remaining petitions in the *PN* supportive of this the model. This, I believe, is the case. In fact, on considering the remaining petitions even briefly, it becomes clear that they reinforce from a variety of angles what I am suggesting: that Jesus' prayer was specifically designed for a cadre of eschatological priests functioning in the *Sitz im Leben Jesu*.

Second petition: 'Your kingdom come' (Q 11.2c)
In Second-Temple and rabbinic Judaism, prayers that Yahweh might establish his kingdom are common enough.[86] But in summoning his disciples to pray for the advent of the kingdom of God, Jesus is assuredly conscripting his

---

[83] See, e.g., 2 Macc. 7, especially 7.6 with its invocation of Deut. 32.36; also *T. Moses* 9–10.

[84] Carson (1991: 440–1) writes that 'since Ezekiel 36 has already been referred to in John 3:5, it is tempting to think that Ezekiel 36:22, 32 are in mind here, thus subsuming all of Christ's redemptive work and the inauguration of the new covenant under God's solemn Old Testament pledge to glorify his own name'. See also Meier 1991: 361–6 n. 36.

[85] As Lohmeyer (1965: 78) puts it: 'The Lord's Prayer is too brief and deliberate to have room for the flourishes and formulas of a doxology'.

[86] See, e.g., *Sib. Or.* 3.47; *Ass. Mos.* 10.1; *Pss. Sol.* 17.1–4, 21–23; *1 En.* 1.3–9; 1QM 6.6, 12.7; *Tg. Zech.* 14.9. For the rabbinic sources, see Dalman and Kay 1902: 96–101.

followers to take their stations in preparation for an anticipated unfolding of eschatological events.[87] For if the cry of 'Father' reflected the onset of tribulation unleashed against the Jesus community; and if the subsequent phrase 'Hallowed be your name' speaks to the reconsecration of Yahweh's holy space precisely through that tribulation; then 'Your kingdom come' imagines the next step in the sequence when Yahweh deigns to indwell the new temple. The coming of the kingdom would hardly be possible without tribulation and resulting consecration; consecration, the preparation of the holy space, would be pointless without God actually coming into it.

For ancient Judaism, the reign of God was fundamentally grounded in God's identity as Creator. Accordingly, where we find such phrases as 'the Lord is king' (*yhwh mālāk*), it is invariably in connection with an eschatological vision involving Yahweh's rightful rule over the nations *and* the nations' response of submission and worship.[88] Obviously such a vision would be absurd so long as Israel, Yahweh's vice-regent, remained in exile. In this sense, the coming of the kingdom has geopolitical implications. At the same time, it can hardly be overemphasized that Yahweh's assumption of his rightful throne as Creator could only be contemplated within a cultic context, which presupposed Israel's right relationship to the land. Return from exile was not an end in itself but a means to a higher, cultic end.

That 'end' was Yahweh's reinhabiting the temple and assuming the throne, positioned as it was directly between the cherubim within the Holy of Holies.[89] To be sure, the enthronement of God was metaphorical for the ancient Jews on some level, but this little changes the fact that for the same Jews, Yahweh's real presence within the temple was the bedrock of all realities. Although Yahweh's rule was universal, as ancient Judaism understood it, the administration of the rule was exercised from within the confines of the temple. The most sacred space was the nexus point between heaven and earth.

Accordingly, Jesus' prayer for the coming of the kingdom – together with his proclamation of the kingdom of God – would have anticipated not simply a divinely initiated reality but also a convergence of events. It would have at least entailed Israel's return from exile, the re-establishment of its political autonomy, and the nations' recognition of Yahweh's superiority over the gods. These moments in turn would have been subsidiary to a larger climactic moment when the Creator God would finally take his rightful place within a duly consecrated temple. The divine presence would have also created the

---

[87] The literature surrounding the kingdom of God in the proclamation of Jesus is immense of course. See Dodd 1961; Ridderbos 1962; Norman Perrin 1963; 1976; Schnackenburg 1963; Brandon 1967; Jeremias 1972; Ladd 1974; Chilton 1979; 1984; 1996; Camponovo 1984; Allison 1985; Beasley-Murray 1986; Chilton and McDonald 1987; Collins 1987; Willis 1987; Selman 1989; Hengel and Schwemer 1991; Harrisville 1993; Mays 1993; O'Neill 1993; Rowe 2002; Horsley 2003; Beavis 2006; Smith 2009; Wright 2012.

[88] E.g. 1 Chron. 16.31; Pss. 10.16; 93.1; 96.10; 97.1; 99.1.

[89] 1 Sam. 4.4; 2 Kings 19.15; 1 Chron. 13.6; Pss. 80.1; 99.1; Isa. 37.16; etc.

conditions by which Israel might fulfil its vocation, namely the discharge of its ongoing priestly service through worship. The ensuing harmony between heaven and earth would continue undisturbed unto eternity, and then, and only then, could Israel say, with overtones of Robert Browning, 'God's in his earth as he is in his heaven; all's right with the world.' The broad and long-standing scholarly disagreement regarding Jesus' own conception of the coming of the kingdom does not diminish the fact that for Second-Temple Judaism the phrase 'your kingdom come' could only be unpacked with reference to this eschatological drama staged on temple grounds.[90] Had Jesus meant something else altogether when he spoke of the coming of the kingdom, he would have been best served using another term.

Falling on first-century ears, the prayer 'Your kingdom come' therefore builds on the same restoration scenario as 'Hallowed be your name'. But it is decidedly unlikely that with this phrase Jesus imagines a return to pre-exilic conditions *simpliciter*. Instead, mindful of Yahweh's promise to establish a final, eschatological temple, he must be referring to that long-awaited moment when the cosmic throne room, the heavenly prototype of the earthly cultus, would descend and finally supplant the temple made by human hands (Dan. 2.34).[91] Therefore Raymond Brown is right on track when in reference to the second petition he writes: 'The Christians are not primarily asking that God's dominion come into their own hearts . . . but that God's universal reign be established – that destiny toward which the whole of time is directed'.[92] When Jesus' followers repeated their master's prayer, they most likely imagined in concrete and realistic terms the establishment of God's kingdom through the implementation of a new and irreplaceable temple cultus.

Third petition: 'Your will be done on earth as it is in heaven' (Matt. 6.10b–c)

Luke lacks the third petition. As a result, many scholars do not ascribe the text back to the historical Jesus and so I will refrain from incorporating it into my larger argument. However, it bears mentioning that the text hardly undermines the eschatological reading as I am presenting it: '[m]ost modern interpreters . . . have taken the line to refer primarily to the eschatological realization of heaven on earth: God's will is done when his salvific purpose – a triumph of grace – is fully accomplished'.[93] Arguably, from Matthew's perspective, that moment occurs when the eschatological temple supplants the earthly temple.

---

[90] This point is properly appreciated in Chilton 1984; 1996.
[91] See Nicholas Perrin 2010: 11, 102.
[92] Brown 2010 (1961): 299.
[93] Davies and Allison 1988–97: 1.605. For a fully developed argument along these lines, see Lohfink 1989.

Fourth petition: 'Give us each day our daily bread' (Q 11.3)

While Matthew 6.11 has 'Give us *this* day our daily bread', the Lukan parallel reads: 'Give us *each* day our daily bread' (Luke 11.3). The differences between the two Evangelists may be explained with recourse to a common Semitic substratum.[94] Meanwhile, the Greek term behind the traditional translation 'daily', *epiousion*, is infamously difficult, having almost no parallel in Greek literature. One commonly adopted reading, going back at least as far as the *Gospel of the Hebrews* (passed down by Jerome), takes *epiousion* as 'coming' (a derivative of *epienai*, 'to come to') and renders the phrase as 'tomorrow's bread'.[95] This opens up the possibility of an eschatological reading, which is exactly how some of our earliest witnesses understood it.[96]

In this case, Jesus may intend either the bread that accompanies the longed-for messianic banquet, which is supported by the Jesus tradition (Matt. 8.11–12; 22.1–14; 25.1–13; Luke 12.35–37; 13.28–29), or the fresh outpouring of manna expected to accompany the eschatological rest, on the model of Exodus 16.[97] It is not impossible that both are simultaneously in view, that is, on the assumption that the messianic feast would be supplied by heaven-sent manna. Either of these explanations would lend support in its own way to the thesis at hand. Given its moorings in Isaiah 25, the messianic banquet was doubtlessly recognized as a priestly meal celebrating the advent of the kingdom.[98] But if Jesus' prayer primarily focused on the eschatological manna and less on the feast itself, more on the menu than on the venue, this hardly detracts from my point. We recall that in the exodus narrative, as part of the ratification of the Mosaic covenant, Yahweh brings Israel's elders into his presence in order to feed them (Exod. 24.11) a cultic meal later memorialized in the practice whereby every Sabbath the priests would consume the previous week's bread and display fresh Bread of the Presence.[99] Divinely sponsored and restricted to priests, the ritualized consumption of the Sabbath presence-bread was an ongoing recapitulation of the founding sacred meal (with intimations of the Passover meal in Exodus 12). Since in the Sinai years

---

94 Grelot 1978–9.

95 So, e.g., Black 1967: 204 (though with qualifications); Brown 2010 (1961): 304–10; Lohmeyer 1965: 134–59; Jeremias 1971: 200; Marshall 1978: 460; Davies and Allison 1988–97: 1.608–10; Green 1997: 443. As Dennis observes (2013: 93), many of these scholars have (rightly) noted that the eschatological interpretation incorporates the *quotidian* interpretation ('Give us bread sufficient for today'), inasmuch as the great eschatological meal entailed the promise of anticipatory, divinely sponsored 'appetizer hours' on earth (cf. also Nicholas Perrin 2014). The earliest interpreters understood the fourth petition on multiple levels such as these with no embarrassment; see Dewailly 1980: 565–88.

96 In addition to the *Gospel of the Hebrews*, also Marcion and the Old Syriac (Curetonian).

97 On the messianic banquet in general, see Zech. 8.12; cf. Isa. 25.6–8; *1 En.* 62.13–16; *2 Bar.* 29.5; 1QSa 2.17–22; 1QS 6.4–6. For manna as the fare at the messianic banquet, see *b. Ḥagigah* 12b; *2 Bar.* 29.9; *Sib. Or.* 7.149; 2 Macc. 2.4–7.

98 Nicholas Perrin 2010: 174–9.

99 The meal of Exod. 24.11 was intended to stand in pointed contrast to the practice of pagan priests who were responsible for feeding bread to their deities (cf. Davies 2004: 135); the Bread of the Presence remained Yahweh's bread at a basic level. On the cultic and covenantal aspects of the meal, see Morales 2012: 240 n. 252.

the Bread of the Presence could only be formed from manna gathered the day before (Exod. 16.5), it was always, in the nature of the case, 'tomorrow's bread'. Therefore (as I will argue more fully in Chapter 6), Jesus' 'tomorrow's bread' referred not to eschatological bread in a general sense but to a Bread of the Presence reserved for the eschatological priests.[100] This future bread would presumably share at least some of the same supernatural properties as manna, which was thought to convey the word of God.[101] Through the fourth petition, Jesus invited his disciples to pray that God would introduce this bread into the here and now.

Fifth petition: 'And forgive us our sins, for we ourselves forgive everyone indebted to us' (Q 11.4a–b)

On the face of it, there is nothing particularly distinctive about Jesus' fifth petition, since there is considerable evidence that first-century Judaism, like the *PN*, grounded eschatological divine forgiveness on the individual's ability to forgive others.[102] But once understood against the backdrop I have been suggesting, the request 'forgive us our sins/debts' (the Aramaic *ḥôbā'* presumed to underlie both connotes a bit of both) begins to take on decidedly sacerdotal overtones. This follows on a closer examination of the field of reference behind Jesus' utterance of Q 11.4a–b.

In his reconstruction of the original wording of the Lord's Prayer, Jeremias hypothesizes that Matthew's aorist verb *aphēkamen* ('we have forgiven') and Luke's present tense *aphiomen* ('we forgive') converge in the Aramaic *šebāqnān*, which was meant as a constitutive perfect, translatable 'as *herewith* we forgive our debtors'.[103] On this reading, the disciples can look forward to God's forgiveness because they have declared themselves, before God and one another in a repeatedly performed speech-act, a community committed to forgiving their enemies' wrongdoing. If this is correct, then the wrongdoings in view are not theoretical transgressions in the abstract and faraway future but rather the particular offences inflicted by the movement's persecutors. As such, the

---

[100] As Lohmeyer (1965: 143) points out, the Old Syriac, Gothic and Armenian versions assume an 'analogy between [the *PN*'s] "our bread" and the Old Testament shewbread', which in Num. 4.7 LXX is designated as 'continual bread' (*hoi artoi hoi dia pantos*). This would be similar to the eschatological vision revealed to Levi in the *Testament of Levi*: 'To you and your posterity will be everything desired in Israel, and you shall eat everything attractive to behold, and your posterity will share among themselves the Lord's table. From among them will be priests . . . and by their word the sanctuary will be controlled' (*T. Levi* 8.16–18). See also Barker 2003: 101–2.

[101] Arguing that the fourth petition alludes to the restoration of Jerusalem and the return of its scattered 'sons' (Psalm 147), Kratz (1992: 22) aptly comments that this bread would have prefigured the realization of the Isaianic promise of return from exile, when 'the "sons", regathered in rebuilt Jerusalem, would have no longer lived on bread alone, but rather on the Word of God – on the word of salvation, which the prophets had proclaimed for Zion'.

[102] Sir. 28.2–5; *T. Zeb.* 5.3; 8.1–2; *T. Jos.* 18.2; *b. Šabb.* 151b; *m. Yoma* 8.9; *t. B. Qam* 9.29; *b. Meg.* 28a. In these instances, there is no necessary inference that the forgiving individual merits divine forgiveness.

[103] Jeremias 1971: 201.

prayer for eschatological forgiveness (which is in some ways already palpable in the present through Jesus) was meant to engender the spiritual and psychological capacity to extend forgiveness to those who played Pharaoh to the Jesus movement's Israel. Thus, in its original setting, the fifth petition was not first and foremost a means of enjoining mutual forgiveness among members *within* the community (Matt. 18.21–35; Mark 11.25; Luke 17.3–4), which could only have been presupposed, but a divinely backed corporate statement of intent to repay with kindness the blistering attacks from *without*.

Although the concrete outworking of such forgiveness – exactly how such forgiveness would look to the outside observer – may leave much to the imagination, it is interesting to consider how the third Evangelist teases out the implications of the fifth petition, first in Jesus' words of forgiveness from the cross ('Father, forgive them; for they do not know what they are doing' (Luke 23.34)) and, second, in Stephen's words of forgiveness as he is being martyred ('Lord, do not hold this sin against them' (Acts 7.60)).[104] Obviously Jesus and Stephen are held out as models, exemplifying the appropriate response to the movement's persecutors in the Evangelist's own day. As models, they do not so much forgive their opponents as intercede for forgiveness on their behalf, in a manner reminiscent of archetypal acts of intercession (Gen. 18.22–33; Exod. 32.7–14). For Luke, 'to forgive those who have sinned against us' finds its supreme expression when believers respond to their enemies by interceding for their forgiveness before God. For Luke's readers in the early Christian community, then, to obey Luke/Q 11.4 was to take up a priestly role.[105]

That the historical Jesus also shared and indeed promulgated this interpretation of his own prayer is not difficult to prove. In Matthew 5.44 ('But I say to you, Love your enemies and pray for those who persecute you'), the authenticity of which is undisputed, Jesus makes clear that one of the distinctive markers of his followers would be a shared commitment to pray for those who bore tangible malice towards the community. Such prayer was to be not a begrudging act, but rather born out of an attitude of love and compassion. This is not to say that Jesus' followers obeyed this injunction with unflinching consistency: on the contrary, the reports that have come down to us record just the opposite.[106] Nevertheless, the prayer embodies an ideal that was central to the movement's *modus operandi*. When Jesus issued the words preserved in Q 11.4a–b to his disciples, he expected them to serve as a prompt for not just forgiveness but also regular intercessory prayer, a characteristically priestly function.

---

[104] Jesus' prayer at Luke 23.34 is textually suspect, but there is sufficient evidence to count it as authentically Lukan. See judicious review of the arguments by Marshall (1978: 867–8), who also comments on the natural ties with 11.4 and Acts 7.60.

[105] If we read Matt. 6.12 in the light of Jesus' instructions to the disciples in Matt. 18.18 ('Truly I tell you, whatever you bind on earth will be bound in heaven, and whatever you loose on earth will be loosed in heaven'), then the forgiveness of 6.12 is ultimately a mediated forgiveness, issued on behalf of the community and on behalf of God.

[106] Luke 9.52–56; Matt. 26.50–52//Luke 22.49–51//John 18.10–11.

In this respect, Jesus' ethical vision marks a significant departure from other sectarian conceptions of the day, especially those which envisaged the latter-day priests as instruments of divine retribution.[107] Here the typical expectation was that Yahweh's priests would mete out justice, sometimes violent justice, to the enemies of God. Intending to install an eschatological priesthood in pursuit of a completely different path, Jesus knew that he would have to reshape his followers' self-understanding accordingly. In this respect, the fifth petition was not only a prayer, but a memorandum of understanding between the disciples as to how they ought to relate to their enemies. As Jesus would have it, this eschatological priesthood-in-the-making would seek to image Yahweh not as a conventional warrior, but rather in his self-revelation as one who is merciful and forgiving.

Sixth petition: 'And do not bring us to the time of trial' (Q 11.4b)

If Jesus is indeed calling on God as 'Father' as part of a re-enactment of the exodus in his own experience and in the experience of his followers, then the plea to be delivered from *peirasmos* ('trial' or 'temptation') fits hand in glove with this distinctive naming of God. The plagues preceding the exodus, not least the tenth Passover plague, were – along with the Aqedah – a kind of paradigmatic *peirasmos*.[108] In retrospect, it was only through this *peirasmos* that true Israel, the Son of God, could be identified and indeed consecrated. The logic of the analogy speaks for itself. By encouraging his disciples to request deliverance from *peirasmos*, Jesus is not simply speaking to the avoidance of sin but, more directly to the point, appealing for safe passage through an anticipated experience of suffering that would make human failure all the more likely.[109] This was not an arbitrary suffering but rather the necessary, appointed means by which Yahweh would define those who were true priestly sons. In scriptural logic, language of trial and testing is associated with the 'fear of the Lord'; the point of *peirasmos* is enhanced obedience.[110]

This at any rate appears to be how Matthew and Luke interpreted it. In Mark, Jesus anticipates *peirasmos* when he prays, 'Watch and pray so that you will not fall into temptation [*peirasmos*]' (Mark 14.38 par., NIV). On Matthew and Luke's retention of this injunction, but now in obvious correlation with the Lord's Prayer, one may be forgiven for wondering whether the linkage between the 'trial' of the PN (Matt. 6.13//Luke 11.4b) and the 'trial' of Gethsemane (Matt. 26.41//Luke 22.46) renders the two occurrences as

---

[107] See for example the *War Scroll*, the *Animal Apocalypse* (*1 Enoch* 89—90), *T. Levi* 3.3, 5.6; *T. Dan.* 6.1–3; etc. The priest-like status of Israel's present-day freedom fighters is presumed throughout 1 and 2 Maccabees. Also see Angel 2010: 196–202; Fletcher-Louis 2013: 698.

[108] Deut. 7.19; 29.2–3. On the Aqedah (the binding of Isaac) as a *peirasmos*, see 1 Macc. 2.52; also Andrews 1942.

[109] So too Lohmeyer 1965: 204–8; Jeremias 1971: 202; Schürmann 1981: 114–18. On the tribulation see Schweitzer 2001 (1906): 315–54; Allison 1985; Dunn 2003: 824; Pate and Kennard 2003; Pitre 2005; McKnight 2005: 145; Nicholas Perrin 2010: 108–16.

[110] Moberly 2000: 78–107.

mutually defining.[111] While it is not impossible that both Evangelists wish us to interpret *peirasmos* in one sense at Matthew 6.13//Luke 11.4b and then in a different sense at Matthew 26.41//Luke 22.46, this is not the most economical reading. In my judgement, for both Matthew and Luke, the 'trial' in view in Gethsemane, the events of the Passion and the dangers which Jesus' arrest would pose to his disciples, is no different from the kind of trial anticipated in the Lord's Prayer. At this point, Carmignac (among others) objects that Jesus never says 'Lead us not into *the* temptation' but rather speaks of temptation without the article and therefore, presumably, in the generic sense.[112] Yet the force of this objection swiftly diminishes once it is recognized how easily *peirasmos* lends itself to synecdoche, so that individual trials may be interpreted in the light of an overarching, divinely mandated trial.[113] From the Gospel writers' perspective, *the* tribulation/temptation included within its scope multiple, isolated instances of conflict with enemies both human and spiritual, resulting in a certain fluidity between the part ('a trial') and the whole ('*the* trial').[114]

In this case, the two earliest receptions of Jesus' prayer understand the sixth petition much as I have described it in the *Sitz im Leben Jesu*.[115] For the Evangelists, despite the obvious differences between how the respective *peirasmoi* of Jesus and the disciples may have been in their particular outworking, both seem to have shared an essential common denominator. If this reading is correct, then Jesus' point is just this: those who intend to validate their status as sons and priests before Yahweh must do so by faithfully passing through the *peirasmos*, the divinely willed crucible of demonically inspired persecution. On analogy with the Passover, the *peirasmos* which the historical Jesus seems to have in mind is the appointed means of consecration unto priesthood (Exod. 13.1).[116]

Seventh petition: 'but rescue us from the evil one' (Matt. 6.13b)

Like the third petition, the seventh petition has often been regarded as a by-product of Matthean ingenuity and thus is excluded from consideration. Nevertheless, if the words are of dominical origin, they would nicely reinforce my case: that Jesus is praying for deliverance from the demonically inspired persecution which he and his followers are facing.[117]

---

[111] The verbal parallels between the Lord's Prayer and the Gethsemane account have been broadly noted; see, e.g., Grelot 1984: 540–1; Davies and Allison 1988–97: 3.497; Luz 1989–2005: 3.394.

[112] Carmignac 1969: 340–1.

[113] Moreover, as Jeremy Otten reminds me, objects of prepositions (even if definite in meaning) are commonly anarthrous.

[114] As non-articular *peirasmos* as an umbrella term for a series of temptations or conflicts, see Andrews 1942: 233–6, 238–40.

[115] This is certainly the way the author of Revelation understood the term: 'Because you have kept my word of patient endurance, I will keep you from the hour of trial [*hōras tou peirasmou*] that is coming on the whole world to test the inhabitants of the earth' (Rev. 3.10).

[116] This topic receives further coverage in Chapter 2.

[117] Popkes (1990) makes an excellent argument for the last petition's integration into the prayer as a whole, connecting particularly with *the* tribulation of the previous petition.

Summary

In this chapter, I have sought to provide a comprehensive reading of the *PN*. On my interpretation, the rationale for Jesus' opening utterance of 'Father' is consistent with the prayer's first petition ('Hallowed be your name'). Thus two lines in turn anchor the subsequent petitions, which are to be understood in the same vein. With each petition Jesus is alluding to a different aspect of a single eschatological reality, all centred around a newly consecrated priesthood and sacred space. One virtue of this overall interpretation consists in its providing a cohesive framework for understanding the *PN* as a whole.[118] Conversely, if (for lack of a better phrase) the so-called 'traditional reading' of the prayer has a debilitating weakness, it is in its failure to offer an integrating point by which the various petitions might be convincingly correlated.[119]

This is not necessarily to say that the traditional reading offers an 'incorrect reading' of the text, as if personal holiness, dependence on God for daily necessities, and the importance of steering clear of temptation are all illegitimate theological inferences from the received text – they are not. But the question we are dealing with is the question of origins. If the historical Jesus first conveyed this prayer in the throes of an exodus-like experience, fraught with danger from the persecutors yet graced by hope of divine redemption, then it seems inherently implausible that Jesus was content to offer the petitions as a kind of generalized wish list covering every conceivable human need for life in the abstract. Rather, given the historical particularity of the Jesus movement with its challenges, the complementary set of asks appears more likely as a blueprint for enduring the hour of tribulation. Understood this way, the prayer comes down to us as a textual artefact of Jesus' sense of vocation, whereby he and his disciples saw themselves as having been called to a task that was soon to present itself.

The task was potentially two-fold. In the first place, if the Ezekielian backdrop to the *PN* is fully cashed out, then Jesus and his movement took it upon themselves to usher in the eschatological kingdom, an event signalled by the return from exile, the fresh indwelling of Yahweh's spirit within a decisively refurbished temple, and the engaging of consistently monotheistic (i.e. idol-free) worship. On this scenario, through praying the *PN*, which specifically included prayer for those who opposed the movement, Jesus and his followers would probably see themselves as giving birth to this new divinely wrought reality. Of course any group which had publicly assigned itself the task of transforming Ezekiel's vision – reconsecrating the land, ordaining new priests, abolishing idolatry and receiving the spirit – into reality would be making a considerable claim. It would also be an essentially priestly claim. Those who were impressed by such aspirations would certainly have con-

---

[118] As noted by Davies and Allison 1988–97: 1.594.

[119] I use the term 'traditional reading' for convenience. The eschatological reading has its own ancient pedigree going at least as far back as Tertullian.

templated attaching themselves to this exciting, heady movement. But those who failed to be persuaded would naturally come to regard the movement as an illegitimate and ultimately dangerous priesthood. And for the politically powerful sceptics, there would have naturally been opportunities for reprisal along social, economic, religious or political lines. All the while, of course, the chief target would have been Jesus himself.

This leads to the second task (that is, if Jesus leveraged the exodus as I have argued): the task of remaining obedient in the face of suffering. As both the larger exodus context and the sixth petition seem to intimate, Jesus anticipated that his movement would endure persecution at the hands of the authorities and that this persecution, once faithfully borne, would have some kind of atoning efficacy. On this reading, by calling God 'Father' and inviting his disciples to do the same, Jesus was ascribing to his movement the priestly status of sonship. This ascription did not originate with any interior experience, whether in Jesus' consciousness or in that of his disciples, but drew directly on the logic of the exodus. Just as Israel was the firstborn son of God, and the firstborn within Israel were to be identified and consecrated as priests through *peirasmos*, so too now Yahweh was poised to bring about a new exodus through a new *peirasmos*, issuing in a new priesthood. As sons of God, Jesus and his disciples were priests, marked off by their shared determination to pray for rather than retaliate against their persecutors. As tried-yet-faithful sons of God, Jesus and his disciples intended to be priests in the truest and fullest sense, even if exactly what that means remains to be seen.

If my reading of the *PN* is on track, then the Lord's Prayer is more than a prayer; it is an unsurpassed summary of all that Jesus had dreamed and hoped for his company of followers. Succinctly worded and to the point, our *PN* was originally issued as the historical Jesus' mission statement; it was the oral charter for a new eschatological priesthood, which was in the process of being formed under Jesus not on the basis of genealogical descent but on his call. Those who wished to affirm their ordination within this new priesthood could only do so by daring to pray the prayer with the community. It was simultaneously the most inclusive and the most exclusive of all prayers.

Whatever the explanatory power of this reading of the Lord's Prayer, we await further corroboration. At the same time, there is still one matter of unfinished business raised in this chapter: the question of Jesus' 'upper-case Sonship' in distinction from the disciples' 'lower-case sonship'. If Jesus and his disciples equally shared in a priestly calling, then one might expect language reflecting a level playing field, at least in the earliest layers of the tradition. Yet on review of the data it appears that the playing field is anything but level: Jesus' sonship is bracketed out as qualitatively superior, unique. If my interpretation of the Lord's Prayer is ultimately to be sustained, this lingering problem of Jesus' unique sonship must also be resolved. I hope to begin to do so in the following chapter.

2

The baptism of Jesus

Introduction

The family of Caiaphas the high priest had long been settled in Jerusalem. As true as this was for the family dynasty, it was all the more true for the institution itself. The high priest was Yahweh's duly appointed, duly installed divine representative to Israel – and by extension to the world. That was at least how the high priest and his extended family thought of it; that too was the presumed theory underwriting the temple organization, a theory the Romans took advantage of as they supported the temple hierarchy in a marriage of political convenience.

But this was *not* exactly how Jesus and his followers viewed things. For Jesus, so I have argued, something new and different was afoot – something from God. While, to be sure, even the most vocal opponents of the high priest would have attributed the person in that office an *ex officio* authority, the opening decades of the first century had only yielded further evidence that Israel's sacred top-brass had corrupted itself.[1] And something had to give. True, the high priest of Jesus' day was not alone in his sacral malfeasance. The office had been breaking bad for years; the chequered history of Israel's priesthood reached all the way back to the Seleucid era of the early second century BCE. But on Jesus' understanding, divine patience had run its course. The present redemptive-historical era was winding down and God was about to do something big, even revolutionary.

How revolutionary? Well, again from Jesus' perspective, the divine timetable required nothing less than a change in the temple economy. According to the band of Galileans, Yahweh was about to sever ties with the established temple and give life to a new priesthood planted in a new cultic space. That cultic space was the very in-breaking of the eschatological temple on earth, the coming of the kingdom of God; *its* priesthood, Jesus' very own following. The resistance which his disciples might expect to endure from the regnant priesthood was in fact part and parcel of their priestly calling. More than that, it was through enduring this opposition that the Jesus movement would discharge its divinely granted vocation.

In the previous chapter, I raised the question as to how we might think of the historical Jesus encouraging his disciples to pray to God as 'Father' without

---

[1] See Nicholas Perrin 2010: 21–45, 92–9.

contradicting his own status as 'Son' in some non-transferable sense. The Old Liberal reading of Jesus, identifying such naming practices with interior experiences of God, admits no categorical distinction between the sonship of Jesus and the sonship of just about everyone else (even if Jesus had a relatively better grasp of his filial status than the rest of us). But, again, this interpretation is undercut by the stubborn fact that Jesus seems to have regarded his disciples as – for lack of better terminology – lower-case 'sons', whereas he himself remained an upper-case 'Son'. Given this quandary, we need either a more nuanced version of the old explanation or a different explanation altogether.

In the present chapter as well as in Chapters 4–6, I want to advance the discussion of Jesus' sonship a few steps. In the latter chapters, I will be arguing that Jesus uses the term 'Son of David' and 'Son of Man' as indicative of a priestly status. Meanwhile, in this the second chapter, I will restrict discussion to what by all accounts seems to have been the originating point of the term 'Son of God' in the Jesus tradition: his baptism. Interrogating this event, I intend to pose two queries: what did it mean for Jesus to be called Son – in the upper-case sense? And how, if at all, did this relate to the disciples' status as sons in the lower-case sense? These are important questions that deserve an answer.

One commonly proposed answer to my first question is that Jesus designated himself as 'Son' with a view to signifying his messianic identity.[2] Certainly, this theory is attractive on several grounds. First, it squares well with the fact that Jesus himself performed a number of actions which could easily have been interpreted as 'messianic' in a broad sense.[3] Second, Jesus' self-identity as messianic Son would explain those dominical pronouncements that in one way or another appear to be indebted to scriptural traditions where messianic son-figures (Son of David and Son of Man) feature prominently. Third, the theory is historically plausible: since 'Son of God' was by the first century already a well-established circumlocution for 'messiah', it does not strain credulity to suppose that Jesus' self-identity as 'Son' was an outworking of a messianic consciousness. If Jesus did see himself as messiah, then his assumed moniker 'Son' would be consistent with this self-perception.

Yet to equate 'Son' with 'messiah' (and vice versa) without further ado is both to say too much and to accomplish too little. It says too much, because we are not so sure that there was a unified first-century expectation for the messiah. If 'Son' is interchangeable with 'messiah', and 'messiah' basically serves as a catch-all designation for an eschatological figure who makes sure the good guys win, then we are hardly better off in our understanding. The

---

[2] While some (e.g. Bultmann 1951: 26–32; Vermes, 1973: 141–3; Crossan 1991: 422–6; Dunn 2003: 652–4) have resisted the notion that the historical Jesus self-consciously prosecuted a messianic programme, others (Manson 1953; Stuhlmacher 1993; Sanders 1985: 307–8 (though with qualification); Wright 1996: 477–539; Keener 2009: 256–67; Bird 2009) have been more sanguine.

[3] On this, see especially Wright 1996: 475–539.

Son-equals-messiah approach also fails to resolve the problem I raised earlier, namely, the incommensurateness between Jesus' filial status and that of his disciples. Again, we are left with one of two options. The first is to maintain the essentially messianic nature of Jesus' sonship but then also to concede that this has no conceptual relationship to the sonship of the disciples – on the face of it, an awkward explanation. A second and inherently more appealing option would be to seize on an explanatory model which, on the one hand, allows for a shared sonship between Jesus and his disciples, but, on the other hand, also allows for some differentiation in how that sonship is worked out, in keeping with the distinction which the tradition consistently posits between Jesus and his disciples.

One such model presents itself on the possibility that Jesus' Sonship and the disciples' sonship shared a common denominator of *priesthood*. If in the previous chapter I sought to argue that the disciples' status of 'sons', implied by the Lord's Prayer, was a function of their priestly calling, in this chapter I will go on to argue that this assignation logically (and chronologically) followed from Jesus' baptism. For at his baptism, a largely recoverable event, Jesus laid hold of his *high-priestly* vocation precisely as the unique 'Son of God', even as he allowed his immediate followers to participate in that sonship indirectly, that is, as they took up their priestly calling.

John's baptism

Given John the Baptizer's stature in the early first century, it is not implausible that the stories about him accrued elements that verged on legendary. All the same, this does not negate the fact that there is indeed much we can know about John and his baptism. First of all, his was a baptism in the wilderness, taking place at the River Jordan.[4] As the wilderness would have not been the most accessible of sites, especially for a public figure interested in attracting large-scale crowds, one suspects that John's choice of venue was motivated more by its symbolic than its practical value. In Judaism, the wilderness was associated with Israel's national origins. By setting up camp there, the Baptizer was not only issuing a thinly veiled protest against the temple authorities but also graphically portraying his own movement as a kind of new Israel in germ form.[5]

I am aware that designating John as a 'movement leader' is controversial.[6] It shouldn't be. It is finally unconvincing to maintain that John called for reform without his ever being a movement leader.[7] Had John's personal

---

[4] Matt. 3.6//Mark 1.5. John reports that John was at Bethany 'on the other side of the Jordan' (1.28).

[5] See Nicholas Perrin 2010: 17–45; Webb 1991: 197–205; also Wright 1996: 160–2; Dapaah 2005: 77; etc.

[6] See, e.g., Taylor (1997: 29–32) who sees John's efforts as reflecting 'a mentality, rather than a movement' (32); also Kraeling 1951: 199–200; Ernst 1989: 349; Chilton 1994: 20–6;

[7] On John as a movement leader, see Webb 1991: 377–8.

identity been so incidental to his baptism or to those gathered around him, it is unlikely that the phrase '*John's* baptism' could have ever become common coinage in early Christianity.[8] Moreover, we have a reasonably secure datum in John 3.26 that John's disciples protested when a baptizing sub-movement under Jesus' name began to drain their own numbers. Such a sensitivity among John's disciples – showing a keen awareness as to who was coming and who was going – would only be explicable in a situation where an identifiable 'John community' was used to drawing some kind of line between who was 'in' and who was 'out'. Those who were 'in' would naturally identify themselves as John's disciples with John himself as their leader. As for those who were 'out', there was always hope that they would one day see the light. Noting these observations, we find that a little common sense can go a long way: if the gathering around John looks like a movement, carries out business like a movement and makes protesting noises like a movement – well, then, it's a movement.

This does not mean that everyone who underwent John's baptism would have been compelled to identify with John's following in the same way. Immensely popular in Judea, the Baptizer had managed to drum up a broad following drawing on all kinds of people. While a subset of this constituency may have given up all kith and kin in order to be with John on a 'full-time basis', the vast majority of the baptized probably returned to their workaday lives. As in Qumran and the later Jesus movement, there seem to have been varying degrees of commitment, or more precisely, various ways in which one's commitment could be expressed. Anyone who was baptized by John would have considered it appropriate for him to have done so and, accordingly, would have also supported his programme.

John's programme was thoroughly eschatological in orientation. He came announcing the imminent arrival of 'one who is more powerful than I', one who would baptize not with water but 'with the Holy Spirit and fire'.[9] Accordingly, the coming one was to be both restorer and judge. Within the context of this announcement, John saw his own role as one of preparing a remnant in anticipation of the soon-to-come eschatological day. Those who responded favourably to his preaching and were thus baptized set themselves apart as the ongoing continuation of that remnant. This is consistent with the Gospel writers' associating John's ministry with Isaiah 40, a passage which announces the return of the forgiven remnant from exile. Because the Baptizer's movement, much like Qumran, identified itself as the fulfilment of the Isaianic return-from-exile, movement members would have naturally regarded themselves as recipients of the same forgiveness which had been promised as both a benefit of and an antecedent condition for the return.[10]

---

[8] Matt. 21.25; Mark 11.30; Luke 20.4; Acts 1.22; 18.25.
[9] Matt. 3.11//Mark 1.8//Luke 3.16.
[10] Isa. 40.1–3. On the use of Isa. 40.3 at Qumran, see 1QS 8.13–16; 9.19–20; Brownlee 1992 (1955).

For this reason, John offered 'a baptism of repentance for the forgiveness of sins'.[11] The baptism was less a service provided to those aspiring to greater piety, and more a national-scale event which called for individual response from all those within Israel; it was not so much a baptism in response to personal repentance, but a repentance-baptism, which effectively sealed one's participation in the newly reconstituted repentant Israel.[12] As a highly symbolic initiation rite, the baptism betokened forgiveness of sins, marking out the baptized as members of the Isaianic remnant who might rightfully expect eschatological vindication. Repentance, baptism and forgiveness would have been ultimately impossible to separate out: John's offer of baptism was essentially equivalent to the offer of divine forgiveness.

Naturally, this kind of standing offer would have created strained relationships with the priestly leaders back in Jerusalem, for they would have taken exception to the masses receiving forgiveness outside the temple apparatus and their prescribed sacrifices. Indeed, by issuing forgiveness and thereby functioning as a gatekeeper for the newly reconstituted Israel, John was already functioning as a priest.[13] In one sense, the role would not be entirely unwarranted, given John's lineage alluded to in Luke 1.5–25. Yet in another sense, by carrying out a priestly ministry outside the confines of Jerusalem holy space and under his own auspices, John would have been regarded by the powerbrokers as a renegade much along the lines of Onias III, the mid-second-century BC priest who had fled to Leontopolis to establish his own temple. In sum, as I and others have argued elsewhere at greater length, John's movement was a counter-temple movement in the making.[14]

Baptism and theophany as history

That Jesus was baptized by John the Baptizer early in his ministry has been established as a non-negotiable datum.[15] The reasons for this judgement are certainly not hard to see. First and foremost, if early Christianity sometimes struggled to temper John the Baptizer's prominence (as part of an effort to pre-empt an 'Early High Baptist-ology'), then inventing a story in which John assumes a superior role and baptizes Jesus would have only aggravated matters. Since this is more or less the opposite of what we would expect

---

[11] Mark 1.4//Luke 3.3; cf. Matt. 3.6. Omitting language of forgiveness, Josephus describes John as one who exhorted the Jews 'to come together for immersion' (*Ant.* 18.5.2 §117). But Josephus's consistent de-eschatologizing of his Jewish heroes, out of deference to Roman sensitivities, qualifies his usefulness as a historical source; see Mason 1992: 179.

[12] So Meyer 2002 (1979): 122–8; Webb 1991: 167. At the same time, to overplay the objective/national element over and against the subjective/personal element (or vice versa) risks quibbling; see the sage remarks of Beasley-Murray 1962: 34–5.

[13] On the priests' crucial role in forgiveness, see Lev. 5.5–10.

[14] For a fuller argument and bibliography, see Nicholas Perrin 2010: 17–45.

[15] See, e.g., Kraeling 1951: 131; Bultmann 1968 (1921): 47; Sanders 1985: 11; Taylor 1997: 4. For an able response to Enslin's argument (Enslin 1975) that John and Jesus were never connected, see Webb 1994: 214–99; Webb 2009: 106–8.

the early Church to invent, historical Jesus scholarship has generally acknowledged this event as historical.

A review of the sources

As to *exactly* what happened at this historical event, we must do some more careful spadework. The sparest account among the synoptics comes down to us via Mark:

> In those days Jesus came from Nazareth of Galilee and was baptized by John in the Jordan. And just as he was coming up out of the water, he saw the heavens torn apart and the Spirit descending like a dove on him. And a voice came from heaven, 'You are my Son, the Beloved; with you I am well pleased.'[16]

Mark records that 'immediately' (*euthys*) after the baptism the 'heavens split open' (*schizomenous tous ouranous*), no doubt anticipating the moment, much later in the narrative, when the temple veil is 'torn asunder' (*eschizthē*) following the crucifixion (1.10a; 15.38). Next, the Spirit is said to descend on Jesus – in a turn of phrase that has puzzled commentators since time out of mind – 'like a dove' (1.10b).[17] Finally, the scene climaxes with an audible proclamation from heaven made up of several scriptural phrases: 'You are my Son, the Beloved; with you I am well pleased' (1.11).

Compared to the second Gospel, Matthew's account of the baptism is more fulsome, occupying the entirety of Matthew 3. While Mark has nothing about the religious elite approaching John or a threshing floor metaphor, the first Evangelist has both (Matt. 3.7–10, 12). Moreover, Matthew adds a brief interchange between Jesus and John, signalling the latter's reluctance to baptize his cousin; his objection is overcome by Jesus' overriding insistence 'to fulfil all righteousness' (3.15). Like Mark, Matthew records a voice from the heavens, albeit in the third person ('This is my Son') rather than Mark's second-person address ('You are my Son').[18] Together Mark and Matthew present a consistent report, even as the latter makes more perceptible use of the event within his own theological agenda, touching on not least the connection between Jesus' baptism and subsequent demands of righteousness, as well as the baptism's integration with the subsequent temptation narrative.[19]

Luke's account is closer to Matthew's than it is to Mark's but is consistent with both. Of course Luke adds his own special material as well. While Matthew's John preaches repentance as a monologue, Luke sets the ethical exhortation within the context of an interchange (Luke 3.10–14). In the third

---

[16] Mark 1.9–11.

[17] On the interpretative possibilities for 'like a dove', see Keck 1970; Gero 1976. For a 'Greek interpretation', see Dixon 2009.

[18] Matt. 3.17//Mark 1.11.

[19] On 'righteousness' in Matthew, see Matt. 5.6, 20; 6.33; 21.32; also Przybylski 1980. The repetition of 'If you are the Son of God . . .' (4.3, 6) in the first two temptations is an obvious echo of 3.17.

Gospel, too, the messianic expectation leading up to the baptism is more explicit (v. 15). Furthermore, Luke picks up on Mark's notice about John's time in prison (Mark 1.14a) and inserts it before the baptism – along with more in-depth elaboration (Luke 3.19–20). Luke's account of the baptism shares elements of Matthew and Mark in its particular wording, but takes pains to cast the event on the stage of a mass gathering (v. 21). The third Evangelist follows Mark in the phrasing, 'You are my Son' (v. 22).

Comparisons across the synoptic Gospels frustrate attempts to identify a singular source (whether Mark or Q) behind Matthew and Luke.[20] There are obvious points where Matthew and Luke agree against Mark.[21] There are also points at which Luke and Mark agree against Matthew, and places too where Matthew and Mark agree against Luke.[22] Such an amalgam of agreements and disagreements must be counted either as evidence against the Two-Source Hypothesis as a whole or, on the assumption of the Two-Source Hypothesis, evidence that Q also contains the baptism scene. Despite the fact that some scholars have eliminated the baptism from Q, a wider lens would seem virtually to require the baptism within the construct Q on two counts. First, the conditional statements at the beginning of Satan's temptations in Q 4.3, 9 ('If you are the Son of God . . .') only make sense given the earlier announcement of Jesus' sonship at Q 3.21–22. Second, in alleging a Q tradition without the baptism (Q 3.21–22), we are hard-pressed to explain the introduction of John's preaching at Q 3.7–9, which would appear as a rather odd and inexplicable rabbit trail. However, bringing up John in a story about Jesus is entirely fitting so long as John's appearance helps us to learn something useful about Jesus, which is exactly what the baptism scene achieves.[23]

---

[20] Such frustrations have spawned creative attempts to think outside the boxes of Q and Mark; see, e.g., Lupieri 1988 who, on canvassing the Minor Agreements which I outline in the present paragraph (1988: 16–19), ultimately advocates for a Markan–Matthean tradition and a Lukan tradition. Either way, the multiplex nature of the Baptist traditions is inescapable.

[21] For Luke and Matthew against Mark, note (1) the double tradition's omission of 'John' and 'Jordan' (Mark 1.9); (2) the mention of Jesus by name in the baptism (Matt. 3.16//Luke 3.21); (3) the change of Mark's finite verb 'he was baptized' (*ebaptisthē*) (Mark 1.9) to passive participial forms (Matt. 3.16//Luke 3.21); (4) a passive form of *anoigō* as opposed to *schizō* (Matt. 3.16//Luke 3.21); (5) *ep' auton* ('on to him') as opposed to *eis auton* ('to him') (Matt. 3.16//Luke 3.22).

[22] For Mark and Luke against Matthew, note (1) *egeneto* ('it was') (Mark 1.9//Luke 3.21); (2) the introductory *kai* ('and') before the description of the baptism (Mark 1.10//Luke 3.22); and (3) *sy ei* ('you are') (Mark 1.11/Luke 3.22) as opposed to *houtos estin* ('this is') (Matt. 3.17), along with corresponding pronouns (*hō* in Matthew; *soi* in Mark and Luke). For Matthew and Mark against Luke, see (1) *apo . . . tēs Galilaias* ('from Galilee') (Matt. 3.13//Mark 1.9); (2) *euthys* ('immediately') (Matt. 3.16//Mark 1.10); (3) a form of *anabainō* followed by the genitive construction *tou hydatos* ('from the water') (Matt. 3.16//Mark 1.10); and (4) plural as opposed to the singular of 'heaven', twice (Matt. 3.16, 17//Mark 1.10, 11).

[23] On both these two points, see especially Webb (2009: 98–9), who is supported by the International Q Project; contra Kloppenborg 2000: 93; Fleddermann 2005: 233–5. Curiously, although Fleddermann (2012: 52) considers Jesus' temptation (Q 4.2b–13) to be a 'flash-forward' to the cross (a story decisively outside the narrative of Q), he inexplicably fails to apply the same narrative-critical logic which would constitute the same temptation as a flashback to the baptism (a story plausibly within Q).

The Fourth Gospel has no baptism scene as such but contains a narrative that presupposes it. The Baptizer's reflection on the baptism affords a unique angle on its meaning in early Christianity:

> The next day he saw Jesus coming towards him and declared, 'Here is the Lamb of God who takes away the sin of the world! This is he of whom I said, "After me comes a man who ranks ahead of me because he was before me." I myself did not know him; but I came baptizing with water for this reason, that he might be revealed to Israel.' And John testified, 'I saw the Spirit descending from heaven like a dove, and it remained on him. I myself did not know him, but the one who sent me to baptize with water said to me, "He on whom you see the Spirit descend and remain is the one who baptizes with the Holy Spirit." And I myself have seen and have testified that this is the Son of God.'[24]

The consistency between the synoptic and Johannine tradition is striking: in both, the Spirit descends as a dove and the event as a whole somehow affords the conclusion that Jesus is 'the Son of God'. Of course there are also differences.[25] While in Mark the focus of the baptism scene is on Jesus' vision of the Spirit, according to the fourth Evangelist it is the Baptizer, not Jesus, who is credited with experiencing this vision. This is no basis for casuistically playing off Mark against John; rather it is only confirmation that, so far as early Christian tradition was concerned, the baptism of Jesus was an inter-subjective experience, that is, perceptible by at least two individuals who were present at the time (Jesus and John). As the tradition would have it, not only was Jesus' baptism a public event, but so too was the heavenly spectacle which closely followed.[26] This is an important point to which we shall return.

Questions surrounding the theophany

The weightier sources report that *something* happened at Jesus' baptism, an occurrence which was perceptible on an auditory and visual level. By common agreement, the sources describe this as an extraordinary event, involving the descent of the Spirit 'like a dove' and a heavenly voice, speaking words of Scripture, so as to confirm Jesus' identity as 'my son'. If we were governed only by the criterion of multiple attestation, the theophany would have secured its place in history without quibble.

History, however, is not always so simple. In addition to the theophany's self-evident uncanny quality, which raises its own set of historiographical concerns, other issues arise. First, given the way in which the rending (*schizomenous*) of the sky (Mark 1.10) foreshadows the rending (*eschisthē*)

---

[24] John 1.29–34.
[25] The successive Gospels posit increasingly starker contrasts between the respective statuses of John and Jesus; see, e.g., Bammel (1971–2).
[26] Although Mark may have intended to describe the vision as something perceptible only by Jesus, the second Evangelist – on analogy with the Transfiguration scene – clearly locates the voice in the public sphere; contra Ernst 1989: 17.

of the temple veil (15.38), and given, too, the crisp parallel between the declaration of Jesus as the Son in 1.11 and the centurion's similar confession in 15.39, Markan scholars often take the theophany to be a poetic fiction, fabricated to establish an *inclusio* bookending the text. Second, for some, the story of the heavenly voice, precisely because it utters scriptural language, must be regarded as a community or redactional invention, designed to establish Jesus' credentials long after the event.[27] Third, on a related point, a number of scholars are quick to ascribe the title 'Son of God' to post-Easter theological retrojection rather than anything connected to the life of Jesus. Thus, even if many are willing to allow Jesus' baptism by John as an unimpeachable fact, the theophany is far more vulnerable.[28]

Although the cumulative weight of the arguments against the theophany's historicity may seem impressive, the individual points are perhaps not as compelling as they initially appear. First, the surmise that the theophany scene was a function of Mark's creativity rather than the facts of history is misguided simply because it replicates the same tired either–or fallacy which needlessly pits history against theology.[29] That Mark intentionally and artfully frames a parallel between the theophany scene and the crucifixion is beyond question. That the theophany is therefore a pure figment of Mark's theological imagination hardly follows. For Mark, as for all the Gospel writers, Jesus' life was not simply to be recounted as a string of disparate episodes, but rather as a carefully shaped narrative, achieving a particular literary and theological effect. If it so happens that the theophany fits nicely within the story, this may legitimately raise the question as to whether such a 'fit' was wholly artificial, but it hardly rules out the possibility that the same effect was achieved by a wordsmith who was as attentive to an accurate account as he was to artful representation.

The second point (that the theophany itself must be secondary because scriptural midrash is by definition secondary) is also less than compelling. We expect that because the historical John and the historical Jesus were the only participants in the baptism experience, they would have also become the foremost interpreters of the same event. Moreover, as self-identified holy persons, they clearly saw themselves as being obliged to a divine mandate, duty-bound to the God of Israel and to the same God's Scriptures. Given these two points, it is most likely that it was neither the Evangelists nor intervening tradents who first associated the baptism with scriptural terms, but these same two historical figures. If we can agree that John and Jesus one day had a religious experience at the River Jordan, we should also be able

---

[27] As argued most fully by Meier 1980; Meier 1994: 106–8.

[28] Those who deny the historicity of the theophany include, e.g., Vögtle 1972: 105–39; Meier 1994: 106–7; Tatum 1994: 148–51.

[29] Maurice Goguel (1933 (1932): 270) provides a parade example: 'Although the fact of the baptism of Jesus by John is an established fact, the accounts of it which we have in the Gospels are not thereby rendered historical. They are theological explanations.' Le Donne (2009) offers an impressive critique of this disjunction.

to agree that they would have required a framework for understanding that experience – and why not Scripture?

The third and related objection to the theophany's authenticity claims an ecclesial ascription of divine sonship to Jesus on the grounds that such a high Christological assertion would have been feasible only after the resurrection. But this point is gravely weakened by the fact that 'son of God' was not a Christian title in the first place, but rather a pre-Christian Jewish one – not to mention a much-used pre-Christian Roman term. Moreover, the wide range of applications for the concept of divine sonship in antiquity gives us lots of room to imagine a first-century person being called a 'son of God' without denoting anything like the package of attributes catalogued in the creeds. Only a narrowly Christian reading of 'Son of God' would force us to see the phrase here as anachronistic.

Back to the theophany

The above discussion should give us some pause before dismissing the theophany as churchly invention, for in scratching the surface of the standard arguments for the theophany's secondary character, one finds less there than meets than eye. A fresh appraisal of the theophany is in order. Did a theophany or a theophany-like event occur that day in the River Jordan? And if so, how do we even begin talking about such an event?

Towards answering such questions, it bears mentioning that the earliest accounts of the baptism/theophany consistently accord Jesus' baptism a legitimizing function, validating his divine sonship on the basis of God's conspicuous penetration of the here and now. As such the event remains inescapably theological in nature. But, to return to an earlier point, this need not reduce the baptism to a mystical event, that is, an event which occurred – or was said to have occurred – strictly within Jesus' consciousness. On the contrary, for the early tradition, it is not as if Jesus' baptism could have just as well occurred on the far side of the moon or, as in the case of Jesus' temptations, in the remote wilderness with only Jesus himself to tell us about it. Instead, for early Christianity, there seems to have been an inner necessity which demanded that Jesus' identity as the 'Son of God' be grounded in a public divine intervention as John and others stood in attendance. And to this extent, the early Church also depended on the legitimacy of the Baptizer's prophetic credentials, as well as on the conviction that John, as God's prophet, spoke willingly to the event.

That the historical John spoke out of his prophetic office to Jesus' baptism is beyond dispute.[30] This finds witness in two places. The first such place is John 1.29–34, where John testifies to Jesus' role as 'lamb of God' in response

---

[30] Bypassing the debate as to how best to classify John's prophetic role, I wish only to note his status as a well-known religious figure. On Jesus' prophetic function, see Becker 1972: 41–62; Webb 1991: 35–55; Tilly 1994; Taylor 1997: 223–34; etc.

to the baptism event. While the authenticity of this passage is sometimes doubted, its thrust is corroborated by a second text of stronger historical claim, which speaks to a brief exchange between Jesus and his opponents in the aftermath of the temple cleansing. Seizing the opportunity to turn Jesus' action in the temple against him, his enemies seek to bait Jesus into going on public record. To that end, they ask him to tease out the implications of the temple act:

> Again they came to Jerusalem. As he was walking in the temple, the chief priests, the scribes, and the elders came to him and said, 'By what authority are you doing these things? Who gave you this authority to do them?' Jesus said to them, 'I will ask you one question; answer me, and I will tell you by what authority I do these things. Did the baptism of John come from heaven, or was it of human origin? Answer me.' They argued with one another, 'If we say, "From heaven", he will say, "Why then did you not believe him?" But shall we say, "Of human origin"?' – they were afraid of the crowd, for all regarded John as truly a prophet. So they answered Jesus, 'We do not know.' And Jesus said to them, 'Neither will I tell you by what authority I am doing these things.'[31]

The passage is an intriguing dialogue in which Jesus and his opponents are jockeying for position in their respective attempts to establish 'authority'. On being asked about his qualifications to cleanse the temple, Jesus retorts with a question of his own, revolving, curiously enough, around John's legitimacy as a messenger from God. Unless Jesus' counter-query was simply an impenetrable *non sequitur*, one supposes that Jesus' response was simply a way of moving the question of his own authority back one step to John's authority, with the suppressed but agreed-upon premise that Jesus' own legitimacy depends on John's attestation to the baptism. Onlookers at the scene very well knew that Jesus' opponents could hardly answer to such a question frankly without sacrificing considerable social capital. Had they gone on record against John the Baptizer at this point, they might have won the rhetorical battle (perhaps!), but it would only have been at the cost of losing the war for public favour. The point of interest for our purposes is this: when pushed to the wall regarding the legitimacy of his own authority as a temple cleanser and movement leader, Jesus appeals to his baptism under John. This appeal would be pointless unless it was already public knowledge that John had baptized Jesus and that their shared report of the baptism was the grounds for Jesus' subsequent claims and ministry.

Of course, notwithstanding the Baptizer's understandable vacillations while in prison (Q 7.18–23), this is exactly what the tradition reports: the Baptizer, in the last few years of his tragically shortened life, took it upon himself to testify that Jesus was a man sent from God. 'Exhibit A' in this testimony was nothing other than Jesus' extraordinary baptism.[32] From this we infer a rather robust oral tradition, springing up very quickly and

---

[31] Mark 11.27–33.
[32] As treated in John 1.29–34.

being broadcast very widely not long after the event. I say 'very quickly' because *whatever* happened on that day must have made a deep impression on John and therefore been difficult *not* to share; I say 'very widely' on account not only of John's wide-ranging popularity, but also his obvious willingness to reflect positively about Jesus' baptism. John's baptism of Jesus and its function in validating Jesus' role were, even in Jesus' own day, matters of street knowledge. All this helps put the reliability of the tradition into proper perspective. By the time Mark picks up pen to relate the details of Jesus' baptism, it had already been old news in Palestine – well established in the communities' oral traditions.

But by 'oral tradition' we cannot in this case mean (as is often meant) a story which is substantively revised as it is handed down. We must suspect fairly tight control here, if only because the two most important reciters of the story, John and Jesus, would have had a vested interest in agreeing on the key components of what they had witnessed. That is, if John and Jesus both perceived the baptism as divine authorization of Jesus (as well as John in its own way), then it would also only be in their respective communities' mutual interest to get their story straight *and* to let others know if and when they failed to get their stories straight. Following the deaths of John and Jesus, their respective bands of followers would have presumably carried on the oral tradition in continuity with their masters' self-credentialling witness. While the essential instability of the Jesus traditions is typically assumed (unless proven otherwise) in contemporary scholarship, in this instance the burden of proof falls on the one who doubts the essential *stability* of the tradition.[33]

Not unexpectedly, then, the synoptic Gospels display a striking consistency in their respective reports of Jesus' baptism. If we choose to chalk up this consistency to a post-Easter conspiracy to rewrite this portion of the Jesus story in post-Easter terms, this still leaves unanswered the question as to how such a rewritten history could pass muster while contradicting the street-level gossip, which would have been heavily stamped by the two intermingling communities' cherished memory. The best path forward is to assume at least a family semblance between the original oral tradition, as first broadcast by John and Jesus and later promulgated by their disciples, and the written Gospels. The broad strokes of the theophany (the opening of the heavens, the descent of the Spirit, and a word of authorization 'You are my son') deserve serious credence as core elements in the history as John and Jesus recalled it.

And why not? After all, as J. D. G. Dunn points out, two distinctive characteristics of Jesus' message revolved around two components of an equally distinctive theophany: Spirit and sonship.[34] The Spirit clearly plays a crucial role in Jesus' self-understanding (Luke 4.1, 14, 18), even as the

---

[33] The intersection between the Jesus traditions and the John traditions is allowed even on the analysis of a scholar as otherwise sceptical as Ernst (1989: 17). On authoritative (eyewitness) tradition, see Dunn 2003: 242–3; Bauckham 2006: 290–318.
[34] Dunn 1975: 62–7.

Spirit is predicted to play as instrumental a role in his disciples' ministry (Matt. 10.20; Mark 13.11; 14.38; Luke 11.13; 12.12). Through the Spirit, Jesus claims his powers as an exorcist (Mark 3.22–30 par.; Luke 11.20), undoubtedly a defining feature of Jesus' self-appointed vocation. Likewise, from the baptism onwards Jesus unflinchingly identifies himself as 'Son' in some extraordinary sense. This designation too, quite obviously, becomes a defining trait of his ministry. As the historian searches for watershed events which may account for Jesus' recurring use of these terms, one cannot do any better than to suggest this single, defining moment. If Jesus brought together texts of Spirit (Ezekiel 36) and sonship (Exod. 4.21–23) in his movement's central prayer (the Lord's Prayer), this move had been anticipated by his personal experience in which Spirit and sonship converged.

Finally, it bears stating that Jesus' baptism was not simply a convenient narrative starting point for the Evangelists, as if it were merely one good option among many. Rather it was *the* most logical starting point simply because – for both Jesus and his biographers – this was Jesus' inaugural moment. *Something* happened that day, something large. From that day forward, Jesus dedicated himself to a new calling, complete with a unique register of narratives and vocabulary, all revolving around his identity as the self-proclaimed 'Son' and his association with the Spirit.[35] When Jesus came to be baptized, his intention may have been nothing more than to align himself publicly with John's counter-temple thrust through the prescribed initiation rite. But through some kind of dramatic event – an event of theophanic proportions – Jesus was immediately set apart as a special figure within that movement, quickly becoming second only to John himself.

In speaking to the historicity of the theophany following Jesus' baptism, I do not mean to suggest that we have access to the events in themselves, as if we were there. Quite obviously we do not and we weren't. But through the Gospels we do have access to a jointly remembered event as it was more or less passed down by the first witnesses. As to what exactly happened on that day is beyond my immediate concern: I am more interested in the *report* of the experience shared by John and Jesus. Whatever happened on that day, together the two men had a story and, as far as we can tell, they stuck to it.[36] It is a story whose basic structure and data points are preserved intact within the Gospel tradition. It is also a story which proved to be a defining moment for Jesus himself. For our purposes, it is actually the interpretation which John and Jesus attached to this extraordinary event that may be even more interesting than the reported facts by themselves.

---

[35] Similarly Hollenbach 1982; Meier 1994: 108–9; Marcus 1995: 512–13; etc. Likewise, Kraeling (1951: 131): 'Not only are we on solid ground in the story of the baptism; we are also on ground that is of the greatest strategic importance' in understanding Jesus' subsequent career and the ultimate dissolution of John's movement.

[36] Or, as Taylor (1997: 269) puts it: 'We cannot know precisely what Jesus experienced, but what we have in Mark's narrative may still reflect how Jesus articulated this experience to his disciples'.

The meaning of Jesus' baptism according to Mark 1.11 par.

When we contemplate Jesus' baptism, we are considering a chain of events: Jesus entered the water, was baptized by John, came up out of the water, the Spirit descended and a voice issued from heaven in reference to Jesus. In reporting back on this remarkable story, John and Jesus would have naturally been tempted to interpret their shared experience in religious terms, which is to say, scriptural terms. Eventually, by the time the baptism event is set down in the synoptic Gospels, each of its constituent elements, the discrete steps in the plotline of this short episode, have already acquired a theological meaning. Whether and to what extent such deep-level interpretation occurred in the first telling of the event is difficult to say apart from digging deeper. Excavation can be a dirty, thankless task, not just for those who work with a pick and shovel, but also for those tasked with sorting out the layers of oral and written traditions beneath the final redaction. For this reason, rather than turn to the archaeological task of determining 'Who said what?' and 'When did they say it?' within the course of the tradition, I take up the more modest project of describing the baptism at the stage of its final redaction and then move backwards to its earliest rehearsals. My goal is to determine each Evangelist's *overall* interpretation of the baptism and whether there is any evidence that the account offered by the Evangelists was rooted in an interpretation offered by John and Jesus themselves.

Towards resolving this issue, we start with the scene's crucial hinge, the declaration from heaven, 'You are my Son, the Beloved; with you I am well pleased' (Mark 1.11 par.). Just what does this quotation mean? And how does it speak to the events which immediately precede it?

The sources of the scriptural quotation (Mark 1.11 par.)

Scholars have typically identified between one and four subtexts embedded within the wording of Mark 1.11 par. The precise relationship between the heavenly declaration and the Hebrew scripture has, as a result, remained a controverted issue. In my view, the most convincing argument on this score will demonstrate clear scriptural allusions in Mark 1.11 on lexical grounds (what kind of verbal correlation obtains between the synoptic text and its alleged precursors?) and explain why the purported echoes make the most sense within their synoptic contexts (what, if any, heuristic value is there in correlating the synoptic tradition and the scriptures in this way?). Therefore, it will be necessary not only to identify the invoked scriptures at Mark 1.11 par. by showing verbal parallels in the Hebrew Bible, but also to examine how these so-identified precursor texts were deployed both in the Jewish and early Christian milieu and by the Gospel writers themselves. Along the way, I will also be addressing the question as to when the scriptural references (Mark 1.11 and Matt. 3.17//Luke 3.22//Q 3.22) entered into the tradition and with what implications. Along the way, too, while building upon some of the more recent scholarship devoted to the intertextual contours of this verse, I will challenge a long-standing line of interpretation, which, so far as I can see, got off on the wrong foot by failing, first, to appreciate the proper significance of a well-accepted subtext and, second, to admit the relevance of another subtext much overlooked.

In surveying scholarly opinion as to which texts stand behind Mark 1.11 par., it is well to begin with one of the less disputed allusions: Psalm 2.7. On comparing but a handful of words, we instantly recognize the resonance. The texts compare as follows:

> *You are my Son* [*su ei ho huios mou*], the Beloved; with you I am well pleased.
>
> (Mark 1.11)

> *You are my son* [*huios mou ei su*]; today I have begotten you.
>
> (Ps. 2.7 LXX)

> *You are my son* [*běnî 'attâ*]; today I have begotten you.
>
> (Ps. 2.7 MT)

Whether we are dealing with the LXX or the Hebrew scriptural tradition is immaterial for our purposes, for both are equally close to the Markan text. Mark's juxtaposition of the key terms ('you', 'my son') through the verb 'to be' finds a unique parallel in Psalm 2.[37] Yet it is also notable that the phrase 'with you I am well pleased [*en soi eudokēsa*]' comes close to 2 Samuel 22.20: 'He brought me out into a broad place; he delivered me *because he delighted in me* [LXX: *hoti eudokēsen en emoi*; MT: *kî-hāpēṣ bî*]'. The language from 2 Samuel is potentially relevant because it highlights David's election, an important premise of Psalm 2.[38] On the first pass of this reading, Jesus' baptism is depicted as an elective act modelled on David's election. That Psalm 2.7 stands behind Mark 1.11, as well as its Matthean and Lukan parallels, is broadly granted.[39]

Another commonly suggested subtext for Mark 1.11 is Isaiah 42.1a, where links are found between the synoptic phrase 'with you I am well pleased' (*en soi eudokēsa*) and 'in whom my soul delights' (LXX: *prosedexato auton hē psychē mou*; MT: *rāṣětâ napšî* (Isa. 42.1a)), as well as between Mark's 'beloved' (*agapētos*) and Isaiah's 'my chosen' (LXX: *ho eklektos*; MT: *běḥîrî*). But there are serious problems here. First, it seems like quite a jump to get from Isaiah's 'in whom my soul delights' to Mark's 'with you I am well pleased': if the Evangelist intended to draw on Isaiah, he certainly went out of his way to hide the fact. Second, the alleged link between the MT's 'my chosen' (*běḥ-*

---

[37] On the uniqueness of the parallel, see Steichele 1980: 147.

[38] On the elective force of the language, see Stegner 1984; Rieske 2012.

[39] So, e.g., Collins 2007: 150 (Mark); Davies and Allison 1988–97: 1.336–43 (Matthew); Nolland 1989: 161–5 (Luke). The connection is disputed by Zimmerli and Jeremias 1957: 80–1; Fuller 1965: 170.

îrî) and the Gospel writer's 'beloved' (*agapētos*) is tenuous at best. Not once in the LXX does the latter Greek translate the former Hebrew. And if appeal is made to Matthew 12.18 where 'beloved' (*agapētos*) is inserted in place of 'my chosen' (LXX: *ho eklektos*; MT: *běḥîrî*), this proves very little, since Matthew is probably rewording Isaiah 42.1 (at Matt. 12.18) so as to secure a connection with the baptism declaration (Matt. 3.17).[40] Finally, if it is argued that Isaiah's 'my servant' (LXX: *ho pais mou*; MT: *abdî*) is somehow equivalent to Mark's 'my son' (*ho huios mou*), this also seems a stretch. All in all, if Mark intended to bring his readers back to Isaiah 42.1, he took the scenic route. The relevance of Isaiah 42 to Mark 1.11 has been long overrated.

The third proposed scriptural invocation comes from Genesis 22. Two key terms here are 'son' and 'beloved'. If Jesus is the 'son' who is also 'the beloved' (*ho agapētos*), then this mirrors the identity of Isaac, at least according to the wording of Genesis 22.2a, where Yahweh commands: 'Take your son [*ton huion sou*], your only [*ton agapēton*] son Isaac, whom you love [*hon ēgapēsas*]'. The verbiage is in fact repeated several times in the Genesis account. Commenting on the Matthean parallel, Leroy Huizenga points out: 'Gen. 22:2, 12, and 16 on one hand and Matt. 3:17 on the other share five words in precise sequence . . . The former verses describe Isaac as the beloved son of Abraham, while the latter verse deems Jesus the beloved Son of God.'[41] Another important phrase is 'from heaven' (*ek tōn ouranōn*) (Mark 1.11), words which fall outside the boundaries of the quotation but which nonetheless parallel Genesis 22.11 and 15, in both instances closely coordinated with 'your son the beloved' (Gen. 22.12, 16).[42] While earlier commentators have tended to overlook intimations of the Aqedah (Genesis 22), perhaps in the interest of giving preference to the Suffering Servant, more recent study seems to have consolidated Genesis 22's position within the Markan – and by extension – synoptic substructure.[43]

There is a fourth possibility. Some 40 years ago Paul Bretscher wrote an article in which he argued that the heavenly voice was appropriating Exodus 4.22–23.[44] The comparison may be drawn up as follows:

You are *my Son, the Beloved* [*ho huios mou ho agapētos*]; with you I am well pleased.[45]

Then you shall say to Pharaoh, 'Thus says the LORD: Israel is *my firstborn son* [LXX: *huios prōtotokos mou*; MT: *běnî běkōrî*]. I said to you, "Let my son go that he may worship me." But you refused to let him go; now I will kill your firstborn son.'[46]

---

[40] So too Bretscher 1968: 303; Luz 1989–2005: 1.214–15; Novakovic 2003: 138; Huizenga 2009: 156–64. The third Gospel makes a similar move at Luke 9.35.
[41] Huizenga 2009: 153.
[42] Huizenga 2009: 154.
[43] See Turner 1926; Dekker 1961; Scattolon 1978; Levenson 1993: 30–1; Boring 2006: 45; Huizenga 2009; Rindge 2012.
[44] Bretscher 1968.
[45] Mark 1.11; emphasis added.
[46] Exod. 4.22–23; emphasis added.

Adducing evidence that 'beloved' and 'firstborn' were sometimes considered equivalents, Bretscher makes an interesting case that the baptism implicates Jesus as the firstborn of Israel. The proposal is intriguing. After all, all three Gospel writers recount the baptism within a string of narrative events that make Jesus out to be the instigator of a new exodus, and so it would be fitting to regard the baptism as a type of exodus, especially when commentators almost universally regard the subsequent scene, Jesus' temptation (Mark 1.12–13//Matt. 4.1–11//Luke 4.1–13), as a type of Israel's wilderness temptations. Moreover, although Bretscher does not point this out, it is striking that *Genesis Rabbah* 97, which takes up Psalm 2, names Exodus 4.22–23 as first among the texts correlating to Psalm 2.7. Nonetheless, as is the case for Isaiah 42.1, the lexical contact is too slight to warrant granting Exodus 4.22–23 the kind of primacy which clearly obtains for Psalm 2.7 and Genesis 22.2.[47]

In summary, I find a clear link between Mark 1.11 (par.), on the one side, and Psalm 2.7 and Genesis 22.2, on the other. While my argument will not crucially depend on this, I am disinclined to grant Isaiah 42.1 and Exodus 4.22–23 the same weight as these as a scriptural backdrop to the heavenly voice. Whatever theological reasons there may be to imagine such a connection, the lexical evidence does not support it. Sharing the seemingly important term 'son', Psalm 2 and Genesis 22 meet each other in the synoptic tradition at just this point.

The meaning of the scriptural quotation (Mark 1.11 par.) in the light of Second-Temple reception

The relevance of these scriptural texts to Jesus' baptism becomes clearer, I think, on examination of the texts themselves and their reception in antiquity. The value of reception in particular should not be minimized. Both Psalm 2 and Genesis 22 yield up many gaps in interpretation. The more we can allow pre-Christian Judaism to fill in some of these gaps, the better our position to make sense of how Jesus applied the same texts and the Evangelists later used them.

Psalm 2 in Second-Temple Judaism

If Psalm 1 describes the righteous individual, Psalm 2 envisages an international, even cosmic scenario in which whole nations array themselves against the righteous community, that is, against the Lord and his Anointed. The decisive resolution of that struggle, according to the biblical texts, consists in the installation of the king on Zion 'my holy hill' (Ps. 2.6). Once installed on the decree of the Lord ('You are my son; today I have begotten you' (v. 7)), the king then stands poised to execute justice against the nations from Zion. The psalm ends with an invitation to the kings of the earth to take heed and respond accordingly (Ps. 2.10–12).

---

[47] Marcus's (2004 (1992): 51–2) dismissal of Bretscher's argument takes no notice of this important piece of rabbinic evidence.

A good deal of scholarship since Gerhard von Rad and Albrecht Alt has regarded Psalm 2 as a coronation psalm that draws on resonances of the Davidic covenant as detailed in 2 Samuel 7.[48] Whatever its exact 'setting in life', the psalm must have been performed in the interest of advancing Davidic ideology, especially as it was understood within the framework of the Davidic covenant. A central piece of this ideology is Yahweh's guarantee of political stability for David's lineage, a promise issued in response to the patriarch's expressed desire to build the temple.

While all this might tempt us to designate Psalm 2 a 'messianic psalm' without further ado, this nomenclature is no warrant for introducing messianic notions that would have been foreign to the author of Psalm 2 – as well as to the author's first-century readers. To be sure, the psalm concerns an 'anointed one' and is certainly 'messianic' in that sense. But we would be very quickly going beyond the evidence if we were to ascribe to this 'messianic figure' a composite profile of character traits associated with messianic figures in other texts, as if every first-century Jew had a crystal-clear idea of what exactly 'messiah' meant. Such ascriptions may have been par for the course when it comes to early Christian interpretation of the synoptic baptism accounts, but to retroject on the basis of Psalm 2 a full-blown, high Christology into the historical Jesus' movement would be a grave anachronism.

We are better off proceeding inductively from the two leading instances of Psalm 2's reception: the sectarian texts 4Q174 and the *Psalms of Solomon*.[49] In the former, Psalm 2.1 occupies an important position within a long chain of scriptural texts, nearly all of which are patently concerned with *the establishment of sacred space*.[50] According to the pesherist, the 'elect ones of Israel' (i.e. members of the Qumran community) stand in for the 'Lord and his Anointed One'; the timing of their conflict with the entrenched temple powers is in the 'last days'.[51] Thus the author conceives of his community's clash with the illicit priesthood as an epic battle between two competing temples: the key to victory is the Qumran community's status as the emerging eschatological temple. For the Qumran covenanteer, as for the psalmist, Psalm 2 provided scriptural assurance that Yahweh was establishing a divine beachhead against evil in the shape of a properly consecrated temple.[52]

The *Psalms of Solomon* employs Psalm 2 in a very similar way. Written in the first-century BCE in response to Pompey's tragic incursion into the temple, which in turn for the author could only have come about on account of the

---

[48] For a nuanced challenge of the von Rad–Alt interpretation, see Roberts 2002: 143–56.

[49] Janse (2009: 51–75) incorporates discussion on some of the more fleeting allusions in 'Early Judaism'; see also O'Brien (2010: 155–60).

[50] The scriptural texts referenced in 4Q174, prior to Ps. 2.1, are as follows in sequential order: Ps. 89.23; Exod. 15.17–18; 2 Sam. 7.11, 12–14; Amos 9.11; Ps. 1.1; Isa. 8.11; Ezek. 44.10.

[51] 4Q174 1 1.19. The interchange between a communal and messianic reading of 'the Son' is also found in *Gen. Rab.* 97 (= Ps. 2.9).

[52] As noted elsewhere (Watts 2007: 309), the centrality of the temple is borne out in *Tg. Ps.* 2.6–7 where the 'beloved' is 'set over my sanctuary' (v. 6).

wickedness of the regnant priesthood, the *Psalms* is part protest literature and part lament over the sorry state of Jerusalem. Yet the text climaxes on a note of hope. Chapter 17, the penultimate chapter, looks ahead to an eschatological day when a messianic figure will appear on the scene:

> See, Lord, and raise up for them their king, the son for David, to rule over your servant Israel in the time known to you, O God.
> Undergird him with the strength to destroy the unrighteous rulers, to purge Jerusalem from gentiles who trample her to destruction; in wisdom and in righteousness to drive out the sinners from the inheritance; to smash the arrogance of sinners like a potter's jar;
> To shatter all their substance with an iron rod; to destroy the unlawful nations with the word of his mouth;
> At his warning the nations will flee from his presence; and he will condemn sinners by the thoughts of their hearts.[53]

A number of words ('nations', 'king', 'son'), phrases ('iron rod', 'potter's jar') and concepts (Davidic ruler, judgement against the Gentiles) hearken back to Psalm 2: the linkage is unmistakable. For the purposes of the present discussion there are two points of interest. First, as in 4Q174, the invocation of Psalm 2 is clearly eschatological in nature. However Second-Temple interpreters understood the second psalm as having been fulfilled in the past, the author of the *Psalms* would have considered such fulfilment to be only partial, pointing forward to a climactic judgement against the nations.[54] Second, although Psalm 2 ostensibly deals with 'the nations', the author of the *Psalms of Solomon* has redefined this category along ethical lines, so that the presenting problem – from the psalmist's perspective – was not the *goyim* outside Israel but the fraudulent priests deep within. The solution to this problem would be in the arrival of a messianic figure who 'will purge Jerusalem [and make it] holy as it was from the beginning' (*Pss. Sol.* 17.30). Leading up to this moment, the same messianic figure shall 'gather together a holy people' and he will know his own, 'that they are all sons of their God' (17.26, 27). For the author of this first-century BCE text, the fundamental problem was not *essentially* geopolitical but cultic in nature. The occupying Roman force was a problem indeed, but it was merely a presenting symptom of the much deeper problem: the temple.[55] The resolution of that problem could only centre on the re-establishment of the rightful eschatological priest (the messianic Son) and his priestly 'sons'.

The last observation should, I hope, lay to rest any false antitheses that suggest that the messiah depicted in the *Psalms of Solomon* was 'royal' *as opposed*

---

[53] *Pss. Sol.* 17.21–25.

[54] Up until the writing of the eleventh-century exegete Rashi, Psalm 2 was regularly interpreted eschatologically, with the installed 'Son' of v. 7 functioning as a messiah. See Signer 1983: 274.

[55] As Embry (2002: 110) helpfully puts it: 'While it is undeniable that the Messiah of *Pss. Sol.* 17 is a political figure, the more central issue for the author is purity, not polity'. Similarly, Watts (2007: 311): 'the very point of the *Psalms of Solomon's* messianic hope is the restoration of the purity of the people, especially as focused on the city, and above all the temple.'

to cultic in nature. For even a cursory reading of the text will show that while the messianic figure inspired in part by Psalm 2 exhibits both royal and priestly qualities, the priestly aspect takes precedence: the messiah's royal rule is not an end unto itself but a means to securing the purity of the temple. This is a crucial point. Whereas many scholarly readings of the *Psalms of Solomon* have laboured under an optic which has been all too quick to categorize figures like these as *either* prophet, *or* priest, *or* king, such trifurcations are more misleading than helpful.[56]

The distinguished theologian Colin Gunton once wrote that when it comes to God, 'it is not a matter of what we *attribute*, but of what he *reveals himself* to be'.[57] If it's appropriate to understand God on God's own terms, we historians might as well extend the same courtesy to God's messiah by focusing on the presenting messiah's instantiated functions rather than a theoretical set of attributes vaguely aligning with our own, often anachronistic, notions of royalty. Though Psalm 2 is normally classified as a 'royal psalm', its royal aspects should not occlude the fact that Second-Temple interpretation seems more interested in its priestly import. Rightful establishment on the holy hill (tantamount to restoring the temple space in Jewish reception) tops the messianic son's agenda as a sacerdotal agenda item.[58]

Genesis 22 in Second-Temple Judaism

Whereas Psalm 2 has left only a modest footprint in the extant literature of Jesus' day, the tracks of Genesis 22 by comparison seem almost ubiquitous. In the rabbinica, the Aqedah is as an event of considerable significance. In the pre-Christian and first-century texts, there is also no short supply of call-outs to Isaac. For the sake of brevity, I will focus on only some of these as representative. Within these texts, there are three rather striking exegetical developments that are not immediately apparent from Genesis 22.

First, by the first century the Aqedah had already been connected with the temple apparatus. The first explicit connection occurs in 2 Chronicles 3.1, where Mount Moriah (the setting of Genesis 22) is identified as the location for Solomon's temple project. The association receives further elaboration elsewhere.[59] This undoubtedly has something to do with the fact that the near-sacrifice of Isaac regularly served as a paradigm of outstanding obedience to Yahweh, and thus acquired its own soteriological significance. Both before and after the time of Jesus, Jewish exegetes went out of their way to emphasize that Isaac was fully aware of what Abraham intended to do, yet faced his death with equanimity – even to the point of embracing his fate.[60]

As to the precise connection between the Aqedah and atonement, various

---

[56] See the helpful critique of much *Psalms of Solomon* scholarship exactly along these lines in Embry 2002: *passim*. David's priestly character will be treated more fully in Chapter 4.
[57] Gunton 2003: 9.
[58] On temple building as a signal aspect of the messiah's role, see Nicholas Perrin 2015.
[59] *Ant.* 1.13.1–2 §§224, 226; *Jub.* 18.13. See Levenson 1993: 111–24; Moberly 2000: 112–8.
[60] See 4Q225 2.2.4; *Gen. Rab.* 56.8; *L.A.B.* 32.3; *Ant.* 1.13.4 §§232–36; *Tg. Ps.-J. Gen.* 22.1; etc.

texts provide their own insight, including the late second-century BCE Judith and the first-century (whether BCE or CE) 4 Maccabees. Beginning with the former, one might think of Judith's address to the elders at Bethulia:

> Therefore, my brothers, let us set an example for our kindred, for their lives depend upon us, and the sanctuary – both the temple and the altar – rests upon us [*epestēristai eph' hēmin*]. In spite of everything let us give thanks to the Lord our God, who is putting us to the test as he did our ancestors. Remember what he did with Abraham, and how he tested [*peirazei*] Isaac, and what happened to Jacob in Syrian Mesopotamia, while he was tending the sheep of Laban, his mother's brother. For he has not tried us with fire, as he did them, to search their hearts, nor has he taken vengeance on us; but the Lord scourges those who are close to him in order to admonish them.[61]

In her call to persevere in the face of trial, Judith claims that their course of action, if obedient, will not only set a good example for the people of Israel, but will also buttress the sanctuary. The testing presently confronting the elders, Judith further claims, is analogous to that faced by Abraham and Isaac. Likewise, in driving home the expiatory significance of the martyrs' death, the author of 4 Maccabees has the seven brothers, in the midst of their tortures at the hands of Antiochus IV, appeal to Isaac: 'Remember where you came from, and the father by whose hand Isaac would have been sacrificed for the sake of devotion'.[62] The point of all this is not hard to miss: in the words of Alan Segal, 'Martyrdom is associated with vicarious atonement, while Isaac is pre-eminent among the martyrs'.[63] As the prime example of a living sacrifice to God, Isaac's sacrifice establishes the basis for all subsequent sacrifice.[64]

Not surprisingly, the Aqedah is also closely aligned with the Passover. This is true not only in the latter rabbinic writings, but in pre-Christian texts like *Jubilees* and 4Q225.[65] The author of *Jubilees* describes Abraham's great trial as occurring on the day of Passover.[66] When the crisis is over, Abraham engages in a seven-day feast, paralleling the seven-day feast of the Passover.[67] Finally, in *Jubilees* both the Aqedah and the Passover envisage a superterrestrial battle between the Angel of the Presence and the demonic

---

[61] Judith 8.24–27.

[62] 4 Macc. 13.12. The translation is my own; the NRSV here is unfortunate.

[63] Segal 1996: 108.

[64] Vermes 1973 (1961): 211.

[65] See, e.g., *Mekilta* on Exod. 12.13. Significantly, the *Targum Pseudo-Jonathan* (*Tg. Ps.-J.*), the *Fragmentary Targum* (*Frg. Tg.*), Paris Manuscript 110 (MS 110) and the *Targum Neofiti* (*Tg. Neof.*) all contain 'The Poem of the Four Nights', an elaboration of Exod. 12.42, which conceives of history as being marked out by four events: creation, the Aqedah, the exodus/Passover and the eschaton. Le Déaut 1963 provides a thorough treatment.

[66] *Jub.* 18.3. While this might strike the modern reader as anachronistic, ancient Jews – including the author of *Jubilees* (*Jub.* 49.7) – would have considered the Passover to have been established before the foundations of the earth.

[67] *Jub.* 18.18–19; cf. Lev. 23.6; Num. 28.17. For the author of *Jubilees*, both Abraham's feast and Passover were to be singularly characterized by joy (*Jub.* 18.18–19; 49.2, 22).

Mastema, who is ultimately shamed through the patriarchs' obedience.[68] In 4Q225 the parallel between the two events is also assumed. Indeed, according to the Qumran writer, the offering of Isaac effectively serves to bind Mastema, thus clearing the way for the Sinai generation to proceed unscathed.[69] From the ancient Jewish point of view, then, the trial of the exodus is but a recapitulation of the trial of the Aqedah.[70] Likewise, just as Israel's trials in Egypt give rise to a 'priestly kingdom and a holy nation' (Exod. 19.6), through his own *peirasmos* Isaac emerges as a true priest, a role he inherits as the firstborn son of Abraham (who was also a priest) and confirms through obedience.[71]

As the seed who also incorporates Israel within himself, Isaac is also the 'son of God' – he is designated as much at least by Philo. This occurs in three separate texts, all in passages concerned with extrapolating the significance of Isaac's name. According to one of these, because Isaac denotes laughter, and God alone is the author of laughter, 'God may with perfect truth be said to be Isaac's father'.[72] To be clear, Philo is not particularly interested in either etymology or laughter but in explaining the young man's distinctive status as 'son of God'. Exactly what Philo means by 'son of God' is difficult to determine. Clearly, Philo regarded Isaac as a figure without parallel; his unique status as 'son of God' cannot be separated from his sacrificial role at the Aqedah.[73]

A final note: in its interpretation of Genesis 22, Jewish exegetical tradition lays emphasis on the theophanic quality of the Aqedah. This becomes evident, for example, in the *Frg. Tg.* on Genesis 22.14 where 'on the mountain of the Temple of the Lord, Abraham offered Isaac his son, and in the mountain – of the Temple – the glory of the Shekinah of the Lord was revealed to him'.[74] Similarly, in 'The Poem of the Four Nights' it is said that 'Isaac (our

---

[68] For the Angel of the Presence at Aqedah and Passover, see *Jub.* 18.9, 48.13; for Mastema at both events, see *Jub.* 17.16; 18.9, 12; 48.2, 9, 12.

[69] See VanderKam 1997a: 254; Huizenga 2009: 91.

[70] So Daly 1977: 55; Davies 1979. Perhaps this point gives added credence to intimations of exodus in the voice of Mark 1.11 par. (Bretscher).

[71] Abraham's priestly status seems to have been taken for granted (cf. Philo, *Abr.* 198); the same holds true for Isaac (*T. Levi* 9.6–14). This patrilineal priesthood becomes almost an *idée fixe* in *Jubilees*, as Kugel (1993: 62) explains: 'One of *Jubilees*' key claims was that the mention of various patriarchs' "building of an altar" in Genesis actually referred to the celebration of various cultic festivals and that the patriarch in question had therefore been a priest. There had thus been a series of priests in ancient times: Adam, Enoch, Noah, Abraham, and Isaac.'

[72] *Det.* 124. See also *Mut.* 131 ('Isaac must not be the man Isaac but the Isaac whose name is that of the best of the good emotions, joy, the Isaac who is the laughter of the heart, a son of God') and *Leg.* 3.219 ('So that what here is said has some such meaning as this, "The Lord has begotten Isaac." For he is the father of perfect nature').

[73] Davies and Chilton's (1978: 519–21) notion that Philo had minimal interest in Isaac is undermined by their inattention to the fuller Philonic corpus as well as their dependence on the now-outmoded premise that the Passover/Aqedah connection was a much later development. Whether Philo's application of 'Son of God' to Isaac has priestly connotations is impossible to determine. At any rate, Philo designates Abraham as the priest (*Abr.* 198).

[74] Vermes 1973 (1961): 195.

father) was not yet 37 years of age when he was offered on the altar. The heavens descended and came down, and Isaac saw their perfections and his eyes were weakened because of their perfections.'[75] The visionary emphasis in the Aqedah, as it was developed in targumic tradition, and undoubtedly current in Jesus' day, only confirms that Gospel writers' theophanic narrative appealed to Genesis 22.

Synthesis

In Second-Temple Judaism, Psalm 2 and Genesis 22 supplied scriptural support for communities and individuals, who – whatever their differences – shared the common dream of a properly functioning sacred space. For the societies behind the Dead Sea Scrolls and the *Psalms of Solomon*, Psalm 2.7 portended the arrival of the eschatological royal priest and the corresponding establishment of the faithful worshipping community. This does not seem to be unconnected to Genesis 22, a passage which Second-Temple Jews broadly regarded as being *the* foundational act of sacrifice. If Psalm 2 held forth a vision of a properly established temple where the unbelievers could finally be put into their place, Genesis 22 promised to foretell how atonement for such a temple could be operationalized. Understood in the light of this background, the tradition preserved in Mark 1.11, blending both scriptures, is centrally concerned with temple-related realities.

All this suggests that when members of the Jesus community reflected on the story of their master's baptism, which included this scripture-citing voice from heaven as a central piece, they ascribed cultic significance to Jesus' baptism and indeed to Jesus himself. More exactly, given the converging sacerdotal concerns of Psalm 2 and Genesis 22, at least as these texts have been interpreted in the milieu, together with the deep-seated apocalyptic quality of the event itself, it would only be natural to speculate that Jesus was a kind of high priest – nothing more and nothing less than a divinely appointed mediator-figure responsible for securing sacred space and undertaking atonement. This does not necessarily rule out the baptism as a 'messianic inauguration', but such a term would be a needlessly imprecise description of the event. On the assumption that Psalm 2 and Genesis 22 stamped this moment as remembered in the earliest days, the story of Jesus' baptism becomes first and foremost a story of consecration. For just as the Aaronic priesthood had been consecrated through water (Lev. 8.6) and anointing oil (Lev. 8.30), Jesus' experience of water and Spirit had been interpreted as setting him apart for a priestly role of a different kind.[76] Framing Jesus as a priest also appears to have been the intention of those who, steeped in the texts of their day, first incorporated the conflated scripture into the tradition.

---

[75] I have translated the (Aramaic to French) translation of Le Déaut 1963: 64–5.
[76] The Spirit is regularly symbolized by oil in the tradition; cf. Isa. 61.1; Zech. 4.1–6; etc.

Jesus' baptism in the context of the synoptic narratives

Whether the meaning ascribed to the baptism, as I have argued it, was recognized and reaffirmed by the time we come to Mark, Matthew and Luke is another question. It is a question worth asking: do the synoptic Gospels betray any recognition of the baptism's sacerdotal thrust, as I have argued it, on the basis of Genesis 22 and Psalm 2? I believe so. The trajectory I have been describing, from the pre-Christian Jewish interpretation of these scriptures to the historic baptism, seems to have been appreciated in the Gospels' presentation of the same event.

On reviewing the synoptic writers' integration of the baptism within their respective stories, we find evidence that the Evangelists were not only aware of the scene's priestly implications but also developed them. Direct and indirect indicators for this fall along three lines. First, if the Evangelists received the baptism story as a consecratory story, we would expect to see this borne out in the surrounding co-text, roughly speaking, Mark 1, Matthew 3 and Luke 3. Second, (if the Evangelists appreciated the baptism as a consecratory event) one would also expect to see indications of a broader cultic concern in each Gospel, in keeping with the baptism's pivotal role in each of the three Gospels. Finally, to sharpen the previous point, if the Evangelists found a cultic significance in Psalm 2 and Genesis 22 as they buttressed the baptism, one might further expect one or both of these texts to recur at other points in the narrative in connection with cultic concerns. If patterns such as these can be established in the synoptic Gospels, we may be one step closer after all to seeing just who the historical Jesus was and how he conceived of his own vocation.

Mark

As the author of the second Gospel sets it up, Jesus' baptism is the complementary piece to John's prediction of the coming one who, far superior to the Baptizer himself, would baptize in the Holy Spirit (Mark 1.7–8), presaging the advent of the Spirit promised in Ezekiel 36. If Mark 1.1 originally contained the phrase 'Son of God' (perhaps a big 'if'), then the recognition of 'my Son' at verse 11 also doubles back to inform the Gospel's incipit, even as it provides an *inclusio*.[77] Moreover, on the assumption that the incipit originally included 'Son of God' and that it retained a programmatic significance for the Gospel as a whole, then the Evangelist's introduction of Jesus as the 'Son of God', associated with Ezekiel's vision of a restored temple space, would serve to frame Mark's entire story.

With its inclusion of the theophanic voice from heaven identifying Jesus as 'Son', the Transfiguration's (9.1–18) connection to the baptism scene is all

---

[77] The inclusion of the phrase 'Son of God' at Mark 1.1 is disputed text-critically; see contrasting viewpoints, e.g. in Gnilka 2010 (1978): 43 (original); Head 1991 (spurious).

but certain.[78] At the same time, with its intimations of Exodus 24, the scene singles out Jesus as a kind of Sinai-situated Moses who takes up an essentially mediatorial role.[79] But to what end is this typology? In a highly illuminating essay, Crispin Fletcher-Louis argues that when the Transfiguration scene is read alongside the preceding confession (Mark 8.27–38), it retrospectively stipulates Peter's declaration as an acknowledgement of Jesus' high-priestly status. Not only did Jewish antiquity have a habit of rendering officiating high priests as shimmering figures, much along the lines of Mark's Jesus, but also the various other details in the scene – Peter's bumbling request to build booths, Jesus' iridescent clothes, the six-day time period – conspire to depict the mount of Transfiguration as a temple mount, with Jesus the presiding high priest perched upon it.[80] On closer inspection, it seems that Mark's emphasis is not so much on the person of Moses but on Moses in his specifically priestly capacity at Sinai.

At the same time, the Transfiguration scene is fraught with multiple connecting points to the Aqedah (Genesis 22). After Peter declares Jesus to be the messiah (Mark 8.27–33), the two men along with James and John – four altogether – ascend a 'high' (*hypsēlon*) mountain, to be sure, somewhat in the manner of Moses, but perhaps even more so in the manner of Abraham's party of four, who are instructed to go to one of the mountains in the 'high' (*hypsēlēn*) land.[81] When Jesus 'takes' (*paralambanei*) his disciples with him up a mountain, this also reminds us of Abraham who 'took' (*parelaben*) Isaac and his two servants.[82] Not unlike the angelic voice issuing from heaven in Genesis 22.11 in regard to Abraham's 'son' (22.16), there is a voice which booms from the cloud as it overshadowed Jesus and his three companions: 'This is my Son, the Beloved; listen to him!' (Mark 9.7). Finally, Abraham 'obeyed' (*hypēkousas*) the voice; so too the disciples are to 'obey' (*akouete*) the Son.[83] Mark's point is that just as Isaac served a priestly function by offering up his own life, so too would Jesus die in an act of atoning self-surrender (Mark 8.31, 34–38).

Mark's deployment of the 'beloved son' motif in these three pivotal scenes, including the insinuations of Aqedah and atonement at 9.1–8, does not exhaust the Evangelist's extension of Genesis 22. In the account of Gethsemane (Mark 14.32–42), much as in the preceding Passover scene (14.22–25), the Gospel writer again interprets Jesus' impending death through the lens of

---

[78] Even the identification of Jesus as 'son' in each passage has very similar wording: Mark 9.7 reads 'This is my Son, the Beloved' (*houtos estin ho huios mou ho agapētos*); Mark 1.11 has 'You are my Son, the Beloved' (*sy ei ho huios mou ho agapētos*).
[79] See Marcus 2004 (1992): 80–4; for Moses as a priest, see Ps. 99.6.
[80] On the iridescence of the high priest's garments, see *2 En.* 22.8–10; *3 En.* 12; *Let. Aris.* 97; *Ant.* 3.8.9 §§216–17; as well as discussion in Fletcher-Louis 2001: 294–5 and Fletcher-Louis 1999.
[81] Gen. 22.2 LXX; Mark 9.2. Philo is emphatic on the point that the Aqedah took place at an elevation; see *Abr.* 32.169. This portion of my discussion, focusing on the parallels between Mark's Transfiguration and the Aqedah, is indebted to Rindge 2012: 766–7, here 766.
[82] Gen. 22.3 LXX; Mark 9.2.
[83] Gen. 22.18 LXX; Mark 9.7.

the Scriptures. Connections with Genesis 22 in particular become obvious, given the parallels shared by both texts. First, the Passover timing of Jesus' test (*peirasmos*) (14.38) finds parallel in the experience of Abraham whom God also puts to the test at the time of Passover.[84] Second, although Jesus has been tested at several points in Mark's Gospel (8.11; 10.2; 12.15), Gethsemane is a final and climactic test. By analogy, the various challenges facing Abraham throughout his life were regarded as but the lead-up to the supreme and climactic test of the Aqedah.[85] Third, just as Jesus instructs his disciples to sit (*kathisate*) while he isolates himself before God (Mark 14.32), so too Abraham instructs the young men accompanying him to sit (*kathisate*) while he leads the lad to go off to take care of his own sacred business (Gen. 22.5 LXX). Fourth, Jesus' cry of 'Abba' (*abba ho patēr*) in Mark 14.36 finds its counterpart in Genesis 22.7a, when on facing the prospect of his sacrifice, Isaac calls out, 'Father!'[86] The comparison between Jesus and Isaac in Mark 14 would have come as no surprise to Mark's readers. After all, in telling the parable of the wicked tenants (Mark 12.1–10), Jesus had already alluded to his impending death, as well as his own role as the Isaac-like 'beloved son' (*huion agapēton*) within that storyline (12.6). Given that that 'son' was also the cornerstone of the temple (v. 10), a role which had in Jewish thought already been assigned to the 'beloved son' of Abraham, Jesus is once again the new Isaac. Haunting Jesus' first and last public acts, the Aqedah of Genesis 22 bookends – to put this in theological terms – the entirety of Jesus' 'active obedience'.

If Mark's Gospel is a like a diptych, with the baptism (Mark 1.9–11) marking off the left edge of the double-panel presentation, and the messianic announcement-plus-Transfiguration serving as the central hinge (8.27—9.13), then the edge of the right-hand panel is marked by the testimony of the Roman centurion in Mark 15. Jesus has been crucified and, on his expiration, a curious turn of events unfolds: 'And the curtain of the temple was torn in two, from top to bottom. Now when the centurion, who stood facing him, saw that in this way he breathed his last, he said, "Truly this man was God's Son!"' (15.38–39). Whatever its precise meaning, the tearing of the temple veil in verse 38 signifies nothing less than Jesus' atoning death having procured new and unprecedented entry through the heavens into the presence of God.[87] Next verse 39, offering the very first commentary on Jesus' passing (issued ironically enough from a Roman centurion), speaks to his identity as 'Son of God'. Whatever a Roman bystander might have meant by calling Jesus 'the Son of God' (or whatever Mark's reader might have *thought* that a Roman bystander meant by calling Jesus 'the Son of God'), the Evangelist capitalizes on the irony of the statement, occurring as it does

---

[84] Gen. 22.1 LXX: 'After all these things God tested [*epeirazen*] Abraham'. See *Jub.* 17.15—18.19; Le Déaut 1963: 179.

[85] *Jub.* 17.16; 18.19. See Grassi 1982: 451; Andrews 1942: 232–6.

[86] MT: *ʾābî*; LXX: *patēr*; Targums: *'abbā'*.

[87] On the rending of the veil as a symbolic rending of heaven, see, e.g., Gurtner 2012: 538–9.

on the heels of an epochal 'veil fail'. In the space of seven Greek words, Mark's centurion unwittingly explains the theological significance of the moment: the rending of the temple veil (collapsing the divide between the sacred and the profane) illustrates that it is Jesus (and not Caiaphas) who is the true priestly Son of God. While Mark may have intended a broad range of intentions in designating Jesus as divine son at Mark 9.1–8 and 15.37–39, Jesus' priestly function remains core.[88]

Pertinent in this connection is Mark's only allusion to Psalm 2 outside the baptism, Transfiguration and crucifixion complex. This is found in a text which is part of the larger scene involving Caiaphas's confrontation with Jesus at the latter's trial:

> But he was silent and did not answer. Again the high priest asked him, 'Are you the Messiah, the Son of the Blessed One?' Jesus said, 'I am; and "you will see the Son of Man seated at the right hand of the Power", and "coming with the clouds of heaven."'[89]

The high priest's question, juxtaposing 'Messiah' (*christos*) from Psalm 2.2. alongside 'Son' plus the second person singular predicate 'you are' from Psalm 2.7, cinches the query within the second psalm.[90] Whether 'Messiah' and 'Son of the Blessed One' are synonymous or merely overlapping categories is not crucial here. My point is simply that Mark brings the escalating conflict between Jesus and the temple hierarchy to climactic pitch with a watershed question worded on the basis of Psalm 2. While many readings of this text have supposed that the high priest and Jesus are sparring about the identity of a third-party royal figure, as I will argue more fully below (Chapter 7) it makes more sense to suppose that Caiaphas is more or less asking, 'Jesus, do you claim to be the rightful eschatological heir of *my* priestly office?' Jesus' answer, now drawn from Psalm 110 and Daniel 7 and extended to include clear messianic claims, is also framed in no uncertain terms. For directly challenging the sanctioned priest's authority, Jesus is found guilty of blasphemy (Exod. 22.28) and executed.

Matthew

Matthew retains Mark's three nodal points (baptism, Transfiguration and rending of the temple veil) in which Jesus is identified as the 'Son of God', as well as the baptism–Gethsemane framing. This may of course simply be explained by Matthew finding the structures to be easily transferable – and

[88] The same point can be made from another angle. It is virtually taken for granted that all three instances of 'son of God' in Mark are mutually interpreting. If the latter two had strong implications of Jesus' priestly role (as is commonly granted) and 1.11 did not, this would be odd indeed.
[89] Mark 14.61–62.
[90] So, e.g., O'Brien 2010.

little more.[91] But the first Gospel gives every indication that its author was not only aware of the cultic significance of the interconnected scenes, but also intentionally developed the idea further. This becomes apparent both in Matthew's reshaping of the baptism scene and in the remainder of the narrative.

Like Mark, Matthew situates the baptism within the context of John's preaching (3.1–12). But here when Jesus requests to be baptized, the Baptizer is resistant (v. 14).[92] Jesus' counter to the Baptizer's objections is as terse as it is puzzling: 'Let it be so now; for it is proper for us in this way to fulfil all righteousness' (v. 15). Exactly how John's baptism of Jesus might 'fulfil all righteousness' is a difficult question occasioning no small cache of possible answers.

On one interpretation, Jesus' baptism fulfils righteousness in that it points to his imminent death, when justification (i.e. the bestowal of righteousness) would take place.[93] There are numerous problems with this reading, not least its failure to explain how both John and Jesus ('it is proper *for us* in this way to fulfil all righteousness' (v. 15)) are *together* required in prefiguring Jesus' atoning death. A second possibility is that 'fulfilling all righteousness' simply means obeying all that is required of God, including submission to the baptism of John. While this approach is virtually impossible to disprove, as an explanation it strikes me as rather lame, voiding as it does any particular connection between the 'fulfilling of righteousness' and the theologically fraught event of Jesus' baptism. A third view, slightly co-extensive with the first, holds that Jesus' baptism fulfils righteousness inasmuch as it allows him to fulfil Scripture, for example, by identifying with sinful Israel as the Suffering Servant.[94] While this reading is an improvement on the first two options, it assumes a meaning of 'righteousness' at 3.15 inconsistent with Matthew's typical sense of 'righteousness'.[95] When it comes to explaining how Jesus' baptism fulfils righteousness, each of these interpretations falls short.

In my view, the most likely reading of Matthew 3.15 is one which coheres with Matthew's use of 'righteousness' elsewhere, including most of all the subsequent usage at Matthew 5.20 ('For I tell you, unless your *righteousness* exceeds that of the scribes and Pharisees, you will never enter the kingdom of heaven'), which is patently connected with Jesus' insistence in 5.17 that he has come to 'fulfil' the law. Consistently using 'righteousness' in its practical sense, the Evangelist would have his readers connect the dots between the baptism of Jesus at 3.15 and the righteous demands of his new moral code at

---

[91] Matt. 3.17; 17.5; 27.54.

[92] The conative imperfect (*diekōluen auton*, 'he kept trying to prevent him') brings this out.

[93] See Cullmann 1950: 15–16; Bornkamm 1963: 140–2; Kammler 2003a: 171–6.

[94] So Davies and Allison 1988–97: 1.326–7.

[95] Elsewhere in Matthew, 'righteousness' refers to the standard of behaviour befitting Israel's covenantal relationship (5.10, 20), as well as, by extension, an eschatological scenario in which such righteous behaviour becomes the norm (5.6; 6.33; 21.32); cf. Przybylski 1980: 91, 98.

5.17, as if to say that Jesus' baptism fulfils righteousness to the extent that it prepares, empowers and equips his followers for righteous living.

Accordingly, the baptism of Jesus 'fulfils righteousness' by functioning not only as a revelatory event, signalling a shift in Yahweh's redemptive purposes, but also as a performative act, making God's saving power unto righteousness available – not fully realized until after the resurrection – in a new way. In recounting the Spirit's visible descent on Jesus, Matthew is symbolically showing that the bundle of righteousness-conferring functions which had hitherto been relegated to the temple and Torah were now being transferred to Jesus. The Evangelist's point then is that now in Jesus, the new locus of divine presence, are met the necessary conditions for the successful establishment of a righteous community – the fulfilment of 'all righteousness' – dedicated to God. In Matthew 4, the same righteousness is exemplified on a personal level in Jesus' temptation (Matt. 4.1–11) and early ministry (vv. 12–25). In Matthew 5—7, righteousness is worked out in practical terms for Jesus' followers in what we today call the Sermon on the Mount.[96] Whereas for Matthew, the Mosaic temple and law may have been preliminary steps towards Israel's 'fulfilling all righteousness', the same objective is now being accomplished through Jesus, beginning with his baptism. Thus, for all practical purposes, as the human repository for the Spirit, Jesus is the temple; as the temple, he is also the repository of the law.

Much of the remainder of Matthew concerns itself with the working out of this new-temple-based righteousness, yet always in relationship to the baptism moment. For example, Jesus' status as the new locus for the Spirit allows him to share the Spirit with his followers in their capacity as messengers (Matt. 10.19–20). Jesus' drawing a corporate priestly following unto himself also positions him to claim that someone (or something) 'greater than the temple' is here (12.6). As high priest of this movement, Jesus extends priestly prerogatives to Peter and the disciples (16.13–20).[97] Then, following acute conflict with the temple authorities (Matthew 21—24), Jesus finally prepares his followers for his departure by repeating Mark's cup-saying ('this is my blood of the covenant, which is poured out for many') and adding to it 'for the forgiveness of sins' (Matt. 26.28) – an essentially priestly task.[98] Instances such as these may be multiplied.

Finally, the closing verses of the first Gospel come back to the baptism as the risen Jesus calls his disciples to baptize, again with all three members of the Trinity in attendance. Having been confirmed as the priestly Son of God in the company of the Trinity, Jesus the Son now invites the Church

---

[96] Reading the Sermon on the Mount in the context of the baptism allows us to navigate its ethical rigour. While Jesus' insistence that the disciples' 'righteousness' exceed that of the scribes and Pharisees (Matt. 5.20) (not to mention the slate of ethics laid out in the Sermon on the Mount as recorded in Matthew 5—7) may seem entirely unreasonable, it has already been hinted that Jesus' baptism secures the disciples' power unto obedience through the Spirit.
[97] In this connection see Barber 2013a: 944–52.
[98] On forgiveness in Matthew, see 6.12; 9.1–8; 12.31–32; 18.21–35.

to discharge its own calling by recapitulating his baptism in a Trinitarian key (28.19–20). Jesus thus links Christian baptismal practice with his own baptism.[99] The analogy is certainly more elegant if we think of Jesus' baptism not as something absolutely unique (as would be the case if we take it to be exclusively messianic in import), but as something which, though unique in some respects, may also be extended. This is possible if both baptisms are consecrations unto priestly service.[100] As far as one can see, this is a Matthean innovation, but an innovation which presupposes a communicable significance to Jesus' baptism, consistent with the interpretation I am offering.

In his handling of the Transfiguration, Matthew provides several touches of his own, two of which are relevant to my argument. First, with Isaiah 42.1 in mind, Matthew adds a phrase to the heavenly utterance: 'with him I am well pleased' (Matt. 17.5). The added allusion to the Suffering Servant is interesting inasmuch as the same figure was sometimes identified with Isaac.[101] Second, Matthew uniquely emphasizes the disciples' fear in reaction to the voice's declaration of Jesus' sonship (v. 6). On perceiving the Transfiguration's tie to the Passion predictions, along with the words 'son of God' and 'fear' in verses 5–6 being matched by the same pairing in connection with the centurion at 27.54 ('Now when the centurion and those with him, who were keeping watch over Jesus, saw the earthquake and what took place, they were terrified and said, "Truly this man was God's Son!"'), A. D. A. Moses reasonably surmises that Jesus' status as endangered son implicitly connects him to Isaac, the *agapētos*, which not only denotes 'beloved' but also, when used, often implies the threat of imminent danger.[102]

Similar Isaac-esque touches accrue in Matthew's Gethsemane account. First, in the midst of Jesus' arrest, the first Evangelist reports: 'Suddenly, one of those with Jesus put his hand on the sword, drew it [*ekteinas tēn cheira apespasen tēn machairan autou*] . . .' (Matt. 26.51). (The underlined words correspond to the wording of Genesis 22.10 where Abraham 'reached out his hand [*exeteinen . . . tēn cheira*] and took the knife [*tēn machairan*]'.)[103] This is immediately followed in Matthew 26.52 by Jesus' admonition that 'all who take the sword [*hoi labontes machairan*] will perish by the sword', a verb–object combination which mimics Abraham's actions as he 'took the sword/knife' (*labein tēn machairan*) (Gen. 22.10 LXX).[104] Granted, these are relatively minor changes on Mark, but they are nevertheless changes that, when taken together, betray Matthew's own consciousness of Gethsemane as an extension of both the baptism and Transfiguration. Undertones of atonement

[99] Nepper-Christensen (1985: 195–8) suggests that Matthew's community intentionally retrieved the Baptizer's practice as a means of self-legitimization; see also France 1994.
[100] For the early Church, baptism signified (among other things) priestly ordination; see Leithart 2000; Nicholas Perrin 2015: 64.
[101] See Rosenberg 1965.
[102] Moses 1996: 140–4; followed by Huizenga 2009: 153.
[103] So Huizenga 2009: 252–3.
[104] Huizenga 2009: 252.

in both the Transfiguration and Gethsemane, as handled by Matthew, are solid evidence that the first Evangelist also conceived of Jesus' baptism in priestly or atoning terms.

Luke

The third Evangelist's interest in priestly themes is no less obvious. Luke has his story begin in the Jerusalem temple; he wraps up his account of what Jesus began to do by depicting the risen Jesus, hands lifted firmly in the air, offering a benediction outside Jerusalem.[105] Between these two bookends, both of which may be characterized as 'temple-centric', the Evangelist offers plenty of other evidence that the story he tells is a story of a newly emerging temple. One need not go any further than the distinctively Lukan scene of Jesus' rejection at Nazareth. Quoting Isaiah 61.1–2, Jesus declares himself to be the one on whom the Spirit of the Lord rests (Luke 4.18–21). Claiming to be the one who would fulfil the mandate for jubilee, Luke's Jesus is essentially taking on a high-priestly role. When Jesus '[sets] his face to go to Jerusalem', he is about to mark out the way in which the duties of this particular priesthood would be discharged.[106]

This role is also tied into Jesus' baptism. In a move unique among the Gospels, Luke inserts before his account of the baptism a section remarking on John's imprisonment, an event which in turn foreshadows the Baptizer's death (Luke 3.19–20). The juxtaposition of John's woes with Jesus' baptism associates the two. In fact, given Luke's pattern of coordinating the two cousins and their respective fates, it would not be going too far to propose that the mention of John's imprisonment, much like the baptism itself, adumbrates Jesus' atoning death.

Right on the heels of Luke's baptism account, there may be further evidence that Luke stylized the theophanic event as a kind of consecration: the remark that Jesus was roughly 'thirty years old' (Luke 3.23) when he began his ministry. To be sure, there are a handful of good exegetical options as to why Luke includes this note. Since the age of 30 was regarded as a kind of golden mean (blending youthful energy with sagacious maturity), and a standard ideal for assuming office in antiquity, Luke may simply be observing Jesus' aptitude for the new vocation in terms of age.[107] Alternatively, as Müller argues, the participle *archomenos* ('when he began') at Luke 3.23 may be a technical term, conventional in ancient bibliography, which had the function of marking off the middle section of a biography.[108] Still another alternative is that Luke is drawing a specific parallel between Jesus' age

---

[105] Luke 1.5–25; 24.50–53.
[106] Luke 9.51.
[107] So, e.g., Bovon 2002: 136; Nolland (1989: 171): 'The most that can be suggested is that such an age denotes an adequate measure of maturity (cf. Num. 4:3)'.
[108] Müller 2003: 499–504; cf. Kurz 1984: 169–71.

when he enters service and the age of one or more Old Testament worthies, including Joseph (Gen. 41.46), Ezekiel (Ezek. 1.1) and, most of all, David (2 Sam. 5.4) – and thus by extension between Jesus and one or more of these figures themselves.[109] A fourth option is this: that in Jewish cultic life, age 30 typically represented the minimum age for priesthood.[110] True, there is some discrepancy on this point within the biblical text itself, since some texts make 25 (Num. 8.24) the threshold age for priestly service; others, 20 (1 Chron. 23.21, 27; Ezra 3.8). But interpreters in Jesus' day were well aware of Scripture's differing age requirements for priestly service, and seem to have resolved this by conceiving of various steps, the first two corresponding to the ages of 20 and 25, the last marking the full rights and responsibilities of priesthood at the thirtieth year.[111]

While it is impossible to adjudicate these options with certainty, the fourth option in my mind seems most promising for two reasons. That Luke's notation of Jesus' tricenarian status was motivated by his determination to cast him as a priest is as strong an explanation as any. First, it is not insignificant that the ensuing genealogy is disproportionately loaded with the names of notable priests; if one function of ancient genealogies was to determine proper lines of priesthood, Luke may well be doing the same here.[112] Moreover, the genealogy climaxes in 'Adam, the Son of God' (3.38), words which form an *inclusio* with the mention of Jesus as the Son of God.[113] This is significant because Adam was also regarded as a priestly figure; in fact, he was the original priest.[114] Whether Luke's overriding interest is in Jesus' Adamic identity or his priestly identity is not crucial to my point: like Adam, Jesus was a priest.

Hints of Jesus' priesthood at the baptism are not unrelated to his status as a new Isaac. Although Luke foreshortens Mark's three-fold declaration of Jesus' sonship by omitting the Roman centurion's confession of faith, he stands by the second Evangelist's decision to bookend Jesus' ministry by placing a baptism in the Jordan at one end and a prayer at Gethsemane at the other. This is no merely mechanical reduplication of Mark's structure. On the contrary, the theological intentionality behind Luke's baptism–Gethsemane *inclusio* is confirmed by his handling of Jesus' final test, which is connected (on a horizontal level) with the baptism and rooted (on a vertical level) in the story of the Aqedah (cf. Mark 10.38). On the horizontal level, Luke

---

[109] So, e.g., Bock 1994: 351–2; cf. Müller 2003: 491–5.

[110] So Sandgren 2003: 284 n. 11. On the watershed significance of 30 for priestly service within the biblical text, see Num. 4.3, 23, 30, 35, 39, 40, 43, 47; 1 Chron. 23.3.

[111] 1Q28a 1.12–16a; 1QSa 1.12–19; 1QM 7.3; *t. Šeqal.* 3.26; *Sipre Num.* 63; *Num. Rab.* 11; *ʾAbot* 5.21. For an excellent discussion, see Milgrom 1990: 64–5.

[112] See Sahlin 1945: 89; Bovon 2002: 134. On the parallel between Luke's genealogy and the priestly genealogy of the *Apocalypse of Weeks*, see Bauckham 1990: 315–26.

[113] On Luke's parallel between Jesus (3.22) and Adam (3.38), see, e.g., Nolland 1989: 167.

[114] On Adam's priestly status, see Fletcher-Louis 2002: 97; Beale 2004: 81–7. This option does not necessarily preclude a focused reference to David (so Marshall 1978: 162). After all, as I have pointed out above, David's role was priestly as well as royal.

reinforces the connection between Gethsemane and the Jordan by adding – a detail without parallel in the other accounts – that Jesus was praying at the baptism, just as he was praying at Gethsemane (Luke 3.21). On the vertical level, the third Evangelist adds certain details which would suggest that he, when compared to his Gospel-writing predecessors, is more rather than less interested in the Aqedah. For example, Luke alone implicates Satan in the *peirasmos* which he and his disciples were about to face, even as Jewish tradition understood the Aqedah to be inspired by Satan (22.31). Second, Luke (and only Luke) describes Jesus' final temptation as occurring on a 'mountain', which in this case happens to be the Mount of Olives (22.39). It is no coincidence that Abraham was also called to a 'mountain' as the venue for his own trial (Gen. 22.2, 14). Thus we have at least two pieces of evidence that Luke took on board the Isaac-esque quality of Gethsemane, as it was handed down to him, and then took minor pains to extend it further.[115]

Expanding our purview into Luke's second volume, Acts, we find further evidence that Luke ascribed cultic significance to the baptism. The first has to do with a much-noted parallel between the Spirit's descent at Jesus' baptism and the Spirit's descent at Pentecost.[116] The mirror imaging of the two events obtains not only by virtue of the fact that the Spirit descends at both events, but also on account of the fact that this parallel is situated within a series of parallels spanning across Luke's two-volume set.[117] There are other points of comparison between Jesus' baptism and Pentecost: both are theophanic events which set the course for the subsequent narrative, both events provide the impetus for mission, and – I wish to maintain – both events lay good claim to symbolizing cultic realities. In a two-part article, Greg Beale has elaborated at length on the connection between Luke's Pentecost narrative in Acts 2 and Jewish expectation of the eschatological temple, arguing that Luke's interest was in showing how the early Church was 'included in and constructed to be part of God's temple . . . by being included in the descending presence of his tabernacling Spirit'.[118] If this is true, then this also has Christological implications, at least in view of the obvious structural parallelism between Jesus' baptism and Pentecost. For Luke, the baptism demonstrated that Jesus was a kind of temple, the human repository for God's 'tabernacling Spirit'. If this is valid, then it reinforces the conclusion that Luke's baptism was intended to reveal Jesus as the human receptacle of God's 'tabernacling Spirit'.

Stepping back to view Luke–Acts in its entirety, we also observe that

---

[115] A third point, though mitigated by the text-critical uncertainty surrounding the verse's authenticity, may also be worth mentioning: the 'angel from heaven' of Luke 22.43, which, if original, may be parallel to the intervening 'angel from heaven' of Gen. 22.11.

[116] Luke 3.22; Acts 2.4.

[117] As has often been noted, various incidents in Luke track with analogous incidents in Acts, and do so in sequential order: Preface (Luke 1.1–4 ≈ Acts 1.1–5); the Spirit descends (Luke 3.22 ≈ Acts 2.4); a lame man is healed (Luke 5.17–26 ≈ Acts 3.1–10); a Roman centurion invites someone to a house (Luke 7.1–10 ≈ Acts 10); a journey to Jerusalem (Luke 9.51–19.28 ≈ Acts 19.21—21.17); an accused man is declared innocent three times (Luke 23.4, 14, 22 ≈ Acts 23.9; 25.25; 26.31).

[118] Beale 2005: 83.

Luke's use of Psalm 2, first invoked at the baptism, goes on to play a key role in Acts in establishing Jesus' priestly identity as the risen Lord. Following initial persecution against its own ranks, including Peter and John, the early Church prays, citing the words of Psalm 2:

> [I]t is you who said by the Holy Spirit through our ancestor David, your servant: 'Why did the Gentiles rage, and the peoples imagine vain things? The kings of the earth took their stand, and the rulers have gathered together against the Lord and against his Messiah.' For in this city, in fact, both Herod and Pontius Pilate, with the Gentiles and the peoples of Israel, gathered together against your holy servant Jesus, whom you anointed . . .[119]

Here Jesus is recognized as the messianic Son of Psalm 2. He comes into the role apparently through his 'anointing' (Acts 4.27), presumably an allusion to Luke's early account of Jesus as the newly consecrated herald of the jubilee (Luke 4.18; cf. Isa. 61.1–2), first among the eschatological 'priests of the Lord' (Isa. 61.6). From Luke's perspective that priestly 'anointing' which Jesus confesses in Luke 4 can only have been actualized at the baptism in Luke 3. It appears that Jesus' baptismal consecration takes full effect only at his exaltation to the Father's right hand, where the risen Jesus may discharge his priestly role on behalf of the Church.[120]

Later, in Luke's treatment of Paul's sermon at Pisidian Antioch, the apostle to the Gentiles alludes to Psalm 2 as having been fulfilled through Jesus' resurrection (Acts 13.33). This is certainly consistent with other citations of Psalm 2 in the early Christian literature. For example, in Hebrews 1, Psalm 2 is coordinated with Psalm 110 to establish the supreme priesthood of the risen Lord.[121] Along roughly similar lines, the author of Revelation finds that Psalm 2 is realized both in the risen Lord but also in his earthly followers, particularly as they continue to witness in the face of persecution.[122] In accordance with the psalm, those who continue 'to do my words to the end' will inherit authority over the nations.[123] The common thread among all these instances is again the thread of a suffering, witnessing priesthood.

Thus, for Luke (as for the *auctor Hebraeos* and the seer of Revelation), Psalm 2 speaks to the establishment of an eschatological temple constituted by the believing remnant who had dared to testify to Jesus as the messiah. While the inheritance envisioned in the psalm would not be fully cashed out until

---

[119] Acts 4.25–27.

[120] See Parsons 1987; Zwiep 1997.

[121] The association between Psalm 2 and the risen Christ's priesthood is made more explicit in Heb. 5.5: 'So also Christ did not glorify himself in becoming a high priest, but was appointed by the one who said to him, "You are my Son, today I have begotten you"'. At the close of a helpful discussion, Lövestam (1961: 37) is led to conclude 'that the proclamation from Ps. 2:7 in Heb. 5:5 refers to Jesus' exaltation as God's Son in power, to which is bound his position and dignity as royal high priest in the heavenly sanctuary'. For Jesus as priestly son in Heb. 3.1–6, see Peeler 2014: 105–39.

[122] Rev. 2.26–27.

[123] Ps. 2.8; Rev. 2.26; Schüssler Fiorenza 1972: 365–8 understands the 'end' here as the parousia.

the future resurrection, these same believers already saw Psalm 2 as being realized through both the risen Jesus and the early believers, particularly as they pursued their roles as witnesses standing toe to toe with an unbelieving and rebellious world. This understanding would hardly be feasible in Luke's mind unless he also assumed that the voice at Jesus' baptism had inaugurated this temple in the person of Jesus.

Synthesis

On reviewing the data, it becomes clear that the synoptic tradition assigned the baptism scene a meaning that has largely, though not entirely, gone unappreciated in the scholarship. To wit, all three Evangelists depict the baptism as an inaugural moment that marks off a priestly career. Mark and Luke leave behind evidence of having read Psalm 2 in priestly terms, a reading shared with at least several early Christian writers (those of Hebrews and Revelation). All three Gospel writers betray awareness of a Jesus–Isaac connection and build on it.[124] Notwithstanding the synoptic writers' unique contributions and interests, they share a common understanding that Jesus' baptism marked his sacerdotal initiation.

The perspective shared across the synoptic tradition thus speaks strongly in favour of the Scripture-citing voice, precisely as a consecrating voice, having roots deep within the early Christian communities. Given our review of the Jewish literature and of the dynamics that must have surrounded the earliest rehearsal of the baptism event, these same roots almost certainly reach back to John and Jesus. Even after the deaths of the two prophetic figures, the baptism tradition continued intact, even as their surviving communities passed on this memory towards corroborating their masters' authoritative claim. This virtually forces us to the conclusion that the origin of the conflated scripture (Ps. 2.7//Gen. 22.2) lies in the *Sitz im Leben Jesu* and, indeed, was somehow bound up in the experience first reported by John and Jesus.

Summary

While we have no sound bite of any heavenly voice on that day, and we have no way of proving what John and Jesus heard or didn't hear, there is no little significance to the fact that we have univocal early tradition as to what the heavenly voice said. Whatever happened that day, John and Jesus were persuaded that Genesis 22 and Psalm 2 were at the bottom of it. This meant as far as both figures were concerned that Jesus was destined to play a priestly role as part of a profound redemptive-historical shift. There is no need to retroject a full-blown post-Easter theology into this historical

---

[124] In connection with Genesis 22, Paul should also not go entirely unmentioned; see, e.g., Hahn 2005 (Galatians 3); Lövestam 1961: 31, 41, 47 (Rom. 1.4); Jipp 2009 (Romans 4). On the Aqedah and Hebrews, see Swetnam 1981.

moment (as has so often been done), any more than we would ascribe this kind of theological cargo to Judith or her Bethulian elders.[125] Nor should we assume that earliest witnesses would have immediately drawn a straight line from 'anointed eschatological priest' to 'messiah'.[126] What we can say is that on account of this baptism experience John and Jesus together expected extraordinary things for the latter, at least nothing less than a role in restoring the temple cultus.

In the previous chapter, I asked how Jesus could both invite his disciples to call on God as 'Father' and retain a unique filial status. Having offered critique of standard answers to this problem, I now propose that Jesus' identification of his disciples as 'sons of God' depended first and foremost on their shared priestly role, a role which entailed suffering for righteousness' sake en route to ushering in the kingdom of God. At his baptism, Jesus became aware of his role as one who, in the spirit of David, would reconstitute the temple (Psalm 2); at his baptism, too, Jesus began to reckon on the possibility that he would have to contribute somehow to the consecration of the same sanctuary (Genesis 22). There is no reason to doubt that Jesus saw both these aspects as falling under his identity as the priestly Son of God. Called to this role by God in the presence of witnesses, Jesus from that point forward saw his singular task as an outworking of that divine mandate, which included the inevitable prospect of suffering as a segue to a new sacred space (even if the details of that suffering might not have been clear). Given Jesus' unique appointment as Son, he probably also surmised that his suffering would be of a unique sort.

At the same time, Jesus seems to have shared certain elements of his priestly office with his immediate followers. This explains why the disciples could claim the title of (lower-case) 'sons', even as Jesus remained the unique (upper-case) 'Son'. The disciples were priests whose vocation was contingent on Jesus' calling as the singular high priest. In one sense, Jesus and his disciples were in the same boat as suffering priestly sons of God; in another sense, precisely on account of his baptism, Jesus was set apart as *the* priestly Son. Between Jesus and his followers there were continuities and discontinuities; the common denominator was their shared ordination for priestly service through the Spirit (and water), their calling as 'sons'.

Again, all this is not to rule out any and all latent messianic implications of the baptism scene, which would later be unpacked as Jesus' ministry progressed. It is to assert that whereas Jesus' baptism has typically been interpreted as an indication of his messianic status in a fairly undefined sense, such an interpretation now proves to be insufficiently specific. In the disciples'

[125] Although to be sure the Evangelists make precisely this move in their interpretation of the baptism, they are of course reflecting on the baptism from a post-Easter perspective.
[126] This answers the objection of Vögtle (1972: 123–4) who finds the baptism inexplicable in the light of the disciples' ignorance of Jesus' messianic status even by the time we reach Mark 8.27–30. That Jesus was anointed as a special priest still left open the possibility that he was more a designate of the messiah than the messiah himself.

earliest perceptions, the baptism was not a clear indication of messiahship; if it was, this messiahship would have been announced much closer to the time of the event. In the original setting, the baptism was first and foremost about priesthood. Consequently, it would be inaccurate to say that in the early Church Jesus was regarded as messiah but one who also happened to have – by the way – some curious if not somewhat distracting priestly functions. Whatever the post-Easter believers meant by 'messiah', their concept included a priestly function as a core component.

Still, the hypothesis I am proposing is not without its challenges – at least in its present form. If Jesus thought of himself as having been declared the priestly, suffering Son of God at this baptism, then this begs for clarification on at least two issues. First, I have admittedly put a good deal of weight on Psalm 2. But on what basis other than Psalm 2 can 'Son of God' be asserted as a priestly role? This is an important question requiring further discussion, especially for readers who are accustomed to locate 'Son of God' in the realm of Davidic ideology, *as opposed to* the realm of the cultic. Second, since time out of mind, intimations of suffering at the baptism have been exactly the kind of thing to persuade scholars of the event's post-Good-Friday setting. But if suffering was somehow integral to Jesus' ministry (as my argument in Chapter 1 has also maintained), where else do we find evidence of this? I will return to the first of these two questions in Chapter 4. But for now, I consider the second, the issue of suffering, even as I seek to show that the most prominent outcomes envisaged by Ezekiel 36, tantalizingly touched on in the Lord's Prayer, were in fact among the key objectives of his ministry.

3

The kingdom of Jesus

At about the age of 30, with only meagre personal resources, Jesus of Nazareth had managed to captivate a sizable following in first-century Palestine, and to be raised to the rank of a well-recognized movement leader. At least one of the secrets of his success was his teaching. By all accounts, Jesus was a rhetorical genius. Whether teaching the crowds out in the open countryside or instructing his disciples in private, he displayed a rare combination of creativity, flair and profundity that made him an unrivalled communicator. Even if Jesus had never been credited with doing a single miracle or healing, the power of his words alone would have undoubtedly carved out his niche in history. It was by the forcefulness of his message that he rose to prominence; it was the same that eventually also proved to be his undoing. For all these reasons, it would be impossible to grasp Jesus' significance without having some sense of his central message. And if there's one thing scholars agree on, it's this: Jesus' central message was the kingdom of God.

In the first chapter of this book, I argued that the Lord's Prayer served as an outline for Jesus' mission and that an important subtext of that mission was Ezekiel 36. From within this prophetic passage, I also teased out four components of the prophetic vision: (1) the restoration of the cultic space, (2) the establishment of a priestly nation, (3) a cleansing from idols and (4) the granting of the Spirit. While the Lord's Prayer's dependence on Ezekiel 36 hardly proves that these four elements were integral to Jesus' vision of the kingdom, their centrality in the prophetic text, together with Jesus' appropriation of that same text, raises the question as to whether he himself imagined the coming of the kingdom as being characterized by the same four strokes.

In the present chapter, drawing from a narrow portion of the large data field of the dominical teachings, I seek to argue that this was indeed the case. Some sensitivity to clues of these four 'Ezekielian points', I believe, will help us to unpack the meaning and notional basis of the kingdom, at least so far as the historical Jesus was concerned. This is not to claim that Ezekiel 36 was *the* leading scriptural source for Jesus' vision of the kingdom. Much less do I intend to argue that Jesus' vision of the kingdom was consciously based on these four abstracted bullet points. Rather, it is to say that this constellation of expectations, scripturally instantiated in Ezekiel 36 and beyond, provides a convenient summary of Jesus' vision. On probing beneath the surface of Jesus' kingdom teachings, we discover that his vision focused on nothing less than a repristinated space, which was to be occupied by an idol-free royal priesthood and overshadowed by the Spirit. For some of my readers, this will appear as a contentious claim, especially insofar as it presupposes a highly biblically literate Jesus. For others, who are willing to grant that the historical Jesus was a Torah-observant Jew expecting the imminent fulfilment of the prophetic promises, this will not be a particularly problematic component of my argument. Perhaps more controversial will be the claim that this vision of the kingdom was essentially a cultic vision, which in turn explains Jesus' emphasis on suffering.

I am principally interested in three passages. The first and third texts, the so-called parable of the sower and the Beatitudes, are regularly regarded as *loci classici* within the Jesus tradition. The second, the parable of salt, has attracted less exegetical attention, but will I think prove no less illuminating. As I hope to demonstrate through a close reading of these texts, those elements which Ezekiel regarded as the tell-tale signs of return from exile turn out to be at the very heart of Jesus' kingdom vision. At the same time, Jesus introduces something not consistently palpable in the prophetic corpus: the element of redemptive suffering. While many scholarly treatments of the kingdom have acknowledged suffering as a catalyst for the kingdom so far as the post-Easter community was concerned, and while a number of others have relegated kingdom-related suffering to Jesus alone, I will maintain that the historical Jesus identified suffering as an essential marker of the community to which he belonged. Faithful suffering was *the* necessary condition for the arrival of the kingdom. Herein lies Jesus' distinctive innovation. While many first-century Jews expected Yahweh to install the kingdom after inflicting suffering on the enemies of God's people, Jesus points to his own movement's marginalization as the conduit by which Israel would finally come into its own.

The apocalyptic framework of the kingdom: the parable of the sower (Mark 4.4–9)

In turning to the parable of the sower, we come face to face with what may be considered the most significant of all of Jesus' parables. By 'significant' I mean not so much its popularity, but its assigned role as the golden key for all other parables. According to Mark, if readers failed to understand this parable, they might as well give up understanding any of them.[1] By the same token, a proper grasp of the parable of the sower promised to open the door to a successful interpretation of all other parables – no small claim indeed! For the second Evangelist, the parable of the sower was a – if not *the* – crucial teaching.[2]

Whether or not the historical Jesus thought of the parable of the sower as a

---

[1] Mark 4.13.
[2] This is essentially the (convincing) argument made by Tolbert (1989) in regard to Mark's Gospel.

crux interpretum is another issue. True, in the past, the important text of Mark 4.13 has often been chalked up to the Evangelist's redaction. But even if one were to adopt this position, it would be a mistake to assume that the parable's elevated role was pure innovation on the Evangelist's part. We have a right to wonder whether Jesus himself attributed this kind of importance to his parable. I for one believe he did. The reason I say this is simply because in this story of the soils we find Jesus' most compressed yet comprehensive account of his understanding of his movement within the timeline of redemptive history.

A complicating factor in any discussion of the sower parable is the array of redaction-critical complexities that create problems for a bald equation between Mark's full version of the parable and its original form as told by Jesus. A good number of scholars have taken offence at Mark 4.11–12, though this erstwhile virtual consensus has long since shown serious signs of erosion.[3] Likewise, many since the days of Jülicher have regarded the interpretation contained in verses 14–20 as late allegorization. Yet these additions are seen as only ancillary detritus layered on what had started off as a rather simple if not homely parable. Convinced that a straightforward story of seeds and soil fits well within Jesus' own agrarian setting, and impressed by its spare parallel in the *Gospel of Thomas* (*Gos. Thom.* 9), scholars of various stripes have come to agree: if there was ever a parable told by Jesus, it was this one – at least in its core form. For the purposes of my argument, it is enough to accept the critical consensus that Jesus spoke the parable of the sower, more or less as it appears in Mark 4.3–9 (presumed to underlie the Matthean and Lukan versions). I will ultimately restrict my treatment of the parable accordingly.

Interpreting the parable of the sower: a first pass

The parable of the sower presents its own natural structure. Once the sower goes out (v. 3), he sprinkles seed in four different areas, each yielding its own distinctive return:

> And as he sowed, some seed fell beside the path, and the birds came and ate it up. Other seed fell on rocky ground, where it did not have much soil, and it sprang up quickly, since it had no depth of soil. And when the sun rose, it was scorched; and since it had no root, it withered away. Other seed fell among thorns, and the thorns grew up and choked it, and it yielded no grain. Other seed fell into good soil and brought forth grain, growing up and increasing and yielding thirty and sixty and a hundredfold. And he said, 'Let anyone with ears to hear listen!'[4]

---

[3] For discussion of the issues, see Evans 1989: 103–6. Though obviously dated, Moule 1969 remains an eminently sensible case for the authenticity of vv. 11–12.

[4] Mark 4.4–9. I have adjusted the NRSV at 4.4 to read 'some seed fell *beside* the path' in place of its questionable rendering of the Greek preposition *para*, yielding 'some seed fell *on* the path'.

Commentaries on this passage teem with questions.[5] Why was the sower so careless in sowing? Did the sower plough the soil? If so, did this ploughing take place before or after the sowing? Is the parable really just about the harvest, with the first three soils merely lending dramatic tension (Dodd, Jeremias)? Or is the story actually about the hearing soil (Marshall)? Or the sower (Ridderbos)? Or the seed (Weder)? Some of these questions may be more pertinent than others, while others may be misframed altogether; nearly all of them are controverted.

Fortunately, when it comes to deciphering the seeds and the sower, we seem to find some comparatively low-hanging fruit. On Mark's interpretation, the seed is the 'word of God', whether preached by Jesus or the early Church.[6] However the Evangelist came to this conclusion, a similar judgement must have been reached by the parable's first hearers, for in the *Sitz im Leben Jesu* it is hard to see how the seed could be anything but Jesus' preached word.[7] Thus, in the parable as it was first spoken by Jesus, the sower is either God or Jesus himself, or perhaps both; the seed is Jesus' teaching and the soils are the members of his audience with their varying levels of receptivity.

To complicate matters, Mark has the seed representing not just the preached word but also human respondents to that word.[8] The latter correspondence is comparable to what we find in a variety of ancient texts where the seed stands for (true) Israel.[9] According to the older commentaries, the metaphoric double-duty which Mark assigns to the seed, representing word *and* hearers, should count as evidence for the secondary nature of the interpretation. After all, so the thinking went, who but our poor Gospel writer could be so muddled so as to suggest that seed could refer to two realities simultaneously? But this critical judgement is problematic for two reasons. In the first place, if we are offended by Mark's two-ply symbolism, there is no reason to assume that what is vexing for us with our delicate semiotic sensibilities would have been equally irritating for his first-century readers. In the second place, the Evangelist's metaphorically modified seed has some precedent. Here we need not go back any further than the apostle Paul who prays that the word of the gospel might bear fruit, even as he prays in the same breath that the Colossian believers might also bear fruit.[10] In a period not long after the composition of Mark, in the closing decades of the first century, we might also consider *4 Ezra* 8.38–41 (where the root-striking seeds among the scattered seeds

---

[5] With sometimes wildly different answers, on comparisons, say, of Dodd 1935: 180–3; Ridderbos 1962: 132; Jeremias 1963: 149–51; Weder 1990 (1978): 99–117; Marshall 1978: 323–4.

[6] Mark 4.14 par.

[7] For Riesner (1981: 370), this much 'had to be clear' to Jesus' hearers; likewise, among others, Bultmann 1975: 30.

[8] Mark 4.20 par.

[9] Ezra 9.2; Isa. 1.9; 6.13; 31.9 LXX; 37.31–32 LXX; 43.5; 44.3; 45.26; 53.10; 54.3; 60.21; 61.9; 65.23; 66.22; Jer. 24.6; 31.27; 32.41; 46.27; Hos. 2.23; Amos 9.15; Zech. 8.9–10; *1 En.* 62.7–8; *Pss. Sol.* 14.2; 1QH 14.14–16; CD 12.20b–22.

[10] Col. 1.6, 10.

symbolize the elect within broader Israel) alongside *4 Ezra* 9.29–37 (where the seed is the law of God). Mark's decision to link the seed with the word and the human receptors puts him in good company.[11]

Before determining whether Jesus himself also belongs in the same company, we should pause to consider Isaiah's role in shaping the trajectory of the seed metaphor well before Mark's first-century setting. Here it would be no overstatement to say that, for the prophet, seed is something of a preoccupation. The canonical text begins on the notice of 'evil seed' (*zer'a měrē'îm*) in Isaiah 1.4, eventually yielding a 'perverse seed' (14.20) and with it a 'false plant' (17.10).[12] In the midst of Israel's horticulturally expressed woes, touched on in such passages as Isaiah 5, the prophet is commissioned to preach to a stubborn exile-bound people, even as he is promised a return from exile in the form of a 'holy seed'.[13] This is undoubtedly one and the same as the 'seed of Abraham' (41.8; 45.19), the remnant of Israel. Then, perhaps surprisingly, in Isaiah 55 the seed represents the word of the Lord, as it continues to symbolize those to whom the word is directed:

> Seek the LORD while he may be found, call upon him while he is near; let the wicked forsake their way, and the unrighteous their thoughts; let them return to the LORD, that he may have mercy on them, and to our God, for he will abundantly pardon. For my thoughts are not your thoughts, nor are your ways my ways, says the LORD. For as the heavens are higher than the earth, so are my ways higher than your ways and my thoughts than your thoughts. For as the rain and the snow come down from heaven, and do not return there until they have watered the earth, making it bring forth and sprout, giving seed to the sower and bread to the eater, so shall my word be that goes out from my mouth; it shall not return to me empty, but it shall accomplish that which I purpose, and succeed in the thing for which I sent it. For you shall go out in joy, and be led back in peace; the mountains and the hills before you shall burst into song, and all the trees of the field shall clap their hands. Instead of the thorn shall come up the cypress; instead of the brier shall come up the myrtle; and it shall be to the LORD for a memorial, for an everlasting sign that shall not be cut off.[14]

On this vision of return from exile, the word of the Lord goes forth in seed form only to give rise to an eschatological forest, symbolizing the transformed remnant; on this vision, too, the divine word and human person coalesce. Apparently, when return from exile occurs, it will coincide with a renewal so profound that the boundaries between divine word and human receptor begin to recede. For Isaiah, this renewal – powerfully symbolized through images of thorns giving way to cypresses along with briers making way for myrtles – is the end goal of Israel's return. The scenario in Isaiah 55 follows up on earlier predictions of Edenic growth in the wilderness (Isa. 51.3) and

---

[11] For further discussion, see Marcus 1986: 50; 2000: 295–6.
[12] The translations here are my own.
[13] Isa. 6.13.
[14] Isa. 55.6–13.

clears the ground for Isaiah 61 (when 'oaks of righteousness' and 'planting of the LORD' crop up), as well as for Isaiah 65 (when 'they shall plant vineyards and eat their fruit . . . for like the days of a tree shall the days of my people be').[15] In these closing chapters, the Isaianic story comes full circle: the problem of the 'evil seed', set out in Isaiah 1, is finally resolved on God bringing his own elect 'seed' (*zer'a*) out of exile (65.9) and into an Edenic state (61.3b). While seed symbolizes the remnant in Isaiah, just as it does in Mark, it also represents — again as in Mark — the word of Yahweh without contradiction.

Yet in this connection we cannot afford to ignore the specific context for this logos–human convergence: return from exile. If we take this context seriously, then the fruitfulness pictured in Isaiah 55 is not an account of individualized human responsiveness to God (as it has often been appropriated), but a situationally specific vision of the restoration. This has two immediate implications. First, when Mark (along with the author of *4 Ezra* and Paul) equates the seed with both God's word and the return-from-exile remnant, he is not introducing a novel synthesis but building on a well-established conceit, the earliest traces of which are already discernible in Isaiah.[16] Second, to the extent that Mark is drawing on Isaiah in its full context (and there is a good deal of evidence in the parable itself that he is), he must have understood the fruitfulness not so much as a subjective psychological reality but as an objective divinely wrought act. Drawing on the metaphor of seed, so familiar to readers of Isaiah, the parable of the sower must have retained a restorational significance in its earliest performance.

Recognizing along with other scholars the importance of Isaiah 55 as an important background to the parable, N. T. Wright reads the historic Jesus' parable as an invitation to return from exile.[17] On this interpretation, the three unproductive seeds, whether 'being eaten by birds (satanic forces, or perhaps predatory Gentiles), or lost among the rocks and thorns of the exilic wilderness', represent those who belong to Israel's protracted state of exile.[18] Meanwhile, the fruitful seed corresponds to the return-from-exile people who respond positively to Jesus' teaching. The parable 'claimed that Israel's history had reached its great climactic moment with the work of Jesus himself. The end of exile was at hand; the time of lost seed was passing away, and the time of fruit had dawned'.[19]

---

[15] Isa. 61.3; 65.21–22.

[16] Along these lines, Bowker (1974: 312) rightly remarks that 'the familiar blurring of the distinction between the word as the seed which is sown, and the people who are sown . . . is far less odd if one realizes . . . the function and purpose of the prophetic word in making unequivocally clear the nature of those who hear it'. Similarly, Ramaroson 1988: 98.

[17] Similarly, Garnet 1983 and Lohfink 1985. Even if one hesitates to accept Jesus' citation of Isa. 6.9–10 (= Mark 4.11–12) in the original setting, Evans (1985: 466–8) makes clear that there's virtually no getting around the naked parable's debt to Isaiah 55 — with or without Mark 4.11–12.

[18] Wright 1996: 234.

[19] Wright 1996: 238–9.

I believe that Wright is on the right track. If Jesus was in fact persuaded that Israel had yet to realize its full return from exile and that this event was now uniquely available in his movement, then his drawing of seed from the silo of Isaiah 55 virtually constitutes a summons to national restoration. Here there is no need to pit eschatological realities against existential decision. The parable was a bid for Jesus' hearers to self-evaluate, locate themselves on the map put before them and respond accordingly. At the same time, it offered a symbolic account as to why so many in Israel were *not* responding to Jesus. If many of Jesus' observers took his cool reception as evidence that he was not who he claimed to be, then this parable explains such unresponsiveness as the wilful choice of those remaining in exile. If some resisted, it was because they lacked the ears to hear, becoming like the mute idols that they worshipped.[20]

Wright is on the right track, but this reading can be sharpened up. In the first place, if the parable was only about exile and return, and nothing more, I think we would expect a much shorter parable involving only two soils: one bad, one good. In the second place, if texts like Isaiah provided Jesus with his seed terminology, then one is bound to ask whether Jesus was interested in not only exile but also the process of tribulation through which, at least on Isaiah's reckoning, this same seed germinates its way out of exile.

The first and clearest connection between tribulation and germinating seed in Isaiah occurs in Isaiah 42.14: 'For a long time I have held my peace, I have kept still and restrained myself; now I will cry out like a woman in labour, I will gasp and pant.' In this text we find return from exile nestled right alongside visions of politico-military distress, expressed through the image of birth pangs and childbirth.[21] When Israel comes out of exile, Isaiah promises, the barren woman will give birth (Isa. 54.1; 66.7–10). Then, strikingly, at the climactic moment of Isaiah 65.23, the theme of childbirth is brought together with the seed motif: 'They shall not labour in vain, or bear children for calamity; for they shall be offspring [*zerʿa*] blessed by the Lord – and their descendants as well.' The metaphorical combination of seed and childbirth is significant, not least because it suggests that there is a redemptive purpose behind Israel's oppression and, indeed, that such redemption cannot take place apart from said tribulation.[22] For Isaiah, Israel's tribulation at the hands of its enemies, the 'pangs of childbirth', will prove to be the mysterious means by which Abraham's seed will finally come to fruition.

The procreative convergence of seed and tribulation in Isaiah, together with the harrowing scenarios which Mark (vv. 17–19) associates with the

---

[20] Beale 1991: 272; Beale 2008: 165–6.
[21] In Isaiah, the connection between birth pangs and political oppression is consistent; whether one considers the threat of Rezin and Pekah (Isa. 7.1—9.6), warriors from 'faraway lands' (Isa. 13.5, NIV), the whirlwind-like Elamites (Isa. 21.1–4), dominating overlords (Isa. 26.12–18) or Sennacherib's siege (Isa. 37.3). See especially Darr 1994: 205–24. Outside Isaiah, a similar pattern obtains: Mic. 4.9–10; Jer. 4.31; 6.24; 13.21; 22.23; 30.5–6; 48.41; 49.22, 24; 50.43.
[22] For more on this point, see Sweeney 2005: 58.

second (shallow) and third (thorny) soils, raises the question as to whether Jesus, standing between Isaiah and Mark, also sought to distinguish different forms of tribulation in describing the second and third soils. Moreover, it remains to be asked whether these two middle soils were intended to symbolize not just possible outcomes of the sown word but, following the narrative logic of Isaiah, destined realities somehow prerequisite to Israel's fruitfulness. For my part, I propose that Jesus did in fact invite his hearers to differentiate the second and third soils as consecutive, even if overlapping, stages of tribulation preparing for eschatological fruitfulness. This proposal, I think, becomes persuasive on comparing Jesus' horticultural story with similar precedents in three near-contemporary (second century BCE) apocalyptic texts. To these I now turn.

The pattern of apocalyptic expectation in three precursor 'seed texts'

The apocalyptic texts of *Jubilees*, *Apocalypse of Weeks* and *Book of Dreams* are appropriate to consider in relation to the parable of the sower, not only because they express traditions current in Jesus' day (and were therefore presumably familiar to him), but also because they employ, much like Jesus' parable, seed/plant imagery within an apocalyptic retelling of Israel's history. Furthermore, as commentator after commentator has noted, whatever the story of the sower is actually about, with its wretchedly disappointing outcomes giving way to spectacular yields, it remains a study in contrasts between neatly compartmentalized categories. This same juxtaposition of starkly segmented realities is of course a leading characteristic of the apocalyptic genre, whether we think of the alternating rhythm between the dark and bright waters (i.e. ages) of *2 Baruch* 53—76, or the gyration of 'weeks' in the *Apocalypse of Weeks*. Whatever reservations one might have in seeing Jesus as an apocalyptic preacher, it can hardly be denied that the parable of the sower situates itself well within an apocalyptic stream that remained vibrant in Jesus' time.

To anticipate my argument, I intend to show that when the communities behind our three texts relayed their storied visions, they did so to express their shared conviction (1) that exile was in some sense still in process but was poised to climax in tribulation with the rise of an apostate generation, (2) that God would respond to this wicked generation by raising up a righteous remnant and (3) that this remnant would become the basis for the eschatological temple. Strikingly, in all three retellings of Israel's story (focusing on past, present and future), seed–plant imagery occupies a central place. The recurring connection between an A-to-Z redemptive storyline and seed is no coincidence. One might even say that scripturally inspired reflection on the history and future trajectory of the Abrahamic seed – the main focus of apocalyptic speculation – left few other options. Once Jesus' parable is mapped on to this commonly shared redemptive-historical template, it is but a short step to show how the story of the sower makes itself at home here. This in turn will entail important implications for our understanding of the parable itself.

Jubilees

One of the more striking features of the second-century BCE text of *Jubilees* is its downplaying of geographical return-from-exile, on the one side of history, and its highlighting of the eschatological temple, on the other side. Although *Jubilees* 1.15–18 may *appear* to make much of the former event, a closer inspection of the passage, with its idealization of life in Israel, reveals a poor fit with any post-exilic reality we are aware of. For this reason, scholars have regularly understood the temple pictured here as the final temple introduced at the new creation, when Yahweh promises to 'build my sanctuary in their midst' and 'dwell with them'.[23]

The installation of the eschatological temple is preceded by the moment at which Yahweh 'transplants' the remnant (or Israel, as the case may be) as 'the righteous plant'.[24] This return from exile is anticipated at three turns. In the first foreshadowing, Abraham blesses the Creator because 'he perceived that from him there would be a righteous planting for eternal generations' (referring to Isaac) and 'a holy seed from him' (referring to Israel).[25] Later, when Abraham blesses Isaac, he warns his son against succumbing to sin lest the seed be uprooted.[26] But if Isaac obeys, the patriarch also promises, God 'will raise up from you a righteous plant in all the earth throughout all the generations of the earth'.[27] Later still, in a similar blessing over Jacob and Esau, it is Isaac who anticipates the day of restoration when God 'will plant you on the earth as a righteous planting which will not be uprooted for all the eternal generations'.[28] Visions of the righteous plant overtaking the earth express the hope of the Abrahamic covenant, namely, that the seed would be a source of universal blessing.[29] The seed, mediated through Isaac, points forward to the eschatological plant, which, as we have seen, immediately sets the stage for the eschatological temple.[30] The step from established plant to eschatological temple is very short indeed.

Yet in *Jubilees* the path to new Eden is hardly a smooth one. For in the lead-up to the eschaton, *Jubilees* 23 warns of an apostate generation of unprecedented wickedness.[31] At that time, some

---

[23] So VanderKam 1997b: 104; van Ruiten 1999: 215–20; Brooke 1999: 294–5. Halpern-Amaru (1997: 140–1) is more cautious on this point; cf. *Jub.* 1.27, 29; 4.26.

[24] *Jub.* 1.16.

[25] *Jub.* 16.26.

[26] *Jub.* 21.22.

[27] *Jub.* 21.24.

[28] *Jub.* 36.6.

[29] Gen. 12.3; 17.4; 18.18; etc.

[30] The specifically Isaacian mediation of the seed is also noted in Tiller 1997: 324.

[31] *Jub.* 23.16–25. For an admirable discussion of tribulation in *Jubilees*, see Pitre 2005: 65–71.

will stand up with bow and swords and war in order to return them to 'the way', but they will not be returned until much blood is shed upon the earth by each (group). And those who escape will not be turned back from their evils to the way of righteousness because they will lift themselves up for deceit and wealth so that one shall take everything of his neighbor.[32]

Eventually, this wicked generation will yield to another – let's just say much more promising – generation: 'in those days, children will begin to search the law . . . and to return to the way of righteousness'.[33] For the author of *Jubilees*, the essential conflict between the searchers of the law and the apostate generation is a conflict over 'the way'. While the future righteous generation will be faithful to it, those who are not on the 'way' are doomed.[34] The latter's failings, providing grist for the mill of tribulation, are characterized by ensnarement in 'deceit' and 'wealth'.[35] Apostasy is the divinely mandated preparation for the establishment of the plant and the final temple.

To summarize: in *Jubilees*, 'seed' represents Abraham's progeny mediated through Isaac; its significance within the unfolding cosmic drama can hardly be overstated. Though enduring a season of tribulation, when the apostate will turn aside from 'the way', the seed finally comes into its own when it is transplanted in the land. Closely coordinated with this moment is the establishment of the eschatological temple.[36] The chronological movement of *Jubilees* is relatively simple and straightforward: first comes the seed, which then suffers through tribulation in order to become a plant, leaving a short step to the eschatological temple.

Apocalypse of Weeks (1 En. *93.1–10; 91.11–17*)

Almost contemporaneous with *Jubilees*, the *Apocalypse of Weeks* sets out a periodized sequence of ten (plus) 'weeks' of history. In the course of the seventh week (at some indeterminate point after the Babylonian exile), an 'apostate generation shall arise', one whose 'deeds shall be many, and all of them criminal'.[37] It is 'a perverse generation' of 'violence' and 'deceit'.[38] This final tribulation can hardly be understood apart from either its antecedents in Israel's history or the alternating pattern of good and evil in which it is embedded. Although one might expect the appearance of a thinly veiled Noah

---

[32] *Jub.* 23.20–21a. Unless otherwise noted, this and subsequent translations of *Jubilees* are from Wintermute 1985.

[33] *Jub.* 23.26.

[34] There is no reason to doubt that this 'way' is the very same 'way' alluded to in the Qumran writings and synoptic tradition, the Isaianic way by which return from exile will take place.

[35] *Jub.* 23.21.

[36] This remains true whether or not that temple stands in continuity with the Second Temple, and whether or not the transition is gradual (as recently argued by Hanneken 2012: 191–4).

[37] *1 En.* 93.9. The community behind this apocalypse seems to believe that even by the second-century BCE (the date of the text's composition) a true return from exile had yet to materialize; see Dexinger 1977: 31–2; VanderKam 1997b: 96–100; Himmelfarb 2007: 234. Unless otherwise noted, this and subsequent translations of *1 Enoch* are from Isaac 1985.

[38] *1 En.* 93.9. For further discussion of these terms as catchwords of tribulation, see Pitre 2005: 45–6.

to have a dampening effect on the 'deceit' of the second week, the reverse actually proves to be the case: injustice only 'becomes greater'.[39] The zig-zag movement from Noah's wicked predecessors, to the righteous patriarch himself, to his very wicked successors and eventually back again conforms to the larger narrative pattern of alternating dark ages and bright, where intensified evil consistently functions as the trigger of divine intervention.

At the end of the seventh week, the 'elect ones of righteousness from the eternal plant of righteousness' come to the rescue with 'sevenfold instruction concerning all his flock'.[40] This future remnant has roots attached to two 'plants' surfacing in the third week, when 'a (certain) man shall be elected as the plant of the righteous judgment and after him one (other) shall emerge as the plant of righteousness' – in short, Abraham and Isaac.[41] Isaac's debut at the beginning of the apocalypse, together with his seminal role at critical turning points throughout the weeks, speaks to the patriarch's importance in the sect's self-understanding. In appropriating Isaac's epithet for itself, the eschatological community behind the *Apocalypse of Weeks* virtually identifies itself as the very embodiment of Isaac himself – both in the present and into the future.

By the time we come to the (second) eight week, the wicked are dispatched and a 'house will be built for the Great King in glory for evermore', referring to the eschatological temple and the messiah, respectively.[42] According to the *Apocalypse of Weeks*, the real return from exile only occurs on the establishment of the final temple.[43] This last phase rounds off a now-familiar pattern. The sequential movement from plant–seed to tribulation, from tribulation to victorious future remnant, from victorious future remnant to eschatological temple is roughly the same as what we find in *Jubilees*. Like the author of *Jubilees*, too, the composer of *Weeks* uses the seed/plant metaphor to symbolize the community's organic continuity through history.

Book of Dreams (1 Enoch *83—90*)

Organic imagery also comes to the fore in Methuselah's vision in the *Book of Dreams*. On the encouragement of his grandfather Mahalalel, the aged patriarch prays for a remnant to be raised up, a prayer which is later realized

---

[39] *1 En.* 93.4.
[40] *1 En.* 93.10.
[41] *1 En.* 93.5. Isaac's epithet 'plant of righteousness' seems to have been derived from a fusion of the same two terms paired at Isa. 61.3b: 'They will be called oaks of *righteousness* [*ḥaṣedeq*], the *planting* [*matta'*] of the LORD, to display his glory'. The same text is also foundational for Qumran's self-understanding as the plantation of God; see Tiller 1997: 313; Swarup 2006: 23–4; M. A. Collins 2009: 94. Another favourite sobriquet at Qumran, 'eternal planting', seems to be more directly tied to Exod. 15.17–18, which was regularly understood as a sneak peek at the eschatological temple; see Brooke 1999: 291–3; Ådna 2000: 90–110 (on Exod. 15.17–18).
[42] *1 En.* 91.12–13b.
[43] Other Second-Temple texts follow suit: Neh. 9.13; Tobit 13:3–6; 2 Macc. 1:27–29; *1 Enoch* 89—90; CD 1.3–11; 1QH^a 12.8–9; 1QS 8.12–14; 9.18–20; 1QM 1.3; 4Q177 5–6, 7–10; 4Q258 frg. 3 3.4; 4Q259 frg. 1 3.19. Also see Knibb 1976; VanderKam 1997b: 96–100; Nicholas Perrin, 2013a.

through Noah's family, which is also a 'plant of eternal seed'.[44] Although neither Abraham nor Isaac is mentioned by name in this context, the 'plant of the eternal seed' anticipates the Abrahamic promise which will centrally focus on *seed*.[45] Once again, where the language of seed/planting occurs, it is a cipher for the remnant.

Similarities between the narrative structure (including the sequence of events as they have already unfolded and are yet to unfold) of this apocalypse and that of the *Apocalypse of Weeks* are easy enough to spot. In a pattern reminiscent of *Jubilees* and the *Apocalypse of Weeks*, the *Book of Dreams* retains a certain redemptive-historical logic, in keeping with but also going beyond the strict demands of the scriptural story. In short, it is a logic that requires apostasy as the necessary and sufficient condition for the emergence of the remnant. When the righteous remnant rises up, it does so not out of a vacuum but in response to apostasy; the form of that remnant is a 'plant of the eternal seed'.

The second of the two visions making up the *Book of Dreams*, the Apocalypse of Animals, expresses not only extreme displeasure in the regnant priesthood but also a certain aloofness to the temple served by it. Here it is not so much that the priesthood takes the brunt of some incriminating invective, but that the temple cultus is passed over in a stonily silent *damnatio memoriae*.[46] This is consistent with the author's allegory involving corrupt shepherds across the pre-exilic and post-exilic eras, all of which presumes the period's essential unity entirely unaffected by the geographical return from exile.[47] For the community of the *Book of Dreams*, the true return from exile was still on the horizon.

En route to that restoration, the remnant will have to travel through the harrowing pass of tribulation.[48] This is a season of apostasy, when the sheep are 'exceedingly deafened' and 'exceedingly dim-sighted', and of intense persecution involving butchery.[49] But at the end of it all, the promise of a new temple remains:

> I went on seeing until the Lord of the sheep brought about a new house, greater and loftier than the first one, and set it up in the first location which had been covered up – all its pillars were new, the columns new; and the ornaments new as well as greater than those of the first, (that is) the old (house) which was gone.[50]

---

[44] *1 En.* 83.8; 84.6.

[45] Gen. 12.7; 13.15–16; 15.3, 13; 16.10; 17.7, 8, 9, 10, 12, etc.

[46] As Himmelfarb (2007: 232) explains, 'the absence of the priests suggests that the Animal Apocalypse is not particularly interested in them because it does not see their behavior as having special significance for the fate of Israel.'

[47] *1 Enoch* 89—90. See Knibb 1976: 256–8.

[48] *1 En.* 90.1–27.

[49] *1 En.* 90.7, 8–12.

[50] *1 En.* 90.29.

While some scholars maintain that this passage speaks only to the rebuilding of Jerusalem and not to that of the eschatological temple, it is difficult to conceive how this passage, with its mention of pillars and ornaments, could exclude the temple.[51] Once again, the trajectory from exile to tribulation culminates in the establishment of God's people and the building of the eschatological temple, in this case under the messiah's auspices.[52]

Synthesis

Given the richness of the sectarians' stories within the story of Israel, a mere recounting of the events would have hardly been sufficient. These communities needed a powerful metaphor that would not only confer the legitimacy of ancient roots, but also offer hope by promising eschatological blessedness. Such a metaphor was found ready-made in the seed/plant motif of the Abrahamic narratives. In each retelling of Israel's story, the seed's vital connection to Abraham through the person of Isaac remains front and centre. The remnant's genealogical connection with Isaac is not simply biological but also ethical. It is only the righteous, who (in the phrasing of *Jubilees*) are 'on the way'. In the Enochic literature, the remnant's connection to the father–son patriarchal duo is so tight that the eschatological remnant is able to identify itself *as* Isaac, that is, as a communal embodiment of his person. The organic motif was convenient because it instantly conveyed the community's future legacy in the revelation of righteousness. Despite conspicuous differences in their respective casting of future events, the three visions are notionally dependent on a shared timeline that begins with the Abrahamic covenant, moves to a scenario of tribulation, and climaxes with the establishment of the eschatological temple. Just as a murder-mystery novel is quickly recognized by a consistent combination of props and formulaic plotline (usually involving a mysterious murder at the beginning, a multiplication of suspects in the middle and an unexpected disclosure scene at the end), so it is for the apocalyptic retellings of Israel's story: the very metaphor of seed invokes a certain narrative grammar, which promises logically successive stages of redemptive history.

The parable of the sower *redux*

The point of these comparisons is not to demonstrate that the communities behind these texts maintained an identical eschatology (they did not), but rather to show a consistent correlation between the seed/plant metaphor and a predictable narrative sequence. It is a sequence which, I propose, Jesus also shared. Like its apocalyptic predecessors, Jesus' parable of the sower seized on

---

[51] For a successful refutation of the judgement that the eschatological temple goes missing in this sequence (so Gaston 1970: 114; Tiller 1993: 376), see Dimant 1981–2.

[52] So also Sanders 1985: 81–2; Ådna 2000: 43; Nickelsburg et al. 2001: 405; Himmelfarb 2007: 229–31.

the organic metaphor in order to link his community back to Abraham via Isaac while at the same time implicating his followers in a three-step process of tribulation, fruit bearing and temple construction. In other words, Jesus' parable deploys specific horticultural images as familiar symbolic placeholders for an equally familiar redemptive-historical plotline. This much, I think, is borne out by the text of Mark 4.3–9.

'A sower went out to sow seed'

We should not be fooled by the simplicity with which this parable begins: a sower goes out to sow *seed*. Certainly, many first-century hearers familiar with the traditions witnessed in the Enochic texts or *Jubilees* would have caught on to intimations of Abraham through a patently metaphorical use of 'seed' within a highly symbolic retelling of Israel's story. Though the parable is obviously a veiled retelling, their 'catching on' was precisely Jesus' intention.[53] His language would have resonated not only with the scriptural texts, but also with recent events and cultural memes *before* the text, as it were, including the teachings of the leading apocalyptic pundit of the day, John the Baptizer. When John publicly declared the importance of bearing fruit and forsaking reliance on one's genetic connection to Abraham, he emphasized that the biological 'seed of Abraham' could lay no automatic claim to Israel's eschatological fruitfulness.[54] On this point, Jesus (as well as his apocalyptic predecessors behind *1 Enoch* and *Jubilees*) would have been in firm agreement. The only difference here is that he, now picking up the conversation where John had left off, is explaining just how such fruitfulness, the cashing out of the Abrahamic promise, will take place.

The Abrahamic context is likewise confirmed on Jesus' specifying that the successful harvest will accrue up to a hundred-fold.[55] Whether or not such a yield is within the realm of possibility (a long-standing if not somewhat extraneous scholarly discussion in its own right), Jesus seeks not just to emphasize the extraordinary output of the good soil, but also to identify it with the singular hundred-fold harvest realized by Isaac in Genesis 26.12: 'Isaac sowed seed in that land, and in the same year reaped a *hundredfold*.'[56] As Jesus' more thoughtful hearers would have pieced together, the sower represents not so much God but Jesus, who as the Isaacian heir of the seed promise, reaps the 'harvest' of the eschatological temple.

---

[53] I reject the commonly touted notion that Jesus' parables were spoken with the intention of obscuring the truth. Rather, '[i]f there is anything that the Evangelists themselves underline in their portrait of Jesus, it is his refusal to be content with spoon-feeding, and his determination to make people think for themselves. The Evangelists' picture in general, therefore, seems to invite us to understand the parables neither as a *disciplina arcani* designed to conceal a secret, nor yet, on the other hand, as merely illustrative, but as provocative and dynamic and creative' (Moule 1969: 98).

[54] Q 3.8.

[55] Mark 4.8 par. Matthew's description of the harvest (13.8) begins with 'a hundredfold'; dropping the numbers 'thirty' and 'sixty', Luke just retains 'a hundredfold' (8.8).

[56] So too, e.g., Cave 1965: 381; Hultgren 2000: 188; Beavis 2011: 78.

'Some seed fell beside the path'

The seed 'beside the path' refers to those within Israel who show no interest in return from exile. We infer this because Jesus' wording is reminiscent of *Jubilees* 23.26, which categorizes people either as belonging to the 'way' or as having departed from it, the righteous returnees and the unrighteous, respectively. Likewise trading on the Isaianic 'way' (Isa. 26.7; 40.3; etc.), the Qumran covenanteers also saw themselves as people who were 'on the way' out of exile.[57] Given such analogies, those 'beside the way' in Jesus' parable must refer to those who by choice are stuck in a state of exile.

Meanwhile, the image of birds plucking up scattered seeds invokes another apocalyptic tradition revolving around Abraham, extrapolated from Genesis 15.11 and discernible in *Jubilees* 11 and *Apocalypse of Abraham* 13.[58] In *Jubilees* 11, the arch-demon 'Prince Mastema sent crows and birds so that they might eat the seed which was being sown in the earth in order to spoil the earth', and it is the 14-year-old Abraham who successfully repels the crows with exorcistic utterances.[59] The young patriarch's success as an exorcist antici-pates his later prayer: 'Save me from the hands of evil spirits which rule over the thoughts of the heart of man, and do not let them lead me astray from following you, O my God; but establish me and my seed forever.'[60] The first threat to the redemptive goal of established seed is the threat of demonic influence. For those who fall prey to such influence, return from exile cannot even get off the ground.

'Other seed fell on rocky ground'

The second soil, we recall, receives seed that produces sprouts, which are then levelled by the scorching sun. The plants shrivel not on account of the heat but on account of their shallow root system. This is the opposite of the experi-ence of Psalm 1's righteous man who, being deeply rooted, stands firm in the midst of 'sinners' and 'mockers'.[61] In Ezekiel 17, withering befalls those who foolishly look to the Egyptians for support against Babylon.[62] This symbol-ism is not inconsistent with Isaiah, where withering is also regularly tied to judgement against the nations.[63] Given such parallels, I believe that Mark's interpretation again preserves the general meaning intended by Jesus on his first performance of the parable: the seed sown on shallow soil refers to those who after a promising start eventually cave to external political pressures.[64]

While Mark's interpretation of the rocky-soil seed is generalized ('when trouble or persecution arises on account of the word, immediately they fall

---

[57] See 1QS 8.12–16; 9.17–21; 10.21; 1QM 1.3; Snodgrass 1980.
[58] As argued by Pesch 1976–80: 1.243; Knowles 1995. See also van Ruiten 2012: 28–30.
[59] *Jub.* 11.11, 18–23.
[60] *Jub.* 12.20.
[61] Ps. 1.1–3, NIV.
[62] Ezek. 17.7–21.
[63] Isa. 1.30; 15.6; 24.4; 33.9; 34.4; 40.7, 8, 24.
[64] Mark 4.17 par.

away' (4.17)), Jesus' hearers would have more immediately connected the imagery to the recent persecution directed against John the Baptizer, as well as the ensuing apostasy which followed.[65] Whereas the Baptizer had in a short time stirred the passions of a sizable following, one suspects the movement was just as quickly pared down following his arrest and execution. I suggest that Jesus' withering plant analogy be understood against this background; it refers in the first place to the conspicuous apostasy that followed the persecution of his mentor. As such, Jesus' symbolic withering plants ask to be interpreted as the first instalment of tribulation, predicted to occur at the closing stages of exile (the first soil) and, now according to Jesus, already precipitated by the death of John. The mental picture of the shrivelling plants is at once a historical reminiscence and a warning to Jesus' followers that they would not be exempt from the very opposition John had faced.

'Other seed fell among thorns'

Although the symbolic multivalence of thorns in the Jewish literature is daunting, the image generally revolves around individuals or systemic realities that impede Israel's pursuit of its vocation. Isaiah 5 provides a good example: 'For the vineyard of the LORD of hosts is the house of Israel, and the people of Judah are his pleasant planting; he expected justice, but he saw bloodshed; righteousness, but heard a cry!'[66] Israel's moral failure is a direct result of 'briers and thorns'.[67] The same metaphor recurs in the reprise of the Song of the Vineyard in Isaiah 27 with much the same meaning:

> On that day: A pleasant vineyard, sing about it! I, the LORD, am its keeper; every moment I water it. I guard it night and day so that no one can harm it; I have no wrath. If it gives me *thorns and briers*, I will march to battle against it. I will burn it up.[68]

The symbolism behind the 'thorns and briers' is further illuminated on comparison with Isaiah 9.18 (MT 9.17) and 10.17. In the first of these two texts, 'briers and thorns' refer to the wicked of Israel who hinder the nation's fruitfulness but who will also be consumed by their own wickedness. In Isaiah 10.17, however, 'thorns and briers' symbolize the Assyrians whom Yahweh had sent to punish Israel. Between these instances there is an inner consistency: thorns and briers appear to refer to individuals or collective entities, internal or external to the commonwealth, which inhibit righteousness and justice.[69]

---

[65] This interpretation is hinted at by Dodd 1935: 182–3. But see also Schweitzer (2001 (1906): 325–6): 'Make of it [i.e. my interpretation of the kingdom] what you will. But one thing is certain: the initial fact to which Jesus points, under the figure of the sowing, must be somehow or other connected with the eschatological preaching of repentance which had been begun by the Baptist'.

[66] Isa. 5.7.

[67] Isa. 5.6.

[68] Isa. 27.2–4; emphasis added.

[69] For full discussion, see Johnson 2011.

It would be difficult to deny the same sense to the thorns in Jesus' parable. In other words, the parabolic briers refer to not only ideological commitments operative within the individual but also any socio-cultural system which undermines Israel's quest for Torah obedience. As such, the parable would apply both to the Roman imposition of certain values and practices, as well as to powerbrokers within Judaism, who operated according to their own idolatrous *modus vivendi*.[70] While, in Jesus' perception, many might have otherwise been inclined to sign on with his newly formed society, they were deterred by socio-political and ideological pressures. Well aware of the radically countercultural nature of his own calling, as well as the gravitational pull of the prevailing cultural norms, Jesus included thorny soil in his parable as part of an open-ended critique of what Walter Rauschenbusch might in his own day have identified as the 'sin [which] is lodged in the social customs and institutions and is absorbed by the individual from his social group'.[71]

The element of the thorny soil was also a sober assessment of Israel's present location within the map of redemptive history. Whereas Isaiah had imagined a future Israel free from thorns, here Jesus takes for granted that the thorns of apostasy were an ever-present reality that all but sealed – by inference from Isaiah 27 – the nation's doom. Jesus' perception of apostasy as an imposing systemic phenomenon would have only been further confirmation that the long-predicted darkness was at hand. That is, for any first-century Jew operating within an apocalyptic framework, widespread and socially destructive apostasy would have been further evidence that the tribulation was underway. One might even construe this third soil as a second layer of tribulation, following yet also building upon the first layer evidenced in the death of John.[72] Though the four soils are presented as concurrent realities, this by itself hardly rules out the possibility that they refer to logically consecutive realities, with the sense of concurrency simply being an unavoidable element of the parable. Indeed, the generic pattern of apocalyptic visions such as we've examined here virtually implies an analogous chronological linearity in Jesus' parable. Unfolding in sequential stages, the spheres of reality represented by the soils do not supplant one another but are presented as successive, overlapping stages.

For better or worse, the interpretation I am offering for the third soil is not inconsistent with the interpretation attached by the synoptic writers themselves. While Mark connects the thorny ground with the 'cares of the world,

---

[70] This comes close to elements of Schottroff and Maloney (2006: 66–78). However, her reconstruction of the parable as 'a critical analysis of the money economy' (68) presumes a social interpretation of history that is without parallel in antiquity (see Auerbach 2003 (1953): 32–9) and is therefore finally implausible.

[71] Rauschenbusch 1987 (1917): 60.

[72] At this point, it is more than tempting to build on Brant Pitre's (2005: 131–218, *passim*; 509–18) case that Jesus saw John the Baptizer and himself as introducing two successive stages of tribulation. Given the persuasiveness of Pitre's argument, it is quite possible that the second and third soils are to be correlated with the stages he has teased out. I raise the point merely as an interesting possibility.

and the lure of wealth' (Mark 4.19), and Luke adds to this the 'pleasures of life' (Luke 8.14), these may be seen as specific instantiations of the same culturally embedded values which Jesus opposed. Of course the Gospel writers would have also been interested in extending the sense of Jesus' parable, as they understood it, to their own context. We should assume no differently here.

'Other seed fell into good soil'

In the above-surveyed apocalyptic narratives, the mere mention of 'seed' can be seen as initiating a redemptive-historical storyline that begins with Abraham and culminates in the establishment of a righteous remnant, setting the stage for the eschatological temple. In Jesus' parable, these very same climactic elements are represented by 'the good soil' and its fruit, respectively.[73] Towards sifting the former phrase, we should not fail to hear the scriptural resonance of 'the good soil', or more exactly, 'the good land'. From the very beginning of the exodus story, Israel is promised it will inherit a 'good land' (Exod. 3.8). Likewise, when Moses' spies report back after their reconnaissance mission, they do so insisting that it is a 'good land' (Num. 14.7). In Deuteronomy the phrase is repeated tirelessly: as Israel stands on the brink of the Jordan, it stands to inherit a 'good land'.[74] The refrain, I believe, is intentionally invoked in Jesus' story of the seed. Simply put, the 'good land' of the parable is not just fertile soil, but the land of inheritance and by extension (from the post-exilic perspective) the land of cultic restoration.

This is consistent with the portrait I have been sketching thus far. If in repeating the Lord's Prayer the disciples understood themselves as recouping lost cultic space through a new exodus (Chapter 1), then the culmination of that exodus would also naturally involve language of inheritance – Israel's real-estate inheritance, to be exact. Whether or not Jesus' construal of 'land' was precisely the same as that of the disciples, the master's parable hints that this 'land' was to materialize in the communal life of those who responded positively to Jesus. This makes sense, especially when we recall that the land was never granted as an end unto itself but was intended to be a set-apart space for worship. Apparently, that 'set-apart space' was the Jesus movement itself.

On the scriptural logic, then, re-entry into 'the good land' of the parable meant not only the installation of a new priesthood responsible for carrying out a new temple service, but also the reintroduction of an Edenic reality, signified by the productive yield. Eden was of course the setting of the very first temple. This is why Second-Temple Judaism understood fruitfulness not only as a metaphor for covenantal obedience, but also (and perhaps more fundamentally) as a metaphor for a truly functional cultus – just as we have it in Isaiah 61. This is the same sort of thinking that allowed the Qumran coven-

---

[73] Mark 4.8 par.
[74] Deut. 1.25, 35; 3.25; 4.21, 22; 6.18; 8.7, 10; 9.6; 11.17; cf. Josh. 23.13, 16; Ezek. 17.8.

anteers to think of themselves as a botanic temple.[75] In the literature, where one finds eschatological plantation, there one finds the eschatological temple.

This interpretation finds confirmation in Jesus' parable of the mustard seed. In this saying, almost certainly dominical, Jesus compares the kingdom to a mustard seed, which, though among the smallest of seeds, eventually yields a magnificent output in the form of a large plant (Mark) or tree (Matthew/Luke).[76] As Mark notes, the mature mustard plant, clearly symbolic of the kingdom, would shelter the Gentiles (= 'birds of the air') and would be 'greater than' all other kingdoms (= 'plants'), including presumably the likes of Rome.[77] That this great kingdom/plant is also the eschatological temple is clear from its scriptural underpinnings. First, the image of the birds 'dwelling' (*kataskēnoun*) in the great tree's branches brings to mind Zechariah's description of the ingathering of the Gentiles on Zion.[78] Second, Jesus' parabolic tree is almost certainly an offshoot of Ezekiel's parabolic tree, planted at the end of exile on 'a high and lofty mountain', that is, on the temple mount.[79] Such allusions combine to suggest that Jesus' full-grown mustard plant is the Zion-based focal point of the Gentiles' pilgrimage – the eschatological temple. So, then, in rehearsing the parable of the mustard seed, Jesus is not merely contrasting the humble beginnings of the kingdom with its future glory; he is also claiming an organic continuity between the community forming under his auspices and the long-awaited final temple. In Jesus' mind, the full-grown mustard plant and the hundred-fold harvest of the parable of the sower were but two images for the same cultic reality.

The parable of the sower and the historical Jesus

A number of implications follow this analysis of the parable of the sower. In the first place, the parable was *analytic*, insofar as it logically broke down – much along the line of its precursor texts – Israel's promise, plight and solution. As Wright has argued, this study suggests that Jesus saw exile

---

[75] The classical passage is 1QS 8.4b–10a: 'When such men as these come to be in Israel, then shall the party of the Yahad truly be established, an "eternal planting", a temple for Israel, and – mystery! – a Holy of Holies for Aaron; true witnesses to justice, chosen by god's will to atone for the land and to recompense the wicked their due. They will be "the tested wall, the precious cornerstone" whose foundations shall neither be shaken nor swayed, a fortress, a Holy of Holies for Aaron, all of them knowing the Covenant of Justice and thereby offering a sweet savor. They shall be a blameless and true house in Israel, upholding the covenant of eternal statutes. They shall be an acceptable sacrifice, atoning for the land and ringing in the verdict against evil, so that perversity ceases to exist.' See also 1QS 11.7–9; 1QHᵃ 13.20—15.6; CD 1.5–8; 4Q266; 4Q418 81; as well as commentary on these passages in Swarup 2006: 15–107.
[76] Mark 4.31–2 par.
[77] Mark 4.32.
[78] 'And many nations will flee for refuge to the Lord in that day, and they will be a people to him. And *they will dwell* [*kataskēnōsousin*] in your midst: then you will know that the Lord Almighty has sent me to you" (Zech. 2.11 LXX; translation is my own). Cf. *Jos. Asen.* 15.6.
[79] Ezek. 17.22.

as the fundamental problem facing the nation. Like the Enochic authors, Jesus' 'ho-hum' take on the geographical return from exile could hardly be separated from his pessimistic take on the regnant priesthood.[80] Yet the relativizing of the Second Temple was also bound up with his forward-looking expectation, fuelled by various prophetic texts, that Yahweh was about to act – and act decisively – in the near future.[81] So if exile was the problem, then 'fruitfulness' in the form of an eschatological temple was the answer. In the terms of Ezekiel 36, Jesus did indeed anticipate his movement brokering a restored cultic space free of ensnaring idols. In fact, participation in this restoration process was one of his key objectives for his movement.

Second, the parable was a Christologically *descriptive* tool, elucidating Jesus' central priestly role in this restoration despite all appearances to the contrary. Convinced that he was both the Isaacian heir of the hundred-fold harvest as well as the agent through which this harvest would be realized, Jesus performed this parable as a way of reasserting his priestly calling in the face of mixed reviews. As would become quickly apparent to observers, whenever Jesus spoke publicly, some would respond and others would not. The parable of the sower was apparently Jesus' go-to explanation as to why. Those who yielded fruit did so, the parable would suggest, because they were the true seed, the true sons and daughters of Abraham. Those who failed to yield fruit did so for reasons that cannot be fully accounted for by narrow categories of existential choice. Like the apocalyptic literature studied in this chapter, the parable of the sower signals a conviction that human responsiveness to the divine was constrained by an unfolding divine drama involving dark spheres of reality finally beyond human control. For those who had trouble conceiving of a messianic priest opposed by his own people, this parable was intended to provide clarification as to why it could not possibly be otherwise.

Third, as a kind of speech-act, the parable maintained an *instrumental* function. Towards advancing the redemptive narrative, from the initial sowing of the word to an Israel still in exile (Isaiah 55) to the experience of a restored Eden (Isaiah 61), Jesus applied the parable of the sower as a kind of spiritual sieve. On offering this retelling of Israel's story he would soon enough be able to differentiate fruit-bearers from non-fruit-bearers, prospective candidates for his movement from the dead wood. In this respect, the parable of the sower *was* the hermeneutical key, a parable of parables, inasmuch as it implied that all his parables, indeed, all his teaching, retained a differentiating function. Whatever verbal encouragement, warning, challenge and comfort Jesus hoped to convey in the course of his ministry, all of these served the larger purpose of identifying a new temple community. Engaging

---

[80] I have documented this at length in Nicholas Perrin, 2010: 92–9.
[81] Especially important in this regard are Jer. 29.10–14 and Dan. 9.24–27. For fuller discussion, see Nicholas Perrin, 2010: 135–7.

with the spoken word of Jesus, the pure would separate themselves from the impure and the unholy from the holy. Because the making of ritual pronouncements of clean and unclean, holy and profane, was fundamentally a sacerdotal task, it follows that Jesus' performance of parables – not to mention his pronouncements, maxims, chreia and so forth – was itself a *priestly activity*. The parable of the sower is good evidence, then, that public preaching was a major means by which Jesus hoped to discharge the terms of his extraordinary ordination.

Fourth and finally, the parable had a *theodicean* agenda, addressing the suffering and marginalization already palpable in the experience of the Jesus community. Against standard interpretations of the parable of the sower which admit no causal relationship between the four soils, I have proposed that Jesus saw the grim circumstances of the first three soils, explicable by their location within a mysterious continuum somehow transcending yet also intersecting with history, as necessary stepping stones to 'the good land' awaiting eschatological Israel. For Jesus, the signs of tribulation – heightened demonic activity, persecution, ensnaring ideologies, and the suffering these inflicted – were not only evidence that construction of the eschatological temple was underway, but also a catalyst for achieving the same. Some would succumb to these *peirasmoi*; those destined to belong to the 'good land' would persevere through them. As Jesus saw it, the negative responses to his movement were not merely unfortunate and largely inexplicable blips on the radar but the necessary complements of a divinely wrought gestation process. The very opposition besetting Jesus' movement had its own teleological explanation. Such suffering, via some mysterious logic, was to be the very means by which the eschatological temple would be realized.

While this analysis of the parable of the sower may answer some important questions, it raises new issues. First, even if we have explained *that* the *peirasmos* was necessary, it still needs to be explained *why* it was necessary. What exactly was supposed to be accomplished by this suffering? Put otherwise: what goes missing in the redemptive plan if suffering is not a part of the process? Second, if Jesus saw himself and his movement as the missing link between present-day exile and future restoration, this does not explain *how* this return from exile was supposed to have taken place. Obviously, Jesus and his contemporaries would have admitted that the return had already occurred on some level, since they were already patently occupying the land of their ancestors. But since the movement from exile to restoration – from the third soil to the fourth – was presumably attended by certain observable conditions, what might those conditions look like? What was, in Jesus' mind, the empirical evidence that restoration was already in progress? Towards answering these two sets of questions ('Why, in Jesus' mind, was suffering necessary?' and 'What, in Jesus' mind, are the distinguishing character traits of restoration?'), we now turn to the remainder of the chapter.

The future trajectory of the kingdom: the parable of salt (Matt. 5.13//Mark 9.50//Luke 14.34–35)

For the ancient Jews no less than for modern theologians, though suffering was a significant component of the divine economy, it remained finally inexplicable. For this reason, we must reckon with the likelihood that in Judaism it was more a reality to be endured than a conundrum to be explained. At the same time, suffering sometimes *did* require explanation. This especially seemed to be the case in instances involving distress at the hands of the unjust, commonly interpreted in redemptive terms on the model of the exodus. In retrospect, although Pharaoh's resistance to Moses had obvious deleterious effects on Israel, such opposition was necessary in forcing the moment to its divinely intended crisis. At the end of the day, it was only through trauma that Israel could be ordained to its destined role as kingdom of priests.

Insight into Jesus' unique vision of oppression – by which the experience of marginalization could be redeemed – now comes by way of one of the more puzzling sayings regularly ascribed to Jesus: the parable of salt.[82] Assigning this pithy aphorism a pink coding (probably dominical), the Jesus Seminar reconstructs it on the basis of Q as follows:

> Salt is good (and salty). But if salt loses its zing, how will it be renewed? It's no good for either earth or manure. It just gets thrown away.[83]

I am aware that in incorporating the parable of salt into my argument I am running with the wind at my back in terms of authenticity but am trudging uphill in terms of perspicuity. Jesus spoke the parable of salt and on many occasions: this is virtually a point of consensus.[84] But as to what Jesus (or for that matter the Evangelists themselves) meant by this enigmatic announcement – that is where the agreement ends.

Interpretation is made all the more difficult by salt's wide-ranging application in antiquity.[85] The compound was utilized as a condiment (Job 6.6), a preservative (Diogenes Laertius 8.1.35; *b. Ketub.* 66b), a cleansing agent (Exod. 30.35; 2 Kings 2.19–23), a fertilizer, an accompaniment to covenantal rituals (Num. 18.19; Lev. 2.13) and a complement to sacrificial offerings (Lev. 2.13; Ezek. 43.24); salt also served as a metaphor for wisdom and wit (Col. 4.5; Dio Chrysostom, *Or.* 18.13).[86] Perhaps something like household duct tape in the modern day, salt was an all-purpose substance, performing

---

82 Matt. 5.13//Mark 9.50//Luke 14.34–35.
83 Funk and Hoover 1993: 354. That Luke 14.34–35 preserves Q with no admixture of Mark is far from certain; see Dunn 2003: 234 n. 254.
84 Persuaded by the criterion of multiple attestation and discernible traces of an Aramaic substratum (see Keener 2009: 158, 480 n. 246; Vattamány 2013), among other factors, most scholars have agreed with the Seminar on the saying's authenticity.
85 For an excellent study on the significance of salt, see Latham 1982.
86 These are nicely catalogued in Davies and Allison 1988–97: 1.472–3; see also Dämmgen 2011.

a variety of functions in a variety of settings. Theoretically, its potential meaning on the lips of Jesus may relate to one, some or all of these
utilities.

Complicating matters further is the fact that the synoptic contexts in which
the salt parable occurs are strikingly different. Like an additive in three very
different dishes, the salt saying takes on a slightly different flavour in each.
In Matthew, the aphorism is ensconced between the Beatitudes (5.3–12), on
the one side, and images of a city on a hill and light (5.14–16), on the other.
Mark situates the metaphor at the tail end of an extended admonition against
sin (9.42–50), where it is linked by catchword connection to intimations of
judgement (9.50). Meanwhile, Luke places the same saying within a context
in which readers are encouraged to consider the cost of discipleship (14.25–
35). Although interpreters are accustomed to interpret isolated sayings like
this with some help from the narrative context, the variety of contexts across
the triple tradition offers – at least at first blush – little help.

The quest for a unified interpretation of the salt parables is hindered still
further by the substantive differences between them. In the first Gospel, Jesus
identifies his disciples as the 'salt of the earth'.[87] By contrast, Mark's
Jesus encourages the disciples to have 'salt *in* [them]selves'.[88] Different from
both of these, Luke neither explicitly identifies the disciples as salt nor speaks
of salt as something to be realized within – 'salt is good' in principle.[89] As if
the salt sayings were not already cryptic enough, these minor differences in
wording hardly help our reconstruction of the metaphor as it may have been
used in the setting of Jesus.

Towards retrieving the dominical intention behind this saline saying, it
will be helpful to consider the logion as it occurs in each of the three Gospels.
As I have noted, the salt maxim shakes out in a different way for each Gospel
writer. Yet these patent differences should not preclude the possibility of
shared and univocal symbolism undergirding each instance. Indeed, given
a closer examination of the Gospel contexts, we find evidence that all three
Gospel writers presuppose a common understanding of the metaphor – and
this despite obvious differences in their respective applications. Where we
find intimations of a common denominator, there we will most likely be
in touch with a basal meaning tacitly shared by the Evangelists. There too,
I suggest, we will most likely be in touch with prior tradition, not least the
tradition originating with the historical Jesus.[90]

---

[87] Matt. 5.13.
[88] Mark 9.50, NIV.
[89] Luke 14.34.
[90] Building on the work of Cecil J. Sharp, J. M. Foley (1991: 6–8) applies the term 'multiform' to
the paradox of 'variations within limits' within oral tradition. Such multiformity is obviously
characteristic of the salt sayings and thus points to a shared metaphorization within the *Sitz im
Leben Jesu*.

Matthew's parable of salt (Matt. 5.13)

If the Beatitudes are the front stairway leading up to the entrance of the Sermon on the Mount, the triad of images making up Matthew 5.13–16 is the landing before the door. The text reads as follows:

> [13]You are the salt of the earth. But if the salt loses its saltiness, how can it be made salty again? It is no longer good for anything, except to be thrown out and trampled by men. [14]You are the light of the world. A city on a hill cannot be hidden. [15]Neither do people light a lamp and put it under a bowl. Instead they put it on its stand, and it gives light to everyone in the house. [16]In the same way, let your light shine before men, that they may see your good deeds and praise your Father in heaven.[91]

When set alongside its synoptic parallels, verse 13 exhibits several distinguishing marks, including (1) the explicit identification of the disciples as salt ('You are the salt of the earth'); (2) the omission of any mention of salt's goodness (retained by both Mark and Luke); and (3) a unique vision of 'de-salted' salt being 'trampled by men'. All three differences are regularly ascribed to Matthean redaction. Matthew's collocation of the three metaphors (salt, light and city) is also distinctive. On the Two-Source Hypothesis, one supposes that the Evangelist composed Matthew 5.13 from Q 14.34–35, and Matthew 5.15 from Q 11.33. Following the syntactical parallelism between the first two logia ('You are the salt of the earth [v. 13a] . . . You are the light of the world [v. 14a]'), the third element, the 'city on a hill' (v. 14b), completes the triad. While it is theoretically possible that the three different images represent three very different realities, the grammatical parallelism, not to mention Matthew's fondness for thematic links in his triads, would lead us to expect otherwise.

It would be a misreading of the two affirmations in this passage ('*You are* [*hymeis este*] the salt of the earth' (v. 13a) and '*You are* [*hymeis este*] the light of the world' (v. 14a)) to interpret them as innocent descriptions of the disciples. The Greek emphasizes the ascription of an exclusive corporate identity, for in both sentences the emphatic second-person plural pronoun occupies first position.[92] Jesus' comments regarding 'a city built on a hill' (v. 14b) follow in train. In other words, Matthew's Jesus is essentially saying, '*You* are the salt of the earth; *you* are the light of the world; *you* are a city on a hill – *you* as opposed to some other group who might stake this same claim for themselves.' Such rhetoric would hardly make sense unless the Matthean community's claim to be these three things was liable to be contested. For the Christian gathering, it was at the blurry boundary line separating itself from the local synagogue that it sensed the keenest challenge to its identity. If this polemical arena helps explain the Sermon on the Mount as a whole (which includes its own

---

[91] Matt. 5.13–16, NIV.
[92] Similarly Davies and Allison 1988–97: 1.471–2.

critique of Pharisaical piety (Matt. 5.20, 21–22, 27–28, 31–32, 33–34, 38–39, 43--44)), then the images of salt, light and city may naturally be understood as a series of metaphorical counterclaims, staked in direct competition with first-century Judaism (whether that Judaism was *intra muros* or *extra muros*).[93] Like a political candidate engaging a rhetorical battle as to who and who does not embody the heart of the nation, Matthew is keen to position members of his own community as the true heirs and guardians of Israel. For the Gospel writer, those who follow Jesus Christ are the true salt, the true light and the true city on a hill. They are all these things in an exclusive sense.

The Matthean context

But what exactly are we to make of the meaning of these metaphors? Working backwards through this triad, it seems evident to me that for any Palestinian Jew of the day the most obvious instance of a 'city on a hill' would have been Jerusalem.[94] The connection is likely given the city's hilltop location, enfolding the temple that was perched on the height of the temple mount, all in keeping with Zion's role as 'light of the nations'.[95] This cannot simply be any city on any hill, or any light. Rather, given the fluidity between the concepts of 'Zion' and 'temple' in Second-Temple Judaism, Matthew's point also seems to be that those who are faithful to the messiah Jesus, precisely by virtue of the qualities just outlined in the Beatitudes (5.3–12), will likewise shine forth as the true Jerusalem and the true temple.

At this point, however, we note that it is pre-eminently in visions of the future, eschatological temple that light comes to play an especially conspicuous role. This occurs not only in the sectarian literature of the day (*Sib. Or.* 3.787; 5.420; *1 En.* 14.8–23; 71.2–47), but more basically within the purview of Israel's eschatological hopes expressed in the ancient Hebrew scriptures. For example, in his apostrophe to Zion, Isaiah foresees the future brilliance of the city:

> Arise, shine; for your light has come, and the glory of the LORD has risen upon you. For darkness shall cover the earth, and thick darkness the peoples; but the LORD will arise upon you, and his glory will appear over you. Nations shall come to your light, and kings to the brightness of your dawn.[96]

Illuminated by the glorious presence of Yahweh within its temple, eschatological Jerusalem will attract the whole world with its light. At

---

[93] So, e.g., Betz and Collins 1995: 160: 'At the time of the New Testament this self-understanding of Jews to be "light of the world" seems to have played an important role.' At the same time, given Cicero's (*Cat.* 4.6) boast that Rome was 'the light of the world', a counterclaim against the Roman imperium can hardly be discounted.

[94] So, e.g., von Rad 1966 (1958): 232–42; Schnackenburg 1964: 379–80; Betz and Collins 1995: 161; Wright 1996: 289; contra Nolland 2005: 214 among others.

[95] The Jewish temple is regularly described as a source of light (Pss. 43.3; 80.1; 132.17), a notion reinforced through certain aspects of its architecture and rituals (see Barker 2003: 19–22; Fletcher-Louis 2000: 142–3; Welch 2009: 72–3).

[96] Isa. 60.1–3.

that time, too, Yahweh himself will render the creational lights redundant through his own presence:

> The sun shall no longer be your light by day, nor for brightness shall the moon give light to you by night; but the LORD will be your everlasting light, and your God will be your glory. Your sun shall no more go down, or your moon withdraw itself; for the LORD will be your everlasting light, and your days of mourning shall be ended.[97]

Like Zechariah's day of perpetual light (Zech. 14.6–7), when 'the LORD will become king over all the earth' (v. 9), this day marks the fullness of the kingdom, when Yahweh will take his rightful place in his temple. The proof of that reality will be the incandescence of the eschatological cultic space.

Following Isaiah's rhetorical lead, the late third-century BCE character Tobit also refers to the future temple, the 'rebuilt tent', as the light of the world:

> Acknowledge the Lord, for he is good, and bless the King of the ages, so that his tent may be rebuilt in you in joy . . . A bright light will shine to all the ends of the earth; many nations will come to you from far away, the inhabitants of the remotest parts of the earth to your holy name, bearing gifts in their hands for the King of heaven.[98]

Tobit's vision of a rebuilt and resplendent temple is but a piece of the larger eschatological picture, which of course includes the full return from exile and the restored glory of the temple. In the Jewish apocalyptic hope, the promise of God's glorious presence indwelling the final temple all but ensured its luminousness.

It is this prophetic hope of an eschatologically radiant Zion that explains Matthew 5.14.[99] By identifying Jesus' followers with the emerging eschatological temple, both in relatively straightforward terms ('You are the light of the world') and obliquely ('A city on a hill cannot be hidden'), Matthew assigns them a role that is at once unique yet in continuity with Israel's vocation. It is also a role that does not necessarily aspire to replace any existing temple structure, but rather seeks to fill out the course of an eschatological future already beginning to take embryonic shape in the present. As the slowly dawning light of the world, the community is called to perform 'good deeds' (v. 16, NIV), much as Israel has been called in its priestly role to be light of the world for the sake of the world.[100] According to the Evangelist, then, those who keep the demands of the Sermon on the Mount are precisely

---

[97] Isa. 60.19–20.

[98] Tobit 13.10–11.

[99] At a late stage in the writing process, my attention has been drawn to Fletcher-Louis 1997a, where I have discovered him making much the same argument.

[100] For all we know, Matthew intended his readers to shed light to 'all in the house' (5.15), namely, Jewish observers. In this case, it is possible that Matthew thought of the early Christian community as a lamp not outside the temple of Judaism but functioning within it.

those who embody the eschatological temple of God. Hardly unique to the Gospel of Matthew, this identification of the early Church as the final temple is broadly expressed across the New Testament literature.[101]

This sacerdotal interpretation of 'light' and 'city' in Matthew 5.14–16 is all the more appealing on account of their placement on the heels of Jesus' warnings of maltreatment at the close of the Beatitudes. Here in verses 10–12, the final two steps of the paradox-clad stairwell of the makarisms (blessings), the sense of paradox is never more elevated, for at this turn predictions of persecution, reviling and slander are conjoined with promises of kingdom inheritance, divine recompense and prophetic status.[102] The predictions are certainly in keeping with Matthew's theology, where the experience of persecution is framed as one of the kingdom's key components.[103] But the promises of reward for persecution are coherent only on the assumption that such suffering retains an intrinsic redemptive value. Once we see verses 14–16 as an attempt to spell out that value, we realize that the epithets 'light of the world' and 'city on a hill' (v. 14), precisely as cultic images, extend rather than abrogate the line of thought developed in verses 10–12. Indeed, given Judaism's integration of persecution within the priestly vocation *à la* the exodus, the step from politico-religious oppression (vv. 10–12) to images of temple (vv. 14–16) is a short step indeed. From Matthew's perspective, the believing community's sense of beleaguerment is most helpfully addressed by setting it in the context of its sacerdotal identity (5.14–16). In the final analysis, it was only the community's identity as the in-breaking eschatological temple that could make sense of such suffering in redemptive terms.

Priestly salt

Once situated within a larger expression of Jewish atonement theology, Matthew's salt saying begins to come into crystal clarity, especially as we recall that in the biblical literature the chemical compound is most commonly tied to the *covenant-making ritual within priestly contexts*.[104] In Numbers 8.8–19, Yahweh entrusts the sacred offerings to Aaron and his offspring 'in perpetuity' (v. 8), even as he reserves the 'devoted things' of Israel for the priestly line. The instructions conclude with reference to a 'covenant of salt':

> All the holy offerings that the Israelites present to the LORD I have given to you, together with your sons and daughters, as a perpetual due; it is a covenant of salt for ever before the LORD for you and your descendants as well.[105]

---

[101] See Nicholas Perrin, 2010: 46–69.
[102] 'Blessed are those who are persecuted for righteousness' sake, for theirs is the kingdom of heaven. Blessed are you when people revile you and persecute you and utter all kinds of evil against you falsely on my account. Rejoice and be glad, for your reward is great in heaven, for in the same way they persecuted the prophets who were before you' (Matt. 5.10–12).
[103] Cf. Matt. 7.13–14; 10.16–22; 13.53–57; 14.1–12; 21.33–46; 24.9–14.
[104] On the covenantal aspects of the salt metaphor, see Garlington 2011.
[105] Num. 18.19.

Because salt is virtually indestructible as well as effective as a preservative, it served well as a symbol of permanence. It was fitting that Aaron and his descendants remain bound to Yahweh through a covenant of salt. In a sense, salt became the defining symbol of the priesthood.

Similarly, in 2 Chronicles 13, when the Judean king Abijah challenges apostate Israel to forsake Jeroboam, he appeals to a 'covenant of salt' made with 'David and his sons' (v. 5). To be sure, while in this passage the king of Judah underscores the permanence of the Davidic covenant (2 Sam. 7.11–16) and thus his own legitimacy over and against Jeroboam, his argument ultimately turns on the cultic faithfulness of his priestly guild in stark contrast to the apostasy of the priests serving under Jeroboam.[106] According to this line of reasoning, obviously approved by the Chronicler, the covenant of salt perpetuated itself not strictly through the Davidic bloodline but through the faithful maintenance of the temple cultus instituted under David. This speaks to the ultimate goal of Yahweh's 'covenant of salt' with David: the maintenance of true worship.

From the earliest days of Israel's sacrificial system, the 'covenant of salt' was ritually memorialized with the inclusion of salt in the sacrifices.[107] Commenting on Leviticus 2.13 ('You shall not omit from your grain offerings the salt of the covenant with your God; with all your offerings you shall offer salt'), one of two basic prescriptions for this practice, Gordon Wenham explains that the 'addition of salt to the offering was a reminder that the worshipper was in an eternal covenant relationship with his God.'[108] As appropriate as Wenham's comments may be to the MT, it should be noted that the LXX, modifying the sense of the Hebrew *wĕ-lōʾ tašbît* ('You [sing.] ought not to omit') to the Greek's *ou diapausete* ('You all [pl.] ought not to omit'), probably reflects what had become standard cultic practice in Hellenistic Judaism, whereby the ritual addition of the salt remained strictly the prerogative of the priests.[109] In the Second-Temple period, as far as we can tell, salt remained a staple of the sacrificing priest's toolkit. Accordingly, one infers that in the first-century context salt was a metonymy for both the sacrifice and the priestly sacrificial attendant.

Salt in Matthew

All this means that when Matthew's Jesus identifies his disciples as salt, intimations of their priestly status are not far below the surface. In a manner reminiscent of Abijah's appeal to the faithful priests under his jurisdiction, the true 'salt of the covenant', Matthew's Jesus employs salt as convenient shorthand for asserting that the true priestly trajectory was now constituted by his disciples. As Matthew would have understood it, the disciples' status

---

[106] 2 Chron. 13.8–12a.
[107] Lev. 2.13; Ezek. 43.24.
[108] Wenham 1979: 71.
[109] As pointed out by Wevers 1997: 20; cited in Garlington 2011: 717.

as 'salt' related not only to their sacerdotal legitimacy, rooted in Jesus' priesthood, but also to their founding function within the mission of the Church (Matt. 16.17–19; 28.18–20).

Nor is this incompatible with the fuller statement that the disciples are 'the salt *of the earth*' (*to halas tēs gēs*). While the seemingly redundant addition of the phrase 'of the earth' has led some commentators to suppose that the salt of earthen ovens or fertilizer salt *for* the earth are in view, it is hard to see how either of these options meaningfully advances the metaphor.[110] In my view, the most illuminating background is provided not by any first-century culinary or agricultural practices but by the theological quandary posed by the profaned land. For if we translate *halas tēs gēs* not as 'salt of the earth' but (with equal warrant) as 'salt for the land [i.e. Israel]', then Matthew's Jesus is holding out the hope that the community of messianic believers will somehow – precisely in their capacity as priests – play a role in re-securing the sacred space of the land, long ago defiled through covenantal disobedience. This interpretation of *gē* as 'land of Israel' is consistent not only with its immediately prior occurrence (Matt. 5.5), but also with the exclusively geographically specific application of the term up to this point.[111] Thus, when Matthew identifies the disciples as 'the salt of the earth', he speaks to their having a role in the restoration of the land but only at personal cost. They are called to play both the priest and in some sense the sacrifice as well.[112]

Of course, Matthew's Jesus is well aware that sometimes the pressure of persecution proves overwhelming. But those who do 'lose saltiness' (v. 13), he goes on to admonish, do so at the cost of their ongoing participation in the priestly covenant. All the same, the dark clouds of persecution retain a silver lining: mysteriously and paradoxically, such persecution would prove to be the very means by which the divine purposes would be achieved. For Matthew, persecution directed against the community can only be explained with reference to the same community's core identity as the eschatological priesthood. This identity is symbolically expressed through three different images: salt of the earth, light of the earth, and city on a hill. The lead image is salt.

Luke's parable of salt (Luke 14.34–35)

The Lukan context

In recounting Jesus' ill-fated journey towards Jerusalem, Luke intends to strike a balance between the egalitarian nature of the kingdom invitation

---

[110] The former possibility is an old interpretation, reasserted most recently by Pilch 2011; on the latter, see also Shillington 2001; Dämmgen 2011.
[111] Matt. 2.6, 20, 21; 4.15.
[112] Similarly Souček 1963; Schnackenburg 1964; Cullmann and Fröhlich 1966: 192–201. Taking the same angle, Minear (1997: 36) offers a succinct summary: 'the metaphor has an ominous overtone, those designated as salt are engaged in a task that leads inevitably to violent rejection'.

(14.14–24), on the one side, and the high cost of discipleship (14.25–33), on the other. Then, as if to round out both concerns, the Evangelist includes the parable of salt:

> [34]Salt is good; but if salt has lost its taste, how can its saltiness be restored? [35]It is fit neither for the soil nor for the manure pile; they throw it away. Let anyone with ears to hear listen![113]

Although interpreters have sometimes struggled to integrate the substance of the Lukan salt saying (vv. 34–35) with its preceding co-text, one obvious connection is the shared focus on issues of inclusion and exclusion – who's 'in' and who's 'out'. Those who are in are those who willingly relinquish their possessions and family ties, and take up their cross; those who are 'out' are those unwilling to make such sacrifices. Notably, the high bar of discipleship is the same thematic backdrop Matthew presents in his staging of the salt logion.

Of particular interest is Luke's decision to join the salt saying to two parabolic stories, the first involving an unfinished building project and the second an ill-conceived battle plan. Both are tales of abortive venture. The two example stories are themselves encased, on the front end, by an introductory pronouncement in which Jesus demands that his followers 'carry the cross' (Luke 14.26–27), and, on the back end, by a statement in which Jesus makes discipleship conditional on relinquishing 'all your possessions' (v. 33). Even if the connection between verses 34–35 and its preceding text may be less than obvious on first blush, it is at least clear that the parable of the foolish builder, the parable of the king going to war and the parable of salt all bear on the topic of discipleship.

But we can be more specific, so long as we get our bearings straight. While the builder and the king in the first two parables have been traditionally interpreted as representing individuals contemplating the cost of discipleship, it makes more sense to interpret the two figures Christologically: that is, by understanding Jesus himself as the builder of the tower and the king going to war. In the first instance, wherever else Luke's Jesus introduces a parable – as he does at verse 28 – with the phrase, 'Who among you' (*tis ex hymōn*), the focus is always on God and/or God's agent, Jesus.[114] Second, the royal character in Jesus' second example story should also give us pause before adopting the standard individualized reading, for both in the Jesus tradition and in the rabbinica, whenever kings are cast in parables they are inevitably made to play the role of God. Third, Jesus' elaboration on the unfinished tower foundation and subsequent ridicule would have almost certainly brought to mind the stop-and-start temple-building project under Herod, not to mention the public ridicule that such a prolonged construction project

---

[113] Luke 14.34–35.
[114] Luke 11.5; 15.4; 17.7. As pointed out by Hunzinger 1960: 214–15; Fletcher-Louis 2000: 127–8.

would have spawned.[115] In this case, the tower is intended as a thinly veiled code for the temple (in the vein of Isaiah 5's vineyard imagery), much as it serves in various Second-Temple Jewish texts.[116]

The allusion to Herod's never-ending construction project would be consistent with Luke's political critique of the ruler as well as his theological agenda. Having unfavourably compared Herod Antipas to John the Baptist (Luke 7.24–25), now Luke's Jesus draws a covert contrast between the Herodian line, which chronically struggled to complete its temple project, and himself, the builder of the true temple tower.[117] This anticipates 20.9–18, where Luke is concerned to present Jesus not just as the true cornerstone of the temple but also as its true builder. Naturally, the tower/temple that Jesus intends to build is not a brick-and-mortar edifice but the temple of his community.

Not only is Jesus the builder; he is also the king going to war in 14.31–33. At this point in the narrative, we have already been informed that he has gathered 'thousands' to himself.[118] Now, after reducing the size of his following by issuing some very challenging sayings, Jesus asks, 'What king, going out to wage war against another king, will not sit down first and consider whether he is able with ten thousand to oppose the one who comes against him with twenty thousand?'[119] Here we cannot help but hear echoes of Gideon, who at God's command reduced his army from twenty-two thousand to ten thousand, by instructing all the faint-hearted to return home.[120] And if the answer to Jesus' *seemingly* rhetorical question ('What king would consider whether he is able to oppose another with ten thousand?') is Gideon, then it is not insignificant that Israel's heroic judge would not command an army of even ten thousand – not because ten thousand was too small a number, but because it was too large! It was only on the further paring down of Gideon's forces that the victory could be secured.[121] The call-out to Gideon is *à propos* because just as the God of Israel sought to de-emphasize the importance of numerical strength in the day of the judges, now Jesus wants to ensure that his own numerical strength not be mistaken as the means by which divine victory would be achieved. To achieve this ideal size, Jesus would reduce his army, much like Gideon, by screening out those of fragile resolve.

But then what of 14.32 (NIV), which reads: 'If he is not able, he will send a delegation while the other is still a long way off and will ask for terms

---

[115] As Crispin Fletcher-Louis (2000: 131–4) convincingly argues in an illuminating essay.

[116] On the relevant primary literature (4Q500; *Sib. Or.* 5.414–33; etc.) or artefacts (Oniad temple at Leontopolis) that presuppose a co-identity between tower and temple, see Brooke 1995; Fletcher-Louis 2000: 135–7; Kloppenborg 2006: 88–96 .

[117] On the allusions to Herod in Luke 7.24–25, see Fitzmyer 1981: 1.673–74; Bovon 2002: 1.283 n. 41.

[118] Luke 12.1.

[119] Luke 14.31.

[120] Judg. 7.3.

[121] Judg. 7.4–23.

of peace'? I take this to mean that Jesus is the far-off king who is far more interested in suing for peace than in fighting. Those proposed 'terms of peace' (14.32) are offered five chapters later when Jesus is about to enter Jerusalem after his disciples:

> When he came near the place where the road goes down the Mount of Olives, the whole crowd of disciples began joyfully to praise God in loud voices for all the miracles they had seen: 'Blessed is the king who comes in the name of the Lord!' '*Peace* in heaven and glory in the highest!' Some of the Pharisees in the crowd said to Jesus, 'Teacher, rebuke your disciples!' 'I tell you,' he replied, 'if they keep quiet, the stones will cry out.' As he approached Jerusalem and saw the city, he wept over it and said, 'If you, even you, had only known on this day what would bring you *peace* – but now it is hidden from your eyes.'[122]

By rejecting the disciples' 'terms of peace' offered by Jesus while he is still at a distance, the Pharisees as representative leaders of Jerusalem miss the opportunity presented by the king Jesus.

On review of these two parables, we find that Jesus' appeal to military imagery – directly alongside another image attributing to him the role of temple-builder – can only be understood as a vision of holy war led by the warrior-priest. In the first century, visions of a newly built temple and holy war were pervasive, stoking the fiery imagination of an oppressed Judaism. But according to Luke, Jesus is the priestly messianic builder, whose tower/temple is composed of disciples; he is also the priestly warrior-chief, whose army is made up of lower-ranking priests.

Salt in Luke

This reading of Luke 14.14–33 has important implications for our interpretation of Luke's parable of salt (vv. 34–35). While commentators have generally read these two verses as an abrupt warning against apostasy and nothing more, such an overly broad interpretation can only be taken, well, with a grain of salt. Against this reading, it appears that Luke, much like his peer Matthew, understands salt to symbolize nothing less than the eternal covenant maintained through the community of priests – in Luke's case warrior-priests – ruling under Jesus' lordship. Salt is 'good' (v. 34) and indeed must be good because priests who are faithful to the covenant are to 'do good' to their enemies who abuse them and curse them.[123] So then, for Luke, as for Matthew, the opposition facing Jesus and his followers becomes the catalyst by which some aspiring 'priests' would seal their place in the covenant and others would be 'thrown out'.

Just where the discarded salt goes or, more exactly, *doesn't* go is also pertinent. According to verse 35a, salt that has lost its saltiness is 'fit neither for the soil nor the manure pile; they throw it away.' While far too many

---

[122] Luke 19.37–42, NIV; emphasis added.
[123] Luke 6.27, 33, 35.

interpreters are content to meet Jesus' 'throw-away comment' with some throwaway comments of their own, dismissing at any rate any especial significance to these earthy materials, this only begs the question as to why Luke's Jesus would identify the inappropriate receptacles for useless salt if he simply meant to say, 'It will be thrown away.'[124] I suggest an interpretative clue lies close at hand, tucked away in the previous chapter in Luke's parable of the fig tree.[125] It is a parable that refers to the fruitlessness of the current temple regime and the foreboding consequences of continued unproductivity:

> Then he told this parable: 'A man had a fig tree planted in his vineyard; and he came looking for fruit on it and found none. ⁷So he said to the gardener, "See here! For three years I have come looking for fruit on this fig tree, and still I find none. Cut it down! Why should it be wasting the soil [*gēn*]?" ⁸He replied, "Sir, let it alone for one more year, until I dig round it and put manure [*kopria*] on it. ⁹If it bears fruit next year, well and good; but if not, you can cut it down."'[126]

Luke 13.8 marks one of only two places in Luke's Gospel (in fact, one of only two places in the New Testament) where either *koprion* (neuter noun: 'dung, manure') or its close cognate *kopria* (feminine noun: 'dung, manure') occur: the other place is our Lukan parable of salt: 'It is fit neither for the soil nor the manure pile [*koprian*]'.[127] Interestingly, with both occurrences, the term *gē* ('soil, earth') is also nearby (13.7; 14.35). This is surely no accident. On the interpretative principle of *intra*textual *gezera shawa*, the Evangelist is inviting his readers to interpret 'fit for neither the soil [*gēn*] nor the manure [*kopria*]' (14.35) with reference to the aforementioned 'soil' (*gē*) and 'manure' (*kopria*) of 13.7–8, where the two materials are helpful additives brought to bear on the flagging fig tree. In the context of Luke 13, that fig tree is quite obviously the temple, while the added soil and manure seems to represent Jesus' best attempts to bring repentance to the established temple system. When the symbolic matrix of Luke 13.6–9 is carried over some five dozen verses later to 14.35, Jesus' meaning speaks for itself: those who renege on the covenant of salt have not only disqualified themselves from his mission of reforming the existent temple ('fit neither for the soil nor for the manure pile'), but also sealed their own disbarment from his community ('they throw it away').

Unlike more traditional interpretations of Luke 14.34–35 involving a generalized warning, this reading has the added advantage of explaining why the Evangelist places this particular saying at this particular juncture. Luke's point in this section is clear: whatever practical requirements Jesus may

---

[124] Refreshing at this point is the cautious remark of Bovon (2013: 396): 'I confess that I do not understand v. 35a.'

[125] Jeremias (1963: 168) and Bock (1994: 1291) connect the parable of the fig tree and the parable of salt in that both parables were directed against Israel.

[126] Luke 13.6–9.

[127] Luke 14.35a.

impose upon his aspiring priests, including the renunciation of social status (taking up one's cross) and personal capital (giving up one's possessions), these all must be carried through to the end, no matter the cost. Failure to persevere on such commitments, so verses 34–35 remind us, would be to opt out of the priestly covenant. Thus, losing one's saltiness refers in the first instance to forgoing the distinguishing mark of those who belong to Jesus' priestly association.

The implications of this for Luke's understanding of Jesus' mission are several. First, this reading suggests that the Evangelist ascribed a two-fold agenda to Jesus, namely, to build a new temple around himself and to wage a strange, holy war where the advantage fell not to a strong and numerous majority, but to a weak but nonetheless committed minority. Second, Luke's noted interest in 'the poor', a point of long-standing interest in New Testament scholarship, can in this instance be explained as his conviction that voluntary poverty was a function of the priestly calling which Jesus imposed. Self-divesture was, in other words, a kind of priestly badge.[128] Third, if, as I have argued, Luke intended to put the parable of salt into narrative conversation with the parable of the fig tree, this suggests, on the Evangelist's vision, that Jesus' *initial* intention was not to supplant the established temple but restore it to repentance. How this point relates to my first above (viz. Jesus' intention to build a new temple) speaks to the inherent tension in Jesus' mission, as Luke conceived it. For Luke, as perhaps for all the Gospel writers, Jesus was a prophet who walked the paradoxical line between offering a genuine call to repentance while at the same time preparing for the contingency of a new future of new wine and new wineskins (5.36–39).

Mark's parable of salt (Mark 9.50)

The Markan context
The Markan version of the parable of salt shows a number of similarities with Matthew and Luke, but also some notable differences:

> Salt is good, but if it loses its saltiness, how can you make it salty again? Have salt in yourselves, and be at peace with each other.[129]

Here the exhortation (unique to Mark), 'Have salt in yourselves', is conjoined with another imperative bearing on the necessity of mutual peace. The saying occurs at the end of an extended discourse, triggered by John's objection to certain strange exorcists who were casting out demons in Jesus' name but 'not following us'.[130] Overruling John's objection, Jesus insists that co-sympathizers are not to be opposed, since they are 'for us'.[131] In this

---

[128] See my fuller discussion in Nicholas Perrin, 2010: 114–48.
[129] Mark 9.50, NIV.
[130] Mark 9.38.
[131] Mark 9.40.

context, then, Jesus' call for metaphorical salt and mutual peace answers the disciples' misgivings over their exorcistic competitors (9.38–41).[132]

Even more so than Matthew and Luke, Mark goes out of his way to situate Jesus' salt sayings within a cultic context. This becomes clear on comparing Mark 9.49 with Leviticus 2.13a LXX:

> For everyone will be salted with fire [*pas gar pyri halisthēsetai*].

(Mark 9.49)

> And every gift of your sacrifice will be salted [*kai pan dōron thysias hymōn hali halisthēsetai*].

(Lev. 2.13a LXX)

Mark's use of *pas* ('every') alongside *halisthēsetai* ('salted') preceded by a dative is simply too close to Leviticus 2.13a to be coincidental. Also noting the close parallel between Mark's language and Leviticus 2.13, Harry T. Fleddermann remarks:

> In the OT salt is a symbol of the covenant. One of the clearest texts is Lev 2:13b: 'Do not let the salt of the covenant of your God be lacking from your cereal offering.' In Num 18:19 an everlasting covenant is called a 'covenant of salt' (see also 2 Chr 13:5). The background of this idea probably lies in the sharing of salt in a meal (Ezra 4:14). To share salt with someone is to share fellowship with him, to be in covenant with him. The discourse began with two situations of conflict and strife, the self-seeking arguing of the disciples about rank and the conflict with the strange exorcist. It went on to discuss the problem of scandal in the community. To all this Mark opposes the peace of covenant fellowship.[133]

Fleddermann's exegesis is convincing so far as it goes. At the same time, one might say that his conclusion raises as many questions as it resolves. For even if Fleddermann is basically right (and I believe he is), we are still left wondering: (1) what exactly does the 'fire' of Mark 9.49 have to do with the invoked covenant of salt, and (2) how is the covenant of salt thematically relevant, if at all, to the hubbub surrounding the strange exorcists in the first place?

Salt in Mark

Towards answering the first of these two questions, we again note the tight verbal connection between Mark 9.49 and Leviticus 2.13a in order to suggest that the salting fire of Mark is to be understood as analogous to the fire prepared for dispatching sacrificial offerings. In this case, the phrase 'For everyone will be salted with fire' (v. 49) pertains not to some post-mortem purgatory but to the socio-political costs facing those who don the new priestly mantle – those in the community as well as those controversial individuals

---

[132] At the same time, the Markan parable of salt must also have at least something to do with the disciples' arrogant competitiveness (9.33–37).
[133] Fleddermann 1981: 73.

outside the Twelve who are nonetheless 'for us' (v. 40). In short, the 'fire' of
Mark 9.49 refers to the persecution soon to be directed against all those who
name the name of Jesus. Those who successfully endure such tribulation will
prove their priestly identity after all, Mark's Jesus says, irrespective of their
tie to the Twelve.

As to why Jesus would respond to the disciples' concern over the strange
exorcists by appealing to a 'covenant of salt' (especially when a simple
exhortation for the disciples to get along better would do), there is at least
one good answer, and one good answer will do. We note that the disciples
are provoked to jealousy by not simply outsiders who invoke Jesus' name but
outsiders who name the name *as they perform exorcisms*. In ancient Judaism,
the social role of exorcist typically fell to the priests. After all, priests were
considered intermediaries of the divine, and only the divine power could
overpower the dark forces.[134] Thus, when Mark's John objects to the 'non-
union exorcists', he feels threatened not because they were doing good in
Jesus' name apart from apostolic authorization, but because they were taking
on a specifically priestly function which, so John thought, ought to be
reserved for the Twelve.

In response to this concern, perhaps not altogether illegitimate on first
blush, Mark's Jesus appeals to the priestly covenant of salt even as he clarifies
its scope. Warning of the persecution which would soon be directed against
all who identify with his movement, Jesus insists that neither demonstrated
exorcistic abilities nor even current membership in his own ranks was surefire
proof of eschatological priestly credentials: only those who retained their
saltiness through the 'fire' would prove themselves as true priests, that is,
as members in good standing within the covenant of salt. In the meantime,
Jesus goes on to admonish, the role of the disciples is to be less concerned
with who is inside and who is outside the circle, and more concerned with
self-examination, along with a charitable commitment to maintaining peace
with sympathizers and other fellow priests. Whatever special privileges the
apostles retained in Mark's mind, true priesthood was measured less by office
and more by faithful perseverance in the face of intense opposition.

The parable of salt and the historical Jesus

The varied rhetorical use of the salt saying across the Gospels speaks to its
elasticity within the tradition.[135] In the Gospel of Matthew, while it falls to
Jesus' disciples to become the eschatological Jerusalem and the light of the

---

[134] Examples include the chief priest Sceva and his seven sons, itinerant exorcists in Asia Minor
(Acts 19.14); the priests at Qumran who conducted public worship while lacing in apotropaic
practices (see Alexander 1997); and perhaps also Eleazar, an exorcist who bore a priestly name
(*Ant.* 8.21.1 §§45–49). In the Greek culture, exorcism was associated with priests (Plato, *Resp.*
364b–65a), though with soothsayers and philosophers as well.
[135] For Jeremias (1963: 107), the salt parable is a parade example of a simile or parable that 'has
been transmitted with divergent applications'.

world, this destiny will only be achieved through the crucible of persecution. Meanwhile, Luke introduces the image of salt to remind his readers that their calling, involving a human temple and an eschatological holy war (though a war on very different terms from what Jesus' peers would have expected), is based on a priestly covenant of salt. Finally, for Mark, the bond of salt is maintained through peaceful relationships between those carrying out such priestly duties as exorcism. In each case, salt is applied in a different direction.

Despite the variation in how this metaphor is worked out in each of the Gospels, the common denominators are significant. To begin with, each Evangelist seems to have shared the assumption that salt was an appropriate metaphor by which the community might assert its own priestly identity. Yet this was not a static identity, for salt symbolized a coalescing society whose boundary lines would take definitive form only on the far side of tribulation. Eschewing any rigid equivalence between community members' present participation in the covenant of salt and their final participation in the eschatological future, the Evangelists agree that the distinguishing mark of the true priests would be their faithful response unto the end.

Moreover, in none of the extant salt sayings is there any attempt to explicate the metaphor, as we find, for example, in the synoptic presentation of the parable of the sower. Rather, for all three Gospel writers, salt as a metonymic equivalent for priesthood is more assumed than asserted. Likewise, the formation of the eschatological priesthood through tribulation seems to be the unspecified premise of the parable's argument, not the argument itself. The unanimity of this premise, as well as the lack of any need to restate it, suggests a vibrant and well-established prehistory reaching back to Jesus himself. All three Evangelists are trading on a well-established biblical tradition which the historic Jesus himself also presupposed. Whatever else might have been said of the disciples, Jesus insisted that his band of followers regard themselves as the heirs of the salt of the covenant, the continuing trajectory of Israel's priesthood into the future, with Jesus himself as the chief priest.

A number of implications follow from this. First, Jesus' identification of his disciples as salt means that the reconfiguring of the priestly office, envisaged in Ezekiel 36, was in fact a crucial element of Jesus' vision of the kingdom. Perhaps this much is to be expected. If Jesus anticipated the rise of an idol-free eschatological temple, in keeping with the prophetic promises, it only makes sense that he also looked forward to that same temple space being staffed by new, duly ordained personnel. Such personnel had no necessary ties to the current priestly organization, but were to be identified by their faithfulness in the face of persecution, the same kind of persecution envisaged in the parable of the sower.

Second, it seems that for Jesus, as for the Gospel writers after him, present participation in the covenant of salt was no automatic guarantee of future tenure in the eschaton. So long as the reality of present and future persecution remained, so too did the prospect of apostasy. According to Jesus, those who did renege on their initial commitments would have little hope of redemption on the far side of tribulation. As dismayed as Jesus must have been by the opposition he faced, he seems to have taken solace in the conviction that this adversity would prove to be the very means by which his community would acquire sharper definition, attaining its fullest form and function. Tribulation, then, had a clarifying function. It served to separate true believers from *faux* believers with a view to establishing a perfected, eschatological community made up of the former, a truly righteous remnant. The introduction of the eschatological temple apparently depended on nothing less.

The Evangelists' respective presentations of the parable of salt also logically depend on a third point, again almost certainly going back to Jesus: namely, as the community took shape on the far side of tribulation, it would then – and only then – lay the groundwork for a properly restored cultic space. This was after all salt 'of . . .' or 'for the land'. If restoration of the defiled land was a necessary step to restoring proper worship, then the persecution of the disciples seems to have been an integral element of that restoration. From out of their collective experience of tribulation, so Jesus reasoned, the God of Israel would give birth to a new spatial reality which would include a new and final priesthood within continuing Israel.

All this not only lines up splendidly with the parable of the sower (as I have presented it), but also helps explain it. If through the parable of the sower, we learn that tribulation was the necessary stepping stone to eschatological salvation, the parable of salt clarifies Jesus' vision for his community within that unfolding process. With the great *peirasmos* underway, Jesus expected his followers essentially to sort themselves out – some would apostasize, others would remain true. In this way, Israel's atonement would be actualized. This conception again allowed Jesus to interpret the opposition he faced not as a basis for calling into question his priestly claims, as his detractors would insist, but rather as confirmation of those claims by virtue of a mysterious, transcendent logic.

The present contours of the kingdom: the Beatitudes (Q 6.20–21)

On surveying the breadth of historical Jesus scholarship, one finds that Luke's first three beatitudes (viz. 'Blessed are the poor'; 'Blessed are those who mourn'; 'Blessed are those who hunger and thirst for righteousness') have as strong a claim as any material in preserving the dominical voice.[136] Strauss was certainly persuaded of this point, as was Bultmann after him, as is the Jesus Seminar today.[137] While there may be some difference of opinion as to *why* Jesus spoke these sayings, most of us can at least agree *that* he spoke them. That fact alone puts the Beatitudes into an elite category of authenticity.

---

[136] Q 6.20 (Matt. 5.3); Q 6.21b (Matt. 5.4); Q 6.21a (Matt. 3.6).
[137] Strauss 1972 (1835): 336–8; Bultmann 1968 (1921): 133; Funk and Hoover 1993: 289.

As it so happens, scholars also regularly regard the Beatitudes as an important component within Jesus' overall kingdom message. Perhaps this is to be expected. After all, when someone goes about saying, 'This kind of person is blessed' and 'This kind of person is accursed', heavily weighted values will come to the forefront soon enough. It's no wonder that the Beatitudes have long been considered a *locus classicus* for Jesus' ethics.

At the same time, any historical-critical investigation of these sayings is burdened with the task of sorting out the voice of the master from the voice of the Church. It is a task which cannot be carried out apart from some consideration of the Evangelists' structure. The material is handed down in Matthew and Luke; the wording of the former Evangelist reads as follows:

> [3]Blessed are the poor in spirit, for theirs is the kingdom of heaven.
> [4]Blessed are those who mourn, for they will be comforted.
> [5]Blessed are the meek, for they will inherit the earth.
> [6]Blessed are those who hunger and thirst for righteousness, for they will be filled.
> [7]Blessed are the merciful, for they will receive mercy.
> [8]Blessed are the pure in heart, for they will see God.
> [9]Blessed are the peacemakers, for they will be called children of God.
> [10]Blessed are those who are persecuted for righteousness' sake, for theirs is the kingdom of heaven.
> [11]Blessed are you when people revile you and persecute you and utter all kinds of evil against you falsely on my account.
> [12]Rejoice and be glad, for your reward is great in heaven, for in the same way they persecuted the prophets who were before you.[138]

Matthew presents us with nine makarisms, that is, nine words of blessing. The first eight are sometimes subdivided into two sets of four (vv. 3–6 and 7–10), on the theory that the first set of four focuses on attitudes, while the second set bears on horizontal relationships. Unfortunately, the hypothesis runs ashore on the simple fact that Matthew finally leaves us with not eight but nine beatitudes, wrecking the symmetry of a 4 + 4 model. Verse 10 is typically regarded as overladen with Matthean enamel; the remaining eight beatitudes, as plausibly pre-Matthean. In any event, the first, second and fourth beatitudes have – as I have said – firmly secured the dominical tag.

Setting aside consideration of verses 7–9 and 11–12, I will take this one step further by maintaining that the first four beatitudes constituted a unity at the very source of the tradition. This is demonstrable on various grounds, not least their shared dependence on Isaiah 61. The Matthean and Isaianic texts may be compared, as shown in Table 1.[139]

In the first beatitude (Matt. 5.3), the coupling of 'poor' (*ptōchos*) and 'spirit'

---

[138] Matt. 5.3–12.
[139] The translations are my own.

Table 1 The dependence of the Beatitudes in Matthew 5 on Isaiah 61

	Matthew 5	Isaiah 61 (LXX)
First beatitude	Blessed are the poor [*ptōchoi*] in spirit [*pneumati*], for theirs is the kingdom of heaven [*basileia tou theou*]. (v. 3)	The spirit [*pneuma*] of the Lord is upon me, because the LORD has anointed me; he has sent me to bring good news [*euangelisasthai*] to the poor [*ptōchois*] (v. 1)
Second beatitude	Blessed are those who mourn [*penthountes*], for they will be comforted [*paraklēthēsontai*]. (v. 4)	to comfort [*parakalesai*] all who mourn [*penthountas*] (v. 2)
Third beatitude	Blessed are the meek [*praeis*], for they will inherit [*klēronomēsousin*] the land [*tēn gēn*]. (v. 5)	to preach good news to the poor [*ptōchois*] . . . [who] shall inherit [*klēronomēsousin*] the land [*tēn gēn*] a second time (vv. 1, 7)
Fourth beatitude	Blessed are those who hunger [*peinōntes*] and thirst for righteousness [*dikaiosynēn*], for they will be filled. (v. 6)	you shall eat up [*katedesthe*] the wealth of the nations, and in their riches you wonder . . . For I am the LORD who loves righteousness [*dikaiosynēn*] (vv. 6, 8)

(*pneuma*) is driven by the convergence of the same two words in Isaiah 61.1. More than that, if the advancement of the 'kingdom of God' (Matt. 5.3) is notionally equivalent to the 'preaching of good news' (Isa. 61.1), then these two verses intersect at not two but three points. In the second beatitude (Matt. 5.4) the comfort issued to mourners seems to have been inspired by the comfort granted in Isaiah 61.2; the Matthean mourners are cut from the same cloth as well. Meanwhile the third beatitude in reference to the meek (Matt. 5.5) is clearly inspired by Psalm 36.11 LXX ('But the meek shall inherit the land, and delight themselves in abundant prosperity'). But since *praeis* ('meek'), like *ptōchos* ('poor'), is a legitimate stand-in for the Hebrew *'ănāwîm* ('poor'), and since, too, the same inheritance awaiting the meek also occurs in Isaiah 61.7, a link back to Isaiah 61 remains probable. Moving down to Matthew's fourth beatitude (Matt. 5.6), we find that whereas Isaiah predicts that the 'poor' will feast in accordance with Yahweh's righteousness (Isa. 61.6), the Evangelist blends the two concepts by presenting his poor as 'hungering for righteousness' (Matt. 5.6). In the light of these considerations, the first four beatitudes may well be regarded as having been inspired by

Isaiah 61.[140] And even if Matthew's third beatitude is slightly weaker, this still leaves at least Matthew's first, second and fourth beatitudes (Q's first three) securely tied together. Dare we propose that Jesus originated these beatitudes under Isaiah's influence?

Robert Guelich thinks not. He argues that the Isaianic elements in these sayings were tacked on by Matthew.[141] But this hardly makes sense. In the first place, if we were to strip away Isaiah's terminology from Matthew 5.3, 4, 6 in order to get back to Jesus' verbiage, what exactly would we be left with? Try as we might to imagine an earlier iteration of these beatitudes without the words 'spirit', 'poor', 'comfort' and 'mourn' (as Guelich would have it), we might as well imagine *Hamlet* without its prince (or without its Claudius or Ophelia, for that matter). Second, in rendering this judgement, this approach ignores the weighty evidence of certain texts outside the immediate pericope, not least Matthew 11.2–15//Luke 7.18–28 (= Q 7.18–28). Commonly thought to reflect accurately on an actual event, Q 7.18–28 records Jesus justifying his ministry to the Baptizer in the words of Isaiah 61, only to cap off his response with a makarism ('Blessed is the one who takes no offence at me').[142] The occurrence of a makarism alongside verbiage from Isaiah 61 at Q 7.18–28, just as we have it in Matthew 5, is strong evidence that crediting the Evangelist with enhanced overtones of Isaiah is to get it backwards: it is not that Matthew has smuggled in elements of Isaiah 61; if anything, it is the Evangelist who has soft-pedalled the prophetic connection.[143] On the most compelling analysis, the bundled sayings in Matthew 5.3, 4, 6 reflect the voice of the historical Jesus as a re-channelling of Isaiah 61.

As I have already pointed out, Isaiah 61 describes a climactic moment in Israel's eschatological future, a glorious time of restoration and a refurbished temple. Given this narrative as a backdrop for Jesus' makarisms, and given, too, the passage's cultic focus (more exactly, its concern with a high-priestly, jubilee-declaring figure leading a band of 'poor' who 'shall be called priests' (Isa. 61.6)), we wonder what implications this might have for our reconstruction.[144] What kind of claims was he making, through the Beatitudes, for himself? And what kind of claims was he making for his hearers?

The meaning of the Beatitudes

The social grammar of blessing

The thrust of Jesus' beatitudes first begins to come clear when we consider the social transaction of blessing. In comparing Matthew with Luke, we discover

---

[140] This is the judgement reached by, among others, Grimm 1976: 68–77; Davies and Allison 1988–97: 1.434–9; Luz 1989–2005: 1.186–7.

[141] Guelich 1976: 427–31; similarly Hengel 1987: 351–3.

[142] Q 7.23 (Matt. 11.6//Luke 7.23). The translation is my own.

[143] So Grimm 1976: 68–77; Davies and Allison 1988–97: 1.437.

[144] On Jesus as the declarer of the eschatological jubilee on the model of Melchizedek, see Nicholas Perrin, 2010: 134–45.

that between the two Evangelists there is some variation between third-person predications ('Blessed are *those*' is generally favoured by Matthew) and second-person predications ('Blessed are *you*' consistently used by Luke). It is not necessary to adjudicate the question as to which of these two forms is original with Jesus. On the likelihood that Jesus offered the Beatitudes on numerous occasions as a kind of stump speech directed *to* 'the poor' and *about* the poor, it is more than possible that Jesus said both 'Blessed are those poor' and 'Blessed are you poor'. Given the latter form, we are forbidden from reducing the saying – in the context of the historical Jesus – to abstract platitude. For Jesus' words 'Blessed are you' engage his hearers in the present moment, implying that the asserted blessing is somehow operative, or at least potentially operative and well within the grasp of the addressee. This is to say, the very form of the beatitude betrays the sense of an interpersonal transaction identifiable with similar acts of publicly staged blessing in antiquity.

In locating the makarisms within the broader context of ancient blessing practices, it is helpful to distinguish the non-technical and technical applications of blessings. In the former, the language of blessings and cursing was part of everyday life, when ordinary people invoked sacred or magical words either as a description of a fortunate or unfortunate state, or as wishful expressions of goodwill and malevolence. By contrast, in their more technical usage, blessings and curses were speech-acts that claimed an inherent efficacy, involving either an appeal to the appropriate divine authorities or the direct agency of a properly credentialled speaker/performer. David Frankfurter expands on this latter category in his analysis of the phenomenon across antiquity:

> Curses and blessings are linked socially through the authority of the one capable of pronouncing them. And to the extent that ritual expertise in some form – that is, the popular sense that a person or type of person is gifted with verbal and gestural powers – is typical to any society, the power both to curse and bless (and remove curses and overwhelm blessings) will be attributed to ritual experts of some sort.[145]

Frankfurter continues: 'the efficacy of these two, ostensibly opposite, types of ritual speech-acts [i.e. blessings and curses]' is directly linked 'to the *authority behind their utterance*', most commonly a priest.[146] This was no less the case in ancient Judaism, where the

> utterance of blessing is the expressed function of the priest (Num 6.23–29; Deut 10:8; 21:5; 1 Sam 2:20). The priestly blessing contains the necessary elements of an effective performative utterance: there is an accepted

---

[145] Frankfurter 2005: 159–60. Also see extended discussion in Kitz 2014: 349–99, where the author distinguishes the relative effectiveness of Ancient Near Eastern priestly curses over and against 'lay curses'.

[146] Frankfurter 2005: 184; emphasis original.

conventional procedure having a certain conventional effect; the particular persona and circumstances in a given case are appropriate for the invocation of the particular procedure, the procedure is executed by all participants both correctly and completely . . .[147]

Given that blessings were typically associated with the priestly role in the daily life of ancient Israel, there is no reason to exclude Jesus' beatitudes, even as they invoked the eschatological high priest of Isaiah 61, as blessings in this technical sense. On this likely scenario, the Beatitudes were originally neither a general description of future blessedness nor a series of detached reflections on life, but rather an efficacious speech-act in which Jesus, functioning as a priest, imparted real blessedness in real time on his hearers. By offering blessings at will and well outside Jerusalem, Jesus had entered into direct competition with the temple.

The Evangelist Matthew seems to have interpreted the Beatitudes just this way. As regularly noted, the very invocation of the jubilary text of Isaiah 61 would have naturally invoked the Day of Atonement (*yom kippur*), since this was the day on which the jubilee was supposed to have been declared.[148] Given the Day of Atonement association with festive joy, we suspect that Matthew's urging of joy at Matthew 5.11–12 (par. Luke 6.22–23) was retained in the interest of reinforcing *yom kippur* as the Beatitudes' conceptual backdrop.[149] In this connection, it should not go unnoticed that the Day of Atonement was also regularly marked off by the high priest's performance of the *birkat kohanim*, the Aaronic blessing (Num. 6.23–26).[150]

Taken together, these observations raise the possibility that Matthew's nine-fold arrangement of the Beatitudes was part of his design to portray Jesus as the eschatological high priest and his beatitudes as his issuing *ex officio sacerdotis* a new Aaronic blessing for an extraordinarily special *yom kippur*, patterned after the standard Aaronic blessing traditionally offered each annual Day of Atonement. Whereas in Judaism the Aaronic blessing was very obviously structured as a three-fold blessing, Matthew's nine beatitudes may well be giving expression to his conviction that Jesus has surpassed Aaron (much as Jesus surpasses Moses; cf. 5.21–42) by offering not three blessings but three sets of three blessings. This would at any rate explain Matthew's otherwise odd choice of presenting nine, as opposed to, say, seven (creation) or ten (Decalogue) makarisms.[151] This would also help explain why Matthew's Jesus famously takes pains to make his pronouncements on an

---

[147] Anderson 2014: 271.
[148] Lev. 25.9–10.
[149] According to *m. Ta'an.* 4.8, 'there were no happier fast days for Israel than the fifteenth of Ab and Yom Kippur'.
[150] *Tamid* 3.8; *Yoma* 6.2. See discussion and some bibliography in Parke-Taylor 1975: 86; also Buchanan 1970: 316 n. 3.
[151] I am not aware of this suggestion having been made in previous scholarship – surprisingly so, given the long-recognized ties between the Beatitudes and the Day of Atonement.

elevated space.[152] Although the Evangelist almost certainly had separate literary and theological reasons for situating Jesus' address on a mountain, it is nonetheless true that the Evangelist's first-century readers would not have missed the fact that, at least while the temple was in existence, the *birkat kohanim* (the Aaronic blessing) would have been consistently pronounced from an elevated platform (*duchenen*).[153] The final strength of this proposal is simply this: the ascription of a specifically cultic context to the Beatitudes (Matt. 5.3–12) is consistent with the cultic implications of Matthew 5.13–16, as I have teased them out above. To put this otherwise, if I am correct about the sacral intimations in 'light of the world', 'salt of the earth' and 'city on a hill', the door is already more than halfway open to construing Matthew's nine blessings as having a specifically cultic context. Given the cumulative force of these considerations, I conclude that Matthew intended the blessings of Matthew 5.3–11 not in some vague and generic sense but as a new *birkat kohanim*. Matthew's carefully arranged beatitudes seek to preserve the memory of a recurring, ritualized speech-act, taking place between, on the one side, Jesus as the eschatological high priest, and, on the other side, 'the poor' as recipients of his blessings.

Though this proposed interplay between the Beatitudes and the Aaronic blessing would be entirely a function of Matthean redaction, I suspect that the Evangelist was inspired by a social memory of Jesus' Aaronic-style performance of the makarisms. This argument is justified on the criterion of coherence. In the first place, we recall that the first petition of the Lord's Prayer ('Hallowed be your name!') amounted to a request for a newly established cultic venue, which would be equivalent to the act – in the language of Deuteronomy – of placing Yahweh's name (*śim śem* or *śikan śem*) on the sacral space.[154] On this logic, inasmuch as the Aaronic blessing was granted for the purpose of 'putting' Yahweh's name on the people (Num. 6.27), one could think of no better complement to Jesus' first-enlisted prayer 'Hallowed be your name!' (a prayer that God might place his name) than Jesus' Aaronic blessing (a blessing in which God places his name). That which the historic disciples were taught to ask for in the first petition of the *PN* Jesus was now somehow being actualized through Jesus' transmogrified *birkat kohanim*. While the audacity of such a gesture might strain our credulity, we need to put this into perspective: if Jesus willingly designated himself as the eschatological high priest and declarer of the final jubilee, updating the Aaronic blessing would be small potatoes – not to mention a natural prerogative of the office.

---

[152] Matt. 5.1. Meanwhile, Luke 6.17 records that 'he came down with them and stood *on a level place* [*epi topou pedinou*]'.

[153] *Soṭah* 15b; 38a. See brief discussion in Philipson and Kohler 1902: 244–6 (245).

[154] Deut. 12.5, 11; 14.23–24; 16.2, 6, 11; 26.2.

The redemptive-historical grammar of blessing

While one might assume, given the above discussion, that Jesus' spoken blessings were directed to individuals strictly as individuals, Qumran parallels to the Beatitudes point us in another direction. In an analysis of the *Community Rule* (1QS) and 4QBerakhot (4Q286–90), Bilha Nitzan remarks on the performative function of ritualized blessings and cursings in the Dead Sea Community.[155] Even as these two documents attest to two separate but related socio-religious functions, Nitzan points out, both are based on the Aaronic blessing and are meant to demarcate those who are inside and those who are outside the covenant. The blessings preserved in 1QS 1—2 in particular were part of an annual covenant-renewal ceremony 'performed in order to strengthen the members of the Community in keeping the Law of Moses according to its strict, Zadokite-priestly halakhic doctrine'.[156] She continues:

> The main peculiarity of the covenantal ceremony of the Rule of the Community is the use of blessings based on the priestly blessing of Num 6:24–26. The circumstances for reciting this blessing are not specified in the Bible, and there is no allusion there to its recitation in a covenantal ceremony. Presumably, the recitation of the Priestly Blessing in the context of the covenantal ceremony was considered equivalent in some respects to that of its recitation in the Temple . . . As the *yaḥad* did not participate in the sacrificial service which atoned for the sins of Israel, but made atonement 'for iniquitous guilt' by means of prayer (1QS ix 4–5; CD xi 18–21), one may assume that the confession in the covenantal ceremony of the Rule of the Community (1QS I 22 – ii 1), preceding the priestly blessings, was considered an act of repentance.[157]

If Nitzan's reconstruction of the social setting behind the *Community Rule* is correct, then the Qumran community had essentially combined two very different kinds of events, seemingly of vastly different scale and significance, into one. Their act of blessing blended the covenant-renewing ceremony, familiar from Israel's history, with the Aaronic blessing, which would receive special prominence on the annual *yom kippur* (in addition to other holidays).

Something very close to this, I suggest, is going on in Jesus' performance of the Beatitudes. On one level, Jesus' travels allowed him, as a matter of routine, to deliver priestly blessings to many different people in many different locations. Yet, on another level, these isolated benedictory transactions were the recurring expression of a fundamental shift that had already taken place in redemptive history. Since Jesus was convinced that the Spirit had descended uniquely on *him*, as the eschatological high priest, this called for a renewal of the covenant according to the newly emerging priestly order.[158] As Jesus issued his blessings, in other words, he saw these as being on a scale

---

[155] Nitzan 2000.
[156] Nitzan 2000: 264.
[157] Nitzan 2000: 264.
[158] Wright (1996: 269, 288–9) similarly finds covenantal renewal in the Beatitudes.

equal to or greater than the blessings issued by Moses when he and the people stood at the cusp of the land (Deuteronomy 28—33).

This deep read of the Beatitudes, like our deep read of the parable of the sower and parable of salt, perhaps speaks less to the historical crowds' understanding than to the historical Jesus' self-understanding. Just how much of all this the crowds would have understood, we can't really say. In any event, it would be difficult to imagine this convergence of theological themes without some careful reflection on Jesus' part. Jesus' beatitudes were no haphazard expression of goodwill, but a carefully constructed 'stump blessing' that clarified – at least for those who dared to follow up – his unique place in Israel's present and future.

But just what did the Beatitudes signify about Jesus, at least as he understood himself? Two things, at least. First, in the light of Jesus' implicit self-designation as the anointed herald of Isaiah 61, we conclude that in his very performance of the Beatitudes Jesus was presenting himself – again for those who 'had ears to hear' – as *the* anointed one, the messiah. In the previous chapter, I expressed my doubts that Jesus' baptism was instantly interpreted as bearing messianic implications, even if the Church eventually attached that significance retrospectively. We do not know when in his ministry Jesus first started speaking beatitudes. But whenever he did so, these blessings were a veiled way of either announcing or reasserting his messiahship. Significantly, Jesus here does not frame his messianic status apart from his priestly election and consequent responsibilities. He comes to us here as a distinctively *priestly* messiah – or, if you will, a messianic priest.

But now between the parable of the sower, which announces epic shifts in Israel's trajectory, and these beatitudes, which were probably pronounced as a way – much like at Qumran – of calling for repentance and renewed obedience, Jesus' job description also begins to look remarkably like that of a prophet. The prophetic role does not stand in competition with Jesus' priestly role, but rather falls under the sacerdotal category. In the Second-Temple period, priests were not uncommonly assigned the prophetic gift by virtue of the office. Here, for example, we might think of Josephus's ascription of prophetic abilities to the priest John Hyrcanus.[159] Or, again, there's Caiaphas's unwitting prophecy of John 11.47–53; or again the Teacher of Righteousness role as priest-cum-prophet (1QpHab 2.8).[160] Other instances may be adduced.[161] The point is this: 'from the time of the Hasmoneans the prophetic endowment was believed to inhere *de jure* if not always *de facto* in

---

[159] *Ant.* 13.10.7 §§299–300. At the same time, Josephus was not opposed to extending the double honour to himself (*J.W.* 3.8.3 §§351–54): it 'is clear from the way he speaks about his priesthood that it is closely associated in his mind with the prophetic gift' (Blenkinsopp 1974: 250).
[160] On John 11.47–53, see Dodd 1962; for the 1QpHab 2.8 reference, I am indebted to Bammel 1997: 134. On the scholarly discussion on the whole concept of prophecy in post-exilic Judaism, see Cook 2011: 10–42.
[161] For further examples from the primary literature, see Dodd 1962; Bammel 1997.

the high priest'.[162] Whereas priestly functions were not in principle intrinsic to the prophetic office, prophetic functions were in principle integral to the high priest's calling. This has direct implications for our study. Whereas it is virtually a truism of contemporary scholarship that Jesus' behaviour corresponded to the social role of prophet, it is probable that his appropriation of this role was foremost related not to any prophetic office but to his priestly vocation, which also carried prophetic entailments. In short, Jesus as priest explains both Jesus as messiah and Jesus as prophet. Whether the converse can also be shown, I am uncertain.

The 'poor' and the historical Jesus

In the original setting, Jesus' blessings were no abstract principles based on personal observation but a verbal transaction involving Jesus himself and a specific set of participants, namely, 'the poor' (*hoi ptōchoi*). In the pre-Christian Greek literature, the word *ptōchos* consistently denotes poverty in an economic sense.[163] Therefore, unless Jesus is being ironic or ridiculous, we infer that by pronouncing blessings on the *poor*, he was either inviting his hearers to become materially poor or validating an audience precisely as the poor – or both. And, in fact, 'both' seems to be the strongest possibility. In the first instance, we know that Jesus invited at least one high-profile figure to forsake his wealth and social standing as a necessary condition for joining the movement, and this invitation was consistent with the movement's goals and practices.[164] We also have good reason to believe that a bulk of Jesus' audience was constituted by impoverished indigents who had the freedom to follow Jesus on a day-to-day basis, even as the Jesus movement itself embodied a life of poverty.[165] For such reasons, it is decidedly unlikely that Jesus used the word 'poor' to indicate something very different from the sense of poverty normally conveyed by the pre-Christian Greek word *ptōchos*. When Jesus said, 'Blessed are the poor', he may have been referring to more than their socio-economic location, but he was not speaking to anything less. For Jesus, the kingdom of God belonged specifically to the socio-economically poor.

But then in what sense could this be so? This is a difficult question, but one which I suggest can be addressed on two levels corresponding to the familiar if not somewhat anachronistic distinction of nature and grace. First, it is possible, perhaps even likely, that Jesus considered the poor naturally blessed or advantaged in the sense that when it came to their potential participation in his return-from-exile movement, they would not incur the same obstacles facing their better situated peers. Unencumbered by social

---

[162] Blenkinsopp 1974: 250.
[163] Hauck 1968.
[164] Mark 10.17–22; for discussion of which, see Nicholas Perrin, 2010: 120–31.
[165] Nicholas Perrin, 2010: 170–1.

pressures bearing down on society's well-positioned, the 'poor' would have a distinct God-given, natural advantage over their more vested counterparts; in this respect, they would have been pre-eminently pre-qualified to join the kingdom movement.[166] In opposition to the controlling narrative of the day, which maintained that the powerful and wealthy held all the cards in life (and that this was in fact the way it was *supposed* to be), Jesus insisted that those at the bottom (not the top) of the ladder are blessed by virtue of their destined station in life. There was, then, a certain providential blessing in poverty, even if this blessing is only actualized on Jesus' benediction.[167]

Yet in directing blessings specifically to the poor, Jesus should not be understood as justifying the state of poverty, much less glamorizing it either as a virtue or as a no-questions-asked pass to eschatological bliss. Instead, on recognizing the performative character of Jesus' speech-act of blessing, we expect that these blessings served less to describe reality than to create a new one. Through the repeated ritualized act of public blessing, Jesus saw himself as setting in motion the very scenario which readers of Isaiah 61 had been expecting for centuries: 'The Spirit of the Sovereign LORD is on me, because the LORD has anointed me to preach good news to the *poor*' (Isa. 61.1, NIV; emphasis added). In the Scriptures and in Isaiah in particular, the 'poor' are victims of oppressive overlords and/or social structures (Isa. 3.14–15; 10.2; 11.4; 25.4; 26.6; 32.7; 58.7; etc.); they are also the pious righteous (Isa. 10.2; 26.6; cf. Pss. 12.5; 14.6; 22.24; 37.14), as well as again the remnant (Isa. 54.11). A composite profile, the 'poor' was simultaneously all of these things without contradiction. Yet when viewed from the eschatological perspective, Isaiah's poor were also priestly beneficiaries of the final jubilee (Isa. 61.6). Convinced of the onset of the redemptive turn, Jesus would have been naturally predisposed to allow this eschatological aspect to dominate. Self-identified as Israel's eschatological high priest, Jesus attracted audiences from the Judean countryside composed largely of the disenfranchised; on these he pronounced blessings that had both a promissory and an invitational quality. As promise, Jesus' blessings intimated that his hearers had been especially poised, as the poor, to participate in his movement; as invitation, the Beatitudes called on others to make good on the promise by throwing in their lot in with Jesus and the way of life he represented. In this respect, Jesus' beatitudes were not only the announcement of a now-unfolding redemptive-historical reality but also a summons for hearers to join his burgeoning movement as it aspired to embody the moral ideals exemplified by Isaiah's quasi-fictive poor.

---

[166] It's also possible that Jesus anticipated that *hoi ptōchoi* would make up the bulk of his movement. If so, he would have been completely right: see Stark 1997: 83–4.

[167] Summarizing blessing as God's activity of providence (distinct from the act of salvation), Patrick Miller (1975: 250) writes: 'In all of this [analysis] we touch base, not with some ancient magical sphere, but with the *providence of God*. That is the theological framework in which we place our reflection on the Aaronic benediction and blessing in general in the Old Testament' (emphasis original).

The Beatitudes and the historical Jesus

To repeat myself, it is not the case that the scriptural rationale undergirding Jesus' blessings would have been perspicuous to one and all. But we can imagine that in their original setting, the Beatitudes retained an almost parable-like function, at first piquing the curiosity of those who self-identified as 'the poor' (or were willing to do so), and then inviting them to investigate how their social station could now be entirely reinterpreted, no longer as a state of cursedness but as an elective point of departure for what God was about to do through his newly appointed high priest. Jesus' phrase 'Blessed are the poor', along with certain other blessings preserved in Matthew's beatitudes, functioned not only as a description of a certain socio-religious reality but also as a declaration of a redemptive-historical transition taking place in the very pronouncement of the blessings. Still further, the Beatitudes were a kind of verbal gauntlet forcing a decision among the broader community as to its own place in God's redemptive plan and among Jesus' enemies as to how they might rebut the claims implicit in the Beatitudes.

The invitation to the poor to become the poor in the full redemptive-historical sense was also coupled, at least for the initiated, with concrete practices that gave visible expression to the movement's core convictions. In my earlier book, *Jesus the Temple*, I argued that Jesus established his community as a kind of social experiment involving a community void not of hierarchy as such but of any social differentiation imposed by the larger culture's value system.[168] Deliberately occupying the bottom rung of the societal ladder, the movement not only identified itself with the socially disenfranchised, but also devoted itself to advancing their socio-economic interests by practising commensality and sharing resources. It did so, again, out of the conviction that the return from exile was presently under way through Jesus, and that the poor of the land, as the contemporary fulfilment of Isaiah's 'poor', had been destined to dramatize this redemptive-historical shift as it was taking shape under Jesus' leadership.

At the same time, Jesus' coalescing society of 'the poor' would have posed an unnerving challenge to powerbrokers, aspiring powerbrokers and all their would-be followers from various quarters. First, by repudiating the very practices and values which had perpetuated the self-serving hierarchies of the day, the Jesus movement posed a stiff challenge to any who stood to gain from such hierarchies. Second, rejecting the path of countless first-century messianic aspirants, Jesus also insisted that his movement sit loose to the acquisition of social and political power, thereby passively disrupting such power. Standing against the tide, he called his followers to a different calculus, one where violence was met with non-resistance (Matt. 5.39) and oppression was met with cheerful cooperation (Matt. 5.40–42). Ultimately,

---

[168] Nicholas Perrin, 2010: 120–30.

so Jesus seems to have reasoned, it was through responses like these that the poor in his midst would display the empowering righteousness of God – all part of its cultic vocation, carried out in protest against business as usual back in Jerusalem. Third, for Jesus, pure devotion to Israel's God as the one true God demanded a corresponding social unity, which could only be practically realized as community members committed themselves to the very ideals expressed in the Beatitudes – a truly 'one people' serving the one true God. (I will say more about this below.) This too would have a destabilizing impact on the first-century social fabric.

The unity which Jesus hoped would characterize his followers found its experiential and objective basis in the activity of the Spirit: 'Blessed are the poor' either 'in' or 'through the Spirit'.[169] We recall that on Isaiah's reckoning the Spirit would be the catalyst for the high priest's anointing, as well as the initial impetus for the proclamation of the good news.[170] On this line of reasoning, Jesus' hearers were not 'poor in spirit' in the sense of being bereft of human spirit or strength; they were poor because the anointing Spirit of God had (through Jesus the appointed messenger) sealed them for a specific redemptive role that was congruent with their social status. By declaring themselves 'in the Spirit', Jesus' disciples were essentially claiming to share in Jesus' role, first acquired at his baptism, of being the human repository for the divine presence, a divine presence which in the past had been restricted to the temple. Appropriately enough, members of the Jesus movement also seem to have recognized the Spirit as having an active role within their own experience. Jesus' baptism, we recall, was marked by the humanly perceptible movement of the Spirit. That the Spirit continued to operate beyond the founding event is evidenced by indications of ecstatic utterances and experiences within the community.[171] It was the empirically verifiable activity of the Spirit among the righteous poor that vouched for the return from exile in the present time. Thus Jesus' kingdom community visibly enacted the kingdom narrative of restoration set out in the Scriptures.

Summary

Through an in-depth study of several of Jesus' key teachings (the parable of the sower, the parable of salt and the Beatitudes), we discover that the four aforementioned components of Ezekiel's return-from-exile vision – restoration of the cultic space, the establishment of a new priestly class, cleansing from idols, and the issuance of the Spirit – were also vital elements for the historical Jesus' mission. These were not so much the explicit focal

---

[169] Matt. 5.3. Flusser (1988: 107) advocates that the Greek dative may be taken as locative or instrumental; he may be right.

[170] Isa. 61.1.

[171] Luke 10.18; Matt. 11.27. On Jesus' ecstatic aspect, see classically Holtzmann 1903; more recently, Borg 1987; Crossan 1991: xii; Schüssler Fiorenza 1994: 123–4; etc.

point of his kingdom message as the unstated narrative premise on which his message depended. While other contemporary accounts of the kingdom may add to this list or describe the same realities with a different vocabulary, I do not believe that it would be possible to omit any one of these four points without doing injustice to the historical reality.

Of course, as Jesus sought to translate the prophets' eschatological vision into present-day reality, the key concepts would have to be creatively transposed. The newly cleared sacred ground, one and the same in the parable of the sower as 'the good land', was at present not a geographical but a socio-religious space, taking shape within the contemporary community but only fully realized on the future construction of the eschatological temple. Within this community, idols and idolatrous ideologies would have to be weeded out, especially as community members self-selected – staying in or getting out as they were inclined – through the season of tribulation. In this manner, as Jesus sought to show through his parable of salt, a new priesthood would progressively emerge even in the midst of opposition. Whereas some within the community might have been tempted to interpret such opposition as an unmitigated evil, Jesus insisted that broader hostility to his movement would in fact prove to be the means by which his followers would be refined and galvanized. Finally, the Beatitudes reflect Jesus' decision to locate his movement socially among the poor, who also maintained first right of refusal in response to the operations of the Spirit in their midst.

Jesus' kingdom teachings also give us some sense of the terms and conditions of his calling. Those who entered his community were predominantly those who, drawn from among the socially marginalized, had accepted his invitation to become the 'poor' in its heightened theological sense. The central condition for remaining in this community was an ongoing commitment to receive the teachings of Jesus (the word of the seed), even as this commitment would come to be challenged by various external and internal pressures, not least persecutions and idolatrous ideologies. And at the centre of this social system was the Twelve, and with the Twelve, Jesus himself, the Isaac-*esque* high priest. Within the broader society Jesus was a controversial figure, especially among the sociopolitically empowered; his movement, hardly less so. But on Jesus' reckoning, as hinted at in the Lord's Prayer, this very opposition would become the means by which the eschatological community would evolve into its true self, all in accordance with a familiar eschatological timetable. And so if the unpopularity of Jesus and his disciples had engendered some doubts within the movement, those doubts could always be redressed by appealing to the long view, which promised that Yahweh would use the suffering of the newly minted priestly guild to usher in the kingdom of God.

As I trust this chapter on Jesus' kingdom teaching (along with Chapter 1) has made sufficiently clear, Jesus recognized suffering and social marginalization as integral components of his movement's experience. Accordingly, as we look back to the previous chapter, we have no reason to suspect that the inaugural baptism, with its intimations of self-sacrifice, was the by-product of some late ecclesial *theologia crucis*. A much simpler explanation is at hand: even as early as his baptism, Jesus already had some idea of the obstacles before him and would have even then acknowledged death as a possible if not likely outcome. The most looming of threats facing Jesus would be the well-ensconced high priest and the temple apparatchiks, together with the Romans. And so from the very beginning, Jesus needed a set of narratives compelling enough to inspire his movement in the face of powerful actors who showed no signs of negotiating Jesus' demands. In the next chapter, we will examine one of those narratives, which, as it so happens, lends important qualification to Jesus' divine sonship and advances our overall understanding of Jesus the priest.

4

Jesus Son of David

Jesus' movement was a society which, so far as we know, never concentrated on any text but the Scriptures. There its members found occupation for the occasional idle hour and consolation in a distressed one; there they found their faculties roused into awe; and there, even while every dream for real change seemed all but hopeless, they could read what was, in a very real sense, their own story with an interest which never failed. In short, the Hebrew scriptures were simultaneously a mirror for the present crisis and a window into a future in which their wildest eschatological imaginations would hopefully become reality, when Israel's story could at long last be closed out with the words, 'and they all lived happily ever after'. We have already observed the extent to which the Hebrew scriptures provided the script for Jesus' self-understanding.

In the opening chapter of this book, I argued that by designating themselves 'sons of God' in the Lord's Prayer, members of the Jesus community were self-consciously asserting their own role within a new exodus. Much as the first exodus looked ahead to the establishment of the temple and the consequent reign of God (Exod. 15.17–18), this new exodus would likewise look forward to the inauguration of the eschatological temple and the uninterrupted reign of God. Then, in Chapter 2, I maintained that Jesus' baptism marked the inception of his vocation as eschatological high priest. From that moment forward, Jesus saw himself, like David, as having a crucial role in the installation of new sacred space; he saw himself, too, like Isaac, as somehow being involved in an atoning transaction. The baptism also explains a distinction, consistent within the tradition, between Jesus' unique role as 'Son of God' and his disciples as 'sons of God': even though Jesus belonged to the same priestly order as his followers, to him alone fell the role of chief priest. Next, in Chapter 3, I set out to show that the substance of Jesus' return-from-exile vision of the kingdom was remarkably consistent with prophetic restoration hope, hinted at through Ezekiel in the Lord's Prayer. Jesus' kingdom vision, like that of the prophets as a whole, revolved around the renewal of sacred space, populated by a new guild of priests, sustained by the Spirit and purged of idols. Yet for Jesus the path to this kingdom was to be paved by suffering. Remaining faithful in the face of persecution, a persecution already palpable in the community's experience, the disciples would conduct themselves in keeping with their identity as Isaiah's eschatological poor, true salt and true priesthood, and the first fruits of the eschatological temple.

So far, so good – perhaps. But the argument I have set forth up to this point would hardly be complete if it did not also account for a certain difficulty raised along the way. If Jesus took on the epithet 'Son of God' as a priestly title (as I have been arguing), how does it line up with sundry indications that this title should be explained otherwise – most promisingly, by relating the phrase either to Jesus' identity as 'Son of David' or to his identity as 'Son of Man'? Towards addressing this question, the following two chapters will be dedicated to examining these two prominent son-related epithets in the Jesus tradition: Son of David and Son of Man. Needless to say, both of these titles by themselves could receive – and indeed have received and deserve to receive – full-blown, monograph-length treatments. Unfortunately, the constraints of space prevent me from attempting something comparable here. To tip my hand, I will maintain, first, that both monikers go back to Jesus himself, and, second, that both retained in Jesus' thinking a radically priestly aspect. Once so understood, the terms 'Son of David' and 'Son of Man' will also help explain the otherwise extremely slippery term 'Son of God', which, again I will argue, spoke first and foremost to Jesus' priestly vocation, at least in his own context. We begin in this chapter with the Son of David.

Jesus as 'Son of David'

The Son of David traditions find their point of departure in 2 Samuel 7.8–16, a passage in which Yahweh counters David's temple-construction bid with a covenantal promise of everlasting lineage to occupy the throne. The promise falls within the broader context of 1–2 Samuel, a narrative which idealizes David as God's righteous warrior-king. While the Psalms (18.50; 78.70–72; 89.3–4, 20–37, 49–51; 132.1–5, 10–18; 144.10) confirm this overall representation of David, the prophetic corpus extends the idea in a different direction by associating Israel's leading royal hero with return from exile (Isa. 55.1–3; Jer. 23.1–5; Ezek. 34.23–24; 37.24–25). Buoyed by these images of eschatological hope, the anticipation of a new and greater David remained vibrant in the post-exilic setting. Even if the expectation of a Davidic messiah was not necessarily a universal expectation within Second-Temple Judaism, it was nevertheless a hope which preoccupied a sizable segment of the population.[1]

Jesus as the Son of David in early Christian tradition

Judging by the fact that the term 'son of David' occurs some 16 times in the Gospels alone, early Christianity seems to have been no stranger to the hope wrapped up in this title. In Mark, Jesus defends his disciples' practice

---

[1] *Pss. Sol.* 17; 4Q161 2.11–25; 4Q174 1 1.7–13; 4Q457b 2.2; 4Q504 1–2 4.5–8; 4Q522 9 2.3–6; 11Q5 27.2–10; *Tg. Isa.* 9.6; 11.1–6, 10; 14.29; 16.5; Jer. 23.3–6; 30.9; 33.15–16; Hos. 3.5.

of gleaning grainfields on the Sabbath by appealing to the precedent set by David.[2] Then at the close of his well-known 'way section' (8.22—10.52), the second Evangelist has blind Bartimaeus shouting out repeatedly after Jesus as the 'Son of David'.[3] Two chapters later, Jesus confronts his adversaries with a puzzle from Psalm 110 regarding the scribes' identification of the messiah as 'the son of David'.[4] Finally, the ensuing Passion narrative is fraught with allusions to Davidic psalms, all of which conspires to frame Mark's Jesus as an analogue to the shepherd-king.[5]

For Matthew, Jesus' status as the son of David is of particular interest.[6] This becomes obvious on the Evangelist's striking introduction of Jesus as 'son of David' (as well as 'son of Abraham').[7] For Matthew the term bears messianic connotations, although the Evangelist does not wholly equate 'son of David' with messiah, as is clear from his tagging Joseph with the same title.[8] Matthew preserves Mark's grainfield incident and doubles up his account of the blind beseeching the 'Son of David'.[9] Mark's Syrophoenician woman also surfaces in Matthew's account, again appealing to his healing capacity.[10] Whereas much of Matthew's Gospel has the crowds merely pondering Jesus as the messianic Son of David, by the time of the triumphal entry they have become convinced of it, a point seemingly capped off by the Psalm 110 puzzler.[11] In Matthew, no less than in Mark, Jesus' status as 'son of David' is front and centre.

Luke shares his colleagues' interest in Jesus' Davidic status.[12] In the programmatic birth narrative, Joseph is introduced as being from 'the house of David', which prepares for the double prediction that Jesus will accede to the dynastic throne.[13] The third Gospel draws attention to Jesus' Davidide roots in his infancy narrative, even as it preserves the grainfield episode, the

---

[2] Mark 2.23–28. On the use of 'son of David' in Markan (and pre-Markan) traditions, see Robbins 1973; Charlesworth 1996; Smith 1996; Bockmuehl 2008; Malbon 2009a; Botner 2017.

[3] Mark 10.47–48.

[4] Mark 12.35.

[5] Mark 14.17–21 (Psalm 40); 14.32–42 (Psalms 41–42); 15.22–39 (Psalms 21 and 68). See Collins 1997; Ahearne-Kroll 2007.

[6] Kingsbury's (1976: 591) statement that 'Matthew alone of the evangelists evinces a keen interest in presenting Jesus as the son of David' is an overstatement (the kind which is often typical of redactional-critical arguments). The most seminal studies on Matthew's use of 'son of David' predate Kingsbury: Bornkamm 1963; Gibbs 1964; Suhl 1968; see more recently Novakovic 2003; Van Egmond 2006; Baxter 2006; Chae 2006; and now Piotrowski 2016.

[7] Matt. 1.1.

[8] Matt. 1.20.

[9] Matt. 9.27; 12.1–8; 20.30–31.

[10] Matt. 15.22.

[11] Matt. 12.23; 21.9, 15; 22.42.

[12] The published dissertations of Strauss (1995) and Miura (2007) together offer an important corrective to the methodologically narrow approach of Burger (1970: 72–91), who minimizes Luke's interest in the title. See also George (1978: 257–82), Tannehill 1991 (1986): 25–6, 38–9, 58–63, 268–70), Bock (1987: 79–82, 234–40); Hahn 2005.

[13] Luke 1.27, 32, 69.

healing of the blind, and the Davidic-messianic conundrum of his source.[14] In his second volume, Acts, Luke also includes three major speeches that focus on Jesus' Davidic status.[15] Notwithstanding the narrative gap between the birth narrative and the explicit expressions of Davidic Christology of Acts, Luke (like Mark and Matthew before him) maintains a healthy interest in Jesus as a Davidic figure.

Later New Testament Christologizing is also haunted by David's spectre. In the Fourth Gospel, Jesus' prediction of his death is set in Davidic terms.[16] The seer behind Revelation twice refers to Jesus in connection with the Davidic promise; in the second instance the risen Christ is identified as 'the descendant of David' (*to genos David*).[17] Likewise, the author of 2 Timothy summarizes the gospel of Jesus Christ with the words, 'raised from the dead, a descendant of David'.[18] The breadth and enduring nature of the tradition linking Jesus with David speak for themselves.

The application of the Davidic title to Jesus is no innovation on the Evangelists' part but predates the Gospels considerably. The clearest evidence for this comes by way of Paul, who unhesitatingly speaks of his gospel 'concerning his [God's] Son, who was *descended from David* [*ek spermatos David*] according to the flesh'.[19] Written within a generation of Jesus' death, and perhaps drawing on a pre-Pauline hymn, the apostle's statement links Jesus' Davidic status with the resurrection.[20] Treading a path initially cleared by Wilhelm Wrede, Burger and Duling maintain that behind Romans 1.3 stands an early Hellenistic community tradition which was the first to ascribe the title to Jesus, and that as a post-Easter 'christologoumenon'.[21] But there are difficulties here, not least the indications that the earthly Jesus' genetic connections with David had some basis in fact, at least as far as Jesus' peers were concerned.[22] If Jesus was widely regarded as a genealogical son of David in his own lifetime, then it would have been extraordinary for the early Church to have nonchalantly extended the same title to the resurrected Jesus for altogether different reasons without at least acknowledging the serendipity of Jesus' lineage.

An alternative reconstruction is put forward by the post-Bultmannian Ferdinand Hahn, who accepts Jesus' genealogical descent from David, but reduces it to a factoid barely relevant to the kerygma of the risen Son of

---

[14] Luke 2.4, 11; 6.1–6; 18.35–43; 20.41–44.
[15] Acts 2.14–41; 13.16–42; 15.13–21.
[16] John 2.17 (Ps. 69.9). For a thorough study of the figure of David in the Fourth Gospel, see Daly-Denton 2000.
[17] Rev. 5.5; 22.16.
[18] 2 Tim. 2.8.
[19] Rom. 1.3; emphasis added.
[20] For a review of issues revolving around the origins of Rom. 1.3–4, see Jewett 1985; Strauss 1995: 60–4.
[21] Burger 1970: 26; Duling 1973: 73.
[22] See Cullmann 1963 (1959): 127–33; Michaelis 1961: 317–30; Brown 1977: 505–12; Chilton 1982: 99.

David. On this theory, Jesus' pre-Easter status as son of David has to do with his 'earthly mission', while his post-Easter assumption of the office of the same name refers quite differently to his eternal reign.[23] Not only is this bifurcating solution patently inelegant, but it also fails to square with passages like Romans 15.7–13, where, as Christopher G. Whitsett has shown, the apostle's argument crucially depends on the suppressed premise of Jesus' physical Davidic ancestry.[24] Even apart from Romans 15, Hahn's theory still awkwardly forces us to imagine two wholly incommensurate 'son of David' roles evinced by one and the same 'Son of David' title. Even Hahn admits that there is 'clearly a tension' here.[25]

But are we really forced to choose between the options of (1) sweeping the historical evidence of Jesus' family tree under the rug (Burger, Duling) or (2) granting this genealogy but imagining two different offices represented by the same title (Hahn)? Hardly. Against these attempts to clarify how the title 'son of David' entered early Christianity, there is a simpler explanation: namely, that the earthly Jesus' Davidic ancestry retained a certain potential theological cache (while he was alive) which was eventually leveraged after his death and resurrection. Thus, whatever Paul meant by the resurrection 'declaring' (Rom. 1.4) the risen Jesus as the Son of David/Son of God (a contentious point), he at least meant that the resurrection had become the catalyst by which Jesus' human ancestry, now retrospectively interpreted through the Easter event, could find its full significance. The ascription of 'son of David' to Jesus was no innovation on the apostle's part; nor did the term originate in some hidden-away Hellenistic community. Well before Paul or even the cross, Jesus was recognized as a biological son of David and this held something more than a purely genealogical significance.

Son of David and the historical Jesus

But just what significance Jesus himself attached to his status as son of David is another question. In answering this question, two extremes are to be avoided. On the one hand, it will not do to attribute to the historical Jesus all that the early Church had come to ascribe to the Jesus as the risen Son of David. On the other hand, given the small crowd of Davidic-messianic claimants rising up in Jesus' own era, it would be inappropriate to pre-empt the possibility of Jesus' self-consciousness as *ben David* in some theologically fulsome sense.[26] Between these two extremes, the significance of Jesus' self-designation as 'son of David' must remain an open question.

It is a question that can be productively renewed along two lines of

---

[23] Hahn et al. 1969: 240–58.
[24] Whitsett 2000: 667–76.
[25] Hahn et al. 1969: 246.
[26] As Horsley (1984: 475) aptly observes: 'David and his movement . . . provided the principal precedent and the historical prototype for subsequent popular messianic movements', including not least the movements of Jesus' own time.

enquiry. In the first place, it might be asked whether Jesus' peers tagged him with the Davidic moniker while he was still alive. In the second place, one might also ask whether Jesus also perceived himself as 'son of David' in some extraordinary sense that transcended genealogy. Here one may begin by appealing to two corresponding lines of evidence: the healings accompanied by the invocation 'son of David' (Matt. 9.27; 15.22; Mark 10.47–48//Matt. 20.30–33//Luke 18.38–39) and the triumphal entry (Mark 11.1–10//Matt. 21.1–11//Luke 19.28–40//John 12.12–19). As for the former question, it is not impossible that the Gospel writers were the first to include the phrase 'son of David' in these healing scenes simply in the interest of framing Jesus as the Davidic messiah. This would be in keeping, at any rate, with a long-standing methodological principle that anything in the Gospels approaching a Christological title must be greeted as post-Easter fancy.[27]

But this approach is not without its problems. In the first place, had the Evangelists been bent on gracing Jesus with the title for purely theological (as opposed to historical) motives, we should, I think, expect a much more far-ranging application of what is actually a sparingly used term. Moreover, the critical impulse to sever the epithet from Jesus' setting should be reconsidered on evidence not only that Jesus' Davidic ancestry was public knowledge, but also that the phrase 'son of David' was commonly employed by ancient Jewish suppliants seeking relief from disease and/or demonic influences.[28] If the physically afflicted of Jesus' day called out to him as 'son of David' simply because they were aware of the famed healer's ancestral roots (and were perhaps hoping that Jesus' DNA could only enhance his therapeutic effectiveness), or because this phrase was a stock address in healing requests, or both, then there is absolutely no reason to doubt the moniker's application to the historical Jesus, though of course without the connotative load that it would come to carry in post-Easter reflection. Along the same lines, there is no basis for supposing that the Gospel writers – insofar as they saw their task as including the recording of biographical facts – thought of the individuals in their accounts as intending some kind of *sensus plenior*. On the contrary, the phrase 'son of David' on the lips of the Canaanite woman and blind Bartimaeus is far more convincingly explained as a cashing out of a potent irony of history than a crude attempt to convince audiences that the historical personages somehow instantly recognized Jesus as *the Son of David* in the fully messianic sense. At the same time, it would be equally rash to suppose that the Evangelists thought of these suppliants as addressing Jesus out of purely genealogical interest. There was *something* about Jesus' reputation or powers that inspired the title, and the desperate were not above, as it were, publicly

---

[27] As far as I know, D. F. Strauss (1972 (1835): 88) first articulated the basic principle: 'If therefore we are told of a celebrated individual . . . that his followers at a single glance recognized him as being all that he actually was . . . we must feel more than doubtful whether it is a real history which lies before us'.

[28] Fisher 1968; Berger 1973: 3–9; Duling 1973; Torijano 2002: 110–28.

drawing attention to Jesus' Davidic calling card for whatever it was worth. This was all part of the point, so far as the Gospel writers were concerned. Yet none of this calls into question the historicity of these encounters. That Jesus was called 'son of David' and did not resist the term is suggested by the historical record: those who wish to deny as much may not be wrong, but on this point they are encumbered by the burden of proof.

The triumphal entry remains the more significant datum.[29] Although this episode is sometimes doubted as a historical event, such a judgement has generally depended less on a rigorous application of the criteria of authenticity and, once again, more on a prior commitment to deny Jesus' messianic consciousness.[30] A more sober assessment of the entry on its own terms yields a more complex picture, one which gives ample enough reason to secure its roots in history. In the first place, the scene is shared across all four Gospels (but not *Thomas*), with all four agreeing that Jesus, much like Solomon en route to his coronation (1 Kings 1.38; cf. also Zech. 9.9), made his way from Bethany into Jerusalem on a colt, while a crowd of indeterminate size laid branches before his path and chanted strains of Psalm 118. On this account, the pericope scores relatively high on the criterion of multiple attestation. Second, the invocation of this particular psalm along with the acclamations 'son of David' is consistent with the Passover setting. Since Psalm 118, one of the standard psalms of the Hallel (Psalms 113–118), would have already been resounding in the streets of Jerusalem in the week leading up to Jesus' death, there is little difficulty in supposing that Jesus' messiah-like appearance in the Holy City was immediately interpreted as a well-timed gesture intimating the imminent fulfilment of that psalm.[31] Third, given the considerable divergences between the Johannine and the synoptic presentation of the occasion, we infer that John depended on a tradition (most likely oral) outside of the synoptics, a point which only strengthens the argument for the event's factual basis.[32] Fourth, assuming with most scholars the historicity of the *titulus*, which explicitly identifies Jesus as 'King of the Jews', it must be asked how such a billboard would have even been possible – in the absence of such a claim on Jesus' part in the course of his last week – without a prior triumphal entry or something like it.[33] To be sure, it is theoretically possible that Jesus made such an explicit claim and it has simply gone unrecorded. Alternatively, it is also conceivable that Jesus' opponents completely invented his assertion of royal status and Pilate bought

---

[29] Mark 11.1–10//Matt 21.1–11//Luke 19.28–40//John 12.12–19.

[30] More recent representative sceptics include Catchpole 1984; Sanders 1985: 306. Advocates for its historicity include Brandon 1967: 350; Dodd 1971: 141–4; Harvey 1982: 120–8; Wright 1996: 491; Tan 1997: 138–43; Theissen and Merz 1998 (1996): 179; Fredriksen 1999: 243–55; Kinman 2009; Keener 2009: 260–1; LeDonne 2011: 191–6.

[31] So Harvey 1982: 127; Kinman 2009: 407. On the messiah's return to the temple during Passover, see Le Déaut 1963: 265–338.

[32] So Smith 1963: 58–64; Coakley 1995: 466–77.

[33] As pointed out by Evans 1993: 470; Kinman 2009: 393–6. On the titulus, see Winter 1961: 107–10; Bammel 1984.

the story, though even here there would presumably still have to have been some kind of factual basis to impress the Romans. Against both of these explanations, it makes far more sense to suppose that the title 'King of the Jews' was stuck to Jesus' cross simply because the crowds had made it stick to Jesus himself only a few days earlier.

In addition to these, a final consideration is in order: while some commentators might regard the crowd's wild vacillating opinion of Jesus during the last week as unrealistic, I would argue just the opposite, namely, that from a socio-psychological point of view there is a realistic link between the crowd's hearty enthusiasm for Jesus in the entry scene and its vindictive disappointment shortly before his crucifixion. On hearing about Jesus' seemingly pathetic capitulation to his Roman arresters, the crowds turned hostile; they had obviously been led to expect a very different outcome.[34] Such expectations would have certainly been generated in Jesus' royal-like entry: bearing all the marks of well-known historical entrances, Jesus' self-conscious staging of his entry would have naturally invited the crowd to regard him as their messianic saviour.[35] Expectations such as these would have been generated in Jesus' royal-like entry – I am not sure where else. The crucial causal link of Jesus' last week, the triumphal entry defies hypotheses of fictive invention.

While the invocation of David/son of David occurs in only two (Mark 11.10; Matt. 11.9) of the four accounts of the entry, this is hardly problematic for my point. After all, as already mentioned, all four Gospels record that the crowds were fixated on Psalm 118, a text which was understood as anticipating the arrival of the eschatological David.[36] Racked with a messianic fever, the people interpreted Jesus' Passover re-enactment of Solomon's coronation as a Davidic-messianic gesture. With or without (so Luke and John) the explicit mention of David, this psalm in the mouth of the crowds amounted to an ascription of Davidic status. It was an epithet which Jesus shows no signs of rejecting.

The best explanation as to why the Gospels' Jesus never declines the Davidic title is simply because it was a title he willingly embraced for himself. In addition to the evidences produced so far, two sets of data point in this direction. First, we consider Jesus' appeal to David in his argument over halakhic protocols relating to Sabbath harvesting (Mark 2.23–28 par. Matt. 12.1–8//Luke 6.1–5).[37] As I will argue more fully below (Chapter 6), Jesus'

[34] Matt. 27.22–23//Mark 15.13–14//Luke 23.21–23//John 18.40; this insight is to be credited to Farmer 1956: 198–201.
[35] Here we think most of all of Judas Maccabeus (*Ant.* 12.7.4 §§348–49) or Simon Maccabeus (1 Macc. 13.50–51). For a survey of historic antecedents to the entry, see Catchpole 1984.
[36] On this point, see discussion in Brunson 2003: 40–2.
[37] The criterion of coherency (the conflict is consistent with an overall trend of halakhic disputes leading up to Jesus' arrest and execution), together with support from the triple tradition, emboldens us to accept the conversation as historically solid; so also, e.g., Pesch 1976–80: 1.183; Chilton 1982: 98.

argument only makes final sense if he is in some sense identifying himself with David. If so, then this is *prima facie* evidence that Jesus thought of himself as the Son of David.

That Jesus willingly appropriated the title 'son of David' is also evidenced by the triple tradition's account of Jesus' disputation over Psalm 110 (Mark 12.35–37 par. Matt. 22.41–54//Luke 20.41–44.).[38] In this fascinating if not perplexing dialogue, Jesus asks how it might be possible that the son of David can be David's son if David himself calls him Lord.[39] Given the implications of Jesus' triumphal entry on a Solomonic beast of burden, such a question would have hardly been of antiquarian or exegetical interest. By this point, the crowds would have been quite settled on Jesus' messianic status. Sensing that the wind of public favour was at his back, Jesus now seeks to outflank his opponents by forcing them to 'go public' on the question of his identity. This identity can only be construed with reference to Psalm 110 – leaving Melchizedek, David and the Son of David as candidates.

From here three observations are in order. First, since Psalm 110 enjoyed currency as a messianic *testimonium* long before Jesus' day, it was clear that Jerusalem's latest hero-in-the-making was now, more clearly than ever, assuming Davidic-messianic status for himself.[40] Second, insofar as the psalm focuses on the meting out of divine justice to David's enemies, Jesus' query tacitly implicates his own opponents – precisely in their opposition to Jesus as the recently acclaimed 'son of David'. On Jesus' interpretation of the psalm, those who reject his messianic claims would be subject to the same judgement which Psalm 110 assigns to all of Yahweh's enemies.[41] Third, by designating his own role along the lines of the priest Melchizedek (Ps. 110.4), Jesus is hinting that his own Davidic role was essentially priestly in nature – after the order of Melchizedek, the quintessential priest. The implicit three-fold claim, bound to delight Jesus' supporters and vex his opponents, forced the hostile entourage to retreat. Leveraging popular sentiments stirred up through the triumphal entry, Jesus' take-no-hostages approach may be the best explanation as to why the temple leadership at this juncture simply breaks off talks with Jesus.

---

[38] Since both Q and Mark chronologically link this dialogue with the entry and temple cleansing, scholars have widely been inclined to grant its authenticity as well as its role in helping to seal the breach between Jesus and his opponents. Wright (1996: 644) is quite correct when he states that the passage has 'a total coherence whose historical force is compelling'. Along similar lines, Dodd: 1952: 110, 126; Beasley-Murray 1986: 299; Chilton 1982; Dunn 2003: 634–5; Keener 2009: 270; contra Bornkamm 1960 (1959): 228; Bultmann 1968 (1921): 66, 136–7, as well as Le Donne (2009: 222–8), who is finally ambivalent on the question.

[39] Mark 12.35 par.

[40] This is patently the case on considering the ways in which Psalm 110 was roundly employed as a theological warrant for the royal-priestly Hasmonean line: 1 Macc. 14.41; *Jub.* 32.1; *T. Levi* 8.3; Sir. 47.8–10. See also Str-B 4.452–60; Davies 1955: 161; Hay 1989 (1973): 24–33; Barber 2013b: 108 n. 27. While some have argued that Jesus invokes Psalm 110 to illustrate the convoluted nature of messianic expectation and therefore why he couldn't be the messiah, I find this unconvincing.

[41] Ps. 110.1–2, 5–6.

To summarize, we have plenty of reason for supposing not only that Jesus' contemporaries accorded him the title 'son of David' (although with different connotations in different circumstances), but also that it was a title which he willingly accepted and indeed capitalized on. While it would fall to post-Easter writers to reiterate this Davidic claim while extending its theological ramifications, they probably did so with some awareness of its dominical origins. The most convincing explanation of the evidence indicates that Jesus thought of himself as the Son of David in a theologically robust manner.

Once this point is granted, it becomes all the more striking that with the exception of the blind calling out for healing (a usage which most likely did not carry much theological freight in the historical situation), each instance of Jesus' Davidic ascriptions connotes a specifically priestly status. This is true not only in relation to the grainfield incident, where Jesus justified his behaviour on the precedent of David's handling of the sanctuary presence-bread, but also on his invocation of Psalm 110, whereby Jesus aligns his own ministry with the arrival of the eschatological high priest. Even Jesus' triumphal entry, acted out to a psalm which envisages a climactic temple entrance through 'the gates of righteousness' (Ps. 118.19) right 'up to the horns of the altar' (v. 27), culminates in a visit to the temple.[42] The evidence has an uncanny consistency. If we had no Old Testament or intertestamental literature, if the only thing we knew about David or the 'son of David' was from the life of Jesus, we would have to infer that this David was renowned not so much for any royal significance but rather for his cultic significance. Given the historically unassailable evidence, this seems to be at least how the historical Jesus interpreted David.

David and the 'Son of David' as priestly figures

Towards explaining this unexpected oddity, we do well to return to the texts which shaped the collective understanding of Jesus' milieu. For although Jesus' intimations of priesthood in connection with his Davidic identity could be merely fortuitous, or could reflect an innovative theological connection in Jesus' mind now lost to history, our best lead is to begin with prior tradition. When we do, we discover – beginning with the historical narratives and then branching out into the imagined future of prophetic expectation – that David and Solomon acquire a priestly function that is more or less without parallel among the later kings.[43] While these functionalities have been variously explained (or explained away, as the case may be), I will maintain that at least

---

[42] Matt. 21.12//Mark 11.11//Luke 19.45. Catchpole (1984: 320–1) rightly points out that Jesus' movement from triumphal entry to temple activity was anticipated by various historical dignitaries, including three different Hasmonean brothers, each of whom (it should be said) nurtured high-priestly aspirations.

[43] The issue has occasioned no small discussion over the decades. See Kraus 1966: 179–88; Cody 1969: 103–5; Armerding 1975; Wenham 1975; Haran 1979; Hahn 2009: 176–83; Deenick 2011; Diffey 2013; Barber 2013b.

certain strands of ancient interpretative tradition not only recognized David and Solomon's priestly tasks *as legitimately priestly tasks* but also associated this capacity with father and son's historically unparalleled position. But first a review of the data and its standard interpretation are in order.

David and Solomon's priestly activity

In the Deuteronomist's narratives, we find three episodes in which David assumes priestly prerogatives.[44] The first occurs in 1 Samuel 21, where David asks the resident priest Ahimelech for the Bread of the Presence to sustain himself and his men; it is a request which Ahimelech grants.[45] While this episode has often been interpreted as a blatant violation of cultic boundaries, implicating both David and Ahimelech, this is counter-indicated by the conspicuous absence of any sense of disapproval from within the narrative. Indeed, when Ahimelech is questioned about the same incident shortly thereafter, he insists without hesitation that none of Saul's servants is more faithful than David.[46] This, together with some sense from the Evangelists that Jesus essentially approved of David's actions, raises the question as to whether modern commentators have been all too quick to assume the shepherd-king's culpability. The striking impression that David had in fact done nothing wrong in partaking of cultic bread raises the possibility that David had certain priestly rights after all.

Later, in 2 Samuel 6, when David has the ark brought into Jerusalem, he carries out several functions exclusively associated with priests: he performs sacrifices (vv. 13, 17), an activity ordinarily relegated to the priests (Num. 3.6–8, 14–38; 4.47; etc.); wears the ephod, a privilege normally restricted to the priest (v. 14; cf. Exod. 28.4); erects the tabernacle (v. 17), a Levitical duty (Num. 1.51; 4.1–33); and blesses the people (v. 18), again, a priestly task (Num. 6.22–27; Deut. 10.8; 21.5).[47] In a parallel account of the same event, the Chronicler is even more conscientious in bringing out David's cultic aspect. Intent on centralizing the worship of Yahweh, David summons all the priests and Levites in the land, that they might be restored to their ancestral lands (1 Chron. 13.2–3). After a failed initial attempt to transport the ark (1 Chron. 13.9–14), David again assumes leadership of the same priests and Levites, and has them consecrated with a solemn charge (1 Chron. 15.3–14). Finally, upon the successful relocation of the ark, David implements a regimen of regular offerings by delegating specific roles to the various

---

[44] Though Martin Noth's judgement for a single author behind 1–2 Samuel and 1–2 Kings now stands under scrutiny, I use his term 'Deuteronomist' out of long-standing convention.
[45] 1 Sam. 21.3–6.
[46] 1 Sam. 22.14.
[47] Kleven (1992: 303) refutes the claim that wearing the ephod was not a uniquely priestly prerogative, in part through his observation that in 1 Sam. 22.18 'the phrase "to wear a linen ephod" is synonymous with being a priest'; cited in Hahn 2009: 181.

Levites and priests.[48] 'So in the Chronicler's expanded retelling of the entry of the ark into Jerusalem', Kenneth G. Hoglund summarizes, 'we see David . . . portrayed as taking on the attributes of the "head priest" of the temple, acting in a priestly role'.[49] In short, if 2 Samuel 6 leaves strong hints of David's priestly function, he 'is presented by the Chronicler as the prototypical high priest'.[50] To the extent that the author of 2 Samuel and the Chronicler shared the same overall goals, his portrayal certainly helps us make sense of the otherwise ethically ambivalent Ahimelech incident.[51]

In 2 Samuel 24, following the announcement of judgement against an ill-advised census, David seeks to stem the tide of divine wrath again by assuming a priestly role. After David prays that God might redirect the punishment on himself, the prophet Gad instructs him to erect an altar on the threshing floor of Araunah the Jebusite.[52] He complies and brings forward cultic sacrifices: 'David built there an altar to the LORD, and offered burnt offerings and offerings of well-being. So the LORD answered his supplication for the land, and the plague was averted from Israel'.[53] The Chronicler notes the location on account of its significance: it is the same space which was thought to be the venue for the near-sacrifice of Isaac, as well as for the foundation of Solomon's temple.[54] In averting the wrath of the census through sacrificial offering, so the Chronicler suggests, David is somehow recapitulating the Aqedah. Echoes of Moses' priestly intercession after the golden calf debacle are also not far below the surface (Exod. 32.11–14, 21–24). This is highly intentional, as the author of our narrative is working up to a parallelism between Moses and Joshua, on the one side, and David and Solomon, on the other. Like Moses, who had initialized the first cultic system, the Chronicler's David was the founder of a cultic system; like Joshua, who had secured the land for the worship of Yahweh, the Chronicler's son of David (Solomon) had united the land into one kingdom with one centralized temple space. If Moses and Joshua were the respective sponsors of the original cultic space and cultic land, David and Solomon take on an analogous task in the post-exilic recapitulation of the same process.[55]

'Like father, like son' – Solomon is depicted in 1 Kings as also wearing the ephod, at least during the consecration of the Solomonic temple. Meanwhile, during this same event, the priests tasked with transporting the ark are glaringly absent.[56] Almost as if to upstage the sacerdotal guild, it is Solomon

---

[48] 1 Chron. 16.1–41.
[49] Hoglund 2002: 187.
[50] Hoglund 2002: 189.
[51] I will discuss this passage further in Chapter 6.
[52] 2 Sam. 24.17–18.
[53] 2 Sam. 24.25.
[54] 2 Chron. 3.1.
[55] The double typology is broadly noted among commentators, e.g. Myers 1965: 193; Ackroyd 1973: 89; Romerowski 1986: 15–16; De Vries 1988; Abadie 1999: 169, 181–2.
[56] 1 Kings 8.1–11. As observed by Davies (2011: 48) in his insightful article relating Solomon's priestly attributes.

who takes up the priestly task of blessing (1 Kings 8.14), Solomon (although perhaps along with the people) who sacrifices (1 Kings 8.5, 62) and Solomon who consecrates the temple court (1 Kings 8.64). While it is possible that the newly crowned king was understood to be delegating all of these activities, this is certainly not the impression left by the narrative. In short, in 1 Kings 8 Solomon is clearly portrayed as a kind of high priest.

This impression is hardly reversed by the Chronicler. Indeed, while in 1–2 Chronicles such priestly activity is not generally associated with the kings of Judea/Israel, it is clearly predicated of David and Solomon.[57] Whatever sacerdotal aura surrounds the son of David in the temple consecration narrative of 1 Kings, it is only accentuated in the parallel account in 2 Chronicles 5—7. As far as the subsequent reception of this point in subsequent Judaism is concerned, Magne Saebø cannot be far from the mark when he concludes that 'this particular form of a Davidic-theocratic messianism represents an important point in the complex history of the Old Testament messianism'.[58] That is to say, the distinctively priestly functions of David and the son of David in the biblical narratives would naturally be expected to play a major role in the expectation of a future David/son of David.

And for all we can tell, it does. In the prophetic literature we find a recurring interest in the eschatological David's priestly function (far more than in any royal functions) and this in connection with the reunification of the tribes. This is exemplified in sundry prophetic texts like Jeremiah 30.21 ('Their prince shall be one of their own, their ruler shall come from their midst; I will bring him near [*qrb*], and he shall approach [*ngš*] me, for who would otherwise dare to approach me?'), which immediately follows a vision of united tribal worship (30.9) and prepares for the promise that 'I will be the God of *all the families* of Israel, and they shall be my people' (Jer 31.1). Here images of reunification are set alongside the insinuation of a sacerdotal role for *David redivivus*; as Michael Barber points out, the very language of Jeremiah 30.21 (*qrb* and *ngš* in particular) 'unavoidably convey the notion that the future Davidic king will have cultic responsibilities'.[59] In Ezekiel 34—37, the eschatological Davidic shepherd is placed 'among them' (Ezek. 34.24; 37.25), just as the sanctuary is placed 'among them' (Ezek. 37.28), suggesting a fluidity between the person of David and eschatological sacred space – a space, again, shared by the unified tribes (Ezek. 37.15–23). Likewise, when the Davidide Zerubbabel (cf. 1 Chron. 3.16–19) appears in Zechariah, his primary significance lies not in his exercise of political power but rather in his cultic activity of rebuilding the temple.[60] At the same time,

---

[57] As noted by Preuss 1996 (1992): 24; Granerød 2010: 181.
[58] Saebø 1980: 103. See also Blenkinsopp 2013: 110–14.
[59] Barber 2013b: 107. On *qrb*, see Exod 29.4, 8; 40.12, 14; Lev. 3.6; 7.35; 8.6, 13, 24; Num. 8.9, 10; 16.5, 9, 10; on *ngš*, Exod. 28.43; 30.20; Lev. 21.22–23; Ezek. 44.13. Likewise, Kaiser 1995: 190–1, in Barber 2013b: 107 n. 25.
[60] The same could be said for Zerubbabel's role in Haggai, where 'cultic concerns seem to take precedence over the issue of civil leadership' (Pomykala 1995: 52); so too Mason 1977: 417.

Zechariah 9—10 'expresses hope for the reunification of the northern and southern kingdoms and for the renewal of the Davidic throne'.[61]

What are we to make of David and Solomon's cultic colouring? A good number of scholars, seeking to maintain a rigid separation between the royal and priestly offices, prefer to explain David and Solomon's priestly gestures in the Deuteronomic writings as outlier occurrences, uniquely if not vaguely connected to the events at hand.[62] As far as I can see, this seems to be the standard solution to the quandary presented by David and Solomon's apparent indiscretions. The initial problem with this analysis of 'priesthood' and 'kingship', however, is its tendency to assume (without justification) that our own modern construction of these 'offices' (a term which is inevitably a modern construct in its own right), posited as immutable entities, was universally operative in the Ancient Near East. In my view, however, such an inflexibly static understanding seems to be driven more by an equally static paradigm of 'Israelite religion' without due sensitivity to ancient Judaism's deeply eschatological character, which implies that Israel's theocratic structure was necessarily responsive to epochal covenantal shifts and was therefore, necessarily again, inherently dynamic. Furthermore, this 'outlier solution' strikes me as something of a dodge, which invariably leads to the kind of equivocation we encounter in de Vaux when he writes that although Israel's king was 'a sacred person, with a special relationship to Yahweh, and in solemn circumstances he could act as the religious head of the people . . . he was not a priest'.[63] On reading assertions such as these, we might be forgiven for arching a suspicious eyebrow, much as we would in response to a trail guide who insists, 'Even though that bird on the water looks like a duck, swims like a duck and quacks like a duck, it's still not a duck.' If de Vaux's account of ancient Israelite notions of kingship and priesthood fails the 'duck test' (and it does), perhaps we would do well to revisit our assumptions. Perhaps the lines separating kingship and priesthood are more fluid than we are accustomed to think.

Shedding some light on this issue, Deborah W. Rooke comments that 'priesthood is primarily about *doing* things, about carrying out rituals and procedures, rather than about *being* a particular kind of person or having a particular genealogical descent'.[64] She continues: because kingship was essentially sacral in nature, 'the king would have had the right, if not the duty, to perform quite a number of ritual observances', even if 'his responsibilities were largely delegated to the senior priest'.[65] So, according to the theory espoused by Rooke, the kings of Israel/Judah maintained an *ex officio* priestly role that was intrinsic to the royal office.[66] Whether or

---

[61] Boda 2015: 35–6.
[62] De Vaux 1961: 114; von Rad 2001 (1962): 1.323. Neither de Vaux nor von Rad (as far as I am aware) discuss the priestly attributes of the eschatological David.
[63] De Vaux 1961: 114.
[64] Rooke 1998: 189; emphasis original.
[65] Rooke 1998: 195.
[66] Rooke 1998: 187–208. Close to this position are Laato 1997: 92–3 and Day 2003 (1992): 100.

not Rooke is correct in all her conclusions, her essay challenges students of Israel's cultus to think of priesthood less as a fixed identity and more as a divinely granted functionality, subject to delegation given certain situational and historical contingencies. If her argument is even close to being on track, then the thick and heavy lines which commentators typically draw between priest and king need to be considerably softened. Rooke's account of Israelite kingship (whereby the royal office also retained priestly prerogatives *ex officio*) is certainly an improvement on de Vaux's description, insofar as it explains those data points which stand out as exceptions to the paradigm. Nevertheless, as a comprehensive model, it remains unsatisfactory in that it fails to explain why, on the one hand, so few Israelite and Judahite kings are recorded as carrying out priestly duties, and, on the other hand, why David and Solomon in particular seem to be singled out in their priestly capacities. Here, to reiterate my above passing critique of the research, I suggest that her argument is not sufficiently responsive to the contours of redemptive history.

Towards an explanation for David and Solomon's exceptional priestly status

The united confederacy as a condition for legitimate royal-priestly rule

In my judgement, the first step towards resolving the problem posed by David and Solomon's seemingly transgressive cultic activities begins by paying closer attention to the correlation between these priestly functions and the (re)unification of the tribes around a common sanctuary in Jerusalem. This is not an arbitrary point of departure. After all, if David and Solomon's assumption of sacred prerogatives marks them off as an exception among Israel's kings, so too does the fact that they both ruled over a united confederacy. Indeed, the bundling together of royal-priestly activity and political unification (with centralized power) seems to be intrinsic to the logic of the Deuteronomist's narrative, not least where David's gathering of the tribes around the cultic centre of Jerusalem (2 Samuel 6) sets the stage for both his building of the temple (2 Samuel 7) and his priestly behaviour in nearby texts. Nor does it seem to be a matter of happenstance that the writer has Solomon consecrating the national temple (1 Kings 8) only after quelling rumblings of internal strife (1 Kings 1—2). In the prophetic literature, meanwhile, Davidic ideology surfaces not so much in connection with hopes of regained political autonomy (although this element is never entirely absent), but in connection with the expectation of a Davidic royal-priestly figure administrating worship amid the reunified tribes in a centralized location.[67] Judging by the prophetic canon, it seems that whatever political

---

[67] Following his brief study of the principal prophetic texts dealing with the eschatological David (Jer. 30.9; Hos. 3.5; Ezek. 34.23–24; 37.23–24), Beauchamp (1999: 229) concludes: 'on our four instances, the theme of reunification far exceeds that of royalty' (my translation). To this list we might also add Isaiah 11.

advantages might have accrued from the regathering of the tribes, such gains seem to have been regarded as secondary to the more important goal of a pan-Israel temple operating under the future David's leadership. Because the future Davidic figure was expected to resolve the twin problems posed by the scattered tribes and consequent disintegrated worship, it comes as no surprise that this same eschatological figure acquires a distinctly priestly cast. But if the eschatological David was expected to be both king and priest, the former role was seen as logically antecedent of and therefore subordinate to the latter.

The close correlation between political unification and a restored cultus in ancient Jewish expectation also comes to expression in the narratives surrounding Hezekiah and Josiah, two David-*esque* Judean kings who approach priestly status while coming as close as anyone to reuniting the tribes. Like David and Solomon before him, Hezekiah implements the regular offering (2 Chron. 30.3) and blesses the people (2 Chron. 30.1, 5; 31.8). Earlier on, in 2 Chronicles 29—30, the same king takes up a decidedly sacerdotal role not only by purging the temple but also by inviting all of Israel for a national Passover. Even though many from the north scorned Hezekiah's overture, the Chronicler's remarks following the event, namely, that 'since the time of Solomon son of King David of Israel there had been nothing like this in Jerusalem', imply that the leading point of comparison between Hezekiah and David/Solomon is their mutual (attempted) leadership over a unified confederation.[68] In the Chronicler's eyes, it was Hezekiah's rare bid to establish centralized worship that provides the warrant for his cultic activity as well as the right to address the priests and Levites as 'sons'.[69]

The linkage between David and Josiah is borne out by the latter's attempt to extend his rule to the northern tribes (2 Kings 23.15–20), an endeavour which is applauded elsewhere as quintessentially characteristic of the Davidic line, past and future.[70] In this connection, it does not go unnoticed that in the broader Hebrew canon Josiah also acquires a distinctively priestly shading. When the text of Zechariah looks forward to the re-establishment of the Davidic dynasty (Zech. 3.8–10), this is promised to occur only after the Davidic shepherd is struck (13.7–9), and only after the piercing of one who is mourned – with overtones of the atoning Isaac – like an 'only child' and 'a firstborn', with a grief comparable only to that experienced at Megiddo (12.10–11). Of course the famed mourning at Megiddo followed the battlefield death of Josiah, mortally pierced by arrow.[71] Thus Zechariah 12—13 not only

---

[68] 2 Chron. 30.26.

[69] 2 Chron. 29.11. So Throntveit 2003: 117–18, followed by Klein 2012: 413–14. Williamson (1982: 351) comes close to saying as much: 'Thus in Hezekiah's recapitulation of Solomon's achievements it is as though the Chronicler is taking us back prior to the point of division where the one Israel is united around a single temple under the authority of the Davidic king.'

[70] As Laato (1992: 188) observes, 'the pan-Israelite ideology presented in Ezek 37:15ff corresponds to Josiah's attempt to restore the Davidic Empire.'

[71] 2 Kings 23.29–30; 2 Chron. 35.22–25.

implicitly depends on a typological correlation between Josiah and the future Davidic messiah, but also seeks to underscore the former's death at Megiddo, itself a theodicean conundrum (how does one explain the death of a good king like Josiah anyway?), as the vicarious absorption of divine wrath.[72] Apart from sheer coincidence, that Hezekiah and Josiah were remembered as stand-out *priestly* exemplars of the Davidic type cannot be unrelated to their shared attempts to reunify the tribes. If these two Judean kings are the lone exceptions to the Hebrew canon's unwritten rule forbidding post-Solomonic kings from wearing the ephod (literally or metaphorically), they are both exceptions which prove 'the rule' as I am now explaining it. The assumption of quasi-priestly roles (in the case of Hezekiah) and the posthumous ascription of priestly atoning functions (as in the case of Josiah) most likely bear some connection to their shared aspirations for a reunified confederacy, after the pattern established by David and Solomon.

To be clear, I am not arguing that the historical David and historical Solomon were the only kings in Israel's history to 'wear the ephod', or that the historical Hezekiah and the historical Josiah were the two kings after Solomon who came closest to doing so. The issue at hand is not what really happened between court and temple in the post-Davidic era, which is historically inaccessible. Rather we are more interested in how Second-Temple Judaism received the story of the Davidic dynasty as it had been shaped by collective redaction. More to the point, we are interested in the potential theological implications of the same story and how these in turn may have shaped first-century thinking.

In this spirit, the sacerdotal behaviour of David and Solomon and the future Davidide, together with the quasi-priestly functions associated with Hezekiah and Josiah, demand some theological explanation – more exactly, a historical reconstruction of Second-Temple Judaism's theological line of reasoning. In my view, the scriptural understanding guiding the depiction of these Davidic figures somehow involved the operative assumption that Israel's *political unity was the sufficient and necessary condition for the convergence of the royal and priestly roles in the idealized kingdom*, the moment at which, according to Zechariah's vision, Joshua's antitype would serve as 'a priest on his throne'.[73] To put this in negative terms, post-exilic Judaism deemed the dissolution of the tribes to be problematic on several levels. First, once the northern and southern tribes separated politically, falling under the rule of two kings as opposed to one king, it was obviously no longer possible to consider Israel as the one people of God. In the scriptural tradition, this fracturing of sociopolitical unity – exacerbated by the exile – had deleterious vertical entailments, insofar as such divisions obviated both the unicity and

[72] So Laato 1992: 290–4; cf. 2 Kings 23.26–30.
[73] Zech. 6.13. I agree with VanderKam (2004: 40–1) that the NRSV's translation of 'by his throne' is 'most unlikely' (40).

reign of God.[74] The text of Zechariah 14.9 ('And the LORD will become king over all the earth; on that day the LORD will be one and his name one'), understood as part of a broader hope for a reunified Judah and Israel (11.7, 14), is particularly instructive. From the ancient Jewish viewpoint, the splintering of the confederation meant nothing less than the kingdom of God's migration from the domain of present historical reality to the realm of future eschatological possibility. Likewise, until the regathering of the tribes, God's status as the one God would remain in question, even as the practical realities associated with Israel's political disarray could not but impinge on divine unicity.

Labouring under our own post-Enlightenment categories, neatly separating what we perceive of God (epistemology) from what is objectively true about God (metaphysics), modern readers may struggle with such concepts. But this should not prevent us from recognizing that in the Jewish mind, pending the full restoration of the scattered tribes, the very worship of the one true and reigning God – national obedience to Judaism's cardinal rule of faith, the Shema – would be forestalled. If the collective submission of a politically unified Israel was prerequisite to the proper worship of the one God Yahweh, then the post-exilic priesthood was by definition a kind of stopgap awaiting an eschatological royal-priestly figure who would in some sense be more priest than the priests themselves. Meanwhile, the perpetuation of the priesthood as an office separate from the royal office was an accommodation to unseemly religio-political circumstances which stood in stark contrast to the ideal which had been tantalizingly realized under David and Solomon.

The priestly David and 'Son of David' according to Psalm 110

To lend further support to this argument, I turn now to the evidence afforded by the post-exilic text of Psalm 110, a psalm which has a central interest in David and the Son of David with specific reference to their priestly roles.[75] Here the psalmist reflects on the nature of that role with reference to the shadowy royal priest of Genesis 14. The full text reads as follows:

> The LORD says to my LORD, 'Sit at my right hand until I make your enemies a footstool for your feet.' [2]The LORD will send out from Zion your mighty sceptre and you will rule in the midst of your foes. [3]Yours is the dominion in the day of your power, in the brilliance of your holy ones. From the womb of the morning I have begotten you. [4]The LORD has sworn and will not change his mind, 'You are a priest for ever according to the order of Melchizedek.' [5]The Lord is at your right hand; he has shattered into pieces kings on the day of his wrath. [6]He will judge among the nations; he shall fill up the corpses; he

---

[74] Mal. 2.10; Zech. 14.9.
[75] Forty years ago, Hay (1989 (1973): 19) declared the pre-exilic origins of Psalm 110 'the majority opinion'. Notwithstanding less-than-convincing attempts to discern Hasmonean fingerprints in the psalm's structure, it seems that no arguments have successfully altered this situation. See Granerød 2010: 181–8; *pace* Nordheim 2008: 5–22. The issue is finally immaterial to my argument.

will shatter heads on the earth. [7]He will drink from the stream by the way; therefore he will lift up his head.[76]

Perhaps the first readers of this psalm were as puzzled as Jesus' first-century hearers when it came to identifying the one whom David addresses as 'my lord'.[77] We suspect that most reasoned, along with a number of modern-day biblical scholars, that there was no better candidate than Solomon, who ascended to the throne during David's lifetime. In this case, the psalm would have been interpreted as a reflection on Solomon's enthronement and, by extension, on the covenant issued in 2 Samuel 7. It is likely that when the psalmist asserts David and Solomon's induction into the order of Melchizedek, this is with some reflection on their cultic initiatives.[78] The LXX's decision to render the Hebrew ('*al-dibrātî malkî-ṣedeq*, 'for the sake of Melchizedek' or 'on account of Melchizedek') of Psalm 110.4 (= Ps. 109.4 LXX) as 'according to the order of Melchizedek (*kata tēn taxin Melchisedek*)' is evidence that as we draw closer to the first-century world of Jesus, interpretative tradition was concerned to reinforce the purple thread stretched between the royal priest Melchizedek and David/Solomon. Whatever connection David was thought to have had with Melchizedek in the original writing of the psalm (when the text must have been composed as part of an attempt to buttress the religio-political position of the Davidic line by connecting it with the legacy of the Jerusalem-based priest-king *par excellence*), its reception in the Hellenistic period betrays intensifying expectation for a coming *priestly* son of David.

At the same time, the key role which Psalm 110 ascribes to Jerusalem could not have been easily missed. Because (for the psalmist) the Davidic king could not take his throne until Yahweh had first properly taken *his* throne at the temple in Jerusalem (Ps. 110.1–2 (Ps. 109.1–2 LXX)), even the most convincingly secured throne would be inconsequential apart from centralized worship in Zion.[79] According to the vision of Psalm 110, the political (re)unification of the tribes, the same tribes' cultic anchoring in Zion and the permanent installation of the Davidic ruler in Zion as priest-king were together the non-negotiable elements of the complete eschatological package.[80] Of course the priestly rule of God's people *from Zion* (the very conditions which uniquely obtained under David and Solomon) was a necessary condition for the full realization of not only Psalm 110, but also Psalm 89 and 2 Samuel 7. All this is to say that, at least according to these texts, the terms of the Davidic covenant could not have finally been realized apart from the Melchizedekian fusion of the royal and priestly roles within the appointed centralized cultus. The issue of space was equally if not more important than

---

[76] Psalm 109 LXX (= Psalm 110 MT/Eng.); the translation is my own.

[77] In the first century, the Davidic origins of the psalm seem to have been unquestioned.

[78] See the excellent discussion in Hahn 2009: 184–95; also, Ishida 1977: 139–40.

[79] Zion's centrality in the Davidic era can hardly be overstated; see, e.g., Hayes 1963.

[80] P. Abadie (1999: 166) essentially makes the same point when he writes: 'The Davidic election and the primacy of Jerusalem are two expressions of the unity of Israel'.

the issue of genealogy.[81] From the Second-Temple perspective, once Israel's worship had been frustrated by the sundering of the kingdom, once too the logical movement from centralization (2 Samuel 6) to worship (2 Samuel 7) had been reversed from worship (1 Kings 8) to decentralization (1 Kings 12), subsequent kings were again obliged to delegate the priestly vocation which would have under more ideal circumstances fallen to them.[82]

If Psalm 110 is any indication (and I think it is), then as far as Second-Temple readers of Scripture were concerned, David and Solomon were seen as uniquely bearing the mantle first carried by the Zion-based priest-king Melchizedek.[83] This of course would have had significant eschatological implications. Because the regathering of 12 tribes would have implied the renewal of the Melchizedekian (Davidic/Solomonic) jurisdiction, as envisaged by Psalm 110, Israel's restoration would have probably also implied a displacement of priesthoods, whereby the familiar present temple hierarchy with its line of succession would be forced to give way to a new priesthood, after the order of Melchizedek.

This helps explains why the supporters of the (second-century BCE) much-disputed Hasmonean dynasty relied so heavily on this text in its flattering descriptions of the high priest Simon and his successors, a dynasty which likewise combined the priestly and royal offices *à la* Melchizedek.[84] Their dependence on Psalm 110 comes to the fore not least through their propensity to identify members of the dynasty as 'priests of the Most High'. The divine epithet 'Most High' is rare in the Jewish scriptures, occurring most frequently in the narrative relating to Melchizedek (Gen. 14.18–20), where it occurs three times. From there it is picked up in Daniel (in reference to the Son of Man), and then by *Jubilees* and Sirach (often in reference to the Hasmoneans).[85] In Genesis, *Jubilees* and Sirach the phrase 'Most High' is consistently used in reference to an officiating priest; as for Daniel, this may or may not be granted, though I will maintain exactly as much below. At any rate, by identifying themselves as 'priests of the Most High', the Hasmonean rulers sought to reinforce the claim that they had achieved Israel's focal hope – a reunited kingdom centred on a Jerusalem-based temple operating under the auspices of a Melchizedekian king-priest. By asserting themselves in this way, the Hasmoneans may have met with stiff resistance (not least from the early Qumran community), but we have no evidence that the theological assumptions undergirding this assertion, the merging of the royal and priestly

---

[81] Similarly, as Jeremias (1969: 134–5) observes, the burden of the prophetic witness against the northern kingdoms pertains not to their decision to secede from the Davidic line but to their choice to eschew worship in the one true temple.

[82] Similarly, Regev 2013: 100.

[83] So also Hahn 2009: 187–94, also citing a number of other supporting voices.

[84] See Nordheim 2008: 221–34, where the author treats 1 Macc. 14.41; *Ass. Mos.* 6.1; *Jub.* 3.1; *Testament of Levi* 8 and 18; see also Sir. 47.8–10.

[85] Dan. 2.18, 19 (OG); 3.23 (OG); 4.14, 24, 34, 37(2) (OG); 7.18, 22, 25, 27 (OG); Sir. 4.10; 7.9, 15; 9.15; 12.2, 6; 17.26, 27, etc.; *Jub.* 7.36; 12.19; 13.16, 29; 16.18, 27; 20.9; 21.20; etc.

offices, were themselves challenged.[86] After all, it was a claim certainly consistent with the trajectory of eschatological expectation articulated by Psalm 110, and supported by the broader witness of Jewish prophetic expectation.

Yet between the royal and the priestly concerns, the priestly remains paramount. This seems to hold true as least as early as the fourth-century (BCE) Chronicles, where, as Ken Pomykala observes, 'neither the text nor the context of Chronicles supports a messianic or royalist interpretation. Instead, in the hands of the Chronicler the Davidic dynasty tradition subserved a particular vision of the Jerusalem *cultic* community in the late Persian period'.[87] The same eclipsing of royal by priestly concerns continues down into the Hasmonean period. This is patently evidenced, for example, in Ben Sira's panegyric dedicated to Simon *in his capacity as high priest* (Sirach 50). As Eyal Regev summarizes, it is not so much the case that the Hasmoneans usurped religious authority as a way of shoring up political power; rather they 'regarded themselves primarily as religious leaders . . . not political or military figures who had invaded the cultic realm, but priests and religious leaders that had been pushed by the hand of God to rule the Jewish people and protect the Temple'.[88] In the Hasmonean period, the priestly and royal roles merged freely in the person of Israel's chief executive.[89] But these rulers were priests first and royal figures second: this was the logic of the Judaism of Jesus' day.

Jesus the priestly Son of David

With these considerations in view, the best explanation for Jesus' self-identification as a distinctively priestly 'son of David' was his conviction that the political conditions which were expected to obtain under the rule of the eschatological Davidide, the restoration of the tribes, was now about to obtain under his own rule. If Jesus in fact operated by this line of reasoning, then this would certainly explain why his acquisition of the 'son of David' title is typically accompanied by intimations of priesthood, just as we have in the synoptic record. For the historical Jesus, to be the 'son of David' was to take on the ephod of the eschatological priest.

---

[86] Assuming that the Qumran community was anti-Hasmonean, it is interesting to note that the covenanters shared the Hasmoneans' two-office conception, but may have expected these roles to be carried by two separate messiahs, a messiah of Aaron and a messiah of Israel (CD 12.23; 14.19; 19.10–11; 20.1; cf. 1QS 9.2); this point has been disputed (see, e.g. Abegg 1995; Hurst 1999). In any event, it cannot be the case that Qumran's eschatological David is altogether emptied of cultic significance, since he remains the 'stone of Zion' (4Q522 9 2.4) and under the advisement of priestly cabinet (11QT^a 56–59). In any event, too, in the community's expectation of the future David, 'the office and role of the king is not greatly emphasized and is overshadowed by the theocratic ideal' (Blenkinsopp 2013: 167). For a review of texts, see Coulot 1999; Chae 2006: 126–53.

[87] Pomykala 1995: 111; emphasis added.

[88] Regev 2013: 102, also 103–28. See also Angel 2010: 257–95; Fletcher-Louis 2016: 221.

[89] VanderKam 2004: 240–393, *passim*.

This account squares with the presentation of the historical Jesus I have advanced to this point. First, if David's anointing (1 Samuel 16) was a symbolic moment that looked forward to the shepherd boy's ascension as king-priest, Jesus must have interpreted his own baptism as playing an analogous role in his own ministry. As the anointed Son of Psalm 2, Jesus saw himself as the rightfully installed Davidic Son, even as he was also the final Isaac, charged with restoring worship in Jerusalem. Second, in reciting the Lord's Prayer, which called for – among other things – the coming of the kingdom, Jesus' disciples must have seen the praying of this prayer as a way of moving towards the realization of Yahweh's promise to David: 'I will establish [your] kingdom'.[90] For Jesus, the coming of the kingdom meant the coming not just of any kingdom but specifically of the Davidic kingdom, which included (per Psalm 110) the installation of a new priesthood designed to supplant the priesthood instituted by Moses. Third, the strategy by which Jesus sought to accomplish this goal also followed on the model of David. If David summoned a new caste of priests and Levites from throughout the land for the purpose of establishing centralized worship (1 Chronicles 13), Jesus' itinerant preaching tour through the Judean countryside was probably, in part, a re-enactment of this very same nationwide gathering process. I have already argued (Chapter 3) that Jesus spoke his parables in order to separate out the holy from the unholy, the clean from the unclean. Now it also becomes clear that those who responded positively to Jesus' teaching would, on the model of the Davidic reordination, distinguish themselves as candidates for the newly emerging priesthood. Through his preaching tours the restoration of the tribes was already underway. Likewise, Jesus' recurring emphasis on suffering and *peirasmos* also finds a suitable match in the life of David. While an earlier generation of biblical scholarship posited the construct of the 'righteous sufferer' as a way of explaining Jesus' own calling of suffering, it must be pointed out that the staple texts supporting this construct are the psalms of lament associated with David.[91] Because David's life was fraught with suffering and opposition, Jesus seems to have surmised, he too was destined to inherit the same lot.[92] This narrative is not unrelated to the narrative of the Son of Man.

Summary

In this chapter, I have argued that the historical Jesus asserted himself as the Son of David. This assertion was not so much a way of affirming any particular ontological status (though such ascriptions would of course later be emphasized by post-Easter believers) but more simply his way of signalling

---

[90] 2 Sam. 7.12.
[91] See Johnson 2009.
[92] Notably, the earliest reference to a Davidic messiah in the rabbinica occurs in the *Mekilta* on Exod. 16.26 and in *Soṭah* 9.15, where emphasis is placed on the 'sorrows of the messiah'.

an eschatological identity involving his priestly oversight of Israel's restoration. This conclusion follows from a fresh exploration of certain Davidic traditions that would have played a major part in informing Jesus' sense of calling. While it is true that Second-Temple Judaism clung to the hope of a future, royal son of David, it is equally true that the chief significance of this eschatological figure was not in his exercise of a political role but rather in his accomplishing the distinctively priestly task for restoring the cultic space. Even if Jesus' peers looked forward to the final enthronement of the messianic David-figure as the turning point at which the Gentiles would be vanquished and Israel's political autonomy restored, these objectives were never ends in themselves. Instead, the establishment of an uncontested Davidic ruler, resulting in the unification of the tribes and guaranteeing a centralized cultic site, was but the necessary political precondition for Israel's fundamentally cultic vocation: one people gathered in one space worshipping the one God. If the bulk of Second-Temple Judaism expected the eschatological Son of David to install a monarchic hagiocracy (i.e. rule by a royal priest), as I have argued, then Jesus' claim to be 'son of David' implies an agenda that is fundamentally oriented to the temple.

5

The identity of the Son of Man

For all we know, Jesus was a handsome and clever young man, with a comfortable home and happy disposition, who united some of the best blessings of existence, while living nearly 30 years in the world with little to threaten him personally. But if he had managed to keep his head down for so many years, all that seems to have changed after his baptism. For at this point, history tells us, Jesus began to draw together his own following, perform miracles and make curious yet compelling assertions. Many of these assertions were flatly enigmatic; others were – once the dots were connected – downright controversial. Of these, perhaps none was more enigmatic or controversial than his association with the Son of Man, an association which, clearly affirmed before the high priest Caiaphas, would ultimately seal his fate. But just what 'Son of Man' meant on the lips of Jesus, well, that's a matter that deserves a chapter or two unto itself.

Almost a century ago, T. W. Manson opined that the problems raised by the enigmatic phrase 'Son of Man' are 'among the most complex and difficult in New Testament study'.[1] Half a century later, Eugene Boring would write that the scholarly discussion surrounding the figure was 'a veritable mine field'.[2] Today, the terrain remains no less complex, no less treacherous. Even many of those mines which seem to have been defused turn out to have been merely repositioned. Much of what used to count as 'the assured results' of Son of Man scholarship has long since been modified even if not altogether rejected; other theories once considered fringe have gained new life. Today, no less than in Manson's day, the field of Son of Man studies continues to be fraught with booby traps.

The traps are countless simply because the questions are as well. What does the phrase 'Son of Man' mean? To whom or to what is the phrase applied? And is it applied by the Evangelists or by Jesus? Is it a title or a circumlocution for something else, perhaps 'I' or humanity in general? If it is a title, is it a messianic title? If so, when was it recognized as such? What scriptural text or texts inform the concept of Son of Man? If Daniel 7 is among such texts, how is that mysterious chapter itself to be understood? Even if we manage to get squared away on this last question, how can we be sure that our reading

---

[1] Manson 1951 (1931): 211.
[2] Boring 1982: 239.

of Daniel 7 is similar to Jesus'? On all these fronts there are questions aplenty but frustratingly few certainties.

Yet the myriad of variables need not translate into a counsel of despair. Even by the end of this chapter I believe it will be possible to hypothe-size a provisional model that addresses such questions while integrating fresh arguments made here with previous Son of Man research. Accordingly, the present chapter is divided into two parts. In the first part, I revive a well-mooted but undersubscribed argument, namely, that in the final recension of the book of Daniel the Son of Man is being symbolically rendered as Israel's eschatological high priest, and that without necessarily any literal ascription of superterrestrial qualities. While this is not to deny potential adumbrations of Davidic messianism in Daniel 7, my point is to show that the book's final redactor advances the Son of Man not so much as a wishful assertion of Davidic ideology (which is at any rate absent from the remainder of the book) but rather as the eschatological resolution to a very specific problem: the defiled temple under Antiochus IV. This finding, when combined with the argument I have been advancing so far (i.e. that Jesus self-consciously took on the role of eschatological high priest), makes it plausible to maintain, as I do in the second part of this chapter, that the historical Jesus at least occasionally uttered the phrase 'Son of Man' in a quasi-titular sense under inspiration from Daniel 7.13. In this section, given indications from Mark 2.1–10 par., the scenario I am hypothesizing is confirmed: the evidence from this isolated pericope suggests that the historical Jesus not only loosely associated himself with the Danielic Son of Man but also did so – at least in this text – in the light of the latter's unique priestly role.

In its favour, my argument need not assume that the Son of Man had already been established as an eschatological apocalyptic figure in the Judaism of Jesus' day. Nor will I be detained by considerations of the Son of Man's presence in such texts as *4 Ezra* and the *Similitudes of Enoch*, texts which in any case cannot be shown to have been material to Jesus' usage. Finally, I will temporarily suspend judgement as to whether Jesus thought of himself as the exalted Son of Man in an exclusive sense. Though, to tip my hand, I would urge for now that the highly symbolic nature of Daniel 7 should in principle make us leery of locking ourselves into a (Lockean) instrumentalist understanding of the prophetic language, which might lead to the rash surmise that Jesus summoned the Danielic Son of Man in order to posit a bald equivalency between sign (the Son of Man) and signified (Jesus himself). While any one of these pre-judgements is bound to enchant some readers who are familiar with the Son of Man discussion, even as it is equally bound to alienate others, I hope to have reduced my assumptions to a bare minimum. And where such assumptions are inevitable, I hope that these in turn will be finally vindicated by the persuasiveness of my conclusions.

The identity of the Son of Man in Daniel

The cultic orientation of the book of Daniel

In order to appreciate the Son of Man within the context of Daniel 7, it is important to appreciate the chapter's context within the book as a whole, beginning with Daniel 1—6, a stretch of text with definite cultic concerns.[3] In the opening verses of the book of Daniel, Nebuchadnezzar is introduced – in striking semblance to Antiochus IV – as one who not only transfers the holy 'vessels of the house of God' into the treasury of his own gods (Dan. 1.2) but also puts the nobility's purity at risk (1.8–16). Following the dream sequence of Daniel 2, the Babylonian tyrant then erects an idolatrous 'image' (MT: *ṣelem*; DanTh: *eikōn*) (3.1), which is 'by decree' (v. 10) to be an object of worship for 'all the peoples' and 'nations' (v. 7). For the thoughtful Jewish reader, the implicit contrast between the pagan image, as the humanly mandated focal point of universal worship, and Israel's temple, as the eschatological focal point of universal worship, is obvious enough. The point is reinforced by the idol's physical dimensions, as Sharon Pace points out:

> [t]he height of the statue is the same as the width of the first temple and is exactly twice the first temple's height (1 Kgs 6:2). In addition, the statue is the same height as the second temple (Ezra 6:3). The choice of the width of the statue similarly recalls the width of the support beams of both the first and second temples (1 Kgs 6:6; Ezek 41:1). In addition to these interesting connotations of the statue's dimensions, the description of its gold recalls the biblical descriptions of the temple as well.[4]

The idolatrous image of the pagan ruler and the true image enshrined in the very architecture of Israel's temple are mutually proportionate, highlighting the former's usurpation of human loyalties more appropriately directed to Yahweh's sacred space.[5] Nor can the Babylonians' competing account of proper worship be detached from concomitant claims of authority – claims which run counter to Yahweh-piety but are eventually refuted. Whereas Nebuchadnezzar had promulgated his own solemn decrees (Dan. 2.5, 8, 13, 15; 3.10), these are answered soon enough by a set of heavenly decrees (4.17, 24). Similarly, Belshazzar's flagrant profanation of the holy vessels (5.1–4) is met by the dooming inscription on the wall (5.24–28). Thus the book of Daniel both poses and resolves outstanding questions revolving around the intrinsic superiority and authority of Yahweh vis-à-vis the counterfeit self-proclaimed deities of the pagan kingdoms. They are questions of course which have direct relevance to the cultic sphere. In fact, given the recurring

---

[3] On this see above all Vogel 2010.
[4] Pace 2008: 90.
[5] On the temple as an image of the 'Glory-Spirit', see Kline 1977: 39–46.

pagan infringement on Israel's cultus in the post-Maccabean context, the issue as to whom and on what basis beleaguered Israel must direct its worship had never been more relevant. I will return to this thematic antithesis and its expression in Daniel's literary structure below (Chapter 7).

The book of Daniel also intimates that faithfulness to Yahweh will be used for redemptive purposes, though not without a price. In Daniel 6, the prophet is thrown into the lions' den on account of his piety, only finally to be delivered. Observing the structural parallel between Daniel's deliverance from persecution and the *todah*-cycle pattern of the temple thanksgiving offering, John Bergsma accurately describes the narrative action of Daniel 6 as a juxtaposition of two mutually opposed liturgies, with the figure of Daniel standing against the 'false cult . . . of the state embodied in the emperor' and maintaining 'fidelity to the true cult, with its ties to the Jerusalem temple and its liturgy'.[6] In retrospect, divine intervention working through Daniel's commitment to the cultus and consequent suffering proves to be instrumental in triggering Darius' volte-face, prompting the pagan ruler even to issue a decree on behalf of Yahweh's kingdom (6.25–28). In retrospect, too, the clash of the two competing liturgies seems to have been almost necessary for God's purposes, for it is precisely through Daniel's agonistic confrontation that Israel's inviolate sacred space is secured. The figure of Daniel is presented not just as a moral exemplar of faithfulness but more specifically as a suffering atoning figure, whose steadfastness unto death has allowed Yahweh's kingdom to triumph over the politically powerful, pagan competition. Given a thin but nonetheless discernible line between Daniel as the Son of Man (8.17) and the Son of Man of 7.13, the reader suspects an intentional parallel between Daniel's atoning conflict in Daniel 6 and the Son of Man's confrontation in Daniel 7.

Backgrounds to the Danielic Son of Man

The central cultic concerns of Daniel 1—6, I believe, lay important groundwork for our understanding of Daniel 7, and within this chapter, Daniel 7.13. The verse and its immediate co-text reads as follows:

> [9]As I watched, thrones were set in place, and an Ancient One took his throne; his clothing was white as snow, and the hair of his head like pure wool; his throne was fiery flames, and its wheels were burning fire. [10]A stream of fire issued and flowed out from his presence. A thousand thousand served him, and ten thousand times ten thousand stood attending him. The court sat in judgement, and the books were opened.
> [11]I watched then because of the noise of the arrogant words that the horn was speaking. And as I watched, the beast was put to death, and its body destroyed and given over to be burned with fire. [12]As for the rest of the beasts, their dominion was taken away, but their lives were prolonged for a season and

---

[6]   Bergsma 2009: 60.

a time. [13]As I watched in the night visions, I saw one like a human being coming with the clouds of heaven. And he came to the Ancient One and was presented before him. [14]To him was given dominion and glory and kingship, that all peoples, nations, and languages should serve him. His dominion is an everlasting dominion that shall not pass away, and his kingship is one that shall never be destroyed.[7]

This passage marks the climax of a highly symbolic narrative, one which, drawing on the familiar imagery and plotline of the Ancient Near Eastern *Chaoskampf*, depicts not only the conflict between the pagan kingdoms represented by the four beasts, but also more pertinently the conflict between these same four and the Son of Man.[8] Once the Ancient of Days takes his seat for judgement, the verdict against the final beast follows soon enough, and dominion is transferred to the Son of Man in the presence of the Ancient One (Dan. 7.9–14). But none of this occurs apart from the sufferings of the 'holy ones' (vv. 21, 22, 25), whose connection with the Son of Man is certain in fact yet ambivalent in detail.

For our purposes, the best way to begin interpreting this surreal drama is by returning to the final form of Daniel itself, which features a fairly obvious analogy between this vision and Nebuchadnezzar's dream in Daniel 2. On comparing Daniel 2 and 7, it becomes clear that the latter chapter, pitting the four antagonistic beasts against the Son of Man, has already been anticipated by the dream sequence of the earlier chapter, which matches up a towering statue of four metallic components against a mountainous stone.[9] The composite statue is patently a symbol for four great kingdoms (the Babylonians, the Medes, the Persians and the Greeks), ultimately yielding to an expanding stone/mountain that fills the whole earth.[10] This stone, the foundation stone 'cut . . . not by human hands' (i.e. an unhewn stone fit for cultic purposes; cf. Deut. 27.6; Josh. 8.31; 1 Macc. 4.47), is none other than the eschatological temple (Dan. 2.35, 44, NIV).

Connecting the dots across the chapters, then, the reader infers that the four unclean beasts of Daniel 7 (including the 'other horn' of Dan. 7.20, the chief desecrator Antiochus IV) are the counterparts to the pagan kingdoms introduced in Daniel 2. More than that, given the structural parallel between Daniel 2 on the one side, where four pagan kingdoms succumb to the temple, and Daniel 7 on the other side, where four unclean beasts meet their match in the Son of Man, we might reasonably expect – especially given the

---

[7] Dan. 7.9–14.
[8] The influence of the *Chaoskampf* tradition on Daniel 7 is all but incontestable; see Anderson 1984: 78; Goldingay 1989: 160; Collins, Cross and Collins 1993: 296; Angel 2006: 100–1. While the precise background to Daniel 7 could possibly be refined further (for example, John Walton (2001) suggests the *Anzu* myth as a backdrop), this would be irrelevant to my argument.
[9] The homology between Daniel 2 and 7 is regularly observed, e.g. Goldingay 1989: 148, 158; Lucas 2002: 185, 188; Boyarin 2012: 153.
[10] Alternatively: Babylon, Media-Persia, Greece and Rome.

Hebrew pun between *'eben* 'stone' and *ben* 'son' – the Son of Man to carry out a role similar to that of the eschatological temple. We might expect in other words that 'one like a Son of Man' is someone like an eschatological high priest waging something like an eschatological war (after all, fighting eschatological battles is what eschatological priests do!).[11] On this surmise, it would seem that the Ancient of Days is God himself; the Son of Man, none other than his high priest.

The surmise gains credence on re-evaluating various lines of evidence which, though marshalled in previous scholarship, have remained curiously overlooked.[12] First, whereas contemporary readers of this chapter have struggled to make sense of what Carsten Colpe describes as the dramatic 'differences between figure and interpretation', not unrelated to the passage's jarring clash of temporal and otherworldly concerns, I suggest there is no better way to account for this than by setting the scene of Daniel 7 in the one space where the mundane and transcendent spheres were thought to converge: the inner sanctuary of the temple. For although Yahweh was regularly understood as being enthroned in heaven (e.g. Ps. 103.19; Isa. 66.1), it was no less true that the God of Israel, paradoxically, was also thought to be seated between the cherubim in the Holy of Holies, the spatiotemporal extension of the heavenly throne room (1 Sam. 4.4; 2 Kings 19.15; 1 Chron. 13.6; Pss. 80.1; 99.1; Isa. 37.16; etc.). Between the invisible kingdom of God on the one side and the visible hierocracy of Israel on the other, the Holy of Holies was the intervening liminal space.

The human agent uniquely associated with that glorious space was of course the high priest himself, who in Second-Temple Jewish accounts takes on a transcendent, even supernatural quality.[13] This is certainly the case, for example, in the *Letter of Aristeas*, where the author declares that any man encountering the accoutred high priest 'would think that he had come out of this world into another one'.[14] Alternatively, consider the sentiments of *Leviticus Rabbah* (16.17), picked up by Philo and Origen, which maintain that on entering the Holy of Holies, the high priest ceases 'to be a man'.[15] Once Daniel 7's metaphysically hybrid quality is set against this thought world, we have grounds for situating this scene within the divine room in heaven – notwithstanding the absence of any explicitly stated *mise en scène*.

Meanwhile Daniel's description of the throne room's uncanny accoutrements, the fiery throne and wheels (Dan. 7.9), are almost certainly tapping into Ezekiel's Merkabah vision (Ezek. 1.15–21; 10.1).[16] While these elements seem to receive relatively scant attention in the secondary literature dedicated

---

[11] See Angel 2010: 196–202.
[12] Notably, Black 1975; Lacocque 1979; Fletcher-Louis 1997b.
[13] As witnessed, say, in 4Q453 2a–b; 4Q545 1.
[14] *Let. Aris.* 99.
[15] For further discussion, see Stökl Ben Ezra 2003: 110–11, 125 n. 243.
[16] This is very similar to *1 En.* 14.22 ('a sea of fire burnt around him and a great fire stood before him'), part of a scene seemingly set in the heavenly temple.

to Daniel 7, in my judgement the significance of the comparison with Ezekiel 1 can hardly be overstated. If Jews of the late Second-Temple period interpreted Ezekiel's chariot as the throne of God, and this throne was also thought to be situated in the heart of the heavenly temple, it then follows that the symbolic action of Daniel 7 conveys not a changing of the royal guards but a changing of the royal high priests.

The temple setting of Daniel 7 is further supported by the likelihood that the conflict between the four anatomically blended beasts and the Son of Man would have been interpreted by Second-Temple audiences as a fundamentally *cultic* confrontation. In a monograph-length study dedicated to the subject, David Bryan demonstrates that the bizarre monsters' composite features are meant to mark them off as *Mischwesen*, embodied transgressions of natural boundaries and therefore emblems of uncleanness.[17] The hybrid character of the beasts would have also underscored that which would have been already quickly acknowledged by Daniel's readers, namely, that *the* issue confronting Israel in the aftermath of Antiochus IV's abominations was the restoration of compromised sacred space.[18] While this point is not uncommonly granted by commentators on Daniel, it is seldom reasoned out that if this is true, then the Son of Man, precisely as the one poised to reverse Israel's ritual uncleanness, is almost certainly assuming a priestly function. After all, in Hebrew tradition, as in the Ancient Near East in general, the task of repristinating the sanctuary required high-priestly oversight as a rule of thumb.[19]

The ascription of Adamic traits to the Danielic Son of Man provides further evidence that the superhero of Daniel 7 was in fact intended to be priestly.[20] The Adam-esque quality of the Son of Man initially follows from several considerations. In the first place, in Daniel 7 the Aramaic phrasing behind the English translation 'Son of Man' includes the word *'ĕnoš*, which in the targums also occurs in Genesis 1.26 in connection with Adam as the 'image of God'. The point becomes more impressive on recognizing the narrative-structural parallelism between the Adamic image of God, who is mandated to have dominion over the beasts 'on the earth' (Gen. 1.26), and the Son of Man, who finally achieves dominion over the four beasts 'on the earth' (Dan 7.17, GkTheo). In much the same way, parallels between Psalm 8 and Daniel 7 – both texts picturing a 'Son of Man' who receives 'glory' and 'dominion' over the 'beasts' – suggest that the Danielic Son of Man figure

[17] See Leviticus 11 and Deuteronomy 14; Bryan 1995: 234–3, 247–8. Adumbrations of the same point are found in Ford 1979: 204–6; Porter 1983: 63–86; 95–118.
[18] Bryan 1995: 213–15.
[19] On the ANE parallels to the restorations of Jehoash and Josiah, and the close involvement of high-priestly leadership in both, see Na'aman 2013; Bedford 2001. Other parade examples of priestly restoration projects include Ezra (Ezra 1—6) and Judas Maccabeus (1 Macc. 4.41–51); though the latter's priestly credentials may have been disputed they were nonetheless clearly asserted by the Hasmoneans themselves (see VanderKam 2004: 241–4; Wise 2005: 352–9).
[20] On the connections between Adam and the Danielic Son of Man in ancient Jewish reception history, see Marcus 2003a and 2003b; also Goulder 2002: 25.

was intended as an extension of the psalmist's Adamic Son of Man.[21] The linking of the two figures implies less of an ontological co-identification and more of a shared functionality. So, then, if much recent scholarship is correct in asserting Adam's priestly role (at least as he was interpreted in Second-Temple Judaism), then Daniel's Son of Man is likewise a strong candidate for a priestly role.[22]

An even more striking and significant point of comparison between the Danielic Son of Man and Adam pertains to their shared role as recipients of worship. In Daniel 7.14 the Son of Man is marked out as one who legitimately receives worship on behalf of Yahweh. Notwithstanding ancient Judaism's strict monotheistic commitments, at least certain currents within ancient Judaism accorded the same right to Adam in his ideal state. Consider the following passage from the *Life of Adam and Eve*:

> The devil replied, 'Adam, what are you telling me? It is because of you that I have been thrown out of there. When you were created, I was cast out from the presence of God and was sent out from the fellowship of the angels. When God blew into you the *breath of life* and your countenance and likeness were made *in the image of God*, Michael brought you and made (us) worship you in the sight of God, and the LORD God said, "Behold Adam! I have made you in our image and likeness." And Michael went out and called all the angels, saying, "Worship the image of the LORD God, as the LORD God has instructed"'.[23]

Here the author of *Life of Adam and Eve* clearly depicts Adam accepting worship by virtue of his status as 'the image'. Such worship was presumably legitimized on the grounds that Adam, precisely as the *imago dei*, was understood as an extension of the godhead into creation. Given the Danielic Son of Man's conceptual moorings in the figure of Adam, borne out not least by structural parallels with Adam (Genesis 1) and the psalter's Son of Man (Psalm 8), we suspect that the worship of the figure depicted in Daniel 7.14 was notionally justified, at least in the minds of many ancient Jews, by the same warrant: both Adam and Daniel's Son of Man appropriately received worship because both bore *the* image.

At the same time, we would miss the mark were we to construe Adam and the Danielic Son of Man as comprising a closed set, for the bearing of the image was in some fashion extended to the high-priestly office.[24] The extension followed on the assumption that Adam served as a prototype for the Aaronic high priest, as suggested by several lines of evidence, including intimations that Aaron's prescribed actions (Exodus 25—31) were a recapitulation of Yahweh's creative activity (much as Adam exercised his priestly role in imitation of Yahweh's creative work). More significant is the high priests'

---

[21] Goulder 2002.
[22] Beale 2004: 66–70; Morales 2015: 52; Brooke 2016; etc.
[23] *L.A.E.* 13.1—14.1.
[24] See especially Fletcher-Louis 1997b; 2004b.

bearing of the ephod, which in the Ancient Near Eastern context was the standard accessory of the divinity's idol or 'image' (*ṣelem*).[25] Because ancient Jews thought of the succession of high priests as bearing the Adamic image *ex officio*, it was even sometimes deemed appropriate for the high priest himself to receive worship on Yahweh's behalf.[26] The tantalizing parallels between Adam and the Son of Man find their principal point of intersection in the high-priestly *imago dei*.[27] But this also means that the Son of Man, for all his apparently unique attributes, equally typifies the relatively mundane office of the high priest.

Having come to terms with the Danielic Son of Man as the high-priestly image of God, we are now in a better position to make sense of the final redactor's interest in the motifs of written edicts and 'image'. As I have already mentioned, the author of Daniel recurs to decretal images in the interest of demonstrating the superiority of Yahweh's authority. Over and against multiple references to Nebuchadnezzar's written 'decrees' (Dan. 2.5, 8, 13, 15), including one which demands that 'all peoples' and nations worship his image on pain of death (3.10), Daniel 7.10 envisages the rolling out of a different set of universal decrees – already anticipated by the writing on the wall in 5.24–28 – contained in the heavenly books. As the eschatological counterpoint to the pagan ruler's wicked policies, these books ensure final judgement together with a scenario in which 'all peoples, nations, and languages' worship the Son of Man (7.14). The final reversal of the misguided, pagan edicts comes by way of the books opened at the resurrection (Dan. 12.1). For the final redactor of Daniel, the point is clear: the pagan rulers' policies will one day be overturned by a wholly different set of books vindicating the righteous and issuing an everlasting judgement. (I will return to this whole business of Daniel's edicts and images in Chapter 7.)

Even so, the question 'Who may rightly authorize worship?' is inseparable from another issue: the appropriate focal point of worship. In this vein, Daniel 7 announces that the Son of Man will emerge as the *true* image, as well as Yahweh's answer to the pagans' impostor 'image', passingly alluded to in the dream vision of Daniel 2 and fully introduced in Daniel 3. According to the author of Daniel, only the Son of Man, the true image and Yahweh's priestly representative, is worthy to receive worship and authorized to issue judgement. But it is only in his capacity as the officiating *priestly* image that such worship is even possible.

The Danielic Son of Man's high priestly credentials also shed much-needed light on his coming 'with the clouds' (Dan. 7.13). Even if this image may have been originally rooted in the Canaanite god Ba'al's iconic posture as 'rider on the clouds', our investigations behind the text need not eclipse the hieratic

---

[25] Provan 1999; Mauser 2000: 92; Fletcher-Louis 2004b: 89–90.

[26] As convincingly argued by Fletcher-Louis 1999; 2004a.

[27] Fletcher-Louis 2004c.

nuances that subsequent ancient Jewish readers would have teased out.[28] In the ancient Jewish imagination, clouds such as we have in Daniel 7 would have probably invoked the 'thick cloud' (Exod. 19.16) hovering over the sacred space of Mount Horeb, a scene which would set precedent for a range of post-Sinaitic theophanies, the majority of which occur in the temple.[29] The point is this: if in ancient Judaism clouds were generally associated with the divine presence, they were even more closely associated with the divine presence as it appeared at the temple. (Scholarship's broad tendency to default to the former point without sufficient consideration of the latter perhaps explains why modern interpretation of Daniel 7 has downplayed the cultic intimations of the throne room scene.) Moreover, as John J. Collins points out, the proposition that the clouds symbolize the Son of Man's unqualified divinity stumbles on the fact that the Son of Man is 'clearly subordinate to the Ancient of Days', resulting in a configuration that 'has no precedent in the biblical tradition'.[30] By reducing the clouds to an 'image of divinity', we are being at best vague and at worst altogether misleading.

In search of an explanation that does better justice to the biblical tradition, I propose the following: the ancient Jewish readers of Daniel 7 would have understood the cloud-carrying Son of Man to be a symbolic representation of a high-priestly figure undertaking rituals associated specifically with *yom kippur*. Within the rhythms of Israel's annual cultic life, clouds artificially generated in the form of incense smoke are the central prop of the Day of Atonement. Prescriptions for this practice are set out in Leviticus 16:

> The LORD said to Moses: Tell your brother Aaron not to come just at any time into the sanctuary inside the curtain before the mercy-seat that is upon the ark, or he will die; for I appear in the cloud upon the mercy-seat . . . Aaron shall present the bull as a sin offering for himself, and shall make atonement for himself and for his house; he shall slaughter the bull as a sin-offering for himself. He shall take a censer full of coals of fire from the altar before the LORD, and two handfuls of crushed sweet incense, and he shall bring it inside the curtain and put the incense on the fire before the LORD, that the cloud of the incense may cover the mercy-seat that is upon the covenant, or he will die.[31]

---

[28] On Daniel 7's background in Ba'alism, see Emerton 1958; Day 1985: 151–78; Collins, Cross and Collins 1993: 286–9. I decline to comment on the merits of this hypothesis. Yet it should be remarked that to write off the clouds simply as an element of Canaanite mythology without consideration of the Jewish redactor's creative repurposing of the image is to make the same category mistake that Collins (1993: 281) discusses, when he writes: 'To say that the one like a son of man "is" Marduk or the Canaanite Ba'al pertains to a different level of meaning than the claim that he should be identified as the archangel Michael or as a symbol for the Jewish people. It is to say that he functions in a manner similar to the way Marduk or Ba'al functions in the pagan myths. This distinction is elementary but is sometimes missed by those who polemicize against religion-historical parallels'.

[29] Lacocque (1979: 146) reckons that out of 'a total of about a hundred occurrences in Scripture, in 70% of the cases, clouds refer to Sinai, or to the Temple (see 1 Kings 8.10–11; 2 Chr. 5.13–14; 2 Macc. 2.; cf. the vision of the *Merkaba* in Ezek. 1.4 and 10.3–4)'.

[30] Collins, Cross and Collins 1993: 290.

[31] Lev. 16.2, 11–13.

On this the most holy of Jewish holy days, when the intersection between heaven and earth was made most tangible, the high priest's billowing incense not only created a firewall of personal protection in the ritual moment but also came to symbolize his unique prerogative to enter the liminal space. It is right along these lines that we can understand the pairing of clouds and high priesthood in Ben Sira's panegyric to the high priest Simon the Righteous (219–196 BCE):

> [5]How glorious he was, surrounded by the people, as he came out of the house of the curtain. [6]Like the morning star among the *clouds*, like the full moon at the festal season; [7]like the sun shining on the temple of the Most High, like the rainbow gleaming in splendid *clouds*; [8]like roses in the days of first fruits, like lilies by a spring of water, like a green shoot on Lebanon on a summer day; [9]like fire and incense in the censer, like a vessel of hammered gold studded with all kinds of precious stones; [10]like an olive tree laden with fruit, and like a cypress towering in the *clouds*. [11]When he put on his glorious robe and clothed himself in perfect splendour, when he went up to the holy altar, he made the court of the sanctuary glorious.[32]

In this collage of creational and hieratic images, the recurring cloud imagery ('among the clouds' (v. 6), 'in splendid clouds' (v. 7) and 'towering in the clouds' (v. 10)) is especially conspicuous. Undoubtedly the symbolism is deployed in the effort to legitimize Simon – pictured as having just emerged 'out of the house of the curtain' (v. 5), that is, the Holy of Holies – as the rightful high priest officiating on the Day of Atonement.[33] Not insignificantly, for the author of Sirach (written close to the time of the final form of Daniel) the most effective rhetorical strategy for confirming Simon's high-priestly status was, as it were, to take a snapshot of him on the Day of Atonement *in* the clouds – much as the Danielic phrasing 'in ['*im*] the clouds' describes the Son of Man.[34] If Sirach 50 provides the closest thing we have to a high-priestly selfie, Daniel 7 comes in as a close second.

More weighty still is the juxtaposition of clouds alongside terminology of cultic procession unique to Daniel and Leviticus. In the former text, we find clear indications of cultic self-presentation in Daniel 7.13b: 'And he came to the Ancient One and *was presented* [MT: *haqrĕbûhî*; DanTh: *prosnechthē*] before him'. On noting the Aramaic term *haqrĕbûh*, one cannot resist pointing out that where we find instances of the related Hebrew cognate (*qrb*) in the Scriptures, it is consistently within a cultic context. For example, in the lead-up to Israel's first formal priestly ordination service, Moses is instructed to take Aaron and the other brothers, and *bring them near* (MT: *haqēb*; LXX: *prosagagou*).[35] Elsewhere, the verb is used to denote the act of cultic offering,

---

[32] Sir. 50.5–11; emphasis added.
[33] The *yom kippur* setting of Ben Sira 50 is granted by the vast majority of commentators, but disputed by Fearghail 1978; Hayward 1996: 50.
[34] As emphasized by Hartman and Di Lella (1978: 206) and Collins, Cross and Collins (1993: 311 n. 297), the Aramaic preposition '*im can* mean 'on' or 'in'.
[35] Exod. 28.1; likewise Exod. 29.4, 8; 40.12, 14; Lev. 8.13; etc.

even where – in the case of young Samuel – the offering is a human being (1 Sam. 1.25).[36] On this basis, it would not be unreasonable to propose that when the Son of Man is being 'presented' before the Ancient of Days, he is either undergoing a symbolic ordination or offering himself as a sacrifice. While not entirely discounting either of these options, I suggest that more to the point is an implied analogy between the Son of Man's 'coming before' (*qrb*) the Ancient of Days 'with the clouds of heaven' in Daniel 7.13, on the one hand, and the high priest's 'coming before' (*qrb*) the Lord amid the cloud of incense in Leviticus 16.1–13, on the other. The two texts deserve full comparison:[37]

> As I watched in the night visions, I saw one like a human being coming with the <u>clouds</u> of heaven. And he came to the Ancient One and <u>was presented</u> [MT: *haqrĕbûhî*; DanTh: *prosnechthē*] before him.
>
> (Dan. 7.13)

> The Lord spoke to Moses after the death of the two sons of Aaron, when they <u>drew near</u> [*bĕqorbātām*] before the Lord and died. ²The Lord said to Moses: Tell your brother Aaron not to come just at any time into the sanctuary inside the curtain before the mercy seat that is upon the ark, or he will die; for I appear in the <u>cloud</u> [*be'ānān*] upon the mercy seat. ³Thus shall Aaron come into the holy place: with a young bull for a sin offering and a ram for a burnt offering. ⁴He shall put on the holy linen tunic, and shall have the linen undergarments next to his body, fasten the linen sash, and wear the linen turban; these are the holy vestments. He shall bathe his body in water, and then put them on. ⁵He shall take from the congregation of the people of Israel two male goats for a sin offering, and one ram for a burnt offering. ⁶Aaron <u>shall offer</u> [*wĕhiqrîb*] the bull as a sin offering for himself, and shall make atonement for himself and for his house. ⁷He shall take the two goats and set them before the Lord at the entrance of the tent of meeting; ⁸and Aaron shall cast lots on the two goats, one lot for the Lord and the other lot for Azazel. ⁹Aaron <u>shall present</u> [*wĕhiqrîb*] the goat on which the lot fell for the Lord, and offer it as a sin offering; ¹⁰but the goat on which the lot fell for Azazel shall be presented alive before the Lord to make atonement over it, that it may be sent away into the wilderness to Azazel. ¹¹Aaron <u>shall present</u> [*wĕhiqrîb*] the bull as a sin offering for himself, and shall make atonement for himself and for his house; he shall slaughter the bull as a sin offering for himself. ¹²He shall take a censer full of coals of fire from the altar before the Lord, and two handfuls of crushed sweet incense, and he shall bring it inside the curtain ¹³and put the incense on the fire before the Lord, that the <u>cloud</u> [*'ānān*] of the incense may cover the mercy seat that is upon the covenant, or he will die.
>
> (Lev. 16.1–13)

Whatever allusions may have been intended by Daniel 7.13, and whatever time-out-of-mind mythologies may have given rise to it, the juxtaposition of *'ānān* and *qrb* in this verse along with the same word pairing in Leviticus

---

[36] Exod. 29.10; Lev. 1.2, 3, 10; 3.1; etc.
[37] Word forms with the root *qrb* are double underlined; the root *'nn* is single underlined.

16.1–13 cannot be easily dismissed. That the author of Daniel 7 self-consciously availed himself of Leviticus 16 is likely, suggesting that the throne room scene is in fact a narrative dramatization of the high-priestly *yom kippur* ritual. To its merit, such an interpretation would at any rate explain the otherwise senseless suffering of the Danielic holy ones. Whereas the presentation of animal blood remained a crucial component in the high priest's Day of Atonement ritual, Daniel 7.13, as a highly symbolic retelling of Leviticus 16.1–13, would imply that the same presentation of blood would be achieved *a fortiori* through the martyrdom of the *hagioi*.[38]

The framing of righteous suffering in Day of Atonement terms would not be unique to Daniel. A similar conception is attested in the Qumran literature, where the 'typology of Yom Kippur as a fight between the good and evil forces [i.e. Qumran's persecutors] must have reinforced the importance of the annual festival in determining the identity of the community', whose 'afflictions by the persecutors were probably perceived as a kind of *flagella Dei*'.[39] Similarly, in 4 Maccabees the martyrdom of the seven sons undoubtedly mines its key terms from Leviticus 16, also suggesting that their righteous deaths were a kind of *yom kippur* blood presentation.[40] This is not necessarily to argue that Daniel 7 directly inspired such texts, but that the Judaism of the day was inclined to interpret the conflict between the righteous and the wicked as a kind of re-enactment of the Day of Atonement ritual, just as we have it in Daniel 7.

Notions of cultic atonement in Daniel 7 emerge in the first place through the implicit parallel between the heroic figure of Daniel 6, who while in the lions' den was destined to become an atoning figure through the throes of pagan opposition, and the Son of Man, who likewise achieves a kind of salvation over the pagan pretenders. Falling on the heels of Daniel 6, Daniel 7 invites its readers to find a similar story of atonement though on a different stage and with differently guised characters. Likewise, looking ahead to Daniel 9, Daniel's readers are led to expect a period 'to atone for iniquity . . . and to anoint a most holy place', at the climax of a 'seventy weeks' (490 years) super-jubilee (9.24) (falling on the great and final Day of Atonement). If this atoning event is any sense a recapitulation of Daniel 7, we must likewise expect the Son of Man's movements to be related to *yom kippur* rituals.

This interpretation of Daniel 7 is certainly consistent with the book's larger purposes, that is, with what we might expect of the final redactor, given the problematic conditions which Daniel 7—12 (and Daniel 7 in particular) seeks to address. Focusing on Antiochus IV's desecration of the Holy Place and his brutal persecution of Torah-observant Jews, these chapters are centrally concerned not only with a theodicean question (why are God's people suffering and what will become of God's enemies?) but also with a

---

[38] I will return to the identity of the *hagioi*, a controverted question in its own right.
[39] Stökl Ben Ezra 2003: 98–9; cf. also Gilders 2012.
[40] Stökl Ben Ezra 2003: 116; cf. 4 Maccabees 5—18.

cultic question (how will the now-defiled temple be restored?). Although the answer to the first question is never entirely spelled out, Daniel's visions are surely intended to situate the suffering of the righteous (Dan. 7.23–25; 8.11–13, 23–25; 9.25–27; 11.28–35) within a divinely ordained chain of events climaxing in eschatological resurrection (Daniel 12). For the final editor of Daniel, then, such seemingly random sufferings are recast as component steps – which later tradition took to be the *peirasmos* or messianic tribulation – in the salvific purposes of Yahweh.[41] The answer to the second question (how will a defiled temple be restored?) is not unrelated to the first. While the text of Daniel 7 appears to be more interested in asserting *that* the Son of Man inherits the throne than in explaining the precise mechanics behind 'the how', it stands to reason that the figure's triumph over the profaning beasts is somehow actualized through the suffering of the 'holy ones'. In the final text of Daniel, the problem of suffering and the problem of a spoiled cultus are coordinated in a causal chain: just as the suffering of Daniel the prophet created protected cultic space for the worship of Yahweh (Daniel 6), so too, as Daniel 7 would have it, the suffering of God's faithful will prove instrumental in restoring the holiness of a new sanctuary, equivalent to the eschatological temple pictured in Daniel 2.

As a final point, the reading I am offering here goes a long way not only towards explaining the extraordinarily transcendent portrayal of the Son of Man, but also towards resolving the nagging question as to whether the same figure is being made out as divine, merely quasi-divine or something even less. Without falling back on an inevitably speculative account of divine ontology, I suspect that the interpretation on offer here would land us somewhere between the first and the second of these three options. This would seem to follow from the premise that whenever the Jewish high priest acted *ex officio*, he was for all intents and purposes an extension of the divine being. On this logic, when the Son of Man finally takes his place beside the Ancient of Days he must have been understood not only as participating in the latter's divinity (as countless scholars now grant on other grounds), but also – and only because he was – functioning as the Ancient of Days' singular high priest.[42]

Who are the 'holy ones'?

Having described compelling hints of the Son of Man's high-priestly identity, we can now get a better read on the second most pressing puzzle of the chapter: the meaning of the 'holy ones' (*hagioi*). But on this issue a few points are in order. First, between the holy ones and the Son of Man we find a

---

[41] Pitre 2005: 51–62.

[42] Those who identify the Son of Man with divinity include Mowinckel 1956: 352–3; Beasley-Murray 1983: 55; Caragounis 1986: 79; Goldingay 1989: 171; Miller 1994: 208–10; Zehnder 2014.

tight-knit correlation that, even if notoriously perplexing, simply cannot be ignored. Just as judgement is issued in favour of the 'holy ones' (Dan. 7.22), so too the same judgement vindicates the Son of Man (vv. 10–14). And just as the 'holy ones' 'receive the kingdom and possess the kingdom for ever' (7.18; cf. 22, 27), so too does the Son of Man (v. 14). Somehow or other, the lots of the Son of Man and the holy ones are intertwined. Second, whereas Daniel 7 never goes into detail as to how the pagan entities, the pagan rulers and the kingdoms they represent, come into power (though an ancient reader's recollection of history just might presumably fill in the backstory quickly enough with mental images of brutal violence), the text at least makes clear that sovereignty is finally transferred to the Son of Man after the tribulation of the 'holy ones'.[43] And so the contrast between *how* the Son of Man and his pagan counterparts ascend to authority remains striking: whereas the beasts *inflict* suffering to secure their power, the holy ones *endure* suffering to secure theirs, bound up as it is with the Son of Man. Because in ancient Jewish thought righteous suffering in the face of pagan violence typically implied a sacerdotal function, the text raises the possibility – indeed the probability – that the holy ones, much like the Son of Man, are being ascribed a priestly role. Third, because we can safely assume that Daniel 7 was meant to be an encouragement for a beleaguered community, we should also assume that the author Daniel is inviting his readers to identify their own suffering with that of the holy ones.[44] As prospective *hagioi*, the faithful are being called to not just the sufferings at the hands of despots like Antiochus IV but also the rewards on the far side of such persecution.[45]

All the while, God's 'holy ones' must continue to play their part in an unfolding cosmic drama, whereby, after discharging their priestly task of faithful endurance, they would one day be requited after the pattern of the Son of Man by inheriting 'thrones' alongside him (Dan. 7.9). Even if the faithful must go so far as to suffer martyrdom, so the symbolic story of Daniel 7 suggests, such tragic events will finally serve to advance a divinely super-intended process, climaxing with the arrival of the kingdom and the vindi-cation of the righteous through resurrection. At a fundamental level, then, Daniel 7 is a reframing of a communal story, a story which, though fraught

---

[43] Dan. 7.18, 21, 22, 25.

[44] While a respectable line of scholarship maintains that the holy ones are not in fact human but angelic beings, this view is gravely undermined by the fact that these same *hagioi* are being 'worn out' (7.24) and ultimately vanquished by the little horn, aka Antiochus IV (7.21). In other words, if the *hagioi* are non-embodied angels, then this still leaves the rather difficult tasking of explaining how such angelic beings could possibly *suffer* the kind of indignities dealt out by Antiochus. Even if *hagioi* more frequently refers to angels than to humans in the Hebrew scriptural corpus, the application of the epithets to righteous humans in the pre-Christian era and especially in early Christianity should not be overlooked (Deut. 33.3; Pss. 16.3; 34.9; 1QM 10.10; Acts 9.13, 32, 41; 26.10; Rom. 1.7; 8.27; 12.3; 15.25, 26, 31; 16.2, 15; 1 Cor. 1.2; 6.1; Heb. 6.10; 13.24; Rev. 5.8, 9; 8.3, 4; etc.).

[45] So most scholars, including, e.g., Hartman and Di Lella 1978: 91; Goldingay 1989: 170–1; Lucas 2002: 192; Boyarin 2012: 152.

with grief and angst, offers itself as an epic of hope. Thus the designation marks off members of the believing community not simply as 'the good guys' (as opposed to the Seleucidian bad guys), but as the righteous endurers who will be rewarded for their participation in the restoration of the sacred space, perhaps even undergoing an angelomorphic transformation (becoming 'like angels' (Mark 12.25 par.)) in the process.

Synthesis

I have been arguing that the vision of Daniel 7 focuses primarily on cultic concerns. But this does nothing to undercut the political quality of the vision. After all, the divine response to the crisis of pagan profanation is nothing less than the establishment of a '*kingdom*' (2.44; 7.12, 14, 18, 22, 24, 27), a kingdom destined to answer the four pagan kingdoms and cash out the covenantal promises. From this simple observation follows a simple caveat, as well as a suggestion. First the caveat: as we prepare to explore the relationship between Daniel 7 and Jesus' understanding of the kingdom of God, we should avoid the trap of assuming that the ancient Jewish concept of kingdom was inherently political *as opposed to* cultic in nature. In the light of Daniel 7, with its vision of an eschatological theocratic kingdom supplanting the religio-political pagan kingdoms, we realize that Jesus and his peers operated with a notion of kingdom that was simultaneously political and cultic. Nor does this proposition stand in tension with the fact that Daniel 7 recounts an enthronement scene (which modern imaginations might strictly associate with a royal office). Consider once again the case of the Hasmonean dynasty, which, provoking controversy in its own day by asserting its royal-priestly role, intentionally drew on the language of Daniel 7 and Genesis 14 in order to style itself as the priesthood of 'the Most High'. Standing in the line of Melchizedek and the Son of Man, the Hasmonean rulers insisted that they were by all rights both Davidic kings and high priests – simultaneously and without contradiction. Such a claim would not have been outlandish, but on the contrary consistent with the Davidic eschatological expectations of the day. Indeed, the Hasmonean claim became increasingly viable as the conditions of a unified, Jerusalem-centric Israel (once operative under David and Solomon) came closer to being realized, especially on the achievement of national independence (142 BCE). The enthronement scene of Daniel 7 is as much ordination as it is coronation.

That the Hasmoneans aligned themselves with both David and the Danielic Son of Man is hardly problematic. On the contrary, seeing as rabbinic commentators tended to interpret the Son of Man as a Son of David (*b. Hag.* 14a; *b. Sanh.* 38b), I believe that the bulk of the Hasmonean supporters would have agreed that a claim to be one figure entailed a claim to be the other as well. Support for this inference comes by way of an illuminating study undertaken about 30 years ago by Paul Mosca, who argued for an essential parallelism between the Son of Man's subjugation of chaos in Daniel

181

7 and David's defeat of the same forces in Psalm 89. The parallelism is initially warranted by the comparison between David's silencing of the ruthless sea creatures (Ps. 89.9–10), on the one side, and our Son of Man's quietening of his sea-originating monsters, on the other. More than that, Mosca argues, when Yahweh promises to set David's 'hand on the sea and his right hand on the rivers' (Ps. 89.25), this is clearly in imitation of Ba'al's suppression of the sea and river gods, Yamm and Nahar, respectively – all paving the way for the images appropriate to Daniel 7.[46] Holding tightly to such texts as Psalm 89, Jews of this era would have almost certainly recognized a *David redivivus* lingering in the shadow of the Danielic Son of Man – and vice versa.[47] This would mean that any first-century figure who self-identified as Son of David would not necessarily have been averse to also claiming some identification with the Danielic Son of Man.

To summarize the more immediate point, I propose that the ancient readers of Daniel 7 would have understood this text as a symbolic story, centring around, first, the re-establishment of sacred space (i.e. clearing the sacred floor of invasive unclean principalities) through a transaction of atonement and, second, an ordination process coinciding with that atonement. The ordinand and the agent of atonement in this case is none other than the Son of Man. At the climax of this process, the Son of Man takes up his position at the right hand of the Ancient of Days within the temple sanctuary, command central within the kingdom of God. Like its pagan counterparts, which depended on ideologies fusing the religious and the royal, the kingdom of God, as presented in Daniel, is equally a politic and a cultic reality. Its titular head is the royal-priestly figure of the Son of Man.

The historical Jesus and the Danielic Son of Man

Preliminary considerations

Having argued that the Son of Man of Daniel 7 leaves himself open to being understood as an eschatological high priest, it is appropriate to enquire as to whether Jesus himself may have shared an interpretation similar to the one being put forth here. In the first four chapters of the present volume, I have argued that Jesus thought of himself as Israel's final high priest. If this is true, and if it is also true that the Danielic Son of Man is a high-priestly figure, then we have more than sufficient warrant for proposing, as a tentative theory anyway, that the historical Jesus invoked the Son of Man precisely as the Danielic and high-priestly Son of Man. For much of the remainder of this chapter, I intend to put this theory to an initial test with reference to Mark 2.1–12 par.

But before doing so, it will be important to disclose a few initial assumptions. The most important of these may be teased out from a certain

---

[46] Mosca 1986: 512.
[47] So, e.g., Beasley-Murray 1983; Gese 1983.

characteristic common to the full range of Son of Man sayings, more specifically, Jesus' unusual tendency to refer to this enigmatic figure in the third person: '*the* Son of Man'. As C. F. D. Moule has strenuously argued, it could hardly be coincidence that whereas the phrase 'the Son of Man' is virtually unknown in pre-Christian Judaism (which consistently prefers the anarthrous 'Son of Man'), the articular form of the phrase occurs in the Gospel tradition without exception.[48] For Moule, this suggests that when Jesus referred to '*the* Son of Man' or perhaps '*that* Son of Man', he was directing his hearers not so much to himself, nor to some expected apocalyptic personage, but to the literary Son of Man figure depicted in the text of Daniel 7. The point is not made redundant by my aforementioned premise that Jesus mined his Son of Man language from Daniel 7. Rather, it is a sharpening of the premise: in referring to '*the* Son of Man', Jesus is primarily if not exclusively directing his hearers to a textual figure, not a historical figure.

For my part, I am persuaded by Moule's line of reasoning for at least two reasons (in addition to those already mentioned). First, by shifting our focus from a hypothesized apocalyptic-historical figure to a literary figure, we can explain why the early Church seldom applied the epithet to Jesus outside the Gospel narratives, as well as why, when the term is used, adumbrations of martyrdom are usually not far removed.[49] If Jesus referred to 'that Son of Man' in order to apply a narrative grid for interpreting hostilities uniquely pertinent to his situation, this would certainly explain the otherwise curious fact that while all other major monikers for Jesus ('Son of God', 'Lord', 'Christ' and 'Saviour') are in abundant supply in the post-Easter tradition outside the Gospels, the 'Son of Man' tag seems to have gone all but missing. Second, on this interpretation, we are also able to explain why Jesus consistently speaks of the Son of Man in the third person. Of course there have been a few explanations for this oddity. For example, much earlier scholarship used to insist that Jesus used the term 'Son of Man' to refer to an apocalyptic figure other than himself.[50] But the main problem here is that if this is true, then none of the Gospel writers seem to have received the memo (though of course Bultmann would hasten to add that they weren't particularly interested in any such memos in the first place), since all four Evangelists regularly

---

[48] The only exception to the Gospel rule (i.e. that the phrase always takes the article) is John 5.27 ('and he has given him authority to execute judgement, *because he is [the] Son of Man [hoti huios anthrōpou estin]*'). But on Cowell's Rule, this is closer to being a near exception, since the indefinite predicate preceding the verb 'to be' must be understood as bearing an articular sense. By contrast, there is a limited number of instances in which the articular phrase occurs in pre-Christian texts. The article is applied in 1QS 11.20, as well as in numerous points in the Similitudes of Enoch (*1 En.* 46.2, 3, 4; 48.2; 62.5; etc.). But in the Enochic texts, the articular use clearly refers back to the first instance which occurs in *1 En.* 46.1, so as to convey 'the aforementioned Son of Man'.

[49] Moule (1977: 17) marshals two instances. The first occurs at Acts 7.56, where the martyr Stephen declares, 'I see the heavens opened and the Son of Man standing at the right hand of God!'; the second case revolves around the martyrdom of James (Eusebius, *Hist. eccl.* 2.23.13).

[50] Strauss (1972 (1835): 281–3) was the first one to suggest this. Bultmann (1968 (1921): 150–2 and *passim*) and Tödt (1965 (1959)) followed suit.

render Jesus' Son of Man sayings as *somehow* self-involving statements. Other scholars, preferring to maintain a simple one-to-one equivalency between Jesus and the Son of Man, explain Jesus' third-person usage as a strategy for avoiding charges of blasphemy. This is not impossible, but it does not sit very well with either Jesus' strident claims freely made (in the first person) elsewhere in the narrative or his continued use of the third-person formulation even after his condemnation has been all but sealed (Mark 14.62). Against both these positions, I am convinced that Jesus referred to 'Son of Man' in the third person simply because he was, strictly speaking, insistently pointing his hearers back to the figures *and* action contained in Daniel 7, though not without sensitivity to the full range of the title's occurrences and nuances in Scripture.[51] With these caveats in place, we turn to one place in the Gospel tradition where 'Son of Man' occurs.

The healing of the paralytic (Mark 2.1–10 par.)

The triple tradition recounts a story of Jesus teaching in a crowded house, only to be interrupted by a paralytic who, having been just lowered down through the ceiling, had been presented for healing. Moments before restoring the man, Jesus explains to the gathered crowd (in wording identical across the three Gospels) the motivation for his impending healing: 'so that you may know that the Son of Man has authority on earth to forgive sins'.[52] Despite Bultmann's influential judgement that Mark had in fact spliced together two separate stories (one involving a healing, the other an act of forgiveness), the essential unity and authenticity of the episode are now more commonly granted than doubted.[53]

Three observations are in order. First, we notice that in combining 'Son of Man', 'authority' and 'on earth' in the same breath, Jesus is couching his explanation of the impending healing in the language of Daniel 7.[54] The three phraseological legs to this Danielic stool make it exceedingly diffi-

---

[51] Thus we cannot rule out the shaping influence of texts like Ps. 80.17, where the Son of Man is connected with Israel's return from exile, or Ps. 8.4, where the phrase seems to signify humanity's paradoxical state of weakness and glory. Along these lines, G. B. Caird (1963: 94–5; cited in Moule 1977: 20.) is not incorrect when he claims that the Galilean used the phrase 'to indicate his essential unity with mankind, and above all with the weak and humble, and also his special function as predestined representative of the new Israel and bearer of God's judgement and kingdom.' Nor, in view of the idealization of human weakness so deeply embedded in the Gospel tradition, can we disagree with Eduard Schweizer (1970: 171) when he writes: 'Perhaps Jesus called himself "Son of Man" in the way Ezekiel did to describe the commission he had received from God to serve in lowliness and suffering'.

[52] Matt. 9.6//Mark 2.10//Luke 5.24.

[53] Bultmann (1968 (1921): 212–13) is followed by, e.g., Taylor 1966: 191; Gnilka 2010 (1978): 96. A different form-critical judgement is registered by Dibelius (1935: 66–7), who ascribes the passage an essential unity; likewise, more recently and on different grounds, Dewey 1979: 66–76; Hampel 1990: 188–90; Sung 1993: 210–15; Collins 2007: 184.

[54] The transfer of 'authority' (*edothē autō exousia* (Dan. 7.14 LXX); cf. 7.6, 12, 26, 27) to the Danielic Son of Man occurs 'on the earth' (*epi tēs gēs* (Dan. 7.17 Theo), *en tē gē* (Dan. 7.23 Theo)).

cult to argue, as many have done, that Jesus is using 'Son of Man' here in a generic or generalizing self-referential sense, as if he were saying: 'So that you might know that we humans have authority on earth to forgive sins'.[55] Nor does it wash to suggest that 'authority' and 'on the earth' have been introduced by Mark. For if we go so far as to sever these phrases from the lips of Jesus, then this only begs the question as to why any of Mark 2.10 should be credited to Jesus.[56] But if we allow with many that Jesus used 'Son of Man' self-referentially, then we are also in a position to agree with the same interpreters that Mark 2.10 is indeed authentic.[57] Considering these factors, it becomes very difficult to deny Jesus' self-framing within the storyline of Daniel 7.

Second, the event is remembered as having been overshadowed by potential charges of blasphemy on the grounds that only God can forgive.[58] Although Mark may be ironically building on a well-established assumption in order to cast Jesus' divinity into ironic relief (the scribes are more right than they knew!), this hardly means that in the original situation Jesus' offer of forgiveness – shocking as it may have been – would have been immediately construed as a claim of divine co-identity. In the Jewish literature, persons depicted as extending forgiveness include the prophet Nathan, who announces Yahweh's forgiveness of David (2 Sam. 12.13); 'an exorcist' whom Nabonidus claims to have 'remitted my sins for Him [i.e. God]' (4Q242); the Suffering Servant of *Targum Jonathan* (Isa. 53.6); the eschatological Melchizedekian high priest (11QMelch 2.4–13), the high-priestly Enoch (*2 En.* 64.5); and Josephus's Samuel (*Ant.* 6.5.6 §92; cf. 1 Sam. 12.16–25).[59] Unfortunately much of the scholarly discussion as to whether these persons themselves are extending forgiveness has failed to recognize the important distinction between distal and immediate agency. When my hand flicks a light switch, I am fully aware that the ultimate source of that light is not my fingers but the local power plant (or, if you prefer, the sun). Nevertheless, my role in providing light is real. Likewise, since Scripture consistently reserves the role of forgiveness to God (Exod. 34.6; Ps. 103.12), it is very unlikely that any of the aforementioned Jewish texts assumed human agency as the 'power plant' of forgiveness. But it is equally clear that these same texts are envisaging a priest-like human agent who by declaration (and perhaps with a motion of their own fingers too) constitutes a state of forgiveness in real time, in anticipation of the separate event of eschatological forgiveness. So, then, even if we have no record of Israel's priests ever muttering '*Ego te absolvo*' or

---

[55] As suggested by Wellhausen 1909 (1903) 16; Vermes 1973: 180; Casey 1979: 228–9; Lindars 1983: 45–6; etc.

[56] Of course, a minority of scholars would hold that Mark 2.10 *is* a later community or Markan interpolation: Percy 1953: 242–3; Higgins 1965 (1964): 26–7; Tödt 1965 (1959): 126–7; Norman Perrin, 1974: 74, 79; Collins 2007: 189. Boobyer (1954: 115–20) suggests that Mark 2.10 is a Markan editorial aside, but this has not garnered support.

[57] Sanders 1985: 272–4; Wright 1996: 393–4; Dunn 2003: 741; Fletcher-Louis 2007b: 74; Keener 2009: 202; Grindheim 2011: 63; Schröter 2014 (2012): 164.

[58] Mark 2.7.

[59] For overviews of discussion see Hägerland 2012: 1–12; Johansson 2011.

its Hebrew equivalent, the priestly rituals relating to atonement itself implied nothing less than full forgiveness – and that apparently without violating the dogma that only God forgives sins. This would suggest that the scribes' vexation over Jesus' declaration pertained to the implication not that he was 'very God of very God' (a notion for which they would have no categories), but that he was God's duly authorized priestly agent (and that without at least first checking in with the official priesthood). This reading of the historical occasion is confirmed by Mark's editorial note that the crowd glorifies not Jesus but God for the paralytic's healing *and* forgiveness.[60] At issue here, then, is Jesus' right to have his hand on the light switch, as it were, a right conferrable only by God as the sole forgiver of sins. At issue is the legitimacy of Jesus' priestly claims.[61]

A third observation: in this episode the act of healing falls closely on the heels of a declaration of forgiveness. The tight connection between forgiveness and healing was in fact a staple notion in the Judaism of Jesus' day, bolstered by texts like Psalm 103, where healing and forgiveness remained divine prerogatives yet were also somehow conjoined with the manifestation of the kingdom.[62] In this vein, it doesn't escape notice that Jesus' address to the paralytic, at least as preserved in Mark 2.5 ('*Son* [*teknon*], your sins are forgiven'), hearkens back to Psalm 103's depiction of Yahweh as Father alongside the forgiven/healed who are his children.[63] For reasons such as these, I am inclined to agree with Otto Betz that Psalm 103 affords 'the key for understanding both the entire, somewhat complicated storyline and the behavior of relevant characters' within the pericope.[64] More than that, Psalm 103 supports the Evangelist's efforts to develop his Christology along new lines while filling out the nature of the kingdom.

Yet this synthesis need not be confined to Mark's creativity. Cognizant of his own role as herald of the very kingdom promised by Psalm 103, the historical Jesus probably saw this moment as an opportunity to indicate that eschatological convergence of healing and forgiveness, a convergence which Psalm 103 associated with the coming of the kingdom, was now coming to the surface in his own ministry.[65] In this case, Jesus extended healing and forgiveness as part of a scripturally informed signal that the kingdom was now at hand. In this case, too, Jesus' encounter with the paralytic was not a strictly interpersonal transaction but retained the character of a prophetic pronouncement that would be stunningly and lastingly inscribed in the body

---

[60] Mark 2.12.
[61] So Wright 1996: 434; Fletcher-Louis 2007b: 71–4; cf. Sanders 1985: 272–4. That the Evangelist understood as much is also supported by numerous commentators, e.g. Marcus 2000: 216; Collins 2007: 186.
[62] Ps. 103.3, 19.
[63] Ps. 103.13 ('As a father has compassion for his children, so the LORD has compassion for those who fear him').
[64] Betz 1984: 266.
[65] The key verse is Ps. 103.19: 'The LORD has established his throne in the heavens, and his kingdom rules over all'; cf. also Isa. 33.17–24.

of the now-healed paralytic. Introduced with a momentous act of forgiveness, the kingdom announced by Jesus retained an indelible sacerdotal stamp. After all, forgiveness is ordinarily the domain of the priest.

Evidence that the Evangelist himself likewise ascribed cultic significance to the event is not hard to come by. But the evidence is in the details. Though the mention that the paralytic is 'carried by four' (Mark 2.3) might ordinarily be shrugged off as extraneous, more studied intentions cannot be ruled out. More exactly, we cannot dismiss the possibility, first, that the four-man team's bearing of the pallet was meant to evoke Ezekiel's four creatures bearing the throne of God (Ezek. 1.5–28) and, second, that Jesus' pronouncement of forgiveness in the direction of the paralytic's supporting box-like frame was intended to invite an almost paronomastic analogy between the wood-frame *krabattos* (i.e. the man's stretcher) and the ark of the covenant's *kibōtos* (i.e. the 'mercy seat' attached as the lid), which was not only, like the paralytic's pallet, the focal physical space of divine forgiveness but also, again like the pallet, a piece requiring four carriers. Alternatively (or perhaps additionally), as a variation of this point, Mark may be hinting that just as Solomon's (four) priests had carted the ark of the covenant into the newly built 'house' of the temple (1 Kings 8.1–6), Jesus is now functioning as the high priest of all places – per a *double entendre* alluding simultaneously to Peter's dwelling and newly created cultic space – 'in the house' (Mark 2.1). In any case, Jesus' parting instructions (Mark 2.11) that the healed man carry his mat and go 'into the house' (*eis ton oikon*) (typically rendered 'go home' in most English translations) not only serves to squeeze the whole scene between the bookends of the 'in the house' *inclusio*, but also may signal that the erstwhile paralytic is now being symbolically tasked with carrying forth his own 'ark of the covenant', as it were, in the guise of a beggar's pallet. On this reading, one wonders whether Mark meant to ascribe to the healed paralytic a missional duty, representing him as one who, having received the forgiveness and healing of Jesus, must now bring that forgiveness and healing to others as he wends his way now to the *house* of the new eschatological temple. To be sure, much of this may be finally imponderable. But my argument that Jesus functioned as an eschatological high priest in Mark 2.1–10 does not depend on Mark interpreting the event just as I have suggested. I only offer this reading of the pericope as potentially supporting evidence.

The key point is this: the historical Jesus' encounter with the paralytic provided occasion for Jesus to associate himself closely with the Son of Man even while simultaneously declaring himself as one charged with ushering in the final temple in the present time. This suggests that Jesus' act of forgiveness, symbolic of more far-reaching eschatological forgiveness, was somehow integral to his mission as the high-priestly Son of Man. If, as I have argued above, the Danielic figure is truly being portrayed as carrying out the atonement appropriate to *yom kippur*, then it seems that Jesus has leveraged this event to show that the reconstitution of sacred space pictured in Daniel was now coming about through the present incarnation of the Son of Man.

At the same time, the scene gives us no reason to assume that Jesus construed an ontological equivalence between himself and the iconic Son of Man. Much less is there any reason to insist that he thought of the characteristic attributes of the Son of Man as being entirely restricted to himself. In fact, the evidence of the Gospels seems to suggest a broader field of reference. After all, the same functions which Jesus predicates of the Son of Man in this episode, again preserved across the triple tradition, are eventually delegated to his disciples, including healing (Matt. 7.22; 10.8; Mark 9.18; Luke 10.17) and the issuance of forgiveness (Matt 6.12; 10.13–15; 16.19; 18.15–20; Mark 6.11; Luke 5.10; 10.5–12) – all in connection with the proclamation of the kingdom per Psalm 103. True, it is possible that the disciples' warrant for undertaking these activities was based exclusively on Jesus' authority as the unique Son of Man (and not in any sense on their own co-participation in that identity). But in that case, it is difficult to know what to make of Mark 2.1–12 as part of a post-Easter charter document, at a time when the early Christian community would have been interested in rehearsing its theological warrant for its own practices of healing and forgiveness.

Indeed, that the believing community shared in the Son of Man's authority to heal and forgive also appears to be how Matthew understood the matter. In his account of this healing the crowds are awestruck because God 'had given such authority to men' (Matt. 9.8, NIV), presumably one and the same as the authority extended to the Church through Jesus (Matt. 18.18). Although Jesus *qua* high priest regarded himself as the priestly Son of Man in a unique sense, this entailed neither, on the one side, his monopolization of priestly authority, nor, on the other side, a radical democratization of priestly authority. Instead, Jesus expected his closest disciples to join him in the trail blazed by the Son of Man. In so doing, they would simply be carrying out their own priestly duty consistent with the arrival of the Day of Atonement.

Summary

If Jesus really did appeal to Daniel 7 as the principal background for his term 'Son of Man', then it is important that we come to grips not just with the Danielic Son of Man (as if he existed in a vacuum), but with the full text of Daniel as well as the Son of Man's place in it. I have sought to undertake this project in the first part of this chapter. On my results, the Son of Man emerges neither as human *simpliciter* nor as divine *simpliciter* but an eschatological high-priestly figure in whom the realms of humanity and divinity converge, even as he performs atoning duties appropriate to the Day of Atonement. From here, in the second part of this chapter, I asked whether Jesus read Daniel 7 in the way that I am suggesting. In other words, do we have any evidence that Jesus himself interpreted the Son of Man as an eschatological high priest? On my analysis of Mark 2.1–12, I propose that we do in fact have such evidence. While Mark 2.1–12 is one of several passages from the synoptic tradition which recounts Jesus offering forgiveness, it is striking that in this passage, which boasts a respectful claim to authenticity, Jesus offers forgiveness in a priestly style precisely while connecting himself with the mysterious figure of Daniel 7.

As intriguing as this finding may be, taken as an isolated instance, Mark 2.1–12 has only limited value in demonstrating Jesus' sacerdotal interpretation of the Son of Man. We need more examples, more evidence. In the following chapter, I intend to provide just that by examining three more Son of Man sayings, all of which are virtually unsurpassed in terms of their claim to dominical roots, at least in the cumulative judgement of the guild. To pre-state the conclusions of this study, I will show that in each instance Jesus invokes a Son of Man, he points to a priestly figure embedded in a narrative highly reminiscent of the one we encounter in Daniel 7. This is not to say that Jesus has a habit of calling up stories directly involving monsters, thrones and smoky clouds. It is to say that once Jesus' Son of Man sayings are understood in their proper context, they point back, no less than Mark 2.9, to his self-appointed role as eschatological priest. Fortunately, as it turns out, by studying each saying on its own terms, we also advance in our understanding of what it means for Jesus to be this final priest.

6

A re-envisaged priesthood

It is unlikely that many who had seen Jesus in his youth would have supposed him to be born a hero, but that's what he became. As to what it was that made him a hero – that's a question that has been debated for years. The same question stands right at the hub of the entire quest for the historical Jesus. Likewise, my study of Jesus would hardly be complete without at least some account of his distinguishing *modus operandi*. If Jesus did in fact pass himself off as the eschatological high priest tasked with installing Israel's final temple, he would have presumably dropped hints of that remarkable role in the course of his ministry – not just in his extraordinary feats but in his workaday life as well. If that is the case, then how did Jesus' priesthood shape his life in the day-to-day? What were the distinguishing traits of his ministry and which, if any, of these can be explained by this special role?

The goal of the present chapter is two-fold. In the first place, I would like to get some answers to questions like these not only to obtain further confirmation of my overall thesis but also to provide added depth to my portrait of Jesus. Up to this point, I have attempted to uncover isolated evidences that Jesus thought of himself as a priest in the making. Is there more that can be said – in addition to what has already been said – in regard to the practical outworking of that vocation? If so, what might that be? Second, given my working hypothesis that the early traditions surrounding Jesus' divine sonship, together with Jesus' traditional designation as Son of David and Son of Man, are likewise rooted in this vocation, I now intend to demonstrate that in at least three instances Jesus used the term 'the Son of Man' as a verbal placeholder for a larger narrative – exceeding the boundaries of Daniel – primarily concerned with the eschatological high priest. My first stated goal for this chapter contributes to the cumulative case I am making for Jesus' priesthood, even as it sharpens the definition of that priesthood. The second goal serves to elucidate a key Christological term which holds promise for shedding light on Jesus' putative divine sonship. Thus the present chapter seeks to advance the two large pieces to my argument.

True to my approach, I will be using a very limited data base, contenting myself with drilling deeply rather than widely. More specifically, I will be turning to three Son of Man sayings which, at least so far as Son of Man sayings go, have earned among the highest marks of authenticity from Jesus scholars: Mark 2.23–28 par. (a grainfield controversy), Q 9.58 (Matt. 8.20// Luke 9.58) (a saying in which Jesus speaks to the homelessness of the Son of

Man) and Q 7.31–35 (Matt. 11.16–19//Luke 7.31–35) (a parable about children calling to each other in the marketplace). Since my concern has been to focus only on Son of Man sayings which would pass muster with even those who hold the highest bars for admissible evidence (short of principled scepticism in regard to the specific material), I hope and trust that my selection of these three texts will avoid charges of tendentiousness. Indeed, precisely when it comes to the Son of Man sayings, my approach hardly does any favours for my argument. (Needless to say, if I were handed a full and uncut deck of 'Son of Man' cards for the purposes of my argument, I would quickly find more than enough aces and kings to put up my sleeve in the form of the so-called 'suffering Son of Man sayings'.) But my goal all along has been to restrict myself to those materials whose authenticity is doubted only by the most radical of sceptics. These now come under consideration in the remainder of this chapter.

Sabbath-day liturgies: the grainfield controversy (Mark 2.23–28 par.)

The first Son of Man saying under review occurs in an account of a Sabbath controversy taking place in a grainfield. While the historical reality of this episode has been commonly granted in recent decades, the exact scope of Jesus' statements at the event has not.[1] The record of the Evangelist reads as follows:

> [23]One Sabbath he was going through the grainfields; and as they made their way his disciples began to pluck heads of grain. [24]The Pharisees said to him, 'Look, why are they doing what is not lawful on the Sabbath?' [25]And he said to them, 'Have you never read what David did when he and his companions were hungry and in need of food? [26]He entered the house of God, when Abiathar was high priest, and ate the bread of the Presence, which it is not lawful for any but the priests to eat, and he gave some to his companions.' [27]Then he said to them, 'The Sabbath was made for the man, and not the man for the Sabbath; [28]so the Son of Man is lord even of the Sabbath.'[2]

---

[1] On the historicity of the event overall, see, e.g., Rordorf 1968: 59–61, 72–5; Roloff 1970: 55–8; Vermes 1973: 180–2; Crossan 1983: 78–85; 1991: 256–7; Borg 1984: 152; Casey 1988; 2010: 361–2; Davies and Allison 1988–97: 2.304–5; Gnilka 1997: 217; Wright 1996: 390–6; Becker 1998: 298–9; Dunn 2003: 742–4; Keith 2014: 120; Crossley 2015: 42–3 (cautiously). The Jesus Seminar gives Mark 2.27–28 a resounding 'That sounds like Jesus!' ranking (Funk and Hoover 1993: 49). Meier (2001: 526) summarizes well the leading reason for conceding the event's authenticity: 'since we have such [Sabbath] disputes multiply attested . . . it seems likely that Jesus was known to have held less-than-stringent views about the extent to which one was obliged to abstain from work on the Sabbath'. Bucking the trend, Sanders (1983: 20) calls the scene 'imaginary' on the grounds that Pharisees did not actually 'spend their Sabbaths patrolling cornfields'; similarly Fredriksen 1999: 105–6; Hultgren 1972: 41. The objection is not without force; I will respond to the point below.

[2] Mark 2.23–28. Translation has been adapted from the NRSV.

In response to allegations that his disciples were desecrating the Sabbath by engaging in 'work', Mark's Jesus first draws an implicit comparison between his followers' behaviour and David's transgressive consumption of the sacred shewbread (vv. 25–26; cf. 1 Sam. 21.1–6); then shifts gears by asserting that 'the Sabbath was made for [the] man' (*ton anthrōpon*) (v. 27); and finally caps off his argument by concluding that 'the Son of Man is lord even of the Sabbath' (v. 28). The main obstacle to accepting all three units as dominical has been their seeming incongruity, tempting scholars to jettison whatever they perceive to be the non-matching baggage. While David's relevance (vv. 25–26) to the incident has sometimes been questioned, most interpreters believe that the historical Jesus in fact appropriated the precedent set by 1 Samuel 21.1–6, since ancient Jewish readers were given to setting the Nob event on the Sabbath.[3] Others have trouble imagining Jesus issuing the rabbinic-*esque* statement regarding man/humankind as beneficiary of the Sabbath and therefore discard verse 27. Meanwhile, many others cannot shake their allergic response to the Son of Man, leading them to drop verse 28. Apparently, when it comes to the convergence of David, 'man' (*anthrōpos*) and the Son of Man in this cosy passage, two's company; but three, so it is generally thought, is a crowd.[4]

In contrast to these atomizing approaches, I maintain that the conjunction of these three elements (vv. 25, 26–27, 28) in Jesus' setting is not only credible, but essential to his basic point. There is nothing intrinsically far-reaching about this assertion. While David, humanity and the Son of Man obviously occupy distinct roles, I believe there is a deeper logic which could have easily induced Jesus to connect these actors. In fact, once these three components of the pericope are properly interpreted alongside one another, they together offer compelling evidence that the historical Jesus traded on the shared roles of all three figures/entities in order to assert the priestly vocation of his own movement – all with the more immediate aim of justifying his disciples' seeming violation of the Sabbath.

In my view, much of the unhelpful dissection of this passage is caused by our misdiagnosing Jesus' self-comparison with David, as it comes to us in Mark. But once we get to the bottom of Jesus' appeal to his royal ancestor (vv. 25–26), we are well on our way towards adopting a framework which makes sense of the episode as a whole. I initially focus on Mark's interpretation not to make it determinative for our reconstruction of Jesus' aims (which would be to get it backwards), but rather to develop an initial hypothesis which will still have to be tested. For obvious reasons, this calls for methodological care. On the one hand, it will not do to foist Mark's interpretation on to the historical Jesus, as if to assume that the Evangelist got history right or even tried to get it right. On the other hand, a close read of the Gospel account could shed light on the community's earliest memory of the event, which in

---

[3]   See *Yalq.* §130 1 Sam. 21.5; *b. Menaḥ.* 95b; cf. also Str-B 1.618–9.
[4]   For a review of options for reconstructions of compositional history, see Neirynck 1975.

turn prepares us to walk backwards in time. A fresh reading of Mark 2.23–28 would seem to hold more promise than the alternative of prematurely dropping one or more elements within the pericope prior to a holistic interpretation, an unfortunate but common enough move which inevitably entails the question-begging procedure of determining what the historical Jesus meant on the basis of a conveniently pared-down version of what he 'really must have said' (which in turn has already been predetermined by 'what Jesus meant').

The grainfield controversy according to Mark

Vexed by Jesus' mysterious invocation of David and his even more enigmatic, double-stranded finish, most interpreters of this passage have fallen back on one (or more) of three principal interpretations.[5] According to the first of these, Jesus is summoning David as a paradigmatic wise man who, when push came to shove, allowed his sabbatarian scruples to take a back seat to human need.[6] This reading is often accompanied by two related judgements: first, that the occurrence of 'Son of Man' in verse 28 is but the vestigial mistranslation of a prior Aramaic tradition (*bar-nāšā*), a self-referential circumlocution referring to humanity in general; second, that verse 27 refers to humanity in this generic sense (so NRSV: 'humankind').

The interpretation has both strengths and weaknesses. To its credit, the approach resonates with certain rabbinic interpretations of 1 Samuel 21.1–6, which also sought to justify David's transgressive behaviour by appeals to human exigency. Yet the interpretation is also deeply problematized on several levels. In the first place, Mark 2.23–28 gives us no hint that the disciples are suffering from dire malnourishment. Indeed, that the disciples are experiencing any discomfort at all is a supposition which has to be introduced into the text. Second, if the point of the passage is to suggest that human hunger trumps law observance, one struggles to square this kind of moral flexibility with – among other factors – the double tradition's account of the temptation, where Jesus forgoes food for 40 days in order to prove his dedication to 'every word that comes from the mouth of God'.[7] True, Mark may not have been aware of the details of the temptation tradition (though this is unlikely), but Matthew and Luke obviously were, and were no less keen to preserve the full-blown temptation scene together with the grainfield incident. It is awkward to say the least to hold that both Matthew

---

5 Doering (1999: 399–400) helpfully lists as many as six positions: (1) Jesus was opposed to the Sabbath in principle; (2) Jesus was not opposed to the Sabbath but to its legalistic interpretation; (3) Jesus was not opposed to the Sabbath, but wished to limit its application; (4) Jesus' understanding of the Sabbath was driven by his eschatological convictions; (5) Jesus was favourably disposed to the Sabbath but sought to uncover its true intent; (6) Jesus was completely fine with the Sabbath as it was generally understood.
6 So, e.g., Marshall 1978: 232; Schottroff and Stegemann: 1984: 124; Yang 1997: 175.
7 Matt. 4.4; cf. Luke 4.4.

and Luke would have their readers emulate a Jesus who came to the brink of starvation out of devotion to the word of God, only later to brush holy writ aside because he and his friends were peckish.[8] Third, if the episodes populating the Gospel's opening chapters (if not the whole Gospel) are consistently marshalled to stake a Christological claim, it would be quite an unexpected detour for Mark to have suddenly decided to make a very different kind of point relating to the sabbatarian freedom his readers share with other humans like David and Jesus himself. The problems accruing to this interpretation are not inconsiderable.

A second approach to 2.23–28 holds that Jesus, in what is essentially an *a fortiori* argument, is claiming the right to transcend the law, because he is at least as great as David.[9] The initial attraction of this reading (over the first option) lies in its taking seriously the intrinsic likelihood that Mark here is interested in Christology as opposed to anthropology. But if the synoptic tradition is giving Jesus *unique* licence to suspend the law on a moment's notice, this not only implies that the messiah's obligation to the law could be arbitrarily suspended at will, but also sits poorly with other indications that Jesus and his followers remained punctilious in their observance of the law in general, and in their sabbatarianism in particular.[10] But perhaps Jesus is taking the opportunity set a new precedent in keeping with the salvation-historical shift. Still, in this case, it is not clear how this eschatological announcement would line up with what appears to be a generally accepted principle articulated in verse 27 ('Sabbath was made for man'). And if Jesus is at this very moment abrogating the Sabbath for one and all, it does not seem to be the case that his followers understood this, at least not until the post-Easter decision to move the Sabbath from the last day to the first day of the week. True, retroactive declarations of this sort do occur in the Gospels (Mark 7.19b), but if this is what he meant, his words would have been next to useless as a defence for his disciples caught yellow-handed in the grainfield. Unsatisfactory resolution of these points does little to enhance the persuasiveness of the overall argument.

Something of a combination of the first two approaches, a third solution proposes that Jesus, much like David before him, is getting at the very heart of the law, which may or may not include a critique of the Pharisees' alleged legalism.[11] On this view, if the Pharisees had erred in laying on rule upon rule, Jesus authoritatively cuts through all such trammels by penetrating to the spirit of the Sabbath. While this is perhaps the strongest option of the three, it too is not without difficulties, the most glaring of which comes in the dilemma posed by the Son of Man (v. 28). On the one hand, if Jesus

---

8 Edwards (2015: 179) makes the point nicely.
9 So, e.g., Grundmann 1959: 70; Hagner 1993: 331.
10 E.g. Matt. 28.1; Mark 16.1; Luke 23.56.
11 Cranfield 1977 (1959): 115; Davies and Allison 1988–97: 2.312; Nolland 1989: 257–8; Green 1997: 253–4.

as the Son of Man is 'Lord of the Sabbath', then he is obviously drawing far more firepower than would be necessary for a halakhic discussion on the Sabbath principle. On the other hand, if we decode 'Son of Man' as Mark's circumlocution for humanity in general, then the Evangelist could not possibly be any more confusing, since elsewhere in the Gospel he typically uses 'Son of Man' with reference to an exalted figure. Even though this interpretation of the *Sitz im Leben Jesu* may be the best of the standard options, it is almost certainly wrong.

Jesus as a type of David

As an initial step towards introducing an alternative to these major options, I begin by focusing on three seemingly minor details on the redactional level. The first is this: when Mark's Jesus first responds to his opponents' criticisms by invoking the case of David, he curiously adds an additional subject alongside David: 'and those with him' (*kai hoi met'autou*) (2.25).[12] While this syntactically isolated tag may have every appearance of being a parenthetical – if not stylistically sloppy – afterthought, its near-equivalent repetition ('and those who were with him' *kai tois syn autō ousin*) in the very next verse (v. 26) raises the possibility that the abrupt grammar was actually meant to attract the readers' attention.[13] The possibility is strengthened on the recurrence of the same phrase just over a dozen verses later, clearly building on 2.25–26 to establish a parallelism between David 'and those *with him* [*met'autou*]' (2.25), on one side of the equation, and Jesus and those disciples he called 'to be *with him* [*met'autou*]' (3.14), on the other. Immediately following 2.25–26, the language of the call scene (3.14) invites a comparison between these two figures and their respective followers. Understood within the broader context of Mark 2—3, then, the phrase 'those with him' in 2.25, 26 hints towards an analogy between David's men and the Twelve.

Yet given the seemingly strategic deployment of *met'autou* ('with him') and *syn autō* ('with him') in the remainder of the Gospel, I think we can be more specific about the nature of this connection. Not insignificantly, the first of these two Greek phrases almost invariably refers to those who are either collaborators in Jesus' mission (1.36; 4.36), or witnesses of extraordinary revelation (5.24, 37, 40; 14.33), or both (3.14; 5.18); *syn autō*, meanwhile, is only used twice in addition to 2.26 and that in reference to the 'thieves' being crucified alongside Jesus (15.27, 32). On this observation, we suspect that Mark uses 'those with him' (*met'autou* and *syn autō*) as umbrella terms, embracing those who partner with Jesus in his paradoxically glorious yet suffering-laden mission. In the Evangelist's theology, to be with Jesus is to share in his sufferings and his glory simultaneously and without contradiction.

---

[12] The translation here is my own.
[13] Luke 6.3 alleviates Mark's grammatical awkwardness by moving the phrase to the front of the clause. Interestingly, the unusual syntax is anticipated in Mark 1.36: *kai katediōken auton Simōn kai hoi met'autou.*

If Mark's readers would have found the disciples' many adverse experiences to be wholly different from what they would normally expect of a messiah's accomplices, the Evangelist's careful deployment of these phrases assures that such experiences have already been anticipated by those who were *with* David, individuals who, as we know from the narrative of 1–2 Samuel, stuck with the anointed king through thick and thin before enjoying the glories of his established kingship.

That Mark intends a general comparison between David and Jesus is supported by at least a handful of typological comparisons, occurring, for example, in Mark's account of the latter's last week in Jerusalem which resembles the Jerusalem-based consolidation of kingship under the former. As he enters the Holy City in the style of Solomon (11.1–8), Jesus is hailed as the Son of David (11.9–10), only later to be identified with David (12.10 (Ps. 118.22–23)). Later still he is crucified as a Davidic 'King of the Jews' (15.26). Finally, in his expiring moments he utters his last prayer in words drawn from a Davidic psalm (15.34 (Ps. 22.1)).[14] Through his shameful death on a Roman cross, Mark insists, Jesus has become Israel's king on the pattern of David.

Yet the Jesus–David analogy also extends to Mark's sequencing of events, as a comparison of their respective careers makes clear. One recalls that in 1 Samuel, David is anointed as king of Israel (1 Samuel 16), thrust into combat with Israel's arch-enemy (Goliath) (1 Samuel 17) and shortly thereafter put to flight by the reigning pretender Saul (1 Samuel 18—20), with an excursion to Nob (1 Samuel 21) marking one of the first stops in his itinerant exile. The early action of the Gospel is parallel in its broad strokes. In the Gospel of Mark, Jesus is anointed the Davidic-messianic king (Mark 1.9–11), thrust into combat with Israel's true arch-enemy (the Satan) (1.12–13) and shortly thereafter embroiled in a series of conflicts (2.1—3.6), complete with its own Nob-like experience (2.23–28). Such structural similarities between the Gospel and the Davidic narrative are not unrelated to more far-reaching thematic comparisons. If David was anointed king but denied any immediate right to reign, so it was with Jesus. If David's band was time and time again forced to go on the run, Jesus and his followers were no less a band on the run. Finally, if David's exile eventually paved the way for securing the throne, the same goes for Jesus – even if in a curious, paradoxical way. Whatever scriptures and traditions shaped Mark's Christology of suffering, the contribution of the Davidic narrative can hardly be denied.

Once Mark's appropriation of the cycle from 1–2 Samuel is brought to bear on our interpretation of his grainfield incident, Jesus' appeal to David (vv. 25–26) quickly comes into view as an effort to frame the controversy as a recapitulation of a distinctively Davidic conflict. Mark 2.23–28's position within a set of post-baptism conflict stories, in grand analogy to David's

---

[14] On the stone of Psalm 118 as a 'Davidic stone', see Kim 1987: 134–48 (136).

experience, points to nothing less. No sooner is David anointed king of Israel than he is ironically persecuted: no sooner is Jesus anointed king of Israel through baptism than he is, with equal irony, persecuted. Meanwhile, if the analogy between the two anointed-but-beleaguered kings effectively links the conflict dialogues of Mark 2.1—3.6 to the travails of David, then Jesus' self-comparison with David at Nob within the episode of 2:23–28 is the weld which seals that link. This is no arbitrary exercise in typology. By embedding Jesus' sufferings within the context of David's suffering, Mark hopes to justify the controverted quality of Jesus' messiahship.

The temple elite as a type of Abiathar

At the same time, we have some indication that Mark exploits the Davidic narrative in order to speak not just to the character of Jesus' messiahship but also to its specific goals. Such evidence emerges in another detail, the surprising identification of Abiathar as high priest at 2.26. It is 'surprising' because the attentive reader of 1 Samuel 21 would expect the Evangelist to name – if anyone at all – not Abiathar but his father, Ahimelech.[15] The Evangelist's apparent error has spawned a handful of explanations. One approach has been to chalk up the received text of Mark 2.26 to a scribal lapse, but this lacks sufficient text-critical support. Another explanation, going back to the eighteenth century and espoused more recently in the twentieth century by J. W. Wenham, is to propose that the prepositional clause beginning with *epi* should not be read 'when Abiathar was high priest' but more along the lines of 'in the passage concerning Abiathar the high priest'.[16] For all its ingenuity this suggestion has not met with wide approval, understandably so since Abiathar's name does not appear until 1 Samuel 22.20, which would make for a pretty large 'Abiathar passage' by any standard. Yet another possibility is that the event at Nob (1 Sam. 21.1–9) was somehow associated with Abiathar for reasons now lost to us.[17] Perhaps, but then it is only our guessing that makes it so. Faced with the weakness of all these proposals, most Markan commentators are content to fault the Evangelist very simply for failing to get his facts straight.[18] Yet despite its appealing simplicity, even this solution is rendered suspect by the ever mounting evidence – surfacing through the last few decades' interest in Mark's use of the Scriptures – of the Evangelist's very detailed knowledge of the Hebrew scriptures.[19] How plausible is it, in other words, that an author so exacting in the composition of his richly allusive Gospel should prove to be so manifestly careless so as to confuse one of the two main characters of the Nob incident? If Mark has indeed made such an unforced and obvious error in regard to 1 Samuel 21, this would be

15 So 1 Sam. 21.1: 'David came to Nob to the priest Ahimelech.'
16 Wenham 1950: 156, who is followed by Lane 1974: 116; Roure: 1990: 14.
17 Rogers 1951; Edwards 2002: 95; Whitelam 1992: 1.13–14; Marcus 2000: 241.
18 Schweizer 1970: 72; Guehlich 1989: 122; Malbon 2009a: 166; Beavis 2011: 63; etc.
19 See now Hays 2016.

painfully ironic since in the very passage the Evangelist has his Jesus chiding his opponents for their inattention to the same chapter: 'Have you never read . . .?' (v. 25)!

In a previously published contribution, I have argued that the inclusion of 'Abiathar' at Mark 2.26 was both intentional on Mark's part and compositionally strategic.[20] To reiterate the thrust of that argument, I maintained, first, that co-regency among Israel's high priests was not unheard of (in which case Abiathar may be appropriately named as high priest instead of his father); and, second, that Mark deliberately names Abiathar rather than Ahimelech on account of the former's dubious distinction as high priest. This merits some review. Abiathar was the son of Ahimelech, who was the son of Ahitub, who in turn was of the line of Phinehas, who in turn, once again, was the son of Eli.[21] For the reader of 1 Samuel, Abiathar's descent from Eli cannot be detached from the divine word of judgement issued against the priestly forebear, who, neglecting to reprimand his sons in his own day (1 Samuel 1—2), had been informed that his priestly lineage would one day be terminated.[22] That termination is finally set into motion when, in the course of Adonijah's rebellion against the heir apparent Solomon, Abiathar throws in his lot with the upstart pretender to the throne.[23] Responding to the coup, David orders that Solomon be crowned in a coronation ceremony involving the ascendant ruler riding on a donkey.[24] As a direct result of what may be deemed the biblical canon's 'first triumphal entry', the rebellion collapses, leaving Solomon to replace the rebel priest Abiathar with Zadok – 'thus fulfilling the word of the LORD that he had spoken concerning the house of Eli in Shiloh'.[25] Failing to back the right horse (or donkey), the disgraced Abiathar would go down in the pages of Hebrew history as the only priest to be deposed.[26]

With this backstory in mind we see the pieces falling into place. Dropping the name 'Abiathar' instead of the expected 'Ahimelech' at Mark 2.26, Mark's Jesus sets up a veiled analogy between the rebellious, ill-fated priest and his priestly opponents. Jesus' subtle comparison functions not only as a clue to his disputants' doom, but also as a map on which his subsequent actions in the narrative may be plotted. Just as Abiathar's fate is all but sealed through Solomon's donkey-style coronation, Mark seems to be saying, so it will be the case in its own mysterious way for the Jerusalem-based priests of the Jerusalem temple as they witness Jesus entering Jerusalem in Solomonic

---

[20] Nicholas Perrin, 2013b.
[21] 1 Sam. 1.3; 14.3; 22.11.
[22] 1 Sam. 2.30–36.
[23] 1 Kings 1.7, 19.
[24] 1 Kings 1.32–40.
[25] 1 Kings 2.27.
[26] 1 Kings 2.27. In Jewish antiquity Abiathar's fall from grace was no obscure historical datum, at least judging by Josephus's elaboration of the same (*Ant.* 8.1.3 §10–12).

fashion.[27] Of course when Solomon mounts his donkey, it is with more than the intention of pre-empting illegitimate royal (Adonijah) and illegitimate priestly (Abiathar) claims: the political deck-clearing would only be the means towards the much more momentous occasion of his consecrating a newly built temple, where he would serve as a royal priest. On the same pattern, even if Jesus' triumphal entry turns out to be only the first instalment of a series of acts and words of judgement against Israel's leaders (11.11—12.37), these scenes are themselves stepping stones to the culminating events: his enthronement through the cross and the building of the temple through resurrection (14.1—16.8). Mark's unexpected inclusion of 'Abiathar' – seemingly gratuitously and off the cuff – reflects his conviction that even as David's struggle had already been recapitulated in the experience of Jesus, so too would his aspirations for a new temple. Anticipating the triumphal entry (11.1–10), the confrontation with Caiaphas (14.53–65), the rending of the temple veil (15.38) and the resurrection of the temple 'not made by human hands' (14.58; 15.29) (my translation), the grainfield incident is the first skirmish of a protracted conflict; this conflict itself is patterned after a well-known earlier struggle which began with David's anointing and came to a close with the consecration of the temple by the Son of David.

The grainfield meal as a sacred meal

It is at this point that one last detail of Mark 2.23–28 becomes especially relevant: Jesus' mention that David took the shewbread and 'gave it to those who were *with him*' (*edōken kai tois syn autō ousin*) (2.26) (my translation). Having already established that those 'with him' in Mark's Gospel are Jesus' followers, we now recognize how the phrase 'gave it to them' in 2.26 anticipates the Last Supper where Jesus took bread 'and gave it to them' (*kai edōken autois*) (14.22), that is, those 'dipping bread into the bowl with me [i.e. Jesus] [*met'emou*]' (14.20; cf. v. 18).[28] Whatever Mark thought was exactly going on in the grainfield that day, he at least seems to have concluded that the disciples' seemingly extemporaneous picnic was actually a solemn anticipation of Jesus' final atoning Passover meal, offered in competition with the temple cultus. This strongly suggests that the Evangelist attached some kind of sacral significance to the grainfield meal, again, like the atoning act of the Last Supper, in direct competition with the official cultus. So then, while the grainfield incident may at first blush appear to be little more than an isolated halakhic disagreement over differing Sabbath practices, when the episode is set within its full narrative context, it serves notice that the disciples are enacting their own sacred meal on the model of David's sacred meal at Nob and in opposition to competing priestly personnel, who belong to the same ill-fated trajectory once occupied by Abiathar. David had a right to

---

[27] Mark 11.1–10.
[28] Luke strengthens Mark's connection by adding *labōn* ('took') in his versions of the grainfield incident and the Last Supper (Luke 6.4; 22.19).

such a meal, after all, because he was the rightful royal priest (as Ahimelech himself seemed to have recognized). Now, Mark's Jesus insists, his disciples have the same right, as heirs of the same office.

To conclude the point, Mark interpreted the grainfield incident as a quasi-sacred meal somehow related to a larger conflict brewing between Jesus and the Jerusalem temple. As a harbinger of the Lord's Supper, the grainfield incident also takes its place alongside the two feeding miracles (6.30–44; 8.1–10), both of which also feature phrasing that recurs in the final Passover meal. In this respect, all four meals are intertwined as 'sacred meals', even if the precise nature of that sacredness is not fully determined. In all this, the scene contained in 2.23–28 stands out on account of its patently oppositional – and therefore controversial – character.

The historical Jesus and the grainfield controversy
Towards an explanation of Mark's handling of the grainfield meal
Even if Mark interprets the grainfield incident as I have argued, this does not mean that the historical Jesus and his immediate followers would have necessarily characterized the original incident in the same way. At the same time, the Evangelist's perception of the episode still requires a historical explanation. The evidence is unimpeachable that Mark, in conveying the fact of Jesus' conflict with the temple, is representing a historical reality. While we might speculate that Mark's decision to situate the grainfield incident within this broader conflict was driven by homiletical as opposed to historical concerns, it would be hard to imagine just what homiletical concerns these might be. A more natural assumption is that the Evangelist's understanding of the episode finds its origins in the earliest memory of the event itself. To put this otherwise, if Mark is seeking to characterize the disciples as participants in some kind of controversial, Sabbath-day *sacred* meal, then it is more likely than not that the disciples did in fact take in a meal of that very kind.

In Chapter 1 above, I argued that the Lord's Prayer functioned as a kind of charter for Jesus' counter-temple movement; its regular re-performance served to remind the community of its unique mission and distinctive practices. There I also argued that a thoroughgoing eschatological orientation permeated each of the carefully worded petitions comprising the *Pater Noster*, including not least the fourth petition (traditionally translated as 'Give us this day our daily bread'), which was actually a plea for the long-awaited eschatological manna. As those who gave themselves to regularly and corporately 'praying in' the messianic feast, the members of the Jesus movement obviously took an especial interest in the eschatological banquet. In part this may be explained by the community's sense that it had been granted a unique role in precipitating the eschaton, and therefore also regarded itself as being at least partially responsible for ushering in the manna's arrival. At the same time, the conspicuous presence of the otherwise unnecessary 'our' within the petition ('Give us this day *our* . . . bread') signals that Jesus and his disciples thought of themselves as having a distinctively vested interest in the future manna: this was *'our* bread', belonging to *us*, as opposed to some other group which might make the same claim. As Jesus' disciples saw it, the eschatological bread was *theirs* in some exclusive sense; the eschatological bread for which they regularly prayed was of 'restricted use'.

Jewish conceptions of the present and future Bread of the Presence

In pre-rabbinic Judaism, the only bread that fell into this kind of 'restricted use' category was the Bread of the Presence, a central feature in the weekly ritual life of the temple. The most fulsome set of instructions surrounding the bread is found in Leviticus 24.5–9:

> You shall take choice flour, and bake twelve loaves of it; two-tenths of an ephah shall be in each loaf. You shall place them in two rows, six in a row, on the table of pure gold. You shall put pure frankincense with each row, to be a token offering for the bread, as an offering by fire to the LORD. Every sabbath day Aaron shall set them in order before the LORD regularly as a commitment of the people of Israel, as a covenant for ever. They shall be for Aaron and his descendants, who shall eat them in a holy place, for they are most holy portions for him from the offerings by fire to the LORD, a perpetual due.[29]

According to Torah prescription, every Sabbath the priests were to lay out two stacks of six loaves of freshly baked bread (a total of 12 loaves corresponding to the 12 tribes) and then consume the bread from the previous week. Through this weekly rite, the priests symbolically re-enacted the covenant meal which Moses and the elders had shared in the divine presence.[30] This was in part a way of giving symbolic expression to the truth that Yahweh feeds and sustains his people; the 12 loaves symbolized divine provision and presence.[31] The priests' weekly bread meal was mandatory for the operation of the cultus; to neglect it would have been a violation of the perpetual covenant. Indeed, the very fact that the table supporting the bread came to be identified as an 'altar' reinforces the fact that this rite was part and parcel of the rubric of sacrifices demanded by Yahweh.[32] Finally, while various sacrificial offerings made outside of the Holy Place were to be shared by the people, this offering within the sanctuary was most holy and accordingly, as Jesus reminds his interlocutors at Mark 2.26, restricted to priests. The shewbread ritual was a sacerdotal rite of immense importance in Israel's cultus.

If, as I have been arguing all along, Jesus and his band thought of themselves as Israel's rightful eschatological priests, then one might expect

---

[29] Lev. 24.5–9. See also Exod. 25.23–30; Num. 4.1–8; 1 Chron. 9.32; 23.29; *Spec. Leg.* 1.168–76; *Ant.* 3.6.7 §§142–43; 3.10.7 §§255–56.
[30] Exod. 24.9–11. Pitre 2015: 125–6.
[31] Flesher 1992: 781; Gane 1992: *passim*; Burer 2012: 31.
[32] Ezek. 41.22; Mal. 1.7, 12; cf. Ezek. 44.15–16. See also Gane 1992: 182; Pitre 2015: 127–8.

them to have developed at least some kind of provisional practice to ensure the perpetuation of the bread-laying rite, important as it was, in real time. Now with Mark's implication that the grainfield supper was not an ordinary Sabbath-day meal but a sacred meal of some sort, together with evidence that the disciples prayed the fourth petition as those who would one day administer the Bread of the Presence, it becomes plausible that the historical event depicted in Mark 2.23–28 was in fact one of many weekly bread-consuming rituals – makeshift as it was – performed by the disciples.

In my view, plausibility turns into probability on considering the pattern of expectation at Qumran, where sectarians saw themselves as the predicted eschatological priests of Ezekiel 44.24, whose duties included stewarding the weekly Sabbath in the future and final temple.[33] This much is made apparent in the War Scroll and a more fragmentary document from Cave II:[34]

> They shall rank the chiefs of the priests after the Chief Priest and his deputy; twelve chief priests to serve in the regular offering before God. The chiefs of the courses, twenty-six, shall serve in their courses. After them the chiefs of the Levites serve continually, twelve in all, one to a tribe. The chiefs of their courses shall serve each man in his office. The chiefs of the tribes and fathers of the congregation shall support them, taking their stand continually at the gates of the sanctuary. The chiefs of their courses, from the age of fifty upwards, shall take their stand with their commissioners on their festivals, new moons, and Sabbaths, and on all days of the year. These shall take their stand at the burnt offerings and sacrifices, to arrange the sweet-smelling incense according to the will of God, to atone for all His congregation, and to satisfy themselves before Him continually at the table of glory.[35]

> [T]hey [shall] go into the temple [. . .] eight sheahs of finest fl[our . . .] and they shall lift the bread [. . .] first upon [the] al[tar . . . two] rows upon [the] ta[ble . . .] two rows of loa[ves . . . every seventh day before God, a memorial offering . . .] the bread. And they shall take [the] bread [outside the temple, to the right of] its west side, and it shall be shar[ed . . .] . . .. And] while I was [watching] one of the two loaves was given [to the high] p[riest . . .] with him. And the other was [g]iven to the deputy who was standing close to him [. . .] *Blank* And while I was watching [one of the two breads [was given to a[ll the priests] . . ..[36]

As the two texts indicate, the Qumran covenanters not only expected the arrival of an eschatological Bread of the Presence at the messianic banquet, but also saw themselves as taking their rightful place as privileged Sabbath-day consumers of the same bread, thus restoring the rite (properly performed

---

[33] Cf. Ezek. 45.17; 46.1–8.
[34] For these references I am indebted to Brant Pitre (2015: 133), who discusses them in relation to Jesus' Last Supper.
[35] 1QM 2.1–2, 4–6. Translation from Abegg, Wise and Cook 2005 (1996).
[36] 2QNJ ar frg. 4.1–10, 14–16; translation from García Martínez and Tigchelaar 2000; cited in Pitre 2015: 133.

this time) of the eternal covenant.[37] While the Dead Sea sect's expectation may not have been universally shared across the spectrum of apocalyptic Judaism, the evidence from Qumran nevertheless attests to a conviction that a restricted priestly class would administer the eschatological Bread of the Presence at the messianic banquet.[38]

Early Christians (and for all we know the historical Jesus himself) were also convinced that qualified priests would be entrusted with perpetuating the bread ritual as part of the ongoing messianic banquet. This is demonstrated by the synoptic accounts of the Last Supper, where Jesus voices his longing to partake of the messianic banquet, the final Passover and the 'fruit of the vine', coinciding with the coming of the kingdom.[39] Given Jesus' rumination on the messianic banquet, precisely as a reprise of the Last Supper with its intimations of atonement, we surmise that the Evangelists regarded the great future feast as an essentially cultic meal and one therefore which would take place under priestly auspices. In another pericope, when Jesus alludes to a day when 'many' would come from the four winds to share an eschatological meal with Abraham, Isaac and Jacob, we are led to envision a banquet essentially comprised of kingdom VIPs.[40] And since all three hosting patriarchs would have also been recognized as priests, this scenario is also consistent with Qumran's vision of a priestly feast – after the pattern of the temple bread-consuming rite, which itself followed the pattern of the Mosaic covenant meal. Early Christians and Qumran sectarians alike, then, seem to have expected the investiture of an eschatological priesthood tasked with implementing some version of the cultic bread-laying/bread-consuming ritual in the eternal temple.

Along these lines, it should also not go unnoticed that an elite class within the Qumran community seems to have connected some of its own present-day eating practices with the eschatological bread-consuming rite. Within the Dead Sea Scrolls literature, a clear distinction is made between pure food and impure food, corresponding to a distinction as to who may and may not eat from the former category. By all accounts, the consumption of pure food at Qumran was a solemnly enacted cultic act – involving ritual bathing, silence, the wearing of linen, etc.[41] Since bread and wine are the foods most prominent in the sect's apocalyptic texts, we would expect the same foods to be staples in their weekly sacred rituals. As it turns out, this is borne out by the archaeological evidence, for

---

[37] In keeping with Ezekiel 40—48, the sectarians clearly assumed that the Sabbath would continue into the eschaton; cf. 1QM 2.4–9. See also, classically, Newsom 1985.
[38] See discussion in Nicholas Perrin 2010: 170–9.
[39] Mark 14.22//Matt. 26.29//Luke 22.16, 18. As Pitre (2015; 133) argues, the bread and wine of the Last Supper correspond to the accoutrements of the table of the presence in the Holy Place, the 12 loaves of bread and the flagons of wine.
[40] Matt. 8.11//Luke 13.29.
[41] *J. W.* 2.8.5 §129–33; 1QS 5.13–14; 6.2–21; 1QSa 2.17–19; 4QMMT B64–5. See discussion in Atkinson and Magness 2010: 329–33.

grinding mills and a plastered shelf (apparently the place for kneading the dough and forming the loaves) were found in close proximity to the ovens, allowing the entire bread-making process to be carried out, from beginning to end, *within a pure enclosure.*[42]

The necessity of keeping bread quarantined as holy bread at Qumran more than suggests that the anticipated bread-laying rite of the eschaton was already being carried out in the sectarians' weekly Sabbath ritual. Given the significance of the same rite within Second-Temple Judaism together with the sectarians' conviction that they were the true stewards of Israel's cultic space, we would almost have to expect nothing less. Very similar practices seem to have obtained for the Therapeutae, with a very similar set of notional implications.[43]

Synthesis

On the basis of the analogy between Qumran and the scenarios which seem to have been envisaged by Mark, I would suggest that when Jesus' disciples entered the grainfield on that particular Sabbath, this was actually part of a weekly practice whereby they would carry out their own bread-consuming rite, substituting the grain from the field for the 12 loaves of the Holy Place. They would do so not in 'the holy place' of the temple, but in some kind of other prescribed sacred space (Lev. 24.9).

This is supported by the following considerations. First, as I have pointed out above, the bread-consuming rite was stipulated in ancient Judaism as part of an inviolable 'eternal covenant'. If Jesus thought of his movement as a counter-temple movement, then the Sabbath-by-Sabbath performance of this ritual might be expected virtually as a matter of course. Second, whereas the Evangelist has Jesus leading his disciples through the grainfields, it is *only* the disciples who are plucking (and consuming) the grain.[44] If by this point in Jesus' ministry he had secured the full slate of 12 disciples (a point of speculation, I grant), then he may well have seen a natural symbolic congruence between 12 disciples and 12 'loaves' of grain (corresponding to the 12 loaves of shewbread), a symmetry which would feasibly explain Jesus' recusal from the eating ritual. Third, unless we are to suppose either that the Pharisees accidentally bumped into Jesus' crew in some out-of-the-way grainfield or that the Pharisees spent – in the wry phrasing of E. P. Sanders – 'their Sabbaths patrolling cornfields', we suspect that Jesus' opponents *anticipated* his disciples' Sabbath-day visit to the grainfields. In this case, one imagines, the disciples maintained a regular pattern of visiting the grainfields every Sabbath and the opponents eventually planned their intervention accordingly.[45] Fourth and most importantly, the interpretation I offer here

---

[42] Pfann 2006: 175; emphasis added.
[43] See Philo, *De vita contemplativa* 1.81–2.
[44] Mark 2.23.
[45] Sanders 1983: 20; cf. Hultgren 1972: 41.

is, I think, the only explanation that finally makes sense of Jesus' invocation of the Davidic example. Jesus' implied syllogism in Mark 2.25–26 is quite simple: if only priests can eat the Bread of the Presence (v. 26b; cf. Lev. 24.9), and if David rightfully ate the bread (despite not being of the established priestly order), then it must mean – suppressed conclusion – that David was a legitimate priest of a different category. Given that chain of logic, Jesus' accusers are now left to connect the dots so far as Jesus is concerned: if the disciples are rightfully partaking of their own makeshift Bread of the Presence on analogy with David's practice, then it must mean that he and his men are also priests (perhaps in the same way that David and his men were). More than this, so the unexpressed conclusion continues, if Jesus and the disciples are priests undertaking temple work, then their activity is in fact God's work and therefore – by standard Jewish definition – immune to charges of Sabbath infraction.[46]

With this piece in place, we are in a better position to make sense of the historical Jesus' closing remarks recorded in 2.27–28. When Jesus declares that the Sabbath was made for 'the man' (*ho anthrōpos*), he is not casuistically asserting that the average Joe has the right to overrule Torah whenever convenient. Rather, the comment must be understood both as an extension of the point regarding David and in the same vein as the rabbinic aphorism: 'The Sabbath is delivered over to you and not you to the Sabbath'.[47] The rabbinic parallel is striking enough that one could suppose that this saying or one like it circulated in Jesus' day, and provided the point of departure for his words in verse 27. If so, then it must also be pointed out that in their context of Exodus 31 these words are directed not to generic humanity but to Israel, precisely as the embodiment of the Adamic 'man', which in turn also explains the presence of the (Adamic) Son of Man in verse 28.[48]

Exactly in what sense the Sabbath is *made* for Adam/Israel comes into focus when we consider the parallelism between divine Sabbath rest and the rest enjoined on Adam. The primordial Sabbath followed six days of creation and marked out Yahweh's rest from battle with chaos, which is also the moment of divine enthronement.[49] By analogy, the Sabbath was created for Adam/Israel in the sense that it was designed to mark off the elect's rest and enthronement. A similar scene of rest and enthronement, in connection with the Son of Man, is also portrayed in Daniel 7 following the vanquishing of the unclean beasts. That Jesus closely links these two narratives is made clear by his drawing inferences about the Son of Man (viz. that he is lord of the Sabbath) on the basis of established truisms regarding the Adamic man (viz. that he is the sole beneficiary of the Sabbath). And yet Jesus seems to make this move with the expectation that the faithful of Israel (aka those

---

[46] On the legitimacy of priestly work on the Sabbath, see Burer 2012: 30, 34.
[47] *Mekilta* Exod. 31.14 (109b).
[48] On Adam as the Son of Man, see Chapter 5 above, pages 172–4.
[49] So, e.g., Sarna 1962.

who corporately embody the Son of Man) would one day attain their destiny as the image of God precisely as they entered into a permanent eschatological Sabbath transcending time and space.[50] More exactly, in asserting that the Son of Man is lord of the Sabbath, Jesus was intimating that the eschaton was already beginning to be realized within his following; this in turn justified the disciples' bread-consuming ritual, notwithstanding its Sabbath-day timing and its location outside the confines of traditional temple space.[51] In a breathtaking stroke, then, Jesus not only framed his movement as the eschatological counterpart to royal-priestly Adam and royal-priestly David, but also suggested in no uncertain terms that the long-awaited enthronement of Daniel 7 was just around the corner.

Even so, I confess my reconstruction of Jesus' intentions still faces what may seem to be a rather daunting objection, namely, that both the Jerusalem cultus and the Qumran community envisioned a *bread*-consuming ritual, not a *grain*-consuming ritual, as I am hypothesizing. Yet the objection is hardly insuperable. As I have just pointed out, Jesus sought to justify his disciples' actions on the grounds that the eschatological era was already at hand, coinciding not only with the imminent lordship of the Son of Man but also the realization of Adam's appointed destiny of sharing in God's eschatological Sabbath. Thus the introduction of the eschatological temple in and through Jesus' own community implied the impending restoration of creational reality. This seems to have been symbolized through nothing less than Jesus' creative reinvention of the bread-consuming ceremony. Whereas God had given Adam 'every plant yielding seed that is upon the fact of the earth . . . for food' (Gen. 1.29), and whereas only after the fall is Adam told 'you shall eat bread' (Gen. 3.19), Jesus' substitution of grain for bread was a highly symbolic way of indicating that the Adamic curse was already being rolled back, in other words that the reversal movement from Genesis 3 to Genesis 1 was all but complete.

Eventually, once the early Church began practising the Lord's Supper not long after Jesus' death, it was only natural that the sacrament would absorb the Bread of the Presence ritual into itself. If the symbolic thrust of the bread-rite was to affirm divine presence and provision, both of these concepts came to be implicitly reasserted in the early Christian Eucharist. In retrospect, perhaps even as Mark realized some decades after the fact, the disciples' rough-and-ready bread-consuming ritual at Jesus' direction was a provisional measure, which had the effect of reminding movement members of their vocation and serving notice to a watching world that the eschaton was now already beginning to materialize. All the while, the same activity (to the extent it was understood by outsiders) would have done little to endear the Jesus movement to the established temple elite or their local representatives.

---

[50] On Sabbath as a day for participating in the image of God, see Hasel 1992: 851.
[51] On the equation of the eschatological Sabbath and eternity, see Philo, *Spec. Leg.* 1.170.

Summary

Not unlike the Qumran community, Jesus' movement regularly undertook certain ritualized practices that were intended to mimic and ultimately supplant the liturgical practices of the Jerusalem cultus. Mark's account of the grainfield incident attests to one such practice (the Lord's Prayer is perhaps another). Although Jesus' followers appeared to be violating the Sabbath by stripping and eating the grain of the field, their 'work' was justified on the grounds that it was priestly work, analogous to the priests' work in the temple every Sabbath.

In its own way, the practice implied a thorough reconfiguring of time and space, which in Ancient Jewish thinking were closely aligned. The Sabbath was the temporal counterpart to the holy space within the temple. On Jesus' reckoning, because the kingdom of God was already pressing into the time–space continuum, it was appropriate to commence practices that would effectively bridge between the temple cultus and the eschatological temple. Under Jesus' auspices the eschatological Sabbath was already underway in the present and sacred space likewise was already being reshaped in line with the new reality. By enacting the restoration of Adamic (prelapsarian) conditions within the confines of their movement, Jesus' followers were boldly and deliberately staking out new dimensions of sacred space and time. Their distinctive temple practices, controversial as they were, symbolized that a new eschatological reality was already taking shape. It was now only appropriate that long-standing cultic practices be adjusted accordingly.

Contrasting priestly approaches: Jerusalem's powerbrokers and Jesus' peripatetics (Q 9.58 = Matt. 8.20//Luke 9.58)

Jesus' off-location cultic practices, involving non-priestly personnel no less, implied nothing less than a radically reshaped universe, one which no longer rotated around the Holy of Holies but himself instead. If this is correct, then it naturally raises the question as to how Jesus conceived of his movement's relationship to Herod's brick-and-mortar edifice.[52] On a practical level this much is sure: once the high priest and his associates caught wind that the budding leader from Galilee was dropping hints that he and his followers – and not the Jerusalem priesthood – marked out the proper temple space, the relationship between the two 'temples' quickly became frayed, eventually resulting in negative consequences for the less empowered Jesus movement. Whatever such 'consequences' might have looked like in the day-to-day, Jesus enjoined his followers to respond not with retaliation but with cheerful humility, gentleness, compassion and forgiveness. Through such responses,

---

[52] On this issue, see also Nicholas Perrin 2010: 46–50.

Jesus taught, the disciples would prove their rightful place in the 'good land', as well as their identity as 'the salt of the earth'. But even if Jesus' ethic of non-retaliation speaks to the 'how' of the disciples' response, it does not entirely clarify either the 'why' or Jesus' understanding of how his own authority related to the authority of the existing powers. Moreover, because issues of contested power were at the very heart of his movement's struggle, it is almost impossible to imagine the master failing to provide some kind of explanation on this matter. Fortunately, as we turn to the second of our three 'critically assured' Son of Man sayings, Q 9.58 (= Matt. 8.20//Luke 9.58), we garner some insight into Jesus' understanding of social power, as it plays out in the geosocial sphere, the realm of social space.

The homeless Son of Man

Preserving material associated with Q and typically ascribed to Jesus, Matthew 8.18–22 and Luke 9.57–62 share a similar story focusing on two (as Matthew has it) or three (as Luke has it) individuals who are contemplating a life of full-time discipleship.[53] The first of these enquirers states his intention to follow Jesus wherever he might go. In a seeming rejection of the man's overture, the master responds (in Greek wording that is identical in Matthew and Luke): 'Foxes have holes, and birds of the air have nests; but the Son of Man has nowhere to lay his head.'[54] Jesus' oblique riposte obviously demands some interpretation.

Common interpretations of Q 9.58

One commonly offered interpretation proposes that Jesus, employing 'Son of Man' as a stand-in term for 'humanity', is contrasting the homeless condition of humankind with the stable habitation of wild animals. This reading is admittedly plausible, but it incurs at least two serious hurdles. First, if Jesus' response is little more than a banal observation about humanity's alienated existence, it is unclear how this would actually make for a meaningful response to the man's request to join *Jesus'* ranks. Second, that humans in general have nowhere to lay their head is patently untrue: in Marshall's words, homelessness 'is not true of men in general'.[55] An alternative, perhaps more popular approach holds that Jesus, using 'Son of Man' as a self-referential title, is discouraging the man by reminding him of the rigours of the movement's itinerant lifestyle. This is certainly an improvement on the first possibility but also faces its own weaknesses, not least the fact that such ascetic ideals do not

---

[53] Though Q 9.58 often passes without comment in treatments of the historical Jesus, its authenticity is safely established by the scholarly consensus: see Vermes 1973: 77; Hengel 1981 (1968): 6 n. 12; Lindars 1983: 29–31; Casey 1985: 15; 2010: 362–3; Smith 1988: 105; Hare 1990: 272–3; Crossan 1991: 256; Funk and Hoover 1993: 316–17 ('probable pink'); Gnilka 1997: 172; Dunn 2003: 744; Brawley 2011: 2.

[54] Matt. 8.20//Luke 9.58.

[55] Marshall 1978: 410; similarly Hooker 1979: 158, among others.

entirely fit the picture of a man who regularly benefited from the hospitality of others.[56] Furthermore, if Jesus is reflecting matter-of-factly on the *modus operandi* of his own movement, one wonders how such a publicly conspicuous fact could possibly be new information for an enquirer who must have done at least some homework on the matter. Finally, on this reading, one may perhaps be forgiven for wondering whether Jesus' succinct but nevertheless elaborate flourish (involving no less than two classes of animals) was really necessary to make a rather simple point.[57] In my view, the problems accruing to both these interpretations outweigh their virtues.[58]

Despite the differences between these two interpretations (which finally turn on the meaning of 'the Son of Man'), both assume a more or less straightforward reading of Jesus' words. The common instinct to take Jesus at face value may well have been encouraged by the spontaneity of the narrative event. According to Matthew and Luke, a certain individual approaches Jesus – quite out of the blue – regarding the prospect of becoming his disciple.[59] In response, we assume, Jesus offers a hastily formulated, *ad hoc* pronouncement. Yet this assumption is hardly necessitated by any of the details in the narrative. Indeed, if both Matthew and Luke considered Q 9.58 worthy of preservation, then it may be surmised that both Evangelists thought of the saying as conveying an important feature of Jesus' aims. But in this case, one might also expect Jesus to have frequently restated the saying in the course of his ministry. In this case, Matthew 8.20//Luke 9.58 is most likely preserving a representative instance of an interaction that replayed itself at least several times over in various contexts. In this case, too, we are better off assuming a degree of thoughtfulness behind the formulation of Q 9.58, perhaps even being open to the possibility that the saying was offered not as an off-the-cuff statement quickly reducible to its most literal sense but as a carefully designed parable.

One of the challenges facing a 'straight reading' of the text involves the seemingly arbitrary nature of the contrast. In other words, if Jesus only needed virtually any one or two examples from the animal kingdom, why does he pick on – of all creatures on earth – 'foxes' (*alōpekes*) and the 'birds of the air' (*ta peteina tou ouranou*)? More than that, on the redactional level, if just about any well-housed fauna will do for the purposes of Luke's Jesus, then his selection of 'foxes' and 'birds of the air' at Luke 9.58 seems especially

---

[56] Vielhauer 1979 (1965): 24. Kingsbury (1988: 50) makes the same point but in respect to Matthew's characterization of Jesus, where 'Jesus is portrayed . . . as domiciled'.

[57] Adopting the standard reading I am describing, Manson (1951 (1931): 73) declares the saying to be 'pure nonsense'. Even if here we have a rare case of a British scholar overstating himself, one gets the point.

[58] Offering an interpretation close to this second reading, Myles (2014) understands Jesus' vagabondage as a forced homelessness. I demur. Whether or not Jesus was homeless in a strict sense, he certainly had access to a network that could support and house him – a point which doesn't sit particularly well with Myles's thesis.

[59] On the question whether or not the enquirer is to be understood as having already become a disciple, see Kingsbury 1988: 47–9.

maladroit, not only because the occurrence of these two species would confusingly invite comparison with the same terms used elsewhere in the Gospel (8.12; 13.9, 19), but also because the same animals often appear as religio-political metaphors in the Second-Temple literature. But perhaps the choice of animals – for Luke, his source and for Jesus – is not arbitrary; perhaps there is something more going on here than meets the eye. In his study of Matthew 8.20//Luke 9.58, Mahlon H. Smith comments that the 'debate about our aphorism boils down to the issue of whether Jesus meant something other than what he superficially seems to have said'.[60] I wholeheartedly agree but I also believe that this debate needs to be freshly re-engaged, starting with a more than superficial consideration of the fauna.

Reviving an overlooked reading: Q 9.58 as socio-political critique

Against the received wisdom surrounding this wisdom saying, I would like to revive an interpretation first offered – as far as I know – by T. W. Manson, who suggested that Jesus juxtaposed foxes, birds of the air and Son of Man not as placeholders on a sliding index of domestic comfort but as scripturally rooted metaphors for political realities.[61] Beginning with the first point of comparison, 'the foxes', we note that ancient Semitic culture did not make a clean linguistic distinction between jackals and foxes, which are indicated by one and the same Hebrew word: *šû'āl*.[62] So, then, in reflecting on Jesus' pairing of *hai alōpekes* ('foxes/jackals') and *ta peteina tou ouranou* ('birds of the air'), there may be some significance to the fact that the same paired sets of creatures finds precedent in Jeremiah 9, a passage in which the prophet laments the fate of the Judean countryside on the far side of approaching exile:

> Take up weeping and wailing for the mountains, and a lamentation for the pastures of the wilderness, because they are laid waste so that no one passes through, and the lowing of cattle is not heard; both the *birds of the air* [*mě-'ôf haššāmayim*] and the animals [*běhēmâ*] have fled and are gone. I will make Jerusalem a heap of ruins, a lair of *jackals* [*tannîm*]; and I will make the towns of Judah a desolation, without inhabitant.[63]

Jeremiah's description of the trauma inflicted on the land not only conveys the extent of the physical destruction but also, drawing on the language of Genesis 1.26 ('the birds of the air . . . and the cattle [*ûbabběhēmâ*]'), seeks to interpret that devastation in theological terms as a reversal of creation.[64] Along these lines, Jeremiah's 'birds of the air' and jackals are also probably taking on specific metaphorical functions. Closely associated with invading armies, divinely charged with 'devouring and destroying', the former creatures

---

[60] Smith 1988: 99.
[61] Manson 1951 (1931): 72–3.
[62] So Casey 1985: 8, 13; cf. Judg. 15.4; Neh. 3.25; Cant. 2.15; Ezek. 13.4.
[63] Jer. 9.10–11.
[64] Cf. also Jer. 4.23–26.

are almost certainly meant to be understood as Gentiles.[65] Similarly, on Jeremiah's accounts, the jackals seem to represent more local opportunists insinuating themselves, in the midst of the socio-political instability, within the upper echelons of the post-exilic Judean political structures.[66] Jeremiah thus takes his place at the beginning of a long tradition which employs these two animalistic images not only to designate the conditions of exile in general terms, but also to establish an allegorical map by which politically aware readers would be able to tell 'who's who in the zoo'.

By the time we come to the apocalyptic texts of the second-century BCE, the two sets of metaphors take on sharpened focus. The Animal Apocalypse, for example, yields up a pattern whereby the birds of the air represent foreign enemies who have hailed from a distance.[67] Meanwhile, in the same text, jackals are also identified with other oppressors of a more homegrown variety.[68] At the same time, both categories of animals are closely connected with the demonic.[69] Such connotations are similar to what we find in Luke. First, the Evangelist uses 'birds of the air' to represent both 'the devil' (8.12) and, if the standard interpretation of the parable of the mustard seed is correct, the Gentiles (13.19). Second, only nine verses earlier, Luke's Jesus characterizes the local puppet ruler Herod Antipas as a 'fox' (Luke 13.9). Thus a metaphorical trajectory spans the years between the exilic period and the late first century CE, connecting jackals and (demonically inspired) local powerbrokers, on the one side, and birds and (demonically inspired) Gentiles, on the other. Although it is difficult to say whether and to what extent birds and jackals would have carried this kind of metaphorical freight in the everyday conversations of Jesus' day, we can at least say that in the post-exilic era whenever these terms are used within the context of a prophetic or apocalyptic discourse, they bear this specific meaning.

Given the apocalyptic leanings of Jesus' language, we conclude that the historical Jesus intended the two terms preserved in Q 9.58 with the very same metaphorical force. That is, working within the standard metaphorical register of Jewish apocalyptic, Jesus' 'foxes' and 'birds of the air' respectively allude to Herod and his temple-based retainers, on the one side, and the occupying Romans, on the other – all of whom, so the metaphor implies, are under demonic thrall. From here we quickly see how this interpretation

---

[65] Jer. 15.3; 16.4; 19.7; 34.20. The conceit also occurs in other post-exilic prophets: Ezek. 31.6, 13; Dan. 2.38; 4.12, 21; Zeph. 1.3.
[66] Jer. 10.22; 14.16; 49.43; 51.37.
[67] *1 En.* 89.10; 90.2–19. Daniel Olson (2013: 136–9) has recently made a convincing case that the four kinds of the birds of the air represented in this apocalypse (eagles, falcons, kites and ravens) correspond to the four different Hellenistic-era powers that occupied Israel (Macedonia, Thrace, Egypt and Syria); his conclusions are anticipated by Bryan 1995: 100.
[68] *1 En.* 89.10, 42, 43, 49, 55.
[69] For the author(s) of 4Q510 (frg. 1.4–5) and 4Q511 (frg. 10), the jackals who have overtaken post-exilic Judea are equated with 'ravaging angels', 'bastard spirits' and 'demons'. On birds as ciphers for the demonic, see *Jub.* 11.11, 18–23, *Apocalypse Abraham* 13, as well as Chapter 7 below.

makes excellent sense of the contrast between these animalistic images and the Son of Man, who can only be the Danielic Son of Man. Whereas Daniel 7 envisages certain powerful, unclean beasts pitting themselves against the Son of Man, Q 9.58 preserves Jesus' attempt to metaphorize his two fronts of opposition, which are also, as far is Jesus is concerned, Israel's true flashpoints of opposition. Yet his saying seeks not so much to assert the fact of such conflict as to assume it en route to establishing a contrast between the religious and political powerbrokers' entrenched position and the Son of Man's unsettledness. The saying, in short, provides historical evidence that Jesus saw his own movement as the homeless Son of Man going up against the Jerusalem-based heavyweights who, inspired by demons to oppose God's purposes, have secured a comfortable niche within the religio-political structures of the day.

Intertextual allusions in Q 9.58

As useful as this background may be for our unpacking of Q 9.58, Jesus' cryptic contrast remains mysterious apart from a better grasp on why the Son of Man/Jesus movement must remain homeless (v. 58b), even while the animals/rulers are comfortably ensconced (v. 58a). To this end, I suggest we explore a handful of scriptural allusions potentially undergirding Jesus' saying. In the final analysis, I believe, just as 'foxes' and 'birds of the air' can be illuminated with reference to the relevant scriptural backgrounds, so too can the saying's other key terms.

We start with Mahlon Smith's proposal that Psalm 8 be understood as one important subtext for Q 9.58.[70] In the targum on Psalm 8.5 MT (8.4 Eng.), the parallel Hebrew terms *'ĕnôš* ('man') and *ben-'ādām* ('son of Adam') are rendered with one and the same Aramaic construction: *bar-nāšā*, that is, 'the Son of Man' (= *huios anthrōpou*). It is equally significant that when the psalmist enumerates the animals subject to the Son of Man, he includes 'the birds of the air' (Ps. 8.9 MT/Targum; 9.9 Eng.). The juxtaposition of these two terms ('Son of Man' and 'birds of the air') in Aramaic Psalm 8 is striking since Jesus invokes the same pairing in Q 9.58, suggesting that his one-liner is to be interpreted with reference to the same psalm. Naturally, for the Aramaic targumist and his Jewish readers, the adversarial relationship between the 'Son of Man' and the 'birds of the air' would have been understood along religio-political lines. On the vision of Psalm 8, the unruly nations (and their gods) represented by the birds would one day be subjugated to Israel and/or its messianic representative, in fulfilment of creation's destiny (Gen. 1.26–27).

Co-opting the birds of the air (together with the jackals) as the standard set of actors within the eschatological scenario depicted by Psalm 8, Jesus seems to have relied on scripturally coded language to issue a politically risky

---

[70] Smith 1988: 94–6, 100.

and therefore necessarily veiled reminder: the demonically inspired power-brokers of the day, of local as well as far-flung and imperialistic origins, would one day be dealt with. All this would happen, in accordance with Psalm 8, when the Son of Man restores the created order. Against the backdrop, Jesus' saying contrasts not only the two divergent eschatological trajectories represented by the Son of Man and the birds of the air (along with the jackals), but also the current situatedness of the two conflicted parties: the well-established state of the demonically driven pagans is set in relief against the more unsettled station of the Son of Man who has nowhere to lay his head.

As important as Psalm 8 may be for understanding Q 9.58, it is short of astonishing that scholarship on this verse has overlooked its retention of another pair of key terms ('lays' and 'head') with equally deep scriptural roots, occurring this time in the dream sequence at Bethel. The passage reads as follows:

> Jacob left Beer-sheba and went towards Haran. [11]He came to a certain place and stayed there for the night, because the sun had set. Taking one of the stones of the place, he put it under his *head* and *lay* down in that place. [12]And he dreamed that there was a ladder set up on the earth, the *head* of it reaching to heaven; and the angels of God were ascending and descending on it. [13]And the LORD stood beside him and said, 'I am the LORD, the God of Abraham your father and the God of Isaac; the land on which you lie I will give to you and to your offspring; [14]and your offspring shall be like the dust of the earth, and you shall spread abroad to the west and to the east and to the north and to the south; and all the families of the earth shall be blessed in you and in your offspring. [15]Know that I am with you and will keep you wherever you go, and will bring you back to this land; for I will not leave you until I have done what I have promised you.' [16]Then Jacob woke from his sleep and said, 'Surely the LORD is in this place – and I did not know it!' [17]And he was afraid, and said, 'How awesome is this place! This is none other than the house of God, and this is the gate of heaven.' [18]So Jacob rose early in the morning, and he took the stone that he had put under his head and set it up for a pillar and poured oil on the top of it. [19]He called that place Bethel; but the name of the city was Luz at the first. [20]Then Jacob made a vow, saying, 'If God will be with me, and will keep me in this way that I go, and will give me bread to eat and clothing to wear, [21]so that I come again to my father's house in peace, then the LORD shall be my God, [22]and this stone, which I have set up for a pillar, shall be God's house; and of all that you give me I will surely give one-tenth to you.'[71]

In this vital turning point of the Jacob cycle, the patriarch 'lays' (LXX: *eko-imēthē*; MT: *wa-yiškab* (v. 11)) his 'head' (LXX: *kephalēs autou*; MT: *mě-ra-'ǎ-šō-ṯāv* (v. 11)) beside a stone, only to be treated to visions of angels ascending and descending a ladder (or staircase), whose top or 'head' (LXX: *kephalē*; MT: *wě-rō'šô* (v. 12)) penetrates heaven.[72] The only place in the Hebrew scriptures where 'laying' occurs alongside 'head', Genesis 28.10–22 presents

[71] Gen. 28.10–22; emphasis added.
[72] Gen. 28.11–17.

itself as a possible subtext to Jesus' phrase 'lay his head' (Q 9.58). In this connection, it may be worth mentioning that the word 'place' (LXX: *topos*; MT: *maqom*) also features prominently in this same patriarchal scene, occurring six times (in the LXX) in the space of ten verses (vv. 10–19). Although *topos* ('place') does not occur in the received Greek text of Matthew 18.20// Luke 9.58, this does not preclude the possibility that the original Aramaic tradition stemming from Jesus passed down the wording 'The Son of Man has no *place*', just as we have it, for example, in the parallel from the *Gospel of Thomas* 86 (Coptic: *ma*) and the earliest Syriac (a cognate of Palestinian Aramaic) translations of the same verse. The point is somewhat speculative but we cannot rule out a scenario in which the tradition behind Q 9.58 drew on not two but three key terms from Genesis 28. While such lexical connections render the Jacob narrative a plausible inspiration for Jesus' saying (Q 9.58), evidence tipping the scales to probability is forthcoming in the Fourth Gospel's report at John 1.51 of Jesus appropriating the Bethel dream in connection with the Son of Man.[73] The relevance of John 1.51 on this issue is not dependent on its authenticity: if the historical Jesus was known to have associated the Son of Man with Genesis 28.10–22 in his own day in sayings like Q 9.58, this would certainly help explain a similar connection in the later text of John 1.51.

The Bethel account is first of all an etiology of sacred space and was interpreted as such in subsequent antiquity. While there may have been minor points of interpretative disagreement between the targums (containing traditions likely going back to the first century) and the rabbinic literature, the ancient interpreters seem to have agreed on the broad strokes: the ladder/ staircase represented the temple; the stone on which Jacob lay his head, the foundation stone for the temple; the ascending and descending angels/ messengers presaged the temple's high priests.[74] Rather than get into further details surrounding these correspondences, including such questions as to whether the angels were more interested in the ladder (*Pseudo Jonathan, Neofiti I*) or in Jacob (*Targum Onkelos*, LXX), my point is simply that in Jesus' day Genesis 28.10–22 would have been understood as one of the earliest intimations of sacred space in Israel's story, not unexpectedly so, given Jacob's declaration that the spot was 'none other than the house of God'.[75]

Of course, Bethel is patently not Jerusalem and on that account Jacob's designation of the area as holy (Gen. 28.17) would have been a point of mild

---

[73] John 1.51: 'And he said to him, "Very truly, I tell you, you will see heaven opened and the angels of God ascending and descending upon the Son of Man."' In addition to the commentaries granting the connection between Jesus' promise (John 1.51) and Jacob's dream (Genesis 28), see Clarke 1974–5; Rowland 1984; Neeb 1992; Bunta 2006; Kerr 2002: 148–54; Kirk 2012; etc.

[74] Clarke (1974–5) provides a review of the primary literature. Clarke (1974–5: 370–5) and Rowland (1984: 498–507) both argue that the traditions preserved in the targums would have dated back to the first century.

[75] Gen. 28.17.

embarrassment for countless Jewish readers, even in Jesus' day, who were adamant in their commitment to Jerusalem as the cultic centre. Towards relieving this tension, a number of traditions conspired to regard the events of Genesis 28.10–22 as marking the place and time for two kinds of ordination: one explicitly connected with Levi, the other less explicitly ascribed to Jacob. Here it was speculated that at Bethel Jacob's son Levi was first designated as a priest, a role to which he later acceded, on having been ordained by his father.[76] This exegetical move is not wholly arbitrary. For on the morning after the vision, Genesis tells us, Jacob makes a vow to build God's house (v. 22), but it is a vow that patently remains unfulfilled. In order to make sense of all this project that never was, the ancient interpreters explained that Jacob's bid to build the house of God was rejected, because – much like David – that honour was due to fall to his son.[77] Yet God's denial of Jacob's desires was not considered absolute, for according to these same interpreters, Jacob's plan to build an earthly temple had been vetoed only because God intended Jacob to build the much more glorious eschatological temple. A story to this effect is told, for example, by the author of *Jubilees*:

> During the next night, on the twenty-second day of this month, Jacob decided to build up that place and to surround the courtyard with a wall, to sanctify it, and make it eternally holy for himself and for his children after him forever. The Lord appeared to him during the night. He blessed him and said to him: 'You are not to be called Jacob only but you will (also) be named Israel.' He said to him a second time: 'I am the Lord who created heaven and earth. I will increase your numbers and multiply you very much. Kings will come from you, and they will rule wherever mankind has set foot. I will give your descendants all of the land that is beneath the sky. They will rule over all the nations just as they wish. Afterwards, they will gain the entire earth, and they will possess it forever.' When he had finished speaking with him, he went up from him, and Jacob kept watching until he had gone up into heaven. In a night vision he saw an angel coming down from heaven with seven tablets in his hands. He gave (them) to Jacob, and he read them. He read everything that was written in them – what would happen to him and his sons throughout all ages. After he had shown him everything that was written on the tablets, he said to him: 'Do not build up this place, and do not make it an eternal temple. Do not live here because this is not the place. Go to the house of your father Abraham and live where your father Isaac is until the day of your father's death. For you will die peacefully in Egypt and be buried honorably in this land in the grave of your fathers – with Abraham and Isaac. Do not be afraid because everything will happen just as you have seen and read. Now you write down everything just as you have seen and read.'[78]

As the writer behind *Jubilees* sees it, Jacob's principal significance lies in his

---

[76] *Jub.* 32.1, 9; *T. Levi* 8–9; *Lad. Jac.* 6–9; 12–13. A full discussion is in Kugel 1993; 2006: 134–5. See also Greenfield, Stone and Eschel 2004: 15–16, 39–40.

[77] Kugel 1993; 2006: Mroczek 2015.

[78] *Jub.* 32.16–24.

role not as a visionary but as a mediator of the covenant which promised something greater than the Mosaic-style temple, namely, the eschatological 'eternal temple'. Again, this does not seem to have been an idiosyncratic view: the author of the *Temple Scroll* (11QT) likewise understood the promise of the eschatological temple to be pursuant 'to the covenant with Jacob at Bethel' (11QT[a] 29.9–10).[79] For both the *Jubilees* community and the community at Qumran, the figure of Jacob emblematizes the tension between the initial ideation of the eschatological temple and its deferred construction in the eschaton.

Exactly what role the authors of *Jubilees* or 11QT imagined for Jacob within this eschatological scenario is not manifestly clear. However, we might hazard a pretty solid guess in the light of one of the more unusual features of Jacob's vision as interpreted by these communities, namely, the fact that a replica of the patriarch's image was inscribed on the 'head' of the ladder (i.e. the heavenly throne, the *merkabah* of Ezek. 1.26–28).[80] In fact, on this interpretation, the Bethel vision included not just one image emblazoned on the 'head' of the ladder but also a second matching image at the bottom of the ladder, on the 'head' of Jacob himself, with angels scurrying up and down between the two 'heads' comparing the likeness in wonder.[81] The supposition of matching 'images', broadly granted in the Judaism of Jesus' day and later maintained by rabbinic and merkabah Judaism, was probably prompted by Adam's double identification as both the 'head' of creation and the primordial *eikōn* of God, together with a double occurrence of 'head' in the dream sequence. Since there can only be one Adamic 'head' and one 'image of God', ancient interpreters of Genesis 28 must have reasoned that the two 'heads' were in fact one head, one image, which also happened to be Jacob's image. From here, because the task of bearing the Adamic image was normally reserved for the high priest, this same line of interpretation almost certainly claimed that Jacob himself retained a high-priestly status, even if not of the Levitical priesthood. Thus, *Jubilees* and the *Temple Scroll* put us in touch with an eschatological expectation of not only Jacob's construction of the eternal temple, but also – precisely in his capacity as the image-bearer – his high-priestly oversight of the same. Although we lack explicit statement of Jacob's priestly administration of the eschatological temple, the point is virtually entailed by the details of Genesis 28's interpretation.

Adam, Jacob and the Son of Man

A second set of inferences is also in order: namely, Jacob's identification with both Adam and the Son of Man. Jacob's linkage to Adam is clearly attested

---

[79] Mroczek 2015: 523.
[80] For this discussion see *Tg. Ps.-J.* on Gen. 28.12; *Tg. Neof.* on Gen. 28.12; *Gen. Rab.* 82.2; *Num. Rab.* 4.15; *Lam. Rab.* 2.1. For secondary sources, see Schwartz 1985; Hayward 1996: 100–1; VanderKam 1997c; Bunta 2006.
[81] A review of the primary literature can be found in Rowland 1984: 504; Fossum 1995: 143 n. 30; Orlov 2004.

in the early rabbinic literature, not surprisingly so.[82] For the rabbinic inter-preters, this connection followed from a handful of considerations, including their shared role as divine image-bearers, their shared connection with the throne, and their double identity as both fragile humans (who undertake the distinctive human activity of sleep) and exalted beings. Simultaneously mocked and adored by the angels (depending on which 'image' the angels were viewing at the time), Adam and Jacob together functioned as handy metaphors for the already-but-not-yet paradox which sought to hold human frailty together with eschatological glory. Though I am not aware of any explicit connection between Jacob and the Danielic Son of Man in the pri-mary literature, one can see why such an association would also be highly inviting in the minds of the ancient interpreters on the basis of a simple syllogism. After all, if Adam and the Danielic Son of Man were already exegetically coordinated in Second-Temple Jewish thought, then Jacob's identification with Adam would seem to imply a triangular relationship – not least in their shared role as bearers of the *eikōn*.

The conflation of Jacob and the Son of Man clearly obtains, again, in John 1.51, with the consensus of Johannine commentators holding that Jesus' mention of angels ascending and descending on the Son of Man is a direct reference to the Bethel dream. To be sure, though these same commentators are divided as to whether Jesus *qua* Son of Man is to be identified with the ladder or Jacob himself, John's broader interest in a Jacob–Jesus typology (evident not least in John 4) leads us to prefer the latter option.[83] If in the Fourth Gospel Jesus is at once the new Jacob and the Son of Man, John's exalted and glorified Son of Man is also clearly the Danielic Son of Man.[84] By the end of the first century, early Christianity made no bones about Jacob and the Danielic Son of Man converging in the person of Jesus.

If we take small liberties in stretching the trajectory a handful of decades earlier, then Q 9.58 must preserve the historical Jesus' attempt to define his own Son of Man movement within this well-established interpretation of the Bethel vision described above. In gesturing to the founding narrative of the eschatological temple, as contained in Genesis 28.10–22, Jesus was not only alluding to his movement's vagabond state, but also explaining it. Even though Jacob was the image-bearing Son of Man in his own day, Jesus and his interlocutors well knew, he would have no place to lay his head (image) until the realization of the final temple at the eschaton. In the same way, so Jesus confirmed, the present Son of Man movement had no immediate aspirations either for building a physical temple to replace Herod's or for asserting raw political power. And just as Jacob would one day take up his

---

[82] This is amply documented in Bunta 2006 with a thorough review of the primary literature.

[83] The Samaritan woman's ironic question to Jesus ('Are you greater than our ancestor Jacob, who gave us the well, and with his sons and his flocks drank from it?') in John 4.12, together with the scene's invocation of Jacob's first meeting of his future bride Rachel (Gen. 29.1–12), confirms Jesus as an antitype of Jacob.

[84] John 8.28; 12.23, 34; 13.31; cf. Dan. 7.10, 14.

glorious priestly mantle, initially denied to him in the present time, so too the same glory would one day accrue to Jesus and his followers. To summarize, if the aspiring disciple described in Q 9.57–58 was entertaining visions of instant results through glorious revolution (we can only guess on this point), then Jesus is responding not with a pithy romantic sentiment about home-lessness (as the text has been commonly interpreted) but a narrative which promises that his priestly movement's rule is at once assured and deferred. Whereas Jacob was 'a wandering Aramean' (Deut. 26.5) in his own day, the same landlessness and social powerlessness would – by divine design – char-acterize Jesus' movement.

An alternative ethic: an excursus on the double commandment (Mark 12.28–34 par.)

Repelled by the rapaciousness and violence of the religious elites who had aligned themselves with the Roman-backed Herod and the high priest Caiaphas, Jesus was resolved to distance his movement from the *Realpolitik* of the first-century world. This is not because Jesus saw power and authority as intrinsically problematic, but because the narratives of the Son of Man and Jacob had outlined a different path, a path where suffering and exile must precede the honour of eschatological priesthood. The *modus operandi* adopted by Jesus' well-entrenched opponents was to be rejected, not least because it involved the kind of predatory attitudes and practices characteristic of the metaphorical 'jackals' and 'birds of the air'. This was the way of destructive self-aggrandizement, the very antithesis of the self-surrendering posture required of Yahweh's priests in the present eschatological crisis.

Jesus famously spoke to this posture in his well-known double love com-mand, which enjoined love for God and one's neighbour.[85] In this passage, the Evangelist recounts a conversation in which a certain scribe approaches Jesus with the question: 'What is the first commandment of all?' Jesus responds by citing not one but two commandments: the Shema (Deut. 6.4–5) and the Levitical command to 'love your neighbour as yourself' (Lev. 19.18b). Impressed by this answer, the scribe agrees with Jesus and adds that the faithful keeping of these commands is 'much more important than all whole burnt-offerings and sacrifices' (v. 33). The scene closes with Jesus congratulating his interlocutor on his insight (v. 34).

While the calls to love God and love humanity are sometimes paired in both pre-Christian and post-temple Jewish texts, and similar attempts to summarize Torah could have quite possibly been current in Jesus' day, neither the former fact nor the latter possibility should detract from the inno-vativeness of this exegetical move.[86] That the double love commandment was

[85] Mark 12.28–34 (par. Matt. 22.34–40//Luke 10.25–28).
[86] For summaries along this line, see, e.g., *Letter of Aristeas* 132; Philo, *Decal.* 65; *Spec. Leg.* 2.63; *b. Shab.* 31a; *T. Dan.* 5.3; *T. Iss.* 5.1–2.

already 'in the air' at the time is rendered unlikely by, among other factors, the fact that the early Christian movement was the first to assert Leviticus 19.18 as *the* summarizing commandment.[87] Nor do we have any traditions prior to Jesus coordinating these two verses, much less elevating either one to the status of a leading principle. Although the point is sometimes disputed, it is generally agreed that the historical Jesus himself was responsible for this distinctive coupling of Deuteronomy 6.4–5 and Leviticus 19.18, only then to combine both in a single transcendent norm.

Jesus' rationale for prioritizing these two commandments remains unstated. But if the scribe agreed on the point, then it is unlikely that he would have done so without having been already persuaded on the point by Jesus himself. For this reason, we should be cautious before ascribing too much ingenuity to the scribe when he injects the notion of sacrificial offerings into the conversation (Mark 12.33). When the unnamed interlocutor freely adds – much to Jesus' approval – that the keeping of the two commandments is greater than the temple sacrifices, he is probably repeating a judgement that Jesus himself had already implied. In other words, he was only connecting the dots which had first been put into place by Jesus.

Following my analysis of Q 9.58 (not to mention Mark 2.23–28), I suggested that Jesus thought of his own temple society as an itinerant movement transcending conventional categories of sacred space. Now in speaking to the double commandment's superiority over temple sacrifices, the scribe in this scene is expressing a judgement which fits hand in glove with the same scenario. The exchange of Mark 12.28–34 also resonates with other religious agendas of Jesus' day, including that of the Qumran community, a sect which likewise sought to create an alternative temple system. Indeed, in commenting on Mark 12.28–34, interpreters will often refer to a well-known passage from the Qumran covenanters' *Community Rule (serekh ha-yahad)*:

> When these become members of the community of Israel according to all these rules, they shall establish the spirit of holiness according to the everlasting truth. They shall atone for guilty rebellion and for sins of unfaithfulness . . . without the flesh of burnt offerings and the fat of sacrifice. And prayer rightly offered shall become an acceptable fragrance of righteousness, and perfection of way as a delectable free-will offering.[88]

The passage attests to the Dead Sea sect's commitment to carrying out distinctively priestly tasks (atoning sacrifice and prayer) yet entirely *outside* of the temple context. Here there is no sense that acts of holiness and prayer were paltry substitutes for 'the real thing' taking place back in Jerusalem: as best as we can tell, the covenanters were convinced that they were very much about 'the real thing', taking care of temple business more effectively than was being done on the official temple grounds. Similar parallels from

---

[87] Rom. 13.8–10; Gal. 5.14; Jas. 2.8; *Did.* 1.2, 2.3; *Barn.* 19.5.
[88] 1QS 8.4–5.

other texts, involving, for example, the study of Torah standing in for temple sacrifices could just as easily be marshalled. As a witness to Jesus' temple-less temple movement, Mark 12.28–34 fits perfectly in the first-century landscape.

But what makes the comparison between Jesus' movement and the Qumran community especially instructive for our understanding of Mark 12.28–34 is the latter's self-identification as the *yahad* (the 'unity' or 'one-ness') of Israel, in connection with its function as Israel's provisional temple through prayer and holiness. At a time when Israel had found itself in the theologically intolerable situation of countenancing multiple temples (here one recalls the surrogate temple operations of Leontopolis and Shechem), and this on top of – what was for the Dead Sea sect – a highly problematic temple in Jerusalem, the 'oneness community' justified its name on the basis of not only its unified mission but also the nature of its objective, that is, to be the *one* converging point at which the once scattered tribes of the southern and northern kingdoms would reunite in return from exile. Whereas the post-exilic prophetic tradition had long yearned for Yahweh-directed worship of 'one accord' (Zech. 3.9) and grieved over the scattering of the tribes that had resulted from Israel's covenantal unfaithfulness (Zech. 11.7–14), the Qumran believers hoped that the 'oneness' of their goals and set-apart life would secure their vocation as eschatological priests. Of course ultimately the sect's aspirations for oneness, borne out by its very name, followed the-ologically on the unicity of Yahweh's very self. Because God's very oneness had been compromised by the emergence of multiple worship sites, with cor-responding worshipping communities to boot, so the Qumran sect believed, the successful completion of their return-from-exile mission would mean nothing less than the restoration of the oneness of God.

This background, I think, further explains not only why Jesus paired Deuteronomy 6.4–5 with Leviticus 19.18b, but also why he seems to have done so within a cultic framework. The Shema (Deut. 6.4–5) was ancient Judaism's cardinal expression of its monotheistic faith, the central affirmation of the oneness of God. In the post-exilic era, because the revealed unic-ity of Yahweh could be no greater than the political and social cohesion of Israel itself, the historical scattering of the tribes and present conditions of social strife were seen as having tragically fractured this oneness (Mal. 2.7–10; Zech. 14.9). For Jesus it was this very logic, which demanded a cor-respondence between horizontal unity and divine unicity that provided the grounds for Jesus' prioritization of love for one's neighbour (Lev. 19.18b) *alongside* the Shema (Deut. 6.4–5). Jesus granted the Shema paramount status because the worship of the one God (and the rejection of idols) was Israel's highest calling; he privileged Leviticus 19.18b alongside the Shema because love for one's neighbour was *the* paramount condition for Israel's self-realiza-tion as one people of the one God. Jesus never seems to have considered love for one's neighbour to be a moral end unto itself, as countless, post-Kantian 'Lives of Jesus' from the nineteenth century onward seem to have assumed.

Instead love for one's neighbour was ultimately a means of honouring Yahweh's oneness, while the communal practice of love was divine unicity's necessary expression. In contrast to the jackal-like and bird-like tendencies of Israel's current leaders, all too consistent with the animalistic behaviour of Israel's earlier leaders which had also threatened the unity of God's people, Jesus sought to model an unconditioned love and expected his followers to follow suit – all with a view to achieving the same kind of 'yahad' which the Qumran community endeavoured to establish through holiness and prayer. Thus love followed divine identity. Jesus and his enquiring scribe regarded love for God and neighbour as superior sacrifices not because the practice of these loves was categorically different from such rituals, but because such loves were the supreme expression of the sacrificial act. In holding to an ethic of love, Jesus was essentially calling his followers to a corporate act of worship.

The double commandment retained both a negative and positive aspect. Sitting alongside Jesus' denunciation of the self-serving jackals and birds, Jesus' ethic of love takes on sharpened definition not as the enjoining of a sentiment or feeling, but as the rigorous rejection of any and all self-serving orientations which are principally aimed at the consolidation of power. (Some hint of this already comes by way of Jesus' beatitudes, where attitudes of inner meekness and gentleness are enjoined as appropriate dispositions for those interested in joining his new temple order.) It was also, at least in part, a calculated response to the official mediators of the divine presence, who according to Jesus were leading Israel's culture in exactly the wrong direction. To state this positively: by issuing the double commandment in cultic terms, Jesus sought to convey that his gathered community would only come into its own as comprising members gave themselves to ongoing and repeated acts of self-surrender – unto God and unto each other. Accordingly, personal and corporate obedience to the two greatest commands would remain the chief means by which the community's identity as the eschatological priesthood would be realized. Jesus' prioritization of love followed not so much from any abstract principles or even from a set of favourite isolated proof texts, but rather from his conviction that a thoroughgoing communal oneness, reflective of divine oneness, was a central entailment of his movement's sacerdotal mission.

Synthesis

Carefully constructed with choice scriptural terms and probably reiterated on numerous occasions, Jesus' statement in Q 9.58 was as much a veiled polemic against temple-based and Roman-backed entities as it was a clarification of his own movement's vocation. Here Jesus intimates his identity as the fulfilment of Jacob, the deferred high priest *par excellence*. Like the revered patriarch, he and the rest of his Son of Man movement had nowhere to lay their heads, because they, again like Jacob, were awaiting the realization of the eschatological temple now already taking place. In positioning himself along this trajectory of expectation, Jesus was disclosing that though he himself was destined to preside over the eternal temple, he and his followers (present and aspiring) would have to content themselves in the present time as temple-less, socially disempowered priests.

Jesus' approach stood in sharp contrast to the strategy adopted by the imperial governance system and the temple authorities local to Jerusalem, metaphorized by the birds and the jackals, respectively. Whereas the Roman-sponsored Herod and leading members of the temple elite had entered into an uneasy alliance in order to consolidate their respective bases of political power, Jesus asked his followers to turn their gaze in an entirely different direction, to a future temple yet to be revealed. For all who had nurtured wild-eyed visions of displacing the godless powerbrokers through messianic revolt, Jesus' words preserved in Q 9.58 came as a chastening caveat, clarifying that his movement had no intentions of becoming a Zealot-style operation with misguided hopes of revolution. Furthermore, unlike Israel's appointed leaders and their revolutionary 'wannabes', Jesus intentionally avoided laying claim to any defining physical space, or to building upon any pre-existing power structures. In a world where power was institutionally and geographically situated, Jesus' rejection of standing structures and standard construals of space was an unusual move, to say the least. According to his vision, the eschatological temple space was to be launched in the present not on the platform of any physical space or on the foundation of pre-established social space but on the basis of his own person. Until the arrival of the eschaton, Jesus himself defined sacred space and sacred structures.

Jesus' critique of Israel's leadership was matched by a positive assertion which demanded that his followers love God and neighbour as the defining feature of their priestly vocation. Only as a loving community could Jesus' movement hope to achieve the practical unity befitting the one God it had claimed to worship. Likewise, in designating the double commandment as greater than all sacrifices, Jesus sought not to trivialize the temple cult but to show that love gave full embodied expression to such prescribed sacrifices. Priesthood required nothing less than absolute self-surrender.

Schweitzer, we recall, had opined that Jesus' ethics were interim in character, situated squarely within the eschatological crisis at hand. If this analysis of Jesus' ethics is correct, then we must acknowledge that Schweitzer was far closer to the truth than most scholars today are willing to admit. Induced by a close reading of Q 9.58 and Mark 12.28–34, and lacking evidence that Jesus was concerned to promulgate a universal ethic for the betterment of humanity in general, I conclude that Jesus' teachings were issued for a specific community holding a special role within the period of eschatological transition. The end point of this transition was nothing less than the eschatological temple. Informed by signal scriptural stories sharing a common schema, the journey to that destination was determined by the overarching imperative of truly monotheistic worship.

Inclusive table practices: the parable of the children in the marketplace (Q 7.31–35 = Matt. 11.16–19//Luke 7.31–35)

Our third and final Son of Man saying comes down to us in Matthew 11.2–19 and Luke 7.19–35, a cohesive chunk of text ordinarily ascribed to Q. In both Gospels, the passage cleanly breaks down into three segments, in which (1) John the Baptizer sends messengers to Jesus querying his putative messianic status (Matt. 11.2–6//Luke 7.19–23); (2) Jesus offers a response along with an addendum regarding John's unique role within the redemptive plan (Matt. 11.7–15//Luke 7.24–30); and finally, (3) Jesus tells a parable, clearly applicable to all the scene's main players, about children playing in a marketplace (Matt. 11.16–19//Luke 7.31–35). My primary concern will be with the third section, the parable and its interpretation:

> [16]But to what will I compare this generation? It is like children sitting in the market-places and calling to one another, [17]'We played the flute for you, and you did not dance; we wailed, and you did not mourn.' [18]For John came neither eating nor drinking, and they say, 'He has a demon'; [19]the Son of Man came eating and drinking, and they say, 'Look, a glutton and a drunkard, a friend of tax collectors and sinners!' Yet wisdom is vindicated by her deeds.[89]

> [29](And all the people who heard this, including the tax-collectors, acknowledged the justice of God, because they had been baptized with John's baptism. [30]But by refusing to be baptized by him, the Pharisees and the lawyers rejected God's purpose for themselves.) [31]'To what then will I compare the people of this generation, and what are they like? [32]They are like children sitting in the market-place and calling to one another, "We played the flute for you, and you did not dance; we wailed, and you did not weep." [33]For John the Baptist has come eating no bread and drinking no wine, and you say, "He has a demon"; [34]the Son of Man has come eating and drinking, and you say, "Look, a glutton and a drunkard, a friend of tax-collectors and sinners!" [35]Nevertheless, wisdom is vindicated by all her children.'[90]

> [31]To what am I to compare this generation and what is it like? [32]It is like children seated in the marketplaces(s), who addressing (the others), say: 'We fluted for you, but you would not dance; we wailed, but you would not cry'. [33]For John came, neither eating nor drinking, and you say: 'He has a demon'. [34]The Son of Man came, eating and drinking, and you say: 'Look, a person who is a glutton and drunkard, a friend of tax collectors and sinners. [35]But Wisdom has been vindicated by her children.[91]

That Jesus spoke a parable like this one is, as far as most scholars are concerned,

---

[89] Matt. 11.16–19.
[90] Luke 7.31–35.
[91] Q 7.31–35. Translation is a modification of Robinson, Hoffmann and Kloppenborg 2000: 140–8.

far more likely than not.[92] As one might expect, other details remain contested, including the parable's original scope. The extant parable breaks down into three parts: (1) the parable proper (Q 7.31–32), (2) its application to John and Jesus (vv. 33–34), and the conclusion (v. 35). A few scholars see the application (vv. 33–34) as a late or independent addition, but most are convinced of its authenticity.[93] More problematic for some is verse 35, which apparently smacks too much of late Wisdom Christology, but this too is a minority report. Rightly so, for although Luke and Matthew may have a demonstrated interest in Wisdom Christology, this does not mean that every trace of sapiential language, including verse 35, must have been inserted late in the game as part of a relentless campaign to rebrand Jesus as embodied Wisdom. Nor should we be so quick to lay this interest, as is so commonly done, at Q's doorstep.[94] Rather, given the fierce clash between the historical Jesus and his opponents over proper Torah interpretation, we would be all the more puzzled if we had no evidence of either side framing the disagreement in the familiar language of the 'two ways tradition' (the way of wisdom and the way of perdition), just as we have it here. Taking on interlocutors who regarded themselves as the true guardians of Torah piety, Jesus countered by characterizing his own movement as the very epitome of Wisdom. All said and done, it is difficult to imagine how the impasse presented by verses 31–34 would even make sense, much less be worth remembering, apart from something like the sapiential tailpiece of verse 35.[95] Accordingly, Q 7.31–35 should be taken as a cohesive unit reflecting Jesus' voice.

Towards unpacking Jesus' intentions in performing the parable of the children, and the meaning of 'the Son of Man' within it, I want to take an approach similar to the one I used in my discussion of the parable of salt (Chapter 3). In my treatment of that passage, I sought to identify shared notional assumptions which emerged through each Evangelist's distinctive handling of the precursor text. So far as the parable of the marketplace children is concerned, if it can be shown that Matthew and Luke (and/or Q) logically depend on certain shared premises which are not necessarily entailed by either text in isolation but stand to explain the differences between both, then this common core puts us in good stead for accessing a much earlier

---

[92] Its historicity is vouched for by Dodd 1961: 15–16; Jeremias 1963: 160–2; Norman Perrin 1967: 12–21; Marshall 1978: 298; Lindars 1983: 31–4; Borg 1987: 131–2; Crossan 1991: 260; Bock 1994: 661; Wright 1996: 149; Becker 1998: 166–7; Schnackenburg 2002: 107; Dunn 2003: 453–4; Blomberg 2009: 48–9; Casey 2010: 363–5; Crossley 2015: 110. True, the Jesus Seminar (Funk and Hoover 1993: 302) reports 'improbable gray' but apparently this was a highly conflicted decision, since were it not for the presence of the phrase 'Son of Man' the seminar 'agreed broadly that these characterizations fit what we otherwise know of John and Jesus' (303).

[93] Vaage (1994: 108–11); Maier and Herzer (2001: 284–5) separate out vv. 33–34.

[94] Robinson 1975: 4–6; Hartin 1995: 153–6; Horsley 1991: 187 (though Horsley himself states that the core materials of Q 7 are 'early' and 'well prior to Q'). Much of this agenda seems to be driven by the *idée fixe* that Q is a 'sapiential text', a construct which has been roundly criticized over the years, not least by Allison 1997: 4–7; Tuckett 1996: 69–75.

[95] As pointed out by Nolland 2005: 346; Légasse 1969: 311.

tradition. And if that early tradition coheres with the setting of Jesus, then we have pay dirt. To illustrate this principle: wherever the two sets of tones emerging from the stereophonic tradition – Matthew's woofer and Luke's tweeter, as it were – converge in a common voice-print, there we are probably hearing the voice of Jesus himself.

Hearing Jesus' voice behind the traditions

There are a number of differences between Luke's and Matthew's respective handlings of the parable of the children. Two are especially significant. First, whereas Matthew moves directly from a discussion of the Baptizer (Matt. 11.7–15) into the parable (vv. 16–19), the third Evangelist inserts a redactional statement that 'all the people . . . including the tax collectors' had justified God (*edikaiōsan ton theon*), but the scribes and tax collectors had not (Luke 7.29–30). Second, whereas Matthew has Wisdom being justified by her works (*ergōn*) (Matt. 11.19), according to Luke, who is said to be following Q, Wisdom is justified by her children (*tōn teknōn autēs*) (Luke 7.35). Whether and to what extent these differences materially affect the meaning of Matthew and Luke's respective version of the parable will require further consideration.

For now, the first order of business is to make sense of the two groups of shouting children in the shared Q tradition. Some commentators identify the flute-playing children with the convivial Jesus community, whereas the dirge-singing youth are the ascetical Baptizer community; meanwhile those who refuse to dance and mourn are the religious leaders.[96] Other interpreters, quite differently, first find a correspondence between 'this generation' (as a pejorative term) and the flautist/dirge-singer children, who are the implacable religious leaders opposed to John and Jesus.[97] While good arguments have been made in support of both readings, in my view the scale of evidence tips gently in favour of the latter – and that for at least two reasons.

First, as Wendy Cotter notes, the fact that the children are *sitting* in a marketplace (*agora*) quite literally positions them as judges, suggesting that John and Jesus are being called to account by peevish listeners who pose as judges but are anything but true judges.[98] Second, as Brian Dennert has more recently pointed out, the saying 'We played the flute for you but you did not dance' was not, as Jeremias mused, a line from a child's game, but a proverbial expression which imagined a socially or politically superior 'flute player' making demands which went unheeded by subordinates who refused to dance.[99] Once this piece is established, the religious authorities fit the bill

[96] Zeller 1977: 252–7; Nolland 2005: 462; Maier and Herzer 2001: 289–92; Wilson 2015: 5.
[97] Linton 1976; Grundmann 1968: 312; Davies and Allison 1988–97: 2.261–2; Carson 1994: 139–41.
[98] Cotter 1987.
[99] Dennert 2015: 51.

as the retainers of socio-political power, while John and Jesus are the ones accused of failing to toe the line, whether by under-stepping it (as in the case of the non-dancing John) or overstepping it (as in the case of the non-mourning Jesus). Jesus' parable, then, paints his and John's critics as having fallen prey to the 'Goldilocks syndrome', thrusting unrealistic demands on God's true messengers. It is not John and Jesus, but the implacable religious leaders, who station themselves in the market square. With these points established, we turn now to Matthew and Luke.

Wisdom and her works (Matt. 11.16–19)

It will be impossible to offer a meaningful interpretation of Matthew 11.16–19 without settling just what Matthew means by 'Wisdom' (*sophia*), 'the works' (*tōn ergōn*) of Wisdom and the manner in which Wisdom is 'justified' (*edikiaōthē*) (v. 19b). Towards resolving the second of these issues, we recall the common observation that 'the works' of Wisdom in verse 19b form an *inclusio* with 'the works [*ta erga*] of the Messiah' (my translation) in verse 2. This bracketing not only marks off verses 2–19 as a discrete unit but also implies some kind of notional kinship between these two sets of 'works'.[100] As a second observation, when John looks into the meaning of the messianic *erga* being wrought under Jesus' leadership (v. 2), Jesus responds by cataloguing a series of activities drawn from conventional messianic *testimonia* inspired by Isaiah (v. 5). Thus Jesus' answer not only confirms his *erga* as messianic works, but also links his messianic identity with these specific activities.[101]

The 'works' of Wisdom – whose works anyway?

Having determined that the activities itemized in verse 5 are instances of the 'works' of verse 2, we can sharpen up our understanding of these 'works'/activities with recourse to the broader Matthean context. While the 'works of the Christ' (*ta erga tou Christou*) (v. 2) prompting John's dispatch certainly include the miracles performed in Matthew 8—9, the timing of the Baptizer's query suggests that it was triggered more immediately by the Twelve's missionary activity (Matthew 10), together with Jesus' preaching activity which enfolds it (9.35, 11.1).[102] And indeed, judging by his response to John (11.5), it seems that Jesus focuses not so much on his own proclamation but on the successfully executed messianic tasks delegated to the Twelve (10.1–8). Whereas the apostles had been instructed to proclaim the kingdom (10.7), Jesus announces to John's messengers that the poor are now being

---

[100] On the *inclusio* created by the repetition of the two terms, see Carson (1994: 134) who comments, 'we need not doubt; that these words were introduced as Matthean redaction is likely'.

[101] Matt. 10.5. Cf. Isa. 29.18; 35.5–6; 42.18; 61.1, also 4Q175. As far as I can see, the point is universally accepted by the commentators.

[102] So, e.g., Edwards 1982: 266; Luz 1989–2005: 2.134. Carson (1994: 134) includes the Sermon on the Mount (Matthew 5—7) in the category of such works, but this seems gratuitous.

'gospelized' (11.5). Whereas the Twelve had been sent out to raise the dead (10.8b), their master is happy to report, the dead are now being raised (11.5). Whereas the apostles had been instructed to cleanse lepers (10.8c), lepers are now being cleansed (11.5). To be sure, each of these apostolic mandates has already been modelled by Christ.[103] But given the fairly obvious parallels between the apostles' assigned activities and Jesus' report to the Baptizer's envoys, we are forced to conclude that Matthew's phrase *erga tou Christou* refers to actions performed by Jesus *and* the Twelve. In this sense, these are not so much 'works of the Christ' (subjective genitive) but 'messianic works' (qualitative genitive). This in turn may explain why John's perplexity had come to a snapping point just here. Perhaps when the Baptizer heard that Jesus was reproducing his ministry through as many as 12 individuals, this would naturally have raised the question as to whether one of Jesus' protégés would become greater than Jesus himself, potentially stretching out the eschatological timetable envisaged by John.

Designated as messianic works in 11.2, the activities of Jesus and his disciples (Matthew 9—11.1) are not unrelated to the metaphorical children's displeasure in 11.16. This becomes clear given the connection between the recurrence of *polis* ('town' or 'city') in Matthew 9—11.2 and the children being specifically – otherwise seemingly gratuitously – located in the marketplaces (11.16). Having sent the Twelve into the cities (10.5, 11, 14, 15, 23 (2x)), Jesus follows up by undertaking his own wrap-up tour of 'their cities' (*polesin autōn* (11.1)). Of course, as anyone with even passing familiarity with ancient urban geography would assume, Jesus and the Twelve would most likely undertake the proclamation of the kingdom and associated activities – including healing and public debate – not in some out-of-the-way alley but in the town's city centre: the *agora*. So, then, when Jesus eventually compares his detractors to children sitting in the city centres (*agorais*) (11.16), his primary focus is not on their rejection of the Baptizer (though this is clearly of a piece) but much more so on the frosty reception incurred by Jesus and the Twelve, precisely as they had been rejected in the marketplaces of the cities (9.1; 10.5, 11, 14, 15, 23 (2x); 11.2). Tragically, though the works performed in Matthew 9—11.2 were intended to harbinger the arrival of the kingdom through Jesus, these nevertheless fail to disabuse the *agora*-based leaders of their negative judgements on Jesus/the Twelve, not to mention John. Though the offence alluded to in 11.16–19 clearly revolves around dining practices, the parabolic children's location in the *agorais* forbids us from finally separating these practices from the messianic activities of 11.2, 5.

The complex interaction between Jesus, John and their disciples

Having shown that Matthew's *erga tou Christou* (11.2) are eschatological works predicated of the entire Jesus movement (rather than of Jesus as an

---

[103] Proclamation of the kingdom (10.7 > 9.35); raising of the dead (10.8b > 9.23–26); cleansing of lepers (10.8c > 8.1–4); etc.

individual), I now want to make the same argument in relation to the 'eating and drinking' attributed to the Son of Man (v. 19a). The argument begins to fall into place once we recognize that the controversy alluded to in verses 16–19 is actually a reprise of an earlier pair of controversy stories contained in 9.9–17: the calling of Matthew (vv. 9–13) and the question about fasting (vv. 14–17). In the first of these two passages from Matthew 9, which portrays Jesus hosting a party for the morally suspect, the Pharisees ask his disciples, 'Why does your teacher eat with tax-collectors?' (9.11). Then, in the following pericope, John's disciples ask Jesus about *his disciples'* decision to forgo fasting (vv. 14–17). With the Pharisees taking the disciples to task for their master's dining practices and John's disciples taking Jesus to task for his disciples' dining practices, the two scenes together comprise back-to-back episodes of triangulated confrontation. Presented as two birds of a common feather, the Pharisees and John's disciples – so Matthew's arrangement emphasizes – find common cause on the matter of the Jesus movement's table practices.[104] And although the two sets of questions each receive provisional resolution of sorts, the rather serious accusation underlying both is only decisively put to rest with the parable of 11.16–19. Here, in closing arguments to the sharp line of questioning occasioned by the Son of Man's eating and drinking (9.9–17), Matthew's Jesus resorts to juridical language by declaring that Wisdom is justified (*edikaiōthē*) by her works (v. 19).

As far as John's role in all this (as Matthew thought of it), we should probably not assume either, on the one extreme, that John's disciples were speaking directly for the Baptizer at 9.14–17 or, on the other extreme, that John would have considered his disciples' interrogation to be entirely rogue. The truth, Matthew's readers suspect, lay somewhere in between. And so Matthew's characterization of John acquires a certain nuance, even ambivalence. After all, though John initially supported Jesus in Matthew 3, by Matthew 11 he is now revisiting this judgement, even as his own disciples raise some serious questions about the dining practices of Jesus and his followers (Matthew 9). At the same time, Matthew's Jesus still affirms John's exceptional role in the redemptive turn of events and does so in glowing terms (11.7–15). Neither unflinchingly virtuous nor measurably diminished by his moment of doubt, Matthew's John emerges as a complex, even paradoxical figure, who nevertheless remains vindicated by his own greatness (v. 15).

Because John is vindicated in 11.15 despite his shortcomings, the point hardly needs repeating in verses 16–19 (John's disciples, however, are perhaps not altogether off the hook!). Indeed, the mention of the ascetical Baptizer in verses 16–19 is designed not to make a fresh assertion about John but to

---

[104] Wilson (2015: 2) rightly comments: 'the incident [of Matt. 9.14–17] also has the effect of aligning John's disciples with Jesus' opponents, both in the way that they include the Pharisees in their question (9, 14) and in the way that they follow the Pharisees' example by posing the question to Jesus while he is at table (cf. 9, 10–11).' Similarly Repschinski 2000: 84.

add one more count to the religious leaders' indictment. And, to be sure, although a blinkered focus on verses 16–19 may yield the initial impression that verse 19b is somehow meant to vindicate both Jesus and John, the fuller context of 9.9—11.19 points us in a very different direction: the obvious correlation between 9.9–17 and 11.16–19, together with the fact that in the former passage John's disciples link arms with the critics of Jesus' dining practices, makes it patently unlikely that John is in any sense a beneficiary of Wisdom's justification (v. 19b). The justification of verse 19b extends neither to John nor, strictly speaking, to Jesus only, but rather to Jesus and his followers who together in their shared dining practices fall under the category of Wisdom. For Matthew, Wisdom is embodied in the whole Jesus movement, even through its habits of eating and drinking.

The double helix of Wisdom and Spirit (Matt. 11.5)

With this insight in mind, we are finally positioned to coordinate the matching 'works' of verse 2 and verse 19b in a more meaningful way by anchoring both in Matthew's appropriation of Isaiah (v. 5). On a very basic level, of course, Matthew's Jesus resorts to the composite quotation of Isaiah 29.18, 35.5–6, 42.18, 61.1 in verse 5 as a handy way of explaining his own movement's activity as messianic activity.[105] In this connection it is surely no coincidence, as Martin Hengel has persuasively argued in a much-neglected essay, that the four Isaianic texts behind Matthew 11.5 (Isa. 29.18; 35.5–6; 42.18; 61.1) comprise a composite *testimonium* which combines the saving movement of Wisdom (Isa. 29.18) with the outpouring of the Spirit (Isa. 35.5–6; 42.18; 61.1).[106] Within the Judaism of the day, the eschatological convergence of Wisdom and Spirit would not have been an unusual notion, since, at least by the time we come to the writing of the first-century BCE Wisdom of Solomon, Wisdom *is* the Spirit.[107] But unlike the author of Wisdom, Matthew maintains that only now through Jesus and his movement are the Isaianic promises of Wisdom and Spirit coming into fruition; only now, too, are the works of Wisdom and Spirit being revealed. So, then, just as Matthew's Jesus seeks at Matthew 11.5 to convince the Baptizer of his messianic credentials by chalking the 'works' of Matthew 9—11.2 up to the

---

[105] So, e.g., Luz 1989–2005: 2.134. In Isa. 29.18, the prophet predicts that 'the eyes of the blind shall see' (*ophthalmoi typlōn blepsontai*) and that the 'deaf shall hear' (*akousontai kōphoi*). Similarly, Isa. 35.5–6 presages the time when the 'eyes of the blind shall be opened' (*anoichthēsontai ophthalmoi typlōn*), the 'ears of the deaf [will be] unstopped' (*ōta kōphōn akousontai*), and 'the lame shall leap' (*haleitai . . . ho chōlos*). Isa. 42.18 commands: 'you that are blind, look up and see!' (*typhloi anablepsate*) and 'Listen, you that are deaf' (*kōphoi akousate*). Moreover, Isa. 61.1 looks forward to the preaching of the good news among the poor (*echrisen me euanglisasthai ptōchoi*). In effect, out of the six categories of marginalized people mentioned in Matt. 11.5, four (the blind, the lame, the dead and the poor) are pulled right out of Isaiah's vision of return from exile. The implications are clear enough: the Isaianic pastiche contained in Matt. 11.5 is clearly meant to show that the eschatological salvation which Isaiah had promised was now unfolding in the ministry of Jesus and the Twelve.

[106] Hengel 1979.

[107] Wisd. 7.21–26.

eruption of Wisdom and the Spirit, so too at verse 19b, in parallel fashion, the Evangelist once again draws attention to the probative 'works' of Wisdom, this time coming to expression in the Son of Man's table practices. Together Jesus and his disciples are Wisdom, even as they are the Son of Man; their activities are the works of Wisdom, as well as messianic works.

Faced with Matthew's habit of defining wisdom in Christological terms, so much interpretation of Matthew 11.16–19 has laboured under the burden of trying to explain how the justification of Wisdom (v. 19b) could possibly extend to the exoneration of both the Son of Man (v. 19a) and John (v. 18) – unnecessarily so. For once we absorb Matthew's clues (via Matthew 9) that John is not to be included in the purview of verse 19b, and once too we recognize the corporate quality of the messianic signs, we can finally accede to a clean-cut parallelism between Wisdom (v. 19b) and the Son of Man (v. 19a), on the one side, and the 'works of Wisdom' (v. 19b) and the 'works of the Christ' (v. 2), on the other.[108]

John's exclusion from the justification of verse 19b should be no cause for exegetical stumbling, since the Baptizer has already been anticipatorily vindicated (vv. 7–15) over and against the later-mentioned criticisms of the Pharisees (v. 18). Once we come to verses 16–19, the point is no longer John's vindication but the vindication of Jesus along with his followers. Building on an important parallel between the messianic 'works' of 11.2 and the 'works' of Wisdom in verse 19, verses 16–19 serve not only to defend the Jesus movement against charges of gluttony and drunkenness, earlier brought by the Pharisees and the disciples of John, but also to assert the same as the Wisdom-embodying Son of Man. Though verses 5 and 19b may speak to the vindication of the Jesus movement in two different ways (the messianic works of Matthew 8.1—11.1 and the meals of Matthew 9) and on two different fronts (John and the Pharisees), both sets of works – again, if the *inclusio* of verses 2 and 19 is to make any sense at all – must be grounded on the same basis of Wisdom/Spirit Christology.

While this exegesis of Matthew 11 may bear numerous implications, it suggests two points for our purposes. First, different from the vast majority of commentators who suggest that the Son of Man is vindicated against charges of gluttony and drunkenness on grounds separate from and completely unrelated to eating and drinking, my reading would suggest that, according to Matthew, the dining practices of the Jesus movement *qua* Son of Man were leading evidence (on par with the kerygmatic *erga tou Christou* alluded to in vv. 2 and 5) for the community's Christologically shaped identity.[109] Second,

---

[108] The correlation between the Son of Man and Wisdom should not be surprising, if only because the Son of Man was, as noted above, thought to be a kind of *Adam redivivus* and the prelapsarian Adam represents the height of human wisdom. Wisdom not only surrounded Adam in a distinctive way (Wisd. 10.1); Adam embodied Wisdom simply because Wisdom and the 'image' are finally inseparable (Wisd. 7.26). For similar instances where the Son of Man is associated with Wisdom, see *1 En.* 48.2, 7; 49.1–3; 51.3.

[109] The exception would be Wilson 2015, with whom I am in substantial agreement.

these same dining practices are seen not only as marking off the Jesus movement as the Son of Man but also as signalling the eschatological in-breaking of divine Wisdom. This is significant. If Jesus' meals with 'sinners' and other social undesirables are to be convincingly interpreted, Matthew and his tradition link those same controversial practices with the eschatological operationalization of Wisdom.

Wisdom and her children (Luke 7.31–35)

Luke's parable of the children in the marketplace in context

While both Matthew and Luke place the scene involving John's messengers (Matt. 11.2–19//Luke 7.19–35) after John's baptism (Matt 3.1–12//Luke 3.1–18), in the latter Gospel the distance separating the two episodes is more compressed, emphasizing the correlation of the two events. This is consistent with what we know of the third Evangelist, who, as his opening chapters (Luke 1—2) suggest, is more keen than Matthew to explore the relationship between John and Jesus. Within this relatively tight accounting of John and Jesus, Luke 7.19–35 presents itself as something of a progress report, whereby Jesus' succinct rehearsal of his proclamation and miraculous deeds in 7.22 virtually becomes a summary of 4.14—7.17.

Perhaps even more important for understanding Luke 7.19–35 are the Lukan parallels to the two previously discussed dining-controversy scenes of Matthew 9.9–13 and 9.14–17: Luke 5.27–31 and 5.33–39. Though there are differences between the Lukan and Matthean versions of these two vignettes (for example, Luke has the Pharisees and scribes making the enquiries in both scenes, not just one as in Matthew), they are substantially similar. When Luke's Jesus is asked about his disciples' 'eating and drinking' (in contrast to the disciples of John and the Pharisees) (5.33), this obviously anticipates his later reference to the Son of Man's eating and drinking in 7.34. Similarly, when Jesus' disciples are being questioned about their keeping company with 'tax-collectors and sinners' (5.30), the interrogation not only refers to the immediate scene, where a large crowd of tax collectors are gathered for a feast (v. 29), but also looks ahead to the sinful woman who anoints Jesus in the scene immediately following our pericope (7.36–50).

The links between Luke 7.31–35 and the subsequent anointing scene (vv. 36–50) are not hard to spot. After responding to insinuations that he is a debauched friend of sinners (v. 34) in the earlier passage, Jesus in the next pericope receives a sinful woman at a banquet meal (vv. 36–37). All the while, the scrutinizing host's inner thoughts (v. 39) betray his common cause with the earlier parable's implacable children (v. 32). By the end of the scene, the woman will have been forgiven and hence justified by Jesus (vv. 47–49). In this manner she proves herself as a child of Wisdom, which also means, per the definition supplied by verses 29–35, that she has justified God (v. 29) and perhaps Wisdom as well (v. 35). By pairing the episodes contained in verses

31–35 and verses 36–50, Luke effects an exquisite paradox: the justified one
is also the justifier – and this is as true for Jesus as it is for the sinful woman.
Meanwhile, Jesus' practice of consorting with tax collectors and sinners, like
the anointing woman, is explained by his close association with the Son of
Man and Wisdom (7.34–35).

The meaning of Luke's Wisdom

In my introduction to this section, I pointed out that Luke differs from
Matthew in two principal respects: (1) by his addition of the editorial verses
7.29–30 (over and against Q) and (2) by claiming (perhaps along with Q)
that Wisdom was justified not by her works (as in Matthew) but by her
children (*tekna*) (v. 35). For a number of commentators, the first of these two
differences warrants our positing a fairly sharp separation between Luke and
Matthew in their respective understanding of Wisdom. It is said, whereas
the first Evangelist forges an exclusive link between Jesus and Wisdom,
Luke by comparison treats Wisdom more as a set of ethical principles than
a hypostasized person. On this reading, too, the 'children of wisdom' (7.35)
are any and all who follow her ways, including perhaps even John and
Jesus.[110] This interpretation finds its support in verses 29–30, which allows
for a parallelism between wisdom (v. 35) and the 'counsel' of God (v. 30),
a wisdom and counsel accepted by the sinners and tax collectors (v. 29) but
rejected by the Pharisees and scribes (v. 30). Following this interpretation,
some commentators go on to suggest that, according to Luke, kinship to
Wisdom is determined by one's responsiveness to divine counsel as an
abstraction.[111]

Though this reading of the passage is certainly plausible, it is unlikely,
not least because it presumes a meaning for Wisdom's *tekna* that is inconsistent with the pattern established by Luke's use of the same term elsewhere,
where it is consistently applied to Jesus' followers and/or the elect. The
parade example occurs in Luke's report of the Baptizer's preaching (Luke
3.1–9). There, when the crowds come to be baptized by John, he warns them
not to presume on being 'children [*tekna*] of Abraham', since God is able to
raise up such children, obviously at some point well *after* their participation
in John's baptism (v. 8). Apparently for Luke, then, submission to John's
baptism did little to guarantee one's status as *teknon* of Abraham.[112] In my
view, this presents a significant tension for the interpretation which holds

[110] The latter option is adopted by Fitzmyer (1981: 678–9), but he is seldom followed on this point.
[111] As we have it, say, in Dunn 1980: 163–76.
[112] This remains the case despite Luke 7.29–30: 'And all the people who heard this, including
the tax-collectors, acknowledged the justice of God, having been baptized [*baptisthentes*] with
John's baptism. But by refusing to be baptized by him, the Pharisees and the lawyers rejected
God's purpose for themselves.' While translations like the NRSV assume that the participle
baptisthentes is causal (i.e. 'because they had been baptized with John's baptism'), the grammar
hardly requires this. In the light of Luke 3.1–9, it seems (contra NRSV) that John's baptism is a
necessary but *insufficient* condition for becoming Wisdom's child.

that 'children of Wisdom' logically include those who have received John's baptism. Meanwhile, from Luke's perspective, the children of Abraham (3.8; cf. 16.25) are almost certainly to be grouped with the 'sons [*huioi*] of the bridegroom' (5.34) (my translation), who are unmistakably Jesus' disciples.[113] Other usages of *teknon* ('child') in other episodes beyond Luke 7 confirm the pattern.[114] Such observations should discourage us from thinking of 'responders to Jesus' and 'responders to John' as virtually two interchangeable categories which together comprise the larger set 'responders to Wisdom'. Unless the concept 'children of Wisdom' is an exception to the rule, it must refer to a subset within the broader category of those baptized by John, namely, Jesus' followers.

Likewise, if Jesus' summary statement in Luke 7.35 ('Wisdom is vindicated by all her children') intends to cast John and Jesus as virtually interchangeable mediators of divine wisdom, then we hardly know what to do with the ensuing anointing scene (vv. 36–50), which is almost certainly set forth as an instantiation of Wisdom being 'vindicated by her children'. Informed that this nameless anointer lived a sinful life in the town (v. 37), Luke's reader is immediately cued up to place the woman in company with the God-justifying tax collectors (7.29). Yet, despite the Baptizer's prominence in 7.18–35, the subsequent anointing account evinces no interest in either John or his baptism. Equally tellingly, if Luke redacted his sources in order to show that one's status as Wisdom's child logically depended on a responsiveness to the 'counsel of God', perhaps as a principle or set of principles articulated through John and Jesus' preaching, then one might have expected at least some verbal articulation of this same 'counsel' prior to the woman's 'conversion'. But that is exactly what we do *not* have. Instead Luke seeks to demonstrate that the wisdom of God embodied in the person of Jesus occasions the woman's faith, and this show of faith in turn reveals her identity. Therefore, whereas Luke (unlike Matthew) does not incorporate the Twelve into either Wisdom or the Son of Man, he does share Matthew's Christological focus. For both Evangelists, Wisdom is personified in Jesus.

This reading is certainly compatible with Luke's redaction contained in 7.29–30. After all, the people and tax-collectors 'justify God' only after hearing (*akousas*) Jesus' words concerning John, making Jesus' speech, as it were, the efficient cause of the people's justification of God. Meanwhile the following participial phrase 'baptized through the baptism of John' (*baptisthentes to baptisma Iōannou*) makes much more sense as a way of clarifying why these people responded positively while others did not. For her part, the woman who anoints Jesus' feet proves herself to be a child of Wisdom by becoming a disciple of Jesus quite apart from John's baptism, and this is also tantamount to being a child of Abraham (3.8; 16.25) and a child of God

---

[113] Luke 3.8; 5.34.
[114] Luke 8.54; 9.48; 16.8; 18.17; 20.36.

(20.36). The critical role falls to Jesus, whom Luke also identifies here with both God (v. 29) and Wisdom (v. 35). In characterizing Jesus as the catalyst for the people's inclusion among Wisdom's progeny, Luke dissolves the notional separation between Jesus and Wisdom.

Of course, this is not to collapse the differences between Matthew and Luke. If Luke claims (perhaps along with his source) that Wisdom is justified by her 'children' and Matthew maintains that Wisdom is justified by her 'works', the divergence in word choice and context generates two different nuances. For Luke the justification of Wisdom takes place through conspicuous response to Jesus, especially as it occurs among 'tax collectors and sinners'. In contrast, Matthew focuses less on the transformative reception of Jesus' kerygmatic activities and more on the activities themselves as Christological signifiers. Perhaps it might be said that whereas Luke reworks his materials to emphasize Wisdom's *opera operata* (the tangible effects), Matthew is more interested in the works of Wisdom on an *ex opere operato* (the works themselves independent of their impact) basis. For all we know, the two differing representations of Wisdom reflect a tension within the early Church's Christological reflection, as it struggled to describe the revelation of Wisdom as both a matter of divine activity and human responsiveness.

Synthesis

This analysis of Matthew's and Luke's respective versions of the parable of the children in the marketplace bears a number of implications. There are at least three directly relevant to my argument. First, the divergent nuances represented by Matthew and Luke seem to presuppose an extended and evolving traditioning process, sustained by scripturally informed speculation – perhaps even animated discussions – on Jesus as Wisdom incarnate. Although each Evangelist obviously leaves his own original mark on the parable as it comes down in tradition, the Gospel writers' theological nuance bespeaks a well-established Jesus-as-embodied-Wisdom tradition that preceded both authors considerably. This 'well-established tradition' may well have started with Q or its alleged community. But an equally if not more compelling argument can be made that the tradition began with Jesus himself. In fact, this makes especially good sense on the larger model I am proposing. At the end of the day, given the correlation between the Spirit's re-entry into the land with the reconstitution of the temple in the prophetic literature and hints of the same in the dominical tradition (Chapter 1), it stands to reason that if Jesus was indeed convinced – as I have been arguing all along – that this reconstitution of sacred space was taking place through his ministry, then he would have presumably worked out a theology of Wisdom, so tightly knit with a late Second-Temple theology of sacred space. Moreover, again on the hypothesis I am setting forth, it is no stretch for us to imagine Jesus virtually collapsing the distinction between Wisdom and his own person. In fact, because ancient Judaism often regarded Wisdom as the special domain of the high priest, we should expect to find nothing less.[115] By all accounts, the historical Jesus identified his own community as the locus of divine Wisdom.

Second, given the strength of Q 7.31–35 as a witness to the historical Jesus, we conclude that Jesus defended his socially suspect dining practices (a datum virtually beyond question) on the basis of his intimate association with Wisdom.[116] At first blush this may not be entirely apparent, for the logic which allowed Jesus to reason from *sophia* to supper may seem hopelessly obscure. Alternatively, one might favour Marcus Borg's suggestion, namely, that Jesus' inclusive table practices generally followed from the way of compassionate Wisdom, broadly if not vaguely considered.[117] But in my view, Jesus took up inclusive table practices as a parabolic act, more specifically as an attempt to dramatize the actions of Lady Wisdom who, according to Proverbs 9.1–6, sets out a banquet for the simple, even as she calls her children to herself. Though commentators are finally divided as to whether the author of Proverbs 9 originally implied the temple as the venue for Wisdom's banquet spread, there is certainly evidence to make just this case.[118]

In Proverbs, whatever the original intentions behind Lady Wisdom's depiction, given the personified figure's increasing tie to the temple and priesthood in the relevant Second-Temple sources (e.g. Sirach 24), I submit that countless eschatologically minded first-century readers of Proverbs 8—9 would have assumed the temple setting of Wisdom's feast as well as its eschatological timing (akin to the eschatological feast of Ezek. 39.17–20), not to mention the high-priestly identity of Wisdom herself.[119] In this light, Jesus' controversial meal practices are best explained by his movement's identification with eschatologically revealed Wisdom and the Son of Man.[120]

Both of these concepts are in turn rooted in and connected by the sect's foundational identity as an emerging eschatological priesthood. To put this otherwise, if Jesus was renowned (and notorious) for his inclusive table practices, this inclusivity was a function of his unique priestly self-identity, an identity which he shared with his most immediate followers. This is not to deny the possibility – indeed the likelihood – that Jesus' meals were carried out in anticipation of the messianic feast, but to suggest that the historical

---

[115] E.g. Mal. 2.6–7; 4Q543.
[116] That Jesus distinguished himself by his dining practices is a thesis that has been registered most forcefully by Sanders (1985: 174–99) and Crossan (1991: 332–53). In the past two decades, a few (Klinghardt 1996; K. E. Corley 2002; Smith 2003) have expressed their dissent with this view, but these have been met – decisively in my mind – by Blomberg 2009.
[117] Borg 1984: 93–4.
[118] As have, e.g., McKane 1970: 362–4; Perdue 2000: 150–2; Longman 2006: 217, 222.
[119] The rabbinic text *Lev. Rab.* 11.1–4 offers these two interpretations (temple and eschatological) simultaneously; cf. Wilson 2015: 12. On the connection between Wisdom and priesthood/cultus, see, e.g., Fournier-Bidoz 1984: 4; Deutsch 1990: 24.
[120] So rightly Merklein (1989 (1983)): 80: 'The fact that Jesus is fond of turning to sinners, with the result that he is branded as "a friend of sinners and tax-collectors" (Luke 7.34b par. Mt 11.19b), has nothing in the least to do with social criticism, as many like to read into the text, but is rather a symbolic eschatological communicative act in the context of the eschatological mission of Jesus.'

Jesus had notionally subsumed the messianic feast under the category of his priesthood. In its capacity as the priestly and atoning Son of Man, Jesus' movement had reopened the sacred space; in its capacity as high-priestly Wisdom, it initiated the process of inviting the wayward into that same sacred space through kingdom meals.

Summary

Jesus' use of 'Son of Man' was rhetorically shrewd, for the Aramaic epithet would have allowed itself to be understood either as an innocuously indefinite reference (where the Aramaic behind 'Son of Man' may be taken merely as 'someone') or as an esoteric, scripturally informed template for interpreting the mounting conflict between his movement on the one side (as the Son of Man/holy ones) and his opponents on the other (as human extensions of the four beasts). As a metonymy for this esoteric narrative, Son of Man was 'not a *title* for Jesus, but a symbol of his vocation to be utterly loyal, even to death, with the confidence of ultimate vindication in the heavenly court'.[121] In mapping experiences of persecution on to the narrative of Daniel 7, Jesus gave his followers a much-needed theological rationale for remaining faithful despite the high costs. 'When the going gets tough,' Jesus was more or less reminding his disciples, 'remember what is *really* taking place and remember too what is at stake: for the faithful individual, as well as for Israel.' When Jesus uttered the words 'the Son of Man', he meant it not only as a coy placeholder for an ethical ideal but also as a compressed parable of national aspiration. All the while, the full realization of this ideal and vision would necessarily await some future time.[122]

Jesus' use of 'Son of Man' was especially strategic, for the term could function as coded template for himself and his movement without requir-ing premature and presumptuous self-identifications in the present time. The forward-looking meaning which Jesus attached to 'Son of Man' did not exclude the possibility of his personally realizing certain aspects of the ideal. This makes room for scenarios in which Jesus may have used the phrase in exclusive reference to himself. Yet even in these cases, where his self-identification with the Danielic figure is unambiguously exclusive, such statements never absolved his disciples from embracing the same vocation even as they might expect to do so on somewhat different terms.

Jesus' including his disciples in the Son of Man's vocation follows from a broad overview of the tradition. In the Gospels, when Jesus anticipates his own suffering as the Son of Man, he never does so in such a way as to suggest that his disciples would be entirely shielded from such suffering. On the contrary, when the Jesus of the Gospels makes daily cross-bearing a precondition

---

[121] Moule 1977: 14.
[122] In this respect, my proposal is similar to that of Weiss (1971 (1892)), Higgins (1965 (1964): 199–200) and Jeremias (1971: 275–6).

of discipleship (Luke 9.23) and promises his followers the prospect of public beatings (Mark 13.9), the clear sense is that he saw his own personal suffering as the leading tip of a larger spear: his own tribulation was virtually a guarantee that his followers would have to endure the same. Yet there is a tension here, for paradoxically, the Gospel tradition also leaves the impression that Jesus thought of his own suffering as somehow *sui generis*. How this worked itself out in Jesus' consciousness must perhaps remain a mystery. For all we know, Jesus' sense of needing to actualize Daniel 7 in a distinctive way may have followed from his unique sense of calling gathered at the baptism. But it is equally possible that inklings of a solitary journey progressively dawned on Jesus over time. Along these lines, T. W. Manson may not be entirely off track when he hinted long ago that Jesus proved himself as *the* Son of Man only after the apostasy of the disciples.[123] In any case, if Jesus did indeed think of the Son of Man as an ideal within his own grasp as well as within the grasp of his disciples, then there must also be some sense in which he also thought of his disciples as realizing that ideal, even if imperfectly or at a remove. Perhaps it is our unconscious prioritization of certain formulations of atonement theology over and against the biblical data that has caused us to understate the communal nature of Jesus' suffering.

That which made Jesus' Son of Man movement distinctive was its striking blend of liturgical practice, itinerant movement and inclusive socialization. As the leader of a *liturgical* movement, Jesus believed that the ordinary boundary lines between clean and unclean, holy and unholy were already now breaking down, giving way to a new epoch which gave him and his followers permission to live life as those dwelling in a divinely transfixed reality. Jesus thought of his community as the conduit through which eschatological new creation was coming into view. Since the rights and responsibilities of the priesthood were also about to shift over to Jesus and his followers, they took to mimicking certain rites ordinarily carried out within the temple. Bridging the conventional divide between the sacred and the mundane, the Jesus movement's regular liturgical activities were not just a protest against the temple (though they were), but a pattern of behaviour that almost certainly stamped the community's entire vision of life. With even a modicum of historical imagination, we can only suppose how this conviction must have endowed the everyday realities of life with a certain – for lack of a better term – sacramental character. Jesus' thoroughgoing liturgical orientation transposed worship of Israel's one God into a whole new key.

As an *itinerant* movement, Jesus and his followers flatly rejected the possibility of establishing either a geographical base or a complementary political base. This was by design, and undoubtedly a source of curiosity and frustration for many of Jesus' well-wishers who supported him from a distance. Even so, the mobile nature of Jesus' society, together with its distinctive liturgical practices,

---

[123] Manson 1951 (1931): 232.

ensured Jesus' ability to mark off geographical space, at least in a provisional and proleptic sense, across the breadth of Judea. In this respect Jesus' journeys had both a negative and positive purpose. Negatively, this on-the-go movement was intrinsically resistant to centralization and institutionalization. Positively, by making the rounds throughout the land, Jesus could quite obviously 'get the word out' more effectively. Perhaps most importantly, as Jesus saw it, itinerant movement combined with liturgical practice served to stake out sacred territory in anticipation of what would one day fall under his jurisdiction.

As the leader of an *inclusive* movement, Jesus welcomed table fellowship from both the high and low within society. This meant, on a corporate basis, sitting loose to issues of purity, along with some indifference to the social stigma that came from associating with society's undesirables. Yet even Jesus' table practices were strategically designed to signify his purposes. As soon-to-be high priest, Jesus also claimed the role of embodied Wisdom and demonstrated that office by supping with the 'sinners', all in accordance with the script of Proverbs 8. The socially destabilizing effects of such practices in turn posed a threat to the social order of the day, and would continue to do so as the early Christians followed Jesus' pattern of inclusive table practices – though in a new key with the advent of Paul's ministry to the Gentiles.

Once again, we begin to see that for Jesus the Son of Man was not a title but a story. More exactly, it was a convergence of stories and scriptures, anchored in the story of Daniel 7. There was in Jesus' time no one-to-one equivalency between Son of Man and messiah, for the Son of Man was neither a title nor a tag, but the tip of a narrative iceberg, the submerged substance of which embodied a paradoxical trajectory of shame and glory. The added value of this understanding of Jesus' words 'the Son of Man' is that it elucidates the central role of corporate suffering in Jesus' thought, as I have – I hope sufficiently – established in Chapter 3. As far as we can tell, Jesus promised his followers that their allegiance to his cause would entail certain suffering, but that this suffering would prove to be a catalyst for the redemption of Israel. Whatever distinctive roles and responsibilities Jesus would assign to himself from within this larger corporate burden, he considered such suffering to be a principally collective calling and a defining trait of his movement. In their faithful endurance, Jesus promised, his followers would be discharging a specifically priestly calling and thus prove to be the means by which the coming of the kingdom (the overthrow of Yahweh's enemies and the restoration of operative sacred space) would be realized.

By recurring to this phrase, the historical Jesus signalled not so much that he was individually the Son of Man (although something approaching this implication was hardly denied), but that the narrative of Daniel 7 was to be both a model and a map for his own ministry. Strategically employed, the 'Son of Man' tag drew attention to a drama which, as Jesus saw it, was already playing itself out in the experience of his movement. While this Son of Man's conflict was unfolding on earth, a separate but analogous struggle was occurring in a contiguous realm where invisible forces clashed.

7

Final confrontations

Introduction

In the nineteenth-century 'Lives' of Jesus, we meet a clever and attractive person with a happy disposition; we find a Jesus who seemed to unite some of the best blessings of existence, and who had lived nearly 30 years in the world with very little to distress or vex him. That portrait of Jesus, which has percolated in various iconic forms down to the present day, is at once accurate and misleading. It is accurate insofar as Jesus *was* clever; a rhetorical genius, he was an accomplished verbal sparring partner for any who dared take him on. It is misleading to the extent that it papers over the fact that there was much about Jesus' society that vexed him. In giving voice to that vexation, he escalated the conflict brewing between himself and the local authorities, accelerating the process which would ultimately seal his fate. The consistent spark igniting these verbal firestorms was Jesus' recurring hint that he – and not one of the more likely candidates – was the rightful high priest.

In the previous chapter, I attempted to add some colour to my sketch of Jesus' kingdom vision, even while maintaining the sacerdotal role of the Son of Man. On this vision, the kingdom of Yahweh's reign was already breaking into the present cosmos through Jesus' movement, as it dedicated itself to the worship of Israel's God, as well as certain cultic practices and ethical commitments entailed by such worship. All the while Jesus saw himself as the central figure, as would be confirmed soon enough. It was through him as the high-priestly Son of Man that the righteous remnant would finally witness the redemptive end, when God would be rightly worshipped on the throne, when the unruly nations would be subdued, when the tribes would be restored and when righteousness would prevail at last. Jesus did not present allegiance to his movement as one option among many plausible options. As Israel's eschatological high priest and the human embodiment of divine wisdom, he called for a commitment that was at once inclusive in terms of constituency and exclusive in terms of his take-no-prisoners claims.

Towards the end of his life, the exclusive character of Jesus' strident assertions finally caught up with him. Staking out his position with clarity, he put intolerable strain on his relations with both those who supported the empire's high priest (Caesar) and those who backed Judaism's high priest (Caiaphas). This does not mean that either Caesar or even the high priest were personally aware of Jesus' challenges. Certainly Caesar was not; Caiaphas, probably not. But those who were sympathetic with Rome and the reigning temple administration, those who accordingly had grown hostile to Jesus and his movement, knew that the exclusiveness of these claims could become a fulcrum on which to leverage Roman executive power against him. And when opportunity presented itself, they wasted no time.

In this chapter, I am less interested in the full chain of events leading up to Jesus' death than in confrontational attitudes or words which helped precipitate that death. As recorded in Mark, these come to the surface in two separate events. The first involves an entourage of enquirers seeking public comment from Jesus on the paying of taxes to Caesar; the second relates to Jesus' appearance at his own 'trial' before Caiaphas. Illustrating the highly controversial nature of Jesus' public assertions, both episodes shed important light on his aims and self-understanding.

The tribute tax for Caesar (Mark 12.13–17 par.)

According to the synoptic writers, in the days leading up to his trial and execution Jesus is approached by a posse which is interested in his views on taxes. The account is as succinct as it is tantalizing:

> [13]Then they sent to him some Pharisees and some Herodians to trap him in what he said. [14]And they came and said to him, 'Teacher, we know that you are sincere, and show deference to no one; for you do not regard people with partiality, but teach the way of God in accordance with truth. Is it lawful to pay taxes to the emperor, or not? [15]Should we pay them, or should we not?' But knowing their hypocrisy, he said to them, 'Why are you putting me to the test? Bring me a denarius and let me see it.' [16]And they brought one. Then he said to them, 'Whose head is this, and whose title?' They answered, 'Caesar's.' [17]Jesus said to them, 'Give to Caesar the things that are the emperor's, and to God the things that are God's.'[1]

That Jesus said 'Give to the emperor the things that are the emperor's, and to God the things that are God's' (Mark 12.17a) is largely beyond dispute; indeed few 'if any doubts are entertained as to the authenticity of this episode' as a whole.[2] The verisimilitude of the entire scene is also borne out by the details. For example, although the convening of the Pharisees *and* their adversaries, the pro-Roman Herodian retainers (v. 13), may at first glance appear to be a Markan touch (paralleling the cast of characters at 3.6), further consideration renders it as entirely plausible that both parties had in fact collaborated in

---

[1] Mark 12.13–17a (par. Matt. 22.15–22//Luke 20.20–26); NRSV adapted.
[2] Dunn 2003: 636. See also, e.g., Derrett 1970: 313–38; Davies and Allison 1988–97: 3.211; Crossan 1991: 352, 438; Wright 1996: 502–7; Theissen and Merz 1998 (1996): 234; Borg 2011 (2006): 238–40; Horsley 2012: 144–5; Schröter 2014 (2012): 150–1. Contra Meier 1991: 565; Carter 2014.

framing this question about taxes.[3] Had Jesus affirmed the Judeans' duty to pay tribute to Caesar, this would have swiftly extinguished his backing among the populace – much to the Pharisees' delight. On the other hand, if Jesus were to go on record against paying the tax, the Herodians would have quickly reported such sedition back to the palace, probably triggering his arrest. In the historical setting, both the Pharisees and the Herodians would have had a vested interest in hearing Jesus out on this particular question; both parties would have had ample motivation for partnering in this well-orchestrated set-up. Perhaps it was considerations like these that led Bultmann, otherwise generally reluctant to ascribe compositional unity to apophthegms (concise sayings) such as we have in Mark 12.13–17, to regard the entire pericope as historically credible.[4]

Problems with the standard readings of Mark 12.13–17

Agreeing on the historicity of Mark 12.13–17 is one thing; deciding what either the Evangelist or the historical Jesus meant is another. What are we to make of Jesus' interchange with his challengers? Perhaps Jesus is engaging the Zealots' opposition to the Roman tax payment. If so, is he coming out against them without necessarily exculpating the Romans? Or is he rather expressing support for the Zealot position en route to his own revolution? Alternatively, perhaps Jesus is reframing the question altogether. Perhaps, for instance, he is suggesting that there are two realms, one belonging to Caesar and the other to God, and that the first of these two falls outside his purview? Or is he inviting his hearers to renege on their obligation to the Roman state, not so much in alignment with the Zealots but in the light of the imminent eschaton? There are further variations on these four options, not to mention completely different options altogether.[5] The shadings of interpretations within and without each of these four camps seem to defy convenient categorization.

Meanwhile, a brisk survey of the commentaries yields up at least two recurring exegetical questions: (1) What is the significance of the image and inscription? (2) What does it mean to give to God the 'things of God' (and to Caesar the 'things of Caesar')? Although each of the aforementioned approaches to the so-called *Steuerfrage* (12.13–17) may admit to slightly

---

[3] Contra Meier 2000; 2001: 562–5. I use the term 'tribute tax' for convention's sake, though it is unclear whether Mark is attempting to describe a poll tax, a *tributum capitis*, a *phoros tōn sōmatōn*, or something else altogether. The synoptic writers' use of different terms (*kēnsos* in Matthew and Mark, *phoros* in Luke) likely reflects the fact that they were not all aspiring to technical accuracy in identifying the kind of tax. Nor, contra Udoh (2005: 207–38), should we doubt the account for lack of corroborating evidence for the kind of tax in view. When Josephus (*J.W.* 2.16.5 §403; *Ant.* 14.10.6 §§202–3) reports that a cash *phoros* was due to Caesar in 66 BCE, I am not aware of any historian claiming that the detail was fabricated, even though we have no independent corroborating evidence for this kind of tax at this time.

[4] Bultmann 1968 (1921): 26, 48.

[5] For a catalogue of positions, see Förster 2012: 3–6 (cf. Derrett 1970: 318).

different ways of answering these questions, a standard set of answers tends to surface in contemporary interpretation. Rudolf Schnackenburg's comments on verse 17 ('Give to the emperor the things that are the emperor's, and to God the things that are God's') are, I think, representative. According to this interpreter, Jesus' interlocutors owed Caesar

> the tax and, as the universal form of the reply shows, obedience generally in the duties required of citizens. But of his own accord Jesus also added a second clause, which, by its position, must receive all possible emphasis, 'and render (give) to God the things that are God's'. Just as great, and even greater, is man's duty to God. 'The State can demand what is necessary to its existence, but God claims the whole man, and man has to "give himself back" to him'.[6]

Though the interpretative approach exemplified by Schnackenburg is broadly shared, it suffers from a number of liabilities. First, if, as this reading suggests, Jesus is redirecting his interlocutors' attention away from the 'things of Caesar' to issues far more relevant to God, we must ask ourselves whether this very notion of two self-contained spheres (one belonging to Caesar, and the other belonging to God) is even historically plausible. I confess my suspicions, if only because, as Joel Green remarks, such 'dichotomous thinking would be entirely alien to ancient anthropology'.[7] No less problematic, Schnackenburg's interpretative jump from the 'things of God' to 'God's claim on the whole man' not only receives threadbare support from the text, but actually raises more questions than it answers. For example, if Jesus supposes that paying taxes is somehow separable from the 'whole man', then what other areas of life may be cleanly parcelled out to 'the State' and on what basis?

Second, whereas several important treatments of this passage have persuasively characterized Jesus' interchange as an example of 'forensic interrogation', a particular form of halakhic dispute culminating in a closing scriptural argument, Schnackenburg's interpretation – like many – fails to explain the scriptural climax that never was.[8] Furthermore, if Jesus is indeed making his case in verses 16–17 without at least veiled reference to Scripture, this would make the *Steuerfrage* pericope an exception to the pattern established by the four remaining conflict scenes in 12.1–37, all of which have Jesus capping off his point with an appeal to Scripture.[9]

Third, on a related point, the other conflict scenes in Mark 12 (with the *possible* exception of the question about marriage at the resurrection (vv. 18–27)), together with Mark 11—16 as a whole, are patently Christological in thrust.[10] If Mark's Jesus receives the question about taxes as a welcome

---

[6] Schnackenburg 1965: 117–18; cited in Völkl: 1961: 113–14.

[7] Green 1997: 716. Similarly Cassidy 1978: 223–5.

[8] On this point, see notably Daube 1956: 158–68; Daube 1966: 8–9; Derrett 1970: 320 n. 3; Giblin 1971; Owen-Ball 1993.

[9] 12.1–12 (vv.10–11), 18–27 (v. 26), 28–34 (vv. 29–31), 35–37 (v. 36).

[10] I will briefly argue below that Mark 12.18–27 is in fact Christological in focus.

break from talking about himself, fair enough – but this would be a detour from the Christological trail which the Evangelist is otherwise so intent to blaze. Finally, given the obvious parallel drawn between 'the things of Caesar' and the 'things of God', we might expect Caesar's image *and* inscription also to have their respective analogues – and Schnackenburg's interpretation reveals none.[11] Problems such as these do not altogether invalidate this reading or others like it, but we will be more satisfied if we can lay hold of an interpretation that relieves such tensions.

The significance of the image and inscription

Although countless interpretations of Mark 12.13–17 have conspired to give us a Jesus who pounds a firm wedge between Yahwistic religion and the politics of his day, historical context would lead us to believe otherwise. Given what we know of the first century, we must assume that Jesus and his contemporaries would not have recognized our very separated categories of 'religion' and 'politics', but rather would have seen these realities as two sides of the same denarius. If only because Rome and Zion were theocratic entities, both the historical Jesus and the Evangelist after him would have regarded Caesar and the high priest's claims to authority to be of an equally political *and* religious nature. And so, short of evidence to the contrary, we should generally assume that our categories of 'religious' and 'political' are both in view here.

With this in mind, it is striking that Jesus emphasizes an inscription which, to the best of our knowledge, declared Tiberius's accession to the priestly office of Pontifex Maximus (March 15 CE) as part of his so-called second series.[12] Fortunately, if we can be reasonably confident that this identification is correct, we can be equally confident in reproducing the same coin's inscription. Its obverse reads: TI CAESAR DIVI AVG F AVGVSTSVS (Tiberius Caesar Augustus Son of the Divine Augustus); its reverse, PONTIF MAXIM (= Pontifex Maximus, High Priest).[13] Jesus' numismatic prop was the most visible means by which Rome's subjects would be reminded not just that Tiberius was emperor (which had already been established by the first coin series) but, more particularly, that he was high priest of the empire and son of divinity. By drawing the crowd's attention to the coin's inscription,

---

[11] As noted by Giblin (1971: 522–3); also Owen-Ball 1993.

[12] On this point Finney (1993: 632) states that there 'can be no doubt'; indeed, since unlike his short-lived first series, Tiberius's second series was issued 'at quite extraordinary numbers at intervals throughout . . . [his] reign' (Hart 1984: 243). Against this, Udoh (2005: 232) argues that the Roman denarius did not circulate in Judea prior to 70 CE, rendering the entire account anachronistic. But this judgement is based on data available from the recovery of hoards. That Jesus' interlocutors must work to cough up a single denarius is no evidence for the denarius's broad circulation in Judea (as Udoh's argument seems to assume), but evidence of its rarity.

[13] For details see Koch 2014: 209–10, 216–17; also Hart 1984 (especially p. 243); Finney 1993: 632–3. On the practice of minting ever new lines of coins so as to celebrate imperial achievements, see Zanker 1988: 12–13.

Jesus was inevitably calling attention to Tiberius's claim to be the divinized Pontifex Maximus.[14]

While the role of Pontifex Maximus, together with its scope and responsibilities, underwent its own evolution over the course of Roman history, the early emperors, beginning with Augustus, 'attached great importance to the office . . . vastly expanding . . . its traditional powers and purview'.[15] Hardly the bearer of a nominal title, the Pontifex Maximus was the head of all the priestly colleges throughout the Roman Empire; to this office alone fell the unique responsibility of ensuring the goodwill of the gods (*pax deorum*).[16] So when the third-century CE writer Cassius Dio surveys the office back to the time of Augustus, he can accurately claim that the emperors, in their capacity as supreme pontiffs, maintained 'control [of] all sacred and religious matters'.[17] Nor were the Pontifex's roles and responsibilities in any sense a matter of insider knowledge. Even the more culturally isolated among the Jews would have known that although the Roman chief priest was not necessarily required to participate in ritual events, the office itself was integral to the perpetuation of the imperial cult, fast becoming the mother of all cults.[18] In the eyes of Rome, all religious expression within the boundaries of the empire led back to Caesar Pontifex Maximus.[19] As Rome's great high priest and Son of God, the emperor served as the sole mediator between the human and the divine. Consequently, Tiberius's assertion of self-identity, promulgated in daily life through such objects as the imperial denarii, would have constituted an exclusive and totalizing claim.

As politically and religiously charged as the denarius's inscription would have been, no less offensive to Jewish sensibilities was its *eikōn* (image), which Jesus also mentions. The significance of the noun *eikōn* in Roman religio-political discourse is supported by the well-known Mytilene inscription, which – as a matter of imperial policy – was reproduced on large slabs in the leading city centres a decade or two before Jesus was born. The policy was implemented following the city of Mytilene's request to establish a cult in Caesar's honour, complete with regular celebratory contests and sacrifices, and publicly displayed monuments rhapsodizing over the emperor's qualities. As it turns out, only one inscription (the original one from Mytilene) has survived:

---

[14] In the words of Reed (2006: 42): 'After they brought him a coin he asked first, "Whose portrait is this? And whose inscription?" and then advised to "Give to Caesar what is Caesar's and to God what is God's." The answer becomes much more subversive when one knows that Roman coinage proclaimed Caesar to be God'; similarly Derrett 1970: 329.

[15] Cameron 2007: 341.

[16] Bayet 1973: 161.

[17] *Dio* 53.17.8; cited in Cameron 2007: 359.

[18] Price 1984: 67–8.

[19] Bernett (2007: 338) writes: 'No cult affected civic life in cities and provinces of the Empire more than the imperial cult. In no public arena were relations of power more clearly visualized and symbolized than in the imperial cult.'

For there is to be an oath . . . with the ancestral gods and Sebastos . . . the image [*eikona*] of God . . . that on the altar . . . every month on his birthday and . . . as the same sacrifices, as are offered to Zeus . . . it is consistent with the typical greatness of his mind for us to take note that those things which are humbler by fate and by nature can never attain equality with those who secure a heavenly reputation and possess the station and power of gods. But if anything is discovered in later times more glorious than these decrees, then let not the zeal and the piety of the city come up short in implementing those things that can deify him all the more.[20]

Compelling evidence for a vibrant imperial cult well before Jesus' birth (a devotion which would only burn more fervently and widely over the course of the first century CE), the Mytilene inscription strongly suggests that when the historical Jesus spoke of the emperor's *eikōn*, as recorded in Mark 12.16, he was picking up on a semi-technical term. According to the Romans occupying Judea and their imported imperial cult, Caesar was the unique earthly embodiment of the gods – and that precisely as the 'image of the God'. The coin which Jesus handled, then, bore an image of not simply a political ruler but *the Image*. Referring to the coin's 'image' with sparse elaboration, Jesus would have unavoidably drawn attention to *eikōn* in both its mundane and transcendent senses.

Roman currency itself was a principal means by which imperial ideology placed its own stamp on Roman daily life.[21] On the one hand, coins of the Augustan Age were meant to serve as objects of political propaganda, reminding the empire's subjects as to whom they owed allegiance. On the other hand, the very emblems on the coins – in this case the portraits of Tiberius on the obverse, together with images of PAX (Peace) and JUSTITIA (Justice) on the reverse – were thought to embody the very presence of divine Caesar. Accordingly, denarii such as the one handled by Jesus functioned as objects of worship.[22] Similarly, individuals who impiously handled a coin bearing the emperor's face, or mistakenly brought the same coin into a brothel, were punished accordingly.[23] Given such sensibilities on the part of the Romans, it is hardly remarkable that faithful Jews quickly came to conclude that the imperial coins were 'images' – not merely in the sense of their bearing the emperor's 'likeness' but in the sense of the Hebrew/Aramaic *ṣelem* (LXX:

---

[20] The translation is my own.

[21] The coins were also minted as proof of allegiance, as Chancey (2004: 105) remarks: 'Every issue of civic coinage provides the elites with the opportunity to demonstrate publicly to Roman officials, administrators, and soldiers their loyalty to Rome'.

[22] Though scholarship on Roman imperial religion has undergone major paradigm shifts in recent decades, Grant (1954: 153) is no less correct today than he was more than 60 years ago when he wrote that the images of Peace and Justice 'would be said by the Romans to possess *numen*, that is divine power, but manifest in activity and function; and *numen* was as completely inherent in personifications as it was in a personally conceived god or an inanimate sacred object' – a phenomenon Gupta (2014: 719) neologizes as 'amphicosmic onotology'.

[23] Philostratus, *Vit. Apoll.* 1.15.

eikōn) as we find it generally used in the Scriptures, that is, as an idol.[24] By highlighting the denarius's 'inscription' and 'image' together, Jesus brings out for his Jewish hearers the idolatrous connotations of both features, subtly yet effectively acknowledging the specie as the extension of an illegitimate religio-political power.

While some might find this interpretation of Jesus' coin gesture to be overly subtle, it must be said that in the very nature of the case any criticism of Caesar would have had to have been oblique. Apart from appropriate cautions, like the indirection I am suggesting here, any high-profile figure speaking against the imperium and its sacred objects would risk incurring speedy and dire consequences. Indeed, given the topic's status as a hot-button issue as well as the stakes involved, I think it is more likely than not that Jesus had carefully pre-scripted his audio-visual demonstration ahead of time for just such a question as this, for just such a moment as this. Merely by trading on these two key words, Jesus satisfied his Torah-pious hearers by acknowledging the coin as an idolatrous extension of the pagan Caesar, without so much as saying so. It was a brilliant move.

Reporting the episode years later in a context where the emperor cult had become even more pervasive, Mark seems to reflect awareness of Jesus' leveraging the coin's features as part of an anti-imperial polemic. This awareness comes to narrative expression, I suggest, in his *seemingly* innocent decision to redeploy the lexeme 'inscription' (*epigraphē*) (12.16) at 15.26, where it shows up on the *titulus*: 'The inscription [*hē epigraphē*] of the charge against him read, "The King of the Jews."' I say this move is '*seemingly* innocent' because, on the assumption that Mark knew of Tiberius's minted pretensions to divinity and high priesthood, there is evidence that the Gospel writer intended Jesus' placard to mimic and ultimately parody Caesar's minted inscription. There is nothing inherently implausible about this proposal, especially now that contemporary scholarship has come to appreciate Mark's skilful reshaping of Jesus' Passion into an ironic Roman enthronement ritual. While earlier, politically naive readings of the Gospel have tended to regard the soldiers' hailing of Jesus, their crowning him with thorns and their lifting him up on the cross merely as acts of cruelty, today I think it is beyond doubt that all these details – corresponding respectively to the acclamation, the coronation and the exaltation of the Imperator – are meant to burlesque the honour normally accorded to Caesar on his accession to the throne.[25] Mark's point all along is that even as the Roman soldiers are engaging Jesus in a mock enthronement as 'King of the Jews', Jesus *is* in fact becoming king through these very taunts and torments, and eventually

---

[24] This is not to discount the fact that ancient Judaism's principal objection to pictorial representation of humans was also likely at play at this time; see Förster 2012: 83–143. On the lexical meaning of *ṣelēm* and its cognates in the Ancient Near Eastern literature, see, e.g., Clines 1998 (1968): 464–74; Garr 2003: 117–76; McDowell 2015: 118–24.

[25] See among others Schmidt 1995; Marcus 2006: 73–87; Winn 2008: 129–32.

through his crucifixion too. Given these ironic comparisons between Caesar and Jesus throughout the closing chapters of his Gospel, to interpret the *epigraphē* on Jesus' cross (Mark 15.26) as a divine response to – and judgement of – the *epigraphē* on Caesar's coin (12.26) would be entirely consistent with Mark's literary agenda.

Yet this needs to be stated more strongly, for the correlation between the two Markan inscriptions is not merely formal, but also substantive. The decisive consideration here is the *tertium comparationis* shared by the two inscriptions, gathered from their historical and narrative context. While many of the Evangelist's readers would have recognized the coin's 'inscription' (12.26) as Tiberius's self-identification as Son of God and Supreme High Priest (*filius divi Caesar pontifex maximus*), the more astute of these would have also discovered that this particular claim is ironically mirrored by the *titulus*'s 'inscription' (15.26), likewise offering Jesus as the Son of God (15:39) and atoning great high priest (14.22–25). The Evangelist's point, subtle yet powerful, is just this: while pocket-sized idols declare Rome's imperial high priest the mediator of the gods, as well as the bearer of justice (JUSTITIA) and peace (PAX), a Roman cross announces that Jesus the King of the Jews is the true occupant of this role, unmasking the emperor as an impostor. The strategic repetition of *epigraphē* serves to reframe a seemingly pragmatic question about paying taxes (do we or don't we?) within a much larger scope of concern relating to the antithesis between Jesus and Caesar. Whereas for some interpreters of Mark 12.13–17 Caesar's inscription seems to earn him a kind of diplomatic immunity running alongside the kingdom of God in a separate track, I propose that Mark's two inscriptions asks us to contemplate how Rome's political sovereignty has been relativized by the cross.

Presenting the denarius's inscription and image as props within an anti-imperial polemic was no Markan innovation: the trope must have already been put into play by Jesus himself, precisely as the one who first (indirectly) highlighted the denarius's idolatrous character. That we can trace this conceit along a trajectory stretching between the historical Jesus and the Gospel writer has two implications. First, Mark and Jesus' co-participation in this tradition confirms my theory that 'image' and 'inscription' were meant as verbal signals of resistance, a resistance which sought to avoid, at one extreme, tangling directly with the Roman authorities and, at the other extreme, whitewashing Caesar's blasphemous claims. Second, if according to Mark, Caesar's ascribed status as 'Son of God' and 'Pontifex Maximus' meets its counterpoint in the crucified King of the Jews, even through his act of offering priestly atonement, we must ask whether this juxtaposition of duelling high priests was driven by a post-Easter understanding or by the historical Jesus himself. I will pursue the second question below. For now, the anti-imperial thrust of Jesus' gesture, both on a compositional level and in the setting of Jesus, gives us some important orientation as we move forward.

The 'things of God' in Daniel

As already mentioned, Jesus' encounter at Mark 12.13–17 follows the form of a rabbinic halakhic dialogue, and this should lead us to expect Jesus to crown his response with some scriptural jewel. Yet we are seemingly disappointed. Vexed by this apparent omission, some interpreters have argued that Jesus does 'cite' Scripture after all, namely, by implying the concept of the Adamic image (Gen. 1.26–27) in the phrase 'things of God' (*ta tou theou*).[26] In this case, Jesus' exhortation to give to God the 'things of God' is essentially a plea to 'give' back to God through self-denying obedience. The initial advantage of this reading consists in its sustaining the parallelism between Caesar and his image, on one side, and God and his image, on the other. Nevertheless, this approach runs into two difficulties. First, while Genesis 1.26–27 may present itself as a plausible subtext for 'image', this interpretation has not – despite some ingenious moves – managed to find a convincing scriptural home for the partner term 'inscription'. Second, since in pre-Christian Judaism the 'image of God' is normally applied either to Israel or to Israel's priest, the theory that Jesus invited his hearers to present themselves as individual *imagi dei* strikes me as anachronistic.[27] While the quest for a scriptural backdrop behind 'image' and 'inscription' could hardly be more justified, given rabbinic convention, perhaps we should keep looking for a better match.

To that end, I propose that the focal subtext is to be found not in Genesis 1 but Daniel 1—7, a stretch of text which takes an especial interest in 'image' and 'inscription' – and that in connection with the 'deep and hidden things' known only to God. As I will argue, the key terms of Mark 12.16–17 are in fact scripturally rooted, but the subterranean roots in question extend well beyond the drip line of a single compositional unit. That is to say, if Mark 12.13–17's dependence on Daniel 1—7 has gone unmooted up to this point, it is largely because scholars have restricted their quest for allusions or echoes to a specific set of verbal correspondences within a well-circumscribed precursor text, without sufficiently recognizing that ancient Jewish interpretation gave no less priority to the interaction between significant themes and words occurring throughout the narrative. For my part, in exploring Daniel 1—7 as a potential repository for Mark's 'things of God', 'image' and 'inscription', I will – starting with the 'things of God' – consider these vital terms, as well as associated concepts, as they occur across Daniel's compositional length.

The 'deep and hidden things of God' in Daniel (Dan. 2.20–23)

While the wording 'things of God' never occurs in the book of Daniel, its lead character does praise God in Daniel 2.22 for revealing 'deep and hidden things'. As it turns out, the former phrase would come to enjoy its

---

[26] Giblin 1971; Owen-Ball 1993; Bryan 2005: 46. Other – though less convincing – scriptural options are presented by Förster 2012: 178–86.
[27] Jervell 1960: 119.

own reception in early Christianity, but only as a shorthand version of the latter. By the first century CE the apostle Paul could unhesitatingly put the 'things of God' (1 Cor. 2.11) into synonymous parallelism with the 'deep things of God' (v. 10) (my translation), even while Mark employs 'things of God' not only in our principal text under discussion (Mark 12.17) but also in Mark 8.33 – with obvious connections to Daniel 7.[28] The sheer fact that the 'things of God' and 'the deep and hidden things of God' were virtually interchangeable raises the distinct possibility that both Paul and Mark wrote with Daniel 2.22 and its larger context very much in mind.[29]

Belonging to a hymn which marks the climax of Daniel 2 and, in some sense, the introduction to the book as a whole, Daniel 2.22 announces several programmatic themes. The plot will be familiar to many of my readers: having prayed for supernatural insight into Nebuchadnezzar's secret dream, Daniel now receives a clear answer to his prayer and gives thanks accordingly:

[20]Blessed be the name of God from age to age,	A
for <u>wisdom</u>	B
and <u>power</u> are his.	C
[21]He changes times and seasons,	C^1
deposes kings and sets up kings;	
he gives <u>wisdom</u> to the wise	B^1
and knowledge to those who have understanding.	
[22]He reveals deep and hidden things;	A^1
he knows what is in the darkness,	
and light dwells with him.	
[23]To you, O God of my ancestors,	A^2
I give thanks and praise,	
for you have given me	
<u>wisdom</u> and	B^2
<u><u>power</u></u>,	C^2
and have now revealed to me what we asked of you,	B^2
for you have revealed to us what the king ordered.[30]	

The hymn is carefully organized around the terms 'wisdom' (B, B^1, B^2) and 'power' (C, C^1, C^2).[31] Intricated within the chiastic parallelism, where A^1/ A^2/A^3 mark the main clauses, 'wisdom' involves the mediation of previously

[28] One might also note 'the great things of God' (*ta megaleia tou theou*) in Acts 2.11 or 'the great things concerning the kingdom of God' (*peri tēs basileias tou theou*) in Acts 1.3 (my translation). As helpful as these verses might be for a study of this kind, since Acts post-dates Mark, I will set them aside.

[29] In his study of 'things of God' in the broader Greco-Roman literature, Philo and Josephus, Förster (2012: 213–20) entirely fails to mention Daniel 2 in this regard, even as he summons the same scriptural chapter for quite different reasons as a background for understanding Paul's treatment of taxes in Rom. 13.1–7. In a book that is otherwise so carefully researched, the oversight is short of astounding.

[30] Dan. 2.20–23.

[31] In the quoted passage the former term is underlined, the latter, double underlined.

hidden knowledge (vv. 21b–22); 'power' entails the ability to change times, seasons and political regimes (v. 21a). Both concepts are subsumed under the category of God's 'deep and hidden things' (v. 22a).[32] Both are also directly related to Nebuchadnezzar's dream presaging the rise and fall of four kingdoms (Dan. 2.31–45); whereas the *content* of the king's nightmare involves the exertion of divine *power* to effect regime changes, the encoded *form* of the dream underscores the *wisdom* of God. Yet on a broader level the terms 'wisdom' and 'power' also become the lenses for understanding the entirety of Daniel, not least its cryptic tales of political realignments. So it is little surprise that more than a few commentators regard Daniel 2.20–23 as *the* introduction to the book's most important themes.[33] The crucial terms within this crucial introductory passage, 'wisdom' and 'power', stand to be developed in the course of the narrative.

Soon enough, Daniel's affirmation of divine power is contested by a line of pagan rulers who assert their own brand of power over and against God (Daniel 3—6). This first occurs in Daniel 3 on Nebuchadnezzar's installation of his idol (*ṣelem/eikōn*), a term emphatically repeated throughout the chapter.[34] In keeping with Ancient Near Eastern practice, the Babylonian ruler sets his image into place with a view to not only asserting political sovereignty over local space but also imposing cultic demands.[35] In this vein, the very establishment of Nebuchadnezzar's image, precisely as an extension of the ruler's personal presence, is an assertion of universal power – all of course in patent tension with Daniel 2.20–23, which ascribes such power to God alone.

At the same time, since Nebuchadnezzar's statue in Daniel 3 asks to be interpreted as an instantiation of the ultimately doomed statue of Daniel 2, hints of the project's eschatological futility are already woven in. While divine intervention helps avert the crisis prompted by Nebuchadnezzar's idol in chapter 3 (vv. 19–30), the structure of Daniel points to the final defeat of the image and its power comes only at the arrival of the Son of Man (Daniel 7). There is an arresting appropriateness about this: inasmuch as Daniel's Son of Man comes to us as an Adamic figure (as noted above) and for this reason also appears as an *eikōn* (the human *eikōn* of God; cf. Gen. 1.26–27), and inasmuch too as his *Mischwesen* adversaries correspond to the metallic images of Daniel 2 (which in some sense include Nebuchadnezzar's image of Daniel 3), the Son of Man's struggle with the beasts finally presents itself as a contest between two vying sets of *images*. Read retrospectively in the eschatological light of Daniel 7, Nebuchadnezzar's image (Daniel 3) and in fact all counterfeit *eikōnes* of its ilk are revealed for what they are; as the text assures its readers, both these images and the powers they represent will one day submit to the enthroned *eikōn* of God, the Son of Man.

---

[32] Gladd 2008: 30.
[33] Towner 1969: 317–26; Lacocque 1988: 66; Watts 1992: 150–2; Gladd 2008: 27–38.
[34] Dan. 3.1, 2, 3, 5, 7, 10, 12, 14, 15, 18.
[35] Garr 2003: 141–3; McDowell 2015: 134.

Returning to Daniel 3, we also find that the deified ruler's *eikōn* is coupled with the issuance of an equally illegitimate royal decree (Dan. 3.10) – in contravention of Yahweh's absolute claim to wisdom (Dan. 2.20–23). As a kingdom-wide policy, it is understood, this decree would have naturally been reduced to writing, so as to articulate the practical entailments of Nebuchadnezzar's *eikōn*. Misguided royal decrees like this one crop up again in Daniel 6 (especially vv. 8–14), where Darius is forced to comply with his own edicts, issued against his own better judgement. The author's point all along is that God's decrees are 'victorious over the decrees of kings (2.9, 13, 15, 21; 6.6. 9, 13 16 [5, 8, 12, 15])'.[36] Thus the battle between Yahweh and the pagan pretenders is actually engaged on two fronts: one front occupied by the deities' respective 'images' and another front marked off by clashing decrees.

The narrative's interest in decrees in Daniel 2, 3 and 6 is a piece of the final author's larger concern with images of writing, signalled not least by a double pair of *book*ends, where books surface twice at the beginning (1.4, 17) and twice at the end (12.1, 4) of Daniel. Observing as much, P. R. Davies regards the two sets of paired terms as intentional:

> The 'books' of chapter 1 are those of the Chaldeans, humanly written, learned excellently by the heroes. In 12,1 is a secret book, divinely written, with the names of the righteous inscribed. The final book mentioned (12,4) is presumably the book written by Daniel, something both earthly *and* heavenly, a human book of the secrets of heaven . . . Daniel, then, is a book in which everything significant is done by *writing*. Political power is exercised in writing, including the political power of the deity.[37]

The narrative's interest in writing is most conspicuous in Daniel 5, a scene in which fingers belonging to the hand of a man (Aramaic: *dî yad-'ĕnāš*; OG: *hōsei cheiros anthrōpou*), perhaps the same 'man' (*'ĕnāš*) as the Son of Man in Daniel 7, begin writing on the wall.[38] The mysterious words are words of judgement, written in response to the king's decision to use the accoutrements of Yahweh's temple for his debauched celebrations (5.2). Of course the fuller and more decisive judgement comes in the inscripturation of the vision of the Son of Man (7.1), the opening of divine books for judgement (7.10), and the book of truth (10.21).[39]

In tandem with its critique of pagan power and images, the motif of cosmic chirographic conflict best explains itself as an attempt to position Jewish wisdom (Dan. 2.20–23) over and against its pagan counterpart. Wary of their pagan overlords' deified status, Daniel's readers would have been

[36] Goldingay 1989: 159.
[37] Davies 1993: 353; emphasis original.
[38] Dan 5.5. Words of writing occur some nine times in Daniel 5: Dan. 5.5 *bis*, 7, 8 12, 15, 16, 17, 25.
[39] On this antithetical parallel between the two writings, divine and pagan, see Gooding 1981: 57–8, 63; also Polaski 2004.

painfully aware that these royal edicts were being issued as pronouncements of divine wisdom, thereby posing a direct challenge to Torah-based wisdom. But at the eschaton, the book of Daniel assures its readers, the written decrees of pagan-style wisdom will prove to be no match for the written words of judgement associated with the Son of Man, vindicating the programmatic point set out in Daniel 2.20–23: to God alone belongs true wisdom. Thus the book of Daniel features a double structural analogy, involving on one axis two competing assertions of power, anchored in the respective *eikōnes* of Yahwehish and paganism; the other, along another axis, centred on two sets of counterclaims to wisdom, narratively symbolized through a war of written words. On the final author's presentation, the power of God will be finally made manifest in the eschatological revelation of the Son of Man (Daniel 7), precisely as the *image* of God, who is closely aligned with another image, the temple of God (Daniel 2). At that time, too, the wisdom of God will refute alternative wisdoms on offer in reputedly divinely authorized *inscriptions*. Both the image of God and the inscriptions of God are representations of the 'deep and hidden things of God'.

The 'things of God' in Paul (1 Cor. 2.1–14)

Outside of the Gospels the phrase the 'things of God' (*ta tou theou*) occurs at 1 Corinthians 2.11, where it parallels 'the things granted to us' (v. 11) to one side and 'the deep things of God' (v. 10) to the other – all within a larger section of 1 Corinthians where Paul reflects on his apostolic ministry. As part of a composition predating Mark by roughly two decades, the text and co-text of 1 Corinthians 2.11 hold promise for illuminating the 'things of God', as it is used in Mark as well as in the setting of Jesus:

> [1]When I came to you, brothers and sisters, I did not come proclaiming *the mystery of God* [*to mysterion tou theou*] to you in lofty words or wisdom. [2]For I decided to know nothing among you except Jesus Christ, and him crucified. [3]And I came to you in weakness and in fear and in much trembling. [4]My speech and my proclamation were not with plausible words of <u>wisdom</u>, but with a demonstration of the Spirit and of <u>power</u>, [5]so that your faith might rest not on human <u>wisdom</u> but on the <u>power</u> of God. [6]Yet among the mature we do speak <u>wisdom</u>, though it is not a <u>wisdom</u> of this age or of the rulers of this age, who are doomed to perish. [7]But we speak God's <u>wisdom</u>, secret and hidden, which God decreed before the ages for our glory. [8]None of the rulers of this age understood this; for if they had, they would not have crucified the Lord of glory. [9]But, as it is written, 'What no eye has seen, nor ear heard, nor the human heart conceived, what God has prepared for those who love him' – [10]these things God has revealed to us through the Spirit; for the Spirit searches everything, even the *deep things of God* [*ta bathē tou theou*]. [11]For what human being knows *the things of man* [*ta tou anthrōpou*] except the human spirit that is within? So also no one comprehends *the things of God* [*ta tou theou*] except the Spirit of God. [12]Now we have received not the spirit of the world, but the Spirit that is from God, so that we may understand *the things granted to us by God* [*ta*

hypo tou theou charisthenta hēmin]. [13]And we speak of these things in words not taught by human <u>wisdom</u> but taught by the Spirit, interpreting spiritual things to those who are spiritual. [14]Those who are unspiritual do not receive the gifts of God's Spirit, for they are foolishness to them, and they are unable to understand them because they are spiritually discerned.[40]

On many levels this is a difficult passage, made even more difficult by the controverted question as to which backgrounds might be informing Paul's interest in 'wisdom' and 'power' (which I have underlined and double-underlined, respectively).[41] While I will not attempt a thorough engagement with this issue, I will insist, as many have already, that the passage's double concern with wisdom and power must be inspired at least partially by Daniel 2.[42] The case for this draws support not only from the frequency of 'wisdom' and 'power', a pair of words central to Daniel 2.20–23, but also because in 1 Corinthians 1 Paul has already brought the terms together, much as they are collocated in Daniel, by equating Christ with 'the power of God and the wisdom of God'.[43]

Further parallels are no less impressive.[44] First, Paul credits the Spirit's agency in the granting of mystery (1 Cor. 2.1) and revelation (v. 10), much as the book of Daniel ascribes the revelation of 'mystery' (*mysterion*) to the 'holy spirit of God' (*pneuma theou hagion*) (Dan. 4.9 Theo).[45] Second, whereas Paul identifies himself and the other apostles as 'interpreters of spiritual things' (*pneumatika synkrinontes*) (1 Cor. 2.13), in Daniel the cognate term *synkrisis* signifies the prophet's *pesher* interpretation of the mysteries.[46] Third, Paul's understanding of 'power' (*dynamis*) in this passage is similar to what we find in Daniel: for both the apostle and the prophet, the power of God is associated with the revelation of divinely hidden mysteries (1 Cor. 2.10–14; Dan. 2.20–23, 27–28); both also speak of 'power' as God's capacity to raise up and bring down human kingdoms (Dan. 2.20–23, 27) or in Paul's language, the 'rulers of this age' (1 Cor. 1.26, 27–28; 2.6).

Fourth and finally, if Paul speaks of God's wisdom as 'secret and hidden' (v. 7), Daniel has already beaten him to the punch.[47] Parallels like these do more than suggest that Paul is matching his own apostolic proclamation to the template of Daniel yet with a polemic wink to the 'wise' at Corinth: on the apostle's vision, the mantic trajectory reaching from Daniel to the apostles, as authorized revealers, has locked horns with another trajectory made up of unauthorized revealers, the wise men of Nebuchadnezzar's

---

[40] 1 Cor. 2.1–14. I have adapted the NRSV to match the wording of the Greek more closely.

[41] See focused treatments in Pogoloff 1992; Winter 1997; Kwon 2010; Miller 2013.

[42] For the Danielic concept of mystery as a backdrop to 1 Corinthians, see Harvey 1980: 330–1; Hays 1997: 393; Williams 2001: 166–8; Brodie 2004: 595–9; Grindheim 2002: 697; Gladd 2008: 129–32.

[43] 1 Cor. 1.23–24; see Kammler 2003a: 100–18.

[44] For these connections see above all Gladd 2008: 129–33.

[45] The term 'mystery' occurs in 2.11; 4.18; 5.11, 14.

[46] Dan. 2.5–7, 9, 16, 24–26, 30, 36, 45; 4.6, 9; 7.16.

[47] Dan. 2.23, 30; 5.11, 14; 9.22.

court and the counterfeit *sophoi* ('wise') of this age (1 Cor. 1.19–20). Falling back on Daniel, Paul not only frames his gospel message in continuity with the initial announcement of the kingdom in Daniel 2, but also compares his Spirit-invested office with Daniel's mediation of Spirit-revealed truth.

With an eye to the prophetic book, the apostle traces the Corinthians' struggles to the Danielic antithesis falling along ideological and anthropological lines. The ideological divide receives immediate attention, for early in his epistle Paul contrasts the message of the cross with 'the wisdom of the world' (1 Cor. 1.20). When he first came to the Corinthians, he later insists, he came neither with the 'wisdom of men' (*sophia anthrōpōn*) (2.5) nor with 'things in words . . . taught by human wisdom' (*didaktois anthrōpinēs sophias logois*), but with words proceeding from the Spirit (2.13). The constellation of 'wisdom', 'words' and 'Spirit' brings us into familiar Danielic territory, as does the sharp distinction between the message borne by the Spirit and the 'wisdom of men'.

The same polarity between the 'human' and the 'spiritual' is developed at different points in the epistle, culminating in Paul's treatment of the resurrection, where the apostle contrasts the first (fleshly) Adam with the life-giving Spirit of Christ (15.45).[48] Not insignificantly, this contrast is set within a larger discussion which is introduced by a transitional statement arguably blending Daniel 7.14 with 12.4: 'Then comes the end, when he hands over the kingdom to God the Father, after he has destroyed every ruler and every authority and power.'[49] Later in the same chapter, the apostle mimics the mantic activity of the prophet as he declares the 'mystery' of resurrection.[50] As he does, he draws on – not a proto-Gnostic or Alexandrian but – Daniel's metaphorization of power, that is, image: 'Just as we have borne the *image* of the man of dust, we will also bear the *image* of the man of heaven.'[51] Paul's mutual pitting of these two incommensurate 'images' within an eschatological framework provided by Daniel (cf. 1 Cor. 15.24, 51) not only bespeaks a homology between the Danielic Son of Man with the Adamic image of God, but also suggests that his whole discussion of the true *eikōn*'s resurrection (1 Corinthians 15), rather than introducing an entirely new topic, is actually –

---

[48] I follow Thiselton (2000: 1275–81) and Wright (2013: 2.1400–2), among others, who rightly maintain that *pneumatikos* refers to moral calibre (not the property of being incorporeal).

[49] 1 Cor. 15.24.

[50] 1 Cor. 15.51; see Gladd 2008: 245–9.

[51] 1 Cor. 15.49; emphasis added. Lee (2012) persuasively argues that Paul forged his Adamic Christology on the anvil of early Christian Son of Man traditions which depended in part on Daniel 7. According to Wright (2013: 2.1064–5), texts like Dan. 7.14, 18, 22, and 27 comprise 'the themes in the background of 1 Cor. 15.20–28, joining the dots to complete Paul's scripture-based picture . . . The passage in 1 Corinthians thus gives every indication that Paul had combined these great biblical themes: Adam, creation, and the dominion of the humans over the animals; the Messiah, his victory over the nations and his continuing rule until all are subject to him; the hope of resurrection before all the people of God.' Moreover, for Wright, that Paul was intentionally echoing Daniel is 'highly probable' (1065).

when read against Daniel's *contra idola* theme – intended to be the *coup de grâce* to the Corinthians' flirtation with *eikōnes*.[52]

Once we recognize both 1 Corinthians 1—2 and 1 Corinthians 15's convergence in Daniel, the epistle emerges as having come full circle: at the resurrection the *eikōnes* of the present age (Corinthians 8—10), supported by the 'words' of the *sophoi* (1.17—2.10), will finally be undone by the Son of Man precisely as the *eikōn* of God (15.35–49), all in accordance with the divine words contained in the Gospel (15.1), the Scriptures (15.3–4, 27, 45) and the apostolic declaration of mystery (15.50–51). If this exegesis of 1 Corinthians is near the mark, it means that Paul in his own mind configures the 'things of God', comprised by its constituent components of 'image' (power) and 'words' (wisdom), exactly along the lines which I am proposing for Daniel.

Of course, differently from the author of Daniel, Paul interprets the image of Daniel 7 Christologically. According to the apostle, that which has been granted to him and the other apostles is not the blessings associated with the Christ-event or even, strictly speaking, the person of Christ, but insight into the brute facts of the crucified and risen Christ (1 Cor. 2.12). This chain of events can only be understood by the apostles through the Spirit (2.11), who reveals them as the once hidden but now revealed wisdom and power of God. For Paul, too, due to the close connection between the crucified and risen Christ and the redemptive display of divine wisdom and power, Christ becomes virtually equated with 'wisdom' and 'power' (1.23, 30). With Daniel 2 and 7 squarely in view, the apostle understands the crucifixion and resurrection of the 'heavenly man' to be the means by which the wisdom and power of God, the 'things of God', come into full expression.

The 'things of God' in Mark

The 'things of God' in Mark 1—8 (Mark 8.33)

As relevant as Paul's 'things of God' may be for our interpretation of the same phrase in Mark 12.13–17, we are obviously much closer to home on considering the term's earlier occurrence in Mark 8.33. The verse is part of a pivotal passage set at Caesarea Philippi:

> [29]He asked them, 'But who do you say that I am?' Peter answered him, 'You are the Messiah'. [30]And he sternly ordered them not to tell anyone about him. [31]Then he began to teach them that the Son of Man must undergo great suffering, and be rejected by the elders, the chief priests, and the scribes, and be killed, and after three days rise again. [32]He said all this quite openly. And Peter took him aside and began to rebuke him. [33]But turning and looking at his disciples, he rebuked Peter and said, 'Get behind me, Satan! For you are setting

---

[52] Schmithals 1971: 87–113; Conzelmann 1975 (1969): 249; Jewett 1978; Fee 1987: 713 are among commentators who perceive a sharp disjunction between the content of 1 Corinthians 15 and the rest of the epistle.

your mind not on *the things of God* [*ta tou theou*] but on the things of man [*ta tou anthrōpou*].' [34]He called the crowd with his disciples, and said to them, 'If any want to become my followers, let them deny themselves and take up their cross and follow me. [35]For those who want to save their life will lose it, and those who lose their life for my sake, and for the sake of the gospel, will save it. [36]For what will it profit them to gain the whole world and forfeit their life? [37]Indeed, what can they give in return for their life? [38]Those who are ashamed of me and of my words in this adulterous and sinful generation, of them the Son of Man will also be ashamed when he comes in the glory of his Father with the holy angels.'[53]

Immediately following Peter's confession of his master's messiahship (v. 29), Mark's Jesus chidingly swears (*epetimēsen*) his disciples to secrecy with a rebuke (v. 30), and then relates – in this the first of three Passion predictions – the future suffering of the Son of Man (v. 31). Troubled by the forecast, Peter rebukes (*epitiman*) Jesus and is in turn swiftly rebuked (*epetimēsen*) for focusing on the 'things of man' (*ta tou anthrōpou*) instead of the 'things of God' (*ta tou theou*) (vv. 32–33) – a contrast which seems to approximate the Pauline antithesis between 'spiritual' (*pneumatikos*) and 'human' (*psychikos*). Up to this point in Mark's narrative, this verb of rebuking has been restricted to Jesus' response to the demonic realm.[54] Now here with the three-fold repetition of the same verb (vv. 30, 32, 33), the Evangelist hints that Peter's objections are inspired by the same dark forces.

In Mark's narrative, the last mention of demonic influence is in the interpretation of the parable of the sower.[55] Per the terms of the parable, Peter's inapt response at 8.31 betrays his precarious position on the 'outside' (4.11b); swayed by Satan, the disciple reveals himself as the seed fallen beside the path (4.4, 15), unable to penetrate the mystery of the kingdom (4.11), which is by all accounts the Danielic 'deep things of God'.[56] Ironically, whereas Jesus had once taken his disciples aside to explain the mystery of the kingdom (4.10, 33–34), it is now Peter who takes Jesus privately aside (8.32), this time to confound the same mystery, exposing the disciple's response as a mantic disclosure turned on its head. In failing to discern the 'things of God', Peter takes his place right alongside Nebuchadnezzar's pagan sages.

Should there be any doubt that the Evangelist is appealing to these familiar battle lines, we need only consider 8.31–38's dependence on Daniel, evident not least in the Gospel writer's reference to the Son of Man coming 'in the glory of his Father with the holy angels' – a scene unmistakably reminiscent of Daniel 7.13.[57] Then there is Mark 8.31, where Jesus says that 'it is necessary' (*dei*) for the Son of Man to undergo the appointed trials, prompting Collins'

---

[53] Mark 8.31–38; NRSV adapted.
[54] Mark 1.15; 3.12; 4.39.
[55] Mark 4.15.
[56] Marcus 1984: 569; 2000: 298.
[57] Mark 8.38.

comment that *dei* here 'implies a theological interpretation of the events', partially because it summons Daniel's speech to Nebuchadnezzar, where the same verb occurs in the Old Greek (Dan. 2.28), with its unpacking of eschatological mystery.[58] Finally, there is the centrepiece of our discussion: the 'things of God'.[59] For Mark, as for the author Daniel before him, the 'things of God' pertain not so much to the isolated events leading up to the cross but rather to the facts *along with their proper interpretation*, an interpretation which comes only through divinely granted insight.[60] As Mark relayed and shaped the traditions now contained in 8.31–38, he allowed Daniel to shape his editorial decisions at virtually every turn.

With this in mind, we just begin to see how Daniel's cosmic battle as a war of words/decrees/writings (wisdom) and images (power) impinges on Jesus' two-fold assertion, involving a promise that those who lose their life 'for my sake, and for the sake of the gospel' (*heneken mou and tou euangeliou*) will save it (v. 35), as well as a warning against being ashamed of 'me and my words' (*me kai tous emous logous*) (v. 38). Between the two phrases there is an obvious parallelism with both clauses focusing on the person of Jesus *qua* Son of Man (v. 31) and his 'gospel'/'words' (vv. 35, 38). Once Jesus' double statement is situated within Daniel's tale of two kingdoms, each with their own images and wisdoms, the Evangelist's point begins to crystallize: Mark 8.31–38 reveals Jesus as the true *eikōn* (Son of Man) and true source of wisdom ('gospel' and 'words'). As the *eikōn*/Son of Man, Jesus promises to stand in judgement on all the *eikōnes* of the pagan kingdoms; as the source of divine words, he will answer the ultimately vain decrees of the kingdoms. Foremost among these *faux* kingdoms – judging not least by the scene's setting at Caesarea Philippi – is the one ruled by the latest iteration of Nebuchadnezzar, Caesar himself.[61] If the syntax and wording of verses 35 and 38 have been determined by the Danielic double motif of image and words, then both the crucified Son of Man and his words comprise the '[deep and hidden] things of God' (Mark 8.33). Together the Son of Man and his words are the counter to Caesar's assertion of himself as the Image, and imperial ideology as divine wisdom.

The 'things of God' in Mark 12.17

We have made headway on a handful of issues in our interpretation of Mark 12.13–17. First, in his own setting, the historical Jesus subtly met his audience on their own terms by drawing attention to the denarius not merely as a grim reminder of Israel's subjugation to Rome but also – especially with its 'image' and 'inscription' writ large – as an iconic assertion of scandalous religio-political claims. To be more exact, Jesus introduces the coin as an idol

---

[58] Collins 2007: 403.
[59] Mark 8.33.
[60] Cf. Matt. 16.17.
[61] The presence of the imperial cult temple at Caesarea Philippi is documented by Josephus (*J.W.* 1.21.3 §§404–6; *Ant.* 15.10.3 §§363–64). Its location is still disputed by archaeologists; see e.g. Berlin 1999; Netzer 2003; Overman et al. 2003.

(an *eikōn* according to the standard scriptural sense of the term), pointing to Caesar's self-identification as the divine 'Son of God'. The significance of this gesture would have not been lost on either Mark or Jesus' first hearers. Meanwhile, again for both Jesus and Mark, the denarius's inscription could hardly have been contemplated apart from its equally vexing assertion that Caesar was also the cosmic high priest (Pontifex Maximus). To be sure, the Evangelist understood Jesus' coin demonstration as an anti-imperial gesture and sought to elaborate on that significance in his own narrative rendering, but the claim focus of Jesus' polemic, Mark also understood, was Caesar's claim to divinized high priesthood.

Second, though the Evangelist's Jesus makes no explicit mention of a divine inscription or image, the obvious parallelism between the 'things of Caesar' and the 'things of God' (12.17) invites thoughtful readers to supply an unstated piece or two of the puzzle, under the general heading of the 'things of God', to complement the image and inscription on Caesar's coin. Realizing that Mark 8.31–38 is building on Daniel's story of two competing kingdoms, complete with its climactic finish involving the victorious 'image' aka Son of Man (v. 38), Mark's ideal reader comes to 12.17 prepared to conclude that the unstated image of God is none other than this same Son of Man. By the same token, the analogue to Caesar's inscription must include Jesus' *titulus* (15.26), announcing him as 'King of the Jews', as well as his own spoken words (8.35, 38) – authoritative words spoken by and about Jesus. Whereas Mark 8.31–38 represents Jesus as the suffering yet prevailing Son of Man (such as we have in Daniel 7 and indirectly in Daniel 2) and the author of binding words (such as we find in Daniel 5, 7 and 12), Jesus' command to give to Caesar and to God (Mark 12.17) now becomes a decree of eschatological judgement issued against the imperial order, as well as an open invitation to join the Danielic line by ascribing the 'things of God' – Jesus as the bearer of the divine image and divine words – to God. For Mark, as for Paul before him, because the crucified and risen Jesus is the image-bearer and word-bearer, he is also the final revelation of the divine power and wisdom first revealed by Daniel.

The Daniel motifs underwriting 12.13–17 also have something to do with why, in the immediately following pericope, Jesus answers the Sadducees as he does, when he says, 'Is not this the reason you are wrong, that you know neither the *scriptures* nor the *power* of God?'[62] Responding to their question about the resurrection, Jesus refers to the divine Scriptures and the power as a parabolic way of referring to himself, again as the image- and word-bearing Danielic Son of Man. Mark 12.18–27's placement beside 12.13–17 supports this, as does its obvious allusion to Daniel 12.3 ('they . . . are like angels in heaven') in 12.25. In this way, 'the scriptures' and 'power of God' (12.24), as the eschatological extensions of the divine 'inscription' and 'image' of Daniel

---

[62] Mark 12.24–25; emphasis added.

1—7, are set into effective juxtaposition with the competing 'inscription' and 'image' of Caesar in the previous pericope (12.17). As Mark would have it, to give to God the things of God is to acknowledge the divine origins of Jesus' person and words, all as the final fulfilment of Nebuchadnezzar's eerie dream.

As for what it means to give to Caesar the 'things of Caesar', I confess that my interpretation of the pericope does not resolve this question with utter clarity. But we can suppose that the activity of giving Caesar his things pertains not so much to the specific issue of paying taxes, as to the more fundamental obligation to weigh the emperor's idolatrous claims within the now-unfolding eschatological narrative. To put this differently, it seems that Mark's Jesus shifts focus from the ethics of tax-paying to the notional basis on which such ethical issues must be adjudicated. Still, this does not mean that the question is illegitimate or somehow undeserving of an answer. So, as for the paying of the tribute (do we or don't we?), I suspect that Mark is saying along with Paul before him (Rom. 13.6) that paying the tax itself did not violate the Jewish prohibition against idolatry, since one's true allegiance, whether to Yahweh or idols, would be clarified by prior judgements regarding the true source of power and wisdom.[63]

One of the merits of this reading of 12.13–17 consists in its ability to resolve the problems besetting the traditional reading, advanced by Schnackenburg among others. In my critique of that interpretation, I remarked on its four-fold failure to explain (1) the warrant for assuming that Jesus subscribed to a bifurcated (sacred–secular) view of reality; (2) the absence of a climactic scriptural proof, as we might expect at 12.17, in keeping with halakhic convention; (3) the abrupt departure from Mark's Christological agenda (that is, on the traditional reading's judgement that 12.13–17 has nothing Christological about it); and (4) the incomplete parallelism between the 'things of Caesar', the image and inscription of the coin, and the 'things of God', which evince no obvious counterparts. In contrast, the reading I have presented here offers (1) an integrated religio-political polemic levelled against Caesar which avoids a modernist dualism; (2) an implicit scriptural climax at 12.17, involving two key terms ('image' and 'writing') drawn from Daniel 1—7; (3) a thoroughly Christological thrust in keeping with the surrounding Markan context; and (4) suppressed parallels to the 'image' and 'writing' of Caesar on the divine side of the ledger, again, drawn from Daniel. Lest this interpretation of Mark 12.13–17 be decried as overly subtle, I would point out that Mark is almost certainly building on an interpretation of Daniel which had been circulating orally and perhaps broadly in pre-Markan Christianity and that, for all we know, this interpretation may in turn have been a takeoff on standard first-century midrashic approaches to Daniel. What may be 'overly subtle' to us may have been dead obvious to a first-century Jew within his

---

[63] Most commentators agree that Jesus is deferring to Caesar's authority to tax; see, e.g., Donahue and Harrington 2002: 347; France 2002: 469.

or her universe of discourse. After all, if the Qumran pesherist can identify certain Roman instruments of war as the fulfilment of isolated words from Habakkuk, what's to prevent us from imagining like-minded pesherists of the same time connecting Roman imperial coinage to a few of Daniel's most important terms?[64]

The 'things of God' in the setting of Jesus

Finally, we come back full circle to the question of Jesus' intentions. What did Jesus – as opposed to Mark – mean when he engaged his questioners on the topic of taxes? What did he hope to signify by drawing attention to the coin's image and inscription? And what did it mean in his setting to give to Caesar the things of Caesar, and to God the things of God? Now that we have laid some ample groundwork, we are, I think, in good position to offer answers to these questions.

But let me begin by restating a handful of assumptions and judgements. First, it is difficult to avoid the judgement that when the historical Jesus referred to the denarius's image and inscription, he did so in part as a way of drawing attention to Caesar's *soi-disant* identity as divine image and cosmic high priest. Second, if, as has been confirmed in earlier chapters, Jesus did style himself as a Danielic Son of Man in the making, then we would naturally expect the book of Daniel to occupy a prominent place in his self-understanding. Third, given evidence that both Paul and Mark used 'things of God' as a concise metonymy for one of the battle lines within Daniel's story of cosmic war, it may be surmised that the Danielic antithesis between the 'things of God', together with the corresponding image and words, and the 'things of man', together with its complementary image and words, was already current in Jesus' day and perhaps even already extended to Roman coinage. Though short of unassailable, these three assumptions are certainly credible starting points.

Given these three starting points, the question then is not whether the historical Jesus' handling of the tax question – his intentions, actions and words – were faithfully preserved by Mark, but rather 'How could it be otherwise?' For Jesus, as for Mark after him, whatever religio-political significance was brought to bear by 'image' and 'inscription' as isolated terms, this would have been subsidiary to Jesus' larger goal of pairing these words as a compressed retelling of the Danielic narrative. Creatively interpreting the denarius through the lens of that narrative, Jesus asks his audience to recognize *its* false image and false inscription, along with himself as the true image with true wisdom, as the eschatological fulfilment of Scripture in real time. On this redefinition, the numismatic reminder of Roman oppression becomes a tangible symbol of imperial power underwritten and legitimized

---

[64] 1QpHab 5.12—6.9.

by a corresponding imperial ideology – the 'things of Caesar'. On this redefinition, too, Roman power and ideology would one day be judged and revealed for what they are – and that through the words and person of the Son of Man, who is of a piece with the image of God as represented in the eschatological temple (Daniel 2). Of course not all those listening to Jesus on that day would have tapped into his hidden transcript. Indeed, I suspect that many if not most did not. But those who had 'ears to hear' and picked up Jesus' allusion to Daniel's story would have probably, with further reflection, connected the dots: taxes or no taxes, in view of the Son of Man's eschatological intervention, Rome posed no real threat to the kingdom-establishing purposes of God. Mapping the saints' conflict with Rome on to the Danielic narrative, Jesus issued the call to render unto God and Caesar as part of a plea to recognize that his Son of Man movement was indeed on the side of Daniel and the angels, as would be made clear at the great eschatological assize.

All the while, Jesus' identification with the *priestly* Son of Man proves crucial throughout. His argument only makes sense in the context not just on the assumption that he and his movement are at once the warrior-priest Son of Man and the eschatological temple (Daniel 2), but also on the assumption that he is responding to Tiberius's attempt to tout his role as Pontifex Maximus, the pagan analogue to the Son of Man. At bottom, Jesus' coin demonstration was motivated by his dual concern to level a veiled warning against the high priest Tiberius and to assert – in equally veiled terms – his own destiny of securing the same role claimed by the emperor. In calling his hearers to 'give to Caesar the things of Caesar and give to God the things of God', Jesus was confronting Caesar's usurpation of the high priesthood which by divine right actually belonged to himself, as the Son of Man.

The trial of Jesus (Mark 14.53–65 par.)

If Jesus' baptism was the first announcement of Jesus' priesthood, his trial before Caiaphas included its last. Given the audacious assertions Jesus had been making during the course of his ministry (not to mention the radical implications of his movement's ritual practices, ethos and social composition), a showdown with Jerusalem's high priest was almost inevitable. Jesus probably knew as much. In fact, whatever else might be said about the aims of Jesus' words, actions and activities, he must have seen all these things as the mechanism which would ultimately land him an audience with Caiaphas, and from there perhaps even the Roman authorities. Jesus' appearance before Caiaphas was not a startling and unfortunate turn, but more likely the final step in his determination to confront Israel at the highest levels, and then, if necessary, to shoulder the consequences of such a confrontation.

That Jesus of Nazareth was executed on a Roman cross is virtually indisputable. But determining exactly what circumstances precipitated his death sentence is slightly trickier business, not least because of the various historical problems surrounding the Gospels' account of the trial before Caiaphas. Due to such problems, a number of scholars have come to doubt that anything like the story recorded in Mark 14.53–65 ever happened.[65] And so whether there really was a trial prior and, if so, whether we can access it historically are questions that will require immediate attention. Yet on the far side of this enquiry, I hope to explore the events leading up to Jesus' execution with a view to grasping more about his self-understanding. If Jesus had set himself up as the true Pontifex Maximus, over and against Caesar, how would he position himself against the 'other high priest', the one recognized by the Jews of his day?

The trial narrative in its Markan context

Though all four Gospels present some version of a trial involving the Jewish authorities, Mark's Gospel is normally thought to lay the strongest claim for historical accuracy.[66] At the same time, the Evangelist's aspirations as a historian cannot be separated from his rhetorical agenda, as discerned from the literary shape of his Gospel. How does the narrative lead-up to the trial scene inform our understanding of its function within the story?

Whereas Mark 1—10 recounts Jesus' activities over the course of several years, beginning with his entry into Jerusalem in 11.1 the action begins to slow down considerably. Soon enough, starting with the first day of the Passover week (14.12), the pace slackens again, calling for even closer attention to details, especially to those events taking place during Jesus' final two days. For the Evangelist, the trial scene merited a comparatively slow and careful (re)telling:

> [53]They took Jesus to the high priest; and all the chief priests, the elders, and the scribes were assembled. [54]Peter had followed him at a distance, right into the courtyard of the high priest; and he was sitting with the guards, warming himself at the fire. [55]Now the chief priests and the whole council were looking for testimony against Jesus to put him to death; but they found none. [56]For many gave false testimony against him, and their testimony did not agree. [57]Some stood up and gave false testimony against him, saying, [58]'We heard him say, "I will destroy this temple that is made with hands, and in three days I will build another, not made with hands."' [59]But even on this point their testimony did not agree. [60]Then the high priest stood up before them and asked Jesus, 'Have you no answer? What is it that they testify against you?' [61]But he was silent and did not answer. Again the high priest asked him, 'Are you the Messiah, the Son of the Blessed One?' [62]Jesus said, 'I am; and "you will see the Son of Man seated at the right hand of the Power", and "coming with the clouds of heaven."' [63]Then the high priest tore his clothes and said, 'Why do we still need witnesses? [64]You have heard his blasphemy! What is your decision?' All of them condemned him as deserving death. [65]Some began to spit on him,

---

[65] So, e.g., Lietzmann 1931; Winter 1961; Cohn 1971.
[66] Mark 14.53–65 par. Matt. 26.57–68//Luke 22.54–71//John 18.13–24.

to blindfold him, and to strike him, saying to him, 'Prophesy!' The guards also took him over and beat him.[67]

The passage conveys a confused episode, crowded with disparate characters along with their equally disparate agendas. The action is halting; progress is frustrated by the conflicting testimonies. Yet within this melee the interchange between Jesus and Caiaphas takes centre stage (vv. 61–63), becoming the hinge on which the whole scene turns. At the very centre of this hinge is Jesus' confession, giving the assembly sufficient grounds for condemning him as a blasphemer. The confession is so crucial in fact that it is nigh impossible to imagine the trial apart from it. One might even say that the trial and confession rise or fall together.[68]

The episode's importance in the plotline is borne out by its anticipation, evident in three different *inclusios* straddling the bulk of the Gospel. First, in the passage involving the healing of the paralytic (2.1–12), the Gospel writer foreshadows the trial scene by observing that Jesus' scribal opponents are 'sitting' (as if in judgement against Jesus) and 'questioning in their hearts' (v. 6), much as other religious leaders will sit in judgement, though much more vocally, in 14.53–65. In Mark 2.1–12, Mark's Jesus enters a house in order to undertake the priestly task of forgiving sins, prompting tacit charges of blasphemy (vv. 5–7). Now in 14.53–65, Mark's readers once again find Jesus in a house, where this time it is the high priest who condemns by levelling the explicit charge of blasphemy (v. 64). In 2.10, Jesus associates himself with the Son of Man, the first use of the phrase; in 14.62, he again indirectly identifies himself as the 'Son of Man', this time for the last time with the phrase's last occurrence. The gravitational centre of these two pericopae is Caiaphas's and Jesus' shared claim to Israel's priesthood.

There are also interesting connections between the trial and the episode centring on the healing of the man with the withered hand (3.1–6), two scenes in which Jesus becomes the target of the religious leaders' accusations. His summoning the man with the shrivelled hand to stand up in the middle (*eis to meson*) in 3.3 is paralleled by Caiaphas's standing up in the middle (*eis meson*) (14.60) – the Gospel's only two instances of this prepositional phrase. If in the earlier scene Jesus' questioning is met with stony silence (3.4), now at the trial it is he who remains silent in response to their interrogation (14.60–61a). Finally, it is at the trial that the leaders finally make good on their murderous intentions, initially aired in the follow-up to the healing scene when they first *held counsel* (*symboulion edidoun*) (3.6). Whatever we make of these intriguing parallels, the trial's connection with Mark 3.1–6 is hardly fortuitous. Since Mark 2.1–12 and 3.1–6 together provide a frame around 2.1—3.6, a series of scenes focusing on Jesus' conflict with the temple authorities, the triangulation between 2.1–12, 3.1–6 and 14.53–65 would

[67] Mark 14.53–65.
[68] Similarly Juel 1977: 15.

suggest that the last of these passages closes out the loop initiated by 2.1–12 and 3.1–6: at the trial the conflict between Jesus and the temple personnel comes to climactic resolution.

Still yet, the trial passage also brings to mind another early scene in which Jesus stands accused of collaborating with the demonic (3.20–29). Prominent among the shared features of 3.20–39 and 14.53–65 is the focus on blasphemy and on its punishment (3:28–29; 14:64). Both scenes are also concerned with themes of unity/disunity and/or consensus/dissension. In the trial, the witnesses' failure to agree (14.59) is an emblem of the house divided flimsily against itself (3:25), a house which, as Jesus' temple action (11.12–25) and eschatological discourse (13.1–30) intimate, is none other than the temple. Finally, we note that in 3.20–29, Mark's Jesus speaks of entering the strong man's house (v. 27), which may possibly have something to do with his own entry into the house of the most powerful Jewish figure of the day. The likely point of these combined correspondences verges on the shocking: though dark forces may have infiltrated the house of the temple, causing its division, it is through Jesus' trial and Passion that the strong man will be bound.

The significance of the connections between three pericopae in Mark 2—3 and the trial scene should not be overlooked. If the end of any story only makes sense in the light of its beginning, then Mark 14.53–65 is certainly meant to be the climax of one of Mark's most important subplots, its crucial moment: Jesus' confession as the enthroned, priestly Son of Man – in direct opposition to the regnant high priest.[69] As important as are the hearing before Pilate, the Passion and the resurrection, they are arguably but the specification of how the enthronement announced in Jesus' confession actually takes place, the *denouement* trailing the crisis of verses 60–64.

At the same time, Mark 14.62 connects itself with two earlier sayings alluding to the future coming of the Son of Man (8.38; 13.24–27). Together, all three sayings share a common paraenetic interest in believers' maintaining their faithful witness despite unbelieving resistance (Mark 8.38; 13.10–13; 14.62–65). This homiletical interest takes more pronounced and extended form in the Passion narrative, where the faithfulness of Jesus as the true Son of Man is played off against the faithlessness of Peter, the 'archetype of the Christian who disowns his Lord under persecution'.[70] The contrast between Jesus and Peter is glaring; it is made even more obvious through the Evangelist's swinging the narrative camera from Peter to Jesus, and back again.[71] In contrast to Jesus' three-fold obedience in Gethsemane (14.35–36, 39, 41), Peter rejects three opportunities to identify publicly with Jesus (vv. 68, 70, 71). Towards the end of Mark 14, whereas the once insightful Peter (8.29)

---

[69] So also Dibelius (1935: 193) who calls 14.61–62 the 'first high point' of the Passion narrative. Juel's (1977: 127–39) point regarding Mark's *contra templum* interest has never been refuted.
[70] Lampe 1973: 119. See also Donahue 1995: 15–23.
[71] See the full-length study of Borrell 1998.

has now been downgraded through his conspicuous failure, Jesus moves on from one set of identities (as a teacher, debater, healer, miracle worker or exorcist) to his more important identity: faithful witness.[72] For Mark, it is through his faithful witness that Jesus proves to be the true, suffering Son of Man and in this sense *becomes* the Son of Man. Embracing this identity at last, Jesus comes to embody fully the ideal that had eluded Peter's even most sincere efforts. The Evangelist's pastoral agenda is correspondingly clear: when faced with a crisis of confessions, the faithful will have to endure the synagogues' charges of blasphemy in order to avoid true blasphemy. Their model: the paradigmatic faithfulness of Jesus, who was crucified for blasphemy yet vindicated through the resurrection.

Mark's homiletical agenda puts the significance of Jesus' final declaration into historical perspective. While some have argued that the confession is a dubious datum of history (either as a mere fact of history or in terms of its exact content), this judgement stumbles on the credence which the Evangelist seems to have granted it *as a historically grounded account*. The surmise of credence becomes clearer on considering the improbable scenarios which a knowingly fictive trial scene – fictive either because Mark never had access to the trial or because it never occurred in the first place – requires. On the possibility that the early Christian community was never made privy to the details of the trial (an issue I will return to momentarily), Mark's trial narrative would be received as a patent fiction, embarrassingly cold comfort for any of his first-century readers forced to choose between self-protecting denial and self-sacrificing confession. That an undeterred Evangelist should invite his readers to expend their lives on account of a myth (as the Old Liberal account has proposed) is simply far more improbable than Markan ignorance of the trial. Alternatively, again, if there never was a trial in the first place, the same logic applies: given the human stakes, it is inherently unlikely that the Evangelist would couch Jesus' trial as *the* template of Christian faithfulness had he and his readers known very well that it never happened. This is not to say that the two scenarios I have just considered are impossible, but to point out that in going any of these routes it must be conceded that we are, in historiographical terms, essentially cutting off our nose to spite our face. Given the confession's crucial function for Mark's homiletical purposes, it makes most sense to assume, short of compelling evidence to the contrary, that the Evangelist and his antecedent community had some report of the proceedings and considered it factually trustworthy. Unless the trial happened roughly along the lines of the Gospel account, the basis of his exhortation to unto-death faithfulness – so central to his interests in writing the Gospel in the first place – quickly crumbles.

---

[72] Though argued deftly, Gundry's recent thesis (2015) that Matthew (though obviously a different concern from Mark) seeks to depict Peter as a permanent apostate falls short of persuasion; see reviews by, e.g., Carter 2016: 376; Gurtner 2016: 211.

The trial as a historical problem

Of course, one can hardly ignore the thorny historical problems surrounding the trial, all of which have been compiled and reiterated in a sub-specialized literature. Rather than recount the conversation in full, it will be sufficient to set forth the presenting difficulties, as recognized by scholarship in this area. Assuming (1) that Jesus was being tried before Caiaphas for a capital crime, and (2) that the regulations of mishnaic Judaism would have been in force in Jesus' day, sceptics have mainly stumbled on seven points:

1. Whereas the ancient Jews only tried capital cases during the day (*m. Sanh.* 4.1), Mark relates that Jesus was tried at night.
2. Whereas Jewish practice forbade capital cases on Sabbath or feast days (*m. Sanh.* 4.1; *m. Besah* 5.2), Mark's story has Jesus being tried during Passover week.
3. Whereas Jewish prescription required deferring the passing of sentence to a separate hearing (*m. Sanh.* 4.1), Jesus is tried and sentenced in the same convening.
4. Whereas blasphemy by definition requires the pronouncing of the divine name (*m. Sanh.* 4.1), the Jesus of Mark's Gospel never does so, yet still incurs the indictment of blasphemy.
5. Whereas trials were required to be held in the council meeting room of the Sanhedrin (*m. Sanh.* 11.2), the Gospel accounts set Jesus' trial at Caiaphas's home.
6. Whereas cases of this nature would require the defendant to make an initial response to the staged charge, bringing in supporting witnesses as appropriate (*m. Sanh.* 4.1), Jesus makes his only statement towards the end of the proceedings.
7. Finally, whereas the high priest's role would typically involve his serving as judge rather than prosecutor, Mark's account likewise falls short of historical verisimilitude.

On the face of it, these considerations seem to comprise damning evidence against Mark's reliability as a historian. Such evidence might suggest either that the Evangelist wilfully set out to deceive his hearers, or that Mark expected his readers to receive his report as fictive mythology (a position which, as I have just pointed out, has its own set of problems).

While several scholars have made plausible cases as to why in fact scepticism regarding Jesus' trial is finally unwarranted, for my part, I am convinced that the root problem stems from the way in which the whole issue has been framed.[73] More to the point, while over the course of the past 80 years

---

[73] Blinzler (1959), for example, stresses that Jesus' trial would have been carried out with a Sadducean procedure, not the Pharisaic protocol preserved in the rabbinica. Lohse (1961) agrees but argues that the argument against the trial's historicity falls apart once it is granted that certain elements of the trial *were* in violation of Jewish law. Two other important advocates

scholars have been busily weighing in on the historicity or non-historicity of
Jesus' trial, the evidence suggests that this event was actually not a trial at all
but in fact something more akin to a preliminary hearing, convened with the
view to eliciting Roman charges of sedition. Such a hearing would not obvi-
ate the necessity of employing many of the same procedures typically used in
a trial, but so long as the convening body did not presume to pass sentence,
the ordinary rules of a capital trial need not apply.

That Jesus' 'trial' was actually an informal hearing follows from at least
four considerations. First, as best as we can tell, the Jews of the period did not
retain the right to try capital cases.[74] Had the Sanhedrin actually attempted
a formal trial resulting in the death penalty, this itself would have been an
illegal act, running a risk with the Romans that would have far outweighed
the benefit accrued in sidelining Jesus. Second, the historical clues suggest
that from the start, the Jewish leaders adopted a strategy whereby they would
seek to entrap Jesus, first, by making him run afoul of Jewish sensibilities
and, second, by portraying him as a disrupter of the *pax Romana*.[75] On the
best-case scenario, the Jewish leadership would drum up sufficient evidence
against Jesus to justify handing him over to Rome (thereby staying in reasonably good graces with internal constituencies), then allow the magistrate
to implement the punishment.[76] This would also explain why Jesus' accusers
are especially fixated on getting the witnesses to line up regarding his alleged
statements against the temple (14.55–59). If a clear-cut statement against the
temple would have been solid grounds for bringing charges of blasphemy, it
would also have been meeting the Romans at their 'sweet spot' for actionable
behaviour. Third, while several of the elements in Mark's account do not fit a
capital trial (e.g. the intrusive participation of the high priest, the absence of
any initial plea and defence), they are consistent with an informal proceeding. These are weighty considerations.

Yet in addition to these there is a compelling and perhaps decisive point:
not once does Mark's Sanhedrin see itself as being in a position to hand
down a sentence. Instead, Jesus is merely declared to be worthy of death
(*enochon einai thanatou*) (14.64). Where we do find technical legal language of
condemnation, it is only in Pilate's term *aition* ('guilty') in one of his earlier
statements about Jesus: 'I have examined him in your presence and have not
found this man guilty of any of your charges against him' (*egō enōpion hymōn*

---

for the essential historicity of the trial in the twentieth-century discussion are Wellhausen 1909
(1903): 124 (less the confession) and Benoit 1969.
[74] Sherwin-White 1963: 35–43.
[75] Many if not all of Jesus' halakhic disputes with the scribes must have been set up with the
long view of drawing up indictments on theological grounds; the question of paying taxes to
Caesar (Mark 12.13–17 par.), as I have argued, was also patently motivated to find some basis
for charges of sedition. As far as I am aware, Kilpatrick (1953: 8–11) is the first to really pick up
on the temple leaders' two-step strategy.
[76] Juel's (1977: 67) objection to this reconstruction ('nothing is ever said about making formal
charges to Pilate based on what was decided at the trial') rings hollow.

anakrinas outhen heuron en tō anthrōpō toutō aition hōn katēgoreite kat'autou).[77] In the scriptural record, the closest we come to such language being predicated of the Jews is in Acts 13.27 ('Because the residents of Jerusalem and their leaders did not recognize him or understand the words of the prophets that are read every sabbath, they fulfilled those words by *condemning* [*krinantes*] him'), but even here the exception actually confirms the rule, for the next verse carefully qualifies its antecedent text by denying probative *aitia* ('cause') for adverse judgement: 'Even though they found no cause for a sentence of death [*mēdemian aitian thanatou*], they asked Pilate to have him killed.'[78] According to Luke, the Jewish leaders were seeking *aitia* but failing to secure it, despite having in hand a charge of blasphemy. Thus, the Jewish leaders were under no illusion that blasphemy could pass muster with the Romans as a capital crime: if Jesus was to be executed, it would have to be the Romans who, convinced by the early fact-finding mission of the Jewish hearing, would take responsibility for handing down the formal death sentence.[79]

As remarkable as it sounds, if so many historical-critical scholars have come to view Mark's trial as a Christian fiction, it is largely because of the unwarranted assumption that the event described in Mark 14:53–65 was a trial. The truth of the matter seems to be that it was not, nor was it ever intended to be.[80]

So much for the potential snags of Mark's 'trial account', but what about the question of access? Jesus obviously did not have the opportunity to share with his disciples the details of the proceedings before his execution, and Peter, the disciple physically closest to the hearing, was still too far away (and too preoccupied with his own conversations) to qualify as an eyewitness. How can we account for the information of what had happened on the inside eventually making its way into the early Christian Passion narrative? While these are legitimate questions, their force should not be exaggerated. After all, assuming some continuity between the hearing of Jesus and the trial of James (both events spanning the high-priestly reign of the Annas family), and noting that individuals like Josephus were obviously positioned to report a great deal of detail about the latter (*Ant.* 20.9.1 §§197–203), we have no basis for insisting that the details of Jesus' interrogation would have been kept under lock and key. That Caiaphas arranged to have the proceedings take place at night was an attempt not to ensure permanent confidentiality, but to take care of business expeditiously out of public view, with the hope – if everything went smoothly – of shunting Jesus over to the Romans as soon possible. Furthermore, despite our having been unconsciously conditioned to think of Jesus' trial as an intimate meeting (think, for example, of Matthias Stom's famous seventeenth-century painting of Caiaphas and Jesus huddled

---

[77] Luke 23.14b.
[78] Mark 14.28.
[79] On the non-legal nature of the terms associated with the trial, see Catchpole 1971: 254–60; Bock 2007: 64–8.
[80] All the same, for the sake of convention I will continue to use the term 'trial' throughout the remainder of my discussion.

around the high priest's work desk), we have to remember that the Sanhedrin was made up of dozens of men, some of whom, including probably Joseph of Arimathea and Nicodemus, would have held varying levels of sympathy for the Jesus movement. Within weeks after the crucifixion, as the post-Pentecostal Church began to make inroads with the Jewish priesthood (Acts 6.8), the already permeable social boundary between the temple leadership structure and the Jesus movement would become even more porous with the exchange of information.

This all adds up to one thing: given the size of the gathering, the highly controversial nature of its focus, and the less than watertight cohesion of the Sanhedrin on the matter at hand, Caiaphas must have regarded ongoing confidentiality as a practical impossibility. Whether there was any attempt to keep the hearing confidential, it is doubtful; whether such an attempt would have even been feasible, we can only say 'no'.

The verbal exchange at the trial

Questions surrounding Jesus' final statement (Mark 14.62)

Even if the report of Jesus' defiant confession sooner or later made its way back to his movement, this does not exclude the possibility that the content of the confession was lost, only later to be reinvented. In the past, in part because of the reigning paradigm which emphasized the historically problematic nature of the trial, many historical-critical scholars had regarded the confession as the product of churchly imaginations. For example, Norman Perrin, having been convinced that all the Son of Man sayings originated with the post-Easter community, argues that Mark 14.62 is the culmination of a process which began with the community generating two discrete pesher interpretations, emerging out of their experience of Jesus' resurrection and Passion as these events came to be understood through the lens of Scripture.[81] The first interpretation (which Perrin calls pesher 1) sought to make scriptural sense of the resurrection by combining the Ascension pictured in Psalm 110 with Daniel 7's vision of the Son of Man going *to* God. At a later stage, a second interpretation (pesher 2) attempted to make sense of the crucifixion with some help from Zechariah 12.10, only to combine this, again, with the Danielic Son of Man. But this time the interpreters appealed to Daniel 7 on the understanding that the Son of Man was coming *down* to the earth in the parousia – not unlike what we find in Revelation 1.7. According to Perrin, the composition finally recorded in Mark 14.62 memorializes the moment at which these two interpretations have been brought together.[82]

Although Perrin's interpretation had its supporters in earlier years, contemporary discussants of the points seem less convinced.[83] They should be.

---

[81] Norman Perrin, 1974.
[82] Norman Perrin, 1974: 10–14.
[83] Such supporters include Boers 1972: 310–15; Walker 1972; 1983.

In the first place, scholarship is no longer in a position (as it was in the 1960s when Perrin wrote his essay) where with a wave of the magical traditio-critical wand we can so effortlessly consign the Son of Man to the imaginary world of early Christianity. Second, if there's ever a place in the Jesus tradition where 'the Son of Man' makes sense as a dominical expression, it is here. Echoing Schweitzer and Schweizer, James D. G. Dunn explains:

> The fact is that the Dan. 7:13–14 vision was a high point in the tradition of the suffering righteous and their vindication. If Jesus was indeed arraigned before Caiaphas's council, then any previous thought that he might escape death (cf. Mark 14:33–36) would have soon disappeared. In these circumstances Daniel's vision of one like a son of man exalted in heaven and interpreted in reference to the 'saints of the Most High' in their vindication after terrible suffering (Dan 7:17–18, 21–27), would have provided a powerful solace and assurance for Jesus. We need not attempt to resolve the tricky question as to whether Jesus referred in this phrase ('the son of man') to himself or to another. The text remains open on this issue. What the text does imply is that Jesus drew on this text to express his confidence that God would not abandon him and would vindicate him following the suffering and death which must have been looming ever more likely by the minute.[84]

Dunn is right: were we to imagine a scripturally conversant Jew contemplating being put to death as a result of commitments to Yahweh, it would be hard to think of a text more relevant to the situation than Daniel 7. And why not say it aloud, as Jesus does, so as to capitalize on one last opportunity to confirm one's own resolve, defy the detractors and – once word got out – galvanize the supporters? Up to this point, I have been arguing that Jesus appropriated Daniel 7 as his primary script for his vocation. By reinserting himself in the story of the heavenly scene one last time, he reasserts one last time his summative vision of eschatological events – even as those events were now about to unfold precisely on account of his assertion.

Now if Daniel 7 fits the situation to a tee, the historical Jesus' mention of Psalm 110 is more probable than improbable. This follows from a series of considerations. First, as Craig Evans notes, in early rabbinic exegesis Daniel 7 and Psalm 110 were exegetically coordinated.[85] Though this interpretation is obviously post-Christian, it probably depends on pre-Christian traditions that could not possibly have been influenced by Mark 14.62. Second (as Evans also notes), Jesus' collocation of Daniel 7 and Psalm 110 should not be surprising, given a handful of shared thematic correspondences between the two passages, to wit, Gentile subjugation, righteous rule and divinely backed judgement.[86] As best as we can tell, the integration of Daniel 7 and Psalm 110 was already firmly part of the interpretative landscape well before the

---

[84] Dunn 2000: 14.
[85] *Midr. Ps.* 2.9; cited in Evans 1991: 220.
[86] Evans 1991: 220. Evans might have also mentioned the first-century's tendency to identify the Danielic Son of Man with the Son of David, the focal figure of Psalm 110.

early Christians made it one of their key Christological focal points. On top of all this, we already have evidence of Jesus' interest in Psalm 110, and that, no less, during the last week of his life (Mark 13.35–37). The question as to whether Psalm 110's intersection with Mark 14.62 is to be chalked up to late redaction (as N. Perrin once argued) or to early tradition (as this N. Perrin now argues) needs to be re-asked with reference to the *Davidssohnfrage*'s increasingly strong claim to authenticity.[87] Which is easier – to believe that the historical Jesus made repeated reference to the same psalm in the space of a few days, or to believe that the believing community smuggled Psalm 110 into its own homespun version of the trial scene for reasons that have absolutely nothing to do with the historically credible occurrence of the same psalm in Mark 13.35–37? I think the choice is clear enough. If along with most we accept the *Davidssohnfrage* (Mark 13.35–37 par.) as authentic, on the criterion of coherence we are virtually obliged to allow both Daniel 7 and Psalm 110 their shared moment in Caiaphas's court.

While I believe that the fatal flaw in Perrin's argument regarding Mark 14.62 is in his prematurely discounting the possibility of dominical provenance, others have seen the essay's greater weaknesses as being his inclusion of Zechariah 12.10b ('when they look on the one whom they have pierced, they shall mourn for him, as one mourns for an only child, and weep bitterly over him, as one weeps over a firstborn') as a viable subtext alongside Daniel 7.13 and Psalm 110.1.[88] On Perrin's judgement, the Markan verb 'you will see' (*hopesethe*) aligns with Zechariah's vision of those who will look (LXX: *hopsetai*) on the one they have pierced. Though the slenderness of the connection between Mark 14.62 and Zechariah 12.10 makes it impossible to form a strong judgement on this matter, Perrin may be on target for two reasons at least. First, Zechariah 12 makes excellent sense in the mouth of Jesus at this time (though Perrin himself would have disagreed on this point), simply because we find Jesus recurring to Zechariah 9—13 throughout the last week of his life.[89] Second, among the thematic interests shared by Daniel 7 and Psalm 110, one of these is the twin theme of exoneration and exaltation (including the divine agent's vindication over his enemies) – an idea that crops up in Zechariah 12 as well. That the historical Jesus appealed to all three texts simultaneously is more probable than a complex theory involving multiple stages of tradition. To put a finer point on it, in Jesus' response to Caiaphas, the evidence is very strong that he appealed to Daniel 7, reasonably strong that he invoked Psalm 110, and only somewhat less strong that he also called up Zechariah 13.

---

[87] According to Norman Perrin (1974: 13), following Lindars' (1961: 47), the *Davidssohnfrage* (Mark 12:35–37) is likewise the product of community *pesher* activities and thus is no evidence that the historical Jesus alluded to Psalm 110 at Mark 14.62.

[88] E.g. Juel 1975: 94.

[89] See Kim 1987: 138–40; Evans 1999: 388; Nicholas Perrin, 2010: 159–63.

The interrogation (Mark 14.55–59)

According to the Gospel record, Caiaphas's enquiry initially focused on Jesus' alleged stated intention to destroy the temple (Mark 14.55–59). The high priest's interest in this issue becomes clearer when we consider his goals, which were two-fold. On the one side of the equation, Caiaphas needed to provide the Romans with a compelling and legal rationale as to why they ought to do away with Jesus. The best chances of achieving this result, the high priest well understood, would be to undertake a discovery process that would unmask Jesus as a dangerous fomenter of sedition. On the other side of the equation, the temple leadership, despite its seemingly unlimited power, remained sensitive to its reputation among the Jewish populace. If the Sanhedrin was about to turn over a leader as popular as Jesus, it would have to be for reasons that would command deference from all quarters. And so Caiaphas must have been looking to stick Jesus with charges involving a clear violation of Jewish law, as interpreted by both the Sadducee-heavy Sanhedrin and the popularly supported Pharisees. If the hearing could somehow get Jesus on record for making public statements against the temple (with statements relating to contemplated acts of terrorism against the temple, to boot), that would allow the Jewish leadership to tick both boxes at once.

While no one would seriously argue that the participants in Jesus' trial approached their investigation without prejudice, the hearing – if we take 14.55–59 as fairly accurate historical reportage – was not quite the kangaroo court it has often been made out to be in so much scholarship. Under Caiaphas's leadership, it was important to pin Jesus with charges of sedition through a reasonably fair process, one in which the witnesses' stories would at least have to line up. Of course with a little backstage rehearsing, the witnesses probably could have been *made* to line up, but as the hearing unfolds, the high priest was not ready to wink at either the disparate testimony or the appearance of collusion resulting from badly rehearsed lines. In any case, when Mark relates that the witnesses had failed to achieve a consistent story, he also gives the impression that the trial was beginning to stall. Apparently, even within an informal Jewish hearing, the rules of argument and evidence still mattered. At least for this proceeding, Caiaphas's concern for orderly procedure probably had less to do with a principled commitment to due process and more to do with his interest in remaining immune to potential objections that Jesus had been executed unjustly.

Frustrated by the lack of traction in the current line of questioning, Caiaphas takes over the interrogation (14.60–61). The high priest's first question is met with silence (vv. 60–61a). But then comes the turning point of the hearing, when he asks Jesus whether he is 'the Messiah, the Son of the Blessed One' (v. 61b). Although this query is often interpreted to be introducing an entirely new line of interrogation, this does not seem to be the case.[90] Determined to get Jesus on record for threatening the temple's destruction, Caiaphas approaches the same issue from another angle: Jesus' putative messiahship. The high priest's internal line of reasoning is not difficult to reconstruct. Because Caiaphas suspected that Jesus was making himself out to be the messiah (as demonstrated not least by the temple action), and because, too, such a role virtually implicated him, according to so much Jewish thought, in a conspiracy to destroy the temple with a view to building a new one, a messianic confession would be the shortest route to proving his intentions against the temple.[91] Of course an unequivocal messianic claim on Jesus' part would be construed as an even more direct threat to Roman interests. So if Caiaphas could get Jesus to agree that he was the messiah, this would not only practically confirm rumours of his having publicly slandered the temple, but also give the temple leadership ample ammunition when it came to explaining to the Romans how politically dangerous Jesus really was.

Perhaps to his own surprise, Caiaphas got what he bargained for – and much more. On hearing Jesus' response in Mark 14.62 ('I am; and "you will see the Son of Man seated at the right hand of the Power", and "coming with the clouds of heaven"'), Caiaphas immediately tears his robes, declares blasphemy and abruptly concludes the proceedings. Clearly the high priest was convinced that he now had more than enough evidence both to secure just cause in the Jewish mind and to persuade the Romans that they now needed to run with the ball in more formal proceedings.

The nature of Jesus' blasphemy (Mark 14.62)

That Jesus decisively incriminated himself in Caiaphas's eyes is patently clear. The precise nature of that self-incrimination, however, is less so. In what sense did Jesus' statement to the high priest attain to the level of blasphemy – not just potential grounds of blasphemy requiring some further connecting of the dots, but a cut-and-dry reason for Caiaphas to terminate the proceedings on the spot? While this question has provoked no small amount of discussion, the leading answers seem to boil down into three or four possibilities.

First, it is sometimes said that Jesus incurs the charge of blasphemy simply on his affirmation of messianic identity, that is, with the words 'I am' (*egō eimi*) (14.62).[92] On this reading, any claim to be the messiah would be a blasphemous claim. Unfortunately, this interpretation is gravely undermined by the absence of any supporting historical evidence. In first- and second-century Judaism, messiahs would come and go, and not once do we have

---

[90] See the still useful discussion of the difficulties attending these verses in Marcus 1989.

[91] On the connection between messianic identity and eschatological temple building, see Juel 1977: 178–9; Nicholas Perrin, 2015: 263–73.

[92] So, e.g., Blinzler 1959: 105–12; O'Neill 1969: 153–67; Lane 1974: 536. A variation of this position proposes that Jesus' offence lay in his pronouncing the word *egō eimi*; so e.g. Stauffer 1960: 121–8.

intimations that their messianic claims, even when they were proved to be patently false (for example, in the case of Simon ben Kosiba), amounted to blasphemy. For good reason, scholars have now discarded this as an option.

A second option, proposed by Robert Gundry, focuses on the rabbinic technical definition of blasphemy, which restricts the infraction to the illicit pronouncement of the divine name.[93] On this reconstruction, Mark sought to preserve a tradition that Jesus had pronounced the divine name but then, rather than repeat the offence by putting it in writing, inserted a circumlocution ('the Power', *tēs dynameōs*) for 'Yahweh', all the while assuming that his readers would gather the essential gist of the scene. The primary strength of this position lies in its ability to draw a straight line between the textbook rabbinic definition of blasphemy (*m. Sanh.* 7.5) and the historic event. Its weaknesses, however, are at least two-fold. In the first place, while Gundry's interpretation assumes that the bar for blasphemy in the rabbinic period applied equally to Jesus' day, the truth is that early first-century Judaism was much more theologically differentiated than rabbinic Judaism, presumably with the result that there was considerable variation in Jesus' day as to what did and did not constitute blasphemy.[94] In this respect, Gundry's straight line between mishnaic legislation and the first-century reality is perhaps *too* straight. A second weakness of Gundry's argument is its inability to adduce any hint that Mark intended to sanitize Jesus' words. In fact, given the high stakes that Mark attaches to this climactic scene (a point which I have already emphasized), it would be surprising, not to mention decidedly anti-climactic, if Mark was inviting his readers to model their faithful witness on a self-defence where Jesus sparked controversy not on account of any Christological claim, but on account of his inexplicable use of an offensive word. On Gundry's scenario, we would be hard-pressed to explain why the Evangelist holds this up as an exemplary crowning moment when he himself is too embarrassed to repeat Jesus' *faux pas*.

A third solution, the traditional and most commonly touted approach, goes something like this: Jesus had incurred the charge of blasphemy by quoting Daniel 7 and Psalm 110, two texts which insinuated his own right to share privileges reserved strictly for God.[95] The obvious strength of this option lies in the stray bits of evidence, largely associated with Philo and Josephus, that in the first century claims to act or be like God were regarded as tantamount to blasphemy.[96] Quite clearly, if Jesus is claiming to be the Son of Man coming on the clouds, he is arrogating to himself the remarkable role of divinely appointed judge. It is perhaps the case that this co-identification was the trigger for Caiaphas's response.

---

[93] Gundry 2005, 2008.
[94] See the study of Collins 2004. For a discussion of differing definitions among the Pharisees and Sadducees, see Bauckham 1999: 223.
[95] Betz 1982: 565–647; Marcus 1989; Bock 1997; 2007; Collins 2004.
[96] Philo, *Somn.* 2.18; *Decal.* 13–14, 61–64; *Legat.* 45; Josephus, *Ant.* 4.8.6 §202.

On the other hand, this explanation for the blasphemy charge is undermined by three observations. The first pertains to the complicating fact that certain swathes of first-century Judaism had considerable tolerance for pushing the boundaries of divinity beyond the person of Yahweh.[97] This is eminently the case in what may count as the earliest instance of *merkabah* mystic literature, the third-century BCE *Exagoge of Ezekiel*, which depicts the Almighty handing over sceptre and crown to Moses. In the same category, we might also consider the Son of Man of *1 Enoch*, a highly transcendent, Enoch-*esque*, messianic figure clearly based on the figure of Daniel 7. Beyond these, the literature offers enough other instances in which either the primordial worthies (Adam, Abel, Noah, Shem) or the patriarchs (Abraham, Isaac, Jacob) or the vindicated righteous rise to take their place alongside Yahweh's throne.[98] Between Josephus and Philo on the one side and early *merkabah* witness on the other side, the boundary between divine and human seems to have been somewhat fluid. In the light of such ambivalence, this account of Jesus' blasphemy must actually limit itself to one of two possible scenarios. One such scenario is that Jesus was liable for blasphemy not because his utterance was blasphemous in principle, but because he, a mere Galilean upstart, was brazenly reaching for a status normally assigned only to such worthies as Moses and Enoch.[99] Another possibility is that Jesus was found guilty of blasphemy on certain theological principles which would have *not* been universally shared by Jews of the day. On either scenario, Caiaphas's sudden denunciation would be subject to scrutiny, thereby risking the possibility of alienating stakeholders who held out hopes of a coming human figure who just *might* attain to the right hand of God. Given Caiaphas's interest in a verdict that would be unimpeachable before a broad constituency, this explanation seems less compelling.

The second problem with this interpretation lies in the assumption that Jesus is identifying himself personally with the Son of Man, when in fact – as Dunn points out in the above-cited quote – there is nothing in his statement to require such identification.[100] In Mark 14.62, after admitting to a messianic self-consciousness, Jesus then goes on, characteristically, to refer to the Son of Man in the third person, a statement which certainly leaves open the possibility that the Son of Man is a distinct collective entity to which he belongs. Again, though we have every reason to believe that Caiaphas sought to steer the hearing in a particular direction, he still felt obligated to ensure a reasonably fair process or at least make a good show of it before making the controversial move of turning over a popular Jewish leader to be crucified by the Romans. If Jesus' offence consists in his self-identification with a divine

---

[97] Segal 1977; Hurtado 1988: 17–92; Bock 1997: 122–45; Eskola 2001: 91–123.
[98] Eskola 2001: 128. See *T. Isaac* 2.7; *T. Job* 33.2–4; *T. Ab.* 10; *T. Benj.* 10.5–6; *Apoc. Mos.* 19.2.
[99] Bock (1997: 152) comes close to this when he writes: '[a]pproximate seating next to God might be considered for a privileged few . . . But such honor would never be contemplated by the leadership for a humble, rural Galilean, preacher like Jesus.'
[100] Dunn 2000: 12–13.

being, Caiaphas would presumably have wanted to make crystal clear that Jesus did in fact make such a bald equation, a point which cannot be sustained by his choice of words. And yet Caiaphas seems quite clear on the matter.

A third problem: if the scandal of Jesus' confession has mostly to do with implicit claims of divinity, this fits awkwardly within a Gospel in which the Evangelist has been pressing home Jesus' *messiahship* – not so much his divinity – over and against potential counterclaims of the temple hegemony. True, it is not impossible that Caiaphas has gone trawling for Jesus' messiahship only somehow to haul in a far bigger fish than he expected, that is, an extraordinary claim of co-divinity far more far-reaching than any messianic claims. But if so, then this only raises the question as to whether the Evangelist's narrative-length interest in Jesus *as Christ* has not been beside the point after all, and whether the *real* point of all this – as made clear at the trial and despite the Evangelist's concerns up to this point – is Jesus' divinity. While I suspect that Jesus' confession has entailments of divinity (more on this below), if the Gospel writer at Mark 14.62 was attempting to emphasize Jesus' divinity in such a way as to relegate his messiahship to a matter of secondary importance, then this basically reduces Mark 1—14.48 to an exercise in walking down a garden path.[101]

Against these three approaches, I recommend a fourth approach, a variation of a commonly offered interpretation which links Jesus' scriptural citation with the alleged blasphemy precisely as a cursing of the high priest – clear grounds for blasphemy according to common Jewish interpretation of Exodus 22.27 (cf. Lev. 24.10–23; Num. 15.30–31).[102] I favour this solution simply because it makes most sense both of Mark's narrative (the presumed earliest written interpretation of Jesus' trial) and the historical situation behind the Gospel. All along, as Mark tells the story, Jesus has been hinting at his own identity as the royal-priestly Son of Man, in flat contradiction to the high priest's *de facto* tenure. And so his account is a tale of two competing priestly powers, whose intermittent clashes lie strewn across the Gospel, with hints of judgement against the temple establishment arranging themselves in a crescendo. Following the penultimate judgement against the temple leadership in the thinly veiled parable of the wicked tenants, now in Mark 14.53–65 Jesus finally comes into direct confrontation with Caiaphas, declaring the latter's doom in unmistakable scriptural terms. One can hardly afford to overlook the intended homiletical punch Mark hopes to land. Whereas modern interpretation of Mark 14.62 (and the Gospels in general) has tended to treat the Evangelist's Christological claims as

---

[101] Making essentially the same point regarding Mark's narrative argument, Burkill (1970: 2) concludes that the Evangelist must have misunderstood Caiaphas's charge of blasphemy as a response to a messianic claim, when Jesus was actually claiming divinity for himself.

[102] Evans (1991: 222) and Bock (1997: 156–60; 2007: 82–5) accept this reading but in combination with the outrage of claiming to share Yahweh's throne. In distinction from their position, I would see connotations of divinity, but denotations of usurpation. For references in Philo and Josephus, see Collins 2004: 389–94.

theological truisms, Mark and his readers would have been keenly aware of these assertions' sharpest and most controversial edge, namely, that Jesus is the true high priest *and* Caiaphas and his heirs are not. Therefore, without minimizing Mark 14.62's import as a climactic Christological summary, we cannot fail to see how Mark's incorporation of the confession is calculated to address a question that would have been burning in the minds of his first-century readers: 'If Jesus really is the messiah, then what about temple-based Judaism and the fate of those who stand by its leadership?'

This lines up with the scriptures Jesus had quoted. According to Evans, as I have mentioned, Daniel 7 and Psalm 110 share more than a few themes: subjugation, rule and judgement.[103] To this list of mutual themes, I would add one more common thread: priesthood. I have already argued that Daniel's Son of Man is actually a priestly figure; an exalted sacerdotal office is also manifestly in view in Psalm 110 with the mention of Melchizedek. In short, both Daniel 7 and Psalm 110 present visions of a priestly figure who is in conflict with God's enemies yet proves to be ultimately victorious. None of this is lost on the Evangelist. Up to this point in the narrative, Mark has presented Jesus as the priestly Son of Man, most recently in his account of the Last Supper with Jesus' indicating his forthcoming sacrifice on the cross (Mark 14.22–25). But now at Mark 14.62 the Evangelist offers Jesus as the coming Son of Man and the Melchizedekian Davidide, who will one day displace and judge Caiaphas and his supporters. The common denominator is eschatological priesthood.

In this vein, Mark fully exploits the irony that Caiaphas should condemn Jesus the true high priest for blasphemously insinuating divine judgement against the official high priest.[104] Paradoxically, in the very act of accusing Jesus of blasphemy the high priest has made himself potentially liable to the same charge.[105] Later at Jesus' crucifixion those who pass by verbally abuse (*eblasphēmoun*) him.[106] Assuming that this last use of *blasphemeō* hearkens back to the 'blasphemy' allegedly committed before Caiaphas, we notice the extension of the same irony, this time with passers-by speaking blasphemously against the allegedly blaspheming Jesus, even as he is carrying out the high-priestly task of atoning for Israel's sin. Thus Mark's Caiaphas and Jesus become mirror images of each other: both are blasphemed yet blaspheming and both are supported by (allegedly) blaspheming followers. But the mirror only succeeds as a literary device if we assume that Jesus' blasphemy was an offence not against divine prerogative but against sacerdotal office. While interpretations of Jesus' confession have generally focused on its significance for either Jesus' divine identity or an underdetermined messianic status, both of these accounts short-circuit the conceptual path which Mark expects

---

[103] Evans 1991: 220.
[104] Mark 14.64.
[105] Cf. Mark 3.28–29.
[106] Mark 15.29.

his readers to take: tagging Jesus as the Davidic Son of Man, Mark 14.62 asserts Jesus in his role as messianic high priest, a role with its full bundle of theological entailments.

That Mark's Jesus is also an *eschatological* high priest is confirmed by the presence of *hopsesthe* ('you will see') in his promise to Caiaphas's assembly. Whether or not Zechariah 12.10 is in view here, in Mark 14.62 the verb is key: Jesus informs Caiaphas and his colleagues that they 'will *see* the Son of Man . . .', even as, according to 13.26, people 'will *see* [*hopsontai*] the Son of Man' with great power. As Bock and others have pointed out, similar such seeing has a strong eschatological aspect, regularly predicated of those who oppressed God's people, only one day finally to realize the truth, and suffer shame and condemnation as a result.[107] By promising the ruling priests in this context that they 'will see . . .', the Evangelist's Jesus indicates their imminent condemnation at the great assize.

Now as to the object of that seeing, what exactly the Evangelist would have understood by Caiaphas *seeing* the coming of Son of Man – on this point scholars have been divided. Some have suggested that the resurrection is in view; others, the destruction of the temple; still others, the parousia. For my money, I don't see any reason to separate out any of these options. Jesus' acquittal as the Son of Man need not be reduced to any one event; on the contrary, since all three events each in their own way confirm Jesus' vindication, and all three would be visible to Caiaphas's assembly in some sense, there is nothing to prevent us from supposing that for Mark the 'coming of the Son of Man' applies both to the entire redemptive historical process (entailing Ascension, temple's destruction and parousia) and to any one of these singular events within that process. In any case, the Evangelist's main point is the radically confrontational nature of Jesus' confession, tracing out Jesus and Caiaphas's respective trajectories, as well as the respective trajectories of those who may identify with one of these two figures. In Mark's theology, the destruction of the temple was not a way for a vindictive God to get even with the Jews who had rejected Jesus, but the divine resolution of a conflict between two competing temple systems.

Yet if this is true, there still remains a niggling but important detail: on the historical Jesus' reckoning, at what point would the Sanhedrin 'see' the Son of Man 'seated at the right' and 'coming with the clouds'? Or what would have the historical Caiaphas understood, if anything, by this assertion? It does not seem likely that the answer to this question is anything like what later Christians would mean by the parousia. For if the historical Jesus did mean something like a 'Second Coming', how could this possibly have been relevant to Caiaphas and his peers in the Sanhedrin? More probable, though by no means certain, is the possibility that for Jesus, 'seeing' the enthroned Son of Man had to do with his prediction of the destruction of the temple,

---

[107] Bock 2007: 82–3 (who cites Wisd. 5.2; *Apoc. El.* 35.17; and *1 En.* 62.3–5). See also Pesch 1976–80: 2.439.

or perhaps his expectation of his own future resurrection and exaltation, perhaps as part of the great eschatological event broadly expected by first-century Pharisees. But still stronger than these possibilities is what I believe to have been the heart of the matter: Jesus' expectation that he would ascend to the priestly throne in order to atone for Israel's sin. After all, for any first-century Jew, as for the later *merkabah* mystics, to see the throne would have been to see the space (over the ark of the covenant) where sin is atoned for.[108] In other words, by promising his confronters that they would see him 'seated at the right hand' and 'coming with the clouds', activities reserved for the Melchizedekian high priest (Psalm 110) and the *yom-kippur*-officiating Son of Man (Daniel 7), respectively, the historical Jesus affirms that they would see him providing atonement for God's people – even through the tribulation he was about to endure as a result of their condemnation. As Jesus prepared to die, he went on record that he was preparing to die as a martyr for Israel's sins.[109] He would die, in other words, as the true priest.

In retrospect, Jesus' final confession was the perfect culmination – and probably well-rehearsed culmination at that – of his priestly career, traces of which have been uncovered in the preceding chapters. To retrace our steps, I first argued in Chapter 1 that Jesus enlisted his disciples in praying the Lord's Prayer as a signature prayer for his counter-temple movement. As a publicly and regularly prayed prayer, it would only be a matter of time before its thrust would have eventually come to Caiaphas's attention. No less significant, and no less unsettling for the high priest, would have been Jesus' baptism, understood at the time to have been fraught with sacral implications (Chapter 2). In his teaching, Jesus called his followers to remain true to his return-from-exile temple movement despite the costs of severe persecution, issuing not least from the local guardians of the temple hegemony (Chapter 3). Such persecution did little to deter the movement, for Jesus promised that these afflictions were the very means by which the true priests would sort themselves out from false adherents. Meanwhile, Jesus came to designate himself both as Son of David and as Son of Man, two terms underscoring Jesus' identity as the eschatological high priest in the making, provided he endure the test of his divinely appointed suffering (Chapters 4–6). Now at last before Caiaphas the test is administered, and Jesus, more conscious than ever of his vocation as Son of David and Son of Man, reasserts himself in the very same terms, sealing his elective destiny, as well as his doom, by publicly embracing both titles. At its core such an assertion meant that Jesus was high priest and Caiaphas was not (nor for that matter was Caesar), and that the latter would one day have to answer to the former. Jesus himself nurtured no illusions regarding the likely consequences of such a claim; this kind of affront, made publicly and directly to the high priest, would almost certainly

---

[108] 1 Sam. 4.4; 2 Kings 19.15; 1 Chron. 13.6; Pss. 80.1; 99.1; Isa. 37.16; etc. See Eskola 2001: 55–8, 146–51.
[109] Similarly de Jonge 1988; Vines 2006.

merit the judgement of blasphemy. And because an attack on the high priest was by extension an attack on the temple which the high priest represented, the Romans too would have all they would need to prosecute a capital case against Jesus. Standing on the gallows, as it were, the historical Jesus knew that his fate was all but sealed, and thus considered it of utmost importance that he go down as the simultaneous Son of David and Son of Man – and be remembered as such. This was the epitome of his self-understanding: Jesus the priest.

Summary

In this chapter, we examined Jesus' conflict with two sets of adversaries: the Romans and the Jerusalem temple elite. Against the pretensions of Tiberius, Jesus insisted that he himself – and not Caesar – was the true Pontifex Maximus, the mediator of all reality. He and his followers were the image of God (not Caesar), even as they (again, not Caesar) were also the source of divine wisdom. At the same time, Jesus insisted in the very presence of Caiaphas that the high priest would be removed and that Jesus himself would become the source of atonement, as the quintessence of the priestly Son of Man. In the very act of confronting the soon-to-be-demoted high priests of the world, Jesus sensed that he would finally discharge his vocation as the true priest through his death.

This brings us full circle to the question set out in Chapter 1: how do we historically explain the historical Jesus' identity as the unique Son of God and his followers' identity as sons of God, in a different sense? In Chapter 2, our study of Jesus' baptism revealed a connection between Jesus' incipient experience as divine son and his self-consciousness as a priest; this priestly vocation, we learned in Chapter 3, had strong entailments of suffering. From there in Chapter 4 we teased out the sacerdotal implications that the title Son of David carried; in Chapters 5–6, the priestly identity of the suffering Son of Man came into view, both in the context of Daniel 7 and in the context of Jesus' own setting. Finally, in this chapter, we see Jesus putting himself into direct competition with the high-priestly ruler whom the Romans called 'Son of God', even as we also see Jesus bringing the Melchizedekian Davidide and Son of Man titles together, in connection with his anticipated act of atonement. On the basis of such considerations, I suggest that when the earliest Christians began reflecting on Jesus as the 'Son of God', this was consistent with Jesus' recommended prayer and baptism, even as it was consistent with Jesus' dual claim to stand in for Tiberius and Caiaphas, as the one in whom Son of Man and son of David converge.[110] That is to say, when the earliest Christians first spoke of Jesus as 'the Son of God', they were referring in the first instance to his *soi-disant* role as the divinely appointed

---

[110] Mark certainly makes this dual correlation; see, e.g., Chronis 2005: 462–3; Tuckett 2014: 190–1.

priestly mediator. Thus if there is any one cord that runs through Jesus' prayer, baptism, teachings, titles and final confrontations, it is the brightly coloured cord of the eschatological high priest's ephod. In his final confrontations, quite literally to his dying day, Jesus thought of himself as the bearer of this ephod and wished to be remembered as such.

Conclusion

The effort to portray the historical Jesus as I have done in this book is not entirely new. But up to this point the project has remained far too piecemeal. In this respect, the portrait I have rendered is less a haunting Pollock than a community mosaic, the scraps and shards of which have already been cut. I have written this book in the conviction that the time has come for a fresh assembling of those pieces, especially those which had been cast back on the scrapheap of history so easily, with some important new pieces thrown in as well. And yet, notwithstanding the present volume, I confess that conspicuous gaps still persist and that the task of completing that full-sized mosaic still remains: there is much more that can be said and, I believe, should be said about Jesus the priest. My project does not pretend to be the last word on the topic but seeks rather to be an invitation for pursuing a new direction of exploration. And if we are in fact – as many fear – coming up to a disciplinary cul-de-sac in both substance and method, then perhaps this is no bad time for 'a new direction'.

From his baptism under John until the day of his trial, Jesus of Nazareth positioned himself as Israel's long-awaited eschatological high priest. Together with his lower-ranking 'priests', he aimed to make his movement the catalyst through which sacred space would be restored, idols vanquished and the Spirit made manifest. On this reconstruction, we can elucidate not only the implicit premises of Jesus' ministry, but also the notional hub around which seemingly disparate dominical traditions (the Lord's Prayer, the baptism, the parable of the sower, the Beatitudes, to name a few) may be integrated. The thesis of Jesus' priesthood furthermore clarifies three titles which the tradition repeatedly attributes to him: Son of God, son of David and Son of Man. In the course of twentieth-century and early twenty-first-century research, these titles' mutual relationship has remained as problematic as their putative ascription to the earthly Jesus. But on discerning the sacerdotal entailments of each, even within a reduced database of authentic Jesus sayings, we find compelling evidence that Jesus himself embraced all three epithets as an expression of his vocation. In the Second-Temple period, it was widely agreed that Israel would only be finally redeemed from its labyrinthic exile, that is, once it found itself safely within the portals of the eschatological temple. By self-identifying as the 'beloved Son' at his baptism, by representing himself as the rising son of David and the emerging Son of Man *par excellence*, Jesus held himself out as a kind of human cord capable of leading Israel out of its maze and away from its menacing antagonists, the contemporary incarnations of Daniel's defiling *Mischwesen*.

Son of David, Son of Man and Son of God were the mutually reinforcing threads of one and the same royal-priestly skein which led to the coming of the kingdom, the return from exile, and the establishment of a new and final temple. Meanwhile, those most closely aligned with Jesus took on aspects of each of these titles (sons of God, Son of Man, sharers of the Davidic throne) as part and parcel of their own vocation and eschatological destiny. While so much historical research over the years has distortedly focused on Jesus and his titles in isolation from his movement, a helpful corrective step consists in appreciating a limited transferability between Jesus – in his capacity as Son of God, Son of Man and son of David – and his disciples. Likewise, while the same field of research has forced us to choose, in Platonic fashion, between a super-celestial Jesus come down to earth and a purely immanent Jesus who would be reinvented as a super-celestial being after his death, this polarity has occluded the mysterious space in between, the inner sanctuary of the temple and the body of the high priest, realities at once transcendent and immanent.

As the eschatological priesthood, Jesus' movement took its principal cues from various scriptural stories; prominent among these was the narrative surrounding the Danielic Son of Man. By devoting themselves fully to the one true God and loving one another in accordance with this monotheistic commitment, Jesus and his followers sought to 'image' God as the renewed humanity who corporately embodied the Adamic Son of Man. In polemical competition with the official cultus, he asked his followers to live out an alternative vision for Israel, thereby mediating a revelation of the godhead. At the same time, in aspiring to become the Son of Man, the movement also aimed to represent Israel to God, as an interceding and finally atoning priesthood. The bidirectional focus of the Jesus movement (from God to humanity and vice versa), implicit in the Christological titles and borne out by certain practices, was also meant to mark off this society as the human venue through which the transition to the eschatological temple would commence.

The obviously controversial nature of this vocation demanded that Jesus resort to indirect modes of communication, preferring symbolic actions and parabolic performances to straight-up propositional discourse. In this regard, Jesus' oblique language has rightly been often explained as a self-protective shield of ambiguity which would only finally be let down in confrontation with Caiaphas. Yet Jesus' indirect teachings equally retained a mantic character, conveying mysteries that fell on the deaf ears of the human 'chaff' but engaged the 'wheat' – to use the Baptizer's dichotomy. Although Jesus was convinced that a spiritual–epistemic divide finally separated the curious from those who responded with passive disengagement or active hostility, he equally offered his teachings in order to provoke existential crisis among his hearers – in Bultmann's terms, 'a call for decision', all part of a cosmic separating process. But even this sorting procedure, not without analogy to the creational account (Genesis 1), was intrinsically priestly in nature. The business of distinguishing the clean from the unclean, the holy from the profane, was after all a priestly business; parables were this business's most suitable mode of discourse.

Notwithstanding Jesus' attempts to force a decision among the rank and file of Israel, the social borders of his following proved to be dynamic, with the more loosely affiliated moving in and out of his gravitational field during the course of his ministry. This helps explain Jesus' emphasis on the provisional character of his society's boundaries. Just as the community confessed itself to be the preliminary stepping stone to the final cultic reality, its members were also taught that the authenticity of one's standing within the movement could only be finally validated at the eschaton; meanwhile present status was determined by one's enduring solidarity – expressed in certain continuing practices and confessions – with the movement. Divine election was predicated on the tension between present commitments and future perseverance.

As for the substance of his teachings, Jesus held forth an alternative, scripturally shaped world, one in which the conventional barriers between the holy and the mundane no longer obtained. For here the present order was already being transfigured by an emerging reality, paving the way for a newly coalescing humanity. The social context for this coalescence was the poor, society's marginalized. Jesus' attraction to this demographic was consistent with not only his self-identity as Isaiah's high-priestly herald (Isa. 61.1), but also his vision of a new space unencumbered by existent social hierarchies. As one familiar with such marginalization, Jesus called his followers to a corporate life carried along by experiences 'in the Spirit' (Isa. 61.1) and utter dependence on God. Having shed those conventional props of power which framed humanity's horizontal and vertical interactions, and that with ruinous effects, Jesus' followers – so he promised – could now avail themselves of a different kind of power, a mysterious power from God. Once this power had been realized in their own midst, Jesus' community would image God's person with the hope of becoming a catalyst for redemptive transformation well beyond the confines of the immediate movement. The platform for that transformation was the now-expanding sacred space, emerging out of the sacred intersection between the divine presence and the worship of God's self-surrendering elect.

As a counter-temple society, Jesus' movement was characterized by at least three traits. First, his was a *liturgical* movement. Having translated the traditional temple rites (the high-priestly blessing and the bread-laying ceremony, for example) into a new vernacular, Jesus aimed to enact the ongoing liturgy of the heavenly temple in everyday time and space. The compelling historical evidence of such liturgy, I think, discredits the tired but still-lingering Romantic saw that Jesus summoned his hearers to a spontaneous religion of the heart as opposed to a religion of external rites. Obviously, Jesus did call for a radical obedience reaching deep into the heart. But, in the master's mind, this interior experience was to be matched externally by corporately enacted rhythms that would underwrite the very meaning of this new life on offer. Furthermore, the liturgical character of Jesus' ministry calls into question the instinct, common among New Testament researchers, to ascribe the early Church's ritual practices to post-Easter settings. The assumptive contrast between a free-spirited religion of Jesus and a more formally constrained religion of the apostolic and sub-apostolic Church is no longer sustainable.

As participants in an *itinerant* movement, Jesus and his followers established certain practices that would eventually carry over into the early Church's missiology. It is almost impossible to resist the conclusion that Jesus and the Twelve moved from place to place partially in the interest of maintaining a decentralized base of power. While other messianic aspirants of Jesus' day summoned their backers in a snowballing fashion, Jesus, though certainly attracting crowds in his own day, seems to have deliberately thwarted any hopes for these aggregations achieving any permanence and fixity. Rather, by establishing a very loosely connected network of sympathizers, Jesus left it to his supporters far-flung across Palestine to work out the implications of his teaching with minimum oversight. Interestingly, this approach bears some semblance to the missionary strategy adopted by the apostle Paul, who though obviously never part of Jesus' movement, may well have sought to emulate the earthly Jesus' commitment to granting high levels of autonomy to converted followers. From a historical point of view, one suspects that the DNA for the early Church's rapid expansion went right back to Jesus himself.

Third, Jesus and his followers demonstrated a degree of *inclusivity* that was unprecedented among the sects of his day. That Jesus and the Twelve enjoyed controversial table fellowship with 'sinners' is beyond historical question. The rationale for that inclusivity, so I have argued, was the master's conviction that he and his followers embodied temple-dwelling Wisdom, who had set a table for the sinful and foolish. Thus Jesus' inclusivity was also finally a function of his sacerdotal calling. Though the early Church's subsequent mission to the Gentiles was obviously justified on a very different line of theological reasoning, it does not escape notice that the Jerusalem church's memory of Jesus' transgressive table practices, understood as intrinsically messianic practices, would have facilitated the transition to a widening mission oriented towards Jews and Gentiles alike. Once again the seeds for the early Church's vision and practices seem to have already been sown by the self-identified sower himself.

All three of these distinguishing marks proceeded from Jesus' claim to be the high-priestly Son of Man designate. This was an absolute claim. And it was this element, Jesus' implicit, incorrigible assertions on his own behalf, along with a variety of hints that Jerusalem was not taking care of business as it should, that provoked progressively fierce resistance from the authorities. As the crucible of persecution burned ever hotter, and as the more casual among Jesus' supporters began to distance themselves from the beleaguered sect, the continuing movement would naturally consolidate, growing steadily more galvanized in conviction. All the while, Jesus continued to appeal to texts like Daniel 2 and 7 in the expectation that the full revelation of the kingdom of God would one day witness the defeat of the pagan powerbrokers including the 'birds of the air' and the 'jackals'. Meanwhile, in accordance with Second-Temple apocalyptic visions of tribulation, the precursor to the final cultic space, Jesus explained the challenges facing his followers as the inevitable effects of the appointed *peirasmos*. Such suffering, as his parable of the sower makes clear, was designed to refine not only the final constituency of his counter-temple movement, but also the personal character of its adherents. By appealing to these symbolic stories of atonement through suffering, Jesus insisted that the official establishment's mounting opposition hardly undermined his narrative of atonement but rather only reinforced it.

Jesus' convictions surrounding this *peirasmos* provide an important qualification to the generally helpful already-but-not-yet paradigm of the kingdom of God. If the already-but-not-yet interpretation of the kingdom has typically characterized the so-called 'intermediate period' between the advent of Jesus and the parousia as a composite amalgamation of traits germane to 'this age' and 'the age to come', this stands to be corrected by an understanding of the *peirasmos* which appreciates its distinctive epochal character, just as apocalyptic thought would have it. Along these lines, 'tribulation' was not merely a chain of dire events situated somewhere within the twilight zone between full exile and full kingdom, but a unique sphere of existence of temporal and spatial dimensions, demanding that God's people adopt a new self-understanding along with a correspondingly new set of ethics. This tribulation period did not mark the termination of either Israel or creation itself, but was the birth canal through which renewed Israel and renewed creation would emerge. From here on out, Jesus taught, he and his followers would have to negotiate life in this darkness before the dawn.

Far from offering a set of universal principles for all people at all times, Jesus' ethics retained an indelibly eschatological stamp – as a totality, they are best understood as a 'tribulation ethic'. As the final high priest in the making, he urged others – through prescribed prayers, mysterious parables and moral teachings – to follow his lead by taking up an analogous but subordinate priestly calling in anticipation of participating in full redemption. In this regard, Jesus' teachings were at once a Christological assertion and (with Bultmann) a demand for decision in the face of the eschaton. Yet (against Bultmann) Jesus' interest was not in decision for decision's sake, but in the daily choices which would either confirm or betray one's participation in the divinely scripted drama. And although Schweitzer was quite right to describe Jesus' ethic as an interim ethic, uniquely oriented to the present crisis, we have no indication of the master ever having stipulated a terminus for this crisis, either for himself or his followers. In contrast to Schweitzer and Bultmann's different attempts to synthesize eschatology and ethics, I propose that Jesus called his followers to work out personal and corporate ethics as those who even now worshipped the one God within the highly conflicted space between the cultic kingdom of God and the kingdoms of this world. This was at the heart of what it meant for Jesus' disciples to call themselves the sons (and daughters) of God.

Mindful that Israel the son of God had seized its elective destiny as a kingdom of priests only on the far side its trials, so too Jesus reasoned, the same dynamic would apply to himself and his followers. A humanity shaped for service in the guild of eschatological priests could only emerge through the crucible of the fully God-honouring life. Thus for Jesus, atonement was not so much a singular act of self-giving but a divinely ordained process by which Jesus' true humanity would come into full expression and realize its full potential. Just as in ancient Judaism atonement was assumed to be ineffective apart from the perfection of the priest, so too the fullness of humanity was inconceivable apart from atoning self-surrender. The life lived utterly unto God was the life of atonement – and vice versa.[1] All the while, for Jesus and his followers, the priestly atoning life was worked out within the tension of eternal election and temporal *peirasmos*.

The elective yet emerging character of Jesus' messianic priesthood, I think, provides the best point of departure for grasping the paradoxical nature of his kingdom. If scholarship has fallen into the bad habit of posing a false alternative between an immanent and a transcendent Jesus, the same dichotomous thinking has unfortunately also plagued our understanding of the kingdom, reducing us to choosing between a radically transcendent kingdom and a radically immanent one. In the course of the modern-day quest for Jesus, not to mention in the course of twentieth-century theology in general, both extremes have wrought their own mischief. On the one side, those who have emphasized the kingdom's radical transcendence have struggled to retrieve any meaningful, contemporary significance from Jesus' person or teachings. On the other side, those amenable to a radically immanent kingdom have sought to replace the void, left vacated by transcendence, by smuggling in some anachronistic philosophical or socio-political agenda as a coordinating principle – all too often, again, on a very selective use of the data. As consequence, we are left with either a de-ethicized Jesus who has very little if anything to say to our world or a de-eschatologized Jesus who has a lot to say but all the while gives the impression of channelling suspiciously contemporary voices. It can hardly be denied that the dualism operative in our modern-day understanding of Jesus and kingdom has conveniently served a variety of agendas.

Without pretending to have transcended such tendentiousness altogether, I hope at least to have shown why pitting the immanence of the kingdom over and against its transcendence does such grave injustice to Jesus' vocation of *being* and *becoming* the Yahweh-embodying high priest. The historical Jesus thought of himself as the Son of God, son of David and the Son of Man, but he did not pass himself off as these things *strictly* in a static sense. Rather he sought to function in these roles in the present even as he aspired to become all these things, as the divinely prescribed course played itself out. For Jesus, divine sonship was as much a destiny as a datum. In the former respect, he

---

[1]   As Marinus de Jonge (1998: 26) puts it, 'Jesus' death cannot be separated from his life. His death could not have served God's purpose had his life not been dedicated to the service of God and humankind all along'.

must have thought of his life as the progressive attainment of a transcendent reality. In the latter respect, Jesus was convinced that the godhead was already fully and uniquely present in his person and this not least on account of his election, confirmed through baptism. The paradoxical nature of Jesus' vocation in turn sets the pattern for the paradoxical experience of those who would participate in his in-breaking kingdom.

To whatever extent all this was perceived by Jesus' contemporaries in his lifetime, it eventually became obvious to the regnant priesthoods that his priestly claims were incompatible with their own interests. If his moral teachings and symbolic actions hadn't done enough to challenge the major stakeholders of Rome and Jerusalem, his increasingly direct assertions of high priesthood eventually forced the hand of the political apparatus. Such absolute claims eventually led to a swift and brutal response. Ever conscious of the Son of Man's destiny to renew Israel's sacred space, Jesus at length came to the conclusion, announced in so many words at his 'trial', that that vocation would have to fall to himself alone. Having denounced Caesar and Caiaphas for infringing on the wisdom and power of the one God, he now sought to seal his identity as God's Son and high priest by surrendering himself in the midst of *peirasmos*. In this way Jesus courageously embraced the fate that had already been hinted at through his baptism and idealized in the first petition of the *Pater Noster*, 'Hallowed be your name'. (Whereas so much scholarship over the years has insisted that Jesus' execution took him by surprise, I hope we can now finally discard that outmoded notion.) Even unto his death, Jesus carried out his vocation with an unflinching consistency. I will have more to say about the meaning of this hallowing in my sequel to this book, *Jesus the Sacrifice*.

But for now, in closing this book, it may be worthwhile to discuss that which has distinguished Jesus as a figure of history. There was, by all accounts, a certain *something* about the historical Jesus that was at once magnetizing and provocative. Just what that 'something' was will on some level always remain a mystery. Even in his own time, the power of Jesus' personality was probably regarded as beyond description. Nevertheless, is there anything that we today can say about this something? Maybe in this regard I can do no better than recall Cornell West's prayer-like apostrophe to Jane Austen by way of dim comparison:

> Jane Austen, allow us to enter this other world that you as a poet provide in stark contrast to so much of the nightmarish, catastrophic world that we inhabit every day. Not in the form of cheap escape . . . but of an alternative world that allows us to get critical distance so we can reengage the real world. And by reengaging that world we have a power, a power of self, a power of soul, a power of mind, and most importantly courage. Most importantly, courage. When we think of the towering figures from Sophocles to Chekhov, mediated with the Austens and Shakespeares and others, we are talking about those who not only have highly cultivated talent, craft, technique, but also something inexplicable, something mysterious. They are on fire.[2]

---

[2] West 2012: 118.

In looking back to the historical Jesus, we see a man who – to trade on West's description for Austen – was 'on fire'. Having been set aflame by God's call at his baptism, Jesus announced an alternative and beckoning world, aflame with eschatological hope. Infused with a different kind of power, even as he was sustained by profound experiences of God's presence, he offered this reality as Israel's only hope for getting much-needed critical distance on the so-called 'real world' offered by Rome, which of course, as Jesus insisted, was not the real world at all. Yet his proffered world was not a world of the mind nor even of the heart but a world of worship where the immanent and transcendent converged. Yet in order to enter this world, more real than any world ever known, in order to participate in Jesus' fire, it was first necessary to descend into a fire of a different kind – marginalization, oppression and even self-surrendering death. Declaring himself as Israel's final high priest, as the last mediator straddling the human and the divine, Jesus was the fire who also invited others to join him – join him in his vocation of bringing together heaven and earth. The call '*into* the fire' reverberated throughout the course of the early Christian movement and has reverberated down to the present day. If we fail to account for this fire at the interface of heaven and earth, we have failed to understand Jesus altogether. And if we have failed to understand Jesus on this point, perhaps it is because that fire is far too threatening.

Bibliography

Abadie, P. (1999), 'La figure de David dans le livre des chroniques', in L. Desrousseaux (ed.), *Figures de David à travers la Bible: XVIIe congrès de l'ACFEB, Lille, 1er-5 septembre 1997* (LD 177; Paris: Cerf): 157–86.

Abegg, M. G. (1995), 'The Messiah at Qumran: Are We Still Seeing Double?', *DSD* 2: 125–44.

Abegg, M. G., M. O. Wise and E. M. Cook (2005 (1996)), *The Dead Sea Scrolls: A New Translation* (San Francisco: HarperSanFrancisco).

Ackroyd, P. R. (1973), *I & II Chronicles, Ezra, Nehemiah: Introduction and Commentary* (London: SCM Press).

Ådna, J. (2000), *Jesu Stellung zum Tempel: Die Tempelaktion und das Tempelwort als Ausdruck seiner messianischen Sendung* (WUNT 2/119; Tübingen: Mohr Siebeck).

Ahearne-Kroll, S. P. (2007), *The Psalms of Lament in Mark's Passion: Jesus' Davidic Suffering* (SNTSMS 142; Cambridge/New York: Cambridge University Press).

Alexander, P. S. (1997), '"Wrestling against Wickedness in High Places": Magic in the Worldview of the Qumran Community', in S. Porter and C. A. Evans (eds), *Scrolls and the Scriptures* (Sheffield: Sheffield University Press): 318–37.

Allison, D. C. (1985), *The End of the Ages Has Come: An Early Interpretation of the Passion and Resurrection of Jesus* (Philadelphia: Fortress).

Allison, D. C. (1997), *The Jesus Tradition in Q* (Harrisburg, PA: Trinity Press International).

Allison, D. C. (2010), 'How to Marginalize the Traditional Criteria of Authenticity', in T. Holmén and S. E. Porter (eds), *Handbook for the Study of the Historical Jesus: Vol. 1* (Leiden: Brill): 3–30.

Anderson, J. S. (2014), *The Blessing and the Curse: Trajectories in the Theology of the Old Testament* (Eugene, OR: Cascade).

Anderson, R. A. (1984), *Signs and Wonders: A Commentary on the Book of Daniel* (Grand Rapids: Eerdmans).

Andrews, M. (1942), '*Peirasmos*: A Study in Form-Criticism', *AThR* 24: 229–44.

Angel, A. R. (2006), *Chaos and the Son of Man: The Hebrew Chaoskampf Tradition in the Period 515 BCE to 200 CE* (LSTS 60; London: T. & T. Clark).

Angel, J. L. (2010), *Otherworldly and Eschatological Priesthood in the Dead Sea Scrolls* (STDJ 86; Leiden/Boston: Brill).

Armerding, C. E. (1975), 'Were David's Sons Really Priests?', in G. F. Hawthorne (ed.), *Current Issues in Biblical and Patristic Interpretation: Studies in Honor of Merrill C. Tenney Presented by His Former Students* (Grand Rapids: Eerdmans): 75–86.

Atkinson, K., and J. Magness (2010), 'Josephus's Essenes and the Qumran Community', *JBL* 129: 317–42.

Auerbach, E. (2003 (1953)), *Mimesis: The Representation of Reality in Western Literature* (Princeton: Princeton University Press).

Bammel, E. (1971–2), 'The Baptist in Early Christian Tradition', *NTS* 18: 95–128.

Bammel, E. (1984), 'The Titulus', in E. Bammel and C. F. D. Moule (eds), *Jesus and the Politics of His Day* (Cambridge: Cambridge University Press): 353–64.

Bammel, E. (1997), 'ΑΡΧΙΕΡΕΥΣ ΠΡΟΦΗΤΕΥΩΝ', in *Judaica et Paulina* (WUNT 91; Tübingen: Mohr): 133–9.

Bammel, E., and C. F. D. Moule (1984), *Jesus and the Politics of His Day* (Cambridge: Cambridge University Press).

Barber, M. (2013a), 'Jesus as the Davidic Temple Builder and Peter's Priestly Role in Matthew 16:16–19', *JBL* 132: 935–53.

Barber, M. (2013b), 'The New Temple, the New Priesthood, and the New Cult in Luke-Acts', *LtSp* 8: 101–24.

Barker, M. (2003), *The Great High Priest: The Temple Roots of Christian Liturgy* (London/New York: T. & T. Clark).

Barr, J. (1988), '"Abba" Isn't "Daddy"', *JTS* 39: 28–47.

Bauckham, R. (1990), *Jude and the Relatives of Jesus in the Early Church* (Edinburgh: T. & T. Clark).

Bauckham, R. (1999), 'For What Offence Was James Put to Death?', in B. D. Chilton and C. A. Evans (eds), *James the Just and Christian Origins* (NovTSup 98; Leiden: Brill): 199–232.

Bauckham, R. (2006), *Jesus and the Eyewitnesses: The Gospels as Eyewitness Testimony* (Grand Rapids: Eerdmans).

Bauckham, R., J. R. Davila and A. Panayotov (2013), *Old Testament Pseudepigrapha: More Noncanonical Scriptures: Vol. 1* (Grand Rapids: Eerdmans).

Baxter, W. S. (2006), 'Healing and the "Son of David": Matthew's Warrant', *NovT* 48: 36–50.

Bayet, J. (1973), *Histoire politique et psychologique de la religion romaine* (Paris: Payot).

Beale, G. K. (1991), 'Isaiah 6:9–13: A Retributive Taunt against Idolatry', *VT* 41: 257–78.

Beale, G. K. (2004), *The Temple and the Church's Mission: A Biblical Theology of the Dwelling Place of God* (NSBT 17; Leicester: Apollos; Downers Grove, IL: InterVarsity).

Beale, G. K. (2005), 'The Descent of the Eschatological Temple in the Form of the Spirit at Pentecost: Part 2: Corroborating Evidence', *TynBul* 56: 63–90.

Beale, G. K. (2008), *We Become What We Worship: A Biblical Theology of Idolatry* (Downers Grove, IL: InterVarsity; Nottingham: Apollos).

Beasley-Murray, G. R. (1962), *Baptism in the New Testament* (London: St Martin's; New York: Macmillan).

Beasley-Murray, G. R. (1983), 'The Interpretation of Daniel 7', *CBQ* 45: 44–58.

Beasley-Murray, G. R. (1986), *Jesus and the Kingdom of God* (Grand Rapids: Eerdmans).

Beauchamp, P. (1999), 'Pourquoi parler de David comme d'un vivant?' in L. Desrousseaux (ed.), *Figures de David à travers la Bible: XVIIe congrès de l'ACFEB, Lille, 1er-5 septembre 1997* (LD 177; Paris: Cerf): 225–41.

Beavis, M. (2006), *Jesus and Utopia: Looking for the Kingdom of God in the Roman World* (Minneapolis: Fortress).

Beavis, M. (2011), *Mark* (Paideia; Grand Rapids: Baker Academic).

Becker, J. (1972), *Johannes der Täufer und Jesus von Nazareth* (BibS[N] 63; Neukirchen-Vluyn: Neukirchener Verlag).

Becker, J. (1998), *Jesus of Nazareth* (New York: de Gruyter).

Bedford, P. R. (2001), *Temple Restoration in Early Achaemenid Judah* (JSJSup 65; Leiden/Boston: Brill).

Benoit, P. (1969), *The Passion and Resurrection of Jesus Christ* (New York: Herder; London: Darton, Longman & Todd).

Ben-Sasson, H. H. (1972), 'Kiddush Ha-Shem and ḥillul Ha-Shem', *EncJud* 10: 978–86.

Berger, K. (1973), 'Die königlichen Messiastraditionen des Neuen Testaments', *NTS* 20: 1–44.

Bergsma, J. (2009), 'Cultic Kingdoms in Conflict: Liturgy and Empire in the Book of Daniel', *LtSp* 5: 47–83.

Berlin, A. M. (1999), 'The Archaeology of Ritual: The Sanctuary of Pan at Banias/Caesarea Philippi', *BASOR* 315: 27–45.

Bernett, M. (2007), 'Roman Imperial Cult in the Galilee: Structures, Functions, and Dynamics', in J. Zangenberg, H. W. Attridge and D. B. Martin (eds), *Religion, Ethnicity, and Identity in Ancient Galilee: A Region in Transition* (WUNT 210; Tübingen: Mohr Siebeck): 337–56.

Betz, H., and A. Collins (1995), *The Sermon on the Mount: A Commentary on the Sermon on the Mount, Including the Sermon on the Plain (Matthew 5:3–7:27 and Luke 6:20–49)* (Hermeneia; Minneapolis: Fortress).

Betz, O. (1982), 'Probleme des Prozesses Jesu', in H. Wolfgang (ed.), *Principat 25/1; Vorkonstantinisches Christentum: Leben und Umwelt Jesu; Neues Testament* (Berlin/New York: de Gruyter): 565–647.

Betz, O. (1984), 'Jesu Lieblingspsalm: Die Bedeutung von Psalm 103 für das Werk Jesu', *TBei* 15: 253–69.

Bird, M. (2009), *Are You the One Who Is to Come? The Historical Jesus and the Messianic Question* (Grand Rapids: Baker Academic).

Black, M. (1967), *An Aramaic Approach to the Gospels and Acts: With an Appendix on the Son of Man* (3rd edn; Oxford: Clarendon).

Black, M. (1975), 'Die Apotheose Israels: Eine neue Interpretation des danielischen "Menschensohns"', in R. Pesch and R. Schnackenburg (eds), *Jesus und der Menschensohn: Für Anton Vögtle* (Freiburg: Herder): 92–9.

Blenkinsopp, J. (1974), 'Prophecy and Priesthood in Josephus', *JJS* 25: 239–62.

Blenkinsopp, J. (2013), *David Remembered: Kingship and National Identity in Ancient Israel* (Grand Rapids: Eerdmans).

Blinzler, J. (1959), *Trial of Jesus: The Jewish and Roman Proceedings against Jesus Christ Described and Assessed from the Oldest Accounts* (Westminster, MD: Newman).

Block, D. I. (1997), *The Book of Ezekiel: Chapters 1–24* (NICOT; Grand Rapids: Eerdmans).

Blomberg, C. L. (2009), 'Jesus, Sinners, and Table Fellowship', *BBR* 19: 35–62.

Bock, D. L. (1987), *Proclamation from Prophecy and Pattern: Lucan Old Testament Christology* (JSNTSup 12; Sheffield: JSOT Press).

Bock, D. L. (1994), *Luke* (BECNT 3; Grand Rapids: Baker).

Bock, D. L. (1997), 'Key Jewish Texts on Blasphemy and Exaltation and the Jewish Examination of Jesus', SBLSP 36: 115–60.

Bock, D. L. (2007), 'Blasphemy and the Jewish Examination of Jesus', *BBR* 17: 53–114.

Bock, D. L., and R. L. Webb (2009), *Key Events in the Life of the Historical Jesus: A Collaborative Exploration of Content and Coherence* (WUNT 247; Tübingen: Mohr Siebeck).

Bockmuehl, M. (2008), 'God's Life as a Jew: Remembering the Son of God as Son of David', in B. Gaventa and R. B. Hays (eds), *Seeking the Identity of Jesus: A Pilgrimage* (Grand Rapids: Eerdmans): 60–78.

Boda, M. J. (2015), *The Book of Zechariah* (NICOT; Grand Rapids: Eerdmans).

Boers, H. (1972), 'Where Christology Is Real: A Survey of Recent Research on New Testament Christology', *Int* 26: 300–27.

Boobyer, G. H. (1954), 'Mark II, 10a and the Interpretation of the Healing of the Paralytic', *HTR* 47: 115–20.

Borg, M. J. (1984), *Conflict, Holiness and Politics in the Teachings of Jesus* (SBEC 5; New York: Mellen Press).

Borg, M. J. (1987), *Jesus, a New Vision: Spirit, Culture, and the Life of Discipleship* (San Francisco: Harper & Row).

Borg, M. J. (2011 (2006)), *Jesus: Uncovering the Life, Teachings, and Relevance of a Religious Revolutionary* (London: SPCK).

Boring, M. E. (1982), *Sayings of the Risen Jesus: Christian Prophecy in the Synoptic Tradition* (SNTSMS 46; Cambridge/New York: Cambridge University Press).

Boring, M. E. (2006), *Mark: A Commentary* (NTL; Louisville, KY: Westminster John Knox).

Bornkamm, G. (1960 (1959)), *Jesus of Nazareth* (New York: Harper, 1960).

Bornkamm, G. (1961), 'Enderwartung und Kirche im Matthäusevangelium', in G. Bornkamm, G. Barth and H. J. Held (eds), *Überlieferung und Auslegung im Matthäusevangelium* (2nd edn; WMANT 1; Neukirchen-Vluyn: Neukirchener Verlag): 13–47.

Bornkamm, G. (1963), *Tradition and Interpretation in Matthew* (Philadelphia: Westminster).

Borrell, A. (1998), *The Good News of Peter's Denial: A Narrative and Rhetorical Reading of Mark 14:54.66–72* (Atlanta: Scholars Press).

Bosworth, E. (1924), *The Life and Teaching of Jesus according to the First Three Gospels* (New York: Macmillan).

Botner, M. (2017), 'What Has Mark's Christ to Do with David's Son? A History of Interpretation', *CBR* 16: 50–70.

Bousset, W. (1892), *Jesu Predigt in ihrem Gegensatz zum Judentum: Ein religionsgeschicht-licher Vergleich* (Göttingen: Vandenhoeck & Ruprecht).

Bovon, F. (2002), *Luke 1: A Commentary on the Gospel of Luke 1:1–9:50* (Hermeneia; Minneapolis: Fortress).

Bovon, F. (2013), *Luke 2: A Commentary on the Gospel of Luke 9:51–19:27* (Hermeneia; Minneapolis: Fortress).

Bowker, J. (1974), 'Mystery and Parable: Mark 4:1–20', *JTS* 25: 300–17.

Boyarin, D. (2012), 'Daniel 7, Intertextuality, and the History of Israel's Cult', *HTR* 105: 139–62.

Brandon, S. G. F. (1967), *Jesus and the Zealots: A Study of the Political Factor in Primitive Christianity* (New York: Scribner).

Braun, F. M. (1960), 'Les Testaments des XII Patriarches et le problème de leur origine', *RB* 67: 516–49.

Brawley, R. L. (2011), 'Homeless in Galilee', *HvTSt* 67: 1–6.

Bretscher, P. G. (1968), 'Exodus 4:22–23 and the Voice from Heaven', *JBL* 87: 301–11.

Brodie, T. L. (2004), *The Birthing of the New Testament: The Intertextual Development of the New Testament Writings* (NTM 1; Sheffield: Sheffield Phoenix).

Brooke, G. J. (1995), '4Q500 1 and the Use of Scripture in the Parable of the Vineyard', *DSD* 2: 268–94.

Brooke, G. J. (1999), 'Miqdash Adam, Eden and the Qumran Community', in B. Ego and A. Lange (eds), *Gemeinde ohne Tempel: Zur Substituierung und Transformation des Jerusalemer Tempels und seines Kults im Alten Testment, antiken Judentum und frühen Christentum* (WUNT 118; Tübingen: Mohr Siebeck): 285–301.

Brooke, G. J. (2016), 'Patterns of Priesthood, Priestliness and Priestly Functions in Some Second Temple Period Texts', *JudAnc* 4: 1–21.

Brown, R. E. (1977), *The Birth of the Messiah: A Commentary on the Infancy Narratives in Matthew and Luke* (Garden City, NY: Doubleday).

Brown, R. E. (2010 (1961)), 'The Pater Noster as an Eschatological Prayer', in R. E. Brown, *New Testament Essays* (New York: Doubleday): 270–320.

Brownlee, W. H. (1992 (1955)), 'John the Baptist in the New Light of the Ancient Scrolls', *Int* 9: 71–90.

Brunson, A. C. (2003), *Psalm 118 in the Gospel of John: An Intertextual Study on the New Exodus Pattern in the Theology of John* (WUNT 2/158; Tübingen: Mohr Siebeck).

Bryan, C. (2005), *Render to Caesar: Jesus, the Early Church, and the Roman Superpower* (Oxford: Oxford University Press).

Bryan, D. (1995), *Cosmos, Chaos and the Kosher Mentality* (JSPSup 12; Sheffield: Sheffield Academic Press).

Bryan, S. M. (2002), *Jesus and Israel's Traditions of Judgement and Restoration* (SNTSMS 117; Cambridge: Cambridge University Press).

Buchanan, W. (1970), *The Consequences of the Covenant* (NovTSup 20: Leiden: Brill).

Bultmann, R. K. (1951), *Theology of the New Testament: Vol. 2* (New York: Scribner).

Bultmann, R. K. (1958 (1934)), *Jesus and the Word* (New York: Scribner).

Bultmann, R. K. (1968 (1921)), *The History of the Synoptic Tradition* (rev. edn; Oxford: Blackwell).

Bultmann, R. K. (1975), 'Die Interpretation von Mk 4,3–9 seit Jülicher', in E. E. Ellis and E. Grässer (eds), *Jesus und Paulus: Festschrift für Werner Georg Kümmel zum 70sten Geburtstag* (Göttingen: Vandenhoeck & Ruprecht): 30–4.

Bunta, S. (2006), 'The Likeness of the Image: Adamic Motifs and צלם Anthropology in Rabbinic Traditions about Jacob's Image Enthroned in Heaven', *JSJ* 37: 55–84.

Burer, M. H. (2012), *Divine Sabbath Work* (BBRSup 5; Winona Lake, IN: Eisenbrauns).

Burger, C. (1970), *Jesus als Davidssohn: Eine tradionsgeschichtliche Untersuchung* (FRLANT 98; Göttingen: Vandenhoeck & Ruprecht).

Burkill, T. A. (1970), 'Condemnation of Jesus: A Critique of Sherwin-White's Thesis', *NovT* 12: 321–42.

Burney, C. F. (1925), *The Poetry of Our Lord: An Examination of the Formal Elements of Hebrew Poetry in the Discourses of Jesus Christ* (Oxford: Clarendon).

Caird, G. B. (1963), *The Gospel of Saint Luke* (PNTC; Harmondsworth: Penguin).

Cameron, A. (2007), 'The Imperial Pontifex', *Harvard Studies in Classical Philology* 103: 341–84.

Campbell, C. R. (2008), *Verbal Aspect and Non-Indicative Verbs: Further Soundings in the Greek of the New Testament* (SBG 15; New York: Peter Lang).

Camponovo, O. (1984), *Königtum, Königsherrschaft und Reich Gottes in den frühjüdischen Schriften* (OBO 58; Göttingen: Vandenhoeck & Ruprecht).

Caragounis, C. (1986), *The Son of Man: Vision and Interpretation* (WUNT 38; Tübingen: Mohr Siebeck).

Carmignac, J. (1969), *Recherches sur le 'Notre Père'* (Paris: Letouzey & Ané).

Carruth, S., and A. Garsky (1996), *Q 11:2b–4* (Documenta Q; Louvain: Peeters).

Carson, D. A. (1991), *The Gospel According to John* (PNTC; Leicester: Apollos; Grand Rapids: Eerdmans).

Carson, D. A. (1994), 'Matthew 11:19b / Luke 7:35: A Test Case for the Bearing of Q Christology on the Synoptic Problem', in J. B. Green and M. Turner (eds), *Jesus of Nazareth: Lord and Christ: Essays on the Historical Jesus and New Testament Christology* (Grand Rapids: Eerdmans): 128–46.

Carter, W. (2014), 'The Things of Caesar: Mark-ing the Plural (Mk 12:13–17)', *HvTSt* 70: 1–9.

Carter, W. (2016), 'Peter: False Disciple and Apostate According to Saint Matthew', *CBQ* 78: 373–8.

Casey, M. (1979), *Son of Man: The Interpretation and Influence of Daniel 7* (London: SPCK).

Casey, M. (1985), 'The Jackals and the Son of Man (Matt. 8:20/Luke 9:58)', *JSNT* 23: 3–22.

Casey, M. (1988), 'Culture and Historicity: The Plucking of the Grain (Mark 2:23–28)', *NTS* 34: 1–23.

Casey, M. (2010), *Jesus of Nazareth: An Independent Historian's Account of His Life and Teaching* (New York: T. & T. Clark).

Cassidy, R. J. (1978), *Jesus, Politics, and Society: A Study of Luke's Gospel* (Maryknoll, NY: Orbis Books).

Catchpole, D. R. (1971), *The Trial of Jesus: A Study in the Gospels and Jewish Historiography from 1770 to the Present Day* (SPB 43; Leiden: Brill).

Catchpole, D. R. (1984), 'The "Triumphal" Entry', in E. Bammel and C. F. D. Moule (eds), *Jesus and the Politics of His Day* (Cambridge: Cambridge University Press): 319–34.

Cave, C. H. (1965), 'Parables and the Scriptures', *NTS* 11: 374–87.

Chae, Y. S. (2006), *Jesus as the Eschatological Davidic Shepherd: Studies in the Old Testament, Second Temple Judaism, and in the Gospel of Matthew* (WUNT 2/216; Tübingen: Mohr Siebeck).

Chancey, M. A. (2004), 'City Coins and Roman Power in Palestine: From Pompey to the Great Revolt', in D. R. Edwards (ed.), *Religion and Society in Roman Palestine: Old Questions, New Approaches* (New York/London: Routledge): 103–12.

Charlesworth, J. H. (1996), 'Solomon and Jesus: The Son of David in Ante-Markan Traditions (Mk 10:47)', in L. B. Elder, D. L. Barr and E. S. Malbon (eds), *Biblical and Humane: A Festschrift for John F. Priest* (Atlanta: Scholars Press): 125–51.

Chilton, B. (1979), *God in Strength: Jesus' Announcement of the Kingdom* (SUNT B; Freistadt: Plöchl).

Chilton, B. (1982), 'Jesus Ben David: Reflections on the *Davidssohnfrage*', *JSNT* 14: 88–112.

Chilton, B. (1984), *The Kingdom of God in the Teaching of Jesus* (Philadelphia: Fortress; London: SPCK).

Chilton, B. (1992), *The Temple of Jesus: His Sacrificial Program within a Cultural History of Sacrifice* (University Park, PA: Pennsylvania State University Press).

Chilton, B. (1994), *Judaic Approaches to the Gospels* (Atlanta: Scholars Press).

Chilton, B. (1996), *Pure Kingdom: Jesus' Vision of God* (SHJ; Grand Rapids: Eerdmans; London: SPCK).

Chilton, B., and J. I. H. McDonald (1987), *Jesus and the Ethics of the Kingdom* (London: SPCK).

Chronis, H. L. (2005), 'To Reveal and to Conceal: A Literary-Critical Perspective on "the Son of Man" in Mark', *NTS* 51: 459–81.

Clarke, E. G. (1974–5), 'Jacob's Dream at Bethel as Interpreted in the Targums and the New Testament', *SR* 4: 367–77.

Clines, D. J. A. (1998 (1968)), 'The Image of God in Man', in *On the Way to the Postmodern: Old Testament Essays, 1967–1998* (2 vols; JSOTSup 292–3; Sheffield: Sheffield Academic Press): 447–97.

Coakley, J. F. (1995), 'Jesus' Messianic Entry into Jerusalem (John 12: 12–19 Par.)', *JTS* 46: 461–82.

Cody, A. (1969), *A History of Old Testament Priesthood* (AnBib 35; Rome: Pontificio Istituto Biblico).

Cohn, H. H. (1971), *The Trial and Death of Jesus* (London: Weidenfeld & Nicolson).

Collins, A. Y. (1997), 'The Appropriation of the Psalms of Individual Lament by Mark', in C. M. Tuckett (ed.), *The Scriptures in the Gospels* (BETL 131; Louvain: Leuven University Press/Peeters): 223–41.

Collins, A. Y. (2004), 'The Charge of Blasphemy in Mark 14.64', *JSNT* 26: 379–401.

Collins, A. Y. (2007), *Mark: A Commentary* (Hermeneia; Minneapolis: Fortress).

Collins, J. J. (1977), *The Apocalyptic Vision of the Book of Daniel* (Atlanta: Scholars Press).

Collins, J. J. (1987), 'The Kingdom of God in the Apocrypha and Pseudepigrapha', in W. Willis (ed.), *The Kingdom of God in 20th-Century Interpretation* (Peabody, MA: Hendrickson): 81–95.

Collins, J. J. (2009), 'The Interpretation of Psalm 2', in F. G. Martínez (ed.), *Echoes from the Caves: Qumran and the New Testament* (STDJ 85; Leiden/Boston: Brill): 49–66.

Collins, J. J., F. M. Cross and A. Y. Collins (1993), *Daniel: A Commentary on the Book of Daniel* (Hermeneia; Minneapolis: Fortress).

Collins, M. A. (2009), *The Use of Sobriquets in the Qumran Dead Sea Scrolls* (LSTS 67; London: T. & T. Clark).

Conzelmann, H. (1975 (1969)), *1 Corinthians* (Hermeneia; Philadelphia: Fortress).

Cook, L. S. (2011), *On the Question of the 'Cessation of Prophecy' in Ancient Judaism* (TSAJ 145: Tübingen: Mohr Siebeck).

Corley, J. (2002), 'God as Merciful Father in Ben Sira and the New Testament', in R. Egger-Wenzel (ed.), *Proceedings of the International Ben Sira Conference, Durham-Urshaw College 2001* (BZAW 321; Berlin/New York: de Gruyter): 33–8.

Corley, K. E. (2002), *Women and the Historical Jesus: Feminist Myths of Christian Origins* (Santa Rosa, CA: Polebridge).

Cotter, W. J. (1987), 'The Parable of the Children in the Market-Place, Q (Lk) 7:31–35: An Examination of the Parable's Image and Significance', *NTS* 29: 289–304.

Coulot, C. (1999), 'David à Qumrân', in L. Desrousseaux (ed.), *Figures de David à travers la Bible: XVIIe congrès de l'ACFEB, Lille, 1er-5 septembre 1997* (LD 177; Paris: Cerf): 315–43.

Cranfield, C. E. B. (1977 (1959)), *The Gospel According to Saint Mark: An Introduction and Commentary* (CGTC 16; Cambridge: Cambridge University Press).

Crossan, J. D. (1983), *In Fragments : The Aphorisms of Jesus* (San Francisco: Harper & Row).

Crossan, J. D. (1991), *The Historical Jesus: The Life of a Mediterranean Jewish Peasant* (San Francisco: Harper SanFrancisco).

Crossley, J. G. (2015), *Jesus and the Chaos of History: Redirecting the Life of the Historical Jesus* (Oxford: Oxford University Press).

Croy, N. C. (2006), *3 Maccabees* (SCS; Leiden/Boston: Brill).

Cullmann, O. (1950), *Baptism in the New Testament* (London: SCM Press).

Cullmann, O. (1963 (1959)), *The Christology of the New Testament* (London: SCM Press).

Cullmann, O., and K. Fröhlich (1966), *Vorträge und Aufsätze, 1925–1962* (Tübingen: Mohr Siebeck; Zurich: Zwingli Verlag).

Dalman, G., and D. M. Kay (1902), *The Words of Jesus Considered in the Light of Post-Biblical Jewish Writings and the Aramaic Language* (Edinburgh: T. & T. Clark).

Daly, R. J. (1977), 'Soteriological Significance of the Sacrifice of Isaac', *CBQ* 39: 45–75.

Daly-Denton, M. (2000), *David in the Fourth Gospel: The Johannine Reception of the Psalms* (AGJU 47; Leiden/Boston: Brill).

Dämmgen, U. (2011), 'Das "Salz der Erde" ist kein "Salz"', *BN* 151: 115–21.

D'Angelo, M. R. (1992a), 'Abba and "Father": Imperial Theology and the Jesus Traditions', *JBL* 111: 611–30.

D'Angelo, M. R. (1992b), 'Theology in Mark and Q: Abba and "Father" in Context', *HTR* 85: 149–74.

Dapaah, D. S. (2005), *The Relationship between John the Baptist and Jesus of Nazareth: A Critical Study* (Lanham, MD: University Press of America).

Darr, K. P. (1994), *Isaiah's Vision and the Family of God* (Louisville, KY: Westminster John Knox).

Daube, D. (1956), *The New Testament and Rabbinic Judaism* (Jordan Lectures in Comparative Religion 2; London: University of London/Athlone Press).

Daube, D. (1966), *He That Cometh* (London: Tolley).

Davies, J. A. (2004), *A Royal Priesthood: Literary and Intertextual Perspectives on an Image of Israel in Exodus 19.6* (JSOTSup 395; London/New York: T. & T. Clark International).

Davies, J. A. (2011), '"Discerning between Good and Evil": Solomon as a New Adam in 1 Kings', *WTJ* 73: 39–57.

Davies, P. R. (1979), 'The Sacrifice of Isaac and Passover', in E. A. Livingstone (ed.), *Studia Biblica 1978: Papers on Old Testament and Related Themes* (JSOTSup 11; Sheffield: JSOT Press): 1.127–32.

Davies, P. R. (1993), 'Reading Daniel Sociologically', in A. S. van der Woude (ed.), *Book of Daniel in the Light of New Findings* (BETL 106; Louvain: Leuven University Press/Peeters): 345–61.

Davies, P. R., and B. D. Chilton (1978), 'The Aqedah : A Revised Tradition History', *CBQ* 40: 514–46.

Davies, W. D. (1955), *Paul and Rabbinic Judaism: Some Rabbinic Elements in Pauline Theology* (London: SPCK).

Davies, W. D., and D. C. Allison (1988–97), *A Critical and Exegetical Commentary on the Gospel According to Saint Matthew* (3 vols; ICC; Edinburgh: T. & T. Clark).

Day, J. (1985), *God's Conflict with the Dragon and the Sea: Echoes of a Canaanite Myth in the Old Testament* (Cambridge: Cambridge University Press).

Day, J. (2003 (1992)), *Psalms* (T. & T. Clark Study Guides; London/New York: T. & T. Clark International).

Deenick, K. (2011), 'Priest and King or Priest-King in 1 Samuel 2:35', *WTJ* 73: 325–39.

Dekker, W. (1961), 'De "Geliefde Zoon" in de Synoptische Evangelien', *NedTTs* 16: 94–106.

Dennert, B. C. (2015), '"The Rejection of Wisdom's Call": Matthew's Use of Proverbs 1:20–33 in the Parable of Children in the Marketplace (Matthew 11:16–18/Luke 7:31–35)', in C. A. Evans and J. J. Johnston (eds), *Searching the Scriptures: Studies in Context and Intertextuality* (LNTS 543; London/New York: T. & T. Clark): 46–63.

Dennis, J. (2013), 'Bread', in J. Brown, J. Green and N. Perrin (eds), *Dictionary of Jesus and the Gospels* (Downers Grove, IL: InterVarsity): 91–5.

Derrett, J. D. M. (1970), *Law in the New Testament* (London: Darton, Longman & Todd).

deSilva, D. A. (2013), 'The Testaments of the Twelve Patriarchs as Witnesses to Pre-Christian Judaism: A Re-Assessment', *JSP* 23: 21–68.

Desrousseaux, L. (1999), *Figures de David à travers la Bible: XVIIe congrès de l'ACFEB, Lille, 1er-5 septembre 1997* (LD 177; Paris: Cerf).

Deutsch, C. (1990), 'Wisdom in Matthew: Transformation of a Symbol', *NovT* 32: 13–47.

De Vries, S. J. (1988), 'Moses and David as Cult Founders in Chronicles', *JBL* 107: 619–39.

Dewailly, L. (1980), '"Donne-nous notre pain": quel pain? Notes sur la quatrieme demande du Pater', *RSPT* 64: 561–88.

Dewey, J. (1979), *Markan Public Debate: Literary Technique, Concentric Structure, and Theology in Mark 2:1–3:6* (Chico, CA: Scholars Press).

Dexinger, F. (1977), *Henochs Zehnwochenapokalypse und offene Probleme der Apokalyptikforschung* (SPB 29; Leiden: Brill).

Dibelius, M. (1935), *From Tradition to Gospel* (New York: Scribner).

Diffey, D. S. (2013), 'David and the Fulfilment of 1 Samuel 2:35: Faithful Priest, Sure House, and a Man after God's Own Heart', *EvQ* 85: 99–104.

Dimant, D. (1981–2), 'Jerusalem and the Temple in the Animal Apocalypse (*1 Enoch* 85–90) in Light of the Thought of the Dead Sea Scrolls', (Hebr.) *Shnaton* 5–6: 178–87.

Dixon, E. P. (2009), 'Descending Spirit and Descending Gods: A "Greek" Interpretation of the Spirit's "Descent as a Dove" in Mark 1:10', *JBL* 128: 759–80.

Dodd, C. H. (1935), *The Parables of the Kingdom* (London: Nisbet).

Dodd, C. H. (1952), *According to the Scriptures: The Sub-Structure of New Testament Theology* (London: Nisbet).

Dodd, C. H. (1961), *The Parables of the Kingdom* (New York: Scribner).

Dodd, C. H. (1962), 'Prophecy of Caiaphas, John 6:47–53', in A. N. Wilder (ed.), *Neotestamentica et Patristica: Eine Freundesgabe, Oscar Cullmann zu seinem 60. Geburtstag* (Leiden: Brill), 134–43.

Dodd, C. H. (1968), *More New Testament Studies* (Grand Rapids: Eerdmans).

Dodd, C. H. (1971), *The Founder of Christianity* (London: Collins).

Doering, L. (1999), *Schabbat: Sabbathalacha und -praxis im antiken Judentum und Urchristentum* (TSAJ 78; Tübingen: Mohr Siebeck).

Donahue, J. R. (1995), 'Windows and Mirrors: The Setting of Mark's Gospel', *CBQ* 57: 1–26.

Donahue, J. R., and D. J. Harrington (2002), *The Gospel of Mark* (Collegeville, MN: Liturgical Press).

Drury, M. A. (2001), 'Anti-Catholicism in Germany, Britain and the United States: A Review and Critique of Recent Scholarship', *CH* 70: 98–131.

Duling, D. C. (1973), 'Promises to David and Their Entrance into Christianity: Nailing Down a Likely Hypothesis', *NTS* 20: 55–77.

Dunn, J. D. G. (1975), *Jesus and the Spirit: A Study of the Religious and Charismatic Experience of Jesus and the First Christians as Reflected in the New Testament* (Philadelphia: Westminster).

Dunn, J. D. G. (1980), *Christology in the Making: A New Testament Inquiry into the Origins of the Doctrine of the Incarnation* (Philadelphia: Westminster).

Dunn, J. D. G. (2000), '"Are You the Messiah?": Is the Crux of Mark 14:61–62 Resolvable?', in D. Catchpole, D. Horrell and C. M. Tuckett (eds), *Christology, Controversy, and Community: New Testament Essays in Honour of David R. Catchpole* (Leiden: Brill): 1–22.

Dunn, J. D. G. (2003), *Jesus Remembered: Vol. 1: Christianity in the Making* (Grand Rapids: Eerdmans).

Dunne, J. A. (2013), 'Suffering in Vain: A Study of the Interpretation of Πάσχω in Galatians 3.4', *JSNT* 36: 3–16.

Dupont, J., and P. Bonnard (1966), 'Le Notre Pere: Notes exégétiques', *FoiVie* 65: 51–79.

Eastman, S. G. (2007), *Recovering Paul's Mother Tongue: Language and Theology in Galatians* (Grand Rapids: Eerdmans).

Edwards, J. R. (2002), *The Gospel According to Mark* (PNTC; Grand Rapids: Eerdmans; Leicester: Apollos).

Edwards, J. R. (2015), *The Gospel According to Luke* (PNTC; Grand Rapids: Eerdmans).

Edwards, R. A. (1982), 'Matthew's Use of Q in Chapter Eleven', in J. Delobel (ed.), *Logia: Les Paroles de Jésus – the Sayings of Jesus* (BETL 59; Leuven: Leuven University Press): 257–75.

Embry, B. (2002), 'The *Psalms of Solomon* and the New Testament: Intertextuality and the Need for a Re-Evaluation', *JSP* 13: 99–136.

Emerton, J. A. (1958), 'The Origin of the Son of Man Imagery', *JTS* 9: 225–42.

Enslin, M. S. (1975), 'John and Jesus', *ZNW* 66: 1–18.

Ernst, J. (1989), *Johannes der Täufer: Interpretation, Geschichte, Wirkungsgeschichte* (Berlin/New York: de Gruyter).

Eskola, T. (2001), *Messiah and the Throne : Jewish Merkabah Mysticism and Early Christian Exaltation Discourse* (WUNT 2/142; Tübingen: Mohr Siebeck).

Evans, C. A. (1985), 'On the Isaianic Background of the Sower Parable', *CBQ* 47: 464–8.

Evans, C. A. (1989), *To See and Not Perceive: Isaiah 6.9–10 in Early Jewish and Christian Interpretation* (JSOTSup 64; Sheffield: Sheffield Academic Press).

Evans, C. A. (1991), 'In What Sense Blasphemy? Jesus before Caiaphas in Mark 14:61–64', SBLSP 30: 215–34.

Evans, C. A. (1993), 'From Public Ministry to the Passion: Can a Link Be Found between the (Galilean) Life and the (Judean) Death of Jesus?', SBLSP 32: 460–72.

Evans, C. A. (2001), *Mark 8:27–16:20* (WBC 34B; Nashville: Thomas Nelson).

Evans, C. A. (1999), 'Jesus and Zechariah's Messianic Hope', in B. Chilton and C. A. Evans (eds), *Authenticating the Activities of Jesus* (NTTS 28/2; Leiden/Boston: Brill): 373–88.

Farmer, W. R. (1956), *Maccabees, Zealots, and Josephus: An Inquiry into Jewish Nationalism in the Greco-Roman Period* (New York: Columbia University Press).

Fearghail, F. O. (1978), 'Sir 50:5–21: Yom Kippur or the Daily Whole-Offering?', *Bib* 59: 301–16.

Fee, Gordon D. (1987), *The First Epistle to the Corinthians* (NICNT; Grand Rapids: Eerdmans).

Fensham, F. C. (1971), 'Father and Son as Terminology for Treaty and Covenant', in H. Goedicke (ed.), *Near Eastern Studies in Honor of William Foxwell Albright* (Baltimore: Johns Hopkins): 121–35.

Finney, P. C. (1993), 'The Rabbi and the Coin Portrait (Mark 12:15b, 16): Rigorism Manqué', *JBL* 112: 629–44.

Fisher, L. (1968), 'Can This Be the Son of David?', in F. T. Trotter (ed.), *Jesus and the Historian: Written in Honor of Ernest Cadman Colwell* (Philadelphia: Westminster): 82–97.

Fitzmyer, J. A. (1981), *The Gospel According to Luke: Introduction, Translation, and Notes* (2 vols; AB 28 and 28A; Garden City, NY: Doubleday).

Fleddermann, H. T. (1981), 'The Discipleship Discourse (Mark 9:33–50)', *CBQ* 43: 57–75.

Fleddermann, H. T. (2005), *Q: A Reconstruction and Commentary* (BTS 1; Leuven/ Paris/Dudley, MA: Peeters).

Fleddermann, H. T. (2012), 'The Plot of Q', *ETL* 88: 43–69.

Flesher, P. V. M. (1992), 'Bread of the Presence', in D. N. Freedman (ed.), *Anchor Bible Dictionary: Vol. 1: A–C* (New York: Doubleday): 780–1.

Fletcher-Louis, C. H. T. (1997a), 'The Destruction of the Temple and the Relativization of the Old Covenent: Mark 13:31 and Matthew 5:18', in K. E. Brower, M. W. Elliott and G. K. Beale (eds), *Eschatology in Bible & Theology: Evangelical Essays at the Dawn of a New Millennium* (Downers Grove, Il: InterVarsity, 145–69)

Fletcher-Louis, C. H. T. (1997b), 'The High Priest as Divine Mediator in the Hebrew Bible: Dan 7:13 as a Test Case', in *Society of Biblical Literature 1997 Seminar Papers* (SBLSP 36; Atlanta: Scholars Press): 161–93.

Fletcher-Louis, C. H. T. (1999), 'The Worship of Divine Humanity as God's Image and the Worship of Jesus', in C. C. Newman, J. R. Davila and G. S. Lewis (eds), *The Jewish Roots of Christological Monotheism: Papers from the St Andrew's Conference on the Historical Origins of the Worship of Jesus* (JSJSup 63; Leiden: Brill): 112–28.

Fletcher-Louis, C. H. T. (2000), 'Jesus Inspects His Priestly War Party (Luke 14.25–35)', in S. Moyise (ed.), *The Old Testament in the New Testament* (Sheffield: Sheffield Academic Press): 126–43.

Fletcher-Louis, C. H. T. (2001), 'The Revelation of the Sacral Son of Man: The Genre, History of Religions Context and the Meaning of the Transfiguration', in F. Avemarie and H. Lichtenberger (eds), *Auferstehung – Resurrection. The Fourth Durham-Tübingen Research Symposium. Resurrection, Transfiguration and Exaltation in Old Testament, Ancient Judaism and Early Christianity (Tübingen, September 1999)* (WUNT 135; Tübingen: Mohr Siebeck): 247–98.

Fletcher-Louis, C. H. T. (2002), *All the Glory of Adam: Liturgical Anthropology in the Dead Sea Scrolls* (STDJ 42; Leiden: Brill).

Fletcher-Louis, C. H. T. (2004a), 'Alexander the Great's Worship of the High Priest', in L. T. Stuckenbruck and W. E. S. North (eds), *Early Jewish and Christian Monotheism* (JSNTSup 263; London/New York: T. & T. Clark): 71–102.

Fletcher-Louis, C. H. T. (2004b), 'The Cosmology of P and Theological Anthropology in the Wisdom of Jesus Ben Sira', in C. A. Evans (ed.), *Of Scribes and Sages: Early Jewish Interpretation and Transmission of Scripture: Vol. 1: Ancient Versions and Traditions* (London: T. & T. Clark): 69–113.

Fletcher-Louis, C. H. T. (2004c), 'God's Image, His Cosmic Temple and the High Priest: Towards a Theological and Historical Account of the Incarnation', in D. T. Alexander and S. J. Gathercole (eds), *Heaven on Earth: The Temple in Biblical Theology* (Carlisle: Paternoster): 81–99.

Fletcher-Louis, C. H. T. (2006), 'Jesus and the High Priestly Messiah, Part 1', *JSHJ* 4: 155–75.

Fletcher-Louis, C. H. T. (2007a), 'Humanity and the Idols of the Gods in Pseudo-Philo's *Biblical Antiquities*', in C. S. Barton (ed.), *Idolatry: False Worship in the Bible, Early Judaism, and Christianity* (T. & T. Clark Theology; New York: T. & T. Clark, 2007): 58–72.

Fletcher-Louis, C. H. T. (2007b), 'Jesus and the High Priestly Messiah, Part 2', *JSHJ* 5: 57–79.

Fletcher-Louis, C. H. T. (2013), 'Priests and Priesthood', in J. Brown, J. Green and N. Perrin (eds), *Dictionary of Jesus and the Gospels* (Downers Grove, IL: InterVarsity): 696–705.

Fletcher-Louis, C. H. T. (2016), *Jesus Monotheism: Vol. 1: Christological Origins: The Emerging Consensus and Beyond* (Cambridge: Clarke).

Flusser, D. (1988), *Judaism and the Origins of Christianity* (Jerusalem: Magnes).

Foley, J. M. (1991), *Immanent Art: From Structure to Meaning in Traditional Oral Epic* (Bloomington: Indiana University Press).

Ford, J. M. (1979), 'Jewish Law and Animal Symbolism', *JSJ* 10: 203–12.

Förster, N. (2012), *Jesus und die Steuerfrage: Die Zinsgroschenperikope auf dem religiösen und politischen Hintergrund ihrer Zeit, mit einer Edition von Pseudo-Hieronymus, De Haeresibus Judaeorum* (WUNT 294; Tübingen: Mohr Siebeck).

Fossum, J. (1995), *The Image of the Invisible God: Essays on the Influence of Jewish Mysticism on Early Christology* (Göttingen: Vandenhoeck & Ruprecht).

Fournier-Bidoz, A. (1984), 'L'arbre et la demeure: Siracide 24:10–17', *VT* 34:1–10.

France, R. T. (1994), 'Jesus the Baptist', in J. B. Green and M. Turner (eds), *Jesus of Nazareth: Lord and Christ: Essays on the Historical Jesus and New Testament Christology* (Grand Rapids: Eerdmans): 94–111.

France, R. T. (2002), *The Gospel of Mark* (NIGTC; Grand Rapids: Eerdmans; Carlisle: Paternoster).

Frankfurter, D. (2005), 'Curses, Blessings, and Ritual Authority: Egyptian Magic in Comparative Perspective', *JANER* 5: 157–85.

Fredriksen, P. (1999), *Jesus of Nazareth, King of the Jews: A Jewish Life and the Emergence of Christianity* (New York: Knopf).

Friedlander, G. (1969 (1911)), *The Jewish Sources of the Sermon on the Mount* (New York: KTAV).

Friedrich, G. (1956), 'Beobachtungen zur messianischen Hohepriestererwartung in den Synoptikern', *ZTK* 53: 265–311.

Fuller, R. H. (1965), *The Foundations of New Testament Christology* (New York: Scribner).

Funk, R. W., and R. W. Hoover (1993), *The Five Gospels: The Search for the Authentic Words of Jesus: New Translation and Commentary* (New York/Toronto: Macmillan).

Gane, R. E. (1992), '"Bread of the Presence" and Creator-in-Residence', *VT* 42: 179–203.

García Martínez, F., and E. J. C. Tigchelaar (2000), *The Dead Sea Scrolls Study Edition* (Leiden/Boston: Brill; Grand Rapids: Eerdmans).

Garlington, D. B. (2011), '"The Salt of the Earth" in Covenantal Perspective', *JETS* 54: 715–48.

Garnet, P. (1983), 'The Parable of the Sower: How the Multitudes Understood It', in E. J. Furcha and G. Johnston (eds), *Spirit Within Structure: Essays in Honor of George Johnston on the Occasion of His Seventieth Birthday* (PTMS 3; Allison Park, PA: Pickwick), 39–54.

Garr, W. R. (2003), *In His Own Image and Likeness: Humanity, Divinity, and Monotheism* (CHANE 15; Leiden: Brill).

Gaston, L. (1970), *No Stone on Another: Studies in the Significance of the Fall of Jerusalem in the Synoptic Gospels* (NovTSup 23; Leiden: Brill).

Gaventa, B. R. (1990), 'The Maternity of Paul: An Exegetical Study of Galatians 4:19', in R. T. Fortna and B. R. Gaventa (eds), *The Conversation Continues: Studies in Paul and John in Honor of J. Louis Martyn* (Nashville: Abingdon): 189–201.

George, A. (1978), *Études sur l'œuvre de Luc* (Paris: Gabalda).

Gero, S. (1976), 'Spirit as a Dove at the Baptism of Jesus', *NovT* 18:17–35.

Gese, H. (1983), 'Die Bedeutung der Krise unter Antiochus IV Epiphanes für die Apokalyptik des Danielbuches', *ZTK* 80: 373–88.

Gibbs, J. M. (1964), 'Purpose and Pattern in Matthew's Use of the Title "Son of David"', *NTS* 10: 446–64.

Giblin, C. H. (1971), '"The Things of God" in the Question Concerning Tribute to Caesar (Lk 20:25; Mk 12:17; Mt 22:21)', *CBQ* 33: 510–27.

Gilders, W. K. (2012), 'The Day of Atonement in the Dead Sea Scrolls', in T. Hieke and T. Nicklas (eds), *The Day of Atonement: Its Interpretations in Early Jewish and Christian Traditions* (TBN 17; Leiden: Brill): 63–73.

Gillingham, S. E. (2013), *A Journey of Two Psalms: The Reception of Psalms 1 and 2 in Jewish and Christian Tradition* (Oxford: Oxford University Press).

Ginzburg, C. (1980), *The Cheese and the Worms: The Cosmos of a Sixteenth-Century Miller* (Baltimore: Johns Hopkins University Press).

Ginzburg, C. (1989), *Clues, Myths, and the Historical Method* (Baltimore: Johns Hopkins University Press).

Gladd, B. L. (2008), *Revealing the Mysterion: The Use of Mystery in Daniel in Second Temple Judaism with Its Bearing on First Corinthians* (BZNW 160; Berlin: de Gruyter).

Gnilka, J. (1997), *Jesus of Nazareth: Message and History* (Peabody, MA: Hendrickson).

Gnilka, J. (2010 (1978)), *Das Evangelium nach Markus* (2 vols; EKKNT; Neukirchen-Vluyn: Neukirchener Verlag).

Goguel, M. (1933 (1932)), *The Life of Jesus* (New York: Macmillan).

Goldingay, J. (1989), *Daniel* (WBC 30; Dallas: Word).

Gooding, D. W. (1981), 'The Literary Structure of the Book of Daniel and Its Implications', *TynBul* 32: 43–79.

Goulder, M. D. (2002), 'Psalm 8 and the Son of Man', *NTS* 48: 18–29.

Granerød, G. (2010), *Abraham and Melchizedek: Scribal Activity of Second Temple Times in Genesis 14 and Psalm 110* (BZAW 406; Berlin: de Gruyter).

Grant, M. (1954), *Roman Imperial Money* (London/New York: Nelson).

Grassi, J. A. (1982), 'Abba, Father (Mark 14:36): Another Approach', *JAAR* 50: 449–58.

Gray, T. C. (2008), *The Temple in the Gospel of Mark: A Study in Its Narrative Role* (WUNT 2/168; Tübingen: Mohr Siebeck).

Green, J. B. (1997), *The Gospel of Luke* (NICNT; Grand Rapids: Eerdmans).

Greenfield, J. C., M. E. Stone and E. Eshel (2004), *The Aramaic Levi Document: Edition, Translation, Commentary* (SVTP 19; Leiden: Brill).

Grelot, P. (1978–9), 'La quatrième demande du Pater et son arrière-plan sémitique', *NTS* 25: 299–314.

Grelot, P. (1984), 'L'arrière-plan araméen du "Pater"', *RB* 91 (1984): 531–56.

Grimm, W. (1976), *Weil ich dich liebe: Die Verkündigung Jesu und Deuterojesaja* (Bern: Peter Lang).

Grimm, W. (1980), 'Die Hoffnung der Armen: Zu den Seligpreisungen Jesu', *TB* 11: 100–13.

Grindheim, S. (2002), 'Wisdom for the Perfect: Paul's Advice to the Corinthian Church (1 Corinthians 2:6–16)', *JBL* 121: 689–709.

Grindheim, S. (2011), *God's Equal: What Can We Know about Jesus' Self-Understanding?* (LNTS 446; London/New York: T. & T. Clark).

Grundmann, W. (1959), *Das Evangelium nach Markus* (THKNT; Berlin: Evangelische Verlagsanstalt).

Grundmann, W. (1968), *Das Evangelium nach Matthäus* (THKNT; Berlin: Evangelische Verlagsanstalt).

Guelich, R. A. (1976), 'The Matthean Beatitudes: "Entrance-Requirements" or Eschatological Blessings?', *JBL* 95: 415–34.

Guelich, R. A. (1989), *Mark 1–8:26* (WBC 34A; Dallas: Word).

Gundry, R. H. (2005), *The Old Is Better: New Testament Essays in Support of Traditional Interpretation* (WUNT 178; Tübingen: Mohr Siebeck).

Gundry, R. H. (2008), 'Jesus' Supposed Blasphemy (Mark 14:61b–64)', *BBR* 18: 131–3.

Gundry, R. H. (2015), *Peter: False Disciple and Apostate According to Saint Matthew* (Grand Rapids: Eerdmans).

Gunton, C. E. (2003), *Act and Being: Towards a Theology of the Divine Attributes* (Grand Rapids: Eerdmans).

Gupta, N. K. (2014), '"They Are Not Gods!": Jewish and Christian Idol Polemic and Greco-Roman Use of Cult Statues', *CBQ* 76: 704–19.

Gurtner, D. M. (2012), 'Interpreting Apocalyptic Symbolism in the Gospel of Matthew', *BBR* 22: 525–45.

Gurtner, D. M. (2016), 'Peter: False Disciple and Apostate According to Saint Matthew', *RelSRev* 42: 210–11.

Hägerland, T. (2012), *Jesus and the Forgiveness of Sins: An Aspect of His Prophetic Mission* (SNTSMS 150; Cambridge/New York: Cambridge University Press).

Hagner, D. A. (1993), *Matthew 1–13* (WBC 33A; Dallas: Word).

Hahn, F., W. Lohff and G. Bornkamm (1969), *What Can We Know about Jesus? Essays on the New Quest* (Philadelphia: Fortress).

Hahn, S. (2005), 'Covenant, Oath, and the Aqedah: *Diatheke* in Galatians 3:15–18', *CBQ* 67: 79–100.

Hahn, S. (2009), *Kinship by Covenant: A Canonical Approach to the Fulfillment of God's Saving Promises* (AYBRL; New Haven, CT: Yale University Press).

Halpern-Amaru, B. (1997), 'Exile and Return in Jubilees', in J. Scott (ed.), *Exile: Old Testament, Jewish, and Christian Conceptions* (JSJSup 56, Leiden: Brill): 127–44.

Hampel, V. (1990), *Menschensohn und historischer Jesus: Ein Rätselwort als Schlüssel zum messianischen Selbstverständnis Jesu* (Neukirchen-Vluyn: Neukirchener Verlag).

Hanneken, T. R. (2012), *The Subversion of the Apocalypses in the Book of Jubilees* (EJL 34; Atlanta: Society of Biblical Literature).

Haran, M. (1979), *Temples and Temple Service in Ancient Israel: An Inquiry into the*

Character of Cult Phenomena and the Historical Setting of the Priestly School (Oxford: Clarendon Press).

Hare, D. R. A. (1990), *The Son of Man Tradition* (Minneapolis: Fortress).

Harrisville, R. A. (1993), 'In Search of the Meaning of "the Reign of God"', *Int* 47: 140–51.

Hart, H. J. (1984), 'The Coin of "Render unto Caesar" (A Note on Some Aspects of Mk 12:13–17; Matt 22:15–22; Lk 20:20–26)', in E. Bammel (ed.), *Jesus and the Politics of His Day* (Cambridge: Cambridge University Press): 241–8.

Hartin, P. J. (1995), '"Yet Wisdom Is Justified by Her Children" (Q 7:35)', in J. S. Kloppenborg (ed.), *Conflict and Intervention, Literary, Rhetorical, and Social Studies on the Sayings Gospel Q* (Valley Forge, PA: Trinity Press International): 151–64.

Hartman, L. F., and A. Di Lella (1978), *Daniel* (AB 23; New York: Doubleday).

Harvey, A. E. (1980), 'The Use of Mystery Language in the Bible', *JTS* 31: 320–36.

Harvey, A. E. (1982), *Jesus and the Constraints of History* (Philadelphia: Westminster).

Hasel, G. F. (1992), 'Sabbath', in D. N. Freedman (ed.), *The Anchor Bible Dictionary: Vol. 5: O–Sh* (New York: Doubleday): 849–56.

Hauck, F. (1968), 'πτωχοί', in G. Kittel (ed.), *Theological Dictionary of the New Testament: Vol. 6: Πε–Ρ* (Grand Rapids: Eerdmans): 886–7.

Hay, D. M. (1989 (1973)), *Glory at the Right Hand: Psalm 110 in Early Christianity* (SBLMS 18; Atlanta: Society of Biblical Literature).

Hayes, J. H. (1963), 'Tradition of Zion's Inviolability', *JBL* 82: 419–26.

Hays, R. B. (1989), *Echoes of Scripture in the Letters of Paul* (New Haven, CT: Yale University Press).

Hays, R. B. (1997), *First Corinthians* (IBC; Louisville, KY: John Knox, 1997).

Hays, R. B. (2016), *Echoes of Scripture in the Gospels* (Waco: Baylor University Press).

Hayward, C. T. R. (1996), *The Jewish Temple: A Non-Biblical Sourcebook* (London: Routledge).

Head, P. M. (1991), 'A Text-Critical Study of Mark 1:1: "The Beginning of the Gospel of Jesus Christ"', *NTS* 37: 621–9.

Heitmüller, W. (1913), *Jesus* (Tübingen: Mohr Siebeck).

Hengel, M. (1979), 'Jesus als messianischer Lehrer der Weisheit und die Anfänge der Christologie', in J. Leclant, J. Bergman and J. Pépin (eds), *Sagesse et Religion: Colloque de Strasbourg* (Paris: Press Universitaires de France): 147–88.

Hengel, M. (1981 (1968)), *The Charismatic Leader and His Followers* (New York: Crossroad).

Hengel, M. (1987), 'Zur matthäischen Bergpredigt und ihrem jüdischen Hintergrund', *TRu* 52: 327–400.

Hengel, M., and A. M. Schwemer (1991), *Königsherrschaft Gottes und himmlischer Kult im Judentum, Urchristentum und in der hellenistischen Welt* (WUNT 55; Tübingen: Mohr Siebeck).

Higgins, A. J. B. (1965 (1964)), *Jesus and the Son of Man* (Philadelphia: Fortress).

Himmelfarb, M. (2007), 'Temple and Priests in the Book of the Watchers, the Animal Apocalypse, and the Apocalypse of Weeks', in G. Boccaccini and J. J. Collins (eds), *The Early Enoch Literature* (JSJSup 121; Leiden: Brill): 219–35.

Hoglund, K. G. (2002), 'The Priest of Praise: The Chronicler's David', *RevExp* 99: 185–91.

Hollenbach, P. W. (1982), 'The Conversion of Jesus: From Jesus the Baptizer to Jesus the Healer', in W. Haase (ed.), *Principat 25/1; Vorkonstantinisches Christentum: Leben und Umwelt Jesu; Neues Testament* (ANRW; Berlin/New York: de Gruyter): 196–219.

Holmén, T. (2002), 'Doubts about Double Dissimilarity: Restructuring the Main Criterion of Jesus-of-History Research', in B. D. Chilton and C. A. Evans (eds), *Authenticating the Words of Jesus* (NTTS 28; Leiden: Brill): 47–80.

Holtzmann, O. (1903), *War Jesus Ekstatiker? Eine Untersuchung zum Leben Jesu* (Tübingen: Mohr Siebeck).

Hooker, M. D. (1979), 'Is the Son of Man Problem Really Insoluble?', in E. Best and R. M. Wilson (eds), *Text and Interpretation: Studies in the New Testament Presented to Matthew Black* (Cambridge: Cambridge University Press): 155–68.

Horsley, R. A. (1984), 'Popular Messianic Movements around the Time of Jesus', *CBQ* 46: 471–95.

Horsley, R. A. (1991), 'Q and Jesus: Assumptions, Approaches, and Analyses', *Semeia* 55: 175–209.

Horsley, R. A. (2003), *Jesus and Empire: The Kingdom of God and the New World Disorder* (Minneapolis: Fortress).

Horsley, R. A. (2012), *The Prophet Jesus and the Renewal of Israel: Moving beyond a Diversionary Debate* (Grand Rapids: Eerdmans).

Huizenga, L. A. (2009), *The New Isaac: Tradition and Intertextuality in the Gospel of Matthew* (NovTSup 131; Leiden/Boston: Brill).

Hultgren, A. (1972), 'Formation of the Sabbath Pericope in Mark 2:23–28', *JBL* 91: 38–43.

Hultgren, A. (2000), *The Parables of Jesus: A Commentary* (BW; Grand Rapids: Eerdmans).

Hunzinger, C.-H. (1960), 'Unbekannte Gleichnisse Jesu aus dem Thomas-Evangelium', in W. Eltester (ed.), *Judentum, Urchristentum, Kirche: Festschrift für Joachim Jeremias* (ZNW 26; Berlin: Töpelmann, 1960): 209–20.

Hurst, L D. (1999), 'Did Qumran Expect Two Messiahs?', *BBR* 9: 157–80.

Hurtado, L. W. (1988), *One God, One Lord: Early Christian Devotion and Ancient Jewish Monotheism* (Philadelphia: Fortress).

Isaac, E. (1985), '1 (Ethiopic Apocalypse of) Enoch: A New Translation and Introduction', in J. H. Charlesworth (ed.), *The Old Testament Pseudepigrapha, Vol. 1: Apocalyptic Literature and Testaments* (ABRL; New York: Doubleday): 5–89.

Ishida, T. (1977), *The Royal Dynasties in Ancient Israel: A Study on the Formation and Development of Royal-Dynastic Ideology* (BZAW 142; Berlin/New York: de Gruyter).

Janse, S. (2009), *'You Are My Son': The Reception History of Psalm 2 in Early Judaism and the Early Church* (Leuven: Peeters).

Jenkins, P. (2003), *The New Anti-Catholicism: The Last Acceptable Prejudice* (New York: Oxford University Press).

Jeremias, J. (1963), *The Parables of Jesus* (New York: Scribner).

Jeremias, J. (1965), *The Central Message of the New Testament* (New York: Scribner).

Jeremias, J. (1969), *Jerusalem in the Time of Jesus: An Investigation into Economic and Social Conditions during the New Testament Period* (Philadelphia: Fortress; London: SCM Press).

Jeremias, J. (1971), *New Testament Theology: The Proclamation of Jesus* (New York: Scribner).

Jeremias, J. (1972), *The Parables of Jesus* (London: SCM Press).

Jervell, J. (1960), *Imago Dei: Gen 1, 26 f. im Spätjudentum, in der Gnosis und in den paulinischen Briefen* (FRLANT 58; Göttingen: Vandenhoeck & Ruprecht).

Jewett, R. (1978), 'The Redaction of I Corinthians and the Trajectory of the Pauline School', *JAAR* 46: 571.

Jewett, R. (1985), 'The Redaction and Use of an Early Christian Confession in Romans 1:3–4', in D. Groh, R. Jewett and E. Saunders (eds), *Living Text: Essays in Honor of Ernest W. Saunders* (Lanham, MD: University Press of America): 99–122.

Jipp, J. W. (2009), 'Rereading the Story of Abraham, Isaac, and "Us" in Romans 4', *JSNT* 32: 217–42.

Johansson, D. (2011), '"Who Can Forgive Sins but God Alone?" Human and Angelic Agents, and Divine Forgiveness in Early Judaism', *JSNT* 33: 351–74.

Johnson, B. J. M. (2011), '"Whoever Gives Me Thorns and Thistles": Rhetorical Ambiguity and the Use of מי יתן in Isaiah 27.2–6', *JSOT* 36: 105–26.

Johnson, V. L. (2009), *David in Distress: His Portrait through the Historical Psalms* (LBS 505; New York: T. & T. Clark).

Jonge, M. de (1960), 'Christian Influence in the Testaments of the Twelve Patriarchs', *NovT* 4: 182–235.

Jonge, M. de (1962), 'Once More: Christian Influence in the Testaments of the Twelve Patriarchs', *NovT* 5: 311–19.

Jonge, M. de (1980), 'The Main Issues in the Study of the Testaments of the Twelve Patriarchs', *NTS* 26: 508–24.

Jonge, M. de (1988), *Christology in Context: The Earliest Christian Response to Jesus* (Philadelphia: Westminster).

Jonge, M. de (1998), 'Jesus' Death for Others and the Death of the Maccabean Martyrs', in A. F. J. Klijn and T. Baarda (eds), *Text and Testimony: Essays on New Testament and Apocryphal Literature in Honour of A. F. J. Klijn* (Kampen: Kok): 142–51.

Joyner, C. W. (1999), *Shared Traditions: Southern Traditions and Folk Culture* (Urbana: University of Illinois Press).

Juel, D. H. (1975), 'The Function of the Trial of Jesus in Mark's Gospel', SBLSP 2: 83–104.

Juel, D. H. (1977), *Messiah and Temple: The Trial of Jesus in the Gospel of Mark* (SBLDS 31; Missoula, MT: Scholars Press).

Kaiser, W. C. (1995), *The Messiah in the Old Testament* (Grand Rapids: Zondervan).

Kammler, H.-C. (2003a), *Kreuz und Weisheit: Eine exegetische Untersuchung zu 1 Kor 1, 10–3, 4* (WUNT 159; Tübingen: Mohr Siebeck).

Kammler, H.-C. (2003b), 'Sohn Gottes und Kreuz: Die Versuchungsgeschichte Mt 4:1–11 im Kontext des Matthäusevangeliums', *ZTK* 100: 163–86.

Keck, L. E. (1970), 'Spirit and the Dove', *NTS* 17: 41–67.

Kee, H. C. (1983), 'The Testaments of the Twelve Patriarchs', *OTP* 1: 777–8.

Keener, C. S. (2009), *The Historical Jesus of the Gospels* (Grand Rapids: Eerdmans).

Keesmaat, S. C. (1999), *Paul and His Story: (Re)Interpreting the Exodus Tradition* (JSNTSup 181; Sheffield: Sheffield Academic Press).

Keith, C. (2014), *Jesus Against the Scribal Elite: The Origins of the Conflict* (Grand Rapids: Baker Academic).

Keith, C. (2016), 'The Narratives of the Gospels and the Historical Jesus: Current Debates, Prior Debates and the Goal of Historical Jesus Research', *JSNT* 38: 426–55.

Keith, C., and A. Le Donne (2012), *Jesus, Criteria, and the Demise of Authenticity* (London: T. & T. Clark International).

Kerr, A. R. (2002), *The Temple of Jesus' Body: The Temple Theme in the Gospel of John* (JSNTSup 220; London: Sheffield Academic Press).

Kilpatrick, G. D. (1953), *The Trial of Jesus* (Oxford: Oxford University Press).

Kim, S. (1987), 'Jesus – The Son of God, the Stone, the Son of Man, and the Servant: The Role of Zechariah in the Self-Identification of Jesus', in G. F. Hawthorne and O. Betz (eds), *Tradition and Interpretation in the New Testament: Essays in Honor of E. Earle Ellis for His 60th Birthday* (Grand Rapids: Eerdmans; Tübingen: Mohr Siebeck): 134–48.

Kingsbury, J. D. (1976), 'The Title "Son of David" in Matthew's Gospel', *JBL* 95: 591–602.

Kingsbury, J. D. (1988), 'On Following Jesus: The "Eager" Scribe and the "Reluctant" Disciple (Matthew 8:18–22)', *NTS* 34: 45–59.

Kinman, B. (2009), 'Jesus' Entry into Jerusalem', in D. L. Bock and R. L. Webb (eds), *Key Events in the Life of the Historical Jesus: A Collaborative Exploration of Content and Coherence* (WUNT 247; Tübingen: Mohr Siebeck): 383–427.

Kirk, D. R. (2012), 'Heaven Opened: Intertextuality and Meaning in John 1:51', *TynBul* 63: 237–56.

Kitz, A. M. (2014), *Cursed Are You! The Phenomenology of Cursing in Cuneiform and Hebrew Texts* (Winona Lake, IN: Eisenbrauns).

Klawans, J. (2006), *Purity, Sacrifice, and the Temple: Symbolism and Supersessionism in the Study of Ancient Judaism* (Oxford/New York: Oxford University Press).

Klein, G. (1906), 'Die ursprüngliche Gestalt des Vaterunsers', *ZNW* 7: 34–50.

Klein, R. W. (2012), *2 Chronicles: A Commentary* (Hermeneia; Minneapolis: Fortress).

Kleven, T. (1992), 'Hebrew Style in 2 Samuel 6', *JETS* 35: 299–314.

Kline, M. G. (1977), 'Investiture with the Image of God', *WTJ* 40: 39–62.

Klinghardt, M. (1996), *Gemeinschaftsmahl und Mahlgemeinschaft: Soziologie und Liturgie frühchristlicher Mahlfeiern* (TANZ 13; Tübingen: Francke).

Kloppenborg, J. S. (2000), *Excavating Q: The History and Setting of the Sayings Gospel* (Minneapolis: Fortress).

Kloppenborg, J. S. (2006), *The Tenants in the Vineyard: Ideology, Economics, and Agrarian Conflict in Jewish Palestine* (WUNT 195; Tübingen: Mohr Siebeck).

Knibb, M. A. (1976), 'The Exile in the Literature of the Intertestamental Period', *HeyJ* 17: 253–72.

Knowles, M. P. (1995), 'Abram and the Birds in Jubilees 11: A Subtext for the Parable of the Sower?', *NTS* 41: 145–51.

Koch, D.-A. (2014), 'Die Kontroverse über die Steuer (Mt 22,15–22 / Mk 12,13–17 / Lk 20,20–26)', in G. van Belle and J. Verheyden (eds), *Christ and the Emperor: The Gospel Evidence* (BTS 20; Leuven: Peeters): 203–27.

Kooij, A. van der (2007), 'The Greek Bible and Jewish Concepts of Royal Priesthood and Priestly Monarchy', in T. Rajak et al., *Jewish Perspectives on Hellenistic Rulers* (Berkeley: University of California Press): 255–64.

Kraeling, C. H. (1951), *John the Baptist* (New York: Scribner).

Kratz, R. G. (1992), 'Die Gnade des täglichen Brots (The Grace of Daily Bread)', *ZTK* 89: 1–40.

Kraus, H-J. (1966), *Worship in Israel* (Richmond, VA: John Knox).

Kugel, J. L. (1993), 'Levi's Elevation to the Priesthood in Second Temple Writings', *HTR* 86: 1–64.

Kugel, J. L. (2006), *The Ladder of Jacob: Ancient Interpretations of the Biblical Story of Jacob and His Children* (Princeton: Princeton University Press).

Kurz, W. S. (1984), 'Luke 3:23–38 and Greco-Roman and Biblical Genealogies', in C. H. Talbert (ed.), *Luke-Acts: New Perspectives from the Society of Biblical Literature Seminar* (New York: Crossroad): 169–87.

Kwon, O.-Y. (2010), 'A Critical Review of Recent Scholarship on the Pauline Opposition and the Nature of Its Wisdom (σοφία) in 1 Corinthians 1–4', *CBR* 8: 386–427.

Laato, A. (1992), *Josiah and David Redivivus: The Historical Josiah and the Messianic Expectations of Exilic and Postexilic Times* (ConBOT 33; Stockholm: Almqvist & Wiksell).

Laato, A. (1997), *A Star Is Rising: The Historical Development of the Old Testament Royal Ideology and the Rise of the Jewish Messianic Expectations* (ISFCJ 5; Atlanta: Scholars Press).

Lacocque, A. (1979), *The Book of Daniel* (Atlanta: John Knox).

Lacocque, A. (1988), *Daniel in His Time* (Columbia, SC: University of South Carolina Press).

Ladd, G. E. (1974), *The Presence of the Future: The Eschatology of Biblical Realism* (Grand Rapids: Eerdmans).

Lampe, G. W. H. (1973), 'St Peter's Denial and the Treatment of the *Lapsi*', in D. Neiman and M. A. Schatkin (eds), *Heritage of the Early Church: Essays in Honor of Georges Vasilievich Florovsky* (AnOr 135; Rome: Pontificium Institutum Studiorum Orientalium): 113–33.

Lane, W. L. (1974), *The Gospel According to Mark* (NICNT; Grand Rapids: Eerdmans).

Latham, J. E. (1982), *The Religious Symbolism of Salt* (Paris: Beauchesne).

Le Déaut, R. (1963), *La nuit pascale: Essai sur la signification de la Pâque juive à partir du Targum d'Exode XII 42* (Rome: Pontificio Istituto Biblico).

Le Donne, A. (2009), *The Historiographical Jesus: Memory, Typology, and the Son of David* (Waco: Baylor University Press).

Le Donne, A. (2011), *Historical Jesus: What Can We Know and How Can We Know It?* (Grand Rapids: Eerdmans).

Lee, Y. (2012), *The Son of Man as the Last Adam: The Early Church Tradition as a Source of Paul's Adam Christology* (Eugene, OR: Pickwick).

Légasse, S. (1969), *Jésus et l'enfant: 'Enfants,' 'Petits' et 'Simples' dans la tradition synoptique* (EBib; Paris: Gabalda).

Lehnardt, A. (2002), *Qaddish: Untersuchungen zur Entstehung und Rezeption eines rabbinischen Gebetes* (TSAJ 87; Tübingen: Mohr Siebeck).

Leithart, P. J. (2000), 'Womb of the World : Baptism and the Priesthood of the New Covenant in Hebrews 10.19–22', *JSNT* 78: 49–65.

Levenson, J. D. (1993), *The Death and Resurrection of the Beloved Son: The Transformation of Child Sacrifice in Judaism and Christianity* (New Haven, CT: Yale University Press).

Lietzmann, H. (1931), 'Der Prozess Jesus', *SPAW* 14: 313–22.

Lindars, B. (1961), *New Testament Apologetic: The Doctrinal Significance of the Old Testament Quotations* (London: SCM Press).

Lindars, B. (1983), *Jesus Son of Man: A Fresh Examination of the Son of Man Sayings in the Gospels* (Grand Rapids: Eerdmans; London: SPCK).

Linton, O. (1976), 'Parable of the Children's Game', *NTS* 22: 159–79.

Lohfink, G. (1985), 'Die Metaphorik der Aussaat im Gleichnis vom Samaan (Mk 4, 3–9)', in F. Refoulé (ed.), *À cause de l'Évangile: Études sur les Synoptiques et les Actes offertes au P. Jacques Dupont, O.S.B.* (LD 123; Paris: Cerf): 211–28.

Lohfink, G. (1989), *Studien zum Neuen Testament* (Stuttgart: Katholisches Bibelwerk).

Lohmeyer, E. (1965), *The Lord's Prayer* (London: Collins).

Lohse, E. (1961), 'Der Prozess Jesu Christi', in Georg Kretschmar and B. Lohse (eds), *Ecclesia und Res Publica: Kurt Dietrich Schmidt zum 65 Geburtstag* (Göttingen: Vandenhoeck & Ruprecht): 24–39.

Longman III, T. (2006), *Proverbs* (Baker Commentary on the Old Testament Wisdom and Psalms; Grand Rapids: Baker Academic).

Lövestam, E. (1961), *Son and Saviour: A Study of Acts 13:32–37* (Lund: C. W. K. Gleerup; Copenhagen: E. Munksgaard).

Lucas, E. (2002), *Daniel* (AOTC 20; Leicester: Apollos; Downers Grove, IL: InterVarsity).

Lupieri, E. (1988), *Giovanni Battista nelle tradizioni sinottiche* (Studi Biblici 82; Brescia: Paideia).

Luz, U. (1989–2005), *Matthew: A Commentary* (Hermeneia; Minneapolis: Augsburg/Fortress).

McDowell, C. L. (2015), *The Image of God in the Garden of Eden: The Creation of Humankind in Genesis 2:5–3:24 in Light of the Mīs Pî Pīt Pî and wpt-r Rituals of Mesopotamia and Ancient Egypt* (Siphrut 15; Winona Lake, IN: Eisenbrauns).

McKane, W. (1970), *Proverbs: A New Approach* (OTL; Philadelphia: Westminster Press).

McKnight, S. (1999), *A New Vision for Israel: The Teachings of Jesus in National Context* (Grand Rapids: Eerdmans).

McKnight, S. (2005), *Jesus and His Death: Historiography, the Historical Jesus, and Atonement Theory* (Waco: Baylor University Press).

Maier, C., and J. Herzer (2001), 'Die spielenden Kinder der Weisheit (Lk 7,31–35 par. Mt 11,16–19): Beobachtungen zu einem Gleichnis Jesu und seiner Rezeption', in C. Maier (ed.), *Exegese vor Ort: Festschrift für Peter Welten zum 65. Geburtstag* (Leipzig: Evangelische Verlagsanstalt): 277–300.

Major, H. D. A., T. W. Manson and C. J. Wright (1938), *The Mission and Message of Jesus* (New York: E. P. Dutton).

Malbon, E. S. (2009a), 'The Jesus of Mark and the "Son of David"', in E. S. Malbon (ed.), *Between Author and Audience in Mark: Narration, Characterization, Interpretation* (Sheffield: Sheffield Phoenix): 162–85.

Malbon, E. S. (2009b), *Mark's Jesus: Characterization as Narrative Christology* (Waco: Baylor University Press).

Manson, T. W. (1951 (1931)), *The Teaching of Jesus: Studies of Its Form and Content* (Cambridge: Cambridge University Press).

Manson, T. W. (1953), *The Servant-Messiah: A Study of the Public Ministry of Jesus* (Cambridge: Cambridge University Press).

Marchel, W. (1963), *Abba, Père! La prière du Christ et des Chrétiens: Étude éxegétique sur les origines et la signification de l'invocation à la divinité comme père, avant et dans le Nouveau Testament* (Rome: Pontificio Istituto Biblico).

Marcus, J. (1984), 'Mark 4:10–12 and Marcan Epistemology', *JBL* 103: 557–74.

Marcus, J. (1986), *The Mystery of the Kingdom of God* (SBLDS 90; Atlanta: Scholars Press).

Marcus, J. (1989), 'Mark 14:61: "Are You the Messiah-Son-of-God?"', *NovT* 31: 125–41.

Marcus, J. (1992), *The Way of the Lord: Christological Exegesis of the Old Testament in the Gospel of Mark* (Louisville, KY: Westminster John Knox).

Marcus, J. (1995), 'Jesus' Baptismal Vision', *NTS* 41: 512–21.

Marcus, J. (2000), *Mark: A New Translation with Introduction and Commentary* (AB 27A; New York: Doubleday).

Marcus, J. (2003a), 'Son of Man as Son of Adam', *RB* 110: 38–61.

Marcus, J. (2003b), 'Son of Man as Son of Adam: Part II: Exegesis', *RB* 110: 370–86.

Marcus, J. (2004 (1992)), *The Way of the Lord: Christological Exegesis of the Old Testament in the Gospel of Mark* (London: T. & T. Clark International).

Marcus, J. (2006), 'Crucifixion as Parodic Exaltation', *JBL* 125: 73–87.

Marshall, I. H. (1978), *The Gospel of Luke: A Commentary on the Greek Text* (NIGTC; Grand Rapids: Eerdmans).

Mason, R. A. (1977), 'Purpose of the "Editorial Framework" of the Book of Haggai', *VT* 27: 413–21.

Mason, S. (1992), 'Fire, Water and Spirit: John the Baptist and the Tyranny of Canon', *SR* 21: 163–80.

Mauser, U. W. (2000), 'God in Human Form', *ExAud* 16: 81–99.

Mays, J. L. (1993), 'The Language of the Reign of God', *Int* 47: 117–26.

Meier, J. P. (1980), 'John the Baptist in Matthew's Gospel', *JBL* 99: 383–405.

Meier, J. P. (1991), *A Marginal Jew: Rethinking the Historical Jesus: Vol. 1: Origins of the Problem and the Person* (ABRL; New York: Doubleday).

Meier, J. P. (1994), *A Marginal Jew: Rethinking the Historical Jesus: Vol. 2: Mentor, Message, and Miracles* (ABRL; New York: Doubleday).

Meier, J. P. (2000), 'The Historical Jesus and the Historical Herodians', *JBL* 119: 740–46.

Meier, J. P. (2001), *A Marginal Jew: Rethinking the Historical Jesus: Vol. 3: Companions and Competitors* (ABRL; New York: Doubleday).

Mell, U. (1994), 'Gehört das Vater-Unser zur authentischen Jesus-Tradition?', *BTZ*

11: 148–80.

Merklein, H. (1989 (1983)), *Jesu Botschaft von der Gottesherrschaft: Eine Skizze* (SBS 111; Stuttgart: Katholisches Bibelwerk).

Meyer, B. F. (1992), *Christus Faber: The Master Builder and the House of God* (PrTMS 29; Allison Park, PA: Pickwick).

Meyer, B. F. (2002 (1979)), *The Aims of Jesus* (London: SCM Press).

Michaelis, W. (1961), 'Die Davidssohnschaft Jesus als historiches und dogmatisches Problem', in H. Ristow (ed.), *Der Historische Jesus und der kerygmatische Christus: Beiträge zum Christusverständnis in Forschung und Verkündigung* (Berlin: Evangelische Verlagsanstalt): 317–30.

Milgrom, J. (1990), *Numbers* [במדבר]*: The Traditional Hebrew Text with the New JPS Translation* (Philadelphia: Jewish Publication Society).

Miller, A. C. (2013), 'Not with Eloquent Wisdom: Democratic *Ekklēsia* Discourse in I Corinthians 1–4', *JSNT* 35: 323–54.

Miller, P. D. (1975), 'Blessing of God: An Interpretation of Numbers 6:22–27', *Int* 29: 240–51.

Miller, S. (1994), *Daniel* (NAC; Nashville: B&H Academic).

Minear, P. S. (1997), 'The Salt of the Earth', *Int* 51: 31–41.

Miura, Y. (2007), *David in Luke-Acts: His Portrayal in the Light of Early Judaism* (WUNT 2/232; Tübingen: Mohr Siebeck).

Moberly, R. W. L. (2000), *The Bible, Theology, and Faith: A Study of Abraham and Jesus* (CSCD 5; Cambridge: Cambridge University Press).

Morales, L. M. (2012), *The Tabernacle Pre-Figured: Cosmic Mountain Ideology in Genesis and Exodus* (BTS 15; Leuven: Peeters).

Morales, L. M. (2014), *Cult and Cosmos: Tilting toward a Temple-Centered Theology* (BTS 18; Leuven: Peeters).

Morales, L. M. (2015), *Who Shall Ascend the Mountain of the Lord? A Biblical Theology of the Book of Leviticus* (NSBT; Downers Grove, IL: InterVarsity).

Mosca, P. G. (1986), 'Ugarit and Daniel 7: A Missing Link', *Bib* 67: 496–517.

Moses, A. D. A. (1996), *Matthew's Transfiguration Story and Jewish-Christian Controversy* (JSNTSup 122; Sheffield: Sheffield Academic Press).

Moule, C. F. D. (1969), 'Mark 4:1–20 Yet Once More', in E. E. Ellis and M. Wilcox (eds), *Neotestamentica et Semitica* (Edinburgh: T. & T. Clark): 95–113.

Moule, C. F. D. (1977), *The Origin of Christology* (Cambridge/New York: Cambridge University Press).

Mowinckel, S. (1956), *He That Cometh* (Oxford: Blackwell).

Mroczek, E. (2015), 'How Not to Build a Temple: Jacob, David, and the Unbuilt Ideal in Ancient Judaism', *JSJ* 46: 512–46.

Müller, C. G. (2003), '"Ungefähr 30": Anmerkungen zur Altersangabe Jesu im Lukasevangelium (Lk 3.23)', *NTS* 49: 489–504.

Myers, J. M. (1965), *I Chronicles* (AB 12; New York: Doubleday).

Myles, R. J. (2014), *The Homeless Jesus in the Gospel of Matthew* (SWBAnt 10; Sheffield: Sheffield Phoenix).

Na'aman, N. (2013), 'Notes on the Temple "Restorations" of Jehoash and Josiah', *VT* 63: 640–51.

Neeb, J. H. C. (1992), 'Jacob/Jesus Typology in John 1:51', *Proceedings* 12: 83–9.

Neirynck, F. (1975), 'Jesus and the Sabbath: Some Observations on Mk II, 27', in J. Dupont (ed.), *Jésus aux origines de la christologie* (BETL 40; Louvain: Louvain University Press): 227–70.

Nepper-Christensen, P. (1985), 'Die Taufe im Matthäusevangelium', *NTS* 31: 189–207.

Netzer, E. (2003), 'A Third Candidate: Another Building at Banias', *BAR* 29: 25.

Newsom, C. A. (1985), *Songs of the Sabbath Sacrifice: A Critical Edition* (HSS 27; Atlanta: Scholars Press).

Nickelsburg, G. W. E., K. Baltzer and C. VanderKam (2001), *1 Enoch: A Commentary on the Book of 1 Enoch* (Hermeneia; Minneapolis: Fortress).

Nitzan, B. (2000), 'The Benedictions from Qumran for the Annual Covenantal Ceremony', in L. H. Schiffman et al. (eds), *Dead Sea Scrolls: Fifty Years after Their Discovery: Proceedings of the Jerusalem Congress, July 20–25, 1997* (Jerusalem: Israel Exploration Society, in collaboration with The Shrine of the Book, Israel Museum): 263–71.

Nolland, J. (1989), *Luke 1–9:20* (WBC 35A; Dallas: Word).

Nolland, J. (2005), *The Gospel of Matthew: A Commentary on the Greek Text* (NIGTC; Grand Rapids: Eerdmans; Bletchley: Paternoster).

Nordheim, M. von (2008), *Geboren von der Morgenröte? Psalm 110 in Tradition, Redaktion und Rezeption* (WMANT 117; Neukirchen-Vluyn: Neukirchener Verlag).

Novakovic, L. (2003), *Messiah, the Healer of the Sick: A Study of Jesus as the Son of David in the Gospel of Matthew* (WUNT 2/170; Tübingen: Mohr Siebeck).

O'Brien, K. S. (2010), *The Use of Scripture in the Markan Passion Narrative* (LNTS 384; London/New York: T. & T. Clark).

Olson, D. C. (2013), *A New Reading of the Animal Apocalypse of 1 Enoch: 'All Nations Shall Be Blessed'* (SVTP 24; Leiden: Brill).

O'Neill, J. C. (1969), 'The Silence of Jesus', *NTS* 15: 153–67.

O'Neill, J. C. (1993), 'The Kingdom of God', *NovT* 35: 130–41.

Orlov, A. A. (2004), 'The Face as the Heavenly Counterpart of the Visionary in the Slavonic Ladder of Jacob', in C. A. Evans (ed.), *Of Scribes and Sages: Early Jewish Interpretation and Transmission of Scripture* (LSTS 51; London: T. & T. Clark International): 59–76.

Overman, J. A., J. Olive and M. Nelson (2003), 'Discovering Herod's Shrine to Augustus: Mystery Temple Found at Omrit', *BAR* 29: 40.

Owen-Ball, D. T. (1993), 'Rabbinic Rhetoric and the Tribute Passage (Mt 22:15–22, Mk 12:13–17, Lk 20:20–26)', *NovT* 35: 1–14.

Pace, S. (2008), *Daniel* (Smith & Helwys Bible Commentary; Macon, GA: Smyth & Helwys).

Parke-Taylor, G. H. (1975), *Yahweh: The Divine Name in the Bible* (Waterloo: Laurier University Press).

Parsons, M. C. (1987), *The Departure of Jesus in Luke-Acts: The Ascension Narratives in Context* (JSNTSup 21; Sheffield: JSOT Press).

Pate, C. M., and D. W. Kennard (2003), *Deliverance Now and Not Yet: The New Testament and the Great Tribulation* (StudBL 54; New York: Peter Lang).

Peeler, A. L. B. (2014), *You Are My Son: The Family of God in the Epistle to the Hebrews* (LNTS 486; London/New York: Bloomsbury T. & T. Clark).

Percy, E. (1953), *Die Botschaft Jesu: Eine traditionskritische und exegetische Untersuchung* (Lund: C. W. K. Gleerup).

Perdue, L. G. (2000), *Proverbs* (IBC; Louisville, KY: John Knox).

Perrin, Nicholas (2010), *Jesus the Temple* (Grand Rapids: Baker Academic; London: SPCK).

Perrin, Nicholas (2013a), 'Exile', in J. Green and L. MacDonald (eds), *The World of the New Testament: An Examination of the Context of Early Christianity* (Grand Rapids: Baker Academic): 25–37.

Perrin, Nicholas (2013b), 'The Temple, a Davidic Messiah, and a Case of Mistaken Priestly Identity (Mark 2:26)', in D. M. Gurtner and B. J. Gladd (eds), *From Creation to New Creation: Biblical Theology and Exegesis: Essays in Honor of G. K. Beale* (Peabody, MA: Hendrickson): 163–77.

Perrin, Nicholas (2014), 'Sacraments and Sacramentality in the New Testament', in H. Boersma and M. Levering (eds), *The Oxford Handbook of Sacramental Theology* (New York: Oxford University Press): 52–67.

Perrin, Nicholas (2015), 'From One Stone to the Next: Messiahship and Temple in N. T. Wright's *Jesus and the Victory of God*', *JSHJ* 13: 255–75.

Perrin, Norman (1963), *The Kingdom of God in the Teaching of Jesus* (London: SCM).

Perrin, Norman (1967), *Rediscovering the Teaching of Jesus* (New York: Harper & Row).

Perrin, Norman (1974), *A Modern Pilgrimage in New Testament Christology* (Philadelphia: Fortress).

Perrin, Norman (1976), *Jesus and the Language of the Kingdom: Symbol and Metaphor in New Testament Interpretation* (Philadelphia: Fortress).

Pesch, R. (1976–80), *Das Markusevangelium* (2 vols; HTKNT; Freiburg: Herder).

Pfann, S. J. (2006), 'A Table Prepared in the Wilderness: Pantries and Tables, Pure Food and Sacred Space at Qumran', in K. Galor, J. Humbert and J. Zangenberg (eds), *Qumran, the Site of the Dead Sea Scrolls: Archaeological Interpretations and Debates* (STDJ 57; Leiden: Brill): 159–78.

Philipson, D., and K. Kohler (1902), 'Priestly Blessing', in I. Singer (ed.), *Jewish Encyclopedia: A Descriptive Record of the History, Religion, Literature, and Customs of the Jewish People from the Earliest Times to the Present Day: Vol. 3: Bencemero–Chazanuth* (New York/London: Funk and Wagnalls): 244–6.

Philonenko, M. (1960), *Les interpolations chrétiennes des Testaments des douze patriarches et les manuscrits de Qoumrân* (CRHP 35; Paris: PUF).

Pilch, J. J. (2011), 'Salt for the Earthen Oven Revisited', *HTS* 67: 91–5.

Piotrowski, N. (2016), *New David at the End of Exile: A Socio-Rhetorical Study of Matthew's Prologue-Quotations* (NovTSup 170; Leiden: Brill).

Pitre, B. (2005), *Jesus, the Tribulation, and the End of the Exile: Restoration Eschatology and the Origin of the Atonement* (WUNT 2/204; Tübingen: Mohr Siebeck; Grand Rapids: Baker Academic).

Pitre, B. (2008), 'Jesus, the New Temple and the New Priesthood', *LtSp* 4: 47–83.

Pitre, B. (2015), *Jesus and the Last Supper* (Grand Rapids: Eerdmans).

315

Pogoloff, S. M. (1992), *Logos and Sophia: The Rhetorical Situation of 1 Corinthians* (SBLDS 134; Atlanta: Scholars Press).

Polaski, D. C. (2004), '*Mene, Mene, Tekel, Parsin*: Writing and Resistance in Daniel 5 and 6', *JBL* 123: 649–69.

Pomykala, K. (1995), *The Davidic Dynasty Tradition in Early Judaism: Its History and Significance for Messianism* (SBLEJL 7; Atlanta: Scholars Press).

Popkes, W. (1990), 'Die letzte Bitte des Vater-Unser: Formgeschichtliche Beobachtungen zum Gebet', *ZNW* 81: 1–20.

Porter, P. A. (1983), *Metaphors and Monsters: A Literary-Critical Study of Daniel 7 and 8* (Lund: Gleerup).

Potterie, I. de la (1976), 'Chrétien conduit par l'Esprit dans son cheminement eschatologique (Rom 8:14)', in L. De Lorenzi (ed.), *The Law of the Spirit in Rom 7 and 8* (Rome: St Paul's Abbey).

Preuss, H. D. (1996 (1992)), *Old Testament Theology: Vol. 2* (OTL; Louisville: Westminster John Knox).

Price, S. R. F. (1984), *Rituals and Power: The Roman Imperial Cult in Asia Minor* (Cambridge/New York: Cambridge University Press).

Provan, I. W. (1999), 'To Highlight All Our Idols: Worshipping God in Nietzsche's World', *ExAud* 15: 19–38.

Przybylski, B. (1980), *Righteousness in Matthew and His World of Thought* (SNTSMS 41; Cambridge/New York: Cambridge University Press).

Rad, G. von (1966 (1958)), *The Problem of the Hexateuch: And Other Essays* (Edinburgh/London: Oliver & Boyd).

Rad, G. von (2001 (1962)), *Old Testament Theology: Vol. 1* (Louisville, KY: Westminster John Knox).

Ramaroson, L. (1988), '"Parole-semence" ou "Peuple-semence" dans la parabole du Semeur', *ScEs* 40: 91–101.

Rauschenbusch, W. (1987 (1917)), *A Theology for the Social Gospel* (Nashville: Abingdon).

Reed, J. L. (2006), 'Archaeological Contributions to the Study of Jesus and the Gospels', in A.-J. Levine, D. C. Allison Jr and J. D. Crossan (eds), *The Historical Jesus in Context* (Princeton, NJ: Princeton University Press): 40–54.

Regev, E. (2013), *The Hasmoneans: Ideology, Archaeology, Identity* (JAJSup 10; Göttingen: Vandenhoeck & Ruprecht).

Repschinski, B. (2000), *The Controversy Stories in the Gospel of Matthew: Their Redaction, Form and Relevance for the Relationship between the Matthean Community and Formative Judaism* (FRLANT 189; Göttingen: Vandenhoeck & Ruprecht).

Ridderbos, H. N. (1962), *The Coming of the Kingdom* (Philadelphia: Presbyterian & Reformed).

Rieske, S. (2012), 'Yahweh the Sadist? An Examination of God's Delight in Destroying Israel in Deuteronomy 28:63', Evangelical Theological Society Annual Meeting, Milwaukee, WI.

Riesner, R. (1981), *Jesus als Lehrer: Eine Untersuchung zum Ursprung der Evangelien-Überlieferung* (WUNT 2/7; Tübingen: Mohr Siebeck).

Rindge, M. S. (2012), 'Reconfiguring the Akedah and Recasting God: Lament and Divine Abandonment in Mark', *JBL* 131: 755–74.

Robbins, V. K. (1973), 'Healing of Blind Bartimaeus (10:46–52) in the Marcan Theology', *JBL* 92: 224–43.

Roberts, J. J. M. (1973), 'Davidic Origin of the Zion Tradition', *JBL* 92: 329–44.

Roberts, J. J. M. (2002), *The Bible and the Ancient Near East: Collected Essays* (Winona Lake, IN: Eisenbrauns).

Robinson, J. M. (1975), 'Jesus as Sophos and Sophia: Wisdom Tradition and the Gospels', in R. L. Wilken (ed.), *Aspects of Wisdom in Judaism and Early Christianity* (SJCA 1; Notre Dame, IN: University of Notre Dame Press): 1–16.

Robinson, J. M., P. Hoffmann and J. S. Kloppenborg (2000), *The Critical Edition of Q: Synopsis Including the Gospels of Matthew and Luke, Mark and Thomas with English, German, and French Translations of Q and Thomas* (Hermeneia; Louvain: Peeters; Minneapolis: Fortress).

Rodríguez, R. (2009): 'Authenticating Criteria: The Use and Misuse of a Critical Method', *JSHJ* 7: 152–67.

Rogers, A. D. (1951), 'Mark 2.26', *JTS* 2: 44–5.

Roloff, J. (1970), *Das Kerygma und der irdische Jesus: Historische Motive in den Jesus-Erzählungen der Evangelien* (Göttingen: Vandenhoeck & Ruprecht).

Romerowski, S. (1986), 'Les règnes de David et de Salomon dans les Chroniques', *Hokmah* 31: 1–23.

Rooke, D. W. (1998), 'Kingship as Priesthood: The Relationship between the High Priesthood and the Monarchy', in J. Day (ed.), *King and Messiah in Israel and the Ancient Near East: Proceedings of the Oxford Old Testament Seminar* (Sheffield: Sheffield University Press): 187–208.

Rordorf, W. (1968), *Sunday: The History of the Day of Rest and Worship in the Earliest Centuries of the Christian Church* (London: SCM Press).

Rosenberg, R. A. (1965), 'Jesus, Isaac, and the Suffering Servant', *JBL* 84: 381–8.

Roure, D. (1990), *Jesús y la figura de David en Mc 2,23–26: Trasfondo bíblico, intertestamentario y rabínico* (AnBib 124; Rome: Pontificio Istituto Biblico).

Rowe, R. D. (2002), *God's Kingdom and God's Son: The Background in Mark's Christology from Concepts of Kingship in the Psalms* (AGJU 50; Leiden/Boston: Brill).

Rowland, C. (1984), 'John 1:51, Jewish Apocalyptic and Targumic Tradition', *NTS* 30: 498–507.

Ruiten, J. van (1999), 'Visions of the Temple in the Book of Jubilees', in B. Ego and A. Lange (eds), *Gemeinde ohne Tempel: Zur Substituierung und Transformation des Jerusalemer Tempels und seines Kults im Alten Testment, antiken Judentum und frühen Christentum* (WUNT 118; Tübingen: Mohr Siebeck): 215–27.

Ruiten, J. van (2012), *Abraham in the Book of Jubilees: The Rewriting of Genesis 11:26–25:10 in the Book of Jubilees 11:14–23:8* (JSJSup 161; Leiden/Boston: Brill).

Saebø, M. (1980), 'Messianism in Chronicles: Some Remarks to the Old Testament Background of the New Testament Christology', *HBT* 2: 85–109.

Sahlin, H. (1945), *Der Messias und das Gottesvolk: Studien zur protolukanischen Theologie* (ASNU 12; Uppsala: Almqvist & Wiksell).

Sanders, E. P. (1977), *Paul and Palestinian Judaism: A Comparison of Patterns of Religion* (Philadelphia: Fortress).

Sanders, E. P. (1983), 'Jesus and the Constraint of Law', *JSNT* 17: 19–24.

Sanders, E. P. (1985), *Jesus and Judaism* (Philadelphia: Fortress).

Sanders, J. T. (1998), 'The Criterion of Coherence and the Randomness of Charisma: Poring through Some Aporias in the Jesus Tradition', *NTS* 44:1–25.

Sandgren, L. D. (2003), *The Shadow of God: Stories from Early Judaism* (Peabody, MA: Hendrickson).

Sarna, N. M. (1962), 'Psalm for the Sabbath Day (Ps 92)', *JBL* 81: 155–68.

Scattolon, A. (1978), 'ΛʼΑΓΑΠΗΤΟΣ sinnotteco milla luce della traditione giudaica', *RivB* 26: 2–32.

Schmidt, T. E. (1995), 'Mark 15:16–32: The Crucifixion Narrative and the Roman Triumphal Procession', *NTS* 41:1–18.

Schmithals, W. (1971), *Gnosticism in Corinth: An Investigation of the Letters to the Corinthians* (Nashville: Abingdon).

Schnackenburg, R. (1963), *God's Rule and Kingdom* (Freiburg: Herder; Edinburgh/ London: Nelson).

Schnackenburg, R. (1964), 'Ihr seid das Salz der Erde, das Licht der Welt: Zu Matthäus 5,13–16', in P. Hennequin (ed.), *Melanges Eugène Tisserant* (Città del Vaticano: Biblioteca Apostolica Vaticana): 365–87.

Schnackenburg, R. (1965), *The Moral Teaching of the New Testament* (New York: Herder and Herder).

Schnackenburg, R. (2002), *The Gospel of Matthew* (Grand Rapids: Eerdmans).

Schottroff, L., and L. M. Maloney (2006), *The Parables of Jesus* (Minneapolis: Augsburg Fortress).

Schottroff, L., and W. Stegemann (1984), 'The Sabbath Was Made for Man: The Interpretation of Mark 2:23–28', in W. Schottroff and W. Stegemann (eds), *God of the Lowly: Socio-Historical Interpretations of the Bible* (Maryknoll, NY: Orbis Books): 118–28.

Schröter, J. (2014 (2012)), *Jesus of Nazareth: Jew from Galilee, Savior of the World* (Waco: Baylor University Press).

Schüngel-Straumann, H. (2000), *Tobit* (HTKAT; Freiburg: Herder).

Schürmann, H. (1981), *Das Gebet des Herrn: Als Schlüssel zum Verstehen Jesu* (Freiburg: Herder).

Schüssler Fiorenza, E. (1972), *Priester für Gott: Studien zum Herrschafts- und Priestermotiv in der Apokalypse* (NTAbh 7; Münster: Aschendorff).

Schüssler Fiorenza, E. (1994), *In Memory of Her: A Feminist Theological Reconstruction of Christian Origins*. New York: Crossroad.

Schwartz, J. (1985), 'Jubilees, Bethel and the Temple of Jacob', *HUCA* 56: 63–85.

Schweitzer, A. (2001 (1906)), *The Quest of the Historical Jesus* (Minneapolis: Fortress).

Schweizer, E. (1970), *The Good News According to Mark* (Richmond, VA: John Knox).

Segal, A. F. (1977), *Two Powers in Heaven: Early Rabbinic Reports about Christianity and Gnosticism* (SJLA 25; Leiden: Brill).

Segal, A. F. (1996), 'The Akedah: Some Reconsiderations', in P. Schäfer (ed.), *Geschichte – Tradition – Reflexion: Festschrift für Martin Hengel zum 70. Geburtstag: Vol. 1* (Tübingen: Mohr Siebeck): 99–116.

Selman, M. J. (1989), 'The Kingdom of God in the Old Testament', *TynBul* 40: 161–83.

Sherwin-White, A. N. (1963), *Roman Society and Roman Law in the New Testament* (Sarum Lectures; Oxford: Clarendon Press).

Shillington, V. G. (2001), 'Salt of the Earth? (Mt 5:13/Lk 14:34f)', *ExpTim* 112: 120–1.

Signer, M. A. (1983), 'King/messiah: Rashi's Exegesis of Psalm 2', *Proof* 3: 273–8.

Smith, B. D. (2009), *Jesus' Twofold Teaching about the Kingdom of God* (NTM 24; Sheffield: Sheffield Phoenix).

Smith, D. E. (2003), *From Symposium to Eucharist: The Banquet in the Early Christian World* (Minneapolis: Fortress).

Smith, D. M. (1963), 'John 12:12ff and the Question of John's Use of the Synoptics', *JBL* 82: 58–64.

Smith, M. H. (1988), 'No Place for a Son of Man', *Forum* 4: 83–107.

Smith, S. H. (1996), 'The Function of the Son of David Tradition in Mark's Gospel', *NTS* 42: 523–39.

Snodgrass, K. R. (1980), 'Streams of Tradition Emerging from Isaiah 40:1–5 and Their Adaptation in the New Testament', *JSNT* 2: 24–45.

Souček, J. B. (1963), 'Salz der Erde und Licht der Welt: Zur Exegese von Matth 5:13–16', *TZ* 19: 169–79.

Stark, R. (1997), *The Rise of Christianity: How the Obscure, Marginal Jesus Movement Became the Dominant Religious Force in the Western World in a Few Centuries* (San Francisco: HarperSanFrancisco).

Stauffer, E. (1960), *Jesus and His Story* (New York: Knopf).

Stegner, W. R. (1984), 'The Baptism of Jesus and the Binding of Isaac', in H. O. Thompson and L. E. Toombs (eds), *The Answers Lie Below: Essays in Honor of Lawrence Edmund Toombs* (Lanham, MD: University Press of America): 331-47.

Steichele, H.-J. (1980), *Der leidende Sohn Gottes* (BU 14; Regensburg: Pustet).

Stein, V. A. (2006), *Anti-Cultic Theology in Christian Biblical Interpretation: A Study of Isaiah 66:1–4 and Its Reception* (SBL 97; New York: Peter Lang).

Stökl Ben Ezra, D. (2003), *The Impact of Yom Kippur on Early Christianity: The Day of Atonement from Second Temple Judaism to the Fifth Century* (WUNT 163; Tübingen: Mohr Siebeck).

Strauss, D. F. (1972 (1835)), *The Life of Jesus Critically Examined* (Lives of Jesus Series; Philadelphia: Fortress).

Strauss, M. L. (1995), *The Davidic Messiah in Luke-Acts: The Promise and Its Fulfillment in Lukan Christology* (JSNTSup 110; Sheffield: Sheffield Academic Press).

Stuart, D. K. (2006), *Exodus* (NAC 2; Nashville: Broadman & Holman).

Stuhlmacher, P. (1993), 'Der Messianische Gottesknecht', in I. Baldermann, E. Dassmann, O. Fuchs and B. Hamm (eds), *Der Messias* (JBTh; Neukirchen-Vluyn: Neukirchener Verlag): 131–54.

Suhl, A. (1968), 'Der Davidssohn im Matthäus-Evangelium', *ZNW* 59: 57–81.

Sung, C. (1993), *Vergebung der Sünden: Jesu Praxis der Sündenvergebung nach den Synoptikern und ihre Voraussetzungen im Alten Testament und frühen Judentum* (WUNT 2/57; Tübingen: Mohr Siebeck).

Swarup, P. (2006), *The Self-Understanding of the Dead Sea Scrolls Community: An Eternal Planting, a House of Holiness* (LSTS 59; London/New York: T. & T. Clark).

Sweeney, M. A. (2005), *Form and Intertextuality in Prophetic and Apocalyptic Literature* (FAT 45; Tübingen: Mohr Siebeck).

Swetnam, J. (1972), 'Hallowed Be Thy Name', *Bib* 52: 556–63.

Swetnam, J. (1981), *Jesus and Isaac: A Study of the Epistle to the Hebrews in the Light of the Aqedah* (AnBib 94; Rome: Biblical Institute Press).

Tan, K. H. (1997), *The Zion Traditions and the Aims of Jesus* (SNTSMS 91; Cambridge/New York: Cambridge University Press).

Tannehill, R. C. (1991 (1986)), *The Narrative Unity of Luke-Acts: A Literary Interpretation* (Philadelphia: Fortress).

Tatum, W. B. (1994), *John the Baptist and Jesus: A Report of the Jesus Seminar* (Sonoma, CA: Polebridge).

Taylor, J. E. (1997), *The Immerser: John the Baptist within Second Temple Judaism* (SHJ; Grand Rapids: Eerdmans).

Taylor, V. (1966), *The Gospel According to St. Mark* (London: Macmillan; New York: St Martin's).

Theissen, G., and A. Merz (1998), *The Historical Jesus: A Comprehensive Guide* (Minneapolis: Fortress).

Thiselton, A. C. (2000), *The First Epistle to the Corinthians* (NIGTC; Grand Rapids: Eerdmans; Carlisle: Paternoster).

Thompson, M. M. (2000), *The Promise of the Father: Jesus and God in the New Testament* (Louisville, KY: Westminster John Knox).

Throntveit, M. A. (2003), 'The Relationship of Hezekiah to David and Solomon in the Books of Chronicles', in M. P. Graham, S. L. McKenzie and G. N. Knoppers (eds), *Chronicler as Theologian: Essays in Honor of Ralph W. Klein* (London: T. & T. Clark): 105–21.

Tiller, P. A. (1993), *A Commentary on the Animal Apocalypse of I Enoch* (SBLEJL 4; Atlanta: Scholars Press).

Tiller, P. A. (1997), 'The "Eternal Planting" in the Dead Sea Scrolls', *DSD* 4: 312–35.

Tilly, M. (1994), *Johannes der Täufer und die Biographie der Propheten: Die synoptische Täuferüberlieferung und das jüdische Prophetenbild zur Zeit des Täufers* (BWANT 17; Stuttgart: Kohlhammer).

Tödt, H. E. (1965 (1959)), *The Son of Man in the Synoptic Tradition* (Philadelphia: Westminster).

Tolbert, M. A. (1989), *Sowing the Gospel: Mark's World in Literary-Historical Perspective* (Minneapolis: Fortress).

Torijano, P. (2002), *Solomon the Esoteric King: From King to Magus: Development of a Tradition* (JSJSup 73; Leiden/Boston: Brill).

Towner, W. S. (1969), 'Poetic Passages of Daniel 1–6', *CBQ* 31: 317–26.

Tuckett, C. M. (1996), *Q and the History of Early Christianity: Studies on Q* (Edinburgh: T. & T. Clark).

Tuckett, C. M. (2014), 'Christ and the Emperor: Some Reflections on Method and Methodological Issues Illustrated from the Gospel of Mark', in G. van Belle and J. Verheyden (eds), *Christ and the Emperor: The Gospel Evidence* (BTS 20; Leuven: Peeters): 185–201.

Turner, C. H. (1926), 'Ο ΥΙΟΣ ΜΟΥ ΑΓΑΠΗΤΟΣ', *JTS* 27: 113–29.

Udoh, F. E. (2005), *To Caesar What Is Caesar's : Tribute, Taxes and Imperial Administration in Early Roman Palestine (63 B.C.E.–70 C.E.)* (BJS 343; Providence, RI: Brown University Press).

Vaage, L. E. (1994), *Galilean Upstarts: Jesus' First Followers According to Q* (Valley Forge, Pa: Trinity Press International).

Van Egmond, R. (2006), 'The Messianic "Son of David" in Matthew', *JGRChJ* 3: 41–71.

VanderKam, J. C. (1997a), 'The Aqedah, Jubilees, and Pseudo-Jubilees', in C. A. Evans (ed.), *The Quest for Context and Meaning: Studies in Biblical Intertextuality in Honor of James A. Sanders* (BIS 28; Leiden: Brill): 241–61.

VanderKam, J. C. (1997b), 'Exile in Jewish Apocalyptic Literature', in J. M. Scott (ed.), *Exile: Old Testament, Jewish, and Christian Conceptions* (JSJSup 56; Leiden: Brill): 89–109.

VanderKam, J. C. (1997c), 'From Patriarch to Priest: The Levi-Priestly Tradition from Aramaic Levi to Testament of Levi', *JSP* 16: 128.

VanderKam, J. C. (2004), *From Joshua to Caiaphas : High Priests after the Exile* (Minneapolis: Fortress).

Vattamány, G. (2013), 'Kann das Salz verderben? Philologische Erwägungen zum Salz-Gleichnis Jesu', *NTS* 59: 142–9.

Vaux, R. de (1961), *Ancient Israel: Its Life and Institutions* (New York: McGraw-Hill).

Vermes, G. (1973), *Jesus the Jew: A Historian's Reading of the Gospels* (New York: Macmillan).

Vermes, G. (1973 (1961)), *Scripture and Tradition in Judaism: Haggadic Studies* (SPB 4; Leiden: Brill).

Vielhauer, P. (1979 (1965)), *Aufsätze zum Neuen Testament* (Munich: Chr. Kaiser).

Vines, M. E. (2006), 'The "Trial Scene" Chronotope in Mark and the Jewish Novel', in G. van Oyen and T. Shepherd (eds), *Trial and Death of Jesus: Essays on the Passion Narrative in Mark* (Leuven: Peeters): 189–203.

Vogel, W. (2010), *The Cultic Motif in the Book of Daniel* (New York: Lang).

Vögtle, A. (1972), 'Die sogenannte Taufperikope Mk 1,9–11: Zur Problematik der Herkunft und des ursprünglichen Sinnes', in P. Stuhlmacher (ed.), *Evangelisch-Katholischer Kommentar zum Neuen Testament: Vorarbeiten Heft 4* (Neukirchen/Zurich: Neukirchener Verlag; Einsiedeln: Benziger): 105–39.

Völkl, R. (1961), *Christ und Welt nach dem Neuen Testament* (Würzburg: Echter-Verlag).

Walker Jr, W. O. (1972), 'Origin of the Son of Man Concept as Applied to Jesus', *JBL* 91: 482–90.

Walker Jr, W. O. (1983), 'The Son of Man: Some Recent Developments', *CBQ* 45: 584–607.

Walton, J. H. (2001), 'The Anzu Myth as Relevant Background for Daniel 7?', in J. J. Collins and P. W. Flint (eds), *The Book of Daniel: Composition and Reception* (VTSup 83; Leiden: Brill): 69–89.

Warschauer, J. (1927), *The Historical Life of Christ* (London: Unwin).

Watts, J. W. (1992), *Psalm and Story: Inset Hymns in Hebrew Narrative* (JSOTSup 135; Sheffield: JSOT Press).

Watts, R. (2007), 'The Lord's House and David's Lord: The Psalms and Mark's Perspective on Jesus and the Temple', *BibInt* 15: 307–22.

Webb, R. L. (1991), *John the Baptizer and Prophet: A Socio-Historical Study* (JSNTSup 62; Sheffield: JSOT Press).

Webb, R. L. (1994), 'John the Baptist and His Relationship to Jesus', in Bruce D. Chilton and Craig A. Evans (eds), *Studying the Historical Jesus: Evaluations of the State of Current Research* (Leiden: Brill): 179–229.

Webb, R. L. (2009), 'Jesus' Baptism by John: Its Historicity and Significance', in D. L. Bock and R. L. Webb (eds), *Key Events in the Life of the Historical Jesus: A Collaborative Exploration of Content and Coherence* (WUNT 247; Tübingen: Mohr Siebeck): 95–150.

Wedderburn, A. J. M. (2010), *Jesus and the Historians* (WUNT 269; Tübingen: Mohr Siebeck).

Weder, H. (1990), *Die Gleichnisse Jesu als Metaphern: Traditions- und redaktionsgeschicht-liche Analysen und Interpretationen* (Göttingen: Vandenhoeck und Ruprecht).

Weiss, J. (1971 (1892)), *Jesus' Proclamation of the Kingdom of God* (Minneapolis: Fortress).

Weitzman, S. (1996), 'Allusion, Artifice, and Exile in the Hymn of Tobit', *JBL* 115: 49–61.

Welch, J. W. (2009), *The Sermon on the Mount in the Light of the Temple* (SOTMS; Farnham/Burlington, VT: Ashgate).

Wellhausen, J. (1909 (1903)), *Das Evangelium Marci* (Berlin: Reimer).

Wenham, G. J. (1975), 'Were David's Sons Priests?', *ZAW* 87: 79–82.

Wenham, G. J. (1979), *The Book of Leviticus* (NICOT; Grand Rapids: Eerdmans).

Wenham, J. W. (1950), 'Mark 2.26', *JTS* 1: 156.

West, C. (2012), 'Power and Freedom in Jane Austen's Novels', *Persuasion* 34: 111–18.

Wevers, J. W. (1992), *Text History of the Greek Exodus* (MSU 21; Göttingen: Vandenhoek & Ruprecht).

Wevers, J. W. (1997), *Notes on the Greek Text of Leviticus* (SCS 44; Atlanta: Scholars Press).

Whitelam, K. (1992), 'Abiathar', in D. N. Freedman (ed.), *The Anchor Bible Dictionary: Vol. 1: A–C* (New York: Doubleday): 13–14.

Whitsett, C. G. (2000), 'Son of God, Seed of David: Paul's Messianic Exegesis in Romans 1:3–4', *JBL* 119: 661–81.

Williams, H. H. D. (2001), *The Wisdom of the Wise: The Presence and Function of Scripture within 1 Cor 1:18–3:23* (AGJU 49; Leiden: Brill).

Williamson, H. G. M. (1982), *1 and 2 Chronicles* (Grand Rapids: Eerdmans; London: Marshall, Morgan & Scott).

Willis, W. L. (1987), *The Kingdom of God in 20th-Century Interpretation* (Peabody, MA: Hendrickson).

Wilson, W. T. (2015), 'Works of Wisdom (Matt 9,9–17; 11, 16–19)', *ZNW* 106: 1–20.

Winn, A. (2008), *The Purpose of Mark's Gospel: An Early Christian Response to Roman Imperial Propaganda* (WUNT 2/245; Tübingen: Mohr Siebeck).

Winter, B. W. (1997), *Philo and Paul among the Sophists* (SNTSMS 96; Cambridge: Cambridge University Press).

Winter, P. (1961), *On the Trial of Jesus* (SJ 1; Berlin: de Gruyter).

Wintermute, O. S. (1985), 'Jubilees: A New Translation and Introduction', in J. H. Charlesworth (ed.), *The Old Testament Pseudepigrapha: Vol. 2: Expansion of the 'Old Testament' and Legends, Wisdom, and Philosophical Literature, Prayers, Psalms and Odes, Fragments of Lost Judeo-Hellenistic Works* (ABRL; New York: Doubleday): 35–142.

Wise, M. O. (2005), '4Q245 (PsDan‘ Ar) and the High Priesthood of Judas Maccabaeus', *DSD* 12: 313–62.

Witherington, B. (1994), *Jesus the Sage: The Pilgrimage of Wisdom* (Minneapolis: Fortress).

Wright, N. T. (1996), *Christian Origins and the Question of God: Vol. 2: Jesus and the Victory of God* (London: SPCK; Minneapolis: Fortress).

Wright, N. T. (2012), *How God Became King: The Forgotten Story of the Gospels* (New York: HarperOne).

Wright, N. T. (2013), *Christian Origins and the Question of God: Vol. 4: Paul and the Faithfulness of God* (London: SPCK; Minneapolis: Fortress).

Wu, S. F. (2015), *Suffering in Romans* (Eugene, OR: Pickwick).

Yang, Y. E. (1997), *Jesus and the Sabbath in Matthew's Gospel* (JSNTSup 139; Sheffield: Sheffield Academic Press).

Zanker, P. (1988), *The Power of Images in the Age of Augustus* (Jerome Lectures 16; Ann Arbor: University of Michigan Press).

Zehnder, M. (2014), 'Why the Danielic "Son of Man" Is a Divine Being', *BBR* 24: 331–47.

Zeller, D. (1977), 'Die Bildlogik des Gleichnisses Mt 11:16f/Lk 7:31f', *ZNW* 68: 252–7.

Zimmerli, W., F. M. Cross, F. Moore and K. Baltzer (1979), *Ezekiel: A Commentary on the Book of the Prophet Ezekiel* (Hermeneia; Philadelphia: Fortress).

Zimmerli, W., and J. Jeremias (1957), *The Servant of God* (SBT 20; Naperville, IL: Allenson).

Zwiep, A. W. (1997), *The Ascension of the Messiah in Lukan Christology* (NovTSup 87; Leiden/New York: Brill).

Index of ancient and biblical sources

OLD TESTAMENT

Genesis
1 173, 206, 283
1.26 172, 210
1.26–27 212, 248,
    250
1.28 41
1.29 206
1.35 41 n. 73
3 206
3.19 206
12.3 99 n. 29
12.7 102 n. 45
13.15–16 102 n. 45
14 160, 181
14.18–20 162
15.3 102 n. 45
15.11 105
15.13 102 n. 45
16.10 102 n. 45
17.4 99 n. 29
17.7 102 n. 45
17.8 102 n. 45
17.9 102 n. 45
17.10 102 n. 45
17.12 102 n. 45
18.18 99 n. 29
18.22–33 49
22 69, 70, 73–76,
    77, 78–9,
    88 n. 124, 89
22.1 79 n. 84
22.2 69, 70,
    78 n. 81, 86, 88
22.2a 69
22.3 78 n. 82
22.5 79
22.7a 79
22.10 83
22.11 69, 78,
    86 n. 115
22.12 69
22.14 75, 86
22.15 69
22.16 69, 78
22.18 78 n. 83
26.12 104
28 214, 216
28.7 214

28.10–22 217, 213,
    214, 215
28.11 213
28.12 213,
    216 n. 80
28.22 215
29.1–12 217 n. 83
41.46 85

Exodus
3.8 108
4.21–23 36, 66
4.22–23 14, 69, 70
5.8 29
9.16 32 n. 40
12 47
12.29 31
12.42 31, 74 n. 65
13.1 51
13.14–16 38
15.7 34
15.17 37
15.17–18 71 n. 50,
    101 n. 41, 143
16 47
16.5 48
16.10 34
19.5 37
19.6 14, 37, 75, 175
19.10 39 n. 62
19.14 39 n. 62
22.27 276
22.28 80
23.33 37
24 38, 78
24.8 31
24.9–11 201 n. 30
24.11 47, 47 n. 99
24.16 34
25—31 173
25.23–30 201 n. 29
28.1 176
28.4 153
28.43 155 n. 59
29.4 155 n. 59,
    176 n. 35
29.8 155 n. 59,
    176 n. 35
29.10 177 n. 36
30.20 155 n. 59

30.35 112
31 205
31.13 39 n. 63
32.7–14 49
32.11–14 154
32.21–24 154
34.6 185
40.1–11 39 n. 62
40.12 155 n. 59,
    176 n. 35
40.14 155 n. 59,
    176 n. 35

Leviticus
1.2 177 n. 36
1.3 177 n. 36
1.10 177 n. 36
2.13 112, 118, 125
2.13a 125
2.13b 125
3.1 177 n. 36
3.6 155 n. 59
7.35 155 n. 59
8.6 76, 155 n. 59
8.13 176 n. 35,
    155 n. 59
8.24 155 n. 59
8.30 76
10.3 40 n. 68, 44
11 172 n. 17
11.44 39 n. 63
16 178
16.1–13 177–8
16.2 175
16.11–13 175
19.18 219
19.18b 218, 220
21.22–23 155 n. 59
22.32 40 n. 68
23.5–9 201 n. 29
23.6 74 n. 67
24.5–9 201
24.9 204, 205
24.10–23 276
25.9–10 133

Numbers
1.51 153
3.6–8 153
3.14–38 153

4.1–8 201 n. 29
4.1–33 153
4.3 84 n. 107,
    85 n. 110
4.7 48 n. 100
4.23 85 n. 110
4.30 85 n. 110
4.35 85 n. 110
4.39 85 n. 110
4.40 85 n. 110
4.43 85 n. 110
4.47 85 n. 110, 153
6.22–27 153
6.23–26 133
6.23–29 132
6.24–26 135
6.27 134
8.5–13 42 n. 75
8.8 117
8.8–19 117
8.9 155 n. 59
8.24 85
14.7 108
15.30–31 276
18.19 112, 117, 125
28.17 74 n. 67

Deuteronomy
1.25 108 n. 74
1.35 108 n. 74
3.25 108 n. 74
4.21 108 n. 74
4.22 108 n. 74
4.34 31, 32 n. 40
4.37 32 n. 40
6.4–5 218, 219, 220
6.18 108 n. 74
7.19 31
8.7 108 n. 74
8.10 108 n. 74
9.6 108 n. 74
10.8 132, 153
11.17 108 n. 74
12.5 134 n. 154
12.11 134 n. 154
14 172 n. 17
14.23–24 134 n. 154
16.2 134 n. 154
16.6 134 n. 154
16.11 134 n. 154

21.5 132, 153
26.2 134 n. 154
26.5 218
26.8 32 n. 40
27.6 170
28—33 136
29.2 31
32 32, 32 n. 41, 33
32.6 32
32.36 44 n. 83
33.3 180 n. 44
34.12 32 n. 40

Joshua
8.31 170
23.13 108 n. 74
23.16 108 n. 74

Judges
7.3 121
7.4–23 121
15.4 210 n. 62

1 Samuel 144
1 198
1—2 196, 198
1.3 198 n. 21
1.25 177
2.20 132
2.30–36 198 n. 22
4.4 45 n. 89, 171,
    279 n. 108
12.16–25 185
14.3 198 n. 21
16 164, 196
17 196
18—20 196
21 196, 197
21.1 197 n. 15
21.1–6 192, 193
21.1–9 197
21.3–6 153
22.11 198 n. 21
22.14 153
22.20 197

2 Samuel 144
5.4 85
6 157, 162
6.13 153
6.14 153
6.17 153
6.18 153
7 71, 157, 161, 162
7.8–16 144
7.11 71 n. 50

7.11–16 118
7.12 164
7.12–14 71 n. 50
12.13 185
22.20 68
24.17–18 154
24.25 154

1 Kings
1—2 157
1.19 198 n. 23
1.32–40 198 n. 24
1.38 149
1.7 198 n. 23
2.27 198 n. 25,
    198 n. 26
6.2 168
6.6 168
8 157, 162
8.1–6 187
8.1–11 154
8.10–11 175 n. 29
8.14 155
8.5 155
8.62 155
8.64 39 n. 62, 155
9.3 39 n. 62,
    42 n. 79
9.7 42 n. 79
12 162

2 Kings
2.19–23 112
19.15 45 n. 89, 171,
    279 n. 108
23.15–20 158
23.26–30 159 n. 72
23.29–30 158

1 Chronicles 155
3.16–19 155
9.32 201 n. 29
13 164
13.2–3 153
13.6 45 n. 89, 171,
    279 n. 108
13.9–14 153
15.3–14 153
16.1–41 153–4
16.31 45 n. 88
23.13 39 n. 62
23.21 85
23.27 85
23.29 201 n. 29
23.3 85 n. 110
29.10 23

2 Chronicles 155
3.1 73, 154
5—7 155
5.13–14 175 n. 29
7.16 42 n. 79
7.20 42 n. 79
13.5 118, 125
13.8–12a 118
29—30 158
29.11 158
30.1 158
30.26 158
30.3 158
30.5 158
31.8 158
35.22–25 158

Ezra
1—6 172 n. 19
3.8 85
4.14 125
6.3 168
9.2 94 n. 9

Nehemiah
3.25 210 n. 62
9.13 101 n. 43

Job
6.6 112

Psalms
1 70
1.1 71 n. 50
1.1–3 105
2 68, 70–3, 76, 77,
    80, 87–8, 89, 90,
    164
2.1 71
2.2 80
2.6 70
2.7 68, 70, 76, 80,
    87 n. 121, 88
2.8 87 n. 123
2.9 70 n. 51
2.10–12 70
6 29 n. 30
8 172, 173, 212,
    212–13
8.4 184 n. 51
8.5 212
8.9 212
10.16 45 n. 88
12.5 138
13 29 n. 30
14.6 138

16.3 180 n. 44
18.50 144
19 29 n. 30
21 145 n. 5
21.3 29 n. 30
22.1 196
22.24 138
25 29 n. 30
29 29 n. 30
34.9 180 n. 44
36.11 130
37.14 138
40 145 n. 5
41—42 145 n. 5
43.3 115 n. 95
68 145 n. 5
69.9 146 n. 16
74.2 37
78.70–72 144
79.2 37
80.1 45 n. 89,
    115 n. 95, 171,
    279 n. 108
80.17 184 n. 51
89 161, 182
89.3–4 144
89.9–10 182
89.20–37 144
89.23 71 n. 50
89.25 182
89.49–51 144
93.1 45 n. 88
96.10 45 n. 88
97.1 45 n. 88
99.1 45 n. 88,
    45 n. 89, 171,
    279 n. 108
99.6 39 n. 62,
    78 n. 79
103 186, 188
103.3 186
103.12 185
103.19 171, 186,
    186 n. 65
109 160–61
109.1–2 161
109.4 161
110 80, 87, 145,
    151–52, 160–64,
    270, 271, 274,
    277, 279
110.1 271
110.1–2 151, 161
110.4 151, 161
110.5–6 151
113—118 149

118 149, 150,
  196 n. 14
118.19 152
118.22–23 196
118.27 152
132.1–5 144
132.10–18 144
132.17 115 n. 95
144.10 144
147 48 n. 101

Proverbs
8—9 235
9 235
9.1–6 235

Canticles
2.15 210 n. 62

Isaiah
1 96
1.4 95
1.9 94 n. 9
1.30 105 n. 63
3.14–15 138
5 95, 121
5.6 106
5.7 106
6.9–10 96 n. 17
6.13 94 n. 9,
  95 n. 13
7.1—9.6 97 n. 21
8.11 71 n. 50
9.17 106
9.18 106
10.2 138
10.17 106
11 157 n. 67
11.4 138
11.9 37
13.5 97 n. 21
14.20 95
15.6 105 n. 63
17.10 95
21.1–4 97 n. 21
24.4 105 n. 63
25 47, 76
25.4 138
25.6–8 47 n. 97
26.6 138
26.7 105
26.12–18 97 n. 21
27 107
27.2–4 106
27.13 37
29.18 226 n. 101,

225 n. 101, 229
29.22–24 40
29.23 40
31.9 94 n. 9
32.7 138
33.9 105 n. 63
33.17–24 186 n. 65
34.4 105 n. 63
35.5–6 226 n. 101,
  225 n. 101, 229
37.3 97 n. 21
37.16 45 n. 89, 171,
  279 n. 108
37.31–32 94 n. 9
40 57
40.1–3 57 n. 10
40.3 57 n. 10, 105
40.7 105 n. 63
40.8 105 n. 63
40.24 105 n. 63
41.8 95
42 69
42.1 68, 69, 70, 83
42.14 97
42.18 225 n. 101,
  226 n. 101, 229
43.5 94 n. 9
44.3 94 n. 9
45.19 95
45.26 94 n. 9
51.3 95
53.6 185
53.10 94 n. 9
54.1 97
54.3 94 n. 9
54.11 138
55 96, 97, 110
55.1–3 144
55.6–13 95
56.7 37
58.7 138
59.21 42 n. 78
60.1–3 115
60.19–20 116
60.21 94 n. 9
61 108, 110,
  129–31, 136, 138
61.1 42 n. 78,
  76 n. 76, 129,
  130, 138, 140,
  225 n. 101,
  226 n. 101, 229,
  284
61.1–2 84, 87
61.2 130
61.3 96

61.3b 96, 101 n. 41
61.6 87, 130, 131,
  138
61.7 130
61.9 94 n. 9
63.16 23
64.8 23
65.9 96
65.21–22 96
65.23 94 n. 9, 97
66.1 171
66.1–14 10
66.7–10 97
66.22 94 n. 9

Jeremiah
3.19 38
4.23–26 210 n. 64
4.31 97 n. 21
6.24 97 n. 21
9 210
9.10–11 210 n. 63
10.22 211 n. 66
13.21 97 n. 21
14.16 211 n. 66
15.3 211 n. 65
16.4 211 n. 65
19.7 211 n. 65
20 38
22.23 97 n. 21
23.1–5 144
23.3–6 144 n. 1
24.6 94 n. 9
29.10–14 110 n. 81
30.5–6 97 n. 21
30.9 144 n. 1, 155,
  157 n. 67
30.21 155
31.1 155
31.9 33, 38
31.27 94 n. 9
31.31–37 42 n. 76,
  42 n. 78
32.41 94 n. 9
33.15–16 144 n. 1
34.20 211 n. 65
46.27 94 n. 9
48.41 97 n. 21
49.22 97 n. 21
49.24 97 n. 21
49.43 211 n. 66
50.43 97 n. 21
51.37 211 n. 66

Lamentations
2.8 219 n. 87

Ezekiel
1 172
1.1 85
1.15–21 171
1.26–28 216
1.4 175 n. 29
1.5–28 187
10.1 171
10.3–4 175 n. 29
13.4 210 n. 62
17.7–21 105
17.8 108 n. 74
17.22 109
17.22–23 37
26.23 40
31.6, 13 211 n. 65
34—37 41, 155
34.23–24 144,
  157 n. 67
34.24 155
36 13, 41, 43, 44,
  44 n. 84, 66, 77,
  90, 91, 110, 127
36.8 41
36.11 41
36.12 41
36.22 44 n. 84
36.23 40, 40 n. 70,
  40 n. 71, 41, 42
36.23–28 40 n. 69
36.23–39 40
36.24 40 n. 71, 41
36.25 41, 42
36.26–27 42
36.28 40 n. 71
36.29 40 n. 71
36.33 40 n. 71
37.14 42 n. 78
37.15 158 n. 70
37.15–23 155
37.23–24 157 n. 67
37.24–25 144
37.25 155
37.28 155
38.23 40 n. 68,
  40 n. 70
39.7 40 n. 68
39.17–20 235
39.29 42 n. 78
40—48 203 n. 37
41.1 168
41.22 201 n. 32
43.24 112, 118
44.10 71 n. 5
44.13 155 n. 59
44.16–17 201 n. 32

44.24 202
45.17 202 n. 33
46.1–8 202 n. 33

Daniel
1—6 168, 169
1—7 248, 259
1.2 168
1.4 251
1.8–16 168
2 168, 170, 174,
   179, 250–5, 258,
   261, 285
2.5 168, 174
2.5–7 253 n. 46
2.8 168, 174
2.9 251, 253 n. 46
2.11 253 n. 45
2.13 168, 174, 251
2.15 168, 174, 251
2.18 162 n. 85
2.19 162 n. 85
2.20–23 248,
   249 n. 30, 250–3,
   259
2.21 251
2.21b–22 250
2.22 248, 249
2.22a 250
2.23 253 n. 47
2.27 253
2.27–28 253
2.28 257
2.30 253 n. 47
2.31–45 250
2.34 46
2.35 170
2.38 211 n. 65
2.44 170, 181
3 174, 250, 251
3—6 250
3.1 168, 250 n. 34
3.7 168
3.10 168, 174, 251
3.19–30 250
3.26 162 n. 85
4 251
4.9 253
4.12 211 n. 65
4.14 162 n. 85
4.17 168
4.18 253 n. 45
4.21 211 n. 65
4.24 162 n. 85, 168
4.34 162 n. 85
4.37 162 n. 85

5 250 n. 34, 251, 258
5.1–4 168
5.2 251
5.5 251 n. 38
5.7 251 n. 38
5.8 251 n. 38
5.11 253 n. 45,
   253 n. 47
5.12 251 n. 38
5.14 253 n. 45
5.15 251 n. 38
5.16 251 n. 38
5.17 251 n. 38
5.24–28 168, 174
5.25 251 n. 38
6 169, 178–9, 251
6.5 251
6.6 251
6.8 251
6.12 251
6.13 251
6.15 251
6.19 251
6.25–28 169
7 80, 166–89, 205,
   206, 212, 236–8,
   249–52, 254 n. 51,
   255, 258, 269–71,
   274, 275, 277,
   279–80, 285
7—12 178
7.1 251
7.6 184 n. 54
7.9 171, 180
7.9–14 169–70
7.10 174, 180,
   217 n. 84
7.12 184 n. 54, 181
7.13 167, 169, 174,
   177–8, 256, 271
7.13–14 270
7.13b 176
7.14 173, 174, 180,
   181, 184, 254
7.17 172, 184 n. 54
7.17–18 270
7.18 162 n. 85, 180,
   181, 254 n. 51
7.20 170
7.21 170, 180,
   180 n. 44
7.21–27 270
7.22 162 n. 85, 170,
   180, 181, 254 n. 51
7.23 184 n. 54
7.23–25 179

7.24 180 n. 44, 181
7.25 30 n. 34,
   162 n. 85, 170, 180
7.26 184 n. 54
7.27 162 n. 85, 180,
   181, 184 n. 54,
   254 n. 51
8.11–13 179
8.17 169
8.19 30 n. 34
8.31 257
8.31–38 257
8.35 257
8.35, 38 257
8.38 257
9 178
9.22 253 n. 47
9.24 178
9.24–27 110 n. 81
9.25–27 179
10 250 n. 34
10.21 251
11.6 30 n. 34
11.28–35 179
11.35 30 n. 34
11.40 30 n. 34
11.45 30 n. 34
12 179, 250 n. 34,
   258
12.1 30 n. 34, 174,
   251
12.3 258
12.4 30 n. 34
12.7 259
14 250 n. 34,
   253 n. 47
15 250 n. 34
17 251
18 250 n. 34

Hosea
1.1 33
2.23 94 n. 9
3.5 157 n. 67,
   144 n. 1
11.1 38

Joel
2.28 42 n. 76

Amos
9.11 71 n. 50
9.15 94 n. 9

Micah
4.9–10 97 n. 21

Zephaniah
1.3 211 n. 65

Zechariah
2.11 109
3.8–10 158
3.9 220
4.1–6 76 n. 76
6.13 159
8.9–10 94 n. 9
8.12 47 n. 97
9—10 156
9—13 271
9.9 149
11.7 160
11.7–14 220
11.14 160
12—13 158–9
12 271
12.10 269, 278
12.10–11 158
12.10b 271
13 271
13.7–9 158
14.6–7 116
14.9 116, 160 n. 74,
   220

Malachi
1.7 201 n. 32
1.12 201 n. 32
2.6–7 235 n. 115
2.7–10 220
2.10 160 n. 74
3.17 37

NEW TESTAMENT
(INCLUDING Q)

Matthew
1.1 145
1.20 145
2.6 119 n. 111
2.20 119 n. 111
2.21 119 n. 111
3 59, 77, 228
3.1–12 81, 231
3.6 58 n. 11
3.7–10 59
3.11 57 n. 9
3.12 59
3.13 60 n. 22
3.14 81
3.15 59, 81
3.16 60 n. 21,
   60 n. 22

3.17 59 n. 18,
  59 n. 19, 60 n. 22,
  67, 69, 81 n. 91
4 82
4.1–11 70, 82
4.3 59 n. 19
4.4 193 n. 7
4.6 59 n. 19
4.12–25 82
4.15 119 n. 111
5—7 82
5 227
5.1 133–4
5.3 128, 129, 130,
  131, 140
5.3–6 129
5.3–11 134
5.3–12 113, 115,
  129, 134
5.4 128, 130, 131
5.5 119, 130
5.6 59 n. 19, 81 n. 95,
  128, 130, 131
5.7–10 129
5.10 81 n. 95
5.10–12 117
5.11–12 129, 133
5.13 112–19
5.13–16 114, 134
5.13a 114
5.14 116, 117
5.14–16 113, 117
5.14a 114
5.14b 114
5.15 114,
  116 n. 100
5.16 19 n. 4, 116
5.17 81, 82
5.20 59 n. 19, 81,
  81 n. 95,
  82 n. 96, 115
5.21–22 115
5.21–42 133
5.27–28 115
5.31–32 115
5.33–34 115
5.38–39 115
5.39 139
5.40–42 139
5.43–44 115
5.44 49
5.44–45 31 n. 38
5.45 19 n. 4
5.48 19 n. 4
6.1 19 n. 4
6.4 19 n. 4

6.6 19 n. 4
6.8 19 n. 4
6.9–13 18
6.9b 18
6.9c 40 n. 71
6.10a 40 n. 71
6.10b 40 n. 71
6.10b–c 46
6.11 40 n. 71, 47
6.12 40 n. 71,
  49 n. 105,
  82 n. 98, 188
6.13 40 n. 71, 50, 51
6.13b 51
6.21 19 n. 4
6.32–33 19 n. 4
6.33 59 n. 19,
  81 n. 95
7.13–14 117 n. 103
7.22 188
8.1—11.1 230
8.11 203 n. 40
8.11–12 47
8.18–22 208
8.20 190, 207–22
9 228, 230
9—11.1 227
9—11.2 227, 229
9.1 227
9.1–8 82 n. 98
9.6 184
9.8 188
9.9 228 n. 104
9.9–13 228, 231
9.9–17 228, 229
9.9—11.19 229
9.10–11 228 n. 104
9.11 228
9.14 228 n. 104
9.14–17 228, 231
9.27 145, 148
9.35 225, 226
10 225, 226
10.1–8 225, 226
10.5 225 n. 101,
  226 n. 101, 227
10.7 225, 226
10.8 188
10.8b 227
10.8c 227
10.13–15 188
10.16–22 117 n. 103
10.19–20 82
10.20 66
11 227, 228, 230
11.1 225–227

11.2 225–227, 229
11.2–15 131
11.2–19 223, 225,
  226, 231
11.5 225–7, 229
11.6 131
11.7–15 223, 225,
  228
11.9 150, 225
11.15 228
11.16 223, 227
11.16–18 225
11.16–19 191, 223,
  225, 226, 228–30
11.16b 226
11.19 228
11.19a 228, 230
11.19b 225, 229,
  230, 235 n. 120
11.25 19 n. 5
11.25–27 19 n. 4, 24,
11.26 19 n. 5
11.27 19 n. 4,
  19 n. 5, 24,
  140 n. 171
12.1–8 145
12.6 82
12.18 69
12.23 145
12.31–32 82 n. 98
12.50 19 n. 4
13.8 104 n. 55
13.53–57 117 n. 103
14 227
14.1–12 117 n. 103
15 227
15.13 19 n. 4
15.22 145, 148
15.22–39 145
16.13–20 82
16.17 19 n. 4,
  257 n. 60
16.17–19 119
16.19 188
17.5 81 n. 91,
17.5–6 83
18.15–20 188
18.18 49 n. 105,
  188
18.21–35 49,
  82 n. 98
20.1–8 150
20.30–31 145
20.30–33 148
21—24 82
21.1–11 148, 149

21.9 145
21.12 152
21.15 145
21.25 57 n. 8
21.32 59 n. 19,
  81 n. 95
21.33–46 117 n. 103
22.1–14 47
22.15–22 240 n. 1
22.41–54 151
22.42 145
23 227
24.9–14 117 n. 103
24.36 19 n. 4
25.1–13 47
26.28 82
26.29 203 n. 39
26.41 50, 51
26.50–52 49 n. 106
26.51 83
26.52 83
26.57–68 262 n. 66
27.22–23 150 n. 34
27.54 81 n. 91, 83
28.18–20 119
28.19 19 n. 4
28.19–20 83
28.46 19

Mark
1 77
1—10 262
1—14.48 276
1.1 31, 70, 77
1.4 58 n. 11
1.7–8 77
1.8 57 n. 9
1.9 60 n. 21,
  60 n. 22
1.9–11 59 n. 16, 79,
  196
1.10 60 n. 22, 61
1.10a 59
1.10b 59
1.11 59, 59 n. 18,
  60 n. 21, 60 n. 22,
  62, 67, 68, 69,
  75 n. 70, 76, 77,
  78 n. 78, 80 n. 88
1.12–13 70, 196
1.14a 60
1.15 256 n. 54
1.36 195 n. 13
2—3 195
2.1 187
2.1–10 167, 184–8

2.1–12 182, 188–9, 263
2.1–3.6 196, 197
2.3 187
2.5 186
2.7 185
2.9 189
2.10 184–5
2.11 187
2.12 186
2.23 204 n.44
2.23–28 144–5, 150, 190, 191, 193–7, 199–200, 202, 219
2.25 195, 198
2.25–26 192, 195, 196, 205
2.26 195, 197–199, 201
2.27 193, 194
2.27–28 191, 205
2.28 192–4
3.6 240
3.11 31
3.12 256 n. 54
3.14 195
3.22–30 66
3.28–29 277
3.31–35 19 n. 6
4.3 93
4.3–9 93, 104
4.4 93 n. 4, 256
4.4–9 92–111
4.8 104 n. 55, 108
4.10 256
4.11 256
4.11–12 93, 96 n. 17
4.11b 256
4.13 92 n. 1, 93
4.14 94 n. 6
4.14–20 93
4.15 256 n. 55
4.17 105–6
4.17–19 97
4.19 108
4.20 94 n. 8
4.31–32 109
4.32 109
4.33–34 256
4.36 195
4.39 256 n. 54
5.7 31
5.18 194

5.24 195
5.37 195
5.40 195
6.11 188
7.19b 194
8.11 79
8.15–26 258
8.22–10.52 145
8.27–30 89 n. 126
8.27–33 78
8.27–38 78
8.27—9.13 79
8.29 256
8.30 256
8.31 78, 256
8.31–38 256–8, 56 n. 53
8.32 256
8.32–33 256
8.33 249, 255–7
8.34–38 78
8.35–38 258
8.38 256 n. 57, 258
9.1–8 78, 80
9.1–18 77
9.2 78 n. 81, 78 n. 82
9.7 78, 78 n. 78, 78 n. 83
9.18 188
9.31 43 n. 82
9.33–37 125 n. 132
9.38 124
9.38–41 125
9.40 124, 126
9.42–50 113
9.49 125–26
9.50 112–13, 124–6
10.2 79
10.17–22 137
10.35–34 31
10.37 30
10.38 85
10.38–39 30
10.45 43 n. 82
10.47–48 145, 148
11—16 242
11.1 262
11.1–8 196
11.1–10 148, 149, 199 n. 27
11.9–10 196
11.10 150
11.11 152
11.11—12.37 199
11.25 19 n. 4, 49

11.27–33 64 n. 31
11.30 57 n. 8
12 242
12.1–10 79
12.1–12 242 n. 9
12.6 79
12.7a 240
12.10 79, 196
12.10–11 242 n. 9
12.13 240
12.13–17 240, 241, 243, 267 n. 75, 247, 248, 255, 257–9
12.15 79
12.16 246
12.16–17 242, 248
12.17 242, 249, 257–9
12.18–27 242, 258
12.24 258
12.24–25 258 n. 62
12.25 181, 258
12.26 242 n. 9, 247
12.28–34 218–20, 242 n. 9
12.29–31 242 n. 9
12.33 218, 219
12.34 218
12.35 145, 151
12.35–37 151, 242 n. 9, 271 n. 87
12.36 242 n. 9
13.1–3 31
13.9 237
13.11 66
13.26 278
13.32 19 n. 4
13.35–37 271
14.1—16.8 199
14.12 262
14.17–21 145 n. 5
14.18 199
14.20 199
14.21–25 277
14.22 199, 203 n. 39
14.22–25 78, 247
14.24 31
14.27 31
14.28 268 n. 78
14.32 79
14.32–42 30, 78, 145 n. 5
14.33 195

14.33–36 270
14.34 31
14.35 30, 31
14.36 19 n. 4, 19 n. 5, 22, 27, 29, 30, 31, 79
14.37 31
14.38 30 n.35, 31, 50, 66, 79
14.53–65 199, 261, 262 n. 66, 276, 268
14.55–59 267, 272
14.58 199
14.60–61 272
14.60–61a 272
14.61–62 80 n. 89
14.61–63 263
14.61b 272
14.62 184, 269–71, 273, 275–8
14.64 267, 277 n. 104
14.66–72 30 n.35
15 256
15.13–14 150 n. 34
15.26 196, 246, 247
15.27 194
15.29 199, 277
15.32 194
15.34 19, 196
15.37–39 80
15.38 59, 62, 199
15.38–39 79
15.39 31, 62, 247
16.1–8 31
17.62 278

Luke
1—2 231
1.1–4 86 n. 117
1.5–25 58, 84 n. 105
1.27 145
1.32 145
1.69 145
2.4 145–6
2.11 145–6
3 77, 87
3.1–9 232 n.112
3.1–18 231
3.3 58 n. 11
3.8 233
3.10–14 59
3.15 60
3.16 57 n. 9

3.19–20 60, 84
3.21 60, 60 n. 21,
  60 n. 22, 86
3.22 60, 60 n. 21,
  60 n. 22, 67,
  85 n. 113,
  86 n. 116, 86 n.
  117
3.23 84
3.38 85
4.1 65
4.1–13 70
4.4 193 n. 7
4.14 65
4.14—7.17 231
4.18 65, 87
4.18–21 84
5.10 188
5.17–26 86 n. 117
5.24 184
5.27–31 231
5.29 231
5.30 231
5.33 231
5.33–39 231
5.34 233
5.36–39 124
6.1–5 150
6.1–6 145–6
6.3 195 n. 13
6.4 199 n. 28
6.17 134 n. 152
6.22–23 133
6.27 122
6.33 122
6.35 122
6.36 19 n. 4
7 233
7.1–10 86 n. 117
7.18–28 131
7.18–35 233
7.19–35 223, 231
7.22 231
7.23 131
7.24–25 121
7.24–30 223
7.29 231–34
7.29–30 225, 231–3
7.29–35 231
7.30 232
7.31–35 191, 223,
  231–2
7.32 231
7.34 231
7.34–35 232
7.34b 235 n. 120

7.35 221, 225,
  231–4
7.36–37 231
7.36–50 231–3
7.37 233
7.39 231
7.47–49 231
8.8 104 n. 55
8.12 210, 211
8.14 108
8.54 233 n. 114
9.23 237
9.35 69
9.48 233 n. 114
9.51 84 n. 106
9.51—19.28
  86 n. 117
9.52–56 49 n. 106
9.57–62 208
9.58 190, 207–2
10.5–12 188
10.17 188
10.18 140 n. 171
10.21–22 19 n. 4
10.22 19 n. 4
10.25–28 218 n. 85
11.2–4 18
11.2b 18, 40 n. 71
11.3 40 n. 71, 47
11.4 49 n. 104
11.4a 40 n. 71
11.4b 40 n. 71, 50, 51
11.5 120 n. 114
11.13 66
11.20 66
12.1 121
12.12 66
12.30 19 n. 4
12.35–37 47
13 123
13.6–9 123
13.7 123
13.7–8 123
13.8 123
13.9 210
13.19 210, 211
13.28–29 47
13.29 203 n. 40
14.14–24 120
14.14–33 122
14.25–33 120
14.25–35 113
14.26–27 120
14.28 120
14.31 121
14.31–33 121

14.32 121–2
14.33 120
14.34 113, 122
14.34–35 112,
  119–24
14.35 123
14.35a 122, 123
14.38 50
15.4 120 n. 114
16.8 233 n. 114
16.25 233
17.3–4 49
17.7 120 n. 114
18.17 233 n. 114
18.35–43 145–6
18.38–39 148
19.28–40 148, 149
19.37–42 122
19.45 152
20.4 57 n. 8
20.9–18 121
20.20–26 240 n.1
20.36 233 n. 114,
  234
20.41–44 145–6,
  151
22.16 203 n. 39
22.18 203 n. 39
22.19 199 n.28
22.29 19 n. 4
22.31 86
22.34 19 n. 5
22.35 43 n. 82
22.39 86
22.42 19 n. 4
22.43 86 n. 115
22.46 19 n. 5, 50,
  51
22.49–51 49 n. 106
22.54–71 262 n. 66
23.4 86 n. 117
23.14 86 n. 117
23.14b 268 n. 77
23.21–13 150 n. 34
23.22 86 n. 117
23.34 19 n. 4, 49,
  49 n. 104
23.46 19 n. 4
24.29 19 n. 4
24.50–53 84 n. 105

Q 17
3.7–9 60
3.8 104
3.21–22 60
3.22 67

4.2b–13 60 n. 23
4.3 60
4.9 60
6.20 128
6.20–21 128–40
6.21a 128
6.21b 128
7.18–23 64
7.18–28 131
7.23 131
7.31–32 224
7.31–34 224
7.31–35 191,
  223–4, 235
7.33–34 224
7.35 224
9.57–58 218
9.58 190, 208 n. 53,
  208–18, 219
11.2a 43
11.2b 39, 40, 43
11.2c 44
11.3 47
11.4 39 n. 67, 44,
  49
11.4a–b 48, 49
11.4b 50
11.33 114
14.34–35 114

John
1.29–34 61 n. 24,
  63, 64 n. 32
1.51 214, 217
2.17 146
3.5 44 n. 84
3.26 57
4 217
4.12 217 n. 83
4.23 19 n. 4
5 24
5.16–18 24–5
5.17 19 n. 4
5.18 25
5.19 19 n. 4
5.19–47 25
5.20 19 n. 4
5.20–30 25
5.27 183 n. 48
6.32 19 n. 4
6.40 19 n. 4
8.19 19 n. 4
8.28 217 n. 83
11.41 19 n. 5
11.47–53 136
12.12–19 148, 149

12.23, 34 217 n. 84
12.28 19 n. 5, 44
13.31 217 n. 84
17.1 19 n. 5
17.5 19 n. 5
17.11 19 n. 5
17.21 19 n. 5
17.24 19 n. 5
17.25 19 n. 5
18.10–11 49 n. 106
18.13–24 262 n. 66
18.40 150
20.17 19 n. 4

Acts
1.1–5 86 n. 117
1.22 57 n. 8
2 86
2.4 86 n. 116, 86 n. 117
2.14–41 146
3.1–10 86 n. 117
4.25–27 87 n. 119
4.27 87
6.8 269
7.56 183 n. 49
7.60 49, 49 n. 104
9.13 180 n. 44
9.32 180 n. 44
9.41 180 n. 44
10 86 n. 117
13.16–42 146
13.27 268
13.33 87
15.13–21 146
17 8
18.25 57 n. 8
19.14 126 n. 134
19.21—21.17 86 n. 117
23.9 86 n. 117
25.25 86 n. 117
26.10 180 n. 44
26.31 86 n. 117

Romans
1.3 146
1.4 88 n. 124, 147
1.7 20 n. 8, 180 n. 44
4 88 n. 124
6.4 20 n. 8
8 29
8.3 30
8.15 20 n. 8, 27, 29,
8.15–18 29 n. 28

8.27 180 n. 44
8.35–36 29
12.3 180 n. 44
13.6 259
13.8–10 219 n. 87
15.7–13 147
15.25 180 n. 44
15.26 180 n. 44
15.31 180 n. 44
16.2 180 n. 44
16.15 180 n. 44

1 Corinthians
1 253
1—2 255
1.2 180 n. 44
1.3 20 n. 8
1.17—2.10 255
1.19–20 254
1.20 254
1.23 255
1.23–24 253 n. 43
1.26 253
1.27–28 253
1.30 255
2.1 253
2.1–14 252
2.5 254
2.6 253
2.7 253
2.10 249, 252, 253
2.10–14 253
2.11 249, 252, 255
2.12 255
2.13 253, 254
6.1 180 n. 44
8—10 255
15 255, 255 n. 52
15.1 255
15.20–28 254 n. 51
15.24 254 n. 49
15.27 255
15.35–49 255
15.45 254, 255
15.49 254 n. 51
15.51 254 n. 50

Galatians
1.4 30
1.7 30
3 88 n. 124
3.29—4.7 30
4 30
4.6 27, 29, 30

4.19 30
4.29 30
5.11 30
5.14 219 n. 87

Ephesians
1.3 20 n. 8

Philippians
2.6 25 n. 26

Colossians
1.6 94 n. 10
1.10 94 n. 10
4.5 112

2 Timothy
1.2 20 n. 8
2.8 146

Hebrews
1 87
2.11 20 n. 8
3.1–6 87 n. 121
5.5 87 n. 121
5.8 31 n.38
6.10 180 n. 44
13.24 180 n. 44
17.1–3 44

James
1.17 20 n. 8

1 Peter
1.2–3 20 n. 8

2 Peter
1.17 20 n. 8

1 John
1.2 20 n. 8

Revelation
1.6 20 n. 8
1.7 269
2.26 87 n. 123
2.26–27 87 n. 122
3.10 51 n. 115
5.5 146
5.8 180 n. 44
5.9 180 n. 44
8.3 180 n. 44
8.4 180 n. 44
22.16 146

APOCRYPHA

Judith
8.24–27 74

1 Maccabees
50 n. 107
2.52 50 n. 108
4.41–51 172 n. 19
4.47 170
13.50–51 150 n. 35
14.41 151 n. 40

2 Maccabees
50 n. 107
1.27–29 101 n. 43
2 175 n. 29
2.4–7 47 n. 97
2.17 37
7.6 44 n. 83

3 Maccabees
2.21 32
5.8 32
6.3 32
6.8 32

4 Maccabees
5—18 178
13.12 74

Sirach 162
4.10 162 n. 85
7.9 162 n. 85
7.15 162 n. 85
9.15 162 n. 85
12.2 162 n. 85
12.6 162 n. 85
17.26 162 n. 85
17.27 162 n. 85
22.24 21, 32
23.1 32
23.1–4 22–3
23.4 32
24 235
28.2–5 48 n. 102
47.8–10 151 n. 40
50 163
50.5 176
50.5–11 176
50.6 176
50.7 176
50.10 176
51.10 32

Tobit
13.1–5 32
13.3–6 101 n. 43
13.4 23, 32
13.6 32
13.10–11 116

Wisdom
2.16–20 35
5.2 278 n. 107
7.21–26 229 n. 107
7.26 230 n. 108
10.1 230 n. 108
14.2–3 35
14.3 23

OLD TESTAMENT
PSEUDEPIGRAPHA

*Apocalypse of
Abraham*
13 105, 211 n. 69

Apocalypse of Elijah
5.28 278 n. 107

Apocalypse of Moses
19.2 275 n. 98

Assumption of Moses
10.1 44 n. 86

2 Baruch
29.5 47 n. 97
29.9 47 n. 97
53—76 98

1 Enoch 104, 275
1.3–9 44 n. 86
14.8–23 115
14.22 171 n. 16
46.1 183 n. 48
46.2 183 n. 48
46.3 183 n. 48
46.4 183, n. 48
48.2 183 n. 48,
    230 n. 108
48.7 230 n. 108
49.1–3 230 n. 108
51.3 230 n. 108
62.3–5 278 n. 107
62.5 183 n. 48
62.7–8 94 n. 9
62.13–16 47 n. 97
71.2–47 115
83—90 101

83.8 102
84.6 102
89—90 50 n. 107,
    101 n. 43,
    102 n. 47
89.10 42, 43, 49,
    55, 211 n. 67,
    211 n. 68
90.1–27 102
90.2–19 211 n. 67
90.7 102
90.8–12 102
90.29 102
91.11–17 100–1
91.12–13b 101 n. 42
93.1–10 100–1
93.4 101 n. 39
93.5 101 n. 41
93.9 100
93.10 101 n. 40

2 Enoch
22.8–10 78 n. 80
64.5 185

3 Enoch
12 78 n. 80

4 Ezra 96, 167
8.38–41 94
9.29–37 95

Jubilees 75 n. 71,
    99–100, 101, 102,
    103, 104, 162
1.15–18 99
1.16 99
1.19 33
1.27 99 n. 23
1.29 99 n. 23
4.26 99 n. 23
7.36 162 n. 85
8.19 79 n. 84
11 105
11.11 105, 211 n. 69
11.18–23 105,
    211 n. 69
12.19 162 n. 85
12.20 105
13.16 162 n. 85
13.29 162 n. 85
16.18 162 n. 85
16.26 99
16.27 162 n. 85
17.16 75 n. 68,
    79 n. 85

18.3 74 n. 66
18.9 75 n. 68
18.12 75 n. 68
18.13 73 n. 59
18.18–19 74 n. 67
18.19 79 n. 85
20.9 162 n. 85
21.20 162 n. 85
21.22 99
21.24 99
23 99
23.16–25 99 n. 31
23.20–21a 99–100
23.21 100
23.26 100, 105
32.1 215 n. 75,
    151 n. 40
32.16–24 215
36.6 99
48.2 75 n. 68
48.9 75 n. 68
48.12 75 n. 68
48.13 75 n. 68
49.2 74 n. 67
49.7 74 n. 66
49.22 74 n. 67

Ladder of Jacob
6–9, 12–13
    215 n. 76

*Liber antiquitatum
biblicarum
(Pseudo-Philo)*
32.3 73 n. 60

*Life of Adam and
Eve*
13.1—14.1 173

Letter of Aristeas
97 78 n. 80
99 171

Psalms of Solomon
71, 76
14.2 94 n. 9
17 72 n. 55, 144
    n. 1
17.1–4 44 n. 86
17.21–23 44 n. 86
17.21–25 72
17.26, 27 72
17.30 72

Sibylline Oracles
3.47 44 n. 86
3.787 115
7.149 47 n. 97

*Testament of
Benjamin (T. 12
Patr.)*
10.5–6 275 n. 98

*Testament of Dan
(T. 12 Patr.)*
5.3 218 n. 86
6.1–3 50 n. 107

*Testament of
Issachar (T. 12
Patr.)*
5.1–2 218 n. 86

*Testament of Joseph
(T. 12 Patr.)*
18.2 47 n. 102

*Testament of Judah
(T. 12 Patr.)*
23.1–5 34
24.1–6 34
24.3 34

*Testament of Levi
(T. 12 Patr.)*
48 n. 100
3.3 50 n. 107
5.6 50 n. 107
8.3 151 n. 40
8.16–18 48 n. 100
9.6–14 75 n. 71
17.11 34
18.1–2 34
18.6 34

*Testament of
Zebulun (T. 12
Patr.)*
5.3 48 n. 102
8.1–2 48 n. 102

*Testament of
Abraham (T. 3
Patr.)*
10 275 n. 98

*Testament of Isaac
(T. 3 Patr.)*
2.7 275 n. 98

Testament of Job
33.2–4 275 n. 98

Testament of Moses
9—10 44 n. 83

DEAD SEA SCROLLS

CD 219
1.3–11 101 n. 43
1.5–8 109 n. 75
9.18–21 135
12.20b–22 94 n. 9
12.23 163 n. 86
14.19 163 n. 86
19.10–11 163 n. 86
20.1 163 n. 86

1Q28a
1.12–16a 85 n. 111

1QH
14.14–16 94 n. 9
17.8–10 34 n. 48
17.34–46 34 n. 49

1QHª
12.8–9 101 n. 43
13.20—15.6
   109 n. 75

1QM
1.3 101 n. 43,
   105 n. 57
2.1–2, 4–6
   202 n. 35
2.4–9 203 n. 39
6.6 44 n. 86
7.3 85 n. 111
10.10 180 n. 44
12.7 44 n. 86

1QpHab
2.8 136
5.12—6.9 260 n. 64

1QS 135
1—2 135
1.22—2.1 135
5.13–14 203 n. 41
6.2–21 203 n. 41
6.4–6 47 n. 97
8.4b–10a 109 n. 75
8.12–14 101 n. 43
8.12–16 105 n. 57
8.13–16 57 n. 10

9.2 163 n. 86
9.4–5 135
9.17–21 105 n. 57
9.18–20 101 n. 43
9.19–20 57 n. 10
10.21 105 n. 57
11.7–9 109 n. 75
11.20 183 n. 48

1QSa
1.12–19 85 n. 111
2.17–19 203 n. 41
2.17–22 47 n. 97

2Q24 (2QNJ ar)
4.1–10, 14–16
   202 n. 36

4Q161
2.11–25 144 n. 1

4Q174 71, 72
1 1.7–13 144 n. 1
1 1.19 71 n. 51

4Q175 226 n. 101

4Q177
5–6, 7–10 101 n. 43

4Q225 74, 75
2.2.4 73 n. 60

4Q242 185

4Q258
1.3.4 101 n. 43

4Q259
1.3.19 101 n. 43

4Q266 109 n. 75

4Q286–90 135

4Q418
81 109 n. 75

4Q453
2a–b 171 n. 13

4Q457b
2.2 144 n. 1

4Q504
1–2 4.5–8 144 n. 1

4Q510 211 n. 69

4Q511 211 n. 69

4Q522
9 2.3–6 144 n. 1
9 2.4 163 n. 86

4Q543 235 n. 115

4Q545
1 171 n. 13

4QMMT 203 n. 41

11Q5
27.2–10 144 n. 1

11QMelch
2.4–13 185

11QT
29.9–10 216

11QTª
56–59 163 n. 86

PHILO

***De Abrahamo* (On
   the Life of
   Abraham)**
32.169 78 n. 81
198 75 n. 71,
   75 n. 73

***De decalogo* (On the
   Decalogue)**
13–14 274 n. 96
61–64 274 n. 96
65 218 n. 86

***De mutatione
   nominum* (On
   the Change of
   Names)**
13 75 n. 72

***De somniis* (On
   Dreams)**
2.18 274 n. 96

***De specialibus
   legibus* (On the
   Special Laws)**
1.168–76 201 n. 29

1.170 206 n. 51
2.63 218 n. 86

***De vita
   contemplativa*
   (On the
   Contemplative
   Life)**
1.81–82 204 n. 43

***Legatio ad Gaium*
   (On the Embassy
   to Gaius)**
45 274 n. 96
46 sec. 368 274 n. 96

***Legum allegoriae*
   (Allegorical
   Interpretation)**
3.219 75 n. 72

***Quod deterius
   potiori insidari
   soleat* (That the
   Worse Attacks the
   Better)**
124 75 n. 72

JOSEPHUS

Jewish Antiquities
*1.13.1–2 §§224,
   226* 73 n. 59
1.13.4 §§232–36
   73 n. 60
3.6.7 §§142–43
   201 n. 29
3.8.9 §§216–17
   78 n. 80
3.10.7 §§255–56
   201 n. 29
4.8.6 §§202
   274 n. 96
6.5.6 §92 185
8.1.3 §§10–12
   198 n. 26
8.2.1 §§45–49
   126 n. 134
12.7.4 §§348–49
   150 n. 35
13.10.7 §§299–300
   136 n. 159
14.10.6 §§202–3
   241 n.3
15.10.3 §§363–64
   257 n. 61

18.5.2 §117 58 n. 11
20.9.1 §§ 197–203
    268

Jewish War
1.21.3 §§404–6
    257 n. 61
2.8.5 §§129–33
    203 n. 41
2.16.5 §§403
    241 n. 3
3.8.3 §§351–54
    136 n. 159

MIDRASH, TALMUD
AND RELATED
LITERATURE

Avot
5.21 85 n. 111

Bava Qamma
9.29 48 n. 102

Betzah
5.2 266

Hagigah
12b 47 n. 97
14a 181

Ketubbot
66b 112

Megillah
28a 48 n. 102

Menaḥot
95b 192 n. 3

Sanhedrin
4.1 266
7.5 274
11.2 266
38b 181

Shabbat
31a 218 n. 86

151b 48 n. 102

Sheqalim
3.26 85 n. 111

Soṭah
9.15 23, 36,
    164 n. 92
15b 134
38a 134

Ta'anit
4.8 133 n. 149

Yoma
8.9 23, 48 n. 102

TARGUMS

**Fragmentary
    Targum**
74 n. 65

Targum Isaiah
9.6 144 n. 1
11.1–6 144 n. 1
11.10 144 n. 1
14.29 144 n. 1
16.5 144 n. 1

Targum Neofiti
74 n. 65

**Targum Pseudo-
    Jonathan**
2.6–7 71 n. 52
22.1 74 n. 65

Targum Zechariah
14.9 44 n. 86

OTHER RABBINIC
WORKS

Mekilta
12.13 74 n. 65
16.26 164 n. 92
20.6 36

Genesis Rabbah
56.8 73 n. 60
97 70, 71 n. 51

Exodus Rabbah
34.1 36

Leviticus Rabbah
16.17 171

Numbers Rabbah
11 85 n. 111

Sifre Numbers
63 85 n. 111

Yalqut
§130 192 n. 3

APOSTOLIC FATHERS

Barnabas
19.5 219 n. 87

1 Clement
8.3 20 n. 8

Didache
1.2 219 n. 87
2.3 219 n. 87
8.2 17

Ignatius
To the Ephesians
4.2 20 n. 8

NEW TESTAMENT
APOCRYPHA

Gospel of Hebrews
47, 47 n. 96

Gospel of Thomas
9 93

OTHER EARLY
CHRISTIAN
LITERATURE

**Apostolic
    Constitutions**
7.44 17

Cyprian
The Lord's Prayer
9 17

Eusebius
Ecclesiastical History
2.23.13
    183 n. 49

Tertullian
Prayer
1 17

CLASSICAL
LITERATURE

Cassius Dio
Roman History
53.17.8 244 n. 17

Cicero
Cataline Orations
4.6 115 n. 93

Dio Chrysostom
*Training for Public
    Speaking (Or. 18)*
13 112

**Diogenes
    Laertius**
*Lives and Opinions
    of Eminent
    Philosophers*
8.1.35 112

Philostratus
Life of Apollo
1.15 245

Plato
Republic
364b–65a
    126 n. 134

Index of modern authors

Abadie, Phillipe 154 n. 55, 161 n. 80
Abegg, Martin 183 n. 86, 202 n. 35
Ackroyd, Peter R. 154 n. 55
Ådna, Jostein 101 n. 41, 103 n. 52
Ahearne-Kroll, Stephen P. 145 n. 5
Alexander, Philip S. 126 n. 34
Allison, D. C. 11 n. 11, 39 n. 66, 45 n. 87, 46 n. 93, 47 n. 95, 50 n. 109, 51 n. 111, 52 n. 118, 68 n. 39, 81 n. 94, 112 n. 86, 114 n. 92, 131 n. 140, 131 n. 143, 191 n. 1, 194 n. 11, 224 n. 94, 225 n. 97, 240 n. 2.
Alt, Albrecht 71
Anderson, Jeff S. 133 n. 147
Anderson, Robert A. 170 n. 8
Andrews, Mary 50 n. 108, 51 n. 114, 79 n. 85
Angel, Andrew R. 170 n. 8
Angel, Joseph L. 50 n. 107, 163 n. 88, 171 n. 11,
Armerding, C. E. 152 n. 43
Atkinson, Kenneth 203 n. 41
Auerbach, Erich 107 n. 70

Bammel, Ernst 61 n. 25, 136 n. 160, n. 161, 149 n. 33
Barber, Michael 9 n. 5, 82 n. 97, 151 n. 40, 152 n. 43, 155
Barker, Margaret 48 n. 100, 115 n. 95
Barr, James 22
Bauckham, Richard 65 n. 33, 85 n. 112, 274 n. 94, 33 n. 46
Baxter, W. S. 145 n. 6
Bayet, Jean 244 n. 16
Beale, G. K. 85 n. 114, 86, 97 n. 20, 173 n. 22
Beasley-Murray, G. R. 45 n. 87, 58 n. 12, 151 n. 38, 179 n. 42, 182 n. 47
Beauchamp, Paul 157 n. 67
Beavis, Mary Ann 45 n. 87, 104 n. 56, 197 n. 18
Becker, Jürgen 63 n. 30, 191 n. 1, 224 n. 92
Bedford, Peter R. 172 n. 19
Benoit, Pierre 266-7 n. 73
Ben-Sasson, H. H. 43 n. 81
Berger, Klaus 148 n. 28
Bergsma, John S. 169 n. 6
Berlin, Andrea M. 257 n. 61
Bernett, Monika 244 n. 19
Betz, Hans 18 n. 1, 115 n. 93, 115 n. 94
Betz, Otto 186, 274 n. 95
Bird, Michael 55 n. 2
Black, Matthew 47 n. 95, 171 n. 12
Blenkinsopp, Joseph 136 n. 159, 137 n. 162,

155 n. 58, 163 n. 86
Blinzler, Josef 266 n. 73, 273 n. 92
Block, Daniel I. 41 n. 74, 42 n. 77
Blomberg, Craig L. 224 n. 92, 235 n. 116
Bock, Darrell L. 85 n. 109, 123 n. 125, 145 n. 12, 224 n. 92, 268 n. 79, 274 n. 95, 275 n. 97, n. 99, 276 n. 102, 278 n. 107
Bockmuehl, Markus 145 n. 2
Boda, Mark J. 156 n. 61
Boers, Hendrikus 269 n. 83
Bonnard, Pierre 39 n. 66
Boobyer, G. H. 185 n. 56
Borg, Marcus 191 n. 1, 224 n. 92, 235 n. 117, 240 n. 2
Boring, M. E. 69 n. 43, 166 n. 2
Bornkamm, Günther 81 n. 93, 145 n. 6, 151 n. 38
Borrell, Agusti 264 n. 71
Bosworth, Edward 21
Botner, Max 145 n. 2
Bousset, Wilhelm 21
Bovon, François 84 n. 107, 85 n. 112, 121 n. 117, 123 n. 124
Bowker, John 96 n. 16
Boyarin, Daniel 170 n. 9, 180 n. 45
Brandon, S. G. F. 45 n. 87, 149 n. 30
Braun, F. M. 33 n. 46
Brawley, Robert L. 208 n. 53
Bretscher, Paul G. 69 n. 40, 69-70, 70 n. 47, 75 n. 70
Brodie, Thomas L. 253 n. 42
Brooke, George J. 99 n. 23, 101 n. 41, 121 n. 116, 173 n. 22
Brown, Raymond E. 39 n. 65, 39 n. 66, 46, 47 n. 95, 146 n. 22
Browning, Robert 46
Brownlee, William H. 57 n. 10
Brunson, Andrew C. 150 n. 36
Bryan, Christopher 248 n. 26
Bryan, David 172, 172 n. 18, 211 n. 67
Bryan, Stephen M. 9 n. 5
Buchanan, Wesley 133 n. 150
Bultmann, Rudolf 3-6, 4 n. 3, 9-10, 9 n. 7, 21 n. 10, 55 n. 2, 58 n. 15, 94 n. 7, 128, 151 n. 38, 183 n. 50, 183-4, 241, 283, 286
Bunta, Silviu 214 n. 73, 216 n. 80, 217 n. 82
Burer, Michael H. 201 n. 31
Burger, Christoph 145 n. 12, 146 n. 21, 147
Burkill, T. Alec 276 n. 101
Burney, C. F. 18 n. 1

Caird, George B. 184 n. 51
Cameron, A. 244 n. 15, n. 17
Campbell, Constantine R. 39 n. 67
Camponovo, Odo 45 n. 87
Caragounis, Chris 179 n. 42
Carmignac, Jean 51
Carruth, Shawn 18 n. 1
Carson, D. A. 44 n. 84, 225 n. 97, 226 n. 100, 226 n. 102
Carter, Warren 240 n. 2, 265 n. 72
Casey, Maurice 185 n. 55, 191 n. 1, 208 n. 53, 210 n. 62, 224 n. 92
Cassidy, R. J. 242 n. 7
Catchpole, David R. 149 n. 30, 150 n. 35, 152 n. 42, 268 n. 79
Cave, C. H. 104 n. 56
Chae, Young S. 145 n. 6, 163 n. 86
Chancey, M. A. 245 n. 21
Charlesworth, James H. 145 n. 2
Chilton, Bruce 9 n. 5, 45 n. 87, 46 n. 60, 56 n. 6, 75 n. 73, 146 n. 22, 150 n. 37, 151 n. 38
Chronis, Harry L. 280 n. 110
Clarke, Ernest G. 214 n. 73, 214 n. 74
Clines, David J. A. 246 n. 24
Coakley, J. F. 149 n. 32
Cody, Aelred 152 n. 43
Cohn, Haim Hermann 262 n. 65
Collins, A. Y. 18 n. 1, 27 n. 27, 115 n. 93, 115 n. 94, 145 n. 5, 170 n. 8, 175 n. 28, 175 n. 30, 176 n. 34, 184 n. 53, 185 n. 56, 186 n. 61, 256–7, 274 n. 94, 274 n. 95, 276 n. 102
Collins, J. J. 18 n. 1, 175, 175 n. 28, 175 n. 30, 176 n. 34
Collins, Matthew A. 101 n. 41
Conzelmann, Hans 255 n. 52
Cook, E. M. 202 n. 35
Cook, L. Stephen Jr 136 n. 160, 202 n. 35
Corley, Jeremy 32 n. 43
Corley, Kathleen E. 235 n. 116
Cotter, Wendy J. 225 n. 98
Coulot, Claude 163 n. 86
Cranfield, C. E. B. 194 n. 11
Crossan, John Dominic 55 n. 2, 140 n. 171, 191 n. 1, 208 n. 53, 224 n. 92, 235 n. 116, 240 n. 2
Crossley, James G. 191 n. 1, 224 n. 92
Croy, N. Clayton 33 n. 44
Cullmann, Oscar 81 n. 93, 119 n. 112, 146 n. 22

Dalman, Gustav 44 n. 86
Daly, Robert J. 75 n. 70
Daly-Denton, Margaret 146 n. 16
Dämmgen, Ulrich 112 n. 86, 119 n. 110

D'Angelo, Mary Rose 19 n. 3, 27 n. 27
Dapaah, Daniel S. 56 n. 5
Darr, Katheryn P. 97 n. 21
Daube, David 242 n. 8
Davies, John A. 38, 39 n. 62, 47 n. 99, 154 n. 56
Davies, Philip R. 75 n. 70, 75 n. 73, 251
Davies, W. D. 39 n. 66, 46 n. 93, 47 n. 95, 51 n. 111, 52 n. 118, 68 n. 39, 75 n. 73, 81 n. 94, 112 n. 86, 114 n. 92, 131 n. 140, 131 n. 143, 151 n. 40, 191 n. 1, 194 n. 11, 225 n. 97, 240 n. 2
Davila, James R. 33 n. 46
Day, John Davies 156 n. 66, 175 n. 28
Déaut, Roger L. 74 n. 65, 76 n. 75, 79 n. 84, 149 n. 31
Deenick, Karl 152 n. 43
Dekker, Wisse 69 n. 43
Dennert, Brian C. 225 n. 99
Dennis, J. 47 n. 95
Derrett, J. Duncan M. 240 n. 2, 244 n. 14
deSilva, David A. 33 n. 46
Deutsch, Claudia 235 n. 119
De Vries, Simon J. 154 n. 55
Dewailly, Louise-Marie 47 n. 95
Dewey, Joanna 184 n. 53
Dexinger, Ferdinand 100 n. 37
Dibelius, Martin 184 n. 53, 264 n. 69
Diffey, Daniel S. 152 n. 43
Di Lella, Alexander 176 n. 34, 180 n. 45
Dimant, Deborah 103 n. 51
Dixon, Edward P. 59 n. 17
Dodd, C. H. 94 n. 5, 106 n. 65, 136 n. 160, n. 161, 149 n. 30, 151 n. 38, 224 n. 92
Doering, Lutz 193 n. 5
Donahue, John R. 264 n. 70, 259 n. 63
Drury, Marjule Anne 10 n. 8
Duling, Dennis C. 146 n. 21, 147, 148 n. 28
Dunn, J. D. G. 121 n. 12, 27 n. 27, 50 n. 109, 55 n. 2, 65, 65 n. 33, 112 n. 83, 151 n. 38, 185 n. 57, 191 n. 1, 208 n. 53, 224 n. 92, 232 n. 111, 240 n. 2, 270, 275
Dunne, John A. 30 n. 31
Dupont, Jacques 39 n. 66

Eastman, Susan G. 30 n. 33
Edwards, James R. 194 n. 8, 197 n. 17
Edwards, Richard A. 226 n. 102
Embry, Brad 72 n. 55, 73 n. 56
Emerton, John A. 175 n. 28
Enslin, Morton S. 58 n. 15
Ernst, Josef 56 n. 6, 61 n. 26, 65 n. 53
Eshel, Esther 215 n. 76
Eskola, Timo 275 n. 97, 275 n. 98, 279 n. 108
Evans, Craig A. 31 n. 37, 93 n. 3, 96 n. 17, 149 n. 33, 270 n. 85, 86, 271 n. 89, 276 n. 102, 277 n. 103

Farmer, William R. 150 n. 34
Fearghail, Fearghas O. 176 n. 33
Fee, Gordon D. 255 n. 52
Fensham, F. C. 19 n. 7
Finney, Paul C. 243 n. 12, n. 13
Fisher, Loren 148 n. 28
Fitzmyer, Joseph A. 121 n. 117, 232 n. 110
Fleddermann, Harry T. 60 n. 23, 125 n. 133
Flesher, Paul V. M. 201 n. 31
Fletcher-Louis, Crispin H. T. 9 n. 5,
    50 n. 107, 78 n. 80, 85 n. 114, 115 n. 95,
    116 n. 99, 120 n. 114, 121 n. 115, n. 116,
    163 n. 88, 171 n. 12, 173 n. 24, 174 n. 25,
    n. 26, n. 27, 185 n. 57, 186 n. 61
Flusser, David 140 n. 169
Foley, John M. 113 n. 90
Ford, J. Massyngberde 172 n. 17
Förster, Niclas 241 n. 5, 246 n. 24, 248 n. 26,
    249 n. 29
Fossum, Jarl 216 n. 81
Fournier-Bidoz, Alain 235 n. 119
France, R. T. 259 n. 63
Frankfurter, David 132 n. 145, n. 146
Friedlander, Gerald 40 n. 71
Friedrich, Gerhard 9 n. 5
Fredriksen, Paula 149 n. 30, 191 n. 1
Fröhlich, K. 119 n. 112
Fuller, R. H. 68 n. 39
Funk, Robert W. 18 n. 2, 112 n. 83,
    128 n. 137, 191 n. 1, 208 n. 53, 224 n. 92

Gane, Roy E. 201 n. 31, 201 n. 32
García Martínez, Florentino 38 n. 48,
    202 n. 36
Garlington, Don B. 117 n. 104, 118 n. 109
Garnet, Paul 96 n. 17
Garr, W. Randall 246 n. 24, 250 n. 35
Garsky, Albrecht 18 n. 1
Gaston, Lloyd 103 n. 51
Gaventa, Beverly R. 30 n. 33
Gero, Stephen 59 n. 17
Gese, Helmut 182 n. 47
George, Augustin 145 n. 12
Gibbs, James M. 145 n. 6
Giblin, Charles H. 242 n. 8, 243 n. 11,
    248 n. 26
Gilders, William K. 178 n. 39
Ginzburg, Carlo 13–14
Gladd, Benjamin L. 250 n. 32
Gnilka, Joachim 27 n. 27, 77 n. 77, 184 n. 53,
    191 n. 1, 208 n. 53
Goguel, Maurice 62 n. 29
Goldingay, John 170 n. 8, 170 n. 9, 179 n. 42,
    180 n. 45, 251 n. 36
Gooding, David W. 251 n. 39
Goulder, Michael W. 172 n. 20, 173 n. 21

Granerød, Gard 155 n. 57, 160 n. 75
Grant, Michael 245 n. 22
Grassi, Joseph A. 27 n. 27, 79 n. 85
Gray, Timothy C. 31 n. 36
Green, Joel B. 47 n. 95, 194 n. 11, 242 n. 7
Greenfield, Jonas C. 215 n. 76
Grelot, Pierre 47 n. 94, 51 n. 111
Grimm, W. 131 n. 140
Grindheim, Sigurd 185 n. 57, 253 n. 42
Grundmann, Walter 194 n. 9, 225 n. 97
Guelich, Robert A. 131 n. 141
Gundry, Robert H. 265 n. 72, 274 n. 93
Gunton, Colin E. 73
Gupta, Nijay K. 245 n. 22
Gurtner, Daniel M. 79 n. 87

Hägerland, Tobias 185 n. 59
Hagner, Donald A. 24 n. 24, 194 n. 9
Hahn, Ferdinand 146–7
Hahn, Scott 88 n. 124, 145 n. 12, 152 n. 43,
    153 n. 47, 162 n. 83
Halpern-Amaru, Betsy 99 n. 23
Hampel, Volker 184 n. 53
Hanneken, Todd R. 100 n. 36
Haran, Menahem 152 n. 43
Hare, Douglas R. A. 208 n. 53
Harnack, Adolf von 4
Harrington, Daniel J. 259 n. 63
Harrisville, Roy A. 45 n. 87
Hart, H. J. 243 n. 12
Hartin, Patrick J. 224 n. 94
Hartman, Louis F. 176 n. 34, 180 n. 45
Harvey, Anthony E. 149 n. 30, 149 n. 31,
    253 n. 42
Hasel, Gerhard F. 206 n. 50
Hauck, F. 137 n. 163
Hay, David M. 151 n. 40, 160 n. 75
Hayes, John H. 161 n. 79
Hays, Richard B. 41 n. 72, 253 n. 42
Hayward, C. T. R. 176 n. 33, 216 n. 80
Head, Peter M. 77 n. 77
Heidegger, Martin 4
Heitmüller, Wilhelm 21 n. 11
Hengel, Martin 45 n. 87, 131 n. 141,
    208 n. 53, 229 n. 106
Herzer, Jens 224 n. 93, 225 n. 96
Higgins, A. J. B. 185 n. 56, 236 n. 122
Himmelfarb, Martha 100 n. 37, 102 n. 46,
    103 n. 52
Hoffmann, Paul 223 n. 91
Hoglund, Kenneth G. 154 n. 50
Hollenbach, Paul W. 66 n. 35
Holmén, Tom 11 n. 11
Holtzmann, Oskar 2, 140 n. 171
Hooker, Morna D. 208 n. 55
Hoover, Roy W. 18 n. 2, 112 n. 83,

128 n. 137, 191 n. 1, 208 n. 53, 224 n. 92
Horsley, Richard A. 45 n. 87, 147 n. 26,
   224 n. 94, 240 n. 2
Huizenga, Leroy A. 69, 75 n. 69, 83 n. 102,
   83 n. 103
Hultgren, Arland 104 n. 56, 191 n. 1,
   204 n. 45
Hunzinger, Claus-Hunno 120 n. 114
Hurst, L. D. 163 n. 86
Hurtado, Larry W. 275 n. 97

Ishida, Tomoo 161 n. 78

Janse, S. 71 n. 49
Jenkins, Philip 10 n. 8
Jeremias, Joachim 21–3, 27–8, 39 n. 66,
   45 n. 87, 47 n. 95, 48, 50 n. 109, 68 n. 39,
   94, 123 n. 125, 126 n. 135, 162 n. 81,
   224 n. 92, 225, 236 n. 122
Jervell, Jacob 248 n. 27
Jewett, Robert 146 n. 20, 255 n. 52
Jipp, Joshua W. 88 n. 124
Johansson, Daniel 185 n. 59
Johnson, Benjamin J. M. 106 n. 69
Johnson, Vivian L. 164 n. 91
Jonge, Marinus de 33 n. 46, 279 n. 109,
   287 n. 1
Joyner, Charles W. 12
Juel, Donald H. 263 n. 68, 264 n. 69,
   267 n. 76, 271 n. 88, 273 n. 91

Kaiser, Walter C. 155 n. 59
Kammler, Hans-Christian 81 n. 92, 253 n. 43
Kay, D. M. 44 n. 86
Keck, Leander E. 59 n. 17
Kee, Howard Clark 33 n. 46
Keener, Craig S. 21 n. 12, 55 n. 2, 112 n. 84,
   149 n. 30, 151 n. 38, 185 n. 57
Keesmaat, Silvia C. 29 n. 29
Keith, Chris 191 n. 1, 11 n. 11
Kennard, Douglas W. 50 n. 109
Kerr, Alan R. 214 n. 73
Kilpatrick, G. D. 267 n. 75
Kim, Seyoon 196 n. 14, 271 n. 89
Kingsbury, Jack D. 145 n. 6, 209 n. 56,
   209 n. 59
Kinman, Brent 149 n. 30, 149 n. 31, 149 n. 33
Kirk, David R. 214 n. 73
Kitz, Anne Marie 132 n. 45
Klawans, Jonathan 9 n. 5
Klein, G. 40 n. 71, 158 n. 69
Kleven, Terence 153 n. 47
Kline, Meredith G. 168 n. 5
Klinghardt, Matthias 235 n. 116
Kloppenborg, John S. 60 n. 23, 121 n. 116,
   223 n. 91

Knibb, Michael A. 101 n. 43, 102 n. 47
Knowles, Michael P. 105 n. 58
Koch, Dietrich-Alex 243 n. 13
Kohler, K. 134 n. 153
Kooij, Arie van der 337 n. 55, 337 n. 56
Kraeling, Carl H. 56 n. 6, 58 n. 15, 66 n. 35
Kratz, Reinhard G. 48 n. 101
Kraus, Hans-Joachim 152 n. 43
Kugel, James L. 75 n. 71, 215 n. 76, 215 n. 77
Kurz, William S. 84 n. 108
Kwon, Oh-Young 253 n. 41

Laato, Antti 156 n. 66, 158 n. 70, 159 n. 72
Lacocque, Andre 171 n. 12, 175 n. 29,
   250 n. 33
Ladd, G. E. 45 n. 87
Lampe, G. W. H. 264 n. 70
Lane, William L. 197 n. 16, 273 n. 92
Latham, James E. 112 n. 85
Le Déaut, Roger 74 n. 65, 76 n. 75, 79 n. 84,
   149 n. 31
Le Donne, Anthony 11 n. 11, 62 n. 29,
   151 n. 38
Lee, Yongbom 254 n. 51
Légasse, Simon 224 n. 95
Lehnardt, Andreas 40 n. 70
Leithart, Peter J. 83 n. 100
Levenson, Jon D. 38 n. 59, 69 n. 43, 73 n. 59
Lietzmann, Hans 262 n. 65
Lindars, Barnabas 185 n. 55, 208 n. 53,
   224 n. 92, 271 n. 87
Linton, Olof 225 n. 97
Lohfink, Gerhard 46 n. 93, 96 n. 17, 47 n. 95,
   48 n. 100, 50 n. 109
Lohmeyer, Ernst 44 n. 85
Lohse, Eduard 266 n. 73
Longman III, Tremper 235 n. 118
Lövestam, Evald 87 n. 121, 88 n. 124
Lucas, Ernest 170 n. 9, 180 n. 45
Lupieri, Edmondo 60 n. 20
Luz, Ulrich 39 n. 64, 51 n. 111, 69 n. 40,
   131 n. 140, 226 n. 102, 229 n. 105

McDonald, James I. H. 45 n. 87
McDowell, Catherine L. 245 n. 24,
   250 n. 35
McKane, William 235 n. 118
McKnight, Scot 21 n. 12, 50 n. 109
Magness, Jodi 203 n. 41
Maier, Christl 224 n. 93, 225 n. 96
Malbon, Elizabeth Stuthers 145 n. 2,
   197 n. 18
Maloney, L. M. 107 n. 70
Manson, T. W. 21 n. 12, 55 n. 2, 166,
   209 n. 57, 210, 237
Marchel, Witold 19 n. 7

Marcus, Joel 66 n. 35, 70 n. 47, 78 n. 79,
    172 n. 20, 186 n. 61, 197 n. 17, 246 n. 25,
    256 n. 56, 273 n. 90, 274 n. 95
Marshall, I. Howard 47 n. 95, 49 n. 104,
    85 n. 114, 94 n. 5, 193 n. 6, 208 n. 55,
    224 n. 92
Mason, R. A. 155 n. 60
Mason, Steve 58 n. 11
Mauser, Ulrich W. 174 n. 95
Mays, James L. 45 n. 87
Meier, J. P. 44 n. 84, 62 n. 27, 62 n. 28,
    66 n. 35, 240 n. 2, 241 n. 3
Mell, Ulrich 18 n. 2
Merklein, Helmut 235 n. 120
Merz, Annette 149 n. 30, 240 n. 2
Meyer, Ben F. 9 n. 5, 58 n. 12
Michaelis, W. 146 n. 22
Milgrom, Jacob 85 n. 111
Miller, Anna C. 253 n. 41
Miller, Patrick D. 138 n. 167
Miller, Stephen 179 n. 42
Minear, Paul S. 119 n. 112
Miura, Yuzuru 145 n. 12
Moberly, R. W. L. 50 n. 110, 73 n. 59
Morales, L. Michael 8 n. 5, 47 n. 99, 173 n. 22
Mosca, Paul G. 181
Moses, A. D. A. 83
Moule, C. F. D. 93 n. 3, 104 n. 53, 183 n. 49,
    184 n. 51, 236 n. 121
Mowinckel, S. 179 n. 42
Mroczek, Eva 215 n. 77, 216 n. 79
Müller, Christoph G. 84 n. 108, 85 n. 109
Myers, Jacob M. 154 n. 55
Myles, Robert J. 209 n. 58

Na'aman, Nadav 172 n. 19
Neeb, John H. C. 214 n. 73
Neirynck, F. 192 n. 4
Nepper-Christensen, Poul 83 n. 99
Netzer, Ehud 257 n. 61
Newsom, Carol A. 203 n. 57
Nickelsburg, George W. E. 103 n. 52
Nitzan, Bilha 135 n. 155, 135 n. 156,
    135 n. 157
Nolland, John 68 n. 39, 84 n. 107, 85 n. 113,
    115 n. 94, 194 n. 11, 224 n. 95, 225 n. 96
Nordheim, Miriam von 160 n. 75, 162 n. 84
Novakovic, Lidija 69 n. 40, 145 n. 6

O'Brien, Kelli S. 71 n. 49, 80 n. 90
Olson, Daniel C. 211 n. 67
O'Neill, J. C. 45 n. 87, 273 n. 92
Orlov, Andrei A. 216 n. 81
Overman, J. Andrew 257 n. 61
Owen-Ball, David T. 242 n. 8, 243 n. 11,
    248 n. 26

Pace, Sharon 168
Panayotov, A. 33 n. 46
Parke-Taylor, G. H. 133 n. 150
Parsons, Mikeal C. 87 n. 120
Pate, C. Marvin 50 n. 109
Peeler, Amy L. B. 87 n. 121
Percy, Ernst 185 n. 56
Perdue, Leo G. 235 n. 118
Perrin, Nicholas 46 n. 91, 47 n. 95, 47 n. 98,
    50 n. 109, 54 n. 1, 56 n. 5, 58 n. 14,
    73 n. 58, 83 n. 100, 101 n. 43, 110 n. 80,
    110 n. 81, 117 n. 101, 124 n. 128,
    131 n. 144, 137 n. 164, 137 n. 165,
    139 n. 168, 198 n. 20, 203 n. 28,
    207 n. 52, 271, 271 n. 89, 273 n. 91
Perrin, Norman 45 n. 87, 185 n. 56,
    224 n. 92, 269–271
Pesch, Rudolf 27 n. 27, 105 n. 58, 150 n. 37,
    278 n. 107
Pfann, Stephen J. 204 n. 42
Philipson, D. 134 n. 153
Philonenko, Marc 33 n. 46
Pilch, John J. 119 n. 110
Piotrowski, Nicholas 145 n. 6
Pitre, Brant 6 n. 4, 9 n. 5, 30 n. 34, 50 n. 109,
    99 n. 31, 100 n. 38, 107 n. 72, 179 n. 41,
    201 n. 30, 201 n. 32, 202 n. 34, 202 n. 36,
    203 n. 39
Pogoloff, Stephen M. 253 n. 41
Polaski, Donald C. 251 n. 39
Pomykala, Kenneth 155 n. 60, 163
Popkes, Wiard 51 n. 117
Porter, Paul A. 172 n. 17
Potterie, Ignace de la 29 n. 29
Preuss, Horst D. 155 n. 57
Price, Simon R. F. 244 n. 18
Provan, Ian W. 174 n. 25
Przybylski, Benno 59 n. 19, 81 n. 95

Rad, Gerhard von 71, 74 n. 48, 115 n. 94,
    156 n. 62
Ramaroson, Léonard 96 n. 16
Rauschenbusch, Walter 107 n. 71
Reed, Jonathan L. 244 n. 14
Regev, Eyal 162 n. 82, 163 n. 88
Repschinski, Boris 228 n. 104
Ridderbos, Herman N. 45 n. 87, 94 n. 5
Rieske, Susan 68 n. 38
Riesner, Rainer 94 n. 7
Rindge, Matthew S. 69 n. 43, 78 n. 81
Robbins, Vernon K. 145 n. 2
Roberts, J. J. M. 71 n. 48
Robinson, James M. 223 n. 91, 224 n. 94
Rodríguez, Rafael 11 n. 11
Rogers, A. D. 197 n. 17
Roloff, Jürgen 191 n. 1

Romerowski, S. 154 n. 55
Rooke, Deborah W. 156 n. 64, 156 n. 65, 156 n. 66
Rordorf, Willy 191 n. 1
Rosenberg, Roy A. 83 n. 101
Roure, Damià 197 n. 16
Rowe, Robert D. 45 n. 87
Rowland, Christopher 214 n. 73, 214 n. 74, 216 n. 81
Ruiten, J. van 99 n. 23, 105 n. 58

Saebø, Magne 155 n. 58
Sahlin, Harald 85 n. 112
Sanders, E. P. 9, 55 n. 2, 58 n. 15, 103 n. 52, 149 n. 30, 185 n. 57, 186 n. 61, 191 n. 1, 204, 235
Sanders, J. T. 11 n. 11
Sandgren, Leo D. 85 n. 110
Sarna, Nahum M. 205 n. 49
Scattolon, Alfredo 69 n. 43
Schleiermacher, Friedrich 21
Schmidt, Thomas E. 246 n. 25
Schmithals, Walter 255 n. 52
Schnackenburg, Rudolf 45 n. 87, 115 n. 94, 119 n. 112, 224 n. 92, 242 n. 6
Schottroff, L. 107 n. 70, 193 n. 6
Schröter, Jens 185 n. 57, 240 n. 2
Schüngel-Straumann, Helen 32 n. 41
Schürmann, Heinz 50 n. 109
Schüssler Fiorenza, Elisabeth 140 n. 171
Schwartz, Joshua 216 n. 80
Schweitzer, Albert 1 n. 1, 2 n. 2, 50 n. 109, 106 n. 65
Schweizer, Eduard 184 n. 51
Schwemer, A. M. 45 n. 87
Segal, Alan F. 74 n. 63, 275 n. 97
Selman, Martin J. 45 n. 87
Sherwin-White, A. N. 267 n. 74
Shillington, V. George 119 n. 110
Signer, Michael A. 172 n. 54
Smith, B. D. 45 n. 87
Smith, D. E. 235 n. 116
Smith, D. M. 149 n. 32
Smith, M. H. 208 n. 53, 210 n. 60, 212 n. 70
Smith, S. H. 145 n. 2
Snodgrass, Klyne R. 105 n. 57
Souček, Josef B. 110 n. 112
Stark, Rodney 138 n. 166
Stauffer, Ethelbert 273 n. 92
Stegemann, W. 193 n. 6
Stegner, William R. 68 n. 38
Steichele, Hans-Jörg 68 n. 37
Stein, Valerie A. 10 n. 10
Strauss, David Friedrich 128 n. 137, 148 n. 27, 183 n. 50
Strauss, Mark L. 145 n. 12, 146 n. 20

Stökl Ben Ezra, Daniel 178 n. 39
Stone, Michael E. 215 n. 76
Stuart, Douglas K. 37 n. 57
Stuhlmacher, Peter 55 n. 2
Suhl, Alfred 145 n. 6
Sung, Chong-Hyon 184 n. 53
Swarup, Paul 101 n. 41, 109 n. 75
Sweeney, Marvin A. 97 n. 22
Swetnam, James 40 n. 71, 88 n. 124

Tan, Kim Huat 9 n. 5, 149 n. 30
Tannehill, Robert C. 145 n. 12
Tatum, W. Barnes 62 n. 28
Taylor, Joan E. 56 n. 6, 58 n. 15, 63 n. 30, 66 n. 36
Taylor, Vincent 184 n. 53
Theissen, Gerd 149 n. 30, 240 n. 2
Thiselton, Anthony C. 254 n. 48
Thompson, Marianne Meye 21 n. 9, 24 n. 22
Throntveit, Mark A. 158 n. 69
Tigchelaar, Eibert J. C. 38 n. 48, 202 n. 36
Tiller, Patrick A. 99 n. 30, 101 n. 41, 103 n. 51
Tilly, Michael 63 n. 30
Tödt, Heinz E. 183 n. 50, 185 n. 56
Tolbert, Mary Ann 92 n. 2
Torijano, P. 145 n. 28
Towner, W. Sibley 250 n. 33
Tuckett, Christopher M. 224 n. 94, 280 n. 110
Turner, C. H. 69 n. 43

Udoh, Fabian E. 241 n. 30, 243 n. 12

Vaage, Leif E. 224 n. 93
VanderKam, James C. 75 n. 69, 99 n. 23, 100 n. 37, 101 n. 43, 159 n. 73, 163 n. 89, 117 n. 19, 216 n. 80
Van Egmond, Richard 146 n. 6
Vattamány, Gyula 112 n. 84
Vaux, Roland de 156 n. 62, 156 n. 63
Vermes, Geza 55 n. 2, 74 n. 64, 75 n. 74, 185 n. 55, 191 n. 1, 208 n. 53
Vielhauer, Philipp 209 n. 56
Vines, Michael E. 279 n. 109
Vogel, Winfried 168 n. 3
Vögtle, Anton 62 n. 28, 89 n. 125
Völkl, Richard 242 n. 6

Walker, William O. Jr 269 n. 83
Walton, John H. 170 n. 8
Warschauer, J. 21 n. 11
Watts, James W. 250 n. 33
Watts, Rikki E. 71 n. 52, 72 n. 55
Webb, Robert L. 56 n. 6, 56 n. 7, 58 n. 12, 58 n. 15, 60 n. 23, 63 n. 30
Weder, Hans 94 n. 5

Wedderburn, A. J. M. 11 n. 11
Weiss, Johannes 236 n. 122
Weitzman, Steven 32 n. 41
Welch, John W. 115 n. 95
Wellhausen, Julius 185 n. 55, 266–7 n. 73
Wenham, Gordon J. 118 n. 108, 152 n. 43
Wenham, J. W. 197
West, Cornel 288 n. 2
Wevers, John W. 37 n. 55, 118 n. 109
Whitelam, K. 197 n. 17
Whitsett, Christopher G. 147 n.24
Williams, H. H. Drake 253 n. 42
Williamson, H. G. M. 158 n. 69
Willis, Wendell L. 45 n. 87
Wilson, Walter T. 225 n. 96, 228 n. 104, 230 n. 109, 235 n. 119
Winn, Adam 246 n. 25

Winter, Bruce W. 253 n. 41
Winter, Paul 149 n. 33, 262 n. 65
Wise, Michael O. 202 n. 35, 272 n. 19
Wright, N. T. 9 n. 5, 29 n. 29, 45 n. 87, 55 n. 2, 55 n. 3, 56 n. 5, 96 n. 18, 96 n. 19, 115 n. 94, 135 n. 158, 149 n. 30, 151 n. 38, 185 n. 57, 186 n. 61, 191 n. 1, 224 n. 92, 240 n. 2, 254 n. 48, 254 n. 51
Wu, Siu Fung 29 n. 30

Yang, Yong-Eui 193 n. 6

Zanker, Paul 243 n. 13
Zehnder, Markus 170 n. 42
Zeller, Dieter 225 n. 96
Zimmerli, Walther 42 n. 75, 68 n. 39
Zwiep, A. W. 87 n. 120

Index of subjects

Aaron, Aaronic priesthood 39 n. 62, 76,
117–18, 163 n. 86, 173–4, 175, 176, 177,
201; Aaronic blessing 133–4, 135–6,
138 n. 167
Abiathar 197, 198, 199
Abraham 73, 74, 75, 78, 79, 83, 86, 99, 102,
104, 105, 108, 145, 203, 275; children of
232–3; seed of 95, 97–9, 100, 101, 103–4,
110
Adam 85, 205, 206, 216–18, 230 n. 108, 248,
250, 254, 275; *see also* Son of God
Ahimelech 153, 197, 198, 200
Amidah 17
Ancient of Days 170, 171, 175, 179
Angel of the Presence 74–5
anti-cultic theology 10–11
anti-Judaism 9–10, 11
Antiochus IV 74, 167, 168, 170, 172, 178,
180, 180 n. 44
Aqedah 50 n. 108, 69, 73–6, 78, 79, 85, 86,
88 n. 124, 154
Aramaic 39, 47, 176, 212, 214, 236
ark of the covenant 153, 154, 187, 279
atonement 29–30, 43, 73–4, 76, 78, 79, 81,
84, 128, 135, 159, 169, 176, 182, 187,
199, 203, 236, 277, 279, 280, 283, 286,
287

beasts, of Daniel 170, 172, 180, 205, 250
beatitudes 92, 113, 114, 115, 117, 140–2, 221
Bethel 214–15, 217
birds 209, 212, 221, 285; as demons 105; as
Gentiles 109
blasphemy 80, 185, 263, 264, 265, 266, 267,
268, 273, 273–80
blessing 131–4, 153, 155, 158
Bread of the Presence 47–8, 47 n. 99, 153,
192, 199, 201, 202, 206

Caesar 248, 257, 258, 260, 279, 280; and
Jesus' anti-imperial critique 246–7, 257,
260–1; as Pontifex Maximus 244, 247,
258, 260, 261, 262; Tiberius 243–4,
246–7, 261, 280
Caiaphas 54, 80, 136, 166, 199, 218, 239–40,
261, 263, 266, 268, 271, 272–3, 273–80
Christology xiii, 26, 31, 71, 86, 110, 120,
146, 148, 186, 190, 194, 233, 234, 242–3,
255, 271, 276–7, 286
conquest 29, 41

consecration 39, 41–2, 45, 51, 52, 76, 77, 83,
84, 87, 108, 143, 153, 155, 177, 181, 182,
199
covenant 203, 216; Abrahamic 88, 103,
104; Davidic 118, 161–2; new 42; of salt
(eternal) 117, 125, 135
criteria of authenticity xiii, 11, 61, 134, 149,
150

Daniel, prophet 169, 174, 179
David, king 68, 71, 73 n. 56, 85, 85 n. 114,
89, 118, 143. 144, 145, 150–1, 152, 153–4,
155–7, 157–60, 154, 161–3, 164, 167,
181–2, 185, 192, 193, 194, 195, 196, 198,
199, 205, 206, 215
Day of Atonement (*yom kippur*) 133, 135,
175, 176, 178, 187, 188, 279
demons *see* Satan
Docetism xiv, 11

early Church/early Christianity 17, 19, 28,
57, 58–9, 63, 83, 86, 87, 89, 92, 119, 129,
146, 147, 206, 265, 270, 271, 280, 285, 289
Eleazar, high priest 32, 33, 126
eschatological high priest 34, 42, 43, 48, 50,
52, 54, 56; Jesus as xiv, 6–8, 14–15, 76,
78, 80, 82, 89–90, 110, 122, 126, 133–4,
135, 138, 139, 141, 143, 151, 152, 163,
164, 167, 182, 187, 190, 203, 221–2,
235–6, 238, 239, 263, 277, 278, 279,
282, 285, 287–8, 289; in Second-Temple
expectation 162, 171, 216–17
eschatological temple 46, 52, 54, 86, 99, 100,
101, 171, 221–2; Jesus movement as 82,
86–8, 98, 104, 108, 111, 128, 141,
143, 188–9, 203, 204, 206, 261; in
Second-Temple expectation 102, 103,
108–9, 110–11, 115, 170, 179, 187, 203,
215–16, 234–5

exile 32, 33, 42, 45, 98, 105, 106, 110, 210
exodus, story of 14, 29–31, 32, 33, 34, 36–7,
38, 43, 47, 50, 52, 53, 70, 74 n. 76, 75, 108,
112, 117, 143

fatherhood of God: in early Church 20, 26,
27, 28, 29–32, 36, 89; in Jesus' teaching
14, 19–28, 43, 44, 53, 54–5, 89; in
Second-Temple Judaism 20, 21, 22–5, 27,
28, 32–8, 41

forgiveness 48–9, 57–8, 82, 184, 185, 187, 207
foxes 208–9, 211–12; and jackals 210

Gentiles, nation 32, 33, 41, 45, 70, 72, 109,
165, 174, 210, 211, 239, 270, 285
God: name of 40, 134; unicity of 160, 165,
220

Herod Antipas 120, 211, 222
Hezekiah 158
high priest 37, 54, 78, 136–7, 142, 214, 266
historical Jesus studies xv, 2, 3, 10–11, 13
history xiv, 1, 2, 11–14
Holy of Holies 32, 45, 171, 176, 182, 207
holy war 122, 124, 127, 171, 261
Horton, Teri 1, 3, 9

idols/idolatry 42, 52, 91, 107, 217, 140, 143,
168, 244–6, 250, 254–5, 257–8, 260, 282
images/imagery, of God, emperors, etc. 174,
216, 217, 230 n. 108, 244–6, 248, 250–3,
254, 258–9, 280, 283, 284
imperial cult 244–6
inheritance 29–30, 31, 37, 38, 41, 87–8, 108
interim ethic 3, 6
Isaac 34, 50, 69, 73–6, 78, 79, 83, 84, 85, 86,
88, 99, 100, 102, 103, 104, 110, 141, 142,
154, 158, 164, 203, 275

jackals 221, 285; *see also* foxes
Jacob 40, 99, 203, 213, 214–18, 221, 275
James, the apostle 30, 78
Jerusalem (Zion) xiv, 2, 48 n. 101, 54, 58, 70,
72, 85, 109, 115–17, 119, 122, 126, 140,
149, 157, 158, 161–2, 164, 181, 280, 285,
288
Jesus: anti-temple polemic 80, 82, 133, 196,
199, 200, 206, 207, 212, 221, 236, 239,
263, 272, 276, 283; arrest of 83; authority
of 64, 184, 188; baptism of 8, 14, 55–6,
58–73, 76–90, 140, 142, 143, 164, 166,
237, 261, 282, 288, 289; cross of 31, 199,
247, 254, 261; death of 2, 31, 43, 44, 78,
80, 84, 142, 146, 195, 196, 240, 246–7,
255, 261, 265, 268, 272, 277, 278, 279,
280; divinity of 25, 185–7, 186, 274–6,
276, 277–8; ethics of 2–5, 50, 126, 129,
138, 207–8, 218–21, 286; at Gethsemane
27, 30–1, 50–1, 78–9, 83–4, 85–6, 264–5;
homelessness of 190, 208, 209, 212; as
itinerant 135, 164, 208, 219, 237–8, 285;
and Last Supper 31, 82, 199, 200, 203; as
messiah 7, 55–6, 55 n. 2, 78, 79, 87, 89–90,
115, 122, 137, 139, 150–1, 226, 272–3,
273–4, 275, 276, 277, 278, 287; parousia of
278; persecution of 106, 111, 119, 126,

126–7, 141, 142, 143, 279; and prayer 24,
49; as prophet 7, 136, 186; resurrection
of 25, 31, 82, 87, 179, 199, 254, 255, 264,
265, 269, 279; sufferings of 1–5, 30–1,
43, 89–90, 164, 195, 236–7, 238, 265, 280,
286; table practices 228, 229–31, 235–6,
238, 285; and temple action 8, 64,
151 n. 38, 152, 264, 273; temptation of
59, 59 n. 19, 60, 60 n. 23, 63, 70, 82; 193;
titulus of 149, 246–7, 258; transfiguration
of 61 n. 26. 77–9, 80, 83–4; trial of 261–80;
triumphal entry 145, 148–51, 196, 198–9;
understanding of tribulation 87, 98, 106,
107, 111, 126–8, 237, 286; as wisdom 4,
228–89, 238, 239; *see also* Jesus movement,
kingdom of God, Lord's Prayer, parables
Jesus movement 13, 27, 41, 43, 48, 52–3, 54,
56, 76, 92, 137, 140, 142, 143, 200, 212,
220, 229, 239, 284; and apostasy 30 n. 35,
33–4, 98, 99, 100, 102, 107, 119, 122–3; as
priests 93, 107, 108, 110, 111, 116, 119,
122, 124, 125, 128, 131, 140, 164, 201,
218, 282, 283; as remnant 97–8, 98, 105,
108
John, the Baptizer 56–8, 81–2, 88, 107, 121,
223, 224, 225, 226–7, 228–9, 231, 232–3,
282; baptism offered by 57–8, 81; death of
84, 107; imprisonment of 64–5, 84, 106;
as movement leader 56–7; as priest 58
Josiah 158–9, 172
joy 74 n. 67, 133
jubilee 87, 131, 133, 138
Judaism (Second-Temple): and anti-priestly
polemic 110; and apostasy 20 n. 35,
33–4, 102, 103; and messiah 71, 72, 73,
76, 79, 101, 103, 110, 144, 145, 148, 155,
163, 164, 165, 167, 212, 238, 273–4, 275,
285; and resurrection 87–8, 147, 174, 258
judgement (of God) 25, 34, 50, 72, 174, 180,
257, 258, 270, 276, 277
Judith 74, 84

kingdom of God 4, 20, 21, 40, 44–5,
45 n. 47, 89, 92, 116, 117, 129–30, 137–8,
140, 143, 180, 181, 182, 186, 188, 207,
227, 239, 256, 258, 261, 264, 282–3, 285,
286, 289
kingdom of priests 14, 37–8, 75, 91, 112,
286–7

land 41, 42, 52, 100, 108, 111, 119, 136, 141,
154, 208, 238
Levi 33–4, 215
Lord's Prayer 13, 17–28, 21–2, 38–53, 56, 66,
91, 108, 134, 141, 143, 164, 200, 207, 279,
282, 288

martyrdom 43, 180, 183
Mastema *see* Satan
Melchizedek 151, 161–3, 181, 185, 277, 280
messianic banquet 47, 200, 202, 203, 236
microhistory 11–14
Moses 32, 33, 36–7, 39 n. 62, 78, 108, 112, 136, 154, 164, 176, 201, 216, 275

Nebuchadnezzar 168, 170, 249, 250, 256, 257, 259
new creation 31, 41, 95–6, 99, 108, 110, 207, 237, 283
Nicene Creed 25

Old Liberalism 1, 2, 4, 21, 26, 27, 55, 265

parables 1, 104, 110–11, 139, 164, 283
Passover 38, 51, 74–5, 78–9, 149, 150, 158, 199, 200
Paul, the apostle 8, 9, 12, 25 n. 26, 27, 29–31, 87, 88 n. 124, 94, 96, 146, 258, 259, 285
persecution, in Second-Temple
understanding 30, 32, 48, 49, 51, 54, 87, 112, 117 169, 178, 180, 197, 236
Peter, the apostle 18, 30, 72, 78, 82, 87, 187, 255–6, 264–5, 268
Pharisees 122, 191 n. 1, 194, 204, 228, 231, 232, 240, 241, 272, 279
plagues 31, 38
Pompey 37, 71–2
poor, the 124, 29–31, 132, 134, 139–40, 137, 141, 284
priests/priesthood 38, 41–2, 71–2, 76, 235;
age requirements of 85; as exorcists 126
Ptolemy IV 32

Q Community 13
Qaddish 40, 43
Qumran community 57, 71, 76, 105, 108, 135, 136, 162, 163, 178, 202–3, 203, 206, 207, 216, 219–20, 220, 221, 260

repentance 124, 135, 136
restoration, return from exile 7, 33, 40, 41, 42, 43, 44, 48 n. 101, 52, 57, 95, 96–8, 99, 101, 105, 110, 116, 128, 139, 140, 143, 144, 184, 220, 279, 282–3
reunification of tribes 157–60, 159–60, 161, 162, 163, 164, 181, 220
Rome 54, 58 n. 11, 72, 109, 115, 124, 150, 211, 213, 218, 221, 239–40, 243–4, 260–1, 267–8, 272, 275, 280, 288, 289

Sabbath 24, 145, 192, 194, 199, 200, 201, 202, 204, 205, 206, 207, 266
sacred space 8, 13, 37–8, 41, 42 n. 79, 43, 45, 52, 54, 71, 76, 91, 108, 119, 127, 128, 134, 140, 143, 154, 165, 182, 204, 207, 214, 219, 234, 236, 272, 282, 284, 286
sacrifice 76, 78, 117–18, 119, 120, 124, 142, 153, 154, 155, 158, 169, 176–7, 177, 201, 218, 219, 221, 222
Satan 74–5, 86, 196, 211, 256
seed 93–8, 100, 102, 103, 256
Sinai 78, 175
Solomon 35, 39 n. 62, 149, 150, 152, 154–7, 157–60, 161–3, 187, 195, 198, 199
Son of David, Jesus as 14, 55, 142, 144–52, 191, 196, 279–80, 282, 287
Son of God 75, 77, 79, 90; Adam as 85;
Caesar as 247, 258; Israel as 14, 36; Isaac as 75; Jesus as 14, 24–6, 31, 55, 61, 62, 63, 66, 69, 78, 79–80, 83, 85, 89–90, 144, 182–5, 190, 280, 282, 287, 288
Son of Man 116–17, 166–82, 214, 218, 258;
as Adam 173, 183; in Daniel 121, 167, 168–78, 179–81, 181, 250, 252, 260, 269, 274, 288; Jesus as 14, 55, 143, 144, 166, 167, 187, 191, 206, 221, 236–7, 256, 257, 261, 265, 275, 279–80, 282, 285, 287;
Jesus community as 228, 229–31, 236–8;
sayings 191, 208, 209, 223, 256, 269; term 192, 193, 210, 216–18, 224, 236, 238, 270, 275
Spirit, Holy, of God 30, 42, 52, 57, 62, 65–6, 76, 77, 82, 86, 91, 129–31, 135, 140, 143, 229, 234, 253, 254, 255, 282, 284
suffering 29, 31–6, 38, 53, 87, 89, 92, 100, 112, 117, 141, 164, 169, 179, 180
Suffering Servant 69, 81, 83, 185

temple: restoration/rebuilding of 71, 73 n. 58, 89, 108, 110, 124, 134, 158–60, 162, 165; Second 9 n. 5, 10, 37, 46, 54, 71, 73, 79, 82, 115, 116, 121, 123, 133, 168, 169, 170, 175, 187, 206, 214, 216, 235, 252, 272, 278
Tertullian 17, 18
Torah 82
tribes *see* reunification of tribes
tribulation, in Second-Temple Judaism 2, 5, 6, 14, 30–1, 34, 35, 38, 40, 44, 45, 50, 51, 52, 97, 98, 99, 100, 102–3, 164, 179, 180, 197
Trinity 83
Twelve, the 126, 141, 195, 204, 226, 233, 285

wisdom 224, 225, 229–31, 230 n. 108, 233, 234–6, 249–50, 251–2, 253, 255, 259, 260, 280, 288
worship 42, 45, 108, 118, 157–8, 160, 162, 168–89, 173, 179, 220, 221, 222, 239, 284, 286, 289